AA
WHERE·TO·GO
IN·THE
COUNTRYSIDE

AA

WHERE·TO·GO
IN·THE
COUNTRYSIDE

Editors: Michael Cady, Julia Brittain
Art Editor: Peter Davies

Editorial Contributors: Ian Armstrong, Ruth Briggs, Stan Davies,
Michael Everett, Nicholas Hammond, Andrew Heaton, Philip
Llewellin, John O'Sullivan, Franklyn Perring, Peter Schofield,
John Thompson, Peter and Valerie Wenham, Nigel Wood

Index compiled by Gail Harada

The AA would like to thank the staff and officers of the following
organisations, whose help was especially valuable in the preparation of
this book: **The Nature Conservancy Council, The National Trust,
The National Trust for Scotland, The Royal Society for Nature
Conservation, The Royal Society for the Protection of Birds**

Picture researcher: Wyn Voysey
Original photography: Harry Williams
Wildlife illustrations: Terence Dalley
Watercolour illustrations: Bob Partridge
Special photographs of country customs: Doc Rowe

Information checked by the Publications Research Unit of the
Automobile Association

Maps produced by the Cartographic Department of the Automobile
Association

Reprinted 1986

ISBN 0 86145 219 4
AA ref 58036

Filmset by Vantage Photosetting Co Ltd, Eastleigh and London, England
Printed and bound by Purnell & Sons (Book Production) Ltd, Paulton, England
Published by the Automobile Association, Fanum House, Basingstoke, Hampshire
RG21 2EA

*The picture on page 1 is of Ben Lawers; the inset drawing is of a
nightjar. This page: Wensleydale*

CONTENTS

INTRODUCTION
6

ABOUT THIS BOOK
8

WHERE TO GO IN THE COUNTRYSIDE
10–302

Country Calendar, January *20*

Brecon Beacons National Park *38*

Country Calendar, February *48*

Cotswolds *66*

Dartmoor National Park *76*

Country Calendar, March *88*

Exmoor National Park *96*

Country Calendar, April *112*

Country Calendar, May *122*

Country Calendar, June *134*

Isle of Wight *138*

Country Calendar, July *146*

Lake District National Park *148*

London *166*

Country Calendar, August *172*

Country Calendar, September *184*

New Forest *188*

Northumberland National Park *196*

North York Moors National Park *200*

Peak District *210*

Pembrokeshire Coast National Park *218*

Country Calendar, October *238*

Snowdonia National Park *254*

Country Calendar, November *270*

Country Calendar, December *282*

Yorkshire Dales National Park *296*

ATLAS AND PLACE-NAME INDEX
303

SUBJECT INDEX
316

ACKNOWLEDGEMENTS
320

INTRODUCTION

The Shropshire Hills on a crystal-clear day of frost and brilliant sunshine; huge waves crashing against the Cornish cliffs; streams of wildfowl against the East Anglian sky; rooks calling in ancient trees in parkland almost anywhere in Britain; a vast panorama of loch, mountain and moorland in the Highlands. These are a random selection of the lasting images of the British countryside.

Britain, for its size, has a uniquely varied countryside. Within the space of a few miles the proverbial crow can fly over wide river valley, thick woodland, carefully tended estate and bare, open hillside.

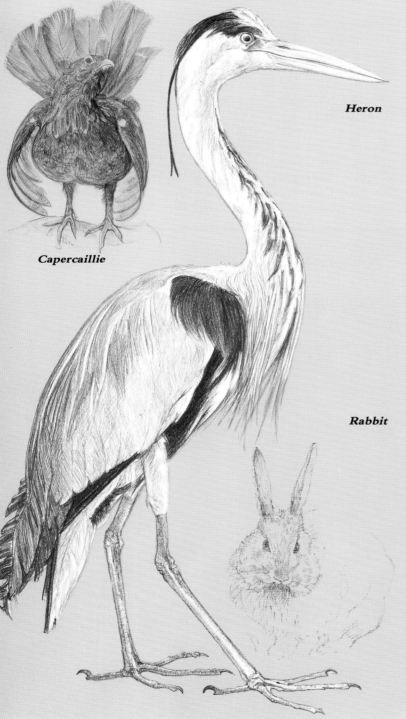

Heron

Capercaillie

Rabbit

The underlying shape of the landscape has been created over millions of years by geological forces and by the weather, but the surface pattern as we see it today is equally a result of the works of men. Heaths, downlands, even great forests like the New Forest and the Forest of Dean appear as they do because of the direct or indirect influence of men.

The cherished notion of the British landscape as somehow timeless and unchanging is quite false. As well as being false, it is a dangerous notion, for it fosters the idea that the countryside, somehow, looks after itself. It does not, and it has not done so since prehistoric men perceived that they could alter the environment to suit their needs.

Hardly any part of Britain is 'wild'; perhaps only sea cliffs and the tops of the highest mountains have never been changed by men. If the entire population of Britain were to be removed, then, after perhaps a hundred years, something like a wild landscape would begin to emerge.

There would be no neat fields, no hedges, no lanes, no parks. All would gradually disappear under a spreading forest. Rivers would burst their banks and great swamps would form. The sea would break through the barriers so carefully erected to keep it at bay and vast mud flats would come into being. If the grazing animals – sheep, cattle, horses, deer – were also removed, then the forests would grow much more quickly, but while those animals remained they would keep some parts of the landscape from becoming overgrown.

After the hundred years had passed, a new Britain would have come into being, but it would not be a Britain that we could recognise, nor, perhaps, is it one that we would like very much. Conceivably, the 'new' Britain would not be so diverse or as rich in wildlife habitats as the one which existed up to the period between the two world wars.

The countryside has always changed, and change has always been essential for its survival, but the changes of the second half of the 20th century are on a frightening scale, and are of kinds once undreamed of. In the last 50 years we have been destroying the British countryside as never before. But surely not: the countryside is still there, you say. This is where chilling statistics make their point: since 1939, 95 per cent of herb-rich meadows have gone or have been damaged, 80 per cent of lowland sheep walks have gone, 60 per cent of the heaths, 50 per cent of lowland fens and mires, and 50 per cent of lowland woodlands have been destroyed. Those figures were not calculated by doom-laden 'greens', but by the Nature Conservancy Council, the government's official nature conservation body.

Where, to paraphrase a famous song, has all that countryside gone? Most of it has been transformed into arable prairies, land where only one crop grows. Such land is inhospitable to wildlife and boring to look at. Many woodlands have been grubbed out and replaced with quick-growing conifers. These modern 'tree factories' are poor in wildlife, partly because many of the trees are foreign, and our native birds, animals and insects are not adapted to live with them.

Red squirrel

Coniferous woodlands are also dark, which means that flowers, which need light to thrive, do not grow in them. Coniferous forests have also been planted over many thousands of acres of previously open moorland and heathland.

Millions of acres have disappeared under developments of one sort or another – housing estates, ring roads and motorways. And then there are all the industrial developments – quarries, open-cast coal mines, power stations and many more.

As is so often the case, nobody realised what was happening until it was too late, or nearly so. Thanks to the efforts of bodies like the National Trusts, the Royal Society for the Protection of Birds, the County Nature Conservation Trusts and others, irreplaceable areas of countryside were saved. But more were lost than were saved, and the destruction goes on relentlessly. Even with much tougher legislation, the litany of losses grows longer every year.

One of the conservationists' worst nightmares is that the only survivors of the 'old' countryside will be nature reserves and other protected areas. That the only way of seeing the great potential richness of the countryside might be in areas fenced off from the landscape as a whole is a prospect almost too depressing to contemplate – but it is a possibility. Already nearly all of the finest and richest sites are protected in some way – in many cases it was the only way of ensuring their survival. One of the great dangers of that course is that people will come to regard the preserved countryside as being in the hands of a few bodies; they will feel, perhaps, that the countryside is something very far from them. So the gap between man and his environment – already almost too wide to cross – will become still wider.

But – unfashionable though the question may be – is the countryside really so very important? What difference would it make if, say, a few species of butterfly that hardly anybody sees anyway became extinct? What harm does it do to our lives if a little piece of woodland in the middle of nowhere is turned over to the production of grain?

For some people the countryside means very little, so why should they care? For others the countryside is only a rather pleasant backdrop for other activities, and they probably won't be much concerned if the countryside is not what it was.

Not for them the argument that we have a responsibility to care for the plants and animals we share our country with; that a varied and fascinating countryside is vital to our very existence; that we might so damage the planet's ecosystems that all life (including our own) would be extinguished.

These are complex issues, and controversial. Understanding the countryside requires work and knowledge, and it is almost always true that those with the deepest love of the countryside are those who have spent longest exploring it.

There is a saying that goes: 'without knowledge there is no understanding and without understanding there is no knowledge'. In order to appreciate great works of art, the observer has to put in much hard work. The same is true of the countryside – it needs to be understood. The rewards for those prepared to make the effort are incalculable indeed, but the effort can only be made while there is a countryside left to discover.

Some of the places described in this book may have changed irrevocably in a few years' time; even as this book goes to press, some are already under imminent threat.

While we have a countryside to nurture and celebrate, this book can function as a kind of signpost to some of the best of it.

Country parks, nature reserves, national parks, country life museums, magnificent estates, and a monthly calendar of traditional customs and events, are all in this book, helping it to provide a marvellously evocative picture of rural Britain today. There are over 500 places to visit, all accessible to the visitor, all seemingly timeless and reassuring, for us all to enjoy.

This book is a permanent record of much we should cherish, and of an irreplaceable heritage we should fight to preserve.

Michael Cady

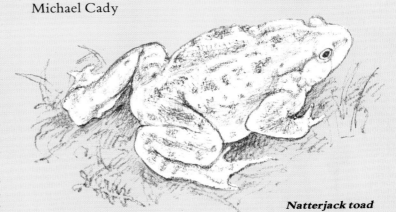

Natterjack toad

ABOUT THIS BOOK

This book contains descriptions of more than 500 places in Britain's countryside. Most are countryside areas – national parks, nature reserves, country parks and the like – but there are also rural life museums, wildlife collections, windmills, watermills and a variety of other places. Of course, the selection is made from the many thousands of areas and places that Britain's countryside offers, but the selection has been made with great care by the book's contributors, all of whom are countryside experts. Most are professional conservationists working with the country's leading conservation organisations, so are perfectly placed to write about the countryside. The book would not have been possible without their help and enthusiasm.

Five leading countryside organisations, the National Trusts, the Royal Society for the Protection of Birds, the Royal Society for Nature Conservation and the Nature Conservancy Council, have given invaluable help and advice throughout the book's production.

Using the Book

The book is organised as an alphabetical gazetteer. Some entries, such as museums, are listed under their town or village. The names of all such places are included in the subject index.

The book also has an atlas index of all the entries in the book. On each double-page spread of maps is an index naming all the places in the book that appear on those maps. The places are located on the maps. (Places which have events described in the Country Calendar features are shown on the maps in a different typeface.)

Large areas, like the national parks, are given ex-tended coverage. Several pages are devoted to these areas, beginning with an introduction to the area. This is followed by a brief gazetteer of particular places to visit within the area. These places are named in the subject index, but not in the atlas index.

Practical Information

At the end of each entry there is a section of practical information. Brief details of the location of places are given; these are not intended to be route directions, but in cases where places may be especially hard to find, more precise details are given. Where special details of access to any place are necessary or potentially helpful, these are given.

Opening times are given where appropriate (see note below). As to the map reference, the page number refers to the atlas pages at the back of the book. The two-figure reference, for example SU23, is a National Grid reference; it can be used to locate places in the book's atlas, or on any map or atlas that uses the National Grid. The first figure is the 'easting', whose corresponding figure can be found either at the top or bottom of the map page. The second figure is the 'northing', which corresponds to figures running up the sides of the map page. By following the lines until they intersect, places can be located.

Some entries in the book, for example long-distance footpaths, have not been given National Grid references as they would not be practical.

A Timely Warning

While every effort has been made to ensure the accuracy of the information in this book, opening times of some locations in the gazetteer may have changed

since the book went to press.

To avoid disappointment it is always advisable to check before making a visit.

Abbreviations

CNT – County Nature Conservation Trusts, including the Manx Nature Conservation Trust and the Scottish Wildlife Trust
FC – Forestry Commission
LNR – Local Nature Reserve
NCC – Nature Conservancy Council
NT – National Trust
NTS – National Trust for Scotland
RSPB – Royal Society for the Protection of Birds
WFT – Wildfowl Trust
WLT – Woodland Trust

Helping to Protect the Countryside

There are many ways in which individual members of the public can help to protect the countryside. It is perhaps an obvious thing to say, but the first thing to do is get to know and love the countryside, so that you feel you have a personal stake in its future.

The best way to support the conservation of the countryside, its wildlife and its rural character, is to join one of the conservation bodies. There are more than enough of these to suit every taste and interest. They range from the biggest, like the National Trust, down to tiny groups of perhaps no more than a dozen individuals. Given below are the addresses of the organisations principally involved in the places described in this book. All such organisations need active members; it's true that they need your money, but sometimes they need your practical help just as much.

The National Trust, 36 Queen Anne's Gate, London, SW1H 9AS

The National Trust for Scotland, 5 Charlotte Square, Edinburgh, EH2 4DU

The Royal Society for Nature Conservation (the national association of the local Nature Conservation Trusts), The Green, Nettleham, Lincoln, LN2 2NR

The Royal Society for the Protection of Birds, The Lodge, Sandy, Bedfordshire, SG19 2DL

The Wildfowl Trust, Slimbridge, Gloucestershire, GL2 7BT

The Woodland Trust, Westgate, Grantham, Lincolnshire, NG31 6LL

(The headquarters of the **Nature Conservancy Council,** the government's official conservation body, is at Northminster House, Peterborough, PE1 1UA.)

The Country Code

Enjoy the countryside and respect its life and work.
Guard against all risk of fire.
Fasten all gates.
Keep your dogs under close control.
Keep to public paths across farmland.
Use gates and stiles to cross fences, hedges and walls.
Leave livestock, crops and machinery alone.
Take your litter home.
Help to keep all water clean.
Protect wildlife, plants and trees.
Take special care on country roads.
Make no unnecessary noise.

Aberlady Bay – a refuge for wildfowl and waders

Afan Argoed Country Park

West Glamorgan

Ravens, herons, foxes, badgers and a herd of about 300 fallow deer are among the creatures which roam the Afon Afan's deep, wooded valley in the hills behind Port Talbot. Japanese larch, Scots pine and other conifers have been planted by the Forestry Commission since 1938, but oak, silver birch, mountain ash and other native trees recall Afan Argoed's original character.

The oldest oaks have witnessed changes typical of South Wales as a whole, because the valley was a coal-mining centre for more than a century. Its return to nature is epitomised at Cwm-yr-Argoed, where what used to be a colliery tip is now a sylvan picnic site. Although the last pit closed in 1970, Afan Argoed's fascinating Welsh Miners' Museum is a tribute to the men who worked deep below the surface hewing 'black gold'. Exhibits range from a domestic scene to memories of the disasters which claimed more than 4000 Welsh colliers between 1837 and 1966.

The park is webbed with waymarked trails from one to just over five miles in length. Some explore the riverside while others climb the steep-sided val-

Aberlady Bay

Lothian

Within easy driving distance of Edinburgh, the nature reserve at Aberlady Bay is as popular with birdwatchers as neighbouring Gullane is with golfers. The tidal mudflats here, on the southern side of the Firth of Forth, attract numerous waders and wildfowl. When the flats are covered at high tide the birds can be seen roosting on the adjoining salt-marsh. Among the commoner species are shelduck, easily distinguished – even from a distance – by their large size, black, white and chestnut plumage, and red bill. They are found round most of Britain's coast except in late summer, when almost the entire British adult shelduck population makes for the Waddensee off northern Holland, where huge numbers of these birds from all over north-west Europe gather to moult. Shelduck breed at Aberlady, but they are most numerous here in January.

In winter Aberlady Bay is also visited by large numbers of pink-footed geese, which come here to roost. These geese usually arrive in Britain in September, having flown in from their nesting grounds in Greenland and Iceland. Wigeon, which also gather in large numbers at Aberlady, are present in Britain all the year round, though their numbers are boosted in winter by many immigrants from Iceland and northern Russia.

The breeding season brings other visitors to Aberlady's salt-marsh and dunes, including dunlins, redshanks and cormorants. The area is especially noted for its breeding terns, which may be watched safely from well outside the colony, where access is restricted.

Neighbouring Gullane Bay, to the north-east, can be reached from Aberlady by walking along the shore round Gullane Point. This whole area is well worth a look in winter, when red-throated divers, grebes, scoters and long-tailed ducks may be seen. Good views of the mudflats may also be had from the coast road east of Aberlady village.

Access: *unrestricted except to ternery in breeding season.*
Location: *N of Aberlady, off A198.*
Map: *page 313, NT48.*

Acton Scott Working Farm Museum

Shropshire

Expertly laid-out and well established, this farm museum gives an excellent introduction to life on a Shropshire farm in the days when most of the work was done by hand or by horse.

It is based round 22 acres of the home farm of a country estate, and has an authentic farmyard which was first laid out in 1769, though much has been altered since. The various buildings now contain such things as a craft shop and display area; demonstrations of butter- and cheese-making are held in the dairy; farm machinery is kept in the barn; carts, harness and tack are on display in the coach house and tackroom. The pig sty's inhabitants are handsome Tamworth pigs – an ancient breed once in danger of extinction – while equally traditional breeds of cow can be seen in the cow house at milking time. Other creatures here are sheep, chickens, ducks, geese and turkeys – all represented by traditional breeds. The museum's land is cultivated on the old rotation system and grows the crops which were common at the turn of the century. All the ploughing and carting is done by Shire horses.

Open: *Apr to Oct daily. Admission charge. Picnic area. Refreshments. Shop. Suitable for disabled visitors. No dogs.*
Location: *Wenlock Lodge, Acton Scott. 3 miles S of Church Stretton, off A49.*
Map: *page 309, SO48.*

A dung cart at Acton Scott Working Farm Museum

Red Squirrel

Almost always shy and usually elusive, the red squirrel is nonetheless one of Britain's best-loved animals. It spends most of its time among the branches of coniferous trees, but its presence can be detected from a litter of stripped pine cone cores over the forest floor. Red squirrels use tree stumps as tables, and these will be surrounded by the debris of cones and carefully removed scales.

Afan Argoed Country Park

ley to viewpoints on the hills. Serious walkers can tackle the Coed Morgannwg Way which crosses Afan Argoed on its 27-mile route from Craig-y-Llyn, north of Treherbert, to Margam Country Park (see page 176).

Open: *country park all year daily; countryside centre and Welsh Miners' Museum Apr to Oct daily, Nov to Mar weekends pm only. Admission charge for museum and countryside centre. Picnic areas. Refreshments. Shop. Parts suitable for disabled visitors. No dogs.*
Access: *country park by waymarked walks.*
Location: *at Cynonville, on A4107, 6 miles NE of Port Talbot.*
Map: *page 305, SS89.*

Alderley Edge & Nether Alderley Mill

Cheshire

Not least among the attractions of Alderley Edge is its easy accessibility from the great towns surrounding it. Many visitors come here for the splendid views of the Cheshire plain from the 600ft-high wooded sandstone ridge, and the Edge also offers historical interest in plenty. There was a large Neolithic settlement here, and tools, weapons and pottery from the Bronze Age have been uncovered. At the highest point of the Edge a pile of stones marks the site of a medieval beacon which was lit in days gone by to convey important news to those living in the surrounding countryside.

A path leading from the car park near the Wizard Inn is a good introduction to the natural history of this beautiful escarpment. Beyond the 40ft deep gash in the sandstone, known as the Engine Vein, from which 19th-century miners extracted metal ore, is a small plantation of Scots pine and larch. It is often possible to see the crossbill here; its unusual double-hooked beak is a splendid tool for extracting seeds from pine cones. Silver birch and bilberry grow above bracken on the left of the path, with glimpses of the view across the plain through the fine beech trees on the right. Storm Point, the exposed area at the top of the hill, fringed by Scots pines, offers the best views.

A mile away from Alderley Edge stands Nether Alderley cornmill. This picturesque Elizabethan water-mill, built in red sandstone from local quarries, is unusual in that it was constructed beside a small stream which was incapable of operating the mill machinery effectively. The builders had to provide reservoirs above the mill to supply sufficient pressure of water, and the mill was built into the dam across the valley. The present machinery dates from the last century and has recently been restored; flour is occasionally ground for demonstrations.

Open: *Alderley Edge at all times; mill Apr to June and Oct Wed, Sun and bank holiday Mon; July to Sep Tue to Sun and bank holiday Mon; all pm only. Admission charge to mill only. NT.*
Location: *Alderley Edge 4¼ miles NW of Macclesfield on B5087. Mill 1½ miles S of Alderley Edge, on E side of A34.*
Map: *page 309, SJ87.*

Allen Banks

Northumberland

Near the junction of two beautiful Northumbrian rivers, the Allen and the Tyne, the National Trust owns almost 200 acres of hill and riverside scenery, with some pleasant trails and more challenging steeper paths. From the top of the eastern bank is a marvellous view northwards through the trees and across the Tyne valley to Hadrian's Wall. On the way to the top is a small tarn, a favourite haunt for several species of duck. Often a solitary heron may be seen here. Along the ravine-like banks of the Allen, mature beech and oak trees still cling – a reminder, in these days of coniferous forestry, of times when this type of woodland, with its variety and grandeur, was much more common.

Roe deer lurk in the woods; but of more particular interest for naturalists is the red squirrel, which has been retreating from so many parts of the country, but is still to be found at Allen Banks. The once widespread belief that the decline in its numbers was caused by the more recent influx of the grey squirrel has now been largely discounted and it seems likely that the grey is simply more resistant to disease than the native red. It may not always be realised that there are still parts of the British Isles where it is possible, with patience, to see the squirrel of our childhood books.

Open: *at all times. Picnic area. NT.*
Location: *3 miles W of Haydon Bridge, ½ mile S of A69.*
Map: *page 313, NY76.*

Alscott Farm Agricultural Museum

Devon

This working farm is the setting for a varied collection depicting North Devon's agricultural past. Farmer Philip Jenkinson began collecting agricultural machinery shortly after the Second World War, because he saw its potential historical value and wanted to prevent it being scrapped. By now his collection, already extensive but still growing, forms the centrepiece of the displays at Alscott. There are tractors, a fine collection of ploughs, a cider press, craftsmen's tools, even enamelled trade advertisements. The exhibits are housed in the farm buildings, including a barn built of cob – a mud and straw mixture – in the traditional West Country manner.

Open: *Easter to Sep daily, pm only. Admission charge. Shop.*
Location: *at Alscott, near Shebbear, 8 miles NE of Holsworthy.*
Map: *page 305, SS41.*

Alvingham Watermill

Lincolnshire

The historic village of Alvingham is known to have had a watermill for at least 900 years. As long ago as 1155, local squire Hugo de Scroteni is recorded as giving the mill – together with the church and one of his daughters – to the Saint Gilbertine Order at Alvingham Priory. The priory is now gone, but the church survives – as one of two which, unusually, share the same churchyard – and the mill grinds corn to this day.

The present mill building dates from the 17th century and its machinery from 1782, when it was installed by the Maddison family, who had acquired the mill after the priory was dissolved by Henry VIII. The mill was at its busiest in the 18th century, when a windmill was built nearby to provide extra power, and a special light gauge railway track was used to haul corn and meal to and from the canal.

One of the two original pairs of Derbyshire peak millstones is still driven by the 11ft waterwheel, and flour is produced regularly.

Open: *Aug and Sep, Mon, Thu, 2nd and 4th Sun in month, pm only. Picnic area. Shop. No dogs.*
Location: *at Alvingham, 2 miles NE of Louth.*
Map: *page 310, TF39.*

Parts of Alvingham Watermill date from the 17th century

Andover: Finkley Down Farm and Country Park

Hampshire

In these days of intensive, specialised agriculture, farming as a way of life is known to fewer and fewer people. Finkley Down Farm and places like it offer valuable opportunities to experience the working of a farm and make contact with farm animals.

Several rare and many common breeds of farm animal can be seen here, including horses, ponies, cattle, sheep, goats, pigs and poultry. A favourite with children are the pets' corners, where rabbits, chicks, kids and lambs may be fed.

An exhibition of historical farm equipment recalls farming life in earlier days, and provides an interesting contrast with the ever larger machinery to be seen in our fields today. Just to see how farming has changed, look at the patterns of agriculture on your way to and from the farm.

Open: *Apr to Sep daily. Admission charge. Picnic area. Refreshments. Shop. Suitable for disabled visitors.*
Location: *on NE outskirts of Andover. From N ring road (A3093) take Walworth exit and follow signs to farm through Walworth Industrial Estate.*
Map: *page 306, SU34.*

Appleby Castle protects threatened animals and birds

Appleby Castle Conservation Centre

Cumbria

Two experiences are offered for the price of one at Appleby Castle. The first, by reason of solid antiquity, is the Norman castle. Its most imposing component is the great square keep, built in stone in about 1100. Massive defensive works were added next and, although the castle was in ruins by the 16th century, an extensive restoration programme has ensured that the castle remains an exciting pageant of architectural history from Norman to Stuart times.

Since 1977, when the castle grounds were opened to the public for the first time, there has been a steadily growing collection of rare animals and birds here, and Appleby Castle is now a centre of the Rare Breeds Survival Trust. This means that it helps to ensure the survival of creatures which were once common on British farms. Among those which can be seen here are white park cattle, descendants of animals introduced to Britain by the Romans; longhorn cattle, descendants of prehistoric cattle; and several breeds of pigs, sheep and goats, including the very rare Bagot goats, of which fewer than 100 survive. A representative selection of European owls is also kept here, as are a number of other kinds of bird, including cranes, rails, pheasants and poultry. An important part of the Appleby collection are the swans, geese and ducks – here can be seen an exciting mix of the world's most attractive and rar-

est kinds. Of these, among the most endearing are the tree ducks – residents of North America with long legs and charmingly bemused expressions.

Open: *Easter, then May to Sep daily. Admission charge. Picnic area. Refreshments. Shop.*
Location: *in Appleby, at top of Boroughgate.*
Map: *page 313, NY62.*

Argyll Forest Park

Strathclyde

Some 100 square miles of forest, rugged mountain country and sea loch shores on the Cowal peninsula make up this, the most westerly of Scotland's Forest Parks. Easily accessible by road, and well served by numerous footpaths, it is a superb area to explore.

The most scenic approach into the park is via the A83 from Arrochar, which climbs to the famous 'Rest-and-be-Thankful' pass, so named because of the roadside inscription carved by the exhausted soldiers who first built the 860ft road pass in 1750. North of this road towers the rocky, 2891ft summit of The Cobbler, which can be reached by a fine hill walk. To the south, along a minor road, is Loch-goilhead, a popular centre for hill-walking, pony-trekking, sailing, fishing and water-skiing. The park's western side surrounds Loch Eck, a long, narrow loch hemmed in by steep, forested hills. The A815 runs along the eastern shore, then continues past the Younger Botanic Garden, which is spectacular at rhododendron time. Further on the road reaches the head of the Holy Loch, where there is a Forest Office and Kilmun Arboretum, a Forestry Commission collection of trees from all over the world.

The park offers many walks of varying length and difficulty from strenuous hill walks requiring map, compass and stout footwear to short circular forest trails taking no more than half an hour. Many of the walks are waymarked by the Forestry Commission, and 165 miles of forest roads are open to walkers, though not to cars. The two car parks off the A815 south of Loch Eck both offer a choice of waymarked trails – one of which leads to the enchanting Puck's Glen, where many kinds of moss, liverwort and fern thrive on account of the moist atmosphere around the tumbling stream.

The Forest Park is a good area to see red deer, found both on the high mountain slopes and in the

plantations, where they find shelter. Other mammals include foxes, badgers, wildcats and even otters – all more likely to be seen at dusk, when they set out on hunting expeditions, or on summer days, when they spend much of the daytime feeding their young, who sometimes emerge to play in the open. Bird-watchers will encounter typical upland birds such as buzzards, ravens, dippers and ring ouzels – with golden eagles a possibility. The woodlands are home to numerous smaller birds, while on the sea loch shores eiders and red-breasted mergansers are common.

Access: *by public roads, footpaths and forest walks. FC. (Car ferry service all year from Gourock to Dunoon and from McInroys Point, near Gourock, to Hunters Quay.)*
Open: *Younger Botanic Garden Apr to Oct daily. Admission charge. Kilmun Arboretum all year daily.*
Location: *W of Loch Long.*
Map: *page 312, NS20.*

Arlington Court

Devon

Arlington had belonged to the Chichesters for over five and a half centuries when Miss Rosalie Chichester died in 1949. In addition to the house, Miss Chichester left to the National Trust an estate of nearly 3000 acres. Her passionate concern for wildlife led her to ring the estate with an eight-mile-long, high iron fence. The 'magical enclosure of pastures, lakes and hanging woods' within is much as she left it.

The parkland surrounding the house is grazed by a flock of Jacob sheep and a herd of Shetland ponies. The lake is a sanctuary for wildfowl and there is also a lakeside heronry. From the lake a two-mile circular walk passes through beautiful oak woods, and alongside the River Yeo. Over the surrounding steeply wooded valleys which seem almost to merge with the parkland, those masters of the air, the buzzard and the raven, can often be seen performing their aerobatics.

Open: *gardens and park all year daily; house Apr to Oct Sun to Fri, and Sat before bank holiday Mon. Admission charge. Refreshments. Shop. NT.*
Location: *8 miles NE of Barnstaple, off A39.*
Map: *page 305, SS64.*

Arnside Knott

Cumbria

Arnside Knott is a wooded promontory at the point where the River Ken flows into Morecambe Bay. Perhaps most striking is the view from the wooded plateau top. The Cumbrian mountains, Shap, the fells of Bowland, the Lancashire plain with the great expanse of Morecambe Bay and the Irish Sea beyond; all this is the backdrop to the quieter surrounding landscape of limestone hills, wooded valleys and the Gilpin estuary.

For the geologist the Knott has both solid and broken limestone with dry valleys, scoured limestone pavements, glacial erratic

Glen Croe, Argyll Forest Park

boulders and innumerable fossils. A unique feature is the south-facing scree area known as the Shilla slopes. Shilla is the local name for the scree, now thought to contain deposits of fine wind-blown dust known as loess, more usually associated with valleys of rivers like the Rhine and Mississippi.

Many species of flowering plant live on the Knott. In spring, thyme and rock-rose grow on the hills made by the wood ant. In late summer yellow hawk-weed and ragwort contrast with the pink and purple of marjoram and knapweed. Bracken, polypody and hard fern abound, but perhaps the jewels of this botanical collection are the six species of orchid now established on the site. The wealth of shrub and tree species include spindle, with its strange bright pink, four-lobed fruit, juniper, rowan, larch and Scots pine. Three walks have been laid out, all starting from the car park. On the low-level walk visitors may see or hear red squirrels, roe deer, bull-finches, meadow pipits, green woodpeckers, warblers, tits, woodcock and tawny owls. There are also numerous species of butterflies, and at night, the bright green lights of glow-worms can be seen. The high-level walk is perhaps the best for geologists and botanists but, most of all, for visitors wishing to enjoy the outstanding views.

Open: *at all times. NT.*
Location: *1 mile S of Arnside.*
Map: *page 309, SD47.*

Arran, Isle of

Strathclyde

Well known to the people of Glasgow and Strathclyde as a holiday island, Arran is relatively quiet, very attractive and of considerable interest to visiting naturalists.

Brodick Castle

The imposing granite peak of Goat Fell (2866ft) dominates the northern half of the island and is one of the most familiar landmarks in the Firth of Clyde; from its summit, the view is breathtaking, covering the firth itself, with the granite hump of Ailsa Craig prominent to the south, Islay and the Paps of Jura visible to the west, and Ben Lomond and many other high peaks discernible to the north. The southernmost breeding ptarmigans in Britain occur here and the rugged hills inland still hold the elusive golden eagle. Goat Fell is reached from Glen Rosa and, with part of the glen and nearby Cir Mhor (2618ft), is owned by the National Trust for Scotland. Glen Rosa is a good area for red deer and as good a place as any to find a typically northern butterfly, the large heath, which is abundant on the island.

Near the mouth of the glen is Brodick Castle, with its country park and gardens. The castle, ancient seat of the Dukes of Hamilton, is well worth a visit for its fine collection of art treasures, while the garden is internationally renowned for its rhododendrons and azaleas, its rare shrubs and maples and its water and rose gardens. Near the castle is the Arran Nature Centre.

At Rosaburn, on the outskirts of Brodick, is the Isle of Arran Heritage Museum, set in a group of buildings which were originally an 18th-century croft farm. One of the features is the 'smiddy', where a blacksmith's business continued until the late 1960s. Many of the tools on show are original and were made on the premises. The cottage has been refurnished in the style of the 1920s, before electricity had reached the island, and in an annexe at the rear is a display of laundry equipment. The stable block houses a variety of interesting objects and 'bygones', while an open-air display of old farm equipment has been arranged around the coach house.

'The String' – the road across the centre of the island – offers good views of the scenery inland, but for many people the essence of Arran is best captured by following the coast road round the island. From it many of the typical coastal birds can be seen – eiders, red-breasted mergansers and oystercatchers almost anywhere, black guillemots around the southern coast and, with luck, the chance of a peregrine in the quieter, more remote stretches. Red-throated divers occur too, breeding on quiet lochans in the interior and flying down to the sea to feed. With Ailsa Craig so near, gannets are a familiar sight offshore and, in late summer and autumn, the waters around Arran can be good for Manx shearwaters and Arctic skuas. Grey seals are quite common around the coast, and in summer there is always the exciting possibility of seeing basking sharks close inshore.

The island is dotted with interesting prehistoric sites. There are stone circles and Bronze Age burial cairns at Auchagallon and Moss Farm Road, both north of Blackwaterfoot. At the head of Kilmory Water is Carn Ban, a famous Neolithic long cairn, while west of Kilmory near Corriecravie Farm, the remains of a circular Iron Age fort are still discernible.

Open: *Brodick Castle – Easter Sun, then Mon, Wed, Sat during Apr; May to Sep daily; all pm only. Garden and country park daily all year. Admission charge. Refreshments. NTS.*
Arran Nature Centre daily (restricted in winter). Bookshop and craft shop.
Isle of Arran Heritage Museum Easter to Sep, Mon to Fri. Admission charge.
Location: *Firth of Clyde. Reached by ferry from Ardrossan to Brodick pier all year daily, and in summer also from Claonaig to Lochranza pier.*
Map: *page 312, NR93.*

Arundel Wildfowl Trust

West Sussex

Opened in 1976, the newest of the Wildfowl Trust's centres is set in the water meadows of the Arun valley, between Swanbourne Lake and the river. Overlooked by Arundel's magnificent castle, the 55-acre reserve hosts a collection of about 1200 wildfowl from Britain and overseas. The clear, spring-fed pools attract various kinds of diving duck, while the damp meadows and the 'wader scrape' are frequented by birds such as the redshank. The reed beds on the reserve provide nesting places for the water rail, similar in size to the redshank but clearly distinguished, chiefly by its slate-grey underparts. Its call is a distinctive grunting squeal – the commonest clue to its presence, for it is a shy, elusive bird. But the Arundel reserve is well equipped with hides, and patient watchers may be rewarded by the sight of this and various other less common species.

Open: *all year daily (except Christmas). Admission charge. Lecture theatre. Exhibition gallery. Refreshments. Shop. Suitable for disabled visitors. No dogs. WFT.*
Location: *on unclassified road to South Stoke, ½ mile N of Arundel.*
Map: *page 306, TQ00.*

tions – but it is the hills and deep valleys covered with bell heather, bracken, gorse and broom that are the most striking. Today the Forest is the second largest area of southern heath in England. This once common type of habitat has disappeared elsewhere at an astonishing rate under the plough or conifer plantation. Heathlands are now among our most threatened habitats.

Writing during the first half of the 19th century, William Cobbett described Ashdown Forest as 'the most villainously ugly spot I ever saw in England'. Although that landscape has changed little, few of today's visitors would agree: one of the few areas in the south-east that approach wilderness, the Forest is an ideal place to get away from it all. There are plenty of small car parks on the heath to allow visitors to park and walk and from East Grinstead to Groombridge there is the Forest Way, a linear country park along nine-and-a-half miles of old railway line now converted to a footpath, bridleway and cycle track.

Location: *4 miles SE of East Grinstead.*
Map: *page 306, TQ43.*

Ashdown Forest

East Sussex

In the Middle Ages Ashdown Forest covered 15,000 acres, surrounded by a five-foot earth bank (some of which can be seen still) topped by a fence of wooden stakes to deter deer from escaping into the surrounding farmland and poachers from entering the Forest.

The medieval lodges in deep valleys where forest rangers cultivated small parcels of land and encouraged the trees, shrubs and ground cover on which deer feed became sites for mansions during the 17th century. During the Commonwealth attempts were made at enclosure by landowners who wished to improve the land and for the next half century there was a running battle between the improvers and the commoners. Eventually a decree in 1693 fixed 6400 acres of common grazing and determined a landscape that has changed little since.

Throughout the Forest there is diversity – small farms, deciduous woodland, conifer planta-

Ashdown Forest heathland

Ashleworth Tithe Barn

Gloucestershire

This magnificent barn was built about 1500 and is still in use. It has large projecting porch bays with carved wooden lintels, through which carts could (and still do) pass with ease. Inside, the high walls, and the dim light filtering along the barn's 120ft length, contribute to an almost church-like atmosphere. Overhead, the massive stone slate roof is supported by great queenpost timbers – vertical posts connecting the ends of a horizontal beam with the rafters above. The barn stands beside a tiny church, a mid-15th-century house, and the River Severn. Close by is a riverside inn and the remains of an old wharf. Altogether the scene seems to have changed little since crops were first brought to Ashleworth Tithe Barn for storage almost 500 years ago.

Open: *all year daily. Admission charge. No dogs. NT.*
Location: *off A417, 4 miles N of Gloucester, 1½ miles E of Hartpury. On W bank of Severn, SE of Ashleworth village.*
Map: *page 305, SO82.*

Ashley Countryside Collection

Devon

Lincoln Longwool, Whiteface Woodland, Lonk and Badger Face are just four of the 48 different breeds of British sheep which can be seen in this unique collection. Tucked away in an unspoilt part of mid Devon, the farm not only offers the opportunity to see sheep of every shape and size – including all Britain's rare breeds – but also displays a collection of more than 1000 rural bygones, including country craftsmen's tools and workshops and many items connected with the age of the horse and the ox on Britain's farms.

Open: *Easter to early Oct Mon, Wed, Sat and Sun (daily, except Thu, in Aug). Admission charge. Picnic area. Refreshments. Shop. Suitable for disabled visitors.*
Location: *at Ashley, 3 miles SW of Chulmleigh, between B3220 and A377.*
Map: *page 305, SS61.*

Ashridge Estate

Hertfordshire

More than 60 years ago a group of local people campaigned for Ashridge to be spared development. Their success will be appreciated by all who nowadays visit this superb 4000–acre stretch of Chiltern countryside.

Excavations at Ivinghoe Beacon, in the northern part of the estate, have established that man was already clearing the original tree and scrub cover here by about 6000 BC. Much of the land was kept open by sheep-grazing until about 1930. In the last 35 years the National Trust has carried out major replanting, with the intention of producing a characteristic English hardwood forest of beech and oak.

Geologically, Ashridge is divided into two distinct soil types: the chalk of Ivinghoe Beacon, Steps Hill and the steep slopes overlooking Aldbury; and the rest of the estate – a variable mixture known as clay–with–flints.

A fascinating aspect of the estate's natural history is the variation between the chalk downland and the plateau. On the chalk soil, hairy violet, horseshoe vetch, kidney vetch and rockrose flower in early spring, followed by gentians, squinancy-wort, restharrow, twayblade, fairy flax and dropwort. Among the many orchids are the fragrant, bee, frog, spotted and pyramidal. Compared with this variety, the species of the plateau are relatively few. Sheep sorrel, heath bedstraw, harebell and tormentil are present, with large areas of heather and bracken. This is because the tops of the hills have a cap of acid soil which supports few plant species. In the woods grow the familiar bluebell, primrose, bugle and dog's mercury, whilst the fungi found include bracket fungus and the deadly bright red-capped fly agaric.

The downlands are home to various butterflies: the dark green fritillary, the adonis and chalkhill blue; with day-flying moths like the five- and six-spot burnets, the aptly named chimney sweeper and wood tiger. In the woods meadow brown, small heath, speckled wood and gatekeeper are plentiful.

The descendants of the fallow deer which escaped from the deer park in 1926, the shy muntjac, and Chinese water deer are established on the estate. Smaller mammals include the water shrew, and even the edible dormouse, while pipistrelle and long-eared bats fly among the trees at night.

Perhaps the best introduction to the natural wonders of the estate is gained by taking the mile-and-a-half nature walk laid out by the National Trust, which starts and finishes at the Bridgewater Monument.

Open: *at all times. Admission charge. NT (except Ashridge House, toll roads and part of park).*
Location: *3 miles N of Berkhamsted, between A41 and B489, astride B4506.*
Map: *page 306, SP91.*

Aston Rowant

Oxfordshire & Buckinghamshire

Aston Rowant is a spectacular National Nature Reserve typical of the Chilterns, with their extensive beech woodlands, mixed scrub and scattered areas of juniper scrub among chalk grasslands. Much of the reserve is on an attractive stretch of the Chiltern escarpment, with impressive views over the Oxfordshire plain. The woodlands extend on to the plateau above the scarp where they continue well outside the reserve into the Chilterns Area of Outstanding Natural Beauty.

One of the Nature Conservancy Council's main objectives at Aston Rowant is to conserve the intricate mixture of different habitats. The grasslands are grazed by sheep on a variable rotation to maintain a variety of structure from close-grazed turf, which favours some of the more spectacular plants, to longer more tussocky grasslands, suitable for the many species of chalk downland butterflies and other insects.

The mixed scrub contains dogwood, hawthorn, blackthorn, spindle, privet, juniper, buckthorn and bramble with beech, yew, wayfaring tree and whitebeam pushing through the scrub canopy. Such diversity is ideal for birds and insects and the juniper has a specialised and rare collection of invertebrates associated with it. Warblers and nightingales abound in summer, and sparrowhawks and kestrels are frequently seen hunting over the reserve. Among the many plants which thrive on the variety of chalky soils are wild candytuft, salad burnet, rock-rose, wild thyme and the rare Chiltern gentian. The woods contain several unusual plants characteristic of the Chilterns such as the violet helleborine, large white hel-

Downland at Ashridge Estate

leborine and wood barley. The many butterflies to be seen on the reserve include the chalkhill blue, common blue, marbled white, brown argus and meadow brown.

Open: *at all times. No dogs. NCC.*
Access: *restricted to waymarked nature trails, except by special permit.*
Location: *S of A40 between Stokenchurch and Lewknor.*
Map: *page 306, SU79.*

Attenborough
Nottinghamshire

This chain of artificial lakes has been created by gravel-digging in the flood plain of the River Trent. Under the joint management of the owners and the Nottinghamshire Trust for Nature Conservation, they form an area rich in animal and plant life.

Large stretches of open water with fringing marshes and willow can attract breeding birds including grasshopper, reed and sedge warblers, greater spotted woodpeckers and kestrels whilst common terns nest on sheltered islands. In some years they are accompanied by a pair of garganey ducks which are among Britain's rarer breeding birds. They migrate from Africa to Europe each year, and a few, perhaps originally bound for Scandinavia, nest in Britain. In winter other ducks are more abundant, including large numbers of mallards, pochards and tufted ducks and occasional shelducks and shovelers.

The lake margins produce a continuous display of colour from the brilliant yellows of marsh–marigold and yellow iris in spring and early summer to the more varied shades of hemp agrimony, water mint, meadowsweet, purple loosestrife and ragged–robin later in the year. To these can be added the multi colours of several species of dragonfly crossing and recrossing the green space or settling on the waterside vegetation. Away from the water's edge patches of herb-rich old grassland with yellow rattle, great burnet and meadow cranesbill are alive with butterflies on sunny days.

Open: *at all times. CNT.*
Access: *by footpaths only.*
Location: *6 miles SW of Nottingham off A6005 Long Eaton road.*
Map: *page 310, SK53.*

Auchindrain Museum of Country Life
Strathclyde

This unique museum is a complete community, whose history can be traced back with certainty for 500 years and probably stretches back 500 years before that. Auchindrain was one of the last communal-tenancy farms, where several families grouped together to run one farm, sharing the hard work, the tools and buildings, and the rewards. All the members had a part to play in the family unit, and were looked after when the need arose. Indeed, one of the houses here was specially built for the aged and the poor; but with a very different atmosphere from that of the dreaded 'poor house'. There are about 20 buildings at Auchindrain, some nearly 300 years old. Some have been restored and contain authentic furniture and other exhibits, some are in the process of being restored, and some are ruined. Round the buildings, the community fields are mostly still cultivated by traditional methods, and support traditional crops and livestock.

Open: *Easter to Sep daily (except Sat in Apr, May and Sep).*
Admission charge. Picnic area. Shop. Suitable for disabled visitors.
Location: *on A83, 6 miles SW of Inveraray.*
Map: *page 312, NN00.*

Fragrant Orchid

Downland, chalk pits and unploughed fields are typical habitats for this orchid. The flowers, which first appear in June, can vary in colour from white through to reddish purple. The scent which gives the plant its name can also vary, sometimes being clove-like, sometimes spicy, and, in a variety found in the Outer Hebrides, rubbery.

Avebury

Wiltshire

Avebury is best known as the site of Britain's largest 'henge' monument. This spectacular stone circle was constructed about 2000 BC by the Beaker people, settlers from the Low Countries, whose name is derived from the distinctive pottery they made.

A massive outer bank of chalk surrounds a vast ditch once 30ft deep but now partially silted up. Entrance to the central area, an astonishing 360yd in diameter, was by one of the four openings cut through the bank. Close to the inner lip of the ditch was the great outer circle of nearly one hundred standing stones. Two smaller circles are enclosed within the great circle.

The stones are of sarsen, a hard sandstone, hauled from the nearby Marlborough Downs. They seem likely to have been chosen for their natural shape – either a tall, thin pillar or a squat diamond. Sadly, many of the stones were knocked over and buried during the Middle Ages, and from the end of the 17th century until as recently as 1925, stones were broken up for use on roads, or as building materials.

Today, concrete posts mark the positions of the missing stones.

Windmill Hill, one and a half miles to the north west, is a famous Neolithic causewayed camp. Estimated to have been settled in 2570 BC by Stone Age farmers from France, the low hill is crowned by three roughly concentric circles. Although unlikely to have been a permanent settlement, the site has yielded much domestic equipment: flint axes, knives, stone querns for milling flour, and the simple deep, round-bottomed vessels known as Windmill Hill pottery.

The Great Barn in Avebury village is a fine thatched building, with a splendid roof structure, surviving from the 17th century and built within the prehistoric stone circle. It houses a museum of Wiltshire folk life, and contains displays on cheesemaking, thatching, saddlery, sheep and shepherds, the work of blacksmiths and wheelwrights and other rural crafts. Regular craft demonstrations and folk dancing are further attractions.

The whole area is rich in ancient monuments, with classic sites such as the Wansdyke, the Ridgeway, the extraordinary mound of Silbury Hill (rich in chalk grassland plants), the West Kennet Long Barrow, and numerous tumuli, barrows, field systems, camps and earthworks.

Avebury – the spiritual centre of Neolithic Britain

Downland flowers, birds and butterflies abound throughout the area, and there are many good walks along bridleways and roads used as public paths.

For those who love to explore the past, or who like a focal point for walks over the quiet downs, Avebury has few equals. It has an air of serene strength, as if secure in the knowledge that it will remain an enigma.

Open: *Avebury Circle and Windmill Hill all year. NT. Great Barn Museum Apr to Oct daily, and most weekends at other times. Admission charge. Refreshments. Shop. Suitable for disabled visitors.*
Location: *6 miles W of Marlborough, off A361.*
Map: *page 305, SU17.*

Avon Gorge & Leigh Woods

Avon

Just across the Clifton Suspension Bridge from Bristol, this woodland reserve offers some fascinating and delightful walks. Most of the trees are common deciduous varieties – chiefly oak – but a true rarity to be found here is the Bristol whitebeam,

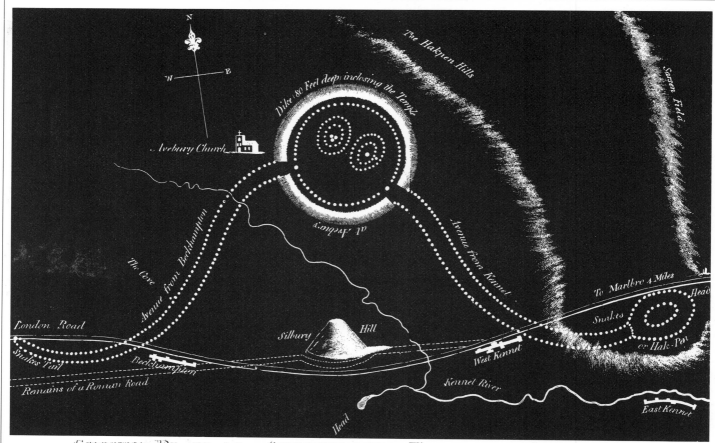

GROUND PLAN of the SERPENTINE TEMPLE at AVEBURY,

The Avon Gorge, rich in plants

which grows nowhere else in the world. In summer especially, the varied tree cover of these woods is home to a great variety of woodland birds. Alert visitors may see or hear woodpeckers and nightingales; part of Leigh Woods is known as 'Nightingale Valley'. The limestone soils, as well as being rich in fossils, encourage many kinds of woodland wild flowers, and other interesting plants grow on the ledges of the cliffs which plunge almost 300ft to the River Avon. The unusual conditions here suit certain very localised species which have attracted botanists for hundreds of years. Between March and May, look out for the sparse, creamy-white flowers of the Bristol rock-cress on their erect purple stems. Other plants which may be seen here include the wild wallflower and the delicate blue autumn squill, which flowers from August to October. The reserve is famous for its fungi, and 110 kinds of moss and liverwort have been recorded here.

For many visitors, pleasure in the reserve is heightened by glimpses of the river far below, with tiny boats bobbing on its surface: heightened too by that masterpiece of bridge-building, the Suspension Bridge, and the knowledge that the very different world of modern Bristol begins a few yards across the river.

Open: *at all times; please keep to footpaths. NCC/NT.*
Location: *on left bank of R. Avon, beside Clifton Suspension Bridge. Entrance off A369, ¼ mile SE of Abbots Leigh.*
Map: *page 305, ST57.*

Avon Valley Woods

Devon

This steep-sided, wooded valley is situated in the heart of the South Hams area of South Devon. The 100 acres of woods extend for almost two miles along the east side of the valley and are owned by the Woodland Trust, a voluntary body dedicated to conserving our native woodlands. They consist of Woodleigh, Titcombe and Bedlime Woods, which together make up one of the largest blocks of broadleaved woodland in the area. The wide variety of trees provides a diverse habitat for birds; typical woodland species found here include nuthatch, treecreeper and great spotted woodpecker. The trees are a rich source of the grubs and insects which these species need – especially in summer, when they are feeding their young.

The River Avon winds through the valley and just to the north of Bedlime Wood is Topsham Bridge, a good spot to watch for dippers – charming chocolate-coloured birds with cream chests – feeding amid the rocks in the swirling river.

Open: *at all times. WLT.*
Access: *by footpath from S end of Woodleigh Wood, near former Loddiswell station.*
Location: *2¼ miles N of Kingsbridge off unclassified Loddiswell road.*
Map: *page 305, SX74.*

Axe Estuary

Devon

This estuary has a shingle bar across its mouth. The small sea-side resort of Seaton is on its western shore, whilst just upstream, on its east bank, lies the village of Axmouth. There are low-lying meadows and reed-marsh on the west side so the best views over the estuary are from the east bank.

Birds on the estuary usually represent a good variety of species, and although their numbers are not usually very great, they can be seen at close range. Curlew, redshank and dunlin are the commonest wading birds, whilst a few shelduck are often to be seen. At migration times there are normally parties of swallows and house martins circling over the fields and scarcer migrants are always a possibility.

From Seaton a tramway runs parallel with the west side of the river. A ride on its open upper deck provides a pleasant way to see this lovely estuary.

Access: *from Axmouth or behind Seaton beach.*
Location: *off B3172 Axmouth to Seaton road.*
Map: *page 305, SY29.*

January

STRAW BEAR FESTIVAL

Whittlesey, Cambridgeshire

In the fenland area on the borders of Huntingdonshire and Cambridgeshire, the day after Plough Monday was known as 'Straw Bear Tuesday' or 'Strawbower Day'. Its name originated in an ancient ceremony said to recall pagan fertility rites associated with the start of spring ploughing.

A version of these rites was revived by the Whittlesey Society in the late 1970s and has continued as an annual event. It entails a man dressed in a straw-covered costume dancing in the streets and outside the village inns, accompanied by at least two teams of Morris dancers, a sword dance team and a 'Molly Dance' team. The festival starts on the Friday night with a lively get-together, then a procession starts at 10.30am on the Saturday in the market square and makes its way round the town. The celebrations continue in the evening with dancing and merrymaking.

When: *Fri and Sat before Plough Monday (Mon after Twelfth Night).*
Map: *page 306, TL29.*

HAXEY HOOD GAME

Haxey, Humberside

Local legend has it that this unique game originated in the 13th century when Lady de Mowbray, then Lady of the Manor, lost her scarlet hood, which was blown away by the wind. This was retrieved with some difficulty by 12 labourers and as a reward she donated to the parish a piece of land, known as Hoodlands, the rent for which was to be used to pay for a leather 'hood' to be contested for annually.

The main players are the 'Boggans' and the Fool, who leads a procession. The contest starts at 3pm with a procession of players to the green, where the Fool welcomes all present and invites them to join the game. The game itself vaguely resembles rugby football, with several minor canvas hoods and one main leather hood, called the Sway Hood, taking the place of the ball. The object of the game is to get the hood, which is thrown in the air by the King Boggan, across the field boundary by eluding not only the other players but also the Boggans. Their aim is to prevent this happening and to touch the hood, making it 'dead' and so necessitating a restart to the game. A player who succeeds in crossing the boundary with a hood keeps it as his prize. After the minor hoods have been disposed of in this way the Sway Hood is tossed into the air and a free-for-all then takes place during which the hood is pushed, pulled and dragged to one of three local inns by the combatant factions. The hood remains at the winners' inn until the next contest.

When: *6 Jan or, if this is a Sun, 5 Jan.*
Map: *page 310, SK79.*

Struggling for the 'hood' during the Haxey Hood Game

PLOUGH STOTS SERVICE

Goathland, North Yorkshire

This event is held on Plough Monday, the first Monday after the Twelve Days of Christmas, so named because it was the day when work on the farms officially resumed, and marked the start of the spring ploughing. Its origins are based on an old tradition where a richly decorated plough was dragged round the villages by young men known as the Plough Stots, 'stot' being a name for a young bullock. The Plough Stots demanded donations of money or in kind from the villagers. Those who refused were liable to have their ground roughly ploughed up as a mark of their meanness.

The present-day version of this event starts in Goathland Parish Church where a service and blessing is held. Then three sets of dancers dressed in either pink or blue uniforms and with 30-inch steel swords perform a traditional long-sword dance. This colourful dancing is of Scandinavian origin and was probably brought to this part of Yorkshire by the Norsemen more than 1000 years ago.

When: *first Mon after 6 Jan.*
Map: *page 310, NZ80.*

BURNING OF THE CLAVIE

Burghead, Grampian

This spectacular ceremony may have its origins in a fire festival brought here by Norsemen. At one time a similar event took place in other Moray Firth fishing villages, but now only this one survives. Its purpose is to drive out evil spirits from the previous year.

The Clavie, or torch, is made by three or four local men. A whisky barrel is sawn in half, one half being broken up for fuel, the other used to contain the fire. This is then supported by a salmon-fisher's stake, known as the 'Spoke'. The 'Clavie Crew' carry the Clavie to Salmon Green where it is lit by a burning peat from a nearby house. Tar is poured on to fuel the flames. The procession then begins, tracing the boundaries of the old town. The Clavie is carried by each member of the 'Clavie Crew' for only a short time because of its weight and heat; it is considered to be a very bad omen should its bearer stumble or fall. Every so often the procession stops to offer firebrands as a sign of good luck to householders and passers-by.

The procession ends at a mound on the headland called Doonie Hill where the Spoke is fitted into a stone pillar. The Clavie is left to burn out and its charred remains can be seen throughout the year.

When: *11 Jan.*
Map: *page 315, NJ16.*

WASSAILING THE APPLE TREES

Carhampton, Somerset

The ancient custom of wassailing orchards used to be widespread in the fruit-growing and cider-making districts of southern and western England. It originated from ceremonies intended to protect the trees from evil spirits which might harm the apple crops. It

An artist's delightful vision of Wassailing the Apple Trees

is rarely performed today, but a version of the rite still takes place in the grounds of the Butchers Arms public house in the village of Carhampton on the evening of the Old Twelfth Night.

The ceremony begins with the local people gathering round an apple tree, then, as an offering, cider is poured on its roots and cider-soaked toast is placed in its branches. An incantation is then sung: 'Old apple tree, old apple tree, We've come to wassail thee–'. When the toasts and singing are over, shots are fired through the branches and over the tree. The object is to make enough noise to drive away the evil spirits and awake the tree from its winter slumber.

When: *17 Jan.*
Map: *page 305, ST04.*

UP-HELLY-AA

Lerwick, Shetland

The origins of this colourful occasion go back to the Viking Yule, a major festival of the pre-Christian era on the Shetlands. The custom has taken its present form – the ceremonial burning of a replica Norse galley – for about 100 years.

The preparations for the festival start months beforehand with the building of the longship. On the morning of Up-Helly-Aa day the longship is escorted through the streets of Lerwick by squads of 'guisers' dressed in magnificent Viking costumes.

At about 7pm, the leader, Guiser Jarl, and his squads muster the main procession at the town hall. A signal is fired to light up the torches – as many as 800, making a spectacular sight in the winter darkness. To the strains of the Up-Helly-Aa song the torch-bearers wend their way through the streets to the quayside, where the guisers surround the longship. They give three cheers, a bugle sounds, and on the last note the burning torches are thrown into the ship. During the ensuing blaze 'The Norseman's Home Song' is sung and, amid much cheering and noise, ships in the harbour sound their sirens in salute. When the flames have abated a night of revels begins.

When: *last Tue in Jan.*
Map: *page 315 for ferry to Lerwick.*

Balmacara

Highland

This huge estate surrounds Kyle of Lochalsh, best known as the main ferry port for the Isle of Skye. Balmacara's 5616 largely untamed acres occupy most of a peninsula between Loch Carron and Loch Alsh, on Scotland's dramatic north-west coast. Balmacara, however, is not dominated by the spectacular mountain peaks often associated with this area. Its network of little roads threads a landscape of low hills, moorland scrub and woodland, nearly always within sight of water. The countryside is punctuated by numerous small lochs or 'lochans', and there are views across broad sea lochs or narrow straits to wild Applecross and to the islands of Skye, Scalpay and Raasay, taking in dozens of small rocky islets.

In the north of the peninsula, a steep hill called Creag nan Garadh gives superb views over Plockton, an attractive coastal village so called because of the odd-shaped peninsula or 'plock' of land on which it sits. This former trading port is now a popular destination for artists and for holidaymakers, who rent cottages here and sail their small boats in the sheltered bay.

The woodlands of Balmacara open to the public include the delightful woodland garden of Lochalsh House in the south.

The house itself is not open to the public, but the garden offers pleasant walks and there is a natural history display in the coach house.

Open: *Lochalsh Woodland Garden all year daily. Admission charge. Coach house Easter to Oct daily. NTS.*
Location: *off A87 Kyle of Lochalsh road.*
Map: *page 314, NG72.*

Bardsea Country Park

Cumbria

Overlooking the great expanse of Morecambe Bay, this strip of the Cumbrian coast combines woodland walks with fine coastal birdwatching country. Morecambe Bay, which has around 100 square miles of tidal sands, is internationally famous for its huge population of wading birds and wildfowl. The best times are in winter, when thousands of birds from northern Europe and Russia move here to feed, or in early spring and early autumn, when migrant birds pass through. Look out for large numbers of curlews, with their down-curving bill and haunting cry, and oystercatchers, with their black-and-white plumage and bright orange bill and legs.

At the south end of the country park is Sea Wood, 60 acres of mixed woodland notable for its spring flowers and wild cherry

trees. About a mile to the north of the country park is Conishead Priory, whose grounds offer three different nature trails.

Open: *all year daily. Picnic area. Car park in Cooper Lane. (Conishead Priory nature trails open Easter to Sep, Sat and Sun pm.)*
Location: *2 miles S of Ulverston on A5087.*
Map: *page 309, SD37.*

Barnwell Country Park

Northamptonshire

Not all the scars that man makes on a landscape remain there. The excavation of sand and gravel is messy, and the raw-edged pits it leaves behind are frankly ugly. But before long the natural growth of water plants and willows softens the margins and the eventual result can be very attractive. Such is the case in this small country park.

The open water is deep and holds several species of fish; these are fed on by various birds. Great crested grebes swim and dive, common terns plunge into the water from the air, whilst herons use their long legs to wade, and kingfishers perch on branches over shallow water before diving in. Each species is built and adapted for its own special way of hunting. Man however, is a clever enough animal to change

Wild and lonely Highland scenery at Balmacara

the habitat to suit himself. Human fishermen, including the disabled, have specially constructed angling stages at Barnwell.

Plants, like animals, tend to specialise. The open water here has white water lilies and the pretty pink spikes of the amphibious bistort. At the margins are reed and reed-mace (whose velvety brown heads are often called bulrushes). In damp areas grow water mint and meadowsweet, while species such as clover and cranesbill prefer the drier areas.

Open: *all year. Picnic areas.*
Location: *on A605, ¼ mile S of Oundle.*
Map: *page 306, TL08.*

Bass Rock

Lothian

This steep-sided islet has served, in its time, as hermitage, prison and fortress, performing all three functions most effectively on account of its inaccessibility. Although it is only one-and-a-half miles offshore, its formidable 350ft cliffs have always protected it from intruders, making the island an ideal nesting site for seabirds.

Especially famous is Bass Rock's colony of gannets,

amounting to anything up to 9000 nesting pairs. These large, stoutly built birds are mainly white and are fascinating to watch. They feed by plunge-diving for fish, plummeting head-first into the sea, often from as high as 100ft, then swallowing their prey greedily. Much of the parent birds' food is regurgitated to feed their chicks, who eat so heartily that they are usually heavier than their parents by the time they are fledged, and are obliged to lose weight before they can take off. Gannets are extremely aggressive, noisy birds, and in summer the air around Bass Rock is filled not only with the noise of their constant squabbling but also by the piercing cries of the many other seabirds who make their homes on the rock, including guillemots, kittiwakes and razorbills.

Access: boat trips round the island operate from North Berwick between Apr and Sep daily, weather permitting.
Location: Firth of Forth, 3 miles NE of North Berwick.
Map: page 313, NT68.

Beachy Head

East Sussex

At Beachy Head the South Downs meet the English Channel. With a height of 575ft, the headland makes a very good viewing point out to sea, along the coast east towards Hastings and west towards Brighton, and inland to the South Downs and the Weald. It is a favourite haunt of romantics for its views, of suicides because of its height, and of birdwatchers to whom its prominent position gives the opportunity to watch seabirds moving up and down the Channel, and to study the migration of birds like swallows, warblers and flycatchers.

Its prominence made it a shipping hazard and in 1831 the Belle Toute Lighthouse was built here. This does not seem to have been entirely successful because in 1853 the East Indiaman *Dalhousie* was wrecked with a total loss of crew. This so moved the Rev. Darby, Vicar of East Dean, that he had a cave cut at the foot of the cliffs so that shipwrecked mariners had a refuge above sea level.

A new lighthouse, 142ft high, was built offshore in 1902.

There are car parks and viewpoints around the Head, and the South Downs Way long-distance footpath (see page 261) follows the clifftop. Other footpaths can be followed inland.

Location: S of A259 between Seaford and Eastbourne.
Map: page 306, TV59.

Beacon Fell Country Park

Lancashire

The distant mountains of Snowdonia, the Ribble Estuary and Blackpool Tower all feature in the panoramic views to be had in clear weather from the 873ft summit at the centre of this country park, set on the western edge of the Forest of Bowland. There was a beacon on the fell as long ago as AD 1002, and for many centuries this site remained part of the chain of beacons built in prominent places and lit to warn of impending danger such as the approach of the Spanish Armada.

It is known that, many centuries earlier, Beacon Fell provided summer grazing for the Vikings' sheep, and farmers continued to eke out a living on its poor soil until the 1930s. Today the area consists mainly of coniferous forest and open moorland, with boggy hollows here and there betrayed by clumps of rushes and the nodding white, fluffy heads of cotton grass. Sphagnum moss also thrives in these places. Bird life includes skylarks and meadow pipits, familiar inhabitants of the open moorland. Footpaths criss-cross the moor and woodlands, and a scenic drive runs right round the perimeter of the park.

Open: at all times. Information centre open daily (situated ¼ mile off the fell, but well signposted). Picnic area. Refreshments at information centre at weekends and most weekday afternoons in summer.
Location: 8 miles N of Preston, 5 miles from A6 on unclassified road.
Map: page 309, SD54.

Wild carrot and knapweed on the cliffs above Beachy Head lighthouse

Beamish: North of England Open-Air Museum

Co. Durham

Set in 200 acres of rolling countryside and woodland, this remarkable museum paints a vivid picture of what life was like in the North of England more than half a century ago. Old buildings are being brought together from all over the north and reconstructed at Beamish, complete with the appropriate furniture or machinery.

The variety is remarkable. From the 19th-century Rowley Station, complete with ladies' waiting room, booking office and wrought-iron footbridge, visitors can take a short ride on a train drawn by an old NER class 'C' locomotive. From the colliery yard a replica of George Stephenson's *Locomotion* hauls wagons across the site, while at the heart of the colliery is a steam winder in its tall stone engine house, the only survivor of a type of engine that was once common in the northern coalfield. In addition there is a row of fully furnished pit cottages, with bread being baked, and coal fires burning.

At the top of the hill stands the Home Farm with pigs, shorthorn cows, ducks, geese and hens, and exhibitions on old farming life.

Open: *all year daily (except Mon, mid-Sep to Easter). Admission charge. Picnic area. Refreshments. Shop.*
Location: *1 mile NE of Stanley off A6076 or A693.*
Map: *page 310, NZ25.*

Beaulieu River

Hampshire

The Beaulieu River drains water from the bogs and heaths of the eastern part of the New Forest and empties into the Solent at Needs Ore Point, between the large Beaulieu and Exbury estates. The river passes through wet alder woods to the north of the village of Beaulieu before it opens out into a wide tidal pool with fringing reedbeds. Behind the alder, on dryer ground, are oakwoods. This great diversity of habitat supports many species of bird, with nuthatches, treecreepers and woodpeckers being seen at the same time as ducks, gulls, coots and moorhens, whilst reed and other species of warbler can be seen in the reedbeds and scrubby habitats during the summer months.

Below the pool and Beaulieu village, the river widens dramatically and, especially at low tide, several species of wading bird may be seen on the mudflats. There is a footpath from the south of the village to Bucklers Hard, from which there are excellent views of the river with its well-wooded shoreline on the east bank. Areas of salt marsh occur on the flat land between the

Bucklers Hard – a good place to begin an exploration of the Beaulieu River

loops of the meanders; here ringed plovers, redshanks, spotted redshanks and curlews may be seen.

Much of the Beaulieu River forms part of the large North Solent National Nature Reserve. The reserve is important for its extensive salt marshes and large nesting colonies of seabirds. The colony of black-headed gulls is the largest in Britain and there are extensive colonies of little, common and sandwich terns. In the autumn and winter there are many species of duck in the area, as well as large numbers of dark-bellied brent geese. On the coastal stretches of the river larger waders such as oystercatchers, godwits and curlews are frequently seen.

Access: *footpath from Beaulieu village to Bucklers Hard. A network of lanes on both sides of the river gives good views of the countryside and the Solent. Permits for bird sanctuary at Needs Ore obtainable from Beaulieu Estate Office. Part NCC.*
Location: *E part of New Forest. Can be reached from Lyndhurst along B3056 to Beaulieu.*
Map: *page 306, SU04.*

Bedgebury Pinetum

Kent

Part of Bedgebury Forest, in the heart of the Kentish Weald, this 100-acre conifer garden is one of Britain's main tree collections. Managed by the Forestry Commission, it was established in 1924. Some of the largest trees seen at Bedgebury today, reaching 100ft or more, were planted the following year – a living demonstration of the rapid growth of many coniferous species, which makes them so popular in modern commercial forestry.

The collection at Bedgebury includes not only the familiar forestry plantation species but many ornamental conifers, as well as slow-growing, and increasingly rare, native conifers like yew and juniper. Altogether more than 200 species of conifer have been planted at Bedgebury, and the collection represents all the temperate regions of the world. Some of the trees seem to have survived against all odds; although most conifers like the poor, acid soils found here, many do not like the severe frosts to which this area is prone. The worst was in January 1940, when an astounding 47 degrees of frost wiped out all but three of the

Oystercatcher

With bright orange bills and feet, and bold black and white plumage, oystercatchers are among our most readily identified waders. They are common round the coast at all times, and it is unusual not to see one or two, at least, probing the mud of estuaries and salt marshes for food. They eat shellfish, but will also take crabs, worms and even the eggs and young of other birds. The oystercatcher gives itself away even when not seen – its 'kleep, kleep, kleep' call is unmistakable.

Pinetum's cypresses. A continual winter planting programme ensures that younger trees will always take the place of older specimens which die from frost, wind or drought damage, disease or simply old age.

Open: *all year daily. Refreshments available at weekends Apr to Oct.*
Location: *3 miles S of Goudhurst on B2079.*
Map: *page 306, TQ73.*

Beecraigs Country Park

Lothian

Good walking country, fine views and plenty to interest the birdwatcher will all be found in this country park in the Bathgate Hills, south of the historic town of Linlithgow. The park was established in an area of old Forestry Commission plantations, the haunt of roe deer, foxes and badgers. The woodland is crisscrossed by various trails. One leads to Goat Fell, from where there are panoramic views eastwards to Bass Rock (see pages 22–3) and north-west to Ben Mor and Ben Vorlich.

At the park's western end is Beecraigs Reservoir, where waterfowl are plentiful, especially in winter. Great crested grebes, teal, pochard and goldeneye are among the birds which can be watched from the observation hides here. The reservoir is stocked with trout from the adjacent fish farm; day permits for fishing are available, and the trout farm is sometimes open to visitors. Close by is a deer farm, where a viewing platform and pedestrian walkway provide good views of the red deer which are kept here. The park also offers orienteering, rock climbing, pony trekking and archery, while the reservoir is used for courses in canoeing and sailing.

Open: *country park at all times. Park centre (at Whitebaulks) daily in summer, closed Tue and Sat in winter. Trout farm open Sun. Picnic area.*
Location: *S of Linlithgow, off unclassified road from Linlithgow to Bathgate.*
Map: *page 313, NT07.*

Beinn Eighe National Nature Reserve

Highland

Established in 1951 as Britain's first National Nature Reserve, Beinn Eighe covers more than 10,500 acres of superb mountain and moorland country. It was set up mainly to preserve important relics of the Old Caledonian pine forest, which once covered large areas of the Highlands.

Visitors to Beinn Eighe will be lucky to see the rare and largely nocturnal pine martens and wildcats which live here, but red and roe deer are more easily seen, and by spending a little time in the area you could encounter many of the birds for which the area is famous – black-throated divers, buzzards, peregrines, golden eagles, dippers, ring ouzels, crossbills and siskins are among those to watch for. The woodlands, the best of which are on the shores of Loch Maree, are composed principally of pine and birch. The poor soils do not support a rich flora, but in some areas where minerals have washed out of the rocks, a variety of flowers grow. On the slopes above the tree line, dwarf species of such plants as juniper can be found, while on the exposed summits flowers such as mossy saxifrage, moss campion and Arctic mouse-ear are survivors of an alpine flora that became established during the Ice Ages.

Access: *restricted in autumn. Visitor centre. Car park with picnic area and two nature trails, beside Loch Maree. No dogs. NCC.*
Location: *off A832, 1 mile NW of Kinlochewe.*
Map: *page 314, NH06.*

Beltring: Whitbread Hop Farm

Kent

Before Flemish traders brought the hop to England in the late 15th century, there were no oast-houses in Kent. Today there are fewer than there were, but oast-houses are still synonymous with Kent and the brewing industry.

Oast-houses are kilns; similar to the pottery kilns of Staffordshire but with the distinctive white cowl on the top. The hops are dried high in the kiln, above a furnace, the vane on the cowl ensuring good ventilation. The hops give beer its bitter taste; help it to clear and keep longer.

The Whitbread Hop Farm is the largest oast and galleried barn complex in Britain. Here, during the hop-picking season from September to mid-October, visitors can see the drying process, then watch the hand-operated hop presses. The methods used

Specimen trees at Bedgebury Pinetum

are traditional, and elsewhere in the long galleried barns can be seen artefacts from an earlier age of hop-farming.

Other barns house a collection of bygones: the tools of blacksmith and wheelwright; dairy equipment; and a country crafts centre where locally made pottery, weaving and other crafts are exhibited.

Outside is a picnic area with a playground. Children will also love the Whitbread Shire horses who either are in permanent retirement or come for a well-earned rest at certain times. Other farm animals can be seen at close quarters and there is plentiful bird life along the banks of the Medway. For the angler there are well-stocked coarse fishing ponds.

Open: *Apr to Oct daily except Mon (but open bank holiday Mon). Admission charge. Picnic area. Refreshments. Shop.*
Location: *at Beltring on W side of B2015 near its junction with B2160, 1¼ miles N of Paddock Wood.*
Map: *page 306, TQ64.*

Ben Lawers

Tayside

On a clear day, it is possible to see both the North Sea and the Atlantic from the 3984ft summit of Ben Lawers. The mountain is one of the most notable botanical sites in Britain, particularly rich in alpine plants. These were already established on the mountain by the Ice Ages, and are mainly confined to the highest and most inaccessible parts of Britain. Ben Lawers has a wide variety of habitats – grassland, wet flushes and rock faces – and lime-rich as well as acidic soils. This diversity has led to a marvellous mixture of flowering, plants, mosses and lichens developing on the mountain. Perhaps the best time to visit is during June and July when the grasslands are bright with the flowers of such plants as moss campion, alpine mouse-ear chickweed and several kinds of saxifrage. Birds likely to be seen include buzzards, kestrels, red grouse, golden plovers, meadow pipits, wheatears and curlews. A large area of the mountain has been in the care of the National Trust for Scotland since 1950 and is managed jointly by the Trust and the Nature Conservancy Council as a National Nature Reserve. The imaginative visitor centre was opened in 1972 and contains interesting geological, natural history and historical displays. Various information leaflets are available here. There is also a nature trail, and guided walks are available in summer.

Open: *visitor centre Easter to Sep daily. Admission charge. NCC/NTS.*
Location: *4 miles NE of Killin, off A827 N of Loch Tay.*
Map: *page 313, NN63.*

Ben Lawers – one of the richest botanical sites in Britain

Bernwood Forest

Oxfordshire

Bernwood Forest is part of a formerly much bigger forest which once covered large tracts of southern central England. In the Middle Ages the forest was claimed by the King as a Royal Hunting Forest. The hunt was more important than timber in the early days, but later wood was produced for building and the smaller material taken for firewood. During the Second World War the wood was almost completely cleared and no replanting was done until the Forestry Commission selected the better trees, cleared much of the remaining bramble, sallow, blackthorn, hazel and birch, and then replanted with oak and Norway spruce. It is because of its location in England and the fact that, for many periods in its history, the wood has had an open character, that it has retained a great diversity of insect life and its collection of butterflies is one of the best in Britain. The best time to visit is on a warm, sunny, windless day in summer when many of the species will be seen, including, if you are lucky, some of our rarest and most spectacular species such as purple emperor, black hairstreak, white admiral, fritillaries, skippers and blues. Over 40 species of butterfly have been recorded in Bernwood Forest in a single year. Much research into insects is carried out in the wood, and collecting is not allowed. The Forestry Commission, in agreement with the Nature Conservancy Council, manage the rides and several extensive areas to protect and encourage butterflies.

Access: *woodland rides open on most days. Some restrictions during shooting. FC/NCC.*
Location: *5 miles E of Oxford on unclassified road between Stanton St John and Boarstall.*
Map: *page 306, SP61.*

Berry Head Country Park

Devon

Set on a dramatic headland, Berry Head Country Park consists of a flat, grassy plateau and extensive cliff and cave systems. The plateau is of special interest and value for its limestone-loving wild flowers such as rock-rose and orchids, some of which are rare. It is partly in order to protect these that Torbay Borough Council has designated the area a local nature reserve. Many species of bird use the plateau as a temporary resting place during migration, while wrens, linnets and stonechats are among the permanent residents. The cliffs are home for sea birds such as guillemots, kittiwakes, shags, cormorants and several species of gull. Another resident is the fulmar. Resembling a gull in plumage, this sea bird is a master glider, but lands clumsily, so needs broad ledges on which to nest. Its population in Britain has boomed in recent decades; little more than a century ago it was found only on remote St Kilda, where it was 'farmed' by the inhabitants. Today there are fulmar colonies all round the coasts of Britain and Ireland.

Berry Head has been used by man since at least as early as Iron Age times, when there was a promontory fort here. Subsequent forts and works have removed most traces of it, and most prominent today are two forts built at the beginning of the 19th century. There are many reminders of the quarrying for building stone which took place until fairly recently. Today, Berry Head offers sporting opportunities in the form of a putting green and sea fishing (at the foot of the cliffs) as well as footpaths and a nature trail.

Open: *all year daily. Picnic sites. Refreshments. Part LNR.*
Location: *directly E of Brixham, reached by Gillard Road.*
Map: *page 305, SX95.*

Bewl Bridge Reservoir

East Sussex & Kent

It takes an energetic walker six hours to walk the perimeter of Bewl Bridge Reservoir: most people would be better to allow eight. Bewl Bridge is the southeast's largest reservoir, constructed between 1972 and 1976 by damming the River Bewl. It now covers 770 acres, has 15 miles of shoreline and holds 6,900 million gallons of water, destined for the people of north and west Kent.

Because it was planned relatively recently this reservoir has been designed from the outset for leisure as well as for water collection. There are marked trails through the woods, special paths for riders and walkers, and a visitor centre with displays about the reservoir and the surrounding High Weald. Throughout the summer special events such as Morris dancing, wildlife exhibitions and guided walks are put on for visitors.

Angling and watersports are the main uses for the water itself. One of the best stillwater trout fisheries in the country, Bewl Bridge has been stocked with brown and rainbow trout. Day and season permits are available and boats may be hired. There are courses for beginners and established flyfishermen. Watersports here are sailing, rowing, canoeing and sub-aqua.

Part of the reservoir has been set aside as a nature reserve, managed by the Sussex Trust for Nature Conservation. Public access is restricted so that it can be an undisturbed refuge for wildlife.

Access: *by marked paths and trails. Passenger cruises on reservoir operate Apr to early autumn daily and in winter at weekends. Visitor centre. Picnic area. Refreshments (Apr to early autumn). Adventure playground. Special waterside car park and toilets for disabled visitors. Part CNT.*
Location: *2 miles S of Lamberhurst off A21.*
Map: *page 306, TQ63.*

Bickleigh Mill Craft Centre and Farm

Devon

A historic village complete with ancient bridge, 14th-century church and fortified manor house, is the setting for this successful project. The mill at Bickleigh is recorded in the *Domesday Book* and, though the age of the present mill is not known, it was in use as a corn mill until the 1950s, when the weir broke. Thirty years later the weir has been repaired and the mill wheels are turning again. Today, they provide power for a working craft centre, set up in 1973 and housed in the fully restored mill buildings.

Adjacent to the mill is a working farm, managed by the traditional methods of a century ago. Shire horses and working oxen are the only source of power in the fields, while in the farmyard the age of mechanised agribusiness is abandoned in favour of hand-milking of cows and goats, hand-shearing of sheep, and a traditionally managed dairy. Visitors can sometimes participate in the work of the farm such as haymaking and milking (4–5pm) and children are sometimes offered rides on the ox-cart or the donkeys. Many of the livestock are traditional or rare breeds; most are

Corn has been milled at Bickleigh since at least as early as the 11th century

very tame, making the farmyard a favourite with children. Farm produce and home-baked bread are on sale in the farm shop and bakery. A bonus in one of the farm buildings is an agricultural museum, with exhibits on thatching, cider-making and lace-making as well as a reconstructed turn-of-the-century farmhouse kitchen.

Open: *daily except Christmas – Apr to Dec all day, Jan to Mar pm only (craftsmen not working Sun am). Admission charged. Picnic area. Mill shop. Restaurant. Farm shop.*
Location: *off A396 at Bickleigh, 3 miles S of Tiverton.*
Map: *page 305, ST90.*

Bix Bottom

Oxfordshire

This large reserve lies in the Chilterns, occupying a typical dry chalk valley with a variety of aspects, slopes and soils. The extensive woodlands here are not the beechwoods so often associated with this area, but mixed broadleaved woodland including oak and birch as well as beech – the result of common land which has, over many years, been invaded by scrub and eventually developed into woodland.

As well as the woodland, the reserve protects areas of scrub and typical dry grassland which supports numerous chalk-loving plants. The summer wild flowers are most spectacular, with 17 different species of orchid on record as well as columbine, wild relative of the garden aquilegia. Gardeners will know the cultivated varieties of two other wild plants found in the woodlands here – green hellebore and Solomon's seal, both spring-flowering. Both had their uses in the days of herbal medicines. Solomon's seal was used to heal bruises and green hellebore as a cure for worms – though, being poisonous, it may well have harmed the patient more than the worms.

Bird life abounds on the reserve, with several species of tit including the willow tit, and breeding birds of prey including kestrels, sparrowhawks and owls. Insect life abounds, while larger creatures to be found include adders, grass-snakes and slow-worms. Badgers and fallow deer may be seen by patient watchers, especially around dusk and dawn.

Open: *all year daily. Information centre open Sat to Wed. CNT.*
Location: *3½ miles NW of Henley-on-Thames, off A423 between Nettlebed and Stonor.*
Map: *page 306, SU78.*

Black Down & Marley Common

Surrey & West Sussex

The outline of Black Down, 'the dark sentinel of the western Weald', has softened since the poet Tennyson regularly walked here a century ago. Then the bleak ridges were only 'flecked with pine'. They have become more sheltered as tree cover has spread, but nonetheless Black Down remains among the wildest of our southern uplands.

The height of this sandstone ridge (second only to that of Leith Hill (see page 156) in this region), and its high rainfall, help to determine its character and wildlife. There is typical moorland vegetation; on the heights grow Scots pine, silver birch and heathers with fine beeches reaching up across the lower slopes. Less than 200 yards from the upper car park are two bog pools where sphagnum mosses, bog asphodel and the insect-feeding sundew grow. In May and June the white cotton-wool tufts of cotton grass surround the pools; its spread in this country has been dramatically curbed by improvements in land drainage. Its fluffy heads were once used in making candlewick and stuffing mattresses.

There is always colour on Black Down – the brilliant yellow of the gorse, the pink and purple heathers with their varied flowering seasons, the pink-flowered whortleberry in early summer and the scarlet berries of the rowan and green, red and black alder buckthorn fruits in autumn. The brimstone butterfly feeds on alder buckthorn leaves and, with the orange-tip and small tortoiseshell, is found on the lower slopes.

The slow change of Black Down from open heathland has affected its bird population. Some once common species such as stonechats and nightjars are on the decline, and others are moving in to take their place. Heathland birds like linnets and yellowhammers still nest in some numbers in the gorse, and small flocks of meadow pipits pass through in autumn. On the lower slopes, woodland birds include both green and great spotted woodpeckers, and in summer the unforgettable trill of the handsome yellow-green wood warbler joins the songs of the chiff-chaff, willow warbler and tree pipit – who, because of his descending flight with wings spread and tail raised as he sings, has been likened to a parachutist.

The finest view from Black Down is to the south, towards the South Downs and – on clear days – to the sea beyond. Views to the west take in Marley Common, about half a mile away. Here, together with some fine Scots pines, grows one of Britain's rarer tree species, the wild service tree. The bark of these trees peels off in rectangular pieces, producing a chequered effect which explains the local name – the 'chequer tree'.

Access: unrestricted. NT.
Location: on Surrey and West Sussex borders, 1 mile SE of Haslemere.
Map: page 306, SU93.

Blackdown Hills

Somerset

The Blackdowns rise to 1000ft over the Vale of Taunton, their slopes thickly wooded, with tracts of ancient oak and ash coppice, and carpeted by a profusion of woodland wild flowers. The wettish clay soil of the lower slopes gives way to wind-baked ground towards the top of the hills.

Those who follow the well-defined tracks to the top are rewarded with superb views of the Vale of Taunton, bordered by the high plain of Exmoor to the north-west and the Quantocks to the north. On particularly clear days it is possible to see the hills of South Wales, 40 miles away across the hazy silver of the Bristol Channel.

The Blackdowns' principal landmark is the slender 175ft obelisk of the Wellington Monument, which stands like a rocket on its launching pad. Visible for many miles, the stone column was built in 1817 to commemorate the military achievements of the Duke of Wellington. The visitor who can face the prospect of a winding climb of 235 steps will find the view from the little chamber at the top of the monument truly breathtaking.

Access: unrestricted, except for farmland restrictions at times. Part NT.
Location: 2 miles S of Wellington, on unclassified road between A38 and B3170.
Map: page 305, ST11.

Blacktoft Sands

Humberside

The flat landscape of the south side of the Humber is intersected by the rivers Ouse and Trent and at their junction lies an extensive system of mudflats, saltmarsh and reed beds. The reeds are nine or ten feet tall and form one of the

largest continuous reed beds in Britain. As the bearded tit flies, with its strange, whirring flight, Blacktoft is not too far from their British breeding stronghold in East Anglia, and about 100 pairs of this delightful species now breed in the reeds. They share this nesting area with that other reed bed specialist, the reed warbler, and small numbers of water

The Wellington Monument in the Blackdown Hills

rails. One of Britain's rarest birds of prey, the marsh harrier, is a regular summer visitor, while in winter merlins and hen harriers hunt in the refuge.

Management of the reserve is designed to maintain the extensive reed bed, but in a number

of areas shallow scrapes have been bulldozed to provide permanent open standing water. These lagoons contain a range of invertebrates as well as eels and sticklebacks which form an important source of food for waders and wildfowl. Up to 1000 teal use the lagoons as a roosting place at high tide and the flighting in of these birds along with thousands of waders is a memorable experience. All of this, and pink-footed geese out on the Humber mudflats, can be watched from hides strategically placed to allow the visitor the chance to appreciate the special atmosphere of this very different part of Britain.

Open: *all year daily. Admission charge to non-members. No dogs. RSPB.*
Location: *7 miles E of Goole off A161, ¼ mile E of Ousefleet.*
Map: *page 310, SE82.*

Black Wood of Rannoch

Tayside

At one time, almost the whole of Scotland, from watersides to mountain summits, was covered by vast forests. The tree cover has gradually been almost entirely destroyed and today only remnants survive. One of the largest remaining areas of ancient pine forest is the Black Wood of Rannoch, on the southern shore of Loch Rannoch. Here the Scots pines are of very many different shapes and sizes; some huddle close together and some stand in solitary splendour – a stark contrast to today's regimented conifer plantations. Even so, the

Blagdon Reservoir, which attracts many wildfowl

Black Wood has been used and abused by man through the centuries and it cannot be described as a 'wild' forest. Because many of the trees are well spaced, plenty of light reaches the forest floor, allowing a variety of plants to grow. Often these are common like heathers and bilberry, but rarer beauties such as coral-root orchid and lesser twayblade can sometimes be found. Birds to be found here include the capercaillie (as big as a turkey and inclined to be fierce), black grouse, crossbills and siskins. On the opposite shore of the loch is oak woodland, and a car journey from Pitlochry to Loch Rannoch, circling the loch, will pass ancient and modern conifer forests as well as broadleaved woodland.

Access: *along tracks and waymarked walks.*
Location: *20 miles W of Pitlochry, off unclassified road round loch from Kinloch Rannoch.*
Map: *page 314, NN65.*

Great Crested Grebe

Great crested grebes prefer to live and breed in large expanses of water with thick vegetation in which to make their nests, but they can also be seen on relatively bare reservoirs. During the breeding season they have some of the most spectacular plumage of all water birds. At this time both sexes have the crests and neck ruffs illustrated here. These are fluffed out during the courtship displays, which consist of much head-shaking and diving.

Blagdon Reservoir

Avon

This reservoir, tucked into the Mendip Hills, was constructed in 1904 and now has all the appearance of a natural lake. It is a mile and a half long by half a mile wide and covers 430 acres. Less well known than nearby Chew Valley Lake, it still has very rich populations of wildfowl in winter. Wigeon, teal and pochard are often numbered in thousands, with a variety of other species occurring. Several species of wading birds visit the shores in spring and autumn, especially if water levels are low. Summer birds include great crested grebes and ruddy duck, and many swallows and house martins come to feed on the insect life, especially on warm evenings.

Access: *good views from public road which crosses the dam. Otherwise access by permit from Bristol Waterworks Company (Woodford Lodge, Chew Stoke, Bristol). This also covers entry to Chew and nearby Cheddar reservoirs.*
Location: *¼ mile N of Blagdon.*
Map: *page 305, ST55.*

Blakeney Point
Norfolk

Statistics such as 260 species of birds and 200 of plants, although impressive, do not tell the full story of Blakeney. The village, a popular yachting centre, is one of the most attractive in Norfolk, and the area is a painter's paradise with that distinctive East Anglian light that ranges from the shimmering gold of summer to the pearly grey of a chill winter morning. The point itself is a long spit of sand dune and shingle beach. The shingle which runs the entire length of the point on its seaward side acts as a barrier to all but the highest tides, protecting the dunes, saltmarshes and mud flats, and making the area a natural bird sanctuary.

Both common and little terns nest in the large ternery, joined in some years by the Sandwich, and small numbers of Arctic and roseate terns. Mallard, gadwall, shelduck, oystercatchers, ringed plovers and other waders breed here, with wheatears, swallows, linnets and reed buntings. But it is perhaps for its visiting birds that Blakeney is best known. Scarce varieties such as long-tailed and eider ducks, wryneck and Lapland bunting are sighted here most years, and large flocks of geese visit in winter.

The shrubby seablite, primarily a shrub of the Mediterranean, grows on the shingle, frequently covered by the sea but seemingly thriving. Yellow horned poppy, sea sandwort, groundsel and rock sea lavender, another Mediterranean arrival, all flourish here. On the dunes, marram grass and red fescue both help to bind the sand. Across the salt marshes, marsh samphire is a pioneering coloniser – joined later by sea aster.

Common and pygmy shrews live on the marsh banks, and stoats are an occasional threat to tern chicks. Seals, both common and grey, are a main attraction, basking on the sands off the point or swimming around visiting boats in high summer.

Access: on foot from Cley or, at high tide, by boat from Blakeney or Morston. Wheelchair walkway from landing stage to bird hide on Point. Exhibition in Lifeboat House. Warden present on Point Apr to Sep. NT.
Location: 2¼ miles NW of Blakeney, off A149.
Map: page 311, TG04.

Blenheim Park, with the palace in the background, as it was in 1787. This landscape is largely the creation of Capability Brown

The salt marshes at Blakeney – good for waders and plants such as sea aster

Blean Woods
Kent

In a well-wooded county, the Blean complex of woods is the jewel in the crown. On minor roads you travel through a sea of green, the illusion enhanced by the fact that you are often looking across the top of the trees, for here there are acres of coppice, where trees are cut to the base on a 15-year cycle, which produces a cluster of straight poles from the stump. Changing demands mean there is now rather more sweet chestnut grown than hazel, which is richer in wildlife.

The bird of the copses is the nightingale, and here it can be heard in abundance. Nightingales by no means only sing at night, and the listener will have to separate the nightingale's song from the babbling of the numerous warblers, drumming woodpeckers, and on still summer evenings the churring of nightjars. Other birds include redstarts and wood warblers, both uncommon in the south-east.

Blean has the usual complement of woodland mammals, among which the dormouse is notable. It is fond of hazel, and you may be lucky enough to come across one in early spring, recently emerged from hibernation and not at all wary. At this time too, spring flowers will be beginning to show, starting with shy violets, moving through primroses to the show of bluebells, which often lasts into the first week of June. These are very much the flowers of the coppices, as the rotational cutting allows plenty of light to reach the ground.

But the Blean woods are not all coppice, and there are fine areas of mature oaks, some heath and conifer plantations. A wide variety of insects can be seen in the forest rides and open parts of the woods, including the rare heath fritillary butterfly.

Access: generally restricted to footpaths on nature reserves, and public rights of way. Picnic site and forest walk at Clowes Wood, 3 miles SE of Whitstable. CNT/FC/NCC/RSPB.
Location: N of A2 between Dunkirk and Canterbury. Extends W to A291 Sturry – Herne Bay road.
Map: page 306, TR16.

Blenheim Park
Oxfordshire

Home of the eleventh Duke of Marlborough and birthplace of Sir Winston Churchill, the magnificent palace, park and gardens were given by Queen Anne to the first Duke following his victory over the French and Bavarians at Blenheim in 1704.

Like the palace, the park, with its broad avenues of trees, is on the 'grand scale', as might be expected of the work of Capability Brown, who created the spectacular lake by damming the River Glyme.

There is a rich and varied wildlife in the park. Great crested and little grebes and many species of wild duck live on the lake, while in the surrounding parkland stand ancient, large and isolated oaks. These support lichens and insects which attract many species of woodland birds. The bird populations are enhanced by the extensive woods and plantations, so woodpeckers, nuthatches and treecreepers, as well as a variety of warblers and tits, can be found. Sparrowhawks and woodcocks also live in the woodlands, while the more open grasslands are habitats for lapwings and winter-visiting fieldfares and redwings.

Open: park all year daily (palace and gardens open Mar to Oct only). Admission charge. Restaurant, shop and garden centre. Suitable for disabled visitors.
Location: off A34, on W edge of Woodstock.
Map: page 306, SP41.

Blithfield Reservoir

Staffordshire

One of the largest lakes in central England, Blithfield Reservoir was completed in 1952 to supply drinking water to part of the nearby conurbation of the West Midlands. It quickly attracted large numbers of wildfowl and by 1963 was the third most important reservoir in Britain for these birds. The best time to see birds here is during the winter months when very large numbers of ducks and gulls use it as a roost. From October to February an average of between 2000 and 3000 ducks are to be seen. These include large numbers of mallard, wigeon, teal, pochard and tufted ducks, and smaller numbers of shoveler and goldeneye. In fact almost every species of duck found in Britain has been seen as well as the various divers, grebes and a great many more. Notable amongst these is the goosander, a large handsome black and pinkish-white duck with a bottle-green head and red bill.

Access: *restricted, but good views from public road (B5013) which crosses reservoir on causeway. Access to birdwatching hides by permit from West Midland Bird Club.*
Location: *4 miles N of Rugeley on B5013.*
Map: *page 309, SK02.*

Boarstall Duck Decoy

Buckinghamshire

Duck decoys – devices for attracting and catching ducks for food – were introduced to Britain in 1665, when one was built for King Charles II in St James's Park, London. Boarstall Decoy first appeared in the 1697 map of the Manor of Boarstall. It is one of the few still functioning in Britain although today ducks are caught, not for eating, but to be ringed for the study of migration.

A decoy is a large shallow pool, usually around 2 to 3 acres in size and surrounded by trees. Between 3 and 8 'pipes', each 60 to 80ft long, curve away from the pool. They are aligned so that at least one can always be approached upwind. The whole 'pipe' is covered with netting over a series of hoops which become successively smaller. The essence of the process is to entice the ducks further and further into the pipe until they cannot escape. Then they are driven into a catch net.

The woods around the decoy are home to several species of butterfly: the speckled wood,

meadow brown, the colourful small tortoiseshell and the beautiful and distinctive peacock. The presence of the tiny muntjac deer may be betrayed by its short bark. Among the fungi in the woods are the honey fungus, bane of the modern gardener, and the Jew's ear fungus; both are edible. Until the 1970s the woods contained many elms and sycamores, but Dutch elm and sooty bark disease respectively have killed many trees. A restocking programme has begun, using

mature trees such as the common oak, wild cherry, hawthorn, hazel and black poplar. Eventually it is hoped that the wood will look much as it did when the decoy was first built.

Visitors in May will enjoy the display of bluebells; other spring flowers include primroses, wood anemones and dog's mercury. Bugle, believed by medieval herbalists to be one of the finest cure-alls, follows with rosebay and great willow-herb among the late summer flowers.

Open: *Good Fri to Aug Wed pm, Sat, Sun and bank holiday Mon. Admission charge. Nature trail suitable for disabled. NT/CNT.*
Location: *6 miles SE of Bicester off B4011.*
Map: *page 306, SP62.*

Bodmin Moor

Cornwall

The bleak and windswept granite plateau which forms Bodmin Moor has a forbidding quality, made famous in the well-known Daphne du Maurier novel *Jamaica Inn*. The grey stone tavern, featured in the novel, is situated on the A30 where it crosses the moor. The highest hills in Cornwall, Brown Willy (1375ft) and Rough Tor (1311ft) dominate the rugged moorland, which is mainly grass-covered and grazed by hardy cattle and sheep. From those tors on a clear day there are superb views across to both coasts of Cornwall.

The moor is much less well known than either Exmoor or Dartmoor, and its heart seems hardly to have been warmed by life or action. But this was not always so, and in prehistoric times it was a thriving and crowded agricultural area. The many remains – field boundaries, enclosures, hut circles and standing stones – bear mute witness to Neolithic and Bronze Age farmers. Indeed, there are few places where a prehistoric landscape can be seen so unchanged.

A changing climate brought a colder and wetter era, leading to changing patterns of population and leaving Bodmin Moor fossilised. Even so, its mineral wealth continued to be extracted until modern times – and remains of these industries still stand against the moorland backcloths.

Virtually all the moorland valleys are boggy and these are good places for plants typical of wet, acid conditions, especially cotton-grass and mare's-tail, but also sundews – well known for their habit of feeding on insects, using their sticky leaves to catch them. Bog asphodel, which is a mass of fragrant golden flowers in mid-summer, also grows in these damp places.

Dozmary Pool, not far from Jamaica Inn, is the only natural lake, but Crowdy and Siblyback reservoirs have increased the area of open water on the moor. A new reservoir at Colliford will provide a further attraction to waders and wildfowl, especially snipe, whose breeding display includes a strange drumming noise produced by extending their tail feathers in flight.

In summer the open moorland is filled with the flight songs of skylarks and meadow pipits, and is also a good place to see and hear cuckoos, which lay their eggs in the nests of the unfortunate pipits.

Location: *NE of Bodmin.*
Map: *page 304, SX28*

**Alder trees on the lake shore
at Bolam Lake Country Park**

Bohunt Manor

Hampshire

Now owned by the World Wildlife Fund, this wildfowl sanctuary was created and maintained by Lady Holman and her late husband, who bought Bohunt in the 1950s. Finding an overgrown garden with a silted-up lake, they set about planning, planting and dredging, and their gardens eventually became home to a collection of wildfowl which today numbers about 40 species.

The collection began with a female shelduck, brought here after it was found in a bedraggled state on a Portsmouth factory site. When she first came to Bohunt the shelduck could not even swim, but with the Holmans' help she survived to become the sanctuary's first resident. Today her descendants share the lake with more than 100 other water birds ranging from British resident species such as pochard and tufted duck to cranes from Africa and the snow goose, pure white with black wing tips and rarely seen in Britain.

The gardens, woodlands and wetlands around the lake are rich in wild flowers, and the trees include the biggest tulip tree in southern England, which blooms in August.

Open: *weekdays, pm only.
Admission charge (proceeds to World Wildlife Fund).*
Location: *off A3 at Liphook.*
Map: *page 306, SY83.*

Bolam Lake Country Park

Northumberland

Owned and managed by Northumberland County Council, this park is less than 20 miles from the centre of the bustling Tyneside conurbation. The combination of large mature deciduous and coniferous trees, open grassland, rhododendrons, and a shallow lake makes this an outstandingly beautiful place to spend a few hours. To go with all this there is a great variety of wildlife, particularly birds.

The easiest place to see the birds is in the small upper car park where large numbers congregate waiting to be fed. Most will come to the hand, and they include blue tits, great tits, marsh tits, and nuthatches. Other exciting species coming to food put out nearby are great spotted woodpeckers and jays.

A system of footpaths winds through the park and gives visitors the opportunity to see some of the mammals which live here, particularly red squirrels. These delightful animals are a special feature of the park. They will even come into the car park to feed on the bird food. A walk through the park passes through a variety of habitats including a reed and willow area at the western end of the lake which is crossed by a boardwalk.

Open: *all year. Picnic area.*
Location: *2 miles N of Belsay on unclassified road off A696; 7 miles SW of Morpeth.*
Map: *page 313, NZ08*

Bookham Commons

Surrey

The London Natural History Society has been conducting a survey of these commons since 1941, and their published reports give a splendidly comprehensive picture of the area. Historically too, much is known of Bookham. Records exist from 666 AD showing the manor of Bocheham in the ownership of Chertsey Abbey. In the Domesday survey the commons are shown as providing pannage – the right to graze pigs on acorns in the oakwoods – for the benefit of the abbey. In the 16th century oak from the commons was used in building the splendid but ill-fated Nonsuch Palace, while in this century the land has been occupied by gypsies, grazed by local farmers and used for military exercises. In the 1970s the land passed to the control of the National Trust.

There are numbers of footpaths and bridleways on the common which may be entered at three main points, each with parking facilities. Because of the wide range of habitats – grassland, scrub, woods, ponds, streams and mossy areas – 500 species of flowering plants have been recorded. Ferns, mosses, lichens and fungi are present in great variety, as are most of the familiar woodland birds. These are augmented by occasional visitors such as kingfishers, herons, and grey wagtails. Although generally less visible, mammals include several species of voles, mice and shrews, as well as weasels and stoats. Grass snakes are common, as are toads (which outnumber frogs) and all three species of newt.

Open: *at all times. Free access. NT.*
Location: *2¼ miles W of Leatherhead, just N of Bookham station between A245 and A246.*
Map: *page 306, TQ15.*

The Border Country, scene of 300 years of recurring strife, possesses many reminders of its centuries of unrest. Any casual foray into the Border Forest Park will uncover ruins of strongholds such as Hermitage Castle in Liddesdale and Dally Castle in Tynedale. Smaller pele towers dot the landscape, and some of the old fortified farmsteads are still occupied today. Evidence of earlier life in the area exists in the many hut circles and hillforts of prehistoric man, and Hadrian's Wall, the northern limit of Roman domination in its time, can be seen from the park.

The border landscapes of today are dramatically different from those known to the early settlers – and from those of a mere 30 years ago. Much of the formerly bare hill country is now clothed with coniferous plantations, but the most drastic change has been the construction of Kielder Water. Occupying a seven-and-a-half-mile length of the North Tyne Valley, the reservoir holds some 44,000 million gallons of water. Built amid great controversy, it nevertheless fits well into the conifer-clad border hills. Its scenic attractions can most easily be appreciated along the road which follows the reservoir's south-west shore. Picnic areas nestle in the trees all the way along this road.

Near the northern tail of the reservoir, close to Kielder village, the Forestry Commission has established a visitor centre at Kielder Castle. Built as a shoot-

Border Forest Park

Northumberland, Cumbria & Borders

Neighbouring forests in England and Scotland have been brought together under one mantle in the Border Forest Park, which extends for over 145,000 acres. Sparsely populated and of low agricultural value, the area was declared a Forest Park in 1955 when the Forestry Commission began to establish the forests which were to supply timber to the nation in years to come. At the heart of the park is the vast expanse of Kielder Water, Western Europe's largest man-made lake.

ing lodge by the Duke of Northumberland in 1775, the castle is now the focal point of the recreational facilities in Kielder Forest. Details of the Border Forest Park's many picnic sites and waymarked walks can be obtained here. The circular waymarked walk known as the Duchess Drive Walk starts from here, while motorists can take a 12-mile scenic route on forest roads, passing through wild and remote forest and moorland to Byrness on the A68. Near the forest drive, on Kielder Burn, there is a wildlife observation hide, and there is also a visitor centre at Tower Knowe, not far from the dam at the reservoir's southern end.

In summer, regular ferry services around and across the reservoir offer a different viewpoint. They link the main centres of Matthews Linn, Leaplish and the Tower Knowe Information Centre with the north shore of Kielder Water, which is inacces-

sible by car. Because it is more difficult to reach, this comparatively peaceful area is the best place for wildlife: Bakethin Reservoir and the surrounding forest has been defined as a nature conservation area. Much of the Border Forest Park consists of moorland and spruce woods, and its wildlife is mostly typical of these habitats. The roe deer, which became scarce in the 1920s, is back again and can sometimes be seen coming down in the evening to browse along the shoreline. The wild goat has been king of the exposed crags of the Cheviots for centuries, sharing its love for the rugged country with the mountain hare, sometimes known as the 'blue hare', which was introduced from the Highlands around 75 years ago. In the older woodlands and in some plantations of spruce red squirrels may be seen. Rabbits are common, as are foxes and badgers, but the latter are not often seen because of their noc-

Displays in Kielder Castle Visitor Centre

Border Forest scenery

turnal habits.

Birds of the Forest Park include the tiny goldcrest, which abounds in the conifers, while less familiar species such as siskins and crossbills prefer to breed in the more mature trees. With a bit of effort, and luck, the walker might well come across the spectacular black grouse at their 'lek' in the spring. The short-eared owl has increased in numbers with the growth of the conifer plantations, which harbour voles, its principal prey.

Because of its leached, acidic soils, this area is not rich in wild flowers, but heather and cowberry flourish in the better-drained areas. Purple moor grass, characteristic of damp soil, dominates the grasslands of the park, and in the bogs are sphagnum moss, cotton grass, bog asphodel, bog rosemary, cross-leaved heath, and round and long-leaved sundews.

Open: *Kielder Castle Visitor Centre Apr to Sep; Tower Knowe Visitor Centre all year. Kielder-Byrness Forest Drive all year (weather permitting); toll charge. FC.*
Location: *reached by unclassified road which leaves B6320 at Bellingham to run for 25 miles NW, skirting Kielder Water, to B6357 at Saughtree.*
Map: *page 313, NY69.*

Bough Beech Reservoir

Kent

About a quarter of the area of this 315-acre reservoir has been set aside as a nature reserve, managed by the Kent Trust for Nature Conservation. Consisting of a bay at the north-eastern corner of the main reservoir, and a smaller lake, the reserve has been extensively managed especially to encourage birds. Nesting islands have been constructed and shallow pools created, and these are used especially by migrant waders and wildfowl. About 60 species of birds breed here annually, usually including great crested grebe, shelduck and tufted duck. Wildfowl numbers are at their greatest during the winter, and waders such as greenshanks and sandpipers are frequent visitors in spring and, especially, autumn.

The KTNC has an information centre in a converted oasthouse close to the reserve. Here there are displays on the flora and fauna of the area, together with information on the water supply functions of the reservoir and on the Kentish hop industry.

Access: *reserve viewable at all times from public road only. No access to lake margins. CNT.*
Open: *information centre Easter to Oct Wed, Sat and Sun.*
Location: *S of Winkhurst Green, 5 miles SW of Sevenoaks, 3¼ miles NE of Edenbridge.*
Map: *page 306, TQ44.*

Box Hill

Surrey

Box Hill rises 400ft above the River Mole, its chalk surface barely covered by shrubs. For two centuries it has attracted visitors, and now, on summer weekends, it is invariably very crowded. Some come to gaze from the heights at the unequalled views across the Weald and others to study the rich and varied plant and animal life.

The tree from which the hill takes its name is making a comeback after a considerable decline in the 19th century; indeed Box Hill is one of the few remaining places where the tree is to be found growing wild. The yellow wood is hard, stable and even-grained; it is also very heavy: 'green' box wood is said to sink in water. It is used for fine wood-carving, inlaid work and in the making of chess pieces. The cause of the tree's decline was probably due to its widespread use for making wood-engraving blocks. The work of the 19th-century artist and naturalist Thomas Bewick stimulated a renewal of interest in wood-engraving, and many tons of boxwood were used in making blocks for engraving illustrations for all the fashionable publications. With the introduction of photo-engraving the demand fell away and the few remaining groves were left to their slow development.

Two nature walks on Box Hill start from the National Trust shop at the summit.

Open: *shop, information room and exhibition Apr to mid Dec Wed to Sun and bank holiday Mon (closed Fri, Nov to mid Dec). Restaurant. Wheelchair access to summit area near main car park only. NT.*
Location: *1 mile N of Dorking, 2¼ miles S of Leatherhead off A24.*
Map: *page 306, TQ15.*

Bradfield Woods

Suffolk

Owned by the Royal Society for Nature Conservation and managed by the Suffolk Trust for Nature Conservation, Bradfield Woods nature reserve is one of the finest examples in the coun-try of a woodland still managed by the ancient practice of coppicing. Since at least the 13th century, the trees and shrubs of this area (totalling 42 native species) have been cut back on a regular cycle, to produce poles for stakes, fencing and tools, etc.

Among the coppice growth are scattered standard timber trees, mainly oaks. The ground flora of the woods is extremely rich, over 370 species of plants having been identified. Among these, on the acid soils, are primroses, wood anemones and bluebells, whilst the more fertile clays support herb paris, dog's mercury, oxlip, water avens and early purple orchid. This great variety of plant life is due to the reduced shade brought about by coppicing: the ground vegetation is at its richest in the second and third summers after the coppice is cut.

The coppicing of woodland also provides suitable habitats for a large variety of animals. During the breeding season, the woods are alive with songs of willow and garden warblers, blackcaps and nightingales, and woodcock, great spotted woodpeckers and tawny owls also nest. Roe deer are resident, and red, fallow and muntjac deer are occasionally seen.

Open: *at all times. CNT.*
Location: *4 miles SE of Bury St Edmunds at Sickesmere; turn off A134 onto unclassified road. Entrance between Little Welnetham and Gedding.*
Map: *page 306, TL95.*

Hurdle-making – once common in Britain's woods

The scarp slope of Box Hill

Bradgate Park & Swithland Woods

Leicestershire

This large country park is part of Charnwood Forest, a rugged area of ancient, hard volcanic rocks which rises dramatically above the gentle Midland plain around it, belying its modest 900ft height.

The park was originally part of the estate of Bradgate House, a 16th-century mansion whose ruins can still be seen. Lady Jane Grey, the ill-fated 'nine days queen', was born here in 1537. The estate remained in the family until 1928, when it was bought by a local businessman and presented to the City and County of Leicester to be preserved as a public recreation area and a haven for wildlife. The park is still home to a herd of about 300

red and fallow deer, which wander freely in the park and raise their young in a special sanctuary which is not open to the public.

The park's visitor centre, known as Marion's Cottage, has a living natural history display in its garden, part of which has been specially planted with a collection of wild flowers – many of them threatened species – and also young trees typical of Bradgate. A 'rock garden' provides a fine introduction to the area's unusual geology, with samples of the different rocks found here.

Nearby Swithland Wood is a rare survival of the oakwoods which once covered much of the Midland landscape. Oaks support more species of insect and bird life than any other British tree, and Swithland Wood is typically rich in wildlife.

Open: *park all year. Parking charge. Picnic area. Suitable for disabled visitors. Ruins Apr to Oct Wed, Thu and Sat pm, Sun am. Visitor centre all year Sat, Sun and*

bank holidays, pm only, also Wed and Thu pm Apr to Oct. Shop.
Location: *6 miles NW of Leicester off B5327 between Newton Linford and Cropston.*
Map: *page 306, SK51.*

Branscombe & Salcombe Regis

Devon

A relatively short distance from the busy 'alternative' route from Lyme Regis to Exeter, Branscombe remains one of the least spoilt villages in South Devon. Its straggling collection of stone and cob cottages, some thatched, follows the lush valley down to the sea through a natural break in the high cliff-wall.

The mill has ceased to operate, but visitors can still see the thatched smithy working, and buy crusty bread fresh from the ash faggot-fired ovens of the bakery. There are rows of converted coastguards' cottages at

both Branscombe and Weston – a reminder of the popularity of smuggling here in earlier times.

At 520ft Weston Cliff is the highest on the South Devon coast and gives panoramic views to Torbay and on to Dartmoor to the west, and Lyme Bay and Portland to the east.

Herring and great black-backed gulls breed in small numbers on the cliffs, together with the fulmar. Wrens, dunnocks, jackdaws and linnets are all residents here, and are joined in summer by migrants such as the chiff-chaff and grasshopper warbler, so-called because of a supposed similarity between its song and that of some grasshoppers. Butterflies find a plentiful food supply on the coastal scrub and grasslands, while the flora is very varied owing to the alkaline nature of part of the soil.

Location: *stretching for 4 miles along coast between Salcombe Regis and Branscombe. NT.*
Map: *page 305, SY28.*

Branscombe village, strung out along its valley

Breamore House Countryside Museum

Hampshire

An unspoilt, tranquil village with a Saxon church and an Elizabethan manor house is the setting for this imaginatively laid-out museum, which traces the changes and advances in farming techniques and machines through several centuries.

The large collection of tools and machinery includes a number of ploughs, ranging from those with one share to those with many. Like many farm implements, ploughs have been the subject of sophistication rather than dramatic change, and have altered little in principle since Saxon times.

The collection also includes tools and machines for harrowing, sowing, rolling, hoeing and harvesting. The work now done in one operation by the combine harvester was once done by a whole series of machines, and examples of each are on display. Many of these machines were horse-drawn, but the age of the tractor is not ignored, and there is a marvellous collection of early tractors – some of which, like the 1917 *Overtime* and the 1919 *Junior*, look more like delightful children's toys.

The wheelwright's shop at Breamore Countryside Museum, with wheels at varying stages of completion

Reconstructions of a blacksmith's shop, a wheelwright's shop, a dairy and a brewery recall the various rural industries which backed up the work of farms in the days when farm life was labour-intensive and an estate such as Breamore employed many skilled individuals.

The Countryside Museum's latest addition is a brick-path maze, completed in 1984 after its design won a nationwide competition. Many centuries older is Breamore's famous Miz-maze, an ancient circular maze cut into the downland turf a mile away from the house.

As well as Breamore House and Countryside Museum, there is also a carriage museum open to the public. Housed in the stables, it features among other things the *Red Rover* – the last stagecoach to run between London and Southampton.

Open: *house, countryside and carriage museums Apr to Sep daily, pm only, but closed Mon and Fri. Admission charge. Refreshments. Shop.*
Location: *on unclassified road off A338 at Breamore, 3 miles N of Fordingbridge.*
Map: *page 305, SU11.*

Brean Down & Axe Estuary

Somerset

Quite apart from its importance as a Site of Special Scientific Interest, the distinctive promontory of Brean Down has a fascinating history. Clearly visible here are the remains of a prehistoric field system and a Roman temple, while at the tip of the Down is a fort, built in 1867 as a defence against possible invasion by Napoleon III, and used in both world wars. Marconi's first radio signals were monitored on Brean Down in 1897.

The Down is an outcrop of the great limestone ridge of the Mendips. Rising to 320ft, it is a fine viewpoint, with Glastonbury Tor, the Quantock and Blackdown Hills, Exmoor and even the Brecon Beacons all visible in clear weather.

The flora is typical of downland, and includes salad burnet, St John's wort and wood sage. Look for the grey-green foliage and papery white flowers of the white rock-rose; between May and July it is common here, yet the only other place where it grows is Torbay in Devon.

The spring and autumn migration of birds past Brean Down has long attracted ornithologists. Migrants like chats and warblers are often accompanied by visiting birds of prey including merlins and the magnificent peregrine falcon, which once nested here. Brean points straight at Steep Holm island, and starlings which roost and nest on this island pour along Brean's ridge on their evening flight home.

Birds are not the only migrant visitors here. The autumn migration of butterflies and moths includes tortoiseshell and red admiral, while common blue, marbled white and meadow brown breed on the Down. The changing pattern of agriculture is adversely affecting many downland butterflies throughout the country, but on Brean there are still quantities of horseshoe vetch, the feed plant of the chalkhill blue caterpillar.

Below the Down is Weston Bay, where the River Axe enters the sea. Various kinds of waders, and many gulls, are usually to be seen along the water as it makes its way across the beach. More waders, particularly redshanks, can be seen in Bleadon Level, to the south of Uphill. There are areas of saltmarsh here. Footpaths lead from Uphill along dykes beside a creek, making good vantage points.

Location: *2 miles SW of Weston-super-Mare; the S arm of Weston Bay. CNT/NT.*
Map: *page 305, ST25.*

Brecon Beacons panorama. The inset picture shows walkers on the slopes of Pen-y-Fan

The Brecon Beacons

Running westwards from the English border to the Vale of Tywi, the mountains of the 519-square-mile Brecon Beacons National Park form a dramatic barrier between Mid Wales and the southern valleys whose character was changed completely during the Industrial Revolution. The 'table top' summit of Pen-y-Fan, 2907ft above sea level, is Britain's highest point south of the Snowdonia National Park. Several roads climb to more than 1500ft, enabling superb views to be enjoyed by motorists as well as walkers.

Although dominated by the Beacons and their neighbours, the Black Mountain to the west and the Black Mountains to the east, the park embraces a rich variety of scenery from lush valleys to vast tracts of open land, such as Fforest Fawr, where sheep and ponies have roamed for thousands of years. The southern slopes are carved by deep, wooded valleys where rivers race over the rocks, vanish into caves and emerge again to thunder over waterfalls. More

contrasts are provided by Llangorse Lake and the park's many forest-flanked reservoirs.

Man has made his mark, but this has always been a region where people are greatly outnumbered by sheep. Even the main towns – Brecon, Crickhowell, Talgarth and Hay-on-Wye – are small by comparison with most British market towns. These towns and scattered villages seem a world apart from the bustling communities just a few miles away in the industrial valleys of South Wales. The area's farmsteads are even more apart; many seem untouched by the sweeping changes of the last 30 years.

Much of the National Park's land would also have been urbanised and industrialised during the 19th century, had it not been for a great stroke of geological good luck. Nature moulded this part of Wales in such a way that the northward march of the coal measures ends along a line which roughly coincides with the 'Heads of the Valleys' road – near the park's southern boundary. Indeed, coal can be seen in the rocks of the Henrhyd Falls, near the village of Coelbren, where the River Llech plunges over a 90ft cliff on its way to join the Tawe.

Rocks and Rivers
If the land south of Brecon could be sliced like a cake it would reveal how the sandstone, formed nearly 400 million years ago, has been forced up to create the national park's long line of dramatic crests. Finishing touches were provided by the last ice age which ended about 10,000 years ago. Glaciers ground relentlessly away at the northern slopes, making them steeper than ever and forming great bowls of rock known as cwms. As the ice melted it left such lonely, crag-clasped lakes as Llyn-cwm-llwch, at the foot of Pen-y-Fan, and Llyn y Fan Fach which lies almost 1700ft above sea level and is overlooked by the highest part of the brooding Black Mountain.

Relatively gentle slopes run southwards from the peaks, and the sandstone vanishes beneath layers of limestone, millstone grit and coal. Miners used to call millstone grit the 'farewell rock' because with it they had reached the strata where the coal seams ended.

Bands of limestone and millstone grit run right across the southern part of the park and are directly responsible for its wealth of caves, waterfalls and gorges. It is an area where nature can be seen at work, slowly but surely changing the landscape, with running water as its most powerful tool.

As many as 100 inches of rain fall on the mountains every year and the water becomes increasingly acidic as it filters down through the peat which carpets much of the high ground. The limestone is eaten away by this acidic water to such an extent that the Mellte, Nedd Fechan and other rivers flow underground for considerable distances.

Sometimes underground streams form curious holes which are a remarkable feature of the park's southern moorland. They look like bomb craters – some are more than 100 yards in diameter – but are created when the ground collapses into large cavities formed by acidic water eating away the limestone. The park has a greater concentration of these holes than any other part of Britain. One of the biggest, Pant Mawr pot, has a vertical shaft 75ft deep.

The gorge south of Ystradfellte is a fine example of how the rivers are cutting deeper and deeper. Porth yr Ogof, where the Mellte vanishes into a cave at the foot of a limestone cliff, is the remains of a long tunnel through which the river ran before the roof collapsed. Lower down the Mellte, and on other nearby rivers, the juxtaposition of hard and relatively soft rocks has combined with geological faults – movements of the earth's crust – to create a series of enchanting waterfalls.

The park's southern valleys are punctuated by such awesome caves as Agen Allwedd, where more than a dozen miles of passages run beneath the limestone plateau of Mynydd Llangattock. Another is Ogof Ffynnon Ddu – 'The Cave of the Black Spring' – in the upper valley of the River Tawe. More than 20 miles of passages extending 850ft below the entrance make it the longest and deepest cave system in the British Isles. It also has the distinction of being the country's only subterranean National Nature Reserve. Most of the caves are in the experts-only category, and permits are required for some of them, but the Dan-yr-Ogof and Cathedral Showcaves, across the valley from Ogof Ffynnon Ddu, are open to visitors.

Early Men
The caves on the Brecons provided shelter for hunters who prowled the area before its first

Moorland slopes above Sennybridge

permanent settlers arrived about 5000 years ago. Their stone axes, fires and domesticated animals began clearing the primeval forest which had spread over all but the highest ground since the ice age ended. Burial chambers near Brecon, Crickhowell, Talgarth and elsewhere are enduring memorials to the people of the New Stone Age.

Bronze Age dwellers also buried their dead beneath circular mounds, but their most impressive additions to the landscape were huge and solitary standing stones, about 30 of which are scattered across the park. One of the biggest, known as Maen Llia, weighs about 20 tons and stands on the lonely moors north of Ystradfellte. Nobody knows how or why the monoliths were erected, but in the Middle Ages they were protected by laws which threatened vandals with the death penalty.

Walkers can explore the weathered banks and ditches of Iron Age hillforts on Carn Goch, Pen-y-Crug, Table Mountain and other summits high above the fertile valleys. Carn Goch, reached through a maze of narrow lanes between Llangadog and Llandeilo, is the biggest hillfort in Wales as well as a fine viewpoint. Later occupiers – the Romans – built Y Gaer, a stone-walled fort in a lovely setting on the River Usk just east of Brecon.

Wildlife

Wild mammals are few and far between on the National Park's mountains, but birds likely to be seen include meadow pipits, ring ouzels and wheatears. The marvellous song of the skylark, which may last for as much as five minutes, is a constant delight from March to high summer.

The most impressive patrollers of the moorland sky are buzzards and ravens. Although absent from most of Britain, they are common sights in the Brecon Beacons area. The buzzard can fly at more than 70 mph, has eyesight at least five times sharper than that of a human, and looks like a small eagle with broad, rounded wings. It is often

seen soaring in slow, wide circles looking for prey that may be anything from a beetle to a small rabbit.

The raven, a voracious scavenger, feeds on dead sheep and other carrion. Glossy black feathers, a wedge-shaped tail and a heavy, flesh-tearing beak make it easy to identify. The raven is also one of nature's most aerobatic birds – males sometimes fly upside-down to impress females in the mating season.

Red grouse, flying close to the ground in a fury of croaking cries and whirring wings, are found on the Black Mountains and in other heather-clad areas. Visitors include hen harriers and sparrowhawks, and there is always a chance of seeing a red kite, one of Britain's rarest birds of prey. Kites breed further north in mid Wales and can be identified by a deeply forked tail.

On the southern slopes, conifer forests criss-crossed by waymarked trails explore the habitats of such creatures as the fox, badger, tree pipit, whinchat, coal tit, goldcrest and barn owl. Woodlands of oak, birch, ash and other native trees – relics of the forests which covered most of the park thousands of years ago – are the haunt of the redstart, wood warbler, pied flycatcher, nuthatch and treecreeper.

The stately heron, stabbing at fish and eels, may be seen on Talybont Reservoir and Llangorse Lake, which also attract pochard, tufted duck, goosander and thousands of black-headed gulls in the autumn and winter months.

The buzzard

The mewing call of the buzzard is one of the most distinctive upland sounds, and the buzzard's habit of gliding on currents of rising air for long periods makes it easy to watch. Buzzards are present in quite large numbers in upland areas like the Beacons.

What to See

AFON MELLTE

Along the lower reaches of this river is a famous series of waterfalls, stretching for some two miles. The most beautiful of them all is Sgwd yr Eira, or 'Fall of Snow', near the Afon Hepste's confluence with the Afon Mellte. Worthy of a fairy tale, it has a path running behind the curtain of cascading water.

There are also falls along the River Neath (Afon Nedd), a little to the west. Both rivers have Forestry Commission woodlands along their banks, and both are good for exploring upland habitats of wood and water. There are pleasant walks, several parking places and picnic spots.

BRECON AND ABERGAVENNY CANAL

Ranking high among Britain's most beautiful inland waterways, the Brecon and Abergavenny (also known as the Monmouthshire and Brecon) Canal runs from Brecon down to Newport. For its entire length it is dominated by hills, especially by the bulk of Blorenge, to the south-west of Abergavenny. For much of its journey the canal follows the Usk valley, and the combination of canal and river, with their bridges, meadows, and tree-shaded lanes, is enchanting. Just to the east of Brecon (near Llanhamlach) the canal crosses the river; this is a good place to explore from, since footpaths follow both river and canal. Near Llangynidr, river and canal are in intimate contact again, and here there is also a flight of locks.

CARREG CENNEN CASTLE

Perched on top of a 200ft limestone bluff, Carreg Cennen is one of the most dramatically sited medieval castles in Britain. It is approached up a steep hill through a farmyard. The sheep-cropped grass around the ruined castle is dotted with primroses and bluebells in spring, and with a variety of lime-loving plants as the year progresses. Outcrops of bare limestone are covered in lichens and mosses, and trees and shrubs have gained a foothold in some of the places inaccessible to sheep. From the ramparts of the castle, looking down to the little Afon Cennen far below, visitors can enjoy the rare sight of birds such as buzzards and jackdaws flying below them.

Open: all year daily, but pm only on Sun Oct to Mar.

CRAIG-Y-NOS COUNTRY PARK

Much of this country park was created from the grounds of Craig-y-nos Castle, an unlikely building which was once the home of Madame Adelina Patti, a famous operatic prima donna of the early 20th century. The castle itself is now a hospital for the elderly, but the grounds offer pleasant walks beside borders of rhododendrons and alongside a mountain stream. There is a lake and many fine trees, and the River Tawe flows through the grounds. Paths lead from here to the Dan-yr-Ogof caves.

Open: all year daily. Voluntary parking charge.

DAN-YR-OGOF AND CATHEDRAL SHOWCAVES

These showcaves are accessible to all, unlike many of the other caves which riddle the limestone along the National Park's southern border. The caves were first discovered in 1912, when they were flooded and had to be explored by coracle. Since then they have been made easy to explore on foot, and lighting brings out the dramatic shapes of the many stalactites and stalagmites. Visitors wishing to explore the caves must join a guided tour.

Open: Easter to Oct daily. Admission charge. Information Centre. Refreshments. Shop.

The Brecon and Abergavenny Canal

GRWYNE FAWR VALLEY

At the head of this remote little valley is the Forestry Commission's Mynydd Ddu Forest, with picnic places and forest trails. Near the source of the river is Grwyne Fawr Reservoir, from where walks can be made across the bare uplands of the Black Mountains. Downstream is the church of Partrishow – a hidden-away gem which is one of the treasures of the National Park. Best visited in spring, when the churchyard is a mass of daffodils, the little church has an exquisitely carved rood screen.

A male whinchat in breeding plumage. These little birds arrive from Africa in April and make their territories in rough grassland

LLANGORSE LAKE

This is the largest natural lake in South Wales, and is an extremely popular leisure venue for boating and water-skiing. There is still room for naturalists, however. The lake's reed-fringed edges are good for birds such as moorhens, coots, grebes and ducks. In the lake is a crannog, a man-made island constructed by early settlers as a water-defended homestead. It is one of the few places in Wales where reed warblers nest.

LLWYN-ON RESERVOIR

This is one of three reservoirs constructed on the Afon Taf Fawr at the beginning of the 20th century to supply Cardiff with water. New forests cloak the hillsides on either side, and among these are several Forestry Commission picnic sites and forest trails. In a group of converted farm buildings close to the reservoir is the Garwnant Forest Centre, which has exhibits on

Llangorse Lake – good for both water sports and wildlife

many aspects of life and work in the Brecon Beacons.

Open: *Garwnant Forest Centre open Easter to Sep daily (but Sat, Sun and bank holiday Mon pm only). Picnic area. Shop.*

MYNYDD ILLTYD MOUNTAIN CENTRE

All aspects of the Brecon Beacons are covered at this information centre. A 2¼-mile circular nature trail starts from the car park and explores a variety of upland habitats. Moors, bogs and streams have an all-year-round bird population which includes herons, buzzards, snipe, whinchats and ravens and summer visitors such as redshanks and wheatears.

Open: *all year daily except Christmas. Picnic area. Refreshments. Suitable for disabled visitors.*

THE SUGAR LOAF

Something of an oddity in the landscape of the Brecons, and

certainly a notable landmark, is the volcano-like profile of Mynydd Pen-y-fal, whose characteristic cone shape has made it better known as the Sugar Loaf. The St Mary's Nature Trail leads up its west side through a steep valley to the summit, from which there are breathtaking views: westwards to the Brecons with the contrasting gentleness of the Usk valley at their feet; north to the Black Mountains; eastwards to the Malverns and Cotswolds; with the Bristol Channel visible beyond Newport in clear weather.

The 'Sugar Loaf' belongs to the National Trust, one of the largest landowners in the National Park.

TAF FECHAN RESERVOIRS

Built to supply the coalfields of South Wales, these reservoirs – Pontsticill, Pentwyn and Neuadd – are beautifully set and are surrounded by Forestry Commission forests. There are numerous picnic places and for-

est trails. Pentwyn Reservoir is a nature reserve of the Brecknock Naturalists' Trust.

Pontsticill Reservoir can be reached by the Brecon Mountain Railway, a narrow-gauge steam line operating from Pant Station, north-east of Merthyr Tydfil.

From the car park near the Neuadd Reservoirs, high up the valley, a track leads to Pen-y-Fan, highest of the Beacons' summits. Much of this range is owned by the National Trust.

TALYBONT RESERVOIR

This long, narrow reservoir – a reserve of the Brecknock Naturalists' Trust – lies in a wooded valley. The water is generally deep with steeply shelving banks, but there are areas with gentler slopes and, at the southern end, there is marshland which is flooded in winter. The range of habitats attracts a wide range of waterfowl and waders, particularly winter visitors. The commonest diving ducks are pochards and tufted ducks, which feed on submerged vegetation, whilst dabbling ducks such as mallard, teal and wigeon feed in the shallows. Here they may be joined by waders such as curlews, redshanks, common and green sandpipers and greenshanks.

Beyond the southern end of the reservoir lies Talybont Forest, where there are picnic places and a forest trail.

Access: *no access to nature reserve, but good viewpoints for birdwatching from road along W shore. CNT.*

VALE OF EWYAS

Hidden away in the heart of this beautiful valley is Llanthony Priory, whose 12th-century ruins could scarcely be in a more evocative setting. Beside them, tucked between the bare hills, are a little parish church and a hotel. The area is usually alive with little birds, particularly pied wagtails and chaffinches, who come to the car park in search of visitors' picnic crumbs.

At the head of the Vale of Ewyas, beyond Capel-y-Ffin with its enchanting roadside chapel, is Gospel Pass, notable for its wide views across moorland towards the Wye valley. Above it is Hay Bluff, with even more panoramic views. Hanggliders can often be seen here. This is the English/Welsh Border, the boundary of the national park, and the route of Offa's Dyke Path. Pipits, skylarks, ravens and buzzards are the wild creatures most likely to be seen on these blustery uplands.

Open: *Llanthony Priory at all reasonable times.*

Brimham Moor & Rocks

North Yorkshire

Brimham Moor has been grazed since monastic times by cattle and sheep; local farms still exercise grazing rights here. Grouse, curlews, plovers and pheasants live on the heather moorland, but they are rarely seen during the tourist season, since the large numbers of visitors drive them away.

The rocks themselves are known for their extraordinary shapes, carved by weather erosion since the thick sandstone layers were formed millions of years ago. These shapes have attracted many different nicknames, such as the Anvil, Eagle Rock, Watchdog and the Flowerpot.

In the 18th and 19th centuries these curious rock formations began to attract an increasing number of visitors; nowadays car-borne visitors come in their thousands each year. These very large numbers were threatening to destroy what they had come to see by trampling and parking on the moor and by causing dust, litter and noise problems. Conservation aims are now being realised by the National Trust's management plan. It has involved installing a warden, building an information centre and laying out car parks. As a result of these measures, bare earth has gradually regained its plant cover, drives and paths

have been repaired and some of the former tranquillity of Brimham is now returning.

Open: *at all times. Parking charge. Information centre. Shop. Special wheelchair path. NT.*
Location: *8 miles SW of Ripon off B6265; 10 miles NW of Harrogate off B6165.*
Map: *page 310, SE26.*

Brockhampton Woods

Hereford & Worcester

Most visitors to this National Trust property come to see Lower Brockhampton's manor house, with its unusual detached Tudor gatehouse. Built around 1400, the house is a most attractive example of a 'black-and-white' moated manor of the Welsh Marches, while the delightful gatehouse, seemingly teetering on the brink of disaster over the moat, is an almost unique survival.

A woodland nature walk has been laid out to the east of the house. The trees include Japanese and European larch (both sweetly scented in spring as the young leaves open), beech and Douglas fir. Cedar of Lebanon, giant redwood and Californian Wellingtonias can also be seen, contrasting with native oaks, willows and alders.

Most of the crow family live on the estate, including the largest, and nowadays the rarest, the raven. At the other extreme of size are tits and finches, while a notable summer visitor is the

pied flycatcher. This striking black-and-white bird is extending its range but is still largely restricted to the west of the country. Among the predators are sparrowhawks, tawny owls and buzzards.

Some of the greatest concentrations of plants are on the lower, damper parts of the walk where lime-loving plants include dog's mercury, enchanter's nightshade, yellow archangel and golden saxifrage. The higher humidity of western Britain provides the right conditions for ferns, and visitors may recognise hart's tongue with its long, narrow, parallel-sided leaves, growing with male and lady fern; the leaves of the latter are more deeply divided and delicate.

Open: *woodland at all times. Medieval hall of manor, Apr to Oct Wed to Sat, Sun am, and bank holiday Mon. Admission charge to hall only. NT.*
Location: *2 miles E of Bromyard on Worcester road (A44).*
Map: *page 305, SO65.*

Brokerswood: Woodland Park & Phillips Countryside Museum

Wiltshire

The Woodland Park and Phillips Countryside Museum is an 80-acre working forest. It is a fine example of how woodland can be successfully managed both to encourage wildlife and to produce a timber crop. Firewood,

bean- and pea-sticks, and rustic poles for garden furniture are all produced by coppicing. This regular cutting every few years prolongs the life of the trees, and enables light to reach the woodland floor, allowing wild flowers to grow.

The woodland here is 'ancient woodland'; that is, an area which has had tree cover for many centuries and probably ever since woodland covered most of Britain. There have been only five owners since the 11th century, so there have been long periods of continuity of ownership and management.

The woods are rich in tree species, some planted, but mostly the trees are allowed to reproduce themselves by seeding or suckering. On the ground many different kinds of woodland flower are to be found and woodland birds and insects abound.

The natural history and forestry museum explains more about the woodland and its plants and animals. The five-acre lake has an interesting collection of wildfowl, and there are many waymarked woodland walks.

Open: *all year daily. Admission charge. Picnic area. Refreshments. Shop. Special trail for the blind.*
Access: *to woodland by paths only.*
Location: *2 miles NW of Westbury and ¼ mile NE of Brokerswood, off unclassified Brokerswood–Southwick road.*
Map: *page 305, ST85.*

Weathered sandstone outcrops at Brimham Rocks

Bromsgrove: Avoncroft Museum of Buildings

Hereford & Worcester

The rural life of seven centuries is revived at this unusual open-air museum. Since 1967 the 10-acre site has become home to a collection of historic buildings which have been rescued from the threat of destruction, painstakingly restored, and reconstructed here. A granary, a cruck-barn, a nail shop, a wagon shed and a working post-mill are among the exhibits. Craftsmen working at the museum have learned traditional skills in order to restore the buildings exactly to their original form. Visitors can sometimes see these skills – such as sawing planks in a saw-pit or building in wattle-and-daub – in practice at the museum as new buildings are restored to be added to the collection. An unusual recent acquisition is an 18th-century ice-house, from Tong Castle in Shropshire. The predecessor of the deep-freeze, it consists of a deep, brick-built pit, insulated so well that ice put inside it on the coldest days of winter remained frozen long enough to keep food chilled in the summer.

Open: *Mar to Nov daily (except Mon in Mar and Nov). Admission charge. Picnic area. Refreshments. Shop.*
Location: *at Stoke Heath, near junction of A38 and B4091, 1 mile S of Bromsgrove.*
Map: *page 309, SO96.*

Brownsea Island

Dorset

Over 100,000 people visit Brownsea each year, yet it is always possible to find seclusion here. The island has an atmosphere of timelessness – a world by-passed by the 20th century. Visitors can wander along woodland paths, relax on the beautiful beaches, enjoy splendid views of Corfe Castle and the Dorset coast or join a tour of the 250-acre nature reserve managed by the Dorset Naturalists' Trust.

Brownsea possesses a wide range of habitats, including deciduous and coniferous woodland, salt marsh and freshwater lakes, seashore and heathland. An indication of the rich diversity of species which the island enjoys is given by the 1½-mile nature walk.

Red squirrels survive in all the woodland areas, unhampered by the presence of the grey squirrel. Sika deer, first introduced here in 1896, may also be seen in the woods. They are smaller than fallow deer, but similar in that they have faint white spots in summer. Autumn visitors may hear the extraordinary rutting cry of the male – a sharp whistle ending in a grunt.

One transatlantic species which has arrived here is the mink. This dangerous pest was introduced into Britain in 1929, but was first recorded as breeding in the wild on the River Teign in Devon in 1956. Since then it has extended its range considerably to include areas as widespread as Pembroke, East Anglia and southern Scotland. On Brownsea the tern colony has suffered badly in some years from its destructiveness.

The white admiral, with its slow, gliding flight, is one of the many butterflies here. More than 330 species of moth and 20 kinds of dragonfly have been recorded on Brownsea. There are no snakes, but common lizards and slow-worms occur.

The brackish lagoon, which is part of the area managed by the Dorset Naturalists' Trust, supports a Sandwich and common tern colony as well as a great number of waders – oystercatchers, dunlins, curlews, sandpipers, greenshanks, common and spotted redshanks and bar- and black-tailed godwits. Many species are present only in autumn and spring, while in the winter large numbers of ducks, including teal, wigeon and pintail, rest on the lagoon during the day. The heronry is one of the largest in the country. Finally, visitors will be unlikely to avoid hearing the raucous cries of the peacocks which roam, semi-wild, across the island. Their forebears belonged to Mrs Bonham-Christie, the island's last private owner before control of Brownsea passed to the National Trust in 1961. Passionately concerned with wildlife, she became a virtual recluse, maintaining the island as a secret garden where birds, animals and plants flourished unchecked.

Open: *Apr to Sep daily. Refreshments. Shop. No dogs. NT/CNT.*
Access: *by boat from Poole Quay or Sandbanks. Landing fee.*
Location: *in Poole Harbour.*
Map: *page 305, SZ08.*

Slow-worm

Like all reptiles, slow-worms (which are legless lizards, not snakes) need the warmth of the sun to make them active, so the best chance of seeing one is as it lies warming up in some sunny but sheltered spot. Slow-worms are quite harmless; the only defence they have against attackers is the ability to shed their tails.

Burnham Beeches then and now – from workplace to recreational area

Burnham Beeches

Buckinghamshire

Burnham Beeches, with the woods and commons to the north and north-west, forms a fascinating complex of different types of habitat and vegetation from open heath, through scrub and young birch wood, to the ancient pollarded beeches themselves. It is these impressive beeches which give the woods their particular appearance, and which attract thousands of visitors every year.

Pollarding involves cutting trees back to several feet above the ground so that they put out new young shoots which are out of the reach of browsing animals. Originally it was undertaken in many ancient wood pastures, to enable animals to feed in woodlands without threat to the timber crop. For centuries, trees were regarded as a valuable renewable resource and were carefully conserved. Pollarding could supply animal fodder, firewood, poles and many other uses. Trees treated in such ways were not harmed, but rather had their lives considerably extended.

Many of the pollarded beeches here are over 450 years old. Research has shown that pollarding probably started here in the early 16th century and continued for at least 300 years. Much of the wood was used for fuel in neighbouring manors or in London. The decline of pollarding was partly brought about by the advent of shipments of coal to London from the north-east.

Tits, woodpeckers, treecreepers, stock-doves, owls and summer-visiting warblers abound at Burnham Beeches. The wetter parts provide suitable habitats for aquatic insects, particularly several species of dragonfly. Smooth and crested newts can be found in the ponds, and fallow and muntjac deer frequent the woodlands and thickets and visit the stream and ponds for water.

Open: *all year. Picnic areas.*
Location: *3 miles N of Slough on W side of A355; 3 miles S of junction 2 on M40.*
Map: *page 306, SU98.*

Burton Dassett Hills Country Park

Warwickshire

The Burton Dassett Hills rise temptingly out of a level plain between Banbury and Warwick. An outlier of the Cotswolds, the hills are composed of marly limestones (ironstones) which were worked for iron ore from the 1860s until well into this century; this has left the characteristic 'hills and holes' topography. All other traces of the industry have gone, however, and today sheep graze the springy turf alongside walkers, picnickers and kite-fliers.

Features of interest include the 'Beacon', a circular stone tower built in the 14th century (probably as a windmill), and a Saxon burial ground. The grassed hillocks and old quarries support many plants including wild thyme, mallows and bedstraws.

There are magnificent views in all directions, and the AA viewpoint on Magpie Hill identifies a host of distant features which can be seen on a clear day.

Burton Dassett is an example of a deserted medieval village, and has a beautiful 12th-century church.

Open: *all year. Parking charge.*
Location: *off A41 half-way between Banbury and Warwick.*
Map: *page 306, SP35.*

Burton Mere

Dorset

The action of the sea along the wide sweep of Lyme Bay has produced a build-up of shingle which eventually becomes Chesil Beach further east. Near Burton Bradstock it has created the shallow lagoon of Burton Mere, now drained and overgrown by reed swamp.

Inland, open fields rise steeply to 500ft within a short distance and there are superb views along the undulating coast towards Lyme Regis. The exposed nature of this stretch of coastline means there are very few trees, so the reeds and scrub of Burton Mere are important as shelter for migrants in spring and autumn.

In spring wheatears are usually in evidence from early April onwards, showing their white rumps as they fly away when disturbed. Breeding birds in the reeds from May onwards are reed and sedge warblers, summer visitors with harsh repetitive songs. In autumn a wide variety of warblers, flycatchers, finches and thrushes may be found.

Access: *from B3157, 1 mile E of Burton Bradstock. A track leads across Burton Common to beach. Also accessible along beach from Burton Bradstock.*
Location: *1¼ miles SE of Burton Bradstock.*
Map: *page 305, SY58.*

Bwlch Nant-yr-arian Forest Visitor Centre

Dyfed

The native princes who built their castles to guard routes into the wild heart of Wales would have appreciated this Forestry Commission centre's spectacular location. Perched on the brink of a near-vertical slope, it looks westwards down a dramatically deep, steep valley whose wooded slopes frame distant views of Cardigan Bay. The view alone merits a visit, but Bwlch Nant-yr-arian also has exhibits and an excellent audio-visual display which explain man's influence on the landscape and trace the development of the Rheidol Forest. More than 10 million trees – mainly the hardy Sitka spruce – have been planted since 1929 at heights of up to 2300ft.

The area is rich in wildlife. Pine martens, polecats, foxes, badgers and hares roam the land, while buzzards, kestrels and many other birds wheel and hover overhead. Red kites, among Britain's rarest breeding birds, are sometimes seen. Salmon and trout have returned to rivers that were polluted by the spoil from lead mines worked since the Middle Ages.

Waymarked walks of up to five miles start from the centre, making their way through the forest to fine viewpoints and

small lakes. The Jubilee Walk, opened in 1977 to mark the 25th anniversary of Queen Elizabeth's reign, leads to Llyn Pendam, a beautiful pool whose waterside picnic area can be reached by car.

The hamlet of Llywernog, close to Bwlch Nant-yr-arian, has a restored silver and lead mine which flourished from the middle of the 18th century until 1914. Its attractions include old machinery and buildings, a floodlit cavern and an audio-visual programme featuring the voice of Alf Jenkins, the last of the local miners. The old mine in this rural setting is a reminder that our ideas of the division between industry and the countryside are modern. Barely a hundred years ago the whole countryside was regarded as a workshop, with miners, masons, woodworkers, roadbuilders and many others living and working in rural surroundings.

Open: *Forest Visitor Centre Easter to Oct daily (Sat pm only). Admission charge. Picnic sites. Shop. Suitable for disabled visitors. No dogs. Llywernog Silver–Lead Mine Easter to Oct daily. Admission charge. Picnic area. Shop. Refreshments. FC.*
Location: *on A44 10 miles E of Aberystwyth near Llywernog.*
Map: *page 309, SN78.*

Wild thyme – an aromatic herb of grassy banks and dry meadows

JETHART BA'
Jedburgh, Borders

This vigorous game of street handball, played with small leather balls decorated with coloured streamers, is said to date from the days of the border skirmishes when a band of victorious Scottish soldiers once played football with the severed heads of their English enemies. Commemorative football games were eventually replaced by handball.

The only rule in this 'free-for-all' is that the ball must never be kicked. There is no limit on numbers, and no referee. The teams consist of the 'uppies', who hail from the town above the Mercat Cross and play towards Castle Hill, and the 'downies' from the other side of town, who play towards the Townfoot. The aim is for the 'uppies' to place the ball over the castle railings and the 'downies' to carry it over the course of an underground stream. There are generally two games, the 'laddies', at noon, and the men's, at 2pm.

When: *2 Feb (Candlemas Day) and again on Thu nearest 1st Tue after the new moon (Fastern's E'en).*
Map: *page 313, NT62.*

February

Balls used in the hurling ceremonies at St Columb

HURLING THE SILVER BALL
St Ives & St Columb Major, Cornwall

The ancient game of 'Hurling' was once played in many parishes and villages throughout Cornwall, but survives only at St Ives and St Columb. The custom is so old that its origins have been lost, but records of the event go back to beyond the 16th century.

At St Ives the game is held on Feast Monday, which is dedicated to St Ia, the 5th-century Irish missionary after whom the town is said to be named. After a mayoral procession and a ceremony to bless the silver ball at the holy well at Porthmeor, the event starts at 10.30am when the ball is thrown from the wall of the parish church and caught by one of the waiting crowd. It is then passed from one to another on the beaches and in the streets of the town. The person who holds the ball at midday takes it to the Mayor at the Guildhall and receives a crown piece in reward.

At St Columb the game is far more of a contest, with competing teams, one from the town, the other from the surrounding countryside. The 'goals' are two miles apart, each being one mile from the market square where the game starts. All business stops and shop windows are barricaded whilst the teams do battle through the streets and alleyways of the town; the ball is hurled up and down the town with great energy and enthusiasm.

When: *St Ives on Mon following 1st Sun after 3 Feb; St Columb on Shrove Tue and following Sat.*
Map: *St Ives page 304, SW54; St Columb Major page 304, SW96.*

COURT OF PURBECK MARBLERS
Corfe Castle, Dorset

Every Shrove Tuesday for at least 300 years, the Freemen of the Ancient Order of Purbeck Marblers and Stone Cutters have customarily met to elect officers and initiate new apprentices. A bell at the parish church is rung at noon to mark the start of the proceedings, and the Freemen of the order then meet in closed session in the Guildhall. The initiate apprentices must then, as laid down by the ancient articles, 'pay into the wardens for the use of the company six shillings and eight pence (34p), one penny loaf and one quart of beer'. Today's tradition requires that the beer be carried from the Fox Inn to the Guildhall while onlookers attempt to upset it.

After the initiation ceremonies, another custom is observed when a football is kicked through the Halves, two fields behind East Street, in recognition of the Marblers' ancient rights of way. A final tradition is that members of the order make a payment of one pound of peppercorns to the farmer at Ower Farm for use of a track leading through his land to Marblers' Quay, a deep water haven once used for shipping marble.

When: *Shrove Tue.*
Map: *page 305, SY98.*

Jolly contestants in the Olney Pancake Race

OLNEY PANCAKE RACE
Olney, Buckinghamshire

This famous pancake race claims to be the oldest in the world and is probably the original of its kind. It is said to have begun as long ago as 1445 and has continued, with only occasional breaks, ever since.

Competitors must be ladies over 16 years of age who have lived within the parish of Olney for at least three months before Shrovetide. By tradition they must wear skirts, aprons and a hat or scarf when taking part in the race. The Pancake Bell is rung to herald the event and warn the competitors to gather in the Market Place to await the start. The course runs from here, along the High Street, to the Parish Church, a distance of around 415 yards.

The bell is rung again to start the race and the ladies run the course, each carrying her frying pan and a cooked pancake which must be tossed at least three times along the route. If anyone drops her pancake on the road, the rules allow that it may be picked up and tossed again to continue with the race. The winner and the runner-up each receive a prayer book from the vicar and in addition the verger, who rings the Pancake Bell, has the right to claim a kiss from the winner. The race is followed by a Shriving service at the church.

When: *Shrove Tue.*
Map: *page 306, SP85.*

SHROVETIDE FOOTBALL
Ashbourne, Derbyshire & Atherstone, Warwickshire

The tradition of these sometimes riotous games of football goes back many centuries. Many variations of the game are still played in different places across the country, although many were banned as too unruly. Two of the best-known surviving versions are at Ashbourne and Atherstone.

The origins of the football at Ashbourne are unknown, but the game still thrives and is well supported by the local inhabitants. The competing sides are the 'Up'ards' and the 'Down'ards' – those living on opposite sides of Henmore Brook.

There is no limit to the number who can play. The goals are three miles apart, each on the site of a former mill, now marked by a stone on which the ball must be touched three times to be goaled. Between the goals the game can be played anywhere; hence the safeguarding of shops in the main street. The ball used is made from stout leather and filled with cork. Up to four are made each year, hand-painted with some design concerning the person chosen to 'turn it up' – the custom requiring a local worthy or a celebrity to throw the ball into play. The game starts at 2pm and can go on until 10pm.

At Atherstone the custom can be traced to the time of King John, when a contest took place 'betwixt the Warwickshire Lads and the Leicestershire Lads' for the prize of a bag of gold. To accommodate the game traffic is diverted from the town centre and shop windows are boarded up. The ball is specially made each year and decorated with red, white and blue ribbons. The football game usually starts in the afternoon when the ball is thrown out from a window of the Three Tuns Inn by a prominent showbusiness or sporting personality. The two teams – men, women and children – then compete for possession in a free-for-all which usually lasts for about two hours.

Two other well-known venues for Shrovetide Football are Alnwick, Northumberland, and Sedgefield, Co. Durham.

When: *Atherstone on Shrove Tue; Ashbourne on Shrove Tue and Ash Wed.*
Map: *Ashbourne page 310, SK14; Atherstone page 306, SP89.*

The Up'ards and Down'ards struggling in the Henmore Brook in Shrovetide football at Ashbourne

Cairngorms National Nature Reserve

Highland

The Cairngorms range – between Aviemore in Speyside and Braemar in Deeside – forms the largest single tract of uplands over 3000ft in Britain. The area includes four peaks rising to over 4000ft, the highest being Ben Macdui at 4300ft. In winter the Cairngorm slopes provide some of the best skiing in Britain, and resorts such as Aviemore now attract throngs of visitors. But it is still possible to visit numerous lonely, wild and fascinating places; to experience the highest mountain plateaux in Britain; to see relics of the old Caledonian pine forest, with their ancient trees and special wildlife; and to enjoy the magnificent scenery of the many peaceful lochs and unspoilt rivers.

A peregrine falcon – lightning-fast master of the air

The Cairngorms National Nature Reserve is the largest nature reserve in Britain, covering 100 square miles. A large part of it is the great massif of the Cairngorms themselves, bisected by the Lairig Ghru, the pass connecting Speyside and Deeside. Various long walks are possible for the energetic, though intending walkers should be well prepared and aware of the possible hazards. Winds can be ferocious, and the weather can change with startling suddenness.

For most people the best and quickest way up onto the high tops is via the ski road up Cairn Gorm (well signposted from Aviemore and Coylumbridge through the Glen More Forest Park) and then by the chair-lift.

More easily accessible, and well worth a visit, is Loch an Eilein, signposted from the B970, and lying in the northernmost part of the National Nature Reserve. Completely surrounded by pine forest, it offers a small but excellent visitor centre which has a good display on the forest and its wildlife. The loch is perhaps best known for its island: it was here, on the ruins of the Wolf of Badenoch's castle, that one of the last pairs of Scottish ospreys nested until their extirpation early this century. Today, feeding ospreys can again sometimes be seen on the reserve.

A nature trail goes all the way round Loch an Eilein, and those out early, and walking quietly, may see some of the wild creatures which abound. There is even a chance of seeing otters, which live in and around the loch, but which are very shy of man. The forest round the loch is a superb example of the Caledonian pine forests which once cloaked much of Scotland. One of the specialist creatures living here is the crossbill, a bird whose mandibles are crossed so that it can easily extract the seeds from pine cones. In summer, dragonflies hawk across the waters of the loch and butterflies gather in the meadows.

Elsewhere in the Cairngorms there are large tracts of native pinewood, sometimes mixed with birch, rowan or juniper. Ground plants include bilberry, crowberry and heather, as well as the more unusual creeping lady's tresses, chickweed wintergreen and lesser twayblade. Forest mammals include red and roe deer and red squirrels, while sparrowhawks, crested tits, siskins and crossbills are among the typical birdlife. The giant forest grouse, the capercaillie, may also be seen. One of Britain's largest land birds, at nearly three feet long, the capercaillie died out in Scotland and Ireland in the mid 18th century, but was rein-

Wooded slopes and cloud-covered Cairngorm ranges

troduced from Sweden a century later and is now established and breeding again. Capercaillies are rarely found far away from coniferous forests. Look out also for black grouse around the forest edges, and red grouse on the open heather slopes higher up.

Heather-dominated moorland lies above the forest zone, with trailing azalea and mountain crowberry often conspicuous; keep an eye open too for mountain species such as cloudberry, alpine lady's mantle and dwarf cornel and, in wetter areas, alpine meadow rue, starry saxifrage and alpine willowherb. On the high top plateaux and in the glacier-carved corries, ptarmigan replace the red grouse. Here, too, the rare dotterel – a summer-visiting plover which frequents high ground – may sometimes be seen. There is always a chance of golden eagles and peregrines. Red deer occur right up on to the high mountain slopes, where blue hares are also common.

Open: *Nature Conservancy Council Visitor Centre at Loch an Eilein open daily in summer. NCC.*
Location: *SE of Aviemore, with access available from B970.*
Map: *page 314, NH90/NJ00/NN99/NO09.*

Caerlaverock

Dumfries & Galloway

It is barnacle geese which make Caerlaverock so outstanding. Thousands of them fly in from their breeding grounds at Spitsbergen to spend the winter resting and feeding along the waters and marshes of the Solway Firth. The striking black-and-white head of the barnacle goose is a helpful aid in telling it from other geese. Pink-footed and greylag geese can also be seen at Caerlaverock; both are 'grey' geese unlikely to be confused with the barnacle.

Ducks like wigeons and pintails can also be seen here in winter, and birds of prey such as peregrines and merlins may be present. The merse, or salt marsh, of the reserve is home to the rare natterjack toad.

Much of the merse at Caerlaverock is a National Nature Reserve, and a substantial area of adjacent farmland and merse is managed as a refuge by the Wildfowl Trust. Here will be found excellent facilities for watching the wildfowl, including an observatory, watching towers and hides. On the north-west edge of the reserve stand the ruins of Caerlaverock Castle, among the finest examples of medieval secular architecture in Scotland.

Open: *Wildfowl Trust Sep to Apr daily (except Christmas). Admission charge. Warden-escorted visits 11am and 2pm. No dogs. National Nature Reserve open at all times. NCC/WFT. Castle open Mon to Sat all day, Sun pm only. Admission charge.*
Access: *visitors should keep to pathways.*
Location: *on Solway Firth, 7 miles S of Dumfries off B725 Annan to Bankend road.*
Map: *page 313, NY06.*

Caldicot Castle & Country Park

Gwent

Caldicot Castle's sandstone keep, probably built by Humphrey de Bohun in the 13th century, overlooks a 45-acre country park whose proximity to the Bristol Channel attracts herons and many other water-loving birds. The extensive lawns, used for fêtes and fashionable garden parties during the Victorian era, complement informal flower-beds and mature trees where squirrels scamper.

The castle itself is one of many border fortresses built by William the Conqueror's supporters and their heirs. It now houses an art gallery and a museum of costumes and furniture from the 17th, 18th and 19th centuries as well as information on local history.

Open: *country park all year daily; Castle Mar to Oct Mon to Sat all day, Sun pm only. Admission charge (castle only). Refreshments. Shop. Adventure playground.*
Location: *on B4245, 4 miles SW of Chepstow.*
Map: *page 305, ST48.*

Camel Estuary

Cornwall

The Camel is the major estuary on the north coast of Cornwall, its extensive sandbanks and mudflats sheltered by open farmland which slopes up on either shore towards the high ground which forms the coastal cliffs.

The disused Wadebridge–Padstow railway line, on the south side of the estuary, has been converted into a footpath and provides a good opportunity to observe the birdlife on the intertidal areas.

The Cornwall Birdwatching Society has built hides on either shore of the estuary which also provide good views of the waders and wildfowl. Curlews – recognised by their haunting, bubbling cry and long, down-curving bill – are among the more numerous of the waders, but a wide variety of species may be seen. The waders are sometimes put to flight by birds of prey. When flocks of them are circling and wheeling in the sky, look out for the peregrine falcon which could be responsible.

Access: *to N shore via B3314; to S side via disused railway path from Wadebridge to former railway car park at Padstow.*
Location: *NW of Wadebridge.*
Map: *page 304, SW97.*

Caerlaverock Castle – built during the 13th century and now the guardian of a superb nature reserve

Above and below: autumn colours on Cannock Chase

his beloved Maer Hills some years previously.

Crossing the open heathland are several delightful valleys, each containing sphagnum bogs reminiscent of those in the New Forest. In these can be found numerous moisture-loving plants including marsh ferns, marsh orchids and the insectivorous sundew.

A third exciting habitat is the remnants of the former native woodland, the most extensive of which is at Brocton Coppice. Here can be seen an area of ancient gnarled oaks with birches and hollies – similar in character to the Chase woodland described by early historians.

Elsewhere, more than 6000 acres have been planted with pines and other softwood trees by the Forestry Commission and are now a productive forest. As parts mature they are harvested and replanted, great care being taken to develop a varied and attractive landscape as a pattern of old and young crops emerges. In this way an open and degraded landscape has been converted to a productive forest in the modern idiom.

The forest provides numerous walks and other facilities for the visitor as well as a home for a varied and evolving wildlife. This includes fallow deer, badgers, red squirrels and other mammals as well as numerous woodland birds. An exhibition on the forest wildlife can be seen at the Wildlife and Forest Centre, to the south-west of Rugeley on the Penkridge road. Nearby is a three-mile Forestry Commission waymarked walk, which runs through pine forest and down into the open heathland of the Sherbrook valley.

At the northern edge of the Chase is Shugborough Park, home of the earls of Lichfield. This is now owned by the National Trust and managed by the County Council. The house, part of which contains the county museum, is well worth a visit, as is the park, which contains a number of interesting monuments.

Cannock Chase

Staffordshire

The Royal Forest of Cannock was one of three such areas in Staffordshire which were created or enlarged by William I and together covered almost half the county. In 1290 part of the Forest passed to the bishops of Lichfield and became Cannock Chase. By the Reformation much of the woodland had given way to agriculture and was grazed by thousands of sheep. Later, woodland clearance accelerated to supply charcoal for the iron industry, and the pressures of grazing prevented trees re-colonising. As a result, heathland developed on the infertile pebbly soils, while bogs became established in the valleys.

Today much of what remains of the Chase is a country park managed for public recreation by the Staffordshire County Council. They have provided car parks, trails and other facilities including an information centre at Milford, three miles south-west of Stafford on the A513, where the history and wildlife of the Chase are attractively explained.

In fact, the area is a wonderful haven for wild plants and animals. The open heather and bilberry heaths support a wide variety of birds, insects and other animals as well as many heathland plants. One of these – a hybrid between bilberry and cowberry – is particularly noteworthy, having been discovered at Cannock only in 1887. The finder published a description of this 'new British plant', only to find that Charles Darwin had already confirmed its existence in

Open: *information centre (Milford) Sat and Sun, pm only. Wildlife and forest centre open Mon to Fri. Shugborough Hall open mid Mar to late Oct: Tue to Fri and bank holiday Mon all day, Sat and Sun pm only; Admission charge; refreshments; shop; NT.*
Location: *between Stafford, Rugeley, Lichfield and Cannock. Accessible from A513, A51, A460 and A34.*
Map: *page 309, SJ91/SK01.*

Carrbridge: Landmark Visitor Centre

Highland

Established as Europe's first real visitor centre in 1970, Landmark is not just a place for a rainy day. No traveller in the Spey valley and Cairngorms area should miss this complex, with its informative and highly imaginative exhibition and slide shows. The story of Strathspey from its formation in glacial times is told in full, ending with the opportunity to wander along its boardwalk nature trail in the Scots pine wood outside. Watch for red squirrels, crested tits, crossbills and siskins here and around the car park. The shop includes one of the best-stocked bookshops in Scotland for titles covering all aspects of Scottish history, geography, natural history and conservation, and is well worth a browse in its own right.

Open: *all year daily. Admission charge. Picnic area. Refreshments. Shop. Suitable for disabled visitors.*
Location: *on S outskirts of Carrbridge.*
Map: *page 315, NH92.*

Castle Eden Dene

County Durham

At intervals along the Durham coast, steep-sided ravines known locally as 'denes' stretch down to the shore. The largest – nearly four miles in length – is Castle Eden Dene. It is densely clothed by mixed woodland which is managed so as to favour tree and shrub species native to the area.

Nuthatch

Mature woodland, especially with large oaks or beeches, is the favourite haunt of the nuthatch. Its dumpy shape, blue back, orange underparts and white chin, and its ability to walk head-first down trees, make it an easy bird to identify. Nuthatches feed – as their name suggests – on nuts which they lodge in cracks and open with their strong beaks. They also eat insects winkled from

tree bark or foraged for on the ground.

Wild flowers are abundant, with over 300 species recorded in the dene.

Inevitably this rich habitat supports a rich variety of birds and insects. The most notable insect is without doubt the Castle Eden argus butterfly, a sub-species of the brown argus which gets its name from the dene itself.

The resident woodland birds are joined in winter by flocks of redwings, fieldfares and bramblings from Scandinavia. Mammals include red squirrels, roe deer, foxes and badgers. Their presence is often indicated by their footprints in muddy places.

Access: *by marked footpaths. LNR (Peterlee Development Corporation).*
Location: *on S outskirts of Peterlee, N of B1281 and crossed by A19 and A1086.*
Map: *page 310, NZ43.*

Spindle berries, distinctive fruits of woodland and wayside

Castle Woods

Dyfed

This is one of the finest areas of woodland in south-west Wales, and covers a steep, south-facing slope above the River Tywi. At the summit the romantic ruins of Dynevor Castle rise above the trees.

Areas of oak, ash and wych elm probably represent remnants of ancient woodland, though the balance is changing rapidly following a severe attack of Dutch elm disease. The wood lies on limestone, and nearer the ground lime-loving species such as privet, spindle and early dog-violet are found. The reserve is especially noted for its lichens which include tree lungwort, a western variety.

Foxes and badgers frequent the reserve and otters may still occur along the river. Woodland birds include pied flycatchers, redstarts, wood warblers, nuthatches, treecreepers and all three species of woodpecker, while buzzards, ravens and sparrowhawks may be seen overhead, each demonstrating its own acrobatic skills.

The reserve overlooks Dynevor Deer Park, with its fine herd of fallow deer and a few red deer, and the flood meadows of the river valley, which attract large numbers of water birds in winter such as mallard, wigeon, teal and, occasionally, white-fronted geese.

Access: *through gateway from public park. CNT.*
Location: *immediately W of Llandeilo.*
Map: *page 305, SN62.*

Ceiriog Valley

Clwyd

The walls and towers of Chirk Castle, built in 1310 and inhabited ever since, overlook the mouth of this lovely, little-known valley. Steep and narrow, carved by the sparkling River Ceiriog, it wriggles westwards into the heart of the Berwyn mountains above the picturesque little village of Llanarmon Dyffryn Ceiriog.

The valley is a popular base for anglers, pony-trekkers, shooting parties and walkers. Narrow lanes, ancient tracks and footpaths run over the barren Berwyns where, according to legend, the 'Hounds of Hell' roam in search of lost travellers. Much gentler walks start from the Forestry Commission's tranquil picnic place beside a stream at Nantyr, two-and-a-half miles west of Glyn Ceiriog. They explore young plantations and have splendid views of the Berwyns.

Glyn Ceiriog, the valley's focal point, was once a small outpost of the North Wales slate industry. Its years of prosperity are recalled at the Chwarel Wynne or Wynne Quarry, where visitors can tour the underground workings. A short, waymarked walk is devoted to the site's natural history.

Open: *Chwarel Wynne Mine and Museum Easter to Sep daily. Admission charge. Picnic area. Refreshments. Shop.*
Location: *off B4500 between Chirk and Llanarmon Dyffryn Ceiriog.*
Map: *page 309, SJ23.*

Cemlyn

Gwynedd

Some of the oldest rock formations in the world occur along this typical stretch of North Anglesey coast. These metamorphic rocks may be as much as 1500 million years old, and will be of prime interest to geologists.

Of greater significance to naturalists is the large brackish lagoon behind a long shingle bank. Controlled by a weir, the lagoon is a breeding ground for many wild birds, among them the Arctic tern. Although this breeds in greater numbers than any other tern, it is mostly restricted to northern and western Britain. This graceful and delicate bird completes an astonishing annual migration trip from Anglesey to the Antarctic and back – a journey of about 12,000 miles. Not surprisingly, the terns need undisturbed breeding sites, and visitors to Cemlyn are asked by the North Wales Naturalists' Trust, which manages the area, not to go on to the shingle bank, especially during the breeding season from April to July.

The winter visitor may enjoy the sight of great flocks of wildfowl, including wigeon, shoveler and goldeneye, either feeding or seeking sanctuary from the often violent seas off this stormy coast.

Open: *at all times. Free access, but visitors are asked not to disturb wildlife or nesting birds on the nature reserve. Birds can best be viewed from a car on unclassified road W and S of lagoon. NT/CNT.*
Location: *2¼ miles W of Cemaes, on unclassified road off A5025.*
Map: *page 309, SH39.*

At Cenarth, a charming village on the banks of the Afon Teifi

Cenarth Fishing Museum

Dyfed

The Teifi is one of the most attractive rivers in South Wales and a celebrated salmon river. On many Welsh rivers the traditional way to catch these powerful fish was from a coracle, a kind of boat hardly changed in design since prehistoric times. However, coracle fishermen are now few in number, and most salmon are caught by rod and line.

At Cenarth Falls, right beside the Teifi in a cottage specially converted for the purpose, is a museum devoted to rod-and-line tackle. It is unique in Britain, and its collection of antique tackle makes fascinating viewing.

As well as the museum, there is a gallery upstairs which has regular exhibitions, and there are pleasant walks along the river, which cascades in a series of foaming rapids nearby.

Open: *Easter to Oct daily*
Location: *2¼ miles W of Newcastle Emlyn on A484.*
Map: *page 305, SN24.*

The ring of beeches crowning Chanctonbury was as prominent a century ago (above) as it is today (below)

Chanctonbury Ring

West Sussex

The ring of beeches planted on the crest of the South Downs at Chanctonbury by Charles Goring in 1760 can be seen from 30 miles away across the Weald. These beeches make Chanctonbury, at 783ft above sea level, one of the most distinctive summits of the South Downs, and a superb viewpoint, looking northwards across the Weald or south to the English Channel.

Men have made use of Chanctonbury for a variety of purposes for thousands of years. On the summit are holes where flint was mined as long ago as 2000 BC and there is a small three-and-a-half-acre fortified enclosure dating from 300 BC. In the centre of this hill-fort are the remains of two late Roman buildings, one of which was a temple.

The Ring can be approached from all directions. Visitors are advised to park either in Steyning and walk along the Downs or at the picnic area south-east of Washington and walk a steeper but shorter path to the summit.

Location: off A283 2 miles SE of Washington.
Map: page 306, TQ11.

Chalfont St Giles: Chiltern Open Air Museum

Buckinghamshire

The aim of this museum is to preserve vernacular buildings from the Chilterns area. Among buildings so far reconstructed on the site are a toll house, a cart-shed, several granaries and a Victorian privy. Perhaps of greatest interest is the cruck-framed barn. It was originally built at Arborfield, near Reading, in about 1500 and was painstakingly dismantled by volunteers in 1977. It was re-erected in its present position in 1980, and so far as possible the original building methods and materials have been employed in its reconstruction. An Iron Age house, reconstructed from archaeological evidence, can also be seen, and this marks the start of a nature trail. Leading through a variety of habitats, including woodland and chalk grassland, it is a useful introduction to a cross-section of common plants and insects.

Open: Easter to Sep Wed, Sun and bank holidays, pm only. Admission charge. Picnic area. Refreshments. Shop.
Location: at Newlands Park, off Gorelands Lane; reached from B4442 on E side of Chalfont St Giles.
Map: page 306, SU99.

Gough's Cave, Cheddar Gorge

set and Somerset have the same name for this little sedum – 'welcome home husband, though never so drunk'. Some of the loveliest of the reserve's 200 or so species of wild flowers and trees grow in and around Black Rock Quarry with its limestone rocks. One of the most distinctive is the rock-rose, whose yellow, five-petalled blooms appear between May and August.

During the summer the song of the willow warbler is the most common bird-sound at Black Rock, but finches are always present, as are sparrowhawks, kestrels and buzzards – the latter feeding on the re-established rabbit population. Although unlikely to be seen, that most charming and much-loved rodent, the dormouse, lives and sleeps among the bushes.

Cheddar Caves, at the other end of the gorge, offer diversions of a different kind. Of outstanding interest are the stalactites, stalagmites and other formations which have been created over thousands of years by the action of mineral-rich water. The museum here displays finds made in the caves and in the gorge. The most famous exhibit is a prehistoric skeleton, found buried in Gough's Cave.

Open: *caves all year daily except Christmas. Other facilities Easter to Oct daily. Admission charge for caves and museum. Refreshments. Shop. No dogs. Nature reserve accessible by waymarked footpaths. Part NT/CNT.*
Location: *NE of Cheddar, off B3135.*
Map: *page 305, ST45.*

Cheddleton Flint Mills

Staffordshire

On the outskirts of Cheddleton village, just off the main road, stand two brick-built watermills and a group of stone cottages. The mills are very old: one is known to have been in existence in 1253, and was originally built as a corn mill.

In many rural areas, industry developed alongside agriculture. At Cheddleton it took the form of the grinding of flints into a fine powder which was used in making china in the nearby Potteries towns. The flint powder was transported on the Caldon Canal, which runs alongside the mills in the valley of the delightful River Churnet. Leats from the river powered the mills.

The two mills have now been restored with their low breast wheels (which means that the water hits the paddles below the

Cheddar Gorge & Caves

Somerset

This is one of Britain's most famous natural features. The gorge itself is tremendous; its limestone walls rise almost vertically for hundreds of feet, and the trees and shrubs which cling to the sides give it a luxuriant and somehow 'un-English' appearance. As well as being a spectacular sight, the gorge is of great interest for its natural history, especially for the uncommon flowers – including Welsh poppy and bloody cranesbill – which grow on the gorge sides.

Several waymarked nature trails explore the varied habitats in and around the gorge. One leads from Black Rock Gate through the Black Rock nature reserve, which is managed by the Somerset Trust for Nature Conservation. The trail takes in a mixture of limestone grassland, broadleaved woodland, scrub areas and conifer plantations. At the start is a drystone wall, believed to be 200 years old. On it grow lichens, mosses and ferns such as spleenwort; while in June and July the yellow flowers of wallpepper can be found. Interestingly, Suffolk as well as Dor-

axles of the wheels), one in working order. A museum in one mill houses displays relating to the preparation of raw materials for the pottery industry, and an 18th-century mill cottage is open to view. Visitors may also enjoy a very pleasant walk alongside the canal, where the restored 70ft horse-drawn narrow boat *Vienna* is moored on the mill wharf.

Open: *all year, Sat and Sun pm only.*
Location: *2¾ miles S of Leek, on W side of A520 on edge of Cheddleton.*
Map: *page 309, SJ95.*

Chesil & the Fleet

Dorset

From the road west of Abbotsbury and from Portland there are spectacular views of Chesil Beach. This long shingle ridge, which curves for some 8 miles of the Chesil's total 15-mile length, divides the shallow lagoon of the Fleet from the sea and also joins the Isle of Portland to the mainland. The pebbles which form the beach are said to vary in size from west to east and locals can tell where they are by the size of the stones.

Chesil Beach and Abbotsbury

In summer the shingle beach is chosen by terns and waders for nest sites, but disturbance by man and predation by rats has led to a gradual reduction in the colonies of common and little terns. West of the narrows, the only right of way is below the high water mark and it disturbs breeding birds to walk higher up the beach.

The Fleet is one of the oldest nature reserves in the British Isles and its shallow waters, of varied salinity, make it rich in aquatic plants. It is also particularly important for waterfowl, which feed on these plants.

The Ferry Bridge car park overlooks the eastern, most tidal part of the Fleet and the area where good numbers of wading birds may be seen. To the east of the bridge is Portland Harbour, its stone breakwaters creating a sheltered anchorage and attracting a variety of sea birds.

At the Fleet's opposite end is Abbotsbury Swannery, where swans have been kept in a managed herd since at least as early as 1393. In 1543 the Fox Strangways family bought the manor of Abbotsbury; they still own the estate and have managed the

swan herd ever since. Today it is the only large swan herd left in Britain and it is the only such colony in the world that can be visited at nesting time. At this period there are about 350 swans here, but the numbers are substantially boosted in the winter by migrants and may reach around 700. In the nesting season visitors can see the swans and their cygnets at very close quarters, since all are kept in special pens as a protection against predators until September when the young are well grown.

Also part of the estate is a large reed bed, carefully managed as much for the special kinds of wildlife it harbours as for the superb thatching material which the reeds make. Visitors are most likely to see moorhens, but there are also rare birds like the waterrail and bearded tit.

Open: *swannery (weather permitting) May to Sep daily except Sat. Admission charge. Refreshments. Suitable for disabled visitors. No dogs.*
Access: *to Chesil Beach and the Fleet from car parks at Ferry Bridge or Abbotsbury beach.*
Location: *off B3157, reached from either Weymouth or Abbotsbury.*
Map: *page 305, SY67.*

Chew Valley Lake

Avon

One of the largest areas of fresh water in south-west England, this man-made reservoir is partly fringed by reeds and scrub, giving it a generally natural appearance. Parts are set aside as nature reserves and there are a number of birdwatching hides as well as car parks and picnic sites.

Wildfowl are a special attraction, especially diving ducks such as pochard and tufted duck; peak numbers occur in winter. In summer one particularly notable resident is a small duck with an upright tail – the ruddy duck, a North American species which has become established in Britain. It breeds at Chew and also gathers here in large numbers

every autumn. Another resident is the great crested grebe, which provides considerable interest during the breeding season with its spectacular display behaviour.

Access: *good views from lay-bys on A368 at Herriotts Bridge and B3114 at Herons Green. Car parks and picnic areas at the dam and at Denny Wood. Permits from Bristol*

Waterworks Company (see Blagdon Reservoir, page 29) are required to enter the reservoir precincts and visit hides.
Location: *1 mile S of Chew Magna.*
Map: *page 305, ST66.*

Reed beds give Chew Valley Lake a natural appearance and provide shelter for birds

Dunlin

In winter huge flocks of dunlins gather at places like Chichester Harbour, where they probe the mud for a variety of molluscs and other creatures. Their plumage in the winter is dark above and light, almost white, beneath. In summer the plumage changes to dark belly and chestnut and black upper parts. The

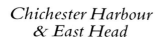

breeding grounds are often places like the moors of the Pennines and Scotland

Chichester Harbour & East Head

West Sussex

Covering an area of some 3000 acres of water, mudflats and salt marsh, Chichester Harbour offers shelter and food to many thousands of waders, wildfowl and seabirds every winter. Generally speaking, the wildfowl seek their vegetable food among the marshes, while the waders search the flats for the countless creatures which live in the mud.

The birds most likely to be seen in this Area of Outstanding Natural Beauty in winter are Brent geese – of which there may be up to 7000 – and dunlin, which may reach numbers in excess of 20,000. The species of Brent goose seen here is the dark-bellied race. This small goose is about two feet long, with a black head and neck, dark-grey underparts and a white rump. It breeds in the far north. Dunlins are the commonest small shore birds; about seven inches long, dark above and almost white beneath in winter. Other birds likely to be seen include shelducks, mallards, ringed plovers, oyster-catchers, redshanks, lapwings, grey plovers and godwits. In summer the salt marshes are rich in coastal plants like sea-aster, glasswort and sea-lavender.

On the east side of the harbour entrance is East Head, a narrow spit of land and shingle beach which runs north-east, like a

finger, into the harbour. Part of its fascination is that it is still changing, influenced by high tide surges and rough weather. Less than a century ago it pointed north, and a century before that north-west, almost touching Hayling Island.

A nature walk at East Head takes visitors along the shingle on the seaward side, returning by the inner saltmarshes. Plant life on the walk includes the salt-resistant sea couch-grass on the seaward side, and sea-rocket on the dunes. Ninety or so species of flowering plants have been recorded at East Head; of note are sea bindweed, the localised evening primrose, rare sea heath and golden samphire. On the beaches are many sea-shells including the pinky-brown slipper limpet, which changes sex as it matures.

Access: *by public footpaths from West Wittering, Bosham, Birdham etc. (Care should be taken to avoid the foreshore at the time of the spring tides.) Good views from A286 West Wittering road and from Hayling Island. East Head NT; free access subject to conservation work in progress.*
Location: *7 miles SW of Chichester.*
Map: *page 306, SU70.*

Child Beale Wildfowl Trust

Berkshire

The Trust was established to preserve a particularly beautiful section of the Thames valley and for the conservation and exhibition

Christchurch Harbour from Hengistbury Head

of creatures such as endangered species of birds, Highland cattle, and rare breeds of British sheep.

Of particular interest are the collections of pheasants and waterfowl. Many of the pheasants are either rare in the wild or spectacular to look at, or both. A flamingo pen contains both Chilean and Caribbean Flamingos. The collections of ducks, geese, swans and cranes contain some spectacular and interesting species. Many species of British duck can be seen at close quarters. Parakeet aviaries, peacocks and a collection of budgerigars add colour and interest to the collections. As well as all these, many species of wild British bird can be seen in the grounds and surrounding woods, downs, river and reed beds.

Open: *Apr to Sep daily except Fri. Admission charge. Shop. Suitable for disabled visitors. No dogs.*
Location: *1¼ miles NW of Pangbourne on A329 Streatley road.*
Map: *page 306, SU67.*

Chillingham Park

Northumberland

In a county with more castles per square mile than any other in Britain it is no surprise to find a place as magnificent as Chillingham Castle, but what really makes this place extra special is about 350 acres of parkland, in which the castle stands. Lovely, rolling countryside, of which a considerable part is woodland, the park is also home to the famous herd of wild white cattle. These interesting animals have lived within the confines of the park since at least the Middle Ages and have fascinated scientists and artists over many years.

Perhaps the most famous artist to depict the herd was Thomas Bewick, whose woodcut of the Chillingham bull is probably the finest of all his works. Much photographed today, the animals are looked after by a warden who escorts all visiting parties, both for the safety of the visitors, and to avoid excessive disturbance to the animals. Originally widespread, and living completely

wild when the countryside was thickly wooded, a group of the cattle became isolated when Chillingham Park was walled, and their descendants now roam the park's extensive woodland. These woodlands are also home to many species of birds with at least one, the nuthatch, at the extreme northern limit of its breeding range. Green woodpeckers like the mature deciduous trees and where cavities occur in some of them, tawny owls can find a nest site.

Open: *park Apr to Oct daily except Sun am and Tue. Admission charge. No dogs. (Castle not open.)*
Location: *at Chillingham, 4½ miles SE of Wooler.*
Map: *page 313, NU02.*

Christchurch Harbour & Hengistbury Head

Dorset

The harbour is the estuary of the Hampshire Avon and Dorset Stour. Sheltered behind the high ground of Hengistbury, it is a superb area for wading birds and wildfowl, with the special quality of being unspoiled by industry and unused by commercial shipping.

The wading birds which feed on the mudflats at low tide can be seen best within a few hours of high tide when Stanpit Marsh, a local nature reserve on the north side, is probably the best place to visit. Dunlins are the most numerous small waders, with numbers reaching several thousand. In flight they form tight flocks which wheel and turn in unison. Wildfowl are also well represented, the large black and white shelduck being the most obvious.

Hengistbury Head is the dominant feature of the harbour, and Warren Hill, its highest point, provides a good vantage point to look over the estuary or out to sea. Its strategic value, both for defence and for ease of trading with the Continent, gave rise to a thriving Iron Age settlement here. These people built two great banks and ditches on the landward side of the Head.

The woodland and scrub which cover parts of the Head provide shelter for many migrant birds in spring and autumn, when rarities such as the exotic hoopoe sometimes occur. A nature trail has been laid out.

Location: *1 mile S of Christchurch.*
Map: *page 305, SZ19.*

Bewick's famous woodcut of a Chillingham bull

Cissbury Ring

West Sussex

All along the great sweep of the South Downs there are tremendous views, but at Cissbury there is also a sense of history. Rising 600ft above sea level, it commands views which stretch from Beachy Head to the Isle of Wight. The history of man at Cissbury is recorded both on and beneath the surface of the hill.

The remains of Neolithic flint mines lie half-hidden among gorse and bracken at the western end of the hill. Some of the shafts were 40ft deep, with interlinking galleries. Cissbury's most prominent ancient monument is its Iron Age hill fort. One of the largest in the country, it was built around 250 BC, though its air of strength and solidarity suggests it could still be used for defensive purposes.

Cissbury was abandoned before the Romans arrived, and there is evidence of an early cultivated Celtic field system within the inner area. At the end of the Roman occupation Cissbury was, briefly, re-fortified – almost certainly against Saxon attack. Today it is a peaceful place best reached through the pretty village of Findon. Almost unceasing winds blow great cloud banks over the hill, the light changes constantly, sheep's sorrel ripples red on the ramparts, and the singing of skylarks is punctuated by the voices of stable lads exercising racehorses on the Findon gallops.

Open: *at all times. NT.*
Location: *1½ miles E of Findon (A24), 3 miles N of Worthing.*
Map: *page 306, TQ10.*

Clayton: Jack & Jill Windmills

West Sussex

There are three striking 19th-century additions to the landscape near the village of Clayton. One is the Clayton Tunnel, built around 1840 to take the London, Brighton and South Coast Railway almost a mile through the chalk of the South Downs. It is not its length that makes it notable, but the castellated and turreted entrance, a legacy of an era when it was considered that even so functional a thing as a railway tunnel entrance could be made to look romantic.

On top of the scarp into which the Brighton line plunges are the other two striking additions – the windmills known as Jack and Jill. Jack, a black tower-mill built in 1866, is not open, but Jill, a white-lead-painted post-mill, can be visited. Jill was built in 1821 and stood in Dyke Road in Brighton until 1852 when it was moved. Moving windmills was no easy task, and to move Jill took 86 oxen – at that time the main draught animals of Sussex. The mill last worked in 1907, and is now being restored by the Jack and Jill Windmills Society.

The rather humble-looking church of St John the Baptist in the village is worth visiting for its unique and extensive 11th- and 12th-century wall paintings.

Open: *Jill only, most Suns Apr to Oct. Donation expected.*
Location: *6 miles N of Brighton on unclassified road, ¼ mile E of A23.*
Map: *page 306, TQ31.*

The Clee Hills

Shropshire

Brown Clee (1792ft) and Titterstone Clee (1749ft) are Shropshire's highest hills. They stand apart from the main mass of the South Shropshire hills and are geologically quite different, being composed of Old Red Sandstone overlain by coal measures and capped by volcanic dolerite.

Titterstone Clee and its associated commons have a remarkably wild character, bearing

in mind that the West Midlands conurbation is only a few miles away. The hill is rugged and exposed, and the croaking sound of ravens can sometimes be heard as they soar overhead. But the hand of man is never far away, whether it be the stone quarries on the flanks, the ruined traces of an ancient hill-fort, or the futuristic radar domes perched on the summit.

Brown Clee is equally wild, but has extensive woodlands all around its eastern slopes. A 1¼-mile forest trail, laid out by the landowner and the Shropshire Trust for Nature Conservation, starts from the picnic area one mile west of Cleobury North. There is also a public footpath which zig-zags up through the woods for about a mile to the summit, where there are three Iron Age hill-forts.

Location: *between Ludlow and Bridgnorth, reached from A4117 or B4364.*
Map: *page 309, SO68.*

Clent Hills Country Park

Hereford & Worcester

Understandably, the edge of the Black Country follows closely the limit of the coal measures. Cross that boundary and it seems like a different land. Nowhere is this more true than on the southern edge, where the bricks and mortar of Stourbridge and Halesowen stop like a frozen wave and the Clent Hills rise to 1000ft out of pleasant rolling countryside.

The National Trust owns a large area of the Clents and part of that is now managed by the County Council as a country park. It offers fresh air, exercise and magnificent views in all directions within a stone's throw of the conurbation.

The rocks (called Clent Breccia) of which the hills are mainly composed give rise to poor, dry soils. These support heathy grassland with few flowers of note. However, the combination of open ground, scrub and woodland attracts a good variety of birds.

Open: *at all times. Part NT.*
Location: *3 miles S of Stourbridge on unclassified road off A491.*
Map: *page 309, SO98.*

Cleveland Way

This 93-mile long-distance path, the second to be opened in England and Wales, follows the western and northern boundaries of the North York Moors National Park (see pages 200–3), then runs along the coast.

Beginning at Helmsley, the path makes its way close to Rievaulx Abbey, one of Britain's most lovely abbey ruins (see page 203). Beyond Rievaulx it follows the scarp of the Hambleton Hills up to Mount Grace Priory. From here it turns eastward, following the Cleveland Hills up to the charmingly named Roseberry Topping, a beautiful hill which looks rather like a volcano. Beyond Guisborough the path makes its way to the sea at Saltburn, from where it follows the coast all the way down to a point near Filey.

Scenery encountered on the way includes moorland, farmland, high pastures and meadows, valleys, and a varied coastline. The best places for flowers are the limestone valleys of the Hambleton Hills and the valleys on the coast. Here a profusion of flowers, including bee orchid, wild thyme, cowslip and primrose can be seen.

Like all long-distance paths, this one can be joined or left at any point where it meets a public road or track.

Location: *runs from Helmsley to the Wyke (1¼ miles NW of Filey)*
Map: *page 310.*

Jack, one of the Clayton windmills

Cley-next-the-Sea

Norfolk

At first glance, Cley looks like any other north Norfolk village. The coast road winds past attractive brick-and-flint cottages which suddenly give way to the open marshes and the distant line of the shingle sea-wall. There is a very attractive windmill with all its sails intact. But there seem to be a lot of people about, even in winter. And why are so many of them carrying binoculars? The answer is, of course, that Cley is one of the most popular bird-watching places in Britain – and arguably the most famous. Rare birds have no doubt made landfall here since Britain became an island. Once they were shot for collections, but today they are much better treated. Indeed, the Norfolk Naturalists' Trust manages its large reserve here especially to encourage birds; it was the first reserve of its kind in the country when it was established in 1926. Rarities such as the avocet, bittern and bearded tit nest; in winter there are large numbers of wildfowl, plus snow buntings; and in spring and autumn ... expect the unexpected! There is a very good visitor centre and fine walking on the East Bank and the sea-wall.

Open: *perimeter paths, banks and public hides at all times. Visitor centre Apr to Oct daily except Mon. Reserve (permit, admission charge) all year daily except Mon. CNT.*
Location: *on A149 coast road N of Cley-next-the-Sea. Reserve is E of Cley village.*
Map: *page 311, TG04.*

Clumber Park

Nottinghamshire

Clumber covers nearly 4000 acres of parkland, farmland, lake and woodlands. Its fine landscapes and serpentine lake were created out of unpromising heathland on the edge of what was once the Royal Forest of Sherwood. Today it is one of Britain's most popular country parks – a tribute to the genius of its 18th-century landscapers.

Great emphasis has been placed on the provision of facilities for visitors. The lake is one of the finest for coarse fishing in the country, and there are special aids for the disabled angler. Many visitors take advantage of the cycle hire scheme to explore the miles of good roads, and riding permits are issued to horse owners. A planned nature walk runs through part of the extensive woodland, passing among fine specimen trees – oak, chestnut and beech. It also follows the longest double lime avenue in Europe, with 1296 trees.

Canada geese, tufted ducks, and grebes live and breed on the lake, and among regular winter visitors is the goldeneye. This comparatively rare duck has an unusual high forehead, giving it a distinctive profile. It dives in its search for food, and if it is disturbed the whistling sound of its wings in flight is unmistakable.

Among Clumber's many other features of interest are the classical bridge over the lake, two garden temples and pleasure gardens. The chapel, described as a 'cathedral in miniature', was built in the 1880s and is a superb example of Gothic Revival style.

Open: *park at all times (chapel daily, pm only). Admission charge for vehicles. Refreshments. Shop. Suitable for disabled visitors. Cycle hire. Fishing permits from Head Warden or Water Bailiff. NT.*
Location: *4½ miles SE of Worksop, 1 mile from A1/A57/A641 junction.*
Map: *page 310, SK67.*

The 18th-century windmill at Cley, overlooking marshland

Coate Water Country Park

Wiltshire

This popular country park has been established around what was originally a buffer lake for the canal locks at Swindon. It offers a wide range of activities including walking, boating, fishing and birdwatching, as well as an agricultural museum. Part of the park is maintained as a local nature reserve, centred on an area of open water with fringing reed beds and swampy ground, and separated from the main lake by a dam. Two hides are available (permits required), and footpaths round the lake offer good views.

Several species of duck can be seen here throughout the year with shoveler, teal, tufted duck and mallard breeding from time to time. Great crested grebes breed here too, and their complex mating displays make them very exciting to watch. Wiltshire's largest colony of breeding reed warblers shares the reserve with many other summer visitors which rear their young here.

The surrounding damp meadows attract such birds as lapwings, redshanks and snipe. In summer, lady's smock, meadow-sweet, ragged robin and other meadow flowers add considerable colour to the scene.

Although this area has changed dramatically since Swindon became a major railway town and business centre, it is still well worth a visit to gain some of the flavour of the countryside written about by the 19th-century naturalist Richard Jefferies. Nearby, at Coate Farm where he was born, there is a museum to commemorate his life and works.

Open: country park and nature reserve all year daily except Christmas; agricultural museum summer Suns, pm only. Picnic and barbecue areas. Refreshments.

Facilities for disabled visitors. Part LNR. Richard Jefferies museum open all year Wed, Sat and Sun, pm only.
Location: SE outskirts of Swindon; entrance off B4006 Marlborough Road.
Map: page 305, SU18.

Cogges Farm Museum
Oxfordshire

Across the River Windrush from Witney is the ancient hamlet of Cogges, with its priory and manor farm. This has recently become the setting for Oxfordshire County Council's farm museum. The medieval farmhouse, dairy, kitchen, garden, farmyard, stables, barns and granary are all restored to reflect the traditional way of life. The museum aims to reconstruct life on a working farm in Edwardian times, and is stocked with breeds of horses, cattle, sheep and pigs appropriate to that period. At weekends in summer many of the old farm and country crafts are demonstrated: cream- and butter-making, threshing, bridle-making, hurdle-making and blacksmithing. A nature trail and a historical trail have been laid out, and include walks beside the Windrush. Cotswold cheese and freshly baked bread from the

Cogges Farm Museum and some of its inhabitants

farm's own bread oven are among the attractions of the restaurant in the old cattle shed.

Open: Apr to Oct daily. Admission charge. Information centre. Refreshments. Bookshop.
Location: off B4022, SE of Witney.
Map: page 306, SP31.

Colwick Park
Nottinghamshire

This popular 260-acre park has been specially planned by Nottingham City Council to cater for all interests. There is a lake set aside for wildlife; one stocked with trout for angling; another reserved for swimming, boating and sailing; and a marina as well. Those who prefer dry land can choose from a network of riding trails and footpaths, and there are picnic sites from where watersports or water-birds may be watched. The winter months are the best time to see waterfowl such as gadwall, goldeneye, wigeon, pochard and teal.

Presiding over the often crowded park is stately Colwick Hall, built 200 years ago and now a restaurant and pub.

Location: 1¼ miles E of Nottingham off B686 Colwick Road.
Map: page 310, SK63.

Coombe Hill

Buckinghamshire

The highest viewpoint in the Chilterns, Coombe Hill rises to 852ft, and on fine days the view extends over a large part of the upper Thames valley to the Berkshire Downs and the Cotswolds. Nearer is the Vale of Aylesbury, while, just to the south-west, and topped by a clump of trees, is Beacon Hill.

The use of Coombe Hill as a public open space is due in good measure to the people of Wendover. In 1906 the owner (the Attorney-General at that time) erected barriers on the property. Local people stormed the hilltop and tore down the obstacles. Public rights of way were established after the ensuing litigation.

The short nature walk is designed to indicate the distinctive forms of vegetation on the chalk hillside and the acid clay of the flat hilltop. The walk passes a natural mixed wood of oak, hornbeam, silver birch and rowan. Yorkshire fog grass, with its characteristic pink-striped stems, grows beneath the trees. A fence on the walk has a badger gate built into it; the badger can push the hinged flap to get in and out of the wood – rabbits are unable to do so and young trees are protected from

their attacks. In 1965 the National Trust re-introduced sheep; among other breeds, visitors may at times see the brown-and-white Jacob sheep grazing on the hillside. On the top of the hill acid-loving plants like sheep's sorrel, tormentil and heath bedstraw grow with heather and gorse.

On the return leg the walk joins the long-distance Ridgeway path for a short section. The kestrel is usually present, hovering over the hill among soaring swifts, housemartins and swallows during the summer.

Open: *at all times. NT.*
Location: *off B4010 1½ miles W of Wendover.*
Map: *page 306, SP80.*

Coombes Valley

Staffordshire

A fast-flowing rocky stream falls 400ft through this wooded valley. Managed jointly by the RSPB and the Staffordshire Nature Conservation Trust, the woodland reserve, with areas of

heath and meadowland, supports a wide diversity of bird life. Over 130 bird species have been recorded, with more than half of these having bred at some time. The flora is equally rich; the woodland, consisting mainly of oak, ash and birch, also includes holly, rowan and wych elm with a mixed understorey of species such as blackthorn, bird cherry, guelder rose and planted rhododendron.

The insect life of the reserve is especially diverse, and among the breeding butterflies is the uncommon high brown fritillary. Badgers are present, and so are great crested newts. There is a nature trail and two bird hides, one beside a pool where various water birds can be seen, and one set in an oak tree, offering views of the smaller insect-feeders in the treetops.

Open: *Apr to Aug Tue, Thu, Sat and Sun; Sep to end Dec Sat and Sun only. Admission charge. Information centre. CNT/RSPB.*
Access: *by nature trail.*
Location: *2¾ miles SE of Leek; 1¼ miles off A523 on unclassified Basford Green-Cheddleton road.*
Map: *page 310, SK05.*

Cornwall's Coast Path crosses much National Trust land

Cornwall Coast Path

Cornwall

Encircling the whole of the Cornish peninsula, this is one of the best-loved of the long-distance footpaths. It forms one of four sections of the South-West Peninsula Coast Path, and, at 268 miles, makes up more than half the total length of this path. It can be joined or left at numerous places, and walks varying in length from a few hundred yards to the complete distance can be planned. The path was designed to hug the coastline as closely as possible, and this it does, following the route of long-established coastguards' paths for much of its length.

Scenery along the path varies from cliffs, hilltops and moors to sand dunes and estuaries, and the wildlife is equally diverse. Particularly wild and dramatic cliffs can be found on the stretches between Marsland Mouth (on the north coast at the county boundary) and Tintagel; from St Ives

right fore paw

round to Mousehole; around the Lizard; and at the Dodman. Long stretches of sand can be had at Newquay and Hayle, while coves and sheltered beaches can be numbered in their hundreds round the entire coast.

The route is marked at intervals by the familiar acorn symbol used by the Countryside Commission on long-distance paths.

Map: *pages 304–5.*

The waterfall at Corrieshalloch

Corrieshalloch Gorge

Highland

Equally notable for its rare plants and its spectacular scenery, Corrieshalloch Gorge is a box canyon, about a mile long and up to 200ft deep, with almost vertical walls. Through it flows the River Droma, which plunges into a 150ft waterfall – the Falls of Measach. Conditions are ideal for a variety of ferns, mosses and liverworts, and dwarf trees including birch, rowan, hazel and sycamore cling to the rocky sides of the ravine. Many typical woodland birds are to be found, and ravens have been known to nest here. Much of the gorge is inaccessible, and it is essential to keep to the footpaths.

Open: *at all times. NCC/NTS.*
Location: *on A835 at Braemore, 12 miles SE of Ullapool.*
Map: *page 314, NH27.*

Cotehele

Cornwall

Few would dispute that Cotehele is as perfect a medieval manor house as any in Britain. Set high above the River Tamar, it has remained a peaceful and beautiful place for many centuries.

Now owned by the National Trust, Cotehele and its grounds are still a constant delight. A path from the beautiful, steeply sloping garden leads gradually into the woods along a deep, narrow valley where sub-tropical plants grow. In spring, flowers carpet the slopes while returning warblers fill the air with song, competing with native birds for nesting places. From the Chapel in the Wood, the view often includes cormorants flying low over the surface of the Tamar to roost on the rocky banks far below.

Cotehele Quay was a busy place full of trading vessels until 1907, when the railway arrived and river trade began to decline. It is now the permanent home of the *Shamrock*, last of the old Tamar sailing barges. Built at Plymouth in 1899, she was laid up and reduced to a hulk in the early 1970s, but is now fully restored. Close by is a small museum illustrating her history. Much of the rigging used in her refitting was made in the Trust's workshops at Cotehele Mill, half a mile away. The mill was a working watermill as early as the 16th century, and has been restored together with the huge horse-drawn cider press beside it. Also worth a visit is the forge and the estate workshops.

Open: *Apr to Oct daily; grounds only also open Nov to Mar daily. Admission charge. Refreshments. NT.*
Location: *8 miles SW of Tavistock, on W bank of R. Tamar. Signposted off A390 Tavistock – Callington road at St Ann's Chapel village. 1 mile W of Calstock by footpath.*
Map: *page 305, SX46.*

The Badger

Almost entirely nocturnal, the badger is probably less frequently seen than any other common British mammal. Badgers live in underground homes called 'setts', which are kept scrupulously clean. When the badger does emerge its first visit is to the latrine – close to the sett – then it goes in search of a drink and food. The badger's diet includes bulbs, roots, worms, slugs and baby rabbits. The best time to watch badgers is in spring, when whole families may play outside the sett.

Badgers
National History Museum, London
31 December . 83

The Cotswolds

Designated an Area of Outstanding Natural Beauty, the Cotswold Hills capture, for many people, the quintessence of the English countryside. A patchwork of arable fields, pasture-land and woodland is complemented by a network of drystone walls, scattered farmsteads and captivating villages whose manor houses, churches and cottages are built of golden Cots-wold stone. Much of the finest architecture is the legacy of a flourishing wool trade which brought tremendous wealth to the area in late medieval times. The sheep grazed the limestone grasslands which, where they remain today, are studded with brilliantly coloured summer wild flowers.

Rising steeply from the lowlands of the Severn valley and the Vale of Evesham, the Cotswold land-scape is one of gently undulating hills dissected by small river val-leys. The topography is domi-nated by the steep, west-facing scarp. The highest point is at Cleeve Hill (1083ft), north-east of Cheltenham. The gentle dip slope to the east is incised by rivers such as the Windrush, Coln and Churn, draining to-wards the Thames valley to the south-east. The Thames itself rises at Thames Head, just a few miles south-west of Cirencester.

The rocks which make up the Cotswolds were deposited some 150 to 130 million years ago. The area was then covered by shallow seas. Gradually, the sea floor be-came covered with layers of shell and bone fragments of dead sea creatures, and these layers are what eventually formed the 'oolitic' limestone – the famous building stone of the Cotswolds. Beneath the oolitic limestones lie clays and sandstones which come to the surface near the foot of the hills. In towns such as Blockley and Winchcombe bricks are made of the clays.

History

Man's influence on the Cotswold landscape is unmistakable. Evi-dence of his presence here dates from Neolithic times and long barrows such as Belas Knap near Winchcombe and Hetty Pegler's Tump near Uley are accessible to the public. One of the most fam-ous archaeological sites is Crick-ley Hill (see page 71), where both Neolithic and Iron Age camps have been excavated. Much later came the Romano-British settle-ments of places such as Cirences-ter and Kingscote, and a visit to the Roman villa at Chedworth

(see page 69) is well worthwhile. Many of the Cotswold villages have their origin in medieval times and evidence of deserted villages and field systems is found, for example, at Coberley, south of Cheltenham.

Throughout the medieval period, Britain was acknowledged as the producer of the finest wool in Europe, and Cotswold wool was the best of British. Legacies of the wool trade are to be found all over the Cotswolds. The landscape itself owes much to generations of grazing sheep, which produced a countryside with few trees and huge tracts of short turf. Today, when many of the sheepwalks have become arable prairies and sheep are confined to much smaller fields, the open character is retained.

Wildlife

The wildlife of the Cotswolds is rich and varied. Habitats such as woods, fields, streams and marshes each have their own characteristic range of plants and animals. The areas of greatest natural history interest are undoubtedly those which have remained least changed throughout history. Thus, as is often the case, it is the ancient woodlands and rough grasslands which support the greatest diversity of wildlife and in some cases are refuges for some of Britain's rarest species.

The woodlands of the Cotswolds are perhaps best seen on the scarp slopes near Painswick. These famous beechwoods are of international renown for the quality of their timber, but are also rich in wildlife. A walk through a Cotswold beechwood on an autumn day when the leaves glow in shades of gold, orange and red is an unforgettable experience. Where the beech is most dense, the ground underneath may be almost bare, but elsewhere there are also trees such as ash, whitebeam, holly and yew. The forest floor in spring may be covered with bluebells, dog's mercury, wood anemones and primroses, while less common plants of these woods include spurge laurel, stinking hellebore and bird's-nest orchid.

Birds of the beechwoods include woodpeckers, titmice, warblers, nuthatch, treecreeper, tawny owl and song thrush, to name but a few. Badgers, foxes and grey squirrels are the commonest mammals and small wood mice and bank voles are also abundant, although rarely seen. A search of the forest floor may yield snails, beetles and fungi, all important components of the woodland ecosystem. Along the forest tracks butterflies such as the speckled wood, the silver-washed fritillary or the rare white admiral may be attracted to the light. Away from the scarp, on the dip slope, there are different types of woodlands. Small copses of oak and hazel are common, while conifers have been introduced in some places. Wild lily-of-the-valley may be found, or a small group of the diminutive yellow star of Bethlehem. Fallow deer may be seen picking their way through the trees, or a buzzard glimpsed soaring overhead.

In complete contrast to the woodlands are the limestone grasslands. Changing farming practices mean that few areas of unimproved grassland remain, but it is those areas untouched by plough or artificial fertiliser which support the greatest range of fauna and flora. Mostly these places occur on the steeper slopes and ancient commons of the Cotswolds. Here, centuries of grazing by sheep or cattle has resulted in a sward rich in grasses, like the delicate quaking grass, and pretty flowers which speckle the ground with yellows, blues and pinks during the summer months. Specialities of the area include the nationally rare pasque flower and orchids such as green-winged, bee, pyramidal and fragrant. On sunny summer days hundreds of butterflies add to the spectacle. The common blue, chalkhill blue, meadow brown, small heath and distinctive marbled white are all closely associated with the limestone grasslands.

The rivers and streams of the Cotswolds provide a quiet refuge for wetland wildlife. Bordered by alders and willows, the water may be covered in summer by the delicate white flowers of the water crowfoot. Crayfish and freshwater shrimps are common, as are fish such as trout, grayling, roach, chub and dace. The most spectacular insects must be the dragonflies and damselflies which course over the rushes and flags at the edges of the streams. Birds such as mallard and moorhen, dipper and kingfisher may be glimpsed.

The Cotswold farmlands are also home for a variety of wildlife. Swallows and house martins nest in and around the farm buildings; barn owls fly over the fields in search of small mammals. Pheasants and partridges are present in abundance and hares are still commonplace.

Finally, some more unusual wildlife habitats. Quarry workings may support another rare plant, the Cotswold pennycress, which grows on the bare rock. Around Nailsworth, the disused stone mines are roosting sites for bats, notably the extremely rare greater horseshoe bat. Disused railway lines, too, are of interest, both for their geological exposures and for the range of species which colonise and thrive in the old cuttings.

Cotswold Stone

The villages, manor houses, churches, farms and walls of the Cotswolds all owe their beauty to the nature of the stone from which they are constructed. The hard oolitic limestone is ideal building material and the buildings are in complete harmony with the landscape. A distinctive style of architecture has developed in the Cotswolds, the houses being characterised by their steep, gable-ended roofs, tall chimneys and casement windows. Slates for the roofs are also derived from the limestone, dug out of the quarries and split into tiles.

Drystone walls are an important and attractive feature of the landscape. In the lowlands, fields are generally bordered by hedges, but here in the more exposed uplands, with a ready supply of rock close to the ground surface, walls have long formed the boundaries, the flat stones neatly laid together without the need for mortar. The walls are also of natural history interest – wrens and wagtails may nest or shelter in the holes and crevices while lichens and stonecrops cover the capping stones.

The colour of the walls reflects the origin of the stone from which they are built – creamy grey in the south, orange-brown in the east and a delicate pale buff everywhere else.

What to See

ARLINGTON ROW, BIBURY
On the River Coln in the pretty village of Bibury stands this lovely terrace of early 17th-century Cotswold stone cottages. Originally timber-framed and once a wool factory, they are now in the care of the National Trust. The weavers hung their wool out to dry on racks in a field nearby; nowadays known as Rack Isle and also owned by the Trust, it is maintained as a nature reserve. Also in Bibury is the Arlington Mill Museum, a collection of old farm implements and domestic bygones set in a former mill.

Open: *exteriors of Arlington Row cottages always viewable; interiors* *not shown. NT. Mill museum open Mar to Oct daily, Nov to Feb weekends only; admission charge.*

BREDON BARN
This aisled Cotswold limestone barn near Tewkesbury was partially destroyed by a fire in 1980, but its restoration has recently been completed.

The barn is 132ft long with an unusually steep stone shingled roof. A small loft, or 'tallat', is sited above one of the gabled porches and is known as the Bailiff's room. It has a fireplace, and is reached by an external staircase.

Open: *Wed and Thu pm only, Sat and Sun all day. Admission charge. NT.*

BROADWAY TOWER COUNTRY PARK

Centred round the tower which gives it its name, this country park offers a wide range of outdoor leisure activities, including adventure playgrounds, nature trails through a variety of Cotswolds scenery, and a collection of animals of various kinds. The tower itself, dating from the 18th century, looks over 12 counties, and houses a series of exhibitions, one of which explains its history; of special interest are its connections with William Morris and the pre-Raphaelites.

Open: *Apr to early Oct. Admission charge.*

CHEDWORTH ROMAN VILLA

In Roman times this villa was built close under a hill in deep woodland north of Cirencester. It was rediscovered in 1864 by a gamekeeper who, seeking a lost ferret, found the now famous mosaic pavement.

The site had been carefully chosen for its proximity to a spring whose waters still run clear and cool through the villa, and were used by the first owner in the all-important villa baths. These baths were, as might be expected, the last word in luxury, incorporating elaborate steam baths and a dry hot bath.

Open: *all year (except for 3 weeks in Dec and Jan) Mar to Oct Tue to Sun and bank holiday Mon (closed Good Fri); Nov to early Dec, and Feb, Wed to Sun. Admission charge. Shop. NT.*

COOPER'S HILL LOCAL NATURE RESERVE

Over 100 acres of deciduous woodland here are protected as a

Bibury, a lovely old village almost entirely built of the local limestone

nature reserve by Gloucestershire County Council. Beech is the dominant tree species and is accompanied by ash, sycamore, birch and holly. Violet, sanicle, bluebell and anemone are among the woodland flowers, and birds include treecreepers, woodpeckers and chaffinches. A break in the woodland cover of the steep scarp slope is the site of the ancient custom of cheese-rolling which still takes place every Whit Monday (see page 122).

Open: *all year. Nature trail. LNR.*

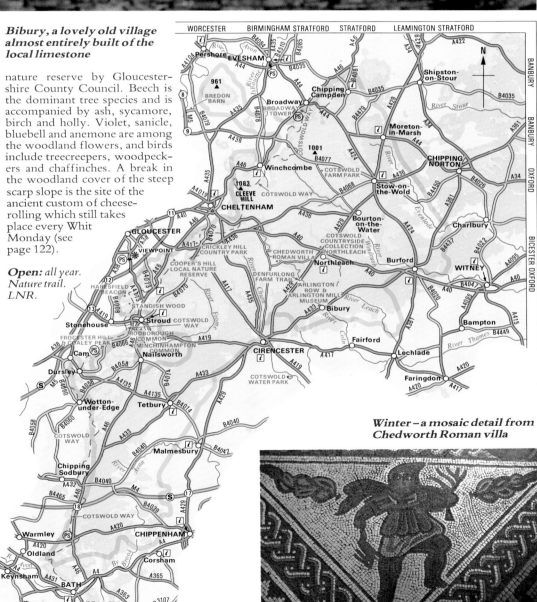

Winter – a mosaic detail from Chedworth Roman villa

COTSWOLD COUNTRY-SIDE COLLECTION

This museum at Northleach combines a collection of agricultural bygones with Northleach's old 'house of correction' which was in danger of demolition. The surviving prison buildings house displays relating to the story of the prison, and a gallery which tells the story of men in the Cotswolds from prehistoric times up to the present day. In the cellar is a display with a 'below stairs' theme with laundry, kitchen, and dairy items on display.

The agricultural collections span the days of horse, steam, petrol and diesel power. Every aspect of rural life is covered here, but outstanding are the Gloucestershire wagons, supreme examples of the wainwrights' art.

Open: *Apr to Sep daily (Sun pm only). Admission charge. Refreshments available weekend afternoons and bank holidays. Shop.*

COTSWOLD FARM PARK

This centre of the Rare Breeds Survival Trust is set in 25 acres of rolling Cotswold grassland, and displays a remarkable cross-section of livestock.

There are Longhorn and White Park cattle – heavy beasts with formidable horns which closely resemble the aurochs, wild ancestors of all domestic cattle. Nearby are Old Gloucester cattle, the rarest breed in Britain.

Numerous breeds of horses and ponies are shown, including huge, gentle Shires, and sturdy Exmoor ponies.

Sheep include Soays, the oldest domesticated breed, and North Ronaldsays, which for generations lived on the seaweed washed up on the shores of the rocky islands on which they grazed. There are many breeds of goat, among which are golden Guernseys, protected by one woman throughout the occupation of the Channel Islands during the Second World War.

Among the pigs are handsome red Tamworths, and 'Iron Age' pigs specially bred at the farm to look like prehistoric pigs. Old-fashioned breeds of poultry are also represented.

Open: *May to Sep daily. Admission charge. Picnic area. Refreshments. Shop.*

COTSWOLD WATER PARK

Lying to the south and south-east of Cirencester, near the headwaters of the River Thames, the Cotswold Water Park is the result of 60 years of gravel extraction. A series of flooded gravel pits of varying ages, depths and sizes has been developed into a major recreational resource offering many forms of water sports including sailing, water

At the Cotswold Farm Park: a fancy cockerel and a Highland cow

skiing, windsurfing and fishing. At Keynes Country Park there are facilities for the whole family, including paddling beaches for young children.

In spite of its recent origin, the Water Park is of national nature conservation interest. Because of the alkaline gravels – derived from the Cotswold limestone – the water is itself alkaline in character. It is exceptionally pure and supports a range of aquatic fauna and flora. Around the lake margins willows and alder soon became established, providing nest sites for birds such as the reed bunting and sedge warbler. In winter the lakes take on another role when they provide a refuge for thousands of wildfowl.

Open: *all year*

THE COTSWOLD WAY

Probably the best way to experience the atmosphere and beauty of the Cotswolds is to walk along all or part of this 100-mile long-distance footpath which follows the length of the scarp between

the fine old market town of Chipping Campden in the north and the elegant Roman and Regency city of Bath in the south. The walk passes through farmland, woods and villages and takes in many of the famous sites and viewpoints of the Cotswolds, for example Broadway Tower, Hailes Abbey and the Devil's Chimney at Leckhampton. Clearly signposted along the whole of its route, the path provides either an excellent day's outing or a week's holiday.

CRICKLEY HILL COUNTRY PARK

On the extreme edge of the Cotswold scarp, Crickley Hill offers visitors 62 acres of Cotswold countryside and scenery to enjoy and explore at leisure. The steep, grassy slopes are rich in flowers and butterflies, while from the edge of the hill there are commanding views across the Severn valley to the Malverns, the Forest of Dean and the mountains of South Wales. On the plateau itself annual archaeological excavations are gradually unravelling the complex story of prehistoric settlement. The Scrubbs, owned by the National Trust, includes part of an Iron Age promontory fort which was re-occupied during the 6th century AD. Present-day quarrying has enhanced its precipitous appearance, and from the top there are fine views over the Severn valley. In contrast to the more exposed hill

top, a pleasant walk can be taken under the trees of the Scrubbs.

Open: *all year. Information centre. Nature trails. Part NT.*

DENFURLONG FARM TRAIL

Here is a chance to see present-day farming on the Cotswolds at first hand. An exhibition in the farm shows aspects of modern agriculture, and there are opportunities to look round the other buildings and watch milking in progress. Two farm trails take the visitor round the fields and show the variety of crops, animals, wildlife and landforms of the area.

Open: *all year. Admission charge. Picnic area. Trail leaflets.*

FROCESTER HILL & COALEY PEAK

13 acres of this high escarpment (778ft) belong to the National Trust – and give beautiful views over the Severn to the Forest of Dean and the Welsh mountains. In spring the flamboyant purple flowers of the pasque flower may be found here.

Picnic area. NT.

HARESFIELD BEACON & STANDISH WOOD

The Beacon is a fine viewpoint on the south-western edge of the Cotswolds, overlooking Gloucester and the Severn valley, with

the Forest of Dean and the mountains of Wales beyond to the west. The Romans built a large encampment on Haresfield and Roman coins have been discovered here in quantity. The National Trust, which owns 354 acres here, has waymarked the footpaths of the Cotswold Way north-east to Cromwell's Siege Stone, commemorating the Battle of Gloucester in 1643, and south-west to Standish Wood past a topograph on Shortwood which provides a useful guide to the area and overlooks the Severn valley.

The pale pink blooms of the dog-rose brighten the waysides here in summer, and the woods are home to little birds such as the nuthatch and the treecreeper.

NT.

MINCHINHAMPTON & RODBOROUGH COMMONS

Rising abruptly from the Nailsworth valley is the picturesque bluff of Rodborough Common and, a little further south, Minchinhampton Common. Both are owned by the National Trust and provide excellent facilities for walking, picnicking or enjoying the views across the Stroud valley, scene of the early wool and cloth industries. Mills are seen alongside the rivers, and in the Frome valley is the Stroudwater Canal.

On the high turfland of Minchinhampton Common are prehistoric earthworks known as the Bulwarks, possibly the headquarters of a tribe which joined Caractacus to defend their land against Rome. Rodborough Common includes part of the site of an early 1st-century enclosure.

Once covered by beech woods, the commons are now among the finest stretches of Cotswold limestone turf, grazed by cattle and with a tremendous diversity of flowers and butterflies, making this an especially splendid place to explore in high summer.

NT.

Left: a cowslip, lovely flower of meadows and pastures

Below: woolly thistle, usually found in dry, grassy places

Flowers on the Commons

Visit one of the famous Cotswold commons on a summer's day and you will find a wealth of wild flowers at your feet. Cleeve Hill, Minchinhampton and Cranham Commons, Painswick Beacon – all command stunning views across the surrounding countryside and are subject to the ancient rights of local people to graze sheep, cattle or ponies.

Flowers here are lime-loving species, well suited to the thin alkaline soils. Harebells waft in the breeze and the related, but rarer, clustered bellflower shows brilliant blue in colour. Yellow rockroses, cowslips and bird's-foot trefoil carpet the ground, while shades of delicate mauve are provided by thyme and milkwort. The giant flowers of the aptly named woolly thistle make this one of the most attractive members of its family. Tway-blade, an early orchid with greenish coloured flowers, occurs in shady areas, while on the sunny south-facing slopes the pink flowers of common spotted and fragrant orchids may catch your eye. Towards the end of the summer come the flowers of the autumn gentian, the rare autumn ladies' tresses and the unmistakable blue heads of the scabious.

The grasslands of the Cotswold commons, with their rare abundance of unusual flowers, are the last remnants of a once widespread habitat. They must be carefully looked after for the future and of course the flowers should not be picked, but left to set seed.

Cragside Country Park

Northumberland

The problem with Cragside is not how much to fit into a day's visit but how many days will be needed to discover its many secrets. The house is fascinating both inside and out, while the azaleas and rhododendrons in the grounds demand to be seen in early summer. There are five lakes, two burns and a canal, three waterfalls and many miles of woodland walks waiting to be explored. There is plenty, too, for the industrial archaeologist: the house was the first in the world to be lit by water-power generated electricity. The delicate iron bridge over the Debdon valley, and the 832ft wooden aqueduct are also worth seeing.

Today it is difficult to imagine Cragside without trees, but until the mid 1860s the whole area lacked them. Then followed a period of spectacular planting of millions of trees, mainly varieties of conifer. Some specimen trees around the house are now among the finest and tallest in the country.

Within the 2300 acres of the country park many animal and bird species live relatively undisturbed. Red squirrels, foxes, badgers and roe deer are all here, though shy creatures and rarely seen. Herons and other water birds can be seen on the lake.

Open: house Apr to Sep daily except Mon (but open bank holiday Mon), pm only; Oct Wed, Sat and Sun pm only. Country park Apr to Oct daily; Nov to Mar Sat and Sun.

Admission charge. Refreshments. Shop. Suitable for disabled visitors. NT.
Location: 1 mile N of Rothbury. Entrance for cars at Debdon Gate on B6341 Alnwick road; for pedestrians at Reivers Well Gate on B6344 Morpeth road.
Map: page 313, NU00.

Craigellachie National Nature Reserve

Highland

No visitor to Aviemore should miss this attractive nature reserve. More than one-third of its

Cragside – created in the 1860s in the Debdon valley

642 acres are birch woodland, and there are many acres of moorland, rising to 1700ft. The steep cliffs visible from the Aviemore Centre – including the famous 'Craigellachie Rock' – are also part of the reserve, as is Loch Puladdern, which is the starting point for a mile-long nature trail. This takes in birch woods and a small reservoir and also provides fine views across to Rothiemurchus Forest and the Cairngorms beyond.

Birch woods are of special value to wildlife, and the insect life of Craigellachie is particularly notable. The birch trees here support several rare moth species with colourful names like the great brocade moth and the angle-striped sallow. Other insects which live in old and dead trees provide food for some of Craigellachie's varied bird species, and some of these birds in turn are preyed on by merlins and peregrine falcons.

Open: at all times. NCC.
Access: by nature trail, with entrance through Aviemore Centre. Trail signposted from centre's car parks.
Location: at Aviemore, opposite Aviemore Centre on W side of A9.
Map: page 315, NH81.

Hawfinch

Although this is Britain's largest finch, it is the least often seen. Hawfinches are retiring by nature, but during the spring they may be seen among the treetops. The hawfinch's enormous bill is its most distinctive feature; it is capable of cracking open the hard stones of such fruits as cherries, sloes and damsons.

Cranborne Chase

Dorset

From Saxon times to 1830 this huge area was set aside as a hunting preserve. By 1830 it had become a haunt of ne'er-do-wells of various sorts and was broken up by Act of Parliament. At that time it consisted of virtually unbroken forest; today most is arable farmland.

That Cranborne Chase was important long before Saxon times can be judged by the impressive earthworks to be found in the area. Three of these can be reached from the A354 Salisbury to Blandford Forum road. The first is called Bokerley Ditch, which crosses the botanically rich National Nature Reserve of Martin Down close to the hamlet of Woodyates. This great earthwork was probably thrown up after the Romans had left Britain, to protect a large Roman farming estate from the Saxons. Today its slopes are studded with downland flowers in the summer months.

Still close to the A354 is the Dorset Cursus, which crosses the B3081 just over half a mile southeast of its junction with the A354. One of the largest prehistoric monuments in Britain, it runs for some eight miles from Bokerley to Thickthorn Down. It consists of parallel banks and ditches, and was built by the Neolithic inhabitants of the Chase. Crossing the Cursus nearby is the line of Ackling Dyke, one of the finest Roman roads in Britain, which ran from Badbury Rings to Old Sarum.

Traditional Manx cottages and enclosures at Cregneash

The B3081 from Sixpenny Handley to Shaftesbury gives excellent views of the Chase's woodlands, downland slopes and arable farmland. A turn off this road three miles north-west of Tollard Royal leads to Win Green Hill, the highest point on the Chase. Crowned by a tree circle and a bowl barrow, this National Trust property offers views stretching as far as the Quantocks and the Isle of Wight.

Location: *between Shaftesbury and A354 Blandford Forum – Salisbury road; crossed by B3081. Part NCC/NT.*
Map: *page 305, ST91.*

Cregneash: Manx Open Air Folk Museum

Isle of Man

Embracing the southern end of the village of Cregneash, which lies in the heart of the Meayl peninsula at the south-western end of the Isle of Man, this fascinating museum comprises a group of traditional Manx cottages with their adjoining gardens and walled enclosures. The village looks down over the Calf Sound from some 450 feet above sea level and is a survival of an ancient Celtic type of farming settlement.

First established in 1938, the museum illustrates the life of a typical Manx crofting community of the last century by preserving homes, furniture and everyday equipment in their original setting. The buildings, mostly thatched, include a crofter-fisherman's home, a farmstead, a weaver's shed complete with

hand loom, a turner's shed with treadle lathe, and a smithy.

Spinning demonstrations are given on certain days each week and a blacksmith works occasionally in the smithy. Normally visitors can also see sheep of the native Manx Loghtan breed in the field adjoining the turner's shed. The rams of this ancient breed, which survives only in very small numbers on the island, have a striking tendency to produce four or even six horns.

Open: *early May to late Sep daily (pm only on Sun). Admission charge. Shop. No dogs.*
Location: *at Cregneash on A31, 1¼ miles W of Port St Mary.*
Map: *page 308, SC16.*

Creswell Crags

Derbyshire

Much of our knowledge of the primitive men who lived in Britain in the early Stone Age comes from Creswell. Here, in a narrow gorge in the magnesian limestone, are a number of caves and fissures of varying sizes containing evidence of occupation as long as 50,000 years ago. Bones, tools and other artefacts gradually accumulated on the floors of the caves and became embedded in layer upon layer of earth. The earliest deposits contain not only evidence of Neanderthal Man (43,000–41,000 BC) and his stone tools, but also bones of the wild animals such as mammoths, wolves and woolly rhinoceros which lived here in the cold tundra conditions of the last ice age.

The caves themselves are not open to the public, but in the visitor centre is an exhibition and

an audio-visual programme showing what life was like for these early people. Footpaths have been laid out through the gorge and there is an informative nature trail. The natural history interest is enhanced by a lake which, though gradually silting up and polluted by local mining, encourages a wide variety of plants and animals.

Open: *visitor centre Mar to Oct Tue to Sun and bank holiday Mon; Nov and Dec Sun only. Picnic site and car park open daily, dawn to dusk in summer; Sun only in winter. Shop. Visitor centre suitable for disabled visitors.*
Location: *4 miles SW of Worksop, ½ mile E of Creswell, off B6042 mid-way between A616 and A60.*
Map: *page 310, SK57.*

Croft Castle

Hereford & Worcester

Originally a Marcher castle largely dating from the 14th or 15th centuries, Croft was transformed into a country house in the 18th century.

Some fine old avenues of oaks and sweet chestnuts survive in the parkland – the chestnuts are said to be 350 years old. In the late 18th century Fishpool Valley was planted with mixed evergreen and deciduous trees, mainly Douglas fir and ash.

Visitors can stroll through Fishpool Valley to the Iron Age hill-fort of Croft Ambrey on its limestone ridge, over 1000ft high, from which there is a view of 14 counties. On the east of the estate is typical open grassland: this is Bircher Common, where local people still enjoy grazing rights and splendid views. Croft's varied habitats shelter a variety of wild creatures; among them fallow deer, rabbits, hares and squirrels. The Forestry Commission controls the deer; stoats, weasels and polecats keep down the others. Polecats have been confined to Wales for much of this century, but following the outlawing of the gin-trap there are signs that they are staging a recovery. Hawfinches, Britain's largest finches, sometimes visit Croft Ambrey during the winter to feed on hornbeam seeds.

Open: *castle Apr and Oct Sat, Sun & Easter Mon, pm only; May to Sep: Wed to Sun and bank holiday Mon, pm only. Park and common land open at all times. Admission charge for castle. Suitable for disabled visitors. NT.*
Access: *by footpaths only.*
Location: *5 miles NW of Leominster, off B4362.*
Map: *page 309, SO44.*

Cudmore Grove Country Park

Essex

Mersea Island, on which this small country park lies, has a real island feel about it, despite being separated from the mainland only by a narrow channel. The visitor arriving via the B1025 crosses 'The Strood', which is, whatever the state of the tide, very obviously an arm of the sea. The road to the park is narrow, yet this is a popular spot for walks or a dip in the North Sea.

Birdwatchers will prefer to look at the wading birds and, particularly, the wildfowl. Shelducks are almost always about and are joined by Brent geese in winter. Early in the year, pairs of eider, goldeneye and red-breasted merganser may well be here, the colourful males tossing their heads, each in its own distinctive display.

Open: *all year. Parking charge Sun and bank holidays.*
Location: *off Bromans Lane in East Mersea, 7¼ miles SW of Colchester.*
Map: *page 306, TM01.*

Culbin Forest & Sands

Grampian

Once an area of huge shifting sand dunes, this is now one of the largest forests in the north-east of Scotland. On the seaward side is the Culbin Sands/Nairn Bar RSPB Reserve.

Culbin Forest was a major achievement for the Forestry Commission: by laying brush-wood 'thatch' an area of about 1600 acres of dunes, which had covered much of the once fertile Barony of Culbin since the end of the 17th century, was stabilised and planted. The huge sand-dune system may no longer be the most extensive in Britain, but it is still well worth seeing.

The pinewoods are home to typical Scottish birds including capercaillies, crested tits and crossbills, while the coastal section is best in winter, when birds likely to be seen include waders and also ducks such as wigeon, common scoter, red-breasted merganser and long-tailed duck. The botanical interest of the area is particularly high, with many plants reaching the north-eastern limits of their British distribution here.

Location: *Forest reached from Kintessack (2¼ miles NW of Forres), on unclassified road N of A96. RSPB reserve reached from Kingsteps, 1 mile E of Nairn on unclassified road past golf course. Admission charge to RSPB reserve for non-members. No dogs on reserve. FC/RSPB.*
Map: *page 315, NJ06.*

Culzean Country Park

Strathclyde

Magnificent seascapes and a varied countryside are the principal attractions of this country park. It looks over towards the Isle of Arran and Kintyre.

This was Scotland's first country park, created in 1969 and managed by the National Trust for Scotland – who own the park and Culzean Castle, one of Robert Adam's masterpieces.

Within the 560 acres are several lakes, large areas of semi-wild woodland, formal gardens, open parkland, cliff scenery and a sandy beach. Breeding birds here include five species of warbler and many resident woodland songbirds. Roe deer and red squirrels are abundant (though both these species need patience

Culzean Castle

to watch), and 200 species of fungi have so far been identified in the park.

The Swan Pond is a 13-acre man-made pond, sheltered on three sides by mature woodland. It provides a wintering area for hundreds of waterfowl.

Open: *all year. Admission charge for vehicles. Interpretation centre open Apr to Oct daily. Refreshments. Suitable for disabled visitors. NTS.*
Location: *10 miles SW of Ayr, off A719.*
Map: *page 312, NS20.*

Cwmcoy: Felin Geri Mill

Dyfed

Ducks, geese, goats and pigs enhance the rustic atmosphere of this ancient flour mill in the River Ceri's secluded valley. Felin Geri dates from the end of the 16th century, but had been derelict for some 30 years before an award-winning restoration project was started in the mid-1970s. The mill, part of a 30-acre smallholding, is powered by a cast-iron waterwheel driving stones which grind about ten tons of wholemeal flour every week. The flour can be purchased by visitors.

Open: *Easter to Oct daily. Admission charge.*
Location: *1½ miles NW of Newcastle Emlyn, signposted from B4333 at Cwmcoy.*
Map: *page 305, SN34.*

Cwmllwyd Wood Nature Reserve

West Glamorgan

Known locally as Bluebell Wood, this 16-acre nature reserve climbs a steep slope less than three miles west of central Swansea. From its highest point, near the car park on Banke Lane, there are broad views which range from the River Loughor's estuary to the distant bulk of the Black Mountain in the Brecon Beacons National Park.

Holly, birch and bracken cover parts of the reserve, but Cwmllwyd is dominated by sessile and pedunculate oaks which have been growing since the middle of the 19th century. They rise above rowan, hazel, alder and other shrubs which provide cover for such woodland birds as coal tits, blue tits and long-tailed tits. Jays and green woodpeckers may also be seen.

Paths run down to the lower part of the valley where a stream, a small pond and an area of boggy ground encourage a variety of water-loving plants. They include yellow flag, ragged robin, guelder rose and bog asphodel. Snipe and woodcock visit the marsh in winter when its alder and sallow also attract flocks of long-tailed tits.

Although its character is now completely rural, Cwmllwyd was a source of coal long before the Industrial Revolution changed the face of South Wales. A fence near the pool surrounds 17th-century workings known as 'bell' pits because of their shape. The technique was to sink a vertical shaft until it reached the coal seam, then dig outwards. The local timber was a convenient source of raw material for ladders and winches. Ponies transported the coal to a wharf at Blackpill, between Swansea and the Mumbles.

Open: *all year.*
Location: *3 miles W of Swansea. Leave B4295 at E edge of Waunarlwydd village, to travel S following unclassified Waunarlwydd Road, then Banke Lane, to reach main car park. LNR.*
Map: *page 305, SS69.*

Danebury Ring

Hampshire

Danebury Ring is an Iron Age fort crowning a small hill on the chalk downs of central Hampshire. The fort is a well-known and important archaeological site, and is managed by Hampshire County Council as a public open space. Apart from its archaeological interest, there are areas of beech wood and scrub which are good for birds. On warm summer days the hobby – a migrant bird of prey usually confined to Hampshire, Sussex and Dorset – can sometimes be seen hunting over the surrounding countryside. Frog and pyramidal orchid are among the rare and beautiful chalkland flowers that can be found in the areas of short grass. In summer there is an abundance of the yellow flowers of horseshoe vetch, which attracts a number of different species of butterfly.

Location: *2 miles NW of Stockbridge, off unclassified road mid-way between A343 and A30.*
Map: *page 306, SU33.*

Above: a shag, a common bird of the coastline. The crest is most prominent in spring and summer

Dart Estuary

Devon

The National Trust has acquired property on both sides of the River Dart in recent years, but the three major areas accessible to the public are Dyer's Hill, Gallants Bower and Little Dartmouth Cliffs, all on the west side of the estuary.

It is not possible to park close to Dyer's Hill, but for those who make the effort there are splendid views of Dartmouth and Kingswear from this steep woodland.

Gallants Bower is an attractively wooded hill, some 400ft high, overlooking Dartmouth Castle. A fine display of bluebells in spring, and superb views over the estuary from the remains of the old fort on the summit, are among its attractions. It is possible to walk from here, along Little Dartmouth Cliffs past Blackstone Point and Compass Cove where a footbridge spans a narrow sea inlet. On the cliffs beyond the cove elder struggles to survive against the elements, while on the rocks off Combe Point cormorants and shags can often be seen, their great black wings spread out to dry.

There are fine views to Start Point across the bay before the path turns away from the cliff towards the alternative car park. The return to Gallants Bower can be made by following an inland path, perhaps taking the opportunity to study the differences in bird and plant species.

Location: *S of Dartmouth, off B3205. NT.*
Map: *page 305, SX84/85.*

Right: a cormorant – bigger than the shag, and with a distinctive white face patch. Cormorants can often be seen inland (some even breed inland), while shags nearly always stay by the sea

Dartmoor National Park

Southern England's 'last unconquered wilderness' – this is how Sir Arthur Conan Doyle, who set his chilling story The Hound of the Baskervilles *in these strange, untamed landscapes, described Dartmoor. His words still ring true today, especially on the lonely heart of the moor.*

Dartmoor, best known for its granite tors, still retains some of its wild and primeval character – especially when contrasted with the gentle farmlands it overlooks (above)

Like most of Britain's landscape, Dartmoor owes its character to the rocks beneath it. Much of the moor is a great mass of granite, forced up in its molten state from deep inside the earth, millions of years ago. Wind and water have done their best, but on many hill-tops the unyielding rock has resisted weathering to form the outcrops called tors, which are such a familiar part of Dartmoor's scenery. The highest just tops 2000ft: not as high as the dramatic mountain peaks of Wales or the Lake District, but high enough to share something of their climate. Dartmoor is known for its mists and rain, and the temperatures here are generally much lower than those of Devon's balmy coastlands barely a dozen miles away. A rainfall of around 80 inches a year, falling on soils which cover impervious rocks, means a vast amount of surface water for most of the year. The majority of Devon's rivers rise on Dartmoor, and their tributaries carry some of this water away in typical fast-flowing streams, with torrents and waterfalls. Much of the soil on the moor is peat, in places up to 12ft deep. This soaks up water like a sponge, forming Dartmoor's notorious bogs. Most of these are confined to the northern part of the moor, a remote, inhospitable area where, as large-scale maps show, there are no roads but, instead, features with sinister names like Ruelake Pit and Gallaven Mire – names which should warn off casual strollers.

Early Settlers

A large-scale map of Dartmoor will also show that the moor is strewn with prehistoric remains. There are hut circles, enclosures, cairns, standing stones, stone rows and many other features. Most of these are relics of the Bronze Age, some 4000 years ago, when there was a considerable population on the moor. This may seem surprising, since there were far richer, more sheltered valleys and lowlands nearby. But the climate was warmer then, and the thin moorland soils would have been much easier to cultivate than the forest and fens of the lower lands.

That there is so much visible evidence of Bronze Age man on Dartmoor is explained by subsequent events. The weather changed, becoming colder and wetter; tools and farming techniques improved, enabling heavy land to be put under the plough; and Dartmoor's soil must have been becoming exhausted in any case. So most of the population moved away, although there were still thriving villages on the moor until the Middle Ages.

One of the best prehistoric set-tlements is Grimspound, north of Widecombe (see page 80). There is another settlement at Standon Down near Willsworthy. A collection of stone rows, cairns, a standing stone and stone circle can be seen at Merrivale, off the B3357.

So much visible history remains largely because the poor soils provided no incentive for subsequent large-scale clearance and ploughing. Even so, during the 18th and 19th centuries, when to be an improving landlord was fashionable, there were attempts to make the moor grow wholly unsuitable crops by wasteful practices. All such schemes failed. Only since the 1950s has there been a possibility that the wild moor might actually disappear for ever – changed beyond recognition by new farming practices, by demands for reservoirs and forests, and by industrial encroachment. The sheer number of visitors also threatens Dartmoor's essential qualities. Lanes which were little-used gravel tracks less than 50 years ago now have to serve vast numbers of car-borne visitors during the summer months.

The Moorland Workshop

Today, strenuous, and not always successful, efforts are made by those who love Dartmoor's wild beauty to keep industry at bay. Yet for hundreds of years the moor was the scene of considerable industrial activity. The fact that the visible remains of those ancient works are often not noticed by the passer-by points up the differences between the relatively small-scale upheavals of yesterday and the potentially horrific destruction wreaked by today's high explosives and huge machines.

Silver, lead, zinc, iron, wolfram (from which tungsten is derived) and arsenic have all been extracted from Dartmoor; but it is tin for which it is most famous. Although tin was essential for the moor's Bronze Age inhabitants, there is no hard evidence that extraction was begun until the middle of the 12th century, when substantial deposits were found near Sheepstor. These were rapidly exploited, and the area soon became the richest source of tin in Europe. It was a boom time, and prospectors flooded in, quickly followed by settlers of other sorts. Farms were established far inside the moorland; many grew good crops of wheat and lasted until the Black Death swept through the country in the middle of the 14th century. The tinners held their own courts of justice, and their gaol was in Lydford Castle.

Traces of the early workings can be found in many places; they are at their most spectacular when great slices have been carved through solid rock in search of the ore. There are excellent examples of this in the West Webburn Valley, near Warren House Inn. Other remains, always found beside streams, are of blowing houses, where the ore was smelted with the aid of water-operated bellows. Mines were not sunk till very much later, and the gaunt engine houses with their tall chimneys were built in the 19th century. Large numbers of these, and of buildings associated with other mining activities, can be seen round Mary Tavy. On the western edge of Dartmoor, the roofless ruin of Wheal Betsy, the engine house of a mine which extracted silver and lead from the moor, is now in the care of the National Trust. The famous clapper bridges, like the ones at Postbridge and Dartmeet, were probably built for the tin trade in medieval times. The most noticeable industrial intrusions on the moor today are the china clay works and their enormous spoil heaps. They lie mainly on Lee Moor, but are slowly encroaching nearer the vulnerable centre of Dartmoor.

Other Memorials

Virtually the whole history of Dartmoor can be discerned upon its surface. Not only are there countless prehistoric monu-

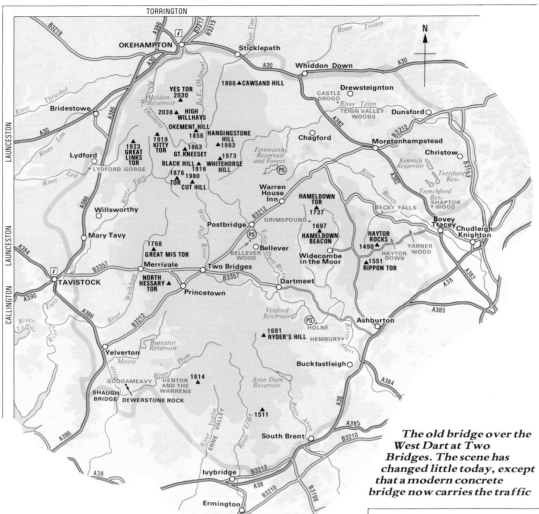

Map labels: TORRINGTON, OKEHAMPTON, Sticklepath, Whiddon Down, Drewsteignton, CASTLE DROGO, Dunsford, TEIGN VALLEY WOODS, Bridestowe, YES TOR 2030, 1806 CAWSAND HILL, 2038 HIGH WILLHAYS, Meldon Reservoir, OKEMENT HILL 1856, HANGINGSTONE HILL 1983, Chagford, Moretonhampstead, Christow, 1919 KITTY TOR, 1923 GREAT LINKS TOR, 1863 GT. KNEESET, BLACK HILL 1916, WHITEHORSE HILL 1973, Fernworthy Reservoir and Forest, Kennick Reservoir, Lydford, LYDFORD GORGE, 1876 TOR 1980 CUT HILL, WARREN HOUSE INN, HAMELDOWN TOR 1737, Tottiford Res., Trenchford Res. SHAPTOR WOOD, BECKY FALLS, Bovey Tracey, Chudleigh Knighton, Willsworthy, Postbridge, GRIMSPOUND, HAMELDOWN BEACON 1697, HAYTOR ROCKS 1490, YARNER WOOD, Mary Tavy, 1768 GREAT MIS TOR, Bellever, BELLEVER WOOD, Widecombe in the Moor, HAYTOR DOWN, 1551 RIPPON TOR, Merrivale, Two Bridges, TAVISTOCK, NORTH HESSARY TOR, Princetown, Dartmeet, Ashburton, Venford Reservoir, HOLNE, 1691 RYDER'S HILL, HEMBURY, Buckfastleigh, Yelverton, Burrator Reservoir, GOODAMEAVY, SHAUGH BRIDGE, HENTOR AND THE WARRENS 1614, DEWERSTONE ROCK, 1511, South Brent, Ivybridge, Ermington

equally fascinating, and in some ways simpler. The high moor, with its poor acid soil, bogs, and peat hags, supports a limited flora and fauna. Birds likely to be seen include pipits and buzzards. Animals are rarely seen except for the hardy Dartmoor pony, but badgers and foxes are present, and the otter still lives in the moorland rivers. The upper reaches of the moorland streams are often devoid of life; being cold, fast-flowing and lacking in nutrients. The middle and lower reaches, in the valleys on the edge of the moor proper, hold a far greater variety of wildlife. Burrator, Fernworthy, and other moorland reservoirs support large wildfowl populations. Lydford Gorge on the moor's western edge, the River Tavy above Tavistock, the Dart Valley, the Bovey Valley and the Teign Valley all have exceptionally beautiful stretches. There are waymarked nature trails along a number of these valleys. The broadleaved woodlands in the valleys add greatly to their interest and beauty. There are other isolated patches of broadleaved woodland on the moor, but the largest woodlands are of conifers planted this century. Much controversy surrounds these plantations; however, they do encourage species that would otherwise be absent. Forestry Commission-owned woodlands often have picnic sites and clearly waymarked nature trails.

The old bridge over the West Dart at Two Bridges. The scene has changed little today, except that a modern concrete bridge now carries the traffic

ments and ruins of the industrial past, but there are a host of other remains and monuments.

Tiny, irregular fields can be seen on some of the moorland slopes. These are associated with the hut circles of ancient villages, and may be fields carved from the wilderness 4000 years ago. Similar fields nearer to existing farm buildings may date from the heyday of the tin trade in the 1500s. Some of the granite farmhouses themselves are of considerable interest and antiquity. The oldest were built to the traditional longhouse pattern, where the people would have their living quarters at one end and the cattle theirs at the other, animals and men all entering the house by the same central door.

Scattered across the moor are numerous warrens, artificial mounds built to house large populations of rabbits. The Normans introduced rabbits to this country shortly after the Conquest, and they soon became a staple source of meat during the winter months. Warren House Inn, on the B3212 north of Postbridge, is named after a large warren which stands close by.

About a mile north on the same road is one of the many worn stone crosses which stand beside roads and tracks all across the moor. The B3212 has been one of the moor's principal thoroughfares since at least as early as the tin boom, and the crosses found at intervals along it were probably erected as waymarkers in an age when the road was no more than a muddy track across a lonely wilderness. Some of the best-known crosses mark the route of the Abbots' Way, which led from Buckfast Abbey to Buckland and Tavistock abbeys.

There is a large military presence on the moor. Much of the north-western part of the moor is used for firing practice and as tank ranges. Today there are barracks and military roads – some of which lead far into the most remote parts of the moor.

Wildlife

Dartmoor is of endless interest for its long and visible human history. Its natural history is

Becky Falls

What to See

BECKY FALLS

Lying just off the B3344, these popular falls are formed by the Becka Brook, which joins the River Bovey little more than a mile downstream. The brook tumbles down a valley strewn with boulders and shaded by oak trees. Although certainly commercialised with the adjacent restaurant and gift shop, this is still a place where something of the character of a Dartmoor valley can be seen.

Refreshments. Picnic area. Shop.

BELLEVER WOOD

The conifer plantations which make up Bellever Wood were established by the Duchy of Cornwall in the years after the First World War and were sold to the Forestry Commission in 1930. Since then further plantings have made the forested area much larger. Typical trees are sitka spruce, Norway spruce and contorta pine, and some Japanese larch. The plantations have

Cotton grass is common in boggy places in May and June

brought birds like blackcaps and garden warblers to Dartmoor, as well as the first breeding siskins to be recorded in Devon. Two waymarked nature trails lead through the woodlands; one making for Bellever Tor, which gives panoramic views across the moor. The East Dart River gives the area further character and interest.

FC.

BURRATOR RESERVOIR

Constructed at the close of the 19th century to supply Plymouth with water, Burrator is a particularly attractive reservoir, closely resembling a natural lake now that it is well established. There are woodlands on the slopes above the reservoir, and beyond them rise the bare slopes of the open moor. This is a good location to see birds of water, woodland and moor.

CASTLE DROGO

After making a fortune in the 1880s from the success of the Home & Colonial Stores, Julius Drewe asked Sir Edwin Lutyens to build him a new home near Drewsteignton on Dartmoor. The result was Castle Drogo, one of Lutyens' most successful creations, and architecturally surely the most remarkable.

Mr Drewe had chosen a superb site, for his castle is set on the very edge of a heather-clad granite bluff, from which the ground falls steeply to the River Teign far below. In addition to the splendours of the house and formal garden there are several walks on either side of the Teign. North of the river the classic walk is through oak woods from Fingle Bridge along the Hunters' Path, and back by way of the Fisherman's Path. South of the Teign the walk is over Whiddon parkland – an ancient deer park, sadly no longer possessing a herd – farmland and oak woodland.

Open: castle Apr to Oct daily. Admission charge. Refreshments. Shop. Suitable for disabled visitors. Parkland accessible at all times. NT.

ERNE VALLEY

The upper Erne Valley is one of the most beautiful parts of Dartmoor, and also the richest in Bronze Age remains. Evidence of tin-mining is also plentiful. Tucked away up the valley is Piles Copse, a wood of stunted oak trees.

FERNWORTHY FOREST & RESERVOIR

Like Bellever, the plantations at Fernworthy were begun by the Duchy of Cornwall to provide employment as well as a source of timber and income. Fernworthy is the largest area of new forest on the moor, and was purchased by the Forestry Commission in 1930. A forest trail winds through it to various viewpoints which give excellent views of Fernworthy Reservoir and the rest of Dartmoor.

FC.

GOODAMEAVY

Two rivers, a wealth of industrial archaeology, fishing, rock-climbing, fine wide-ranging views and an area designated a Site of Special Scientific Interest – all these contribute to the variety of the National Trust's Goodameavy estate, covering 395 acres of typical south-west Dartmoor country.

The Meavy and the Plym rivers meet at Shaugh Bridge in the deep shade of an oak wood. Between the two rivers the ground rises steeply, and the walker along the Plym gains a splendid impression of the towering Dewerstone Rock, on which many novice climbers have started their mountaineering careers.

Prehistoric enclosures and hut circles, a Bronze Age burial chamber and a prehistoric field system can all be seen in a walk of approximately half a mile from the summit of Dewerstone Hill which itself gives extensive views towards Plymouth, and the nearer china clay workings.

Just below Goodameavy Bridge, where the Meavy enters the National Trust's property, is a stone embankment, built to carry a quarry tramway across the river. Close to Shaugh Bridge are the remains of a 19th-

One of the hut circles at Grimspound, a Bronze Age village

century iron mine and just outside the property are other industrial sites.

Although the National Trust suggests a route around Goodameavy, a walk along any path will provide a variety of interest.

NT.

GRIMSPOUND

This famous collection of huts and pens is contained within a ruined stone wall. All 24 of the round dwelling huts have the remains of hearths within them. A stream runs through the pound, which was almost certainly used by Bronze Age pastoralists. Many other prehistoric monu-

ments can be found on the surrounding moorlands.

HAYTOR DOWN

Tors are an essential part of the Dartmoor scene. These enormous natural sculptures of worn granite are an obvious and irresistible goal for most visitors to the moor. Haytor Rocks are among the most unusual in shape, are easily accessible and they provide a superb viewpoint over South Devon to the coast. Further from the road prehistoric hut circles and cairns can be found, as can remains of granite quarrying, and of the Haytor Granite Tramway, opened in 1820 and the earliest railway in Devon. It was operated by horses.

HEMBURY

Between the river Dart and the Holy Brook the National Trust owns 347 acres of wood and open heathland at Hembury, close to Buckfastleigh. Through the coppiced oakwoods run splendid woodland rides and above the woods lies open heath, ablaze from February to July with the yellow flowers of gorse.

The views from the Iron Age castle at Hembury's summit justify the climb to the top, but on a hot summer day the great joy is the cool beauty of the woods below, the air full of birdsong and the sound of the distant, hurrying Dart, to which several of the paths lead. Butterflies are plentiful, their caterpillars feeding on the oaks and other woodland trees – sycamore, hazel and alder buckthorn. On the south side of Hembury public footpaths lead through Burchetts Wood and Beechwood Copse.

NT.

HENTOR AND THE WARRENS

Once, rabbits were intensively farmed in artificial warrens like those at Trowlesworthy and Willings Walls. Today the Trowlesworthy warrener's house is one of the few inhabited buildings in this part of Dartmoor. Rabbits are few, and only the sheep and an occasional bird disturb the scene.

Much of the moorland beside the Plym and up to its headwaters at Plym Head is owned by the National Trust, including the warrens and Hentor, which rises to 1600ft and provides exhilarating views over Dartmoor and down into Cornwall. The Trust is responsible for more than 100 hut circles and many enclosure walls in its 3333 acres here. Almost all the relics in this area can be dated to the Bronze Age and it is strange for the walker to reflect that 3000 years ago there would have been more humans here to observe his progress than there are today!

NT.

HOLNE

Not far from the fine woods at Hembury the National Trust owns almost 2½ miles of woodland at Holne. As at Hembury, the trees are mostly oak and the river – the Dart – is the same.

The Holne property has some delightful woodland paths beside the Dart and continuing high into the woods along the steep valley on the south side of the river.

NT.

LYDFORD GORGE

South of historic Lydford village is Lydford Gorge, a place of steep, wooded slopes, waterfalls, miniature gorges with dripping mossy rocks and a very rich collection of wild flowers.

Postboxes in Strange Places

On Far Tor, as far from track or road as it is possible to be on the moor, there is a postbox. It is one of several that have become essential destinations for keen walkers and explorers. The first was established at Cranmere Pool in 1854 by a Dartmoor Guide to protect a visitors' book. Later the custom began of leaving stamped addressed post cards in the boxes. These are collected and posted by the next visitor to the box.

Technically, Lydford Gorge is an exceptional example of 'river capture', which occurred when the Lyd was breached by a smaller stream and diverted from its own gentle route around the edge of Dartmoor to the route of the smaller stream. The extra weight of water rushing along the steep river bed accelerated the speed of erosion, and this process, which began 450,000 years ago and continued over thousands of years, has created the deep ravine that is Lydford Gorge.

The woods are mainly self-seeding oak with sycamore and beech. The humidity in the narrow valley causes the trees and the sides of the ravine to be covered in ferns, mosses and lichen. In summer the contrasting scents of wild garlic and meadowsweet fill the air, and the sound of birdsong is often drowned by the noisy river. The White Lady waterfall is a major

Dipper

Fast-flowing upland streams are the haunt of this jaunty little bird. As its name suggests, it has a habit of bobbing up and down on stones in the water. Dippers have the ability, unique among perching birds, of being able to hunt for food under water.

attraction, falling 100 feet and described as long ago as 1788 as 'one continued silvery chain'. The best and most dramatic of the pot-holes along the river is the aptly named Devil's Cauldron, where the water does indeed appear to be boiling.

Open: *all year daily, but Nov to Mar from Waterfall Entrance as far as waterfall only.*
Admission charge. Refreshments.
NT.

SHAPTOR WOOD
Much of Dartmoor must once

have been covered in deciduous woodlands, but man and his animals have been removing the natural tree cover for thousands of years. Few broadleaved woodlands remain, and Shaptor is one of the best. It was purchased by the Woodland Trust in 1978 to protect it from possible clear-felling or replanting with conifers. There are areas of oak which was once coppiced (a practice being reintroduced by the Trust), and mature beeches. The woods are home to a wide variety of birds, including wood warblers and tree pipits.

WLT.

TEIGN VALLEY WOODS
One of the most spectacular of Dartmoor's valleys is that of the River Teign, with its magnificent hanging woods.

The National Trust has provided a nature walk through the

Bog pimpernel – a pretty flower of boggy places

Fingle Bridge was built across the Teign in the 16th century

beech and oak woodlands and along the river near Steps Bridge.

NT.

YARNER WOOD NATIONAL NATURE RESERVE
This reserve protects some of Dartmoor's once extensive woodlands. Once it would nearly all have been managed as oak coppice, but changes in land use and other factors have meant that there are also beech trees, birches, conifers and other trees here. The Nature Conservancy Council manages Yarner to ensure that it remains wooded, and to ensure that the wildlife-rich oak woodland is not taken over by other sorts of trees. Woodland walks and a nature trail explore this fascinating place.

NCC.

Daventry Country Park

Northamptonshire

Nowadays, reservoirs are built to supply water for industry and homes or for agricultural irrigation. When Daventry Reservoir was dug at the beginning of the 19th century, it was to provide a head of water for the Grand Union Canal, a vital waterway for the industry of the Midlands. Today, the reservoir is better known for its coarse fishing (day tickets can be bought) and its wildlife. Part of the country park is set aside as a nature reserve, and a nature trail has been laid out.

The water is home in winter to flocks of diving ducks, particularly the tufted duck, males of which are black and white with a drooping crest. The related pochard is more colourful – the males have a dark red head. In spring great crested grebes may build their floating nests alongside a reed bed where sedge and reed warblers sing. The reed warbler has no obvious distinguishing marks, whereas the sedge warbler has an obvious eye-stripe and its song is an impatient, continuous chatter. The reeds and other water-loving plants attract various species of butterflies and dragonflies.

Open: *all year. Picnic areas.*
Location: *1 mile N of Daventry off B4036 Market Harborough road.*
Map: *page 306, SP56.*

Delamere Forest

Cheshire

Although Cheshire is a fertile county renowned for dairying, there are areas of poor, sandy soil which are not suitable for farming and have remained wooded. The most extensive is Delamere Forest, which is all that now remains of the great Forest of Mara and Mondrum that stretched from Nantwich to the Mersey in Norman times. The original natural forest has gone, but in its place are extensive plantations of pine trees, mostly managed by the Forestry Commission. Here the Commission has laid out a variety of well signposted walks among the dense pine woods where, despite the large numbers of visitors, peace and tranquillity can soon be found.

As in many coniferous woodlands, the deep shade allows few wild plants to grow. However, the forest is one of Cheshire's best areas for birds, with the usual woodland species sup-

plemented by owls, kestrels, sparrowhawks and even the occasional buzzard. Crossbills and goldcrests – both lovers of coniferous trees – may be seen, while the forest's mammal population includes foxes, badgers and red squirrels.

The Cheshire Sandstone Trail, a walking route which follows a sandstone ridge for 14 miles, runs through the woodlands at Delamere. Half a mile west of Delamere Station, a one-and-a-half-mile forest trail has been laid

out. It starts from the Forestry Commission Visitor Centre, where a display on the forest's history and management can be seen.

Elsewhere in the forest are bogs and pools occupying hollows in the deposits created during the last ice age. Some of these are 'kettle holes' formed by the melting of large blocks of ice left behind by the retreating ice sheet. Unlike most of Cheshire's famous meres, these lakes are very acid and their margins sup-

The three stacked bridges at Devil's Bridge

port bog plants like sundew, cranberry and cotton grass. The latter is easily recognised by the conspicuous cotton-like tufts attached to the seed heads. One of the most accessible and attractive of these lakes is Hatchmere, on the forest's eastern edge.

Location: *9 miles NE of Chester off B5152. FC.*
Map: *page 309, SJ57.*

Ditchling Beacon & Common

West Sussex

In the days before the telegraph and telephone news of potentially dangerous naval activity in the English Channel was signalled by a series of beacons across high ground through southern England. One of these was at Ditchling, the third highest point on the South Downs at 813ft. The importance of this hill had long been recognised and there are remains of an Iron Age camp and a late Roman camp: the position was easily defended and allowed good all-round vision.

Today, visitors go to Ditchling Beacon for the spectacular views west to Chanctonbury Ring, north-west to Leith Hill and the North Downs on a clear day; and north-east to Ashdown Forest. The National Trust owns a 4½-acre area on the Beacon's north-eastern slope, and another part is looked after by the Sussex Trust for Nature Conservation, which has a 49-acre nature reserve. The old chalk workings here are rich in flowers and shrubs, and the reserve is also noted for its mosses and lichen.

In high summer, a good variety of heathland flowers and butterflies can also be seen at Ditchling Common, two miles north of Ditchling village; it is now a country park with a 1½-mile nature trail. This explores the varying habitats of the common, which range from open heath to scrub, and includes an area of marshy ground centred on a stream and a pond.

Location: *5½ miles N of Brighton; 1½ miles S of Ditchling village, on unclassified road. Part CNT/NT.* **Map:** *page 306, TQ31.*

Ditchling Beacon

Devil's Bridge

Dyfed

Rising on the slopes of Plynlimon, the Afon Rheidol races seawards through a wooded gorge whose spectacular beauty is seen at its best near Devil's Bridge. At this point it is joined by the Afon Mynach, which surges beneath the lowest of three bridges built one above the other, before thundering down in a series of waterfalls.

Despite its name, the oldest of the bridges was probably built in the 12th century by monks from Strata Florida Abbey, between Devil's Bridge and Tregaron. Its replacement dates from the 18th century while the present iron bridge was completed in 1901.

The bridges are best seen by descending the steps known as Jacob's Ladder, which lead deep into the valley. The dramatic gorge, shaded by sessile oaks, can also be explored on foot by following a path which starts by the chapel at Ysbyty Cynfyn, between Devil's Bridge and Ponterwyd. Devil's Bridge itself is the terminus of the narrow-gauge and steam-operated Vale of Rheidol Railway whose line runs inland for nearly twelve miles from Aberystwyth. The journey reveals a different facet of the Rheidol's character as the river wriggles down a valley where herons and kingfishers may be seen.

Location: *8 miles E of Aberystwyth on A4120.* **Map:** *page 309, SN77.*

Dolaucothi

Dyfed

The National Trust owns more than 2500 acres of farmland and woods in the valley of the Afon Cothi, above the village of Pumpsaint. A circular estate walk, taking about an hour, has been laid out here by the Trust. It begins by following a forest track. From a bend early in the walk is a fine view of the Afon Twrch winding through its flat valley towards distant oak woods – little changed from Roman times. The woods through which the walk passes were also once pure oak, used principally for the manufacture of charcoal, and more recently to supply timbers to make pit-props.

The path continues past a hill farm grazed by sheep and beef cattle in contrast to a lowland dairy farm a little further on as the trail curves back eventually to rejoin the track to the starting point. Beyond the farmhouse are the oak woods where the famous Roman gold-mines are to be found. After the Romans conquered Wales it is thought that they used the gold from these mines to provide the mints in France and Rome with bullion.

There are three tours of the mines, of varying lengths, starting at Ogofau Lodge, south-east of Pumpsaint. These show the opencast workings and the ingenious aqueduct system installed by the Roman miners to bring water to wash and separate the ore. Gold was mined here intermittently until 1939.

Open: *estate walk at all times; gold-mine tours in summer only (usually daily July to Sep). Admission charge to mines. Picnic area at Garreg. NT.* **Location:** *S of Pumpsaint, off A482 between Llanwrda and Lampeter.* **Map:** *page 305, SN64.*

Dolebury Warren

Avon

This limestone hilltop at the northern end of the Mendips has a rich chalk grassland flora, but also a variety of other habitats including acid grassland, heathland and mixed scrub.

The variety of wild flowers near the old fortifications of Dolebury Camp includes an abundance of kidney vetch and harebell. To the east is an area of more acid-tolerant plants such as the attractive heath bedstraw. The herb-rich grassland supports a variety of butterflies including several local species, one of which is the dark green fritillary.

To the south lies Rowbarrow Warren, now Forestry Commission woodland. Access here is strictly along the forestry paths, where there is the chance to see woodland birds and the shy roe deer. Further east lies Burrington Combe, with limestone cliffs and several small gorges.

Location: *½ mile S of Churchill, off A38. Part FC/CNT. Restricted parking and access.* **Map:** *page 305, ST45.*

Dollar Glen
Central

This spectacular glen lies on the southern edge of the Ochil Hills, just above the small town of Dollar. Two streams, the Burns of Sorrow and Care, which rise in the moorland heights of the Ochils, have in a much more vigorous era after the ice ages, carved out precipitous ravines following lines of weakness, or faults, in the volcanic rock. Their present small size belies their former strength and they are technically 'misfit' streams in that they now appear to be too small for the gorges in which they flow.

The damp, steep-sided ravines are shady and cool in the summer months, as the sunlight is filtered out by trees growing on the heavily wooded upper slopes. Elm (some still surviving), ash, oak, wild cherry and hazel clothe these slopes, and primroses and bluebells provide a profusion of colour in the spring and early summer. In crevices and ledges on the near-vertical rock walls, a wide variety of liverworts, mosses and ferns thrive in the moist atmosphere.

In places the gorge of the Burn of Sorrow is less than 10 feet wide, but visitors are able to walk through this narrow defile on a specially constructed walkway. The path from Dollar climbs steeply into the gorge and then divides, a branch going up the ravine of each stream. Upstream, where the gradient of path and burn are reduced, the paths merge again at the entrance gate of Castle Campbell, a late 15th-century stronghold, built in a commanding position on the spur separating the streams. Perhaps more in keeping with the names of the two burns is its alternative name, Castle Gloom.

The 60 acres of the glen, and the castle, are owned by the National Trust for Scotland but the castle is under the guardianship of the Scottish Development Department (Ancient Monuments Branch).

Open: *Castle Campbell all year daily except Sun am and Thu pm; also closed Fri Oct to Mar. Admission charge. Dollar Glen open at all times. During or after rain the path can be dangerous; strong footwear and great care are advised. NTS.*
Location: *in Dollar, off A91.*
Map: *page 313, NS99.*

Dornoch Firth & Loch Fleet
Highland

This area on the east coast of Scotland's Highland region is outstanding for wildlife, being particularly rich in estuarine habitats. Although of interest throughout the year, Dornoch Firth is most important for its winter wildfowl and waders. Greylag geese, whooper swans, pintail and scaup are all to be seen in winter, but the most numerous wildfowl are wigeon, which may number over 8000 in autumn. Several thousand waders are usual here, with oystercatchers, bar-tailed godwits, knots and dunlins the most abundant. These large numbers of birds are attracted by the wide sandy foreshore of the firth. Many roost on Morrich More, where there are large expanses of sand dunes and salt marsh. The outer waters of the firth are good in winter for divers, scoters and long-tailed ducks.

About six miles north of the estuary lies Loch Fleet, a sandy,

Dorset Coast Path

Forming the shortest of the four sections of the South-west Peninsula Coast Path (see also pages 64 and 261), the Dorset path runs right round Dorset's seaboard from Poole to Lyme Regis. The whole length of this path is within the Dorset Area of Outstanding Natural Beauty, and much of the actual coastline is of such quality that it is likely to be designated a Heritage Coast.

There is a tremendous diversity of scenery along the path, but it is the stretches of dramatic cliffs that are perhaps the most spectacular. One of the best sections is on the Isle of Purbeck, from Durlston Head (see page 87) to Kimmeridge. A lovely cove, and what is probably Britain's most famous natural arch, Durdle Door, can be seen further west, near Lulworth, while further west still, towards Weymouth, is the headland of White Nothe. On the other side of Weymouth is Chesil Beach, its great sweep of shingle enclosing a stretch of water famous for wildfowl (see page 57). Beyond Burton Bradstock is the great headland of Golden Cap (see page 117), owned by the National Trust, and west of that are the crumbling cliffs of Charmouth and Lyme Regis, famous for their fossils. It was along here that Mary Anning, then a teenage girl, made the discovery of a fossil dinosaur which founded modern palaeontology.

Walking is fairly easy on the path for the most part, but some stretches of cliff are crumbling and need care, and there are well-signed military ranges at Chickerell and near Lulworth, where access to the path is sometimes temporarily interrupted.

An inland section of the path can be followed as an alternative from Osmington to West Bexington. It provides superb views from its upland vantage points.

Location: *between South Haven Point (accessible by ferry from Sandbanks) and Lyme Regis.*
Map: *page 305.*

Claval Tower – a folly built above Kimmeridge Bay in 1820

cliffs that are perhaps the most spectacular. One of the best sections is on the Isle of Purbeck, from Durlston Head (see page 87) to Kimmeridge. A lovely cove, and what is probably Britain's most famous natural arch,

Dorset fossils: a fin spine (left) and an ammonite (right)

Dorset fossils: a bellemnite (left) and an assorted cluster (right)

tidal basin which is managed as a nature reserve by the Scottish Wildlife Trust. It is well worth a look, particularly in winter for divers and sea-ducks. The reserve also has areas of pine wood where redstarts, crossbills and siskins may be seen, and there is a large area of sand dunes and shingle. At the inland end of Loch Fleet, where the A9 crosses, is a fine freshwater marsh with the Mound Alderwoods National Nature Reserve, a complex of alder, willow and birch woodland.

Access: mostly free, except to Mound Alderwoods NNR, which can be seen from the road, and Morrich More, on S side of Dornoch Firth, which is a military testing zone with no access. Part NCC/CNT.
Location: *between Golspie and Tain.*
Map: *page 315, NH78/79/88/89.*

Dunbeath: Laidhay Croft Museum

Highland

This museum offers the visitor a taste of a way of life which has now largely vanished. The thatched Caithness croft buildings at Laidhay are derived from a much earlier style of longhouse or byre dwelling once common in this part of Scotland. The main building measures over 105 ft in length and incorporates a dwelling, byre and stable, all under one roof. The dwelling is furnished in a style typical of about 100 years ago. Exhibits include an extensive collection of early agricultural implements and machinery and interesting contemporary literature.

A fine detached winnowing barn stands nearby, also with a thatched roof which is carried on three 'Highland couples' or crucks. This technique requires each roof-truss to be made up of several members lapped and pegged together and set into the lower third of the side walls, giving a rounded, tunnel-like effect.

Open: *Easter to Sep daily. Admission charge. Picnic area. Shop. Suitable for disabled visitors. No dogs.*
Location: *1 mile N of Dunbeath, off A9.*
Map: *page 315, ND12.*

Dungeness

Kent

Apart from our great dune systems, Dungeness is the nearest thing to a desert you will find in these islands. Like a desert, Dungeness hides its life under an apparently dead surface, and like a desert this windswept place has its own devotees: botanists, entomologists and ornithologists.

Probably the largest shingle foreland in Europe, and possibly the world, Dungeness consists of successive shingle ridges, known as 'fulls', whose changing direction illustrates the gradual formation of the Ness by wave action.

The prevailing south-west wind which directs the waves, also controls the vegetation clinging to the sheltered sides of the fulls and in the hollows. Many of the plants grow in stunted form, and broom has developed its own prostrate form to cope with the unique conditions here. Other local plants occur, including Nottingham catchfly, a national rarity. Because the air is so clean a particularly rich lichen flora exists.

Birds have to adapt as well, and magpies and crows nest close to the ground in bushes or on the electricity pylons that cross the area from the power station. Kestrels, mistle thrushes and wood-pigeons also use these artificial sites.

The furnished dwelling, with 19th-century fittings, at Laidhay Croft Museum near Dunbeath

The RSPB has had an interest in the area since the 1930s when it was given part of Dungeness by a local benefactor, Robert Burrowes. Much of the ornithological interest of the area was destroyed during the Second World War when the whole of the reserve was requisitioned by the War Office. The colonies of black-headed gulls and common terns deserted, and even after the war ended, they never thrived.

In the 1970s a lake was excavated to a laid-down plan in cooperation with a gravel company. The islands created now support healthy colonies of gulls and terns, and large numbers of wildfowl use the open water in winter.

Dungeness has long been famous as a landfall for migrating birds, and it also receives a wide variety of migrant insects. These include the clouded yellow butterfly, common throughout Europe but only seen here as a migrant, and a wide variety of hawk-moths.

Open: *RSPB reserve all year Wed, Sat and Sun; Thu also from Apr to Sep. Admission charge to non-members. No dogs. RSPB.*
Location: *RSPB reserve 1½ miles SE of Lydd, off Dungeness road.*
Map: *page 306, TR01.*

Dunham Massey

Cheshire

There was a castle here in medieval times, but Dunham Massey today is a largely 18th-century house with 20th-century additions. Its fine park is one of the few surviving sites of the type of habitat known as pasture-woodland, once very common, and seemingly very practical since the same land could both support stock and produce a timber crop.

Today part of the estate is a scheduled Site of Special Scientific Interest for its beetle species. Over 180 kinds have been recorded here, living on decaying wood and the wide variety of associated fungi. Nowadays even new deciduous woods are usually planted under what might be termed controlled conditions – planted, grown and felled together – resulting in a relatively limited variety of wildlife. It is because the natural cycle of woodland (young, mature and dying trees together) has been continued at Dunham that insects and their attendant bird predators are so numerous.

A planned walk around the park takes in many points of interest. It includes the Old Mill, the estate sawmill now restored and working; a stand of very old oaks, probably part of the medieval park; and the deer slaughterhouse where carcasses were hung. For centuries deer were an important source of fresh meat, and the Dunham herd of fallow deer has probably been here for over 500 years.

Open: *Apr to Oct daily except Fri, but pm only Mon to Thu; house open pm only. Admission charge. Parking charge. Refreshments. Shop. Grounds, outbuildings and shop suitable for disabled visitors. No dogs. NT.*
Location: *2 miles SW of Altrincham off B5160.*
Map: *page 309, SJ78.*

Dunstable Downs

Bedfordshire

A great arc of chalk extends from the south coast of England through Wiltshire, Berkshire, Oxfordshire, Bedfordshire and up into Yorkshire. Each area has its own characteristics and the Dunstable Downs, running north-south to the south of the town from which they take their name, are no exception.

Here is a fine sweep of downland with many typical downland plants. In these days of 'improved' grassland, downland

which has not been treated with fertilisers and weedkillers is becoming increasingly rare. Where it does survive, it supports a unique and immensely rich flora. Many of the coarse, invasive plants often seen on waste ground do not thrive on the thin, dry soils of chalk downs; in the past, sheep-grazing has also helped keep them at bay, so the more delicate species are not crowded out - provided that scrub is not allowed to invade. Close scrutiny of a patch of downland turf may reveal up to 40 species of plant per square metre. They may include gems like eyebright, the tiny, blue chalk milkwort, or the even smaller fairy flax and squinancy-

wort; grasses like the delicate quaking grass; and herbs such as salad burnet, wild thyme and marjoram.

Areas of scrub on Dunstable Downs add diversity, supporting a population of the diminutive muntjac deer as well as badgers and foxes. The terrain is ideal for downland birds such as skylark and kestrel, with whinchats, and grasshopper and other warblers, as summer visitors.

Location: *1½ miles S of Dunstable off B4541. Part NT.*
Map: *page 306, TL01.*

Dunham Massey house has an estate which includes an ancient mill and a herd of deer

Dunwich Heath

Suffolk

To the north of Dunwich Heath lies the village of Dunwich, all that remains of the 7th-century capital town of Saxon East Anglia. To the south is the famous Minsmere nature reserve (see page 179), where marsh harriers hunt in winter, and avocets breed in summer. With such fascinating neighbours what does the heath offer?

It remains relatively uncrowded, and inland the gorse, bracken and silver birch-covered heathland can often appear totally untenanted except by the typical birds and insects of such areas. Perhaps the great contrasts in climate also help to draw those who love the area to Dunwich again and again. On summer evenings the wind drops, sand martins twist and turn after insects, the sea is a murmur barely heard from the cliff-top car park. In winter, cars in the same car park are rocked by gales, gulls are tossed sideways as they rise above the cliff, while on the shore lie the sad bodies of guillemots killed in a storm.

As the avocet is the symbol of Minsmere, the nightjar is possibly that of the heath. This wonderfully camouflaged bird lies motionless on the ground all day, flying only at dusk. The unmistakable churring song, often lasting five minutes, is the most common method of identifying this bird. The nightjar is unusual, even a little mysterious – words which also apply to Dunwich Heath.

Location: 1¼ miles S of Dunwich off unclassified road. NT.
Map: page 307, TM46.

Durlston Country Park

Dorset

Impressive limestone cliffs, as well as acres of downland and scrub, are features of this coastal country park. The cliffs, once quarried for their stone, now provide nesting sites for seabirds; the area between Tilly Whim caves and Durlston Head has been designated a sanctuary to enable them to breed undisturbed. From April until July the cliffs resound to the cries of not only kittiwakes and other gulls but also a colony of several hundred guillemots. This is one of the few colonies of this attractive member of the auk family on the south coast. A few puffins are also found here, but they are becoming scarce.

The clifftop grassland is studded with flowers in spring and summer, when several types of orchid – once much commoner, when visitors were fewer – may be seen. The downland grasses and herbs attract a variety of butterflies as well as different types of grasshoppers and crickets. Chiff-chaffs and willow warblers are summer visitors to the thicket on the seaward side of the road, while chaffinches, linnets

The Afon Dyfi

and whitethroats find cover for nesting in the valley, with its many species of shrubs and small trees.

Open: at all times; information centre Easter to Oct.
Location: 1 mile S of Swanage.
Map: page 305, SZ07.

Dyfi National Nature Reserve

Dyfed

The mountains on the south-western boundary of the Snowdonia National Park form a dramatic backcloth for the Afon Dyfi's estuary, which drives inland towards Machynlleth like a broad, flat wedge. At low tide the river swirls through deep channels and leaves a 'desert' of glistening sandbanks patrolled by herring gulls and other seabirds. When the waters return, sails bring bold splashes of colour to the estuary.

The Dyfi National Nature Reserve covers over 5000 acres downstream from Dyfi Junction. The beach and sand dunes at Ynyslas – visited by more than 200,000 people every year – contrast with lonely mudflats and saltings overlooked by the single-track railway line. The reserve also includes Cors Fochno, a rare example of a raised bog, for which a visitor's permit is required.

The dunes at Ynyslas are explored by a mile-long waymarked trail. It enables walkers to appreciate the constant battle with natural and human erosion, and also points out many aspects of the dunes' plant, bird and animal life. Creatures range from the yellow-and-black caterpillars of the cinnabar moth to rabbits and lizards. Birds include shelducks and wheatears, which nest in abandoned burrows, skylarks, meadow pipits and stonechats.

Traeth Maelgwyn, the beach immediately east of the dunes, is said to be where Maelgwyn Gwynedd claimed the throne of North Wales in the 6th century AD. According to legend, Maelgwyn and his rivals agreed to a contest in which they defied the incoming tide for as long as possible. Maelgwyn won by making himself a throne that floated.

The northern tip of the dunes faces Aberdyfi, a small resort whose Victorian and Edwardian buildings are mirrored in the estuary at high tide. The mid-channel refuge tower was built in the 1860s for travellers awaiting the ferry.

Location: between Dyfi station and Borth, W of A487. Nature trail and information centre off B4353, ¼ mile N of Borth. NCC.
Map: page 309, SN69.

Guillemot

Guillemots are most likely to be seen on cliffs and rocky islands. It is in such places that the female lays her single egg; there is no nest, but the egg is shaped in such a way that it tends to roll in circles, not roll off the ledge on which it has been deposited. The birds often form huge nesting colonies, with row upon row of guillemots holding eggs between their feet. Between August and January guillemots are birds of the ocean, coming close to land only when the wind blows them off course.

KIPLINGCOTES DERBY

Kiplingcotes Racecourse, Humberside

Dating from 1519, the Kiplingcotes Derby is claimed to be the oldest flat race in the world. It originated when the local gentry agreed to put their horses through a fitness test after the winter to ensure it was worth betting on them. The event was secured in 1619 when a group of gentlemen subscribed £365 in order that 'Kiplingcoates Plate was ridd yearly on the third Thursday in March'.

The rather unusual four-mile course comprises a wide grass verge, two country lanes, one bridge and one major road (the A163). Other peculiarities include the absence of a grandstand and of bookmakers; free viewing by spectators; and only one official judge, known as Clerk of the Course. This position has been held by members of the same family for more than five generations.

Competitors assemble between 10 and 11am to be weighed in – a procedure governed by strict regulations. They must weigh at least 140lb. If anyone is lighter, he is obliged to carry lead weights in his pockets. The horses are led out to the starting post between noon and 1pm. The competitors vie for two prizes. The winner carries off a cup, plus cash, but if there are more than three riders, the competitor who achieves second place receives the entry money – invariably amounting to more than the winner's sum!

When: *3rd Thu in Mar.*
Where: *3½ miles NE of Market Weighton.*
Map: *page 310, SE84.*

TICHBORNE DOLE

Tichborne, Hampshire

With its medieval origins, the Tichborne Dole is claimed to be one of the oldest charities in England. It was founded by the dying Lady Mabella Tichborne who asked her husband, Sir Roger Tichborne, to provide an annual dole of bread for the poor on Lady Day. He was a cruel man and consented to give to the charity only the corn grown on the amount of land his wife could walk round before a burning torch went out. She was of course too ill to walk, but surprised him by managing to crawl round a 23-acre area which is still known as 'The Crawls'. Before Lady Mabella died she muttered a curse upon anyone who should stop the Dole, predicting that the family name would die out, the house would fall down and a generation of seven daughters would be born.

The Dole was regularly distributed until 1796, and in 1803 the curse appeared to come true when part of Tichborne House collapsed and Sir Henry Tichborne fathered seven daughters. As a result the Dole was resumed annually – although loaves are no longer used. Today, following an open-air service, 1½ tons of flour, still made from wheat grown on 'The Crawls', is distributed to the parishioners of Tichborne and Cheriton.

When: *25 Mar.*
Map: *page 306, SU53.*

Ritual confrontation between two participants during the Midgley Pace Egg Play

March

SKIPPING

Alciston, East Sussex

This old custom is associated with fishermen and their families who used to skip along the sea-front at Brighton and Newhaven. It moved inland to the Rose Cottage Inn at Alciston when the beaches were closed during the Second World War. The custom declined, but a group of people known as the Knots of May have recently revived it.

The celebrations begin at mid-day with morris dancing followed by the 'Long Rope Skipping' in which adults and children participate. The custom's link with Good Friday is rather vague, although one theory suggests that the rope represents the one which hanged Judas Iscariot.

When: *Good Fri.*
Map: *page 306, TQ50.*

PACE EGG PLAY

Midgley, West Yorkshire

The name 'Pace Egg' is derived from the Latin 'Pascha', meaning Easter, and this play is really an Easter version of the more popular 'Mummer's Play', which depicts the struggle between good and evil. The 'Pace-eggers', or actors, are selected from the boys at Calder High School. There are eight original characters plus a ninth, known as the Bugler.

Five of the characters – the Fool, St George, Bold Slasher, the King of Egypt and Hector – are dressed similarly in bright red tunics decorated with paper rosettes. They also wear large cardboard helmets covered with tissue paper, on which hang two bells and long strings of coloured beads. The costume of the Black Prince of Paradine resembles these, except the paper rosettes and beads are black and white, and his face is usually blackened. The Doctor wears checked

trousers, a long black frock-coat and a top hat adorned with ribbons. The most ridiculously dressed of all is the Toss Pot, who wears clothes much too big for him and has a long straw tail to emphasise his devilish connections. He carries a basket for donations of eggs or – more popular today – money, from the audience.

When: *Good Fri.*
Map: *page 310, SE02.*

THE NUTTERS' DANCE

Bacup, Lancashire

This dance appears to be linked with the pirate dances brought to Cornwall by Moorish pirates. Numerous Cornishmen took the dance northwards during the 18th and 19th centuries when they went to work in the expanding Lancashire mining industry.

Today the dance is performed through the streets of Bacup by a team of morris dancers known as the Britannia Coconut Dancers. They are accompanied by the town band and their unusual appearance has strong links with that of the Moorish pirates. The dancers have blackened faces and wear white turbans, black long-sleeved jerseys, black breeches, a short red and white skirt, white stockings and black clogs. The 'Coconuts' are not what their name suggests, but wooden discs attached to the hands, waist and knees. Their clattering provides a frenzied rhythm and gives the dance its peculiar name.

When: *Easter Sat.*
Map: *page 309, SD82.*

Left and below: the Nutters' Dance

Earl's Hill

Shropshire

The steep sides of Earl's Hill rise to over 1000ft above the north Shropshire plain; at the summit is an Iron Age hill-fort. The rocks of which the hill is made were formed over 1,200 million years ago and are among the oldest in Britain.

On the eastern side the steep cliffs give way to scree which provides a site for rock stone-crop, navelwort and wood sage. Lower down, on the deeper soils of the Habberley Valley, there is woodland, with uncommon tree species such as large-leaved lime and wild service-tree over which buzzards, merlins and ravens may sometimes be seen and all three species of woodpecker heard.

The long, dry south and south-west slopes are grass-covered with outcrops of bare rock where attractive small plants such as upright chickweed and shepherd's cress flower in early spring, to be followed by mouse-ear hawkweed, carline thistle and the stately yellow spikes of great mullein.

This wide range of habitats attracts large numbers of butterflies: 29 species have been recorded here including four species of skipper, four species of fritillary, green and white-letter hairstreak and holly blue.

Open: *at all times; visitor centre most weekends in summer. Nature trail. CNT.*
Location: *7¼ miles SW of Shrewsbury; 1 mile S of Pontesford take unclassified road off A488.*
Map: *page 309, SJ40.*

The green hairstreak butterfly, found on downs and moors

Earsham: The Otter Trust

Suffolk

The otter is one of our rarest mammals, suffering from the effects of man's use of pesticides and the over-zealous management of rivers and streams. It is extremely difficult to see a wild otter now. At the Otter Trust, however, attractively designed pens make it possible to watch this delightful animal (and some of its relatives from other parts of the world) at close quarters.

Their playful nature and mastery of the water make otters very popular with visitors. But showing the animals to the public is only part of the work of the Trust, which seeks to protect British otters in a variety of ways. For instance, a programme of reintroduction to the wild, using captive-bred animals, has recently been started. The progress of the released animals has been monitored by the use of temporary radio transmitters, and the experiment promises success. This work is explained at the Trust's centre. There is also a collection of wildfowl, aviaries with other water birds, a lake and walks by the River Waveney.

Open: *Apr to Oct daily. Admission charge. Picnic area. Refreshments. Shop. No dogs.*
Location: *1½ miles SW of Bungay (signposted off A143).*
Map: *page 306, TM38.*

A resident of the Otter Trust

Mellow stones and tiles at Preston Mill, East Linton

those jobs now done by tractors. Suffolk Punch stallions can weigh as much as a ton, and are always chestnut in colour. Unlike their cousins – the Shires and Clydesdales – they do not have 'feathered' – or hairy – feet.

The farm park's other attractions include a collection of tools, tractors and other vehicles and a working blacksmith. A nature trail has also been laid out. Passing through damp woodland and pasture and alongside the River Deben, it provides an excellent introduction to some of our best-loved woodland, farmland and wetland plants and animals.

Open: *Easter to Sep daily. Admission charge. Picnic area. Refreshments. Shop. Suitable for disabled visitors.*
Location: *3 miles NW of Wickham Market, off unclassified road SW of Easton village.*
Map: *page 306, TM25.*

Eaves Wood

Lancashire

For generations Eaves Wood has been managed to produce timber crops on the traditional system of coppice-with-standards. Coppiced trees, mainly hazel and ash, are cut back to a stump and then produce shoots which are used for a wide range of purposes. The frequency of cutting depends on the size of timber required. Some trees, the 'standards', usually oak, are left to grow up through the coppice.

The walk around the wood is steep; there are fissures ('grikes') in the limestone away from the paths. A shorter walk covers many natural history features.

After the First World War woodland management declined and the control of species virtually ceased. As a result, one of the particular fascinations of Eaves Wood is the variety of its trees. You will find small-leaved lime, yew, larch, sessile oak, wild privet, a local species of whitebeam, juniper, a wild service tree and wild cherry as well as the coppiced species. There are several varieties of fungi – some poisonous, others simply inedible. The many species of flowers include various orchids, and the expected woodland birds add further interest to a satisfying walk through an example of living and evolving natural history.

Location: *at Silverdale, 1 mile NW of Carnforth, off unclassified road. NT.*
Map: *page 309, SD47.*

East Linton: Preston Mill & Phantassie Doocot

Lothian

Preston Mill is the oldest example of a mechanical water-driven mill in Scotland. It was built in the 16th century and continued to grind oats until 1957. The mill lies in a romantic riverside setting where its conical-roofed kiln and red-pantiled outbuildings are much admired by artists.

Nearby is Phantassie Doocot (or Dovecot), once the nesting place for 500 birds. Doves were not kept in such large numbers for appearances; they were regarded simply as an economical and plentiful supply of food, especially in winter when fresh meat was otherwise unobtainable. The Phantassie Doocot is an especially massive dovecot – its stone walls are four feet thick at the base. It dates from the 18th century, and was given to the National Trust for Scotland in 1961.

Open: *Apr to Oct daily (Sun pm only); Nov to Mar weekends only. Admission charge. NTS.*
Location: *at East Linton, 5½ miles W of Dunbar, off A1.*
Map: *page 313, NT57.*

Easton Farm Park

Suffolk

Modern farming techniques are very different from those of a hundred years ago, a fact the visitor can see clearly at Easton. In about 1870 the Duke of Hamilton established an up-to-date dairy farm here, and it, with much of the equipment of that period, is on display beside a modern operation, where visitors can stand on a raised walkway and watch the milking of a large herd of Friesians. Although very familiar today, these sturdy black and white cows are relative newcomers to the English landscape, and the farm has older breeds of cattle, such as the Longhorn, as well as other animals including Suffolk Punch horses. Like all Britain's heavy horses, the Suffolk Punch is descended from horses bred in the Middle Ages to carry knights encased in very heavy armour. Some idea of the strength of those beasts can be gained from the fact that, by the time of Henry VIII, the only way some knights could mount their horses was to be lowered onto their backs by a kind of crane. The farm horses that followed were equally powerful, performing all

Early spring in Ebbor Gorge

highest point of Mynydd Maen – open country between the forest and Pontypool – stands 1553 feet above sea level and provides splendid views over the Bristol Channel to Gloucestershire, Avon and Somerset. Equally fine views can be admired from the forest's seven-mile Cwmcarn Scenic Drive, which also provides opportunities to leave the car and explore on foot. Walks climbing to 1370 feet reveal much of the forest's bird and plant life.

Open: *scenic drive Easter to Oct. Small charge. Picnic areas. FC.*
Location: *at Cwmcarn, off A467.*
Map: *page 305, ST29.*

Eden Estuary

Fife

Although relatively small, the Eden supports large numbers of wintering wildfowl and waders. It is also good for migrants such as ringed plovers in spring, and spotted redshanks and whimbrels in autumn. With its brown plumage and downcurving bill, the whimbrel is perhaps the only British wader which might be mistaken for the larger and much commoner curlew. However, whimbrels are unlikely to be seen in winter, and can be told from curlews by their pale eye-stripe, which has a distinctive darker band on either side.

Waders in the Eden Estuary may total between 7000 and 10,000 in winter. Oystercatchers (up to 5000) are the most numerous and there are large numbers of bar-tailed godwits and dunlins. The area is of special interest for its small but regular wintering flock of black-tailed godwits. Slightly larger than the bar-tailed, this species has a straight bill, whereas the bar-tailed godwit's bill, almost equally long, curves upwards. In flight they can easily be told apart, for black-tailed godwits have white wing bars, a black-and-white tail and trailing legs.

Wildfowl on the Eden include shelduck, mallard, wigeon, pintail, eider, goldeneye and red-breasted mergansers, with common and velvet scoters and long-tailed ducks in neighbouring St Andrew's Bay. Scoters in particular can be very numerous and scaup may also be seen.

Access: *from Out Head at north end of West Sands, St Andrews, and good viewpoint at lay-by on N side of A91, ¼ mile E of Guardbridge. LNR (North-East Fife District Council).*
Location: *3 miles NW of St Andrews, 1 mile S of Leuchars, off A919.*
Map: *page 313, NO42.*

Ebbor Gorge

Somerset

Sadly, present-day visitors to Ebbor will not see reindeer, bears or lemmings, but it is wild and unspoilt enough for the more romantic to imagine their presence. That they did once live here is certain, since their remains have been discovered, along with artefacts left by Stone-Age man.

Of the two nature walks at Ebbor, the shorter is suitable for disabled visitors, while the other is relatively fierce, climbing to 800ft, with magnificent views across the great Somerset plain with Glastonbury, the Sedgemoors and the Polden Hills in the foreground, and beyond, Exmoor and the Bristol Channel.

Buzzards circle and kestrels hover over the Mendip uplands, while sparrowhawks speed through the woodland. Badgers are always present, if rarely seen; one of their setts is almost beside the path. Wych elm is surviving the ravages of Dutch elm disease, because it reproduces by seed and not by sucker. Both bats of the western hills, greater and lesser horseshoe, live and hibernate in Ebbor's caves.

Open: *at all times. Nature Conservancy Council information centre in car park. NCC/NT.*
Location: *3 miles NW of Wells.*
Map: *page 305, ST54.*

Ebbw Forest

Gwent

This forest takes its name from the Ebbw River and not from the better-known industrial town of Ebbw Vale, some eight miles to the north. The valley echoed to the sounds of industry during the 19th century, but Ebbw Forest is a reminder of what South Wales was like before the age of steelworks and 'King Coal'. Though the present forest dates from the early 1920s, it is in part a re-creation of the 13th-century Forest of Machen.

Streams visited by water-loving birds hurry down deep valleys whose conifer-clad slopes rise to nearly 1500 feet. The

Elan Valley

Powys

The Afon Elan rises in a remote and boggy wilderness, nearly 1700 feet above sea level, then flows through wild country before mingling with the River Wye to the south of Rhayader. It was an unexceptional river until the end of the 19th century, when Birmingham's fast-growing demand for water brought about the construction of the Craig Goch, Pen-y-garreg, Garreg Ddu and Caban Coch reservoirs. They were completed in 1904, 48 years before the huge Claerwen Reservoir in a neighbouring valley was officially opened by Queen Elizabeth. Their combined surface area is about 1500 acres and they send 75 million gallons of water to Birmingham every day. It flows through a 73½-mile aqueduct, taking 36 hours to complete the journey because the average gradient is very gentle.

The reservoirs caused controversy when they were first planned, since they totally changed this part of Wales. However, they are now seen by many as a valuable visual amenity, and have been established long enough to create a 'natural' atmosphere. Certainly, the roads built to serve them enable people to explore the wilderness of central Wales. Walkers can soon leave behind the new landscapes of reservoir and commercial forestry, and reach open moorland where wind soughing through the vegetation, and the calls of buzzard and pipit, are often the only sounds.

Three of the reservoirs are skirted by a narrow road which runs northwards before following the Elan towards its source near the boundary of Powys and Dyfed. A branch turns left after crossing the Garreg Ddu's dam, then runs through trees and follows the Claerwen towards the biggest of the reservoirs. A rough track from the dam snakes alongside the lake and eventually reaches the hamlet of Ffair Rhos, south of Devil's Bridge. It is suitable for energetic walkers, pony-trekkers and four-wheel-drive vehicles. Other tracks link the Claerwen, Elan and Wye valleys to make this a rewarding part of Wales for visitors willing to leave the car behind and explore on foot or horseback. Crossing streams, passing small lakes and climbing to nearly 2000 feet, they traverse one of the wildest tracts of country in Britain.

Location: *reached by B4518 SW from Rhayader or from minor road over mountains between Rhayader and Devil's Bridge.*
Map: *page 309, SN96.*

Elmley Marsh

Kent

Scenically the Isle of Sheppey is dull, but the journey across Kingsferry Bridge is worth making for the bird reserve at Elmley.

When the RSPB took over the lease here in 1973 the place had little to offer but potential, being a low-lying greensward of drained grazing marsh, with the bird life restricted to the ditches and creeks. But therein lay the clue to the future, for by controlling and diverting the water that used to drain to the sea, a 40-acre flood has been produced that has a magnetic effect on birds.

The reserve now holds a vast population of birds in winter and a great variety of breeding species, as well as providing a high water refuge for thousands of waders outside the breeding season.

Recent years have seen national rarities like pintail, garganey and black-tailed godwit breeding, with greatly increased numbers of commoner wetland birds. Not to be missed in summer are the cackling marsh frogs and an abundance of dragonflies.

At Spitend Point a hide overlooks a colony of black-headed gulls and common terns. Winter brings huge concentrations of wildfowl and waders plus a good selection of birds of prey. Rarities can turn up here at any time of the year.

Open: *Wed, Sat and Sun all year. Admission charge to non-members. No dogs. RSPB.*
Location: *3 miles S of Sheerness, off A429. Access from Kingshill Farm, 2 miles along farm track from A249.*
Map: *page 306, TQ96.*

Elan Valley – Craig Goch Reservoir and moorland slopes

Elvaston Castle Country Park

Derbyshire

Elvaston Castle's elaborate ornamental gardens were considered to be among the most remarkable of their kind in the country when they were created in the mid 19th century. The landscaper, William Barron, managed to create the most intricate of topiary gardens, using high hedges, short avenues and trees to give space and depth.

In 1968 the castle and park became one of Britain's first country parks. Derbyshire County Council, who manage it, have extensively renovated the once-neglected gardens and park and provided a great variety of facilities for visitors. Within the former walled kitchen garden, for example, they have created an old English garden, with roses and scented herbs – especially suitable for visually handicapped visitors. The original estate workshops have been restored as a working museum, with joinery, blacksmithing, saddlery and other crafts being practised. There are nature trails and numerous walks, a riding school and a campsite – all presided over by Elvaston Castle, a 17th-century mansion which was later remodelled in neo-Gothic style.

Open: *country park all year daily; estate museum Easter to Oct Wed to Sat pm only, Sun and bank holidays all day. Castle not open. Admission charge for museum. Parking charge weekends and bank holidays. Picnic area. Refreshments Easter to Oct daily (other times weekends only). Shop. Suitable for disabled visitors.*
Location: *6 miles SE of Derby.*
Map: *page 310, SK43.*

High Beach, Epping Forest, as it was at the close of the last century. Then many of its trees (like the hornbeams in the photograph below) were pollarded for crops of poles and other wood. Fewer people gather wood today, but 'Forest people' still have the right to graze their beasts here

Epping Forest

Essex

It is little short of a miracle that an ancient forest of this size should have survived so close to London. Today, Epping Forest covers nearly 6000 acres, and within this area is a magnificent assembly of native trees, particularly oaks. The huge, smooth, pillar-like trunks of beeches lend a cathedral-like air to some areas, while there is something of an Essex Epping speciality, the hornbeam, with its deeply-fissured bark. Until the beginning of this century many of the hornbeams were pollarded, that is their branches were lopped some ten feet from the ground. Since this practice was discontinued the trees have grown into bizarre and contorted shapes.

The forest contains many open areas of grassland and bushes, and here the nightingale still sings in spring and early summer.

Queen Elizabeth's Hunting Lodge, dating from about 1543, houses a museum covering the animals and plants of the Forest, and there is a conservation centre at High Beach.

Open: *Queen Elizabeth's Hunting Lodge Wed to Sun and bank holiday Mon, pm only. Admission charge. Picnic area. Shop. No dogs. Epping Forest Conservation Centre open Easter to Oct Wed to Sun and bank holidays; Nov to Easter Sat and Sun.*
Location: *between Chingford and Epping off A1069, A104 and B1393.*
Map: *page 306, TQ49.*

The Essex Way

Essex

Britain's long-distance paths are not confined to the hills. This walk stretches from the edge of London to the Suffolk border and the beautiful Constable Country around Dedham. The 50-mile walk passes through the well-tended farmlands of East Anglia for much of its length, but there are streams and woods along the way where wildlife flourishes comparatively undisturbed by the activities of modern agriculture.

For those not able to walk the whole distance, there are many places along the Way worthy of a visit, and short walks can easily be made. The path begins in Epping, an attractive market town with many old buildings. Greensted has what is probably the oldest wooden church in the world, while just to the east is Chipping Ongar, which has a Norman castle mound, complete with moat. There are fine views from the village churchyard at Good Easter, and outside its vicarage is a pillory, where 18th-century offenders were pelted for their crimes. A little further northeast, at Pleshey, lie the massive earthworks of a Norman castle which was already in ruins when Shakespeare wrote of it. At Cressing, the Knights Templar, of Crusades fame, had their first English settlement: all that remains now is two interesting barns. The last part of the Way is certainly the most beautiful. The delightful village of Langham was a favourite of Constable's (he was at school here), and just across the border in Suffolk lies the famous Flatford Mill, which Constable painted frequently and which belonged to his father.

Map: page 306.

Etchingham: Haresmere Hall Shire Horses

East Sussex

At the end of a long day behind the plough the horseman probably did not muse very much on the majesty of the Shire horse. To him the Shire was the source of still more work once the sun had gone down – feeding, watering and grooming. Today our view of heavy horses is much more romantic and most of us find them very exciting, which is why Haresmere Hall is a popular family outing.

Once the home of the Prince Regent's Master of the Horse, Haresmere continues its equestrian tradition as a Shire horse centre. On the estate working horses are being reintroduced for farm work and forestry wherever this is economic. The stable-block is an equestrian and breeding centre for the Sussex Shire Horses. As well as a Shire stallion and mares, there are Ardennes mares from France, Welsh cobs, Suffolk punches and colliers. Visitors are encouraged to learn about the horses, with facilities ranging from cart rides for children to handling courses for the real enthusiast.

Open: Apr to Oct Tue to Sun and bank holiday Mon. Admission charge (includes gardens). Picnic area. Refreshments. Suitable for disabled visitors. No dogs.
Location: S of A265 between Etchingham and Hurst Green.
Map: page 306, TQ72.

Exe Estuary and Dawlish Warren

Devon

The Exe Estuary is one of the largest in the West Country. It supports a wealth of wildlife on account of its shallowness and its extensive mudflats. It is bordered on both banks by railway lines, but there are a number of places where excellent views can be had: the riverside villages of Topsham, Exton, Lympstone and Starcross all offer good access points.

Across the mouth of the estuary stretches the 1½-mile dune system of Dawlish Warren. This is a mecca for holidaymakers, but it is also a nature reserve with outstanding birds and flowers. As well as the famous Warren crocus, a diminutive lilac blue flower which has its only mainland Britain site here, Dawlish Warren boasts over 450 other plant species, including several orchids. It is also the site of one of the estuary's high-tide wader roosts, which can be viewed in comfort from a large hide looking back up the estuary. Oystercatchers are very numerous here but it is also a good place for terns in the summer. Many wading birds can be seen, including the small, pale-plumaged sanderling, which runs like a clockwork toy in front of the waves. Upstream on the west side, the deer park at Powderham is another high-tide roosting area for waders and wildfowl, and also boasts an attractive herd of fallow deer. Above Powderham lie the fields of Exminster Marshes, bordered by the Exeter Ship Canal, its towpath providing good vantage points for the upper estuary where curlews and black-tailed godwits are often seen.

Peak numbers of waders and wildfowl occur in mid-winter, when the estuary is host to a large flock of brent geese and also a flock of wintering avocets. A good variety of birds is nevertheless present for most of the year.

Access: car parks at Exmouth and Dawlish Warren (where information on public hide is displayed). Footpath upstream from Powderham follows river bank. Part CNT.
Location: reached from Exeter by A376 Exmouth road or A379 Dawlish road.
Map: page 305, SX98/SY08.

The Exe Estuary, with Dawlish Warren in the middle distance and Exmouth on the far shore

Exmoor National Park

In essence Exmoor is a large plateau of ancient sandstone rocks which have been weathered and worn by millions of years of frosts, rains, and winds. Its position and altitude mean that the moor has a very high rainfall, which runs off the impervious rocks to form fast-flowing streams. These have carved steep-sided valleys over the millennia, forming the combes for which Exmoor is so famous.

Ancient hunting preserve

Like many of England's large tracts of wild or semi-wild land, part of Exmoor was once a royal hunting forest, a huge area set aside as a game preserve. Exmoor's hunting forest, centred round Simonsbath, was actually rarely used by royalty. From 1818 onwards the hunting preserve, mostly used as sheep walks, was purchased by John Knight, who lived in Simonsbath, but who had made his for-

With its mixture of wooded valleys, bracken–covered combes, heathery hills and patchwork of fields, Exmoor is one of the most diverse and attractive areas of southern England. It has the bonus of a dramatically beautiful coastline which is as unspoilt as any round Britain.

Left: an engraving of the Valley of the Rocks

Below: Exmoor is a mixture of farmlands, woods and open moors

tune in the Midland iron industry. He and his son transformed 15,000 acres into productive farmland. The distinctive steep banks of the area, topped by beech hedges, are visible reminders of this remarkable family.

The moor itself, with its associated valleys and farmlands, the Brendon Hills to the east and the superb coastline – in all some 265 square miles – became a National Park in 1954.

At the heart of the National Park is the moorland that once composed the Forest of Exmoor. In historic times the 'forest' was never wooded, the word simply referring to wild and uncultivated land. Fortunately for us, much of the forest still fits that description, and it is on these moorlands that the true essence of Exmoor can be discovered. Much of the soil here is dominated by purple moor grass and deer sedge, with cotton-grass abundant in peatier areas. For most of the year the ground is wet, but the bogs are usually not so much deadly as hazardous. Even so, walkers would be well advised to carry a compass against the fogs and mists which can envelop the area within mi-

nutes. Those who do explore the forest will be rewarded with solitude, silence and peace.

Outside the old forest boundaries are heather moorlands. These have been managed for a very long time to produce fresh young growth for the moor's grazing livestock. Among the heather which, left to itself, would become a tall and straggly plant, can be seen gorse, whortleberry, several grasses, and little flowers such as heath milkwort, heath bedstraw and yellow tormentil.

Wildlife of the combes

In the numerous combes which divide the moor, a greater variety of plants and animals is usually to be found. Trees and shrubs – notably hawthorn, mountain ash and oak – frequently gain a foothold here and are sheltered from the worst of the gales and storms. In these trees buzzards, ravens, kestrels and crows may nest. Ring ouzels – close relations of blackbirds, but with creamy crescents on their chests – are often seen on valley sides with rocky outcrops, and dippers are a constant delight along, and often in, the streams. Grey wagtails are also essential elements in the wildlife of Exmoor streams.

The woodlands in Exmoor's combes are dominated by oaks.

Both British species – sessile and pedunculate – can be found. In the past nearly all the oak woods were coppiced – the bark being used in the tanning industry. Along with oaks there is often holly, hazel, birch and wych elm. The Forestry Commission has huge plantations on the Brendon Hills – nearly all of which are coniferous. The broadleaved woodlands are home to all the usual species of birds, with additions like the redstart. These handsome little birds, with rusty red tail and chest, chocolate-coloured throat and grey head and back, now breed mostly in old woodlands in the west and north of the country.

Arable and pastoral farmland accounts for much of the scenery of the National Park, and these habitats attract particular kinds of birds and animals.

Most famous of Exmoor's wild animals are the ponies and the red deer. The ponies are a very common part of the Exmoor scene – no picnic spot is complete without them. However, they should never be fed, and it is foolish to try to touch foals since this will probably result in your being either bitten or kicked by the mare. There is a continuous debate as to the origins of the ponies. Some claim that they are descended from indigenous wild horses which arrived in Britain after the retreat

of the glaciers. Others, perhaps the majority, say that they were brought here by Neolithic people. Since that would mean they have been here for something like 6000 years, it must surely give them a valid claim to be among Britain's earliest immigrants. Either way, Exmoor would be incomplete without them.

The same is true of the red deer, which really are wild. Man did not introduce them – they have been roaming the combes and tops of Exmoor since the ice ages. They are Britain's largest native animals; a rutting stag, half mad with desire, rage and exhaustion, is an awe-inspiring and formidable sight.

Exmoor in trust

A sizeable area of Exmoor is cared for by the National Trust. Their largest property here is the Holnicote estate. Its 12,443 acres encapsulate all that Exmoor contains. From the height of Dunkery Beacon, the highest point on the moor at 1705ft, the estate stretches out over moorland, mature woods, prehistoric sites and moorland villages to the Bristol Channel. Wild and often lonely country, it lacks the grim harshness of Dartmoor. Summer birds sing in the woods and buzzards wheel over the barrows on the heights. Villages such as Selworthy are known throughout the world for their beauty, appearing in hundreds of photo-

graphs in guidebooks, calendars and on postcards.

Subtle variations in planting add interest to the Holnicote woods. Around Selworthy, the mixture is of oak (with a high percentage of the holm or evergreen oak) chestnut and Scots pine. Tivington Woods are similarly planted but Luccombe Woods are almost exclusively conifer. The National Trust is replanting where necessary with groups of trees similar to those reaching maturity. The aim is to preserve the views so carefully landscaped by the Acland family, who had owned the estate for 200 years before handing it to the Trust.

The immense popularity of the Holnicote estate is fully justified; thousands flock here each week in summer, yet it is not difficult, even at the peak holiday times, to find solitude, walking the many paths which cross and re-cross the estate just a few miles to the south of the 'honeypots'. The National Trust publishes a leaflet giving suggestions for 14 different routes around Dunkery. On most of these the buzzards wheeling and mewing overhead will be the walker's likeliest companions. Many of Holnicote's places of greatest interest will be found in the gazetteer section below.

What to See

ALDERMAN'S BARROW AREA

The unclassified road which follows the little River Exe from Exford towards its source veers northwards across the moor after about two miles and enters some of Exmoor's wildest scenery. Alderman's Barrow was one of the boundary markers of the old Forest of Exmoor, though it is actually older than the Forest by several millennia. From here it is possible to explore the lonely moor, and there is the likelihood of seeing Exmoor ponies, the chance of red deer, and the possibility of upland birds like pipits and curlews. To the west of the barrow are the ruins of two farmsteads – Tom's Hill and Larkbarrow. These steadings, created by John Knight's son Frederick in the 19th century, supported tiny communities for over a century. Larkbarrow was the last to go, literally battered into the ground when the area became an army training ground during the Second World War.

BADGWORTHY WATER

Many who come to Exmoor will know R. D. Blackmore's famous story *Lorna Doone*. His descriptions of scenery are so precise that it is difficult to believe that he did not record exactly what he had seen. Yet although Blackmore used some Badgworthy scenery in his book, some details were taken from other places, while much else was created by his fertile imagination. But those who know the book will find features that they recognise.

There is no road up the Doone Valley, but a footpath from Malmsmead, at the foot of Badgworthy Water, leads for 2½ miles along the deep combe, into the legendary 'Doone country'. In the valley of Hoccombe Water – which enters Badgworthy Water high up the valley – can be found the traces of ancient houses, likely to be the originals on which Blackmore based the Doone settlement. The scenery of Badgworthy and Hoccombe is lovely enough to warrant exploration and enjoyment even without the lure of the Doones.

Closer to the beaten track, in the delightful Oare valley, is Oare Church. This charming building, in a lovely setting, is where Lorna and Jan Ridd were married. A path from the church leads to Alderman's Barrow.

BRENDON HILLS

These gentle hills form the eastern boundary of the National Park. Unlike most of the rest of Exmoor, they are largely pastoral in appearance. The tops of many of the hills are covered in woodlands, most of them coniferous, but woodlands of oak and other broadleaved trees – always more interesting from a wildlife point of view – can be found along the valleys of the Washford River and its tributaries. On the northern edge of the Brendons is Dunster, one of Exmoor's prettiest villages. It has a wide street lined with delightful houses of many periods, set off by a 16th-century market building at one end, a handsome medieval dovecote, and a beautiful hilltop castle at the other. This belongs to the National Trust, which also owns the restored 18th-century watermill on the River Avill below the castle.

Open: castle Apr to early Nov Sat to Wed (pm only during Oct & Nov); admission charge; NT. Mill Apr to Sep, Sat to Wed pm only; admission charge; NT. Dovecote Easter to mid Oct daily.

Malmsmead, in the Doone Country

THE CHAINS

One of the wildest parts of Exmoor, this area north-west of Simonsbath is also particularly rich in prehistoric remains. The numerous tumuli, barrows and standing stones remain as silent memorials to ancient peoples who lived on what appears to us to be inhospitable moorland.

The blanket bog which covers much of The Chains is dominated by one plant – deer grass – and it is thought that this vegetation has altered little since the late Bronze Age, and will probably not change again unless there is some dramatic change in the climatic conditions.

Of the prehistoric memorials on The Chains, the Long Stone is surely the most dramatic. It stands quite alone, a nine-foot pillar of slate, hidden from casual gaze in a natural depression in the moorland. It almost certainly dates from the same period – the Bronze Age – as the barrows which dot the hilltops all around. The best group of these is Chapman Barrows, a group of 11 which command superb views.

There are two stretches of open water on The Chains – Challacombe Reservoir, and Pinkworthy Pond. The latter was built by John Knight in the early 19th century. No one is sure what its function was; it was probably constructed simply to beautify an otherwise gaunt area.

DUNKERY BEACON & WEBBER'S POST

It is possible to park a car near Webber's Post and take a path in almost any direction. A nature trail along the beautiful East Water Valley to Cloutsham is described in a booklet published by the Exmoor National Park Authority, and several walks either starting from or passing close to Webber's Post are described in a leaflet produced by the National Trust. After leaving Webber's Post the road to Wheddon Cross passes Robin How, where there are round barrows, on the left, and then, to the right, the great mass of Dunkery Beacon, owned by the National Trust. The view from the Beacon, which takes in large parts of Somerset and Devon, justifies the walk to the summit.

NT.

THE HEDDON VALLEY

The approach to Heddon is by steep hills and narrow, difficult lanes, often so overhung as to resemble a tunnel. The Heddon is one of the many small rivers rising on Exmoor which make their way to the sea through steep wooded valleys, or combes, forming great clefts between gentle rounded hills. Several of these rivers, like the West Lyn, make dramatic final dashes to the sea, as if impatient to arrive, and the Heddon is no exception. As spectacular as the Lyn, but on a small scale, it cascades through the valley, creating miniature fjords and tiny waterfalls, ending in a lovely sequence of crystal-clear pools behind a rocky shore. Because of the depth of the valley, Heddon is invariably warm, even humid, and attracts a variety of plant and insect life.

A narrow path runs beside the river down the steeply wooded east side of the valley where oak and sycamore flourish with poplar and some firs. The 18th-century lime kiln, where lime ferried from Wales was burned before being hauled up the valley for use on neighbouring farmland, has survived only as a ruin at the side of the tiny beach.

On the western side of the valley a mass of primeval grey scree, unusual by the coast, forms a neutral backdrop to the beauty of this combe.

NT.

HORNER WOODS

These woods are scheduled as a Site of Special Scientific Interest, and anyone who parks in Horner village, and follows the paths along Horner Water will quickly appreciate the reason for this. The woods are a mixture of 'high forest' and coppiced oak. The latter serve as a reminder of the many uses the oak once had, while the former, on lower ground, protected from the worst of the weather, were allowed to grow to maturity. They provide shelter for animals and birds. For most of the year red deer are in the woods but only the very observant will see them. In autumn it is difficult to avoid hearing the 'belling' or roaring of the stags in woodland or over the moorland; they tend to be less shy at this time. At all seasons Horner Woods are full of sound – Horner Water can be a torrent or a trickle but is never entirely quiet. Summer birds to be found here include blackcaps and willow warblers.

NT.

HURLSTONE POINT

The point is reached by a none-too-gentle path through gorse and heather from Bossington village at the eastern end of Porlock Bay. The walk is highlighted by a series of splendid views: north across the Bristol Channel to South Wales and the distant heights of the Brecon Beacons; to west and east along the coast and over the patchwork fields where once there was marshland. Dunkery dominates the moor to the south. As an alternative to the headland, a winter stroll on Bossington Beach with only waders and gulls for company may be preferable to the same beach in summer – then anything but deserted.

Dunster Castle

LYNMOUTH: COUNTISBURY & WATERSMEET

At Lynmouth, on both sides of the A39, the National Trust manages two adjoining, but quite different properties – Countisbury and Watersmeet. There are several car parks from which a variety of tours may be made. From the car park at Barna Barrow above Countisbury village, there are superb views across the Bristol Channel to the Welsh coast with Lundy on the horizon to the west. A series of footpaths lead round the property. The paths around Foreland Point and leading down to the lighthouse are not for the faint-hearted but they afford spectacular views of sea and cliff. Those who take the route to the lighthouse down Caddow Combe may be rewarded by the sight of gannets diving head first into the sea in search of fish.

Inland, the Watersmeet estate is a very popular tourist attraction. Among the many walks, both banks of the East Lyn River may be explored and two particularly beautiful high-level walks are above Myrtleberry Cleave and a shorter route along Winston's Path. The woods overhanging the river are mostly sessile oak, much of it coppiced, with beech and larch among the younger plantings. Two local species of whitebeam grow in the woods; also the rare and poisonous Irish spurge. An abundance of wild flowers flourishes against a background of ferns and mosses. Seventeen fishing pools lie along this stretch of the East Lyn and lucky visitors may see salmon leaping at several of the falls or rapids.

Open: *Watersmeet House (information point) (off A39) Apr to Oct daily. Refreshments. NT.*

Lynmouth's harbour

SELWORTHY

Photographic suppliers and calendar publishers would show reduced profits without this charming model village. Built in 1828 for estate pensioners, the cottages around the green seem to epitomise the English village for visitors from all over the world. Sheltering in its little combe, Selworthy's thatch and crowded flower gardens never fail to delight the visitor. The church is 15th-century. Above the village is an Iron Age fort.

NT.

STOKE PERO

The 19th-century church at Stoke Pero may claim to be unique in several respects. At 1013ft high, it is said to be the highest and most isolated on Exmoor, and reputed to have been built on a site where a church has stood for almost 1000 years. At Stoke Pero the moor can be seen at its bleakest, with chill winds even on warm days. The long bubbling cry of the curlew, somehow more eerie on the moors than in marshland, drifts over the sparse heather. Both red and black grouse live on these bare uplands, usually observed only as they rise close ahead, exploding away in furious whirring activity with clock-like calls.

TARR STEPS

This well-known Exmoor beauty spot lies about a mile northeast of Hawkridge. Here the River Barle is spanned by an ancient packhorse bridge some 180ft long, with 17 spans.

Purple moor grass – common on parts of the moor

Selworthy is one of Exmoor's prettiest villages

VALLEY OF THE ROCKS
Ever popular with visitors, this remarkable dry valley, which runs parallel with the coast just west of Lynton, is certainly worth visiting. It is most famous for its strange, towering rock formations. As is usual in such cases, the rocks have been given fanciful names – Ragged Jack, Devil's Cheesewring, and Castle Rocks (which is 800ft high). The rocks were probably sculpted in this way during the ice ages by a combination of pressing ice and extraordinarily hard frosts.

WIMBLEBALL LAKE
Completed in the late 1970s, this reservoir lies on the south-eastern edge of the National Park. It lies north of Bampton below Haddon Hill, which is an excellent viewpoint, and from here footpaths lead to the waterside. The Somerset Trust for Nature Conservation has a reserve on the northern arm of the reservoir, approached from the unclassified road between Brompton Regis and the B3190 Brendon Hill road. A number of habitats are protected here, including wet grassland which varies from base rich to acidic, scrubland, and woodland.

Part *NT*.

WINSFORD HILL & SOUTH HILL
Close to the B3223 Exford – Dulverton road, the National Trust owns almost 1300 acres of the gorse and heather-clad moorland of Winsford Hill. On the hill are two fascinating relics of our past. A group of Bronze Age barrows known as the Wambarrows are just a small part of some 350 burial mounds on Exmoor, confirming, with the remains of several hut circles, the existence of a large community of Bronze Age people in the area.

The second relic on Winsford Hill is the Caratacus Stone. Five feet high and clearly of Celtic origin, it appears to commemorate a kinsman of Caratacus but it is not certain whether it is the Caratacus of the Silures who fought the Roman invaders in the first century AD and was deported to Rome around 50 AD. The stone, together with one similar, now at Lynton, is probably of 5th or 6th century origin. Close to the Wambarrows near the summit of Winsford Hill is the Punchbowl, a natural amphitheatre where the ground falls sharply to a small valley in which a stream rises. Near Winsford Hill, and also owned by the National Trust, is South Hill – 93 acres of unimproved moorland.

NT.

WOODY BAY
About two miles from Heddon's Mouth (see page 99), and also owned by the National Trust, is Woody Bay, an area almost as beautiful, but often surprisingly undisturbed by numbers of visitors. Woody Bay has never easily been reached by land and the route to the little beach is by a steep, twisting, narrow road not recommended to the elderly or unfit, and barred to cars, which must park at the top of the hill.

Those who visit the bay on hot summer days will particularly appreciate the walk through an almost continuous archway of trees which create a welcome atmosphere of coolness and shade. Much of the dense woodland in the deep combe is oak, bolstered by beech and sycamore. Foxes and badgers live, unseen by any but the luckiest, in the woods where the small, handsome and fierce merlin nests. It might be seen hunting over the cliffs and moorland.

The tiny shingle beach is framed by a natural amphitheatre of oak, and from it guillemots and razorbills can sometimes be seen, flying to their nesting places on the cliffs which rise 800ft on either side of the bay.

Visitors not exhausted by the journey to and from the bay may take a path from the car parking area of Highveer Point over Wringapeak. The views, both along the coast with its deep, mysterious, wooded combes, or out towards Lundy and the Welsh coast, are magnificent.

NT.

Red Deer
'Full head' is the expression used to describe a stag's complete set of antlers. The antlers are cast every year, usually between the middle of April and the beginning of May. People wonder why the cast or 'mewed' antlers are rarely found; this is because the stags retreat to the deepest, most remote coverts for the 'mewing'. Although there are as many as 1000 red deer on the moor, they are not often seen. This is because they are shy creatures, most active at dusk and very early morning, preferring to spend their days in deep cover. Patience, and knowledge of their hiding places, are required for anything other than chance sightings. Nowhere else in England can truly wild red deer be found – and it can be strongly argued that if the controversial hunting were to be banned farmers would not tolerate their depredations on the crops and they would be exterminated.

Fairburn Ings

West Yorkshire

'Ing' is a local word of old Norse derivation which means low-lying meadow. It sounds promising, but in fact a more unlikely place to find a nature reserve would be hard to imagine, with the ings – a series of flooded depressions alongside the River Aire – bounded by collieries, a power station, and the town of Castleford. The best view of Fairburn Ings is from the A1, which carries traffic thundering past high above the eastern end of the reserve. From here the ings can be seen stretching away for two-and-a-half miles to the west, providing a combination of open water, deciduous woodland and mixed farmland. From the village of Fairburn a footpath (Cut Lane) runs down to the river between two of the main stretches of water, and the trees on both sides are a haven for small birds all year round. The valley of the Aire is a natural flyway for many birds, so the reserve has a great variety of species. During spring and autumn common and Arctic terns and the even more exotic black terns are regularly seen. In the late summer and autumn a large roost of swallows, gathers in the waterside vegetation.

The colder months bring a big influx of wintering wildfowl, when species such as goldeneye and goosander are numerous, and a herd of whooper swans regularly roosts on the reserve after feeding on the nearby farmland. This is the time of year when great use is made of the lay-by on the road to Castleford, by both birds and humans! Lots of the wild waterfowl will come

Fal Estuary

Cornwall

The Fal estuary is really a complex of several rivers which wind seawards along steep valleys with woodland overhanging the shore in places.

The sheltered anchorage of Carrick Roads is the widest part of the estuary. From here the river gradually narrows and various arms lead off on either side.

These Cornish estuaries are rias – drowned valleys caused by a rise in sea level. They still have fairly extensive mudflats with some salt marsh and, at the upper end, even tidal woodland. Their character is unlike most estuaries elsewhere in Britain, the proximity of the woodland to the tidal creeks creating a very enclosed scenery. Wider views can be enjoyed over Falmouth Bay and the Carrick Roads from St Anthony Head, with its lighthouse, and Pendennis Point, beyond 16th-century Pendennis Castle.

The best areas for birds are Devoran Creek and the rivers Fal, Tresillian and Truro. A minor road to Malpas borders the Truro River; while good views of the Tresillian can be had from the riverside footpath from St Clement. A good variety of waders and wildfowl occurs, while in winter species such as greenshank and spotted redshank can still be found, although they may be absent from most other parts of the country.

Location: *coastline between St Anthony Head and Falmouth.* **Map:** *page 304, SW83/84.*

Fal Estuary: Carrick Roads and the lighthouse on St Anthony Head

to be hand-fed, giving visitors close-up views in the process.

Open: all year. Information centre and hide open weekends. No dogs. RSPB.
Location: 2 miles N of Ferrybridge, off unclassified road W of A1.
Map: page 310, SE42.

Falls of Clyde
Strathclyde

The heart of this reserve is the spectacular wooded gorge of the River Clyde with its three separate waterfalls, Bonnington Linn, Cora Linn and Dundaff Linn.

The woods of the gorge are semi-natural, with broadleaved trees and a ground flora associated with ancient woodland: at lower altitudes this includes lesser celandine, dog's mercury, red campion and bluebells. These give way to bilberry, heather and great wood-rush higher up the glen.

Above the uppermost fall the river is deep and flows between overhanging banks with flat sandy areas where minks and otters rest. Badgers, roe deer and red squirrels also occur.

Inaccessible ledges on the gorge sides are the nesting sites of kestrels, while below kingfishers flash across the dark waters. Other birds include such summer visitors as garden warblers, spotted flycatchers and chiffchaffs, while the residents include five species of tit and green and great-spotted woodpeckers.

Open: at all times. Visitor centre. CNT.
Location: At New Lanark, ½ mile S of Lanark.
Map: page 313, NS84.

Farne Islands
Northumberland

Stand among the dunes beside the coast road near Bamburgh on a mild April evening and, by a trick of the light, the Inner Farne island with its lighthouse seems close enough to touch.

The charm of the Farnes lies in their contrasts – between the contemplative life of St Cuthbert, who lived here in the 7th century, and the short, heroic life of Grace Darling in the 19th century; between the destructiveness of the rocks on which so many ships have foundered and the protection they afford to nesting seabird colonies.

Geologically the Farnes form part of the Great Whin Sill and consist of a hard rock called dolerite. Some 115 species of plants are found, the greatest diversity on Inner Farne, where sea campion and thrift are common; the only shrubs are a few stunted elder bushes. The grey seal colony is one of the most important in the world; these lovable creatures, as inquisitive as man, invariably 'greet' visiting boats. But it is for their bird life that the Farnes are most famous. Nearly 250 species have been recorded. Regular breeding birds include cormorants, fulmars, kittiwakes and other gulls, guillemots, razorbills, Sandwich, Arctic, common and roseate terns, and puffins – the most numerous nesting bird on the island. Final mention must be of St Cuthbert's 'chicken' – the delightfully tame eider, probably the first bird in the world to be 'protected' under rules laid down by the saint, and now safe to breed in perpetuity on the Farnes.

Puffin and Grey Seal

The Farne Islands are an ideal place to watch puffins and grey seals. The puffins nest on headlands or cliffs, in tunnels which they may excavate themselves, but they are more likely to use an old rabbit burrow. Their multi-coloured beaks make them unmistakable. Grey seals live and breed mostly in western and northern Britain; their eastern stronghold is the Farnes.

Access: Inner Farne & Staple Island only, Apr to Sep daily; restricted access during the breeding season. Nature walks. Landing fee. Boat trips (weather permitting) from Seahouses harbour. NT.
Location 2–5 miles off Northumberland coast, opposite Bamburgh.
Map: page 313, NU23.

Farway Countryside Park
Devon

This private park is partly a working farm set in picturesque Devon countryside. There are scenic views from the centre, set on a hillside overlooking woods and farmland in the Coly valley.

One of the main interests is a collection of rare farm breeds, especially horses, cattle and sheep; but also a very early breed of pig. There are several species of British deer, including roe deer, which run wild in the park. Children can meet a collection of farm and domestic animals – rabbits, ducks and others – in the pets' enclosure.

Three nature trails prepared by the Devon Trust for Nature Conservation provide an opportunity to explore the variety of wildlife habitats in the area. These include Step Common, where birds of open country including linnets, yellowhammers and smartly plumaged stonechats can be seen.

Open: Good Fri to Sep daily except Sat. Admission charge. Picnic area. Refreshments. Shop. Suitable for disabled visitors.
Location: 4 miles S of Honiton on unclassified road off B3174.
Map: page 305, SY19.

Felbrigg

Norfolk

A sense of continuity is apparent in both Felbrigg Hall and the surrounding landscape. Additions to the interior and exterior of the hall have been made only where necessary, and with unfailing good taste. The same is true of the park landscape; the Great Wood, planted in the 17th century to protect the house from North Sea winds, has been developed and maintained by successive owners of the Hall.

The two circular nature walks at Felbrigg both start from the car park but cover very different terrain.

The mile-long Woodland Walk proceeds through the old deer park with its sycamores and sweet chestnuts to the heath; then on to the conifer plantation where red squirrels live among the Douglas fir and Norway spruce, which are being grown commercially. The walk next enters the Great Wood, planted 300 years ago, although the area has been beech woodland for 10,000 years (since the last Ice Age when it formed part of the great belt along the Cromer Ridge). Most of the older trees are pollarded. The new Victory Woods show the modern trend of planting oak and beech among the faster growing conifers.

The lake at Felbrigg is invisible from all but the attic windows of the hall, but it is the main feature of the one-and-a-half mile Lakeside Walk. Traversing a

Felbrigg Hall – a Jacobean mansion enlarged in the 18th century

small wood and crossing open farmland to the lake, the walk passes a working blacksmith's shop. Canada geese, swans, herons and ducks live on or visit the lake, which is stocked with pike, tench, carp, perch and eels. The return journey across the park passes St Margaret's Church – a favourite of the late Sir John Betjeman – and towards the end of the walk are traces of a sweet chestnut avenue; all that remains of the park's formal layout.

Open: *parkland and walks at all times. House and garden Apr to Oct daily, but open bank holiday Mon. (except Mon and Fri), pm only. Admission charge. Refreshments. Shop. No dogs. NT.*
Location: *2¼ miles SW of Cromer, of A148.*
Map: *page 311, TG13.*

Fence Wood

Berkshire

Fence Wood is part of one of the largest and most diverse areas of woodland in Berkshire. Although much of it is now managed for commercial forestry, it is a relic of ancient woodland and there are signs of man's activities stretching back over thousands of years. They include the ancient fort of Grimsbury Castle, which can be seen on either side of one of the minor roads through the wood.

The diversity of structure and of tree species, together with the wide rides, glades and open spaces over gently undulating ground, make a walk in Fence Wood enjoyable and fascinating. Most kinds of woodland bird to be found in southern Britain, and many woodland butterflies and moths, can be seen here.

Adjoining Fence Wood to the south-east is the Slade, much of which is almost medieval in character, with ancient woods, small open areas and isolated fields, scrubby areas, glades and scattered cottages, many of them thatched, in a mosaic of 'Old England'. Beyond the Slade are Upper Common and Bucklebury Common, where nightjars and woodcock can be found.

Location: *3¾ miles NE of Newbury; ½ mile S of Hermitage, E of B4009.*
Map: *page 306, SU57.*

The Pike

Voracious hunter of rivers and ponds, the pike can grow to over three feet in length and a weight of nearly 50lbs. They will eat almost anything, from small fish, such as perch, to moorhens. Pike like to hide near vegetation, where their mottled, stripey bodies are well disguised and from where they can pounce on unsuspecting prey.

Ferry Meadows Country Park

Cambridgeshire

Ancient and modern come together in this riverside park, which is the focal point of 2000-acre Nene Park, a swathe of greenery stretching six miles from the centre of Peterborough to the A1 at Wansford. The restored foundations of Roman buildings lie not far from a wind-surfing lake and there are steam railways, rowing and sailing, golf, angling and horse-riding. Seclusion is possible in the four miles of walks around the lakes and alongside the River Nene. There are good views of wildfowl, especially in winter, including a large flock of feral geese, and always the chance of a kingfisher flashing by. Outstandingly for a park of this kind, there is a carefully designed bird sanctuary, with lagoons and islands, overlooked by hides. This is interesting all the year round, with ducks in winter and migrant waders in spring and autumn. In the breeding season little ringed plovers, scarce birds in Britain, can be watched in their beautiful, butterfly-flight courtship-displays.

Open: all year. Parking charge at weekends and bank holidays Easter to Oct. Visitor centre. Picnic area. Refreshments. Shop. Suitable for disabled visitors.
Location: 2¼ miles W of Peterborough city centre, signposted off A605 Oundle road between A1260 and A1.
Map: page 306, TL19.

Finchampstead Ridges

Berkshire

Here three adjoining National Trust properties overlook the valley of the River Blackwater which, for much of its length, forms the boundary between

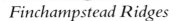

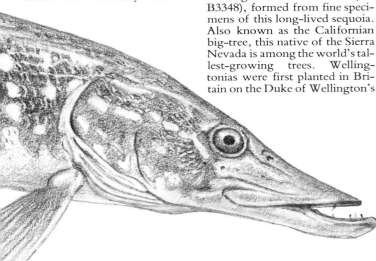

Hampshire, Surrey and Berkshire. From the 300ft-high Ridges are splendid views of all three counties. At the south end of the National Trust land is a topograph indicating the recognisable features.

The Ridges are covered with fine woods, mostly deciduous but with splendid clumps of Scots pine, now over 100 years old. The deciduous trees include oak, birch, beech and sweet chestnut. The higher ground is cloaked with heather and bracken.

A wide range of bird species has been recorded on the Ridges. In the winter siskins join residents like the goldcrest and long-tailed tit, all performing acrobatics in the trees, while blackcap and spotted flycatcher are among summer visitors.

Just to the east of the Ridges is Wellingtonia Avenue (the B3348), formed from fine specimens of this long-lived sequoia. Also known as the Californian big-tree, this native of the Sierra Nevada is among the world's tallest-growing trees. Wellingtonias were first planted in Britain on the Duke of Wellington's estate at Stratfield Saye, about eight miles to the west of the Ridges along the Devil's Highway – the old Roman road from London to Silchester.

Location: 3¾ miles S of Wokingham on either side of B3348, between B3016 and A321. NT.
Map: page 306, SU86.

Findhorn Bay

Grampian

This huge bay has only existed since the 18th century. Before that, the River Findhorn entered the Moray Firth some three miles to the west. A fierce storm on 11 October 1702 breached the shingle barrier at the point where the Findhorn now enters the sea. The river changed course, and the bay gradually developed. At one time it was a flourishing seaport, but commerce has been replaced by the holiday trade, and yachts now lie in the sheltered waters. The bay is especially noted for its winter gatherings of wildfowl and waders. Large numbers of oystercatchers, bar-tailed godwits, curlews, greylag geese, wigeon, goldeneye and red-breasted mergansers can be seen in the bay itself, while on the Firth some of Britain's largest concentrations of sea ducks occur. To the west of the bay is Culbin Forest (see page 74), a vast area of coniferous forest and sand dune systems.

Location: N of Forres, off B9011.
Map: page 315, NJ06.

Finchampstead Ridges

Fingringhoe Wick

Essex

Few places along the Essex coast can match the variety of this reserve of the Essex Naturalists' Trust: a fascinating mixture of beach, saltmarsh, fresh water, scrub and woodland. Variety of habitat usually means variety of wildlife, and so it is here. In early summer nightingales sing in profusion in the woodlands, shore-birds nest beside a man-made lagoon and there is a cliff with a sand martin colony, where something is always going on. Spring and summer bring a variety of colourful plants, which attract butterflies, and dragon-flies and damselflies chase smaller insects over the lake and ponds. In mid-summer the sea lavender turns the saltmarsh to a sheet of mauve. These same marshes look less hospitable in winter, but are home for waders and wildfowl, notably the dark-breasted brent goose. Hen harriers and other birds of prey terrorise the finch flocks over the marshes. The visitor centre is a comfortable vantage point on wild days.

Open: all year Tue to Sun (at bank holidays, Mon not Tue). Visitor centre. Admission charge. CNT.
Location: 4 miles SE of Colchester. (From Fingringhoe follow signs to South Green and reserve.)
Map: page 306, TM01.

Flamborough Head and Bempton Cliffs

Humberside

For anyone following the coastal footpath from Filey in the north or Bridlington in the south, one of the greatest spectacles in Britain lies before them between Flamborough Head and Bempton. Here the great chalk cliffs rise 445ft above the North Sea. Erosion has formed numerous cracks and ledges, which support the largest breeding colony of seabirds in England.

The breeding birds of Bempton were systematically robbed of their eggs for over 250 years by men known locally as 'climmers'. Around 130,000 eggs a year were collected. Many were sold in local markets for food, but the majority went to the West Riding, where the whites were used in the making of patent leather. Shooting the birds on the cliffs was also a popular pastime but this came to an end in 1869 when the Seabirds Preservation Act was passed. 'Climming' was brought to an end by the 1954 Protection of Birds Act.

Today the cliffs support Britain's only mainland colony of gannets, our biggest seabird. Over 300 pairs of these large, mainly white birds nest at Bempton, but by far the commonest breeding bird here is the kittiwake, with over 80,000 pairs. The area at the top of the cliffs is open, windswept and treeless, but a few hawthorns struggle against the salt spray or form low, dense hedges along with crab-apples to form the boundaries between the cliff-top fields. The narrow band between these fields and the clifftop is an excellent place for wild flowers.

Access: *free access along cliff-top path. Part RSPB.*
Location: *4 miles NE of Bridlington off B1259, B1255 and B1229. RSPB reserve 1¼ miles N of Bempton on coast.*
Map: *page 310, TA17/27.*

Fleet Pond

Hampshire

Fleet Pond is a Local Nature Reserve owned by Hart District Council. The large, shallow lake is flanked by extensive reed beds and alder carr, with oak and birch woods beyond. The reed beds are the breeding place of a large colony of reed warblers. This summer visitor, similar in plumage to the rarer marsh warbler, can be distinguished by its unusual 'churring' song. Reed warblers live almost entirely in

reed beds, hopping with great agility from one reed to another and weaving a nest suspended among the reed stems. This protects it from ground predators, but reed warblers' nests are often invaded by cuckoos. Despite frequently losing their eggs to these opportunists, reed warblers are still numerous.

The woodlands around Fleet Pond support a dozen or so different kinds of warbler, tit and finch. Swallows, swifts and martins frequently hunt insects over the water surface. In winter several species of waterfowl and great crested grebes are attracted to the open water both for food and to roost. Siskins and redpolls, together with flocks of mixed tits, feed in the alders in winter. On a warm, windless summer day dragonflies and damselflies can be seen frequently 'hawking' for flying insects over the water and reed beds and through clearings in the trees.

Open: *all year. LNR.*
Location: *car park (on N side of pond) signposted off B3014 Cove road 1½ miles NE of Fleet.*
Map: *page 306, SU85.*

Fontmell Down

Dorset

Fontmell Down was purchased by the National Trust in 1976 as a memorial to Thomas Hardy, and there are magnificent views over 'his' Blackmore Vale to the south-west. No less superb are the views from the clump of trees on the crest to the southeast over Cranborne Chase, and south towards Blandford Forum and the sea beyond.

Fontmell is of particular importance because much of it has never known the plough, or been 'improved' by artificial fertilisers and weedkillers. Unimproved

downland is becoming rarer and rarer, with the result that such areas are of great value botanically. A profusion of traditional downland plants still flourish on Fontmell Down; they include squinancywort, purging or fairy flax, hoary plantain (the only scented plantain) and salad burnet. This cucumber-flavoured herb was for centuries a common component of salads. Rabelais wrote of it in the 1530s and it was part of Napoleon's daily diet on St Helena. It then fell from favour, but in recent years has begun to reappear in recipes.

Summer visitors to Fontmell will find orchids, including the aptly named bee orchid, growing on its flinty soil. Dorset Horn sheep graze, as they have for centuries, across the two Iron Age defensive cross dykes – making the past seem tantalisingly close in this unspoilt spot.

Access: *by public footpaths. NT/CNT.*
Location: *3 miles SE of Shaftesbury, off unclassified road between Shaftesbury and Blandford, which runs parallel with, but to E of, A350.*
Map: *page 305, ST81.*

The cliffs at Flamborough Head

Forest of Bowland

Lancashire

Long gone are the endless trees which once covered this landscape and made it a royal hunting forest. Although the landscape may be very different today, it remains one of the wildest parts of Britain, and has been designated an Area of Outstanding Natural Beauty by the Countryside Commission.

Bowland is now all open fell with very few inhabitants and is among the most inaccessible places left in Britain, although, for those willing to walk, public footpaths give access to some of the most dramatic areas. The solitary road through the area follows the Trough of Bowland from Dunsop Bridge to Abbeystead or on to Lancaster. For sheer spectacle this is a road not to be missed. Unfenced for most of the way, it follows tree-lined rivers, switchbacks across open fells, and plunges between steep-sided, bracken-covered slopes.

The remoteness and vastness of these high fells encourage birds of prey such as merlin and hen harrier. In the valley dippers abound in the rocky and fast-flowing streams, and the plentiful tree cover along these streams provides nest sites for redstarts and pied flycatchers. On Mallowdale Fell is an enormous gullery where about 20,000 pairs of lesser black-backed gulls breed each year.

On the western edge of the Forest is Beacon Fell Country Park (see page 23).

Access: *by public footpaths.*
Location: *NW of Clitheroe, off B6478.*
Map: *page 309, SD65.*

Winter colours in the Forest of Bowland

Forest of Dean

Gloucestershire

The Forest of Dean, like the New Forest, is one of the very few ancient royal forests that have survived as large areas of woodland to the present day. Originally a royal hunting chase, 'The Dean', as it is known to foresters, at one time covered most of the triangle between the picturesque gorge of the Wye and the broad tidal estuary of the Severn. Although much reduced over the centuries, it still covers over 50 square miles. Forestry, mining and grazing have developed side by side since records began, through Roman times and up to the present.

The centre of the forest is a coal-field which, despite its small size, has been important in the economy and history of the area. It has also been a source of iron ore since the early Iron Age and for centuries iron-smelting was carried out here. The early miners earned the exclusive right to work the iron ore and this was later extended to coal and other minerals too. Even today those born in the forest who qualify as 'Freeminers' have the right to dig for coal and other minerals. At the same time the rights of common or free grazing have also been acquired and now affect very large areas of the forest. The removal of timber, the burning of wood to make charcoal for use in smelting, and the common grazing all led to destruction of the trees on such a scale that strict laws came to be introduced. These culminated in an Act of 1668 which authorised the enclosure of 11,000 acres for growing timber. Despite that, the woods continued to dwindle, but in the early 19th century huge plantations were created, causing much local unrest leading to the serious riots of 1831 when 2000 inhabitants took part and 100 miles of fences and walls were destroyed.

Charcoal burning as it was practised in the 18th century

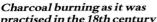

Cannop Ponds

Near Blakeney, on the forest's south–east border

Who would imagine that the majestic oakwoods which grow today originated in such turbulent times? Gone is the smelting and the working of iron ore, but coal is mined at a few pits where freeminers still exercise their rights.

The forest has much to offer the walker and naturalist. Most of the oakwoods and the more recent softwood plantations occupy acid soils over the coal measures. Bracken is widespread, often associated with bluebells, but bilberry thrives where sufficient light reaches the woodland floor. Heather and gorse occur in open areas such as at Wigpool Common, near Mitcheldean. In the many areas where sheep have access, grasses predominate.

The bird life is varied and has been enhanced by the new plantations, whose thickets attract warblers, titmice and that tiniest of British birds, the goldcrest. However, some of the richest bird communities occur in the older oakwoods such as at Nagshead, where the RSPB has a nature reserve. Here the typical birds of mature oak woodland abound, including woodpeckers, nuthatches, redstarts and the pied flycatcher, a black-and-white summer visitor occurring mainly in western counties.

Among the more convenient and interesting places to visit are Soudley Ponds and Cannop Ponds, the Roman road at Blakeney Straights, the ancient iron mines and mock–Gothic castle at Clearwell and the Speech House Hotel, which contains the historic Courtroom of the Verderers of the Forest. The Forestry Commission, which has managed the Forest since 1924, has laid out car parks, picnic sites and waymarked walks.

Location: *S of Ross-on-Wye. FC.*
Map: *page 305, SO60/61.*

Forge Valley & Raincliffe Woods

North Yorkshire

For much of its length the River Derwent flows quietly through low-lying water meadows or 'ings' but here, close to its source on Fylingdales Moor, is a complete contrast. At Forge Valley the river has formed a steep-sided gorge which in some places has almost vertical sides, and is wooded to the top of the escarpment.

Entering the valley from the southern end, off the A170 at East Ayton, and before the woodland begins, a square stone ruin is noticeable in a field on the left. This is all that remains of the 14th-century fortified manor house known as Ayton Castle. There is no sign now of the old forge, demolished around 1800, from which the valley gets its name; the iron industry was established here in the 13th century. The road follows the course of the river and a little further on enters the most picturesque section of the valley. Footpaths wander north at different points on the valley sides,

Places like Fourteen Locks in Gwent were once busy waterways packed with barges like those on the right

Ainsdale Dunes near Formby

and after a mile or so Lady Edith's Drive turns right through Raincliffe Woods to the edge of Scarborough.

Footpaths lead off in various directions among wych elm, oak and ash trees, with a wide variety of the common woodland birds for company.

Location: *3½ miles SW of Scarborough; 1 mile N of A170 at East Ayton. NCC.*
Map: *page 310, SE98.*

Formby & Ainsdale

Merseyside

The coast to the west and north of Formby offers some of the finest examples of sand dunes in Britain. This is a mobile landscape continuously being added to from the sea and changing shape and contour, year by year, so that as recently as 1910 the old fishing village of Formby disappeared under these sands. The present town of Formby is built on a safer site two miles inland. Between it and the sea, north of Formby Point, is an area of National Trust land where footpaths and a nature trail offer an

sive wave, while elsewhere the much larger oystercatchers break open cockles with their chisel-like bills. Gulls and shelduck also form components of the constantly moving black and white carpet of birds.

On the mobile dunes, behind the beach, the vital marram grass traps the sand, beginning the process of stablising the dunes – helped now by brushwood fences. Within the dune system, in the damp, low-lying hollows called slacks, lives one of Britain's endangered species which is specially protected by law – the tiny natterjack toad. The dune systems of north-western England are the stronghold in Great Britain of this scarce amphibian, which is distinguished by a yellow stripe along its back. The wet slacks in the dunes are where the greatest variety of plants and animals is to be found. Other unusual animals include the sand lizard (also protected by law), while the thickets of sea-buckthorn around the slacks attract birds like stonechats and whinchats.

Among the 400 or so species of flowering plants recorded here are many rare or unusual kinds, including some which grow only on this coast. The area is so important as a national wildlife resource that over 1200 acres of the northern part of the system near Ainsdale, comprising dunes, marshes and woodland, has been declared a National Nature Reserve.

Access: free, but keep to marked paths in Ainsdale Sand National Nature Reserve. Part NCC/NT.
Location: coast between Ainsdale and Formby.
Map: page 309, SD20/21.

Fourteen Locks Picnic Area

Gwent

Easy-going waymarked walks of two and three miles start and finish at this fascinating picnic area in an abandoned waterway less than three miles from the bustling heart of Newport. The longer route goes under the M4 and climbs a low, wooded ridge overlooking the town, the shorter crosses fields and passes the Ynysyfro reservoirs formed between 1847 and 1881 to provide water for Newport, a town whose population doubled in the second half of the 19th century. An even shorter trail, just half a mile in length, explores the canal and canal-side ponds near the Fourteen Locks interpretation centre.

The picnic area takes its name from a flight of locks on the Crumlin arm of the Monmouthshire and Brecon Canal. The 'staircase' enabled barges to climb 168 feet in less than 1000 yards and took about two hours to negotiate. Forty thousand gallons of water were needed to fill each lock, but adequate supplies were provided by a series of 'top', 'header' and 'side' ponds devised by the canal's engineer, Thomas Dadford.

The section of canal between Newport and Crumlin was opened in 1798 and carried its last cargo in 1930.

Open: all year. Interpretation centre open for 6 months from Easter daily except Tue and Wed, but open all week during school summer holidays. Picnic area.
Location: off B4591, 3 miles NW of Newport.
Map: page 305, ST28.

Fowey Valley

Cornwall

This wooded valley winds south from Bodmin Moor and eventually joins the route of the A38 for some miles.

The native broadleaved woodland has been replaced in some parts by plantations of conifers, but where the traditional woodlands remain there are good bird populations. One of the larger areas of oak wood is in the upper valley near Golitha Falls, reached by a pleasant woodland walk from the picnic area of Redgate. Here the fast-flowing river is ideal for several interesting birds. The grey wagtail, with its constantly flicking tail, has attractive lemon-yellow underparts and a slate-grey back. The dipper is a plump brown bird, with a white bib, and is always bobbing up and down. It has the remarkable habit of walking into the fastest-flowing sections of the river, and can feed underwater. Because of the unpolluted air of the West Country these woods are rich in lichens and mosses and are highly prized for the wide variety which can be found in them.

The nearby Forest Park and Thorburn Birds Gallery at Dobwalls has an outstanding collection of birds and landscape paintings by one of Britain's most famous bird artists, Archibald Thorburn, who lived from 1860 to 1935.

Open: Thorburn Museum and Gallery Good Fri to early Oct daily. Admission charge. Picnic area at Redgate, 4 miles NW of Liskeard.
Location: between Bodmin Moor and A38, 4 miles NW of Liskeard.
Map: page 305, SX26.

Natterjack Toad

Natterjack toads are not at all common. They prefer to live in sand dunes, and the largest populations are found on England's north-west coast. The male in the picture is croaking to attract a female. Courtship takes place at night in May and June.

excellent introduction to the area. The vast expanses of dunes and beach lend an extraordinary sense of remoteness, and the quiet is often broken only by the far-away sound of waves, and the wind in the pine trees, where red squirrels can sometimes be seen. Yet only eleven miles to the south lies the huge conurbation of Liverpool.

Down on the shore itself, beside the Atlantic waves, tiny sanderlings chase up and down like little clockwork toys catching food brought in by each succes-

Fowlmere

Cambridgeshire

The vast Cambridgeshire fens, with their wealth of wildlife, have long since been drained. Only one or two pockets of wetland survive. One is here, where, because of a line of springs, the land resisted conversion to agriculture. The area did not escape use, however, but was managed as a watercress farm. Part of this remains, and has its own interest, but much of the area became disused and turned into reed bed, with alder and willow trees and scrub. In so intensively farmed an area, it became an oasis for wildlife, particularly birds, and it was bought by the RSPB in 1977, using funds raised by children in the society's Young Ornithologists' Club. Young people are particularly welcome to visit, and use the hides. Visitors may see a variety of such birds as little grebe, water rail, kingfisher and various warblers. There are bee orchids, their flowers extraordinarily bumble-bee like, and many other interesting plants. Frogs and toads are common.

Open: all year. Boardwalk suitable for disabled visitors. Warden in summer. No dogs. RSPB.
Access: along marked trail.
Location: 1½ miles NE of Melbourn, off A10. Access off Shepreth–Fowlmere road.
Map: page 306, TL44.

Frensham Common

Surrey

Frensham Common is now part of a country park offering sailing and fishing, horse-riding and walking. It becomes very busy at weekends and during the summer months but it is a large area – the National Trust alone owns nearly 1000 acres – and it can still offer peace and quiet. It is also a haven for wildlife.

The area around the Little Pond is usually the quietest, and swans glide effortlessly over what can be, on calm summer mornings, a near-perfect mirror surface. Grebes, coots, mallards and other wildfowl frequent this pond (and Great Pond), and a total of over 100 species have been recorded in the heathland and among the mixed woodland. Today's naturalist is in good company: Gilbert White visited Frensham, and pioneering work on bird courtship behaviour was

Frensham Great Pond

carried out by Julian Huxley on the grebes here.

Gorse and several varieties of heather ensure that there is colour on the heath for much of the year, and the water lilies on the Little Pond are a special early summer feature.

Largely because of the degree of urbanisation, there are few prehistoric remains left in Surrey, but a group of bowl barrows runs along the crest of the common overlooking the Great Pond. In more recent history, both ponds were drained early in the Second World War to prevent the Germans using them as navigational aids.

Location: astride the A287. NT.
Map: page 306, SU84.

The bee orchid is one of Britain's loveliest and most unusual flowers

Friston Forest

East Sussex

Before 1926, the 1967-acre area of chalk downland which is now Friston Forest was scrub and barely cultivable farmland. The area is now leased to the Forestry Commission, who made it one of their principal experimental areas for forestry techniques in chalk downland. Downland sites are often very exposed, with thin, dry soils that make special care necessary when young trees are being established. Most of

the trees now growing at Friston are beeches, with Corsican pines planted to 'nurse' the newly planted trees. For 20 to 25 years it is necessary to maintain a shelter belt – of pines or birches for ex-

The Adder

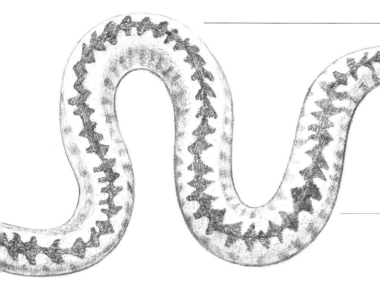

Dry, sunny grasslands and heaths are the best places to see adders, though many people would rather avoid them since they are poisonous. But adders usually only bite if they are threatened or frightened – as a rule they would far rather slip quietly away. Adders can be distinguished from other British snakes by the zig-zag pattern which runs down their backs, and by the V shape behind their heads.

ample – to protect the young beeches from the salt carried by the wind from the nearby sea.

A 2¾-mile trail waymarked in red is available for visitors. As the trail goes along the northern border of the forest there are fine views across Charlston Bottom. Among over 350 species of plant that have been recorded are many typical flowers such as viper's bugloss and travellers' joy.

Hawthorn, gorse and elder scrub adds to the variety, and helps to provide cover for small mammals such as voles. Hares, deer and numerous rabbits are other animals likely to be encountered here. Butterflies to be seen in the summer include chalkhill blue and marbled white. On the open rides adders may be seen basking on warm days; these snakes are poisonous but are not dangerous unless provoked, so if you see one leave it alone.

At the western edge of the forest is Seven Sisters Country Park (see page 246).

Location: *7 miles W of Eastbourne on unclassified road off A259. FC.*
Map: *Page 306, TQ50.*

Fritton Lake Country Park

Norfolk

Like the Norfolk Broads, which lie a little to the north, this large lake is thought to have been formed by medieval peat-digging. Lying so near the coast, it attracts many wildfowl, migrating into Britain in winter from frozen waters further north and east. Once, these birds were trapped here in cleverly constructed funnel traps, known as decoys, but this practice stopped in 1960. In summer, the resident birds share the reed-fringed lake with

water sports and angling: once known as England's finest pike lake, Fritton still contains many kinds of fish including perch, bream, carp, tench and eels. There are pony rides, an adventure playground, pitch-and-putt course and a basket-maker's workshop. The well-stocked flower gardens are attractive and the surrounding woodlands provide good walks. Birds and animals can be difficult to see in summer woods: waiting by a pool or puddle for them to come to drink is often rewarded with close views.

Open: *Apr to Sep daily. Admission charge. Information centre. Picnic area. Refreshments. Shop. Suitable for disabled visitors. No dogs.*
Location: *beside A143, 4 miles S of Gt Yarmouth.*
Map: *page 307, TG40.*

Fritton Lake probably originated as medieval peat diggings

Left: one of the kegs used in the bottle kicking ceremony at Hallaton

BOTTLE KICKING & HARE PIE SCRAMBLE

Hallaton, Leicestershire

This bizarre custom dates back to the early 1770s, when a piece of land was settled upon the Rector of Hallaton on condition that he provided two hare pies, 24 loaves and a quantity of ale to be scrambled for in public. Since then the provisions have changed: the loaves no longer form part of the ceremony, and there is one large pie made from beefsteak or similar meat instead of the two hare pies.

Proceedings commence in the morning with a children's church parade, and during this service the 'hare pie' is blessed. After the service half of the pie is distributed to the villagers at the church gates by the rector and the remaining half is cut into pieces, placed in a sack and carried in procession to Hare-Pie Bank, where it is scrambled for. Once this is over the bottle-kicking event takes place: three small wooden kegs, two containing ale and one empty, are used. The contest is between two teams, of unlimited numbers, one from Hallaton and the other from the neighbouring parish of Medbourne; this team can also include 'strangers'. One full barrel is thrown on top of the bank, and the winning team is the one which succeeds in kicking it over their own line. The contents are then shared amongst the winners before the empty barrel is fought over. When the game ends the second full barrel is carried to the old Market Cross on Hallaton Green where both teams share the ale. The first drink, however, is taken by the leader of the winning team from the top of the cross. Each year the kegs are repainted for the next event unless they are too battered, in which case they are replaced by new ones.

When: *Easter Mon.*
Map: *page 306, SP79.*

BIDDENDEN DOLE

Biddenden, Kent

The Biddenden dole is said to have originated during the 12th century with a bequest of the Biddenden Maids, Elisa and Mary Chulkhurst. They were Siamese twins who lived joined together at the hips and shoulders until the age of 34, when one had a fatal illness and died. The other twin refused to be separated and died only six hours later. By their will they left 20 acres of land – still known as the Bread and Cheese Lands – to the poor of the parish, to pay for an annual 'Dole'.

No-one knows how true this extraordinary story is, but it is still commemorated annually when bread, cheese and tea are distributed to the Biddenden poor. The famous 'Biddenden cakes' – biscuits stamped with a likeness of the twins – also form part of the dole, and are given to all who attend the ceremony.

When: *Easter Mon.*
Map: *page 306, TQ83.*

RUNNING AUCTION

Bourne, Lincolnshire

Matthew Clay of Bourne was responsible for instigating this custom in 1742. His will provided for an annual gift of bread to the poor of Eastgate Ward. To meet the cost a piece of land known as White Bread Meadow would be rented. Since then the land has been let every year at a curious auction: bidding is only valid whilst two boys run up and down a prescribed length of road. Once the auction is concluded the company share in a traditional supper of bread, cheese, spring onions and beer at a local hostelry.

When: *Easter Mon.*
Map: *page 306, TF02.*

The Biddenden Maids

HOCKTIDE FESTIVAL

Hungerford, Berkshire

This festival dates from the 14th century, when John of Gaunt, owner of the Manor of Hungerford, granted certain fishing and grazing rights to the local people. These ancient rights are still protected by the Hocktide Court, which is responsible for electing the governing body of the town.

Proceedings commence at 8am, when the Town Crier, dressed in full livery, sounds his horn to remind people that the court will meet at 9am. Whilst it is in session two Tithingmen or Tutti-Men, armed with decorated staves, plus the Orange Scrambler with his sack of oranges, visit the Common Right houses. They collect a penny from every man of the house and a kiss from every woman and child, who are given an orange in return.

Following the civic luncheon for the officials, another custom known as 'shoeing the colt' takes place. Each stranger at the lunch is approached by the blacksmith, who pretends to drive a horse-nail into the sole of his shoe. He is only released at the cry of 'punch' which indicates his willingness to contribute to the supply of punch. After this he is no longer regarded as a stranger by the Hungerford men.

When: *Easter Tue.*
Map: *page 306, SU36.*

CANDLE AUCTION

Tatworth, Somerset

It is not known when this custom began although it is claimed to be of ancient origin. 'Candle' auctions were certainly well-known events in the 17th and 18th centuries. The idea was that the auction lasted for as long as a candle took to burn down by a measured amount.

The Candle Auction at Tatworth involves the annual renting of a piece of land called Stowell Mead – a procedure undertaken by the Tatworth Stowell Court. This body consists of approximately 25 members, who meet behind closed doors at the 'Poppe Inne'. Business commences with a supper, featuring watercress from the Mead, followed by the lighting of an inch of tallow candle by the clerk of the court. As the candle burns bids are accepted, and the last one made before it burns out has the use of the Mead for the coming year. Members must remain seated throughout the session or pay a 10 pence fine. The event is concluded by a skittles match; this was only introduced in 1950.

When: *first Tue after 6 Apr.*
Map: *page 305, ST 30.*

Yesterday and today at Hungerford's Hocktide festival

Galloway Forest Park

Dumfries & Galloway

Magnificent scenery, 16 hill lochs, rivers, forests and open fells are features of this area. Covering 240 square miles, the park includes much of the Rhinns of Kells and the highest mountain in the Southern Uplands, The Merrick (2764ft).

Rugged scenery around the Black Water of Dee is a feature of the 10-mile Raiders Road Forest Drive, which has been planned by the Forestry Commission along forest roads through Bennan and Clatteringshaws forests. An alternative is the Queens Way – the A712 road from New Galloway to Newton Stewart – which offers a fine series of views and good stopping places.

Perhaps the best way to see the park on foot is to take one of the numerous forest walks. One of the best is the Loch Trool Forest Trail (4½ miles) which starts from Caldon's caravan and camping ground and goes around the loch through mixed woodland and past the Steps of Trool, where Robert the Bruce defeated the English in 1307. The Larg Hill and Bruntis Forest Trail starts at Daltamie Picnic Place, signposted at Palnure on the A75 three miles south-east of Newton Stewart. It leads to a scenic viewpoint above Bruntis Loch. Two others are the Stroan Forest Walk, which starts and ends at Stroan Bridge car park half a mile east of Glen Trool village on the unclassified road from Bargrennan (A714), and the Talnotry Forest Trail, which starts near Murray's Monument on the A712 between Newton Stewart and New Galloway.

The wildlife interest of the park is considerable: both red and roe deer are common and birds likely to be seen include peregrine, hen harrier and sparrowhawk. Buzzards are quite common and around the higher hills there is the chance of golden eagles. Wild goats can be seen in the Goat Park near Talnotry Caravan Park on the A712, and the Galloway Deer Museum is also situated on the A712 beside Clatteringshaws Loch.

Open: *Galloway Deer Museum end Apr to end Sep daily. Toll for Raiders Road Forest Drive. Park FC.*
Location: *between New Galloway and Newton Stewart along A712; bounded by A713 to E, A714 to W and B741 to N.*
Map: *page 313.*

Gelli Aur Country Park

Dyfed

The large and impressive mansion of Gelli Aur (Welsh for 'golden grove') is set on high ground above the broad and beautiful Vale of Tywi. It overlooks a country park whose attractions include an arboretum and a herd of fallow deer whose ancestors have roamed the area since the 17th century.

The arboretum, established in the 1860s, is a splendid collection of mature native and exotic trees; there are many varieties of oak including the curious cork oak, copper beech, Japanese maple, sweet chestnut, Caucasian wingnut, magnolia, Chinese juniper, rowans, hollies, Wellingtonias, Monterey pine and Crimean pine. Rhododendrons, azaleas and many other exotic shrubs add bold splashes of colour to the arboretum.

The trees, shrubs and flowers attract birds such as wrens, flycatchers and woodpeckers. Small mammals provide prey for kestrels and buzzards. Parts of the park are home to lizards, grass snakes and a few adders.

Open: *Easter week; May Sat, Sun and bank holiday Mon; June and early July Thu to Sun; early July to early Sep Tue to Sun and bank holiday Mon. Limited access to mansion July to Sep. Picnic areas. Nature trails.*
Location: *off B4300, 4 miles SW of Llandeilo.*
Map: *page 305, SN51.*

Gibraltar Point

Lincolnshire

In complete contrast to the holiday resort of Skegness just to its north, is this reserve of the Lincolnshire and South Humberside Trust for Nature Conservation. In this wild and beautiful place the sea is still building a series of dunes, and the different stages in the colonisation of these plants (what ecologists call 'succession') is easy to see here. Nearly bare dunes give way to well-vegetated ones, and the densest of all are covered with thick growths of sea buckthorn. The bright orange berries of this plant attract hordes of thrushes from northern countries in the autumn and rare migrants occur regularly. In winter, the sand and shingle spits provide roost-sites for waders, and there is a good chance of a flock of snow buntings, their flashing white wings and tails often the brightest elements in the winter landscape.

Times past: young Somerset peat diggers

Summer is no less exciting. One of Britain's rarest seabirds, the little tern, nests on the beach beside the delightful ringed plover. There are many interesting plants, such as the extraordinary sea holly, and butterflies include the uncommon and brightly coloured green hairstreak. The visitor centre is a particularly good one, with attractive and informative displays.

Open: *all year. Parking charge in summer. Visitor centre open May to Oct daily; weekends only in winter. Picnic areas. Nature trail. CNT.*
Location: *3 miles S of Skegness, reached by unclassified Drummond and Gibraltar roads.*
Map: *page 310, TF55.*

Glamis: Angus Folk Museum

Tayside

Aspects of Scotland's domestic, social and agricultural past are vividly portrayed here in one of the best collections of its kind in Scotland. The museum is in Kirkwynd Cottages, which began life at the start of the 19th century as six single-storey cottages with a communal washhouse. They have been restored and cleverly converted into a single building to house the museum, while retaining their original character. Inside, two centuries of country life are reflected in more than 1000 exhibits. Handlooms and spinning equipment recall traditional cottage crafts, while early kitchen furnishings and equipment can be seen in the reconstructed farmhouse kitchen. Another feature is the Victorian parlour.

Open: *May to Sep daily, pm only. Admission charge. NTS.*
Location: *off A94 in Glamis, 6 miles SW of Forfar.*
Map: *page 313, NO34.*

Glen Coe – a marvellously atmospheric place where a good cross-section of Scotland's wildlife can be seen

Glastonbury: Somerset Rural Life Museum

Somerset

This museum is centred on a magnificent 14th-century barn and contains displays of old-style farming. In the abbey farmhouse the social and domestic life of a farm worker, John Hodges, in Victorian times is described and reconstructed from cradle to grave.

There are also displays of activities associated with the surrounding Somerset Levels and moors; peat-digging, willow-growing and cider-making. The exhibits have an intimacy which makes the past seem very close. From spring until autumn there are regular demonstrations of farming and associated activities: butter-making, bee-keeping, sheep-shearing, basket-making and forge work.

Open: *all year daily, but pm only Sat and Sun. Admission charge. Picnic area. Refreshments (summer). Shop. Suitable for disabled visitors.*
Location: *Abbey Farm, Chilkwell Street, Glastonbury.*
Map: *page 305, ST53.*

Glen Affric

Highland

For a typical example of a Highland glen one could do no better than to drive the length of Glen Affric from Cannich (where there is a Forest Office) to Loch Beinn a' Mheadhoinn. There is a fine mixture of habitats, from river and loch to woodland and forest, with some of the highest hills north of the Great Glen along the northern side. The southern side includes an important relict area of Caledonian pine forest, mixed in places with much birch and rowan. Bilberry is the predominant ground species in dense stands of pine, while heather takes over in the more open areas. The regeneration of the pine trees is hindered by browsing red deer, which are common here. Roe deer and red squirrels are among other mammals likely to be seen, while birds include buzzard, sparrowhawk, golden eagle, capercaillie, dipper, redstart, crested tit, siskin and Scottish crossbill.

Location: *at foot of Strathglass. Reached from Cannich, off A831.*
Map: *page 314, NH 12/22/32/33.*

Glen Coe

Highland

Whether you enter Glen Coe from Loch Linnhe in the west, or from the desolate fastness of Rannoch Moor to the east, it is a startling place – a short, steep-sided glen with impressive peaks and rock scenery, grim and forbidding in its own way and actually at its most spectacular in really bad weather! Famed for its massacre, it is well known as a tourist 'must', and is one of the best areas for hill-walking and mountaineering in Scotland.

The A82 runs right through the glen. The minor road into Glen Etive at the eastern end also gives good access and good scenic views and leads to Dalness, which is included in the 14,200-acre estate owned by the National Trust for Scotland. The visitor centre near Clachaig is the source for all information on the glen. Specially planned forest trails include the Signal Rock Trail (1½ miles) and the Lochan Nature Trail (2 miles).

Red deer, peregrine, raven and hooded crow are all fairly readily seen in Glen Coe, as are buzzards, kestrels and ring ouzels, and when there are not too many people on the hills there is always a chance of seeing a golden eagle. Ptarmigans are present, too, but are only likely to be seen by climbers and mountain walkers. Interesting plants include mossy saxifrage and alpine lady's mantle.

Open: *visitor centre Apr to mid Oct daily. Admission charge. Ranger Service. Picnic area. NTS.*
Location: *A82, 10 miles N of Tyndrum.*
Map: *page 314, NN15.*

Glengoulandie Deer Park

Tayside

At their best in August and September, when the rut is beginning and the stags have lost the velvet from their antlers, red deer are worth seeing at any time: they are very common in many parts of the Highlands, and sometimes not at all difficult to watch at reasonably close quarters. However, a good deer park like this one takes you right in among the animals, especially since it includes a fine scenic drive. Deer are not the only interesting animals at Glengoulandie: there is a fine herd of Highland cattle and there are also two rare breeds of sheep, the little brown Soay from St Kilda, which has existed in its present form since prehistoric times, and the four-horned Jacob, said to be descended from the brown sheep taken from Laban's flock, as related in Genesis in the story of Jacob's departure.

With tame red foxes, donkeys, goats, peafowl, pheasants and guinea-fowl, there is much to interest visitors. Children, especially, will be enchanted by the tamer animals, while for those who prefer their wildlife in the wild, buzzards, sparrowhawks, redstarts, wood warblers and red squirrels may be seen on one of the many walks available.

Open: *Apr to Sep daily. Admission charge. Picnic area. Shop. Pets must be kept in cars.*
Location: *8 miles NW of Aberfeldy on B846.*
Map: *page 314, NN75.*

Glen More Forest Park

Highland

An excellent base for the camper or caravanner seeking to explore Speyside and the Cairngorms, this forest park comprises about 3000 acres of forest and woodland and some 9000 acres of high ground around Loch Morlich. The park contains some good remnants of Old Caledonian pine forest, as well as planted areas, with open moor and hillsides, lake shore, rivers and high mountains.

The shores of Loch Morlich are worth exploring, especially at the quieter western end, and access to the high tops is made easy by the ski road up to Cairn Gorm (see Cairngorms feature, page 50). There are eight walks of varying lengths, including an excellent one from Glen More Lodge up to the bothy at Ryvoan via the extraordinary Green Lochan (An Lochan Uaine). As always on the high tops, sudden changes in weather can make walking hazardous and it is essential to be well prepared.

Although very popular with tourists in summer, this is still a good area for wildlife. Many typical upland creatures are found, and this is the place to

A red deer stag at Glengoulandie Deer Park

look for the famous herd of feral reindeer. Goosanders can often be seen on Loch Morlich, while parties of snow buntings sometimes appear in the car park in winter.

Open: *forest information centre all year.*
Location: *SE of Aviemore, with access from B970.*
Map: *page 315, NH90/91.*

Glenmuick and Lochnagar

Grampian

This large nature reserve begins at the Spittal of Glenmuick car park. Details of the wildlife of the area are available from a small visitor centre nearby. This is the starting point for a variety of walks.

For the less energetic there is a low-level path to Loch Muick which passes through heather moorland with scattered bearberry, bilberry, cowberry, and crowberry. Butterwort and sundew grow in the boggy hollows. Redshank and snipe may be flying overhead, while lizards and adders emerge in warm weather.

For those prepared for a strenuous climb, a rough track leads up the north face of Loch-

Below: male capercaillie in display pose

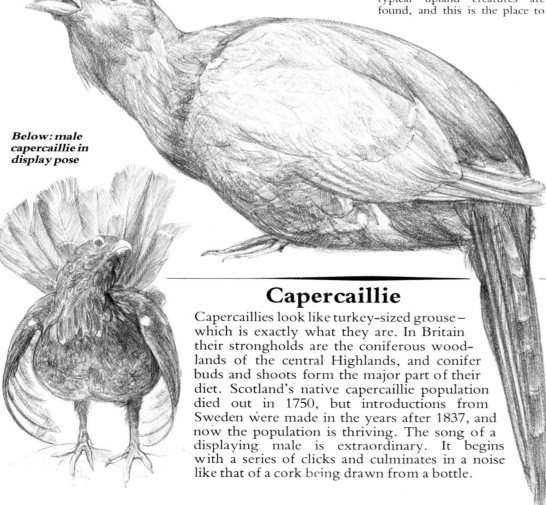

Capercaillie

Capercaillies look like turkey-sized grouse – which is exactly what they are. In Britain their strongholds are the coniferous woodlands of the central Highlands, and conifer buds and shoots form the major part of their diet. Scotland's native capercaillie population died out in 1750, but introductions from Sweden were made in the years after 1837, and now the population is thriving. The song of a displaying male is extraordinary. It begins with a series of clicks and culminates in a noise like that of a cork being drawn from a bottle.

Head of female

Golden Cap Estate

Dorset

From Bridport to Charmouth the route of the A35 is rarely very far from the coast. Here and there between the hills, little valleys run to the sea, and it is possible to glimpse the waters of Lyme Bay. At Eype Mouth, Seaton and Charmouth the coast may be reached, and here, as on Langdon and Stonebarrow Hills, there are car parks from which the large National Trust property of Golden Cap can be explored. The estate takes its name from the gold-coloured sandstone of the hilltop, whose seaward side forms the highest sea cliff on England's south coast, at 618ft.

The best way to enjoy this beautiful area of South Dorset is on foot; indeed it is the only way access may be obtained to some parts of the estate. The 15 miles of footpaths range from gentle rambles to strenuous climbs as

Golden Cap offers an almost infinite variety of routes for the walker to savour. Downlands, narrow combes leading to forgotten villages (Stanton St Gabriel is a gem among these), memorable views inland and along the coast, little rivers, sandy beaches, steep cliffs and cool woods: all this is contained in a six-mile range, crossed by the Dorset Coast Path (see page 84).

On Golden Cap the Trust has been able to preserve some of the older ways of farming and as a result a rich variety of flora and fauna remains. The many typical down and heathland flowers attract a large number of butterflies and other insects. Fox and badger both live on the estate with the rabbit, now recovered from the decimation of the 1960s. Buzzards and kestrels are among the predators, while perhaps the symbol of Golden Cap is the handsome stonechat with his black, red and white plumage. Perched on golden yellow gorse, flicking tail and wings, his pebble-clicking call sounds over the estate.

Location: *Between Charmouth and Eype Mouth, S of A35. NT.*
Map: *page 305, SY39/49*

The Dorset Coast Path, Golden Cap and the sea

nagar where the wild flowers of the steep corrie slopes are exceptionally fine. Many species of alpine saxifrage, speedwell and willow-herbs are found in the wet flushes. In the corrie bottom, where the snow lies long, there are numerous plants of chickweed wintergreen, bog bilberry and dwarf cornel. The summit, at over 3000ft, is dominated by lichens and mosses among which dunlins and ptarmigans breed: mountain hares are frequent and herds of red deer roam freely.

As on any mountain, conditions can change rapidly and all visitors taking the upper path must have proper clothing and footwear.

Open: *at all times when conditions are suitable. Details from visitor centre and from Balmoral Estate Office or their ranger. CNT.*
Location: *11 miles S of Ballater.*
Map: *page 315, NO38.*

Goodwood Park

West Sussex

Goodwood is the setting of a beautiful 18th-century house surrounded by elegant parkland. It also boasts the most attractive race-course in the country, and a 60-acre country park, opened in 1971. The house, which stands at 150ft above sea level, ranges in style from classical to gothic and its kennels, which must have been among the grandest in the country, are now a golf club.

The race-course lies to the north of Goodwood House and was laid out in 1802. Adjacent to it is the country park, an area of woodland and open grassland providing unrivalled views over Sussex, together with the opportunity for walks and picnics. Overlooking both race-course and golf course is the Trundle, a hill-fort and elaborate Neolithic causeway camp. The earthworks

are nearly 1000ft in diameter, and date from 3500 BC.

Open: *park at all times. (Goodwood House May to mid Oct Sun and Mon pm only; also Tue to Thu pm in Aug). Admission charge.*
Location: *3 miles NE of Chichester.*
Map: *page 306, SU80/81.*

Gouthwaite Reservoir

North Yorkshire

Set in Nidderdale, this long, narrow reservoir is managed by the Yorkshire Water Authority as a private nature reserve, largely because of its high ornithological interest. Bounded by high ground, particularly to the north-east, where Hambleton Hill rises to 1331ft, Nidderdale provides a natural flyway for many birds. The shelter provided by the high ground, together with the trees along the

lower slopes and shoreline, make it very attractive for wintering wildfowl.

Although there is no public access to the reservoir surrounds, the unclassified road from Pateley Bridge to Ramsgill, which runs the entire length of the western side, provides excellent opportunities for watching the birds without disturbing them. In spring and summer there is an abundance of small songbirds and even the possibility of seeing the occasional osprey on passage. Canada geese are always to be seen and are joined during the winter months by a wide range of wildfowl including two Icelandic visitors, goldeneye and whooper swans. The bugling call of these beautiful swans is one of the loveliest sounds to be heard in winter.

Location: *2 miles NW of Pateley Bridge.*
Map: *page 310, SE 16/17.*

Gower Peninsula

West Glamorgan

Gower cannot fail to astonish and delight strangers whose stereotyped vision of South Wales is heavy with the smoke and clangour of industry. Instead of collieries and steelworks there are majestic cliffs, huge beaches and lonely shingle coves.

The peninsula is basically a huge slab of limestone formed beneath the sea almost 300 million years ago. It was forced upwards – several 'raised beaches' mark earlier sea levels – and now rises gently from the River Loughor's broad estuary to the long line of cliffs overlooking the Bristol Channel. Rising to 320 feet at Pwlldu Head on the southern coast – only seven miles from central Swansea as the crow flies – the cliffs embrace a series of beautiful bays and snug coves whose sands are flanked by rocks dappled with low-tide pools. Brandy Cove, Pwlldu, Threecliff, Mewslade and several other bays have remained completely unspoiled because they cannot be reached by car.

Several stretches of Gower's southern coast are managed as nature reserves by the Glamorgan Trust for Nature Conservation, the Nature Conservancy Council and the National Trust. The cliffs here in spring support a wide variety of colourful wild flowers – the yellow of rock-roses and golden samphire, the blue of spring squill, purple cranesbills and white daisies. Some of these plants are uncommon in the country as a whole, being restricted to lime-rich areas or places like this where the in-

fluence of salt spray is strong.

More sheltered areas provide a home for typical cliffland birds; linnets, stonechats and yellowhammers are all to be found amongst the gorse and hawthorn scrub. Some of the rocky crags attract ravens. Because of its south-westerly position, the Gower is a staging post for many migrant birds. In winter, thousands of common scoter gather offshore.

Oxwich Bay, halfway along the south coast, is an ideal starting point for visitors eager to learn something about the peninsula's natural history. Approached down steep and narrow lanes flanked by hanging woodlands, the bay is sheltered by the massive limestone headland of Oxwich Point and has been a National Nature Reserve since 1963. Behind the dune-backed shore, groves of oak, ash, elm and beech overlook a reedy wilderness where dragonflies hover above secluded lagoons.

Footpaths run the entire length of the coast to Rhossili, a clifftop village perched 250ft above the sea on limestone cliffs pounded by severe storms in winter. Rhossili is worth visiting for the sheer beauty of its setting alone; for the enormous sweep of sand forming Rhossili Beach backed

by the breathtaking curve of the cliffs which run to Worms Head; or for the exciting walk south over the cliff tops or to the north along the whaleback ridge of Rhossili Down. Other walks, most of which start from the vicinity of the car park in the village, include a circular three-mile Nature Conservancy Council walk over the cliffs. Look for typical limestone flowers like kidney vetch and bird's-foot trefoil, both members of the pea family. Along the cliffs it is possible to see fulmars, while guillemots, razorbills and kittiwakes nest on the tiny ledges. Migrants passing through include terns and skuas, and in winter on the shore the occasional purple sandpiper. Along this walk can be seen an Iron Age village and the outline of a medieval open field system. On fine days – not guaranteed on this coast – the views can be spectacular, and it may be possible to see Hartland Point, 40 miles away on the Devon coast.

Worms Head, beyond Rhossili, is linked to the mainland by a natural, tide-swept causeway. The long arm of turf-topped rock rises to a knife-edge almost 200ft above the sea. Complete with 'head', 'neck', 'body' and 'tail', this geological wonder resembles a fairy-tale monster

Rhossili and Worms Head

forever striving to swim. Like Rhossili Down, Rhossili Beach and many other areas on Gower, it is protected by the National Trust.

Gower's northern coast is in complete contrast to the south. Here tidal saltings as green and flat as the fens of East Anglia contrast with extensive sand dunes where seabirds wheel above rippling carpets of slender marram grass. Cockles are harvested here, while sheep and ponies share the saltings with starlings by the thousand, mallards, teal, oystercatchers, snipe, curlews, knots and geese.

Inland, the sheep and ponies roam free on gorse-gold hills where prehistoric dwellers buried their dead. Although rising to little more than 600 feet, the peninsula's highest points – Rhossili Down, Llanmadoc Hill and Cefn Bryn – have views embracing South Wales, the Bristol Channel, Somerset and Devon. They are as much a part of Gower's magic as the magnificent coastline.

Location: *SW of Swansea. Part CNT/NCC/NT.*
Map: *page 305, SS 48/49/58/59/68/69.*

Grafham Water

Cambridgeshire

Cambridgeshire lacks a coastline, but it does have what amounts to an inland sea in this huge, man-made reservoir. The dam at the eastern end holds back 2¼ square miles of water-surface. There are four car parks, two on the south side and two on the north. Most visitors are content to sit and look out over a sheet of water dotted with sailing dinghies and the rowing-boats of trout-fishermen.

At the western end of the reservoir is a 370-acre reserve of the Bedfordshire and Huntingdonshire Naturalists' Trust. Here two nature trails have been laid out, and there is a hide, overlooking the reserve's creeks, which can be reached on foot from the Mander Park car park, off the B661 west of West Perry Village. The hide is ideal for observing wildfowl and other water birds at close quarters, but binoculars, or better a telescope, will reveal hundreds or even thousands of ducks further out on the water, especially in the winter. Unusual birds, including the occasional osprey, turn up on migration and in the spring the elegant great crested grebes can be seen in their elaborate, head-shaking courtship dances when one bird presents the other with water weeds.

Open: *at all times. Hide available Sep to Mar, Sun only. Charge for hide (except CNT members); permit necessary for hide. Part CNT.*
Location: *5½ miles SW of Huntingdon, 1 mile W of A1 at Buckden, on B661.*
Map: *page 306, TL16.*

Graig Fawr

Clwyd

Over 300 million years ago Graig Fawr was a large reef, and today, in its small quarry, it is possible to find the fossilised shells and skeletons of former marine inhabitants of what is now a limestone hill. Because of the fossils and a large variety of plants Graig Fawr is recognised as a Site of Special Scientific Interest.

On the lower north-eastern slopes of the hill is an area of young trees growing on the deep soil cover. Sycamore, ash and wild cherry are establishing themselves over a carpet of blackthorn and elder. Higher up the slopes on the limestone grassland, bird's-foot trefoil, salad burnet, lady's bedstraw and sheep's fescue are common plants. Near the windswept summit of Graig Fawr – a much-visited viewpoint – a few sturdy blackthorn and hawthorn bushes are established.

Location: *1½ miles SW of Prestatyn off A547. NT.*
Map: *page 309, SJ08.*

Grand Western Canal

Devon

This canal winds for over 11 miles between Tiverton and the Devon/Somerset border at Holcombe Rogus. It was built in 1814 to carry local stone and limestone, and was active for about 100 years.

Since 1971, when it was taken over by the county council, the canal has been completely restored and has been designated a country park. The canal is a haven for wildlife, and it also passes through much delightful Devon countryside.

The starting point for many of the present-day activities is the Canal Basin at Tiverton, which is the base for horse-drawn barge trips and the hire of boats.

The canal is well used by anglers in search of coarse fish, including the ferocious pike. Along the banks grow bulrushes, iris and small sallows, which help to provide cover for nesting birds; mainly moorhens, coots and the occasional pair of mute swans. In summer the canal is a pleasant place to walk and enjoy the sight of dragonflies and see how nature has begun to clothe the remains of jetties and wharves.

East of Sampford Peverell, the halfway stage, there are good views of the Blackdown Hills.

Location: *terminus at Canal Basin, Canal Hill, Tiverton, where there is a car park and a picnic area.*
Map: *page 305, SS91/ST01.*

On the Grand Western Canal

Spring Squill

This delicate little flower can be found in grassy places by the sea, where it blooms in April and May. It grows in profusion on Britain's northern and western coasts, but is not very common elsewhere

Great Coxwell: The Great Barn

Oxfordshire

This beautiful and imposing Cotswold stone building was constructed in the 13th century by Cistercian monks from Beaulieu Abbey in Hampshire – about 150 years after the Manor of Faringdon had been granted to the abbey by King John.

Standing in the majestic and tranquil interior is not unlike being in a cathedral. The barn's shape is cruciform, and although the axis of most tithe barns runs east and west, that of Coxwell runs north and south. Stone lies just beneath the surface of the site, and the barn was laid out to follow the contours of the land.

The walls are reinforced by buttresses faced with ashlar – stone walling with an evenly dressed surface. Two of the original doors remain on the east and west, but those in the end walls are 18th-century and are taller and wider – presumably to admit larger wagons and loads. All the principal roof timbers are original. Twenty years ago the barn was extensively restored by the National Trust. It is still used to house farm machinery and other agricultural equipment.

Open: *all year at reasonable hours. NT.*
Location: *1½ miles SW of Faringdon, between A420 and B4019.*
Map: *page 306, SU29.*

Great Coxwell's superb medieval tithe barn

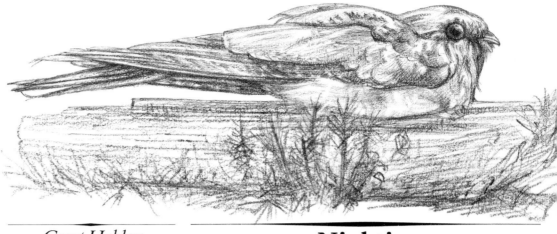

Great Haldon

Devon

This wooded ridge south-west of Exeter has superb views towards the east over the Exe valley and estuary. The woodlands are owned by the Forestry Commission, who have laid out and signposted a number of walks through the plantations. The trees are mainly conifers, but they still support a range of woodland birds – especially where the plantations of trees are less than 15 years old.

Typical birds of this type of plantation are chaffinch, coal tit and the tiny goldcrest. There is a good chance to see birds of prey, especially sparrowhawks, hunting along the woodland rides or soaring overhead, where they are very likely to be joined by the larger buzzards.

Evening walks in summer may be rewarded with a sighting of long-winged nightjars, which fly at dusk and make an unusual 'churring' sound.

Nightjar

This is one of those birds that nearly everyone has heard of, but few have actually seen. That nightjars are largely nocturnal is part of the reason for that, but they are also found in a limited number of habitats, and in any case they are not present in very large numbers.

Location: *5¼ miles SW of Exeter. Main car park at Buller's Hill, reached on unclassified Dunchideock – Ide road from A38 opposite Exeter Race Course. FC.*
Map: *page 305, SX 88/98.*

Gressenhall: Norfolk Rural Life Museum

Norfolk

Norfolk has long been one of Britain's most important agricultural counties. This does not mean that it has remained in any way static. Indeed, the county has always been at the forefront of agricultural changes, whether in methods or machinery. This continuous process is well illustrated in this new museum which covers Norfolk's agriculture, rural crafts and village life over the last 200 years.

The building itself is a very attractive late 18th-century workhouse with adjoining chapel. Inside is a large collection of tools and machinery, including such heavy items as steam engines. It is interesting to guess how these implements were used before reading the accompanying explanations – how bizarre these formerly everyday objects now seem! An interesting feature is Craftsmen's Row, with its painstaking replicas of traditional workshops such as a smithy and a saddlery. There is also a reconstruction of a turn-of-the-century cottage, authentically furnished.

Open: *May to Sep, Tue to Sat and Sun pm; also bank holiday Mon. Admission charge. Picnic area. Refreshments. Shop. Suitable for disabled visitors. No dogs.*
Location: *at Beech House, Gressenhall, 3 miles NW of East Dereham off B1146 Fakenham road.*
Map: *page 306, TF91.*

Grey Mare's Tail

Dumfries & Galloway

The National Trust for Scotland owns this 2383-acre site, where the Grey Mare's Tail waterfall drops 200ft from a superb hanging valley into a spectacular rocky gorge as the Tail Burn makes its way down from Loch Skeen towards Moffat Water.

The delicate watery strands of the Grey Mare's Tail falls

There is a herd of wild goats here; common gulls breed on Loch Skeen; and birds in the area also include raven and peregrine, but without doubt the main natural history interest of the area is botanical. Much of the area is sheep-walk, with some bilberry heath, but generally declining heather areas, and although there are interesting grassland, mire and upland plants, it is on the cliffs that the richest variety of montane and submontane species is to be found. This is the best area for them in the Southern Uplands and among the most notable are downy willow, starry, purple and mossy saxifrages, alpine mouse-ear, globe flower, alpine meadow-rue and rose-root.

Access: *very important to keep to the marked paths. Information point. NTS.*
Location: *10 miles NE of Moffat on A708 Selkirk road.*
Map: *page 313, NT11.*

Gwenffrwd/Dinas Nature Reserve

Dyfed

South of Llyn Brianne, a reservoir completed in 1973, the Afon Tywi races through a spectacular gorge as it sweeps round the steep, wooded, crag-topped hill known as Dinas. A two-mile nature trail, laid out by the Royal Society for the Protection of Birds, circles the isolated hill. A short detour climbs through the lichen-covered oaks to a cave that is said to have been one of Twm Sion Catti's refuges. One of the most colourful characters in Welsh folklore, Twm lived in the 16th century and became the principality's answer to Robin Hood. The cave is little more than a cleft in the rocks, but its setting is superb.

Dinas, like the nearby reserve of Gwenffrwd, attracts a remarkable variety of birds which flourish in what is still, despite the reservoir, one of the wildest parts of Wales. This area is the breeding ground of the red kite, one of Britain's rarest birds of prey. The species came close to extinction at the end of the 19th century, but survived in the lonely hills and valleys north of Llandovery. Kites share the skies with buzzards and kestrels while pied flycatchers and wood warblers flit among the ancient groves of oak. The Tywi and its fast-flowing tributaries are patrolled by dippers, grey wagtails and common sandpipers.

The narrow road which skirts Dinas used to end a little higher up the valley. It now runs above Llyn Brianne's eastern shore before reaching the old drovers' route from Tregaron to Abergwesyn. The moorland road passes Soar-y-mynydd, an isolated chapel of whitewashed stone set amid trees above a clear stream. It was built in the 19th century for families who raised sheep in this remote part of Britain and went to worship on foot or horseback.

Open: *Easter to Aug, Mon, Wed and Sat. Admission charge, except for RSPB members. Dinas information centre open in summer. Dinas nature trail open all year. Car park. No dogs. RSPB.*
Location: *8 miles N of Llandovery, on unclassified Llyn Brianne road about 2 miles N of Rhandirmwyn village.*
Map: *page 305, SN74.*

HOBBY HORSES

Padstow, Cornwall & Minehead, Somerset

According to local legends the Padstow and Minehead Hobby Horses originated several centuries ago, when they were devised to frighten away foreign invaders approaching the coast. They have since become associated with May Day celebrations and their appearance is now believed to welcome in the summer. Festivities in both towns are similar although the structure of the two 'horses' differs.

At Padstow celebrations commence on May Day eve with singing in the town. The 'Obby 'Oss', as it is locally known, does not emerge from its headquarters, the Golden Lion Inn, until the following morning. Its hoop-shaped frame is covered with black tarpaulin, and the 'horse' has a small wooden head, complete with snapper jaws, in front of the hoop, whilst the 'rider's' head is hidden by a grotesque mask with a cone cap.

The Minehead horse, known as 'The Sailor's Horse', has a framework covered by horsecloth painted with different coloured circles. The horseman puts his head through a central opening to rest the frame on his shoulders and, as at Padstow, the man's face is covered by a ferocious-looking mask with a cone cap. Unlike Padstow's 'Oss, the Minehead horse first makes an appearance on May Day eve, known as 'Warning Night'. The following day it emerges again from the Quayside, making one final appearance on the night of 3 May before retiring until the next year.

On May Day both horses caper through the streets of their respective towns, amusing large crowds who gather to watch these singular events.

When: *Padstow 1 May; Minehead 30 Apr to 3 May.*
Map: *Padstow page 304, SW97; Minehead page 305, SS94.*

HELSTON FURRY DANCE

Helston, Cornwall

There are numerous theories as to the origins of this very old and famous dance; the most popular is that it celebrates the victory of St Michael, Patron Saint of Helston, over the Devil. The dance occurs several times on the day of the Feast of the Apparition of St Michael which, owing to the garlands worn, has become known as 'Floral Day'.

Festivities commence at 7am, when young people perform the Early Morning Dance. Then, at 8.30am, the Hal-an-Tow, claimed by many to be the oldest part of the festival, begins at St John's Bridge. This is a boisterous event in which people dance, waving branches of beech and sycamore and sing such lines as 'Summer is a come-O and Winter is a gone-O'. At 10.30am young children dressed in white dance from each school. The main Furry Dance takes place at noon, when the participants dance by invitation only. This is very spectacular, the men wearing morning coats and top hats, and the women adorned in long summer dresses. They dance through the main streets and enter shops, houses and gardens which have all been decorated with flowers and branches. The last dance commences at 5pm, and is led by the young people who danced in the first. Everyone involved in

the dancing wears a spray of lily-of-the-valley, the flower of the festival, and the traditional tune is played by the Helston Band.

When: *8 May.*
Map: *page 304, SW62.*

CHEESE ROLLING CEREMONY

Cooper's Hill, Gloucestershire

This is thought to be among England's oldest surviving customs, possibly dating from pre-Roman times. Four Double Gloucester cheeses, each weighing approximately 9lbs, are enclosed in strong wooden cases decorated with red and blue ribbons. The event begins at 6pm when, at half-hourly intervals, the cheeses are rolled down the steep hill. The Master of Ceremonies, who wears a white smock and a black top hat, adorned with ribbons, starts the ensuing races and the first runner in each to reach the bottom of the hill is given the cheese.

When: *Spring Bank Holiday Mon.*
Map: *page 305, SO81.*

BREAD AND CHEESE DOLE

St Briavels, Gloucestershire

This custom, claimed to be 13th-century in origin, is observed to secure the commoners' rights of grazing and cutting wood in Hudnalls Wood. The Dole is distributed to the villagers after the Evening Service in St Mary's Parish Church and takes place in the narrow lane nearby. Small pieces of bread and cheese are thrown from the top of the high stone wall and are scrambled for by the people waiting in the road below.

When: *Whit Sun.*
Map: *page 305, SO50.*

CASTLETON GARLAND DAY

Castleton, Derbyshire

According to popular belief Garland Day commemorates the restoration of Charles II to the throne in 1660. It is also known as Oak Apple Day because Charles II hid in an oak tree after the Battle of Worcester.

The event starts in the early evening when a procession sets out, headed by the Garland King, dressed in Stuart costume and on horseback. His head and shoulders are hidden by the Garland – a bell-like wooden cone covered with leaves and flowers, weighing about 60lbs and three feet high. On top of this is a smaller posy of flowers known as the 'Queen'. The procession stops at several places including the six village inns, when the Garland Tune fills the air and white-clothed children dance. On arrival at the church the King's Garland is removed and the 'Queen' posy detached. The Garland is then hoisted to the top of the church tower, while the king places the 'Queen' posy at the foot of the war memorial. Festivities continue into the evening with dancing.

When: *29 May (Garland Days are also celebrated at Charlton-on-Otmoor, Oxfordshire on 1 May and Abbotsbury, Dorset on 13 May).*
Map: *page 310, SK18.*

GROVELY FOREST RIGHTS

Great Wishford, Wiltshire

Many claim that this custom existed before 1140, although the official Charter to protect it was not drawn up until 1603. It allows the inhabitants of Great Wishford to go to Grovely Forest at any time to collect 'all kinde of deade snappinge woode Boughes and Stickes', provided it is carried by hand or pulled in a hand cart. This right is enforced on Oak Apple Day.

Proceedings begin at 3am, when a group of young people create a disturbance with bugles and drums shouting 'Grovely, Grovely, Grovely and All Grovely'. As dawn breaks, villagers walk to Grovely Forest to cut green boughs; this is allowed only on Oak Apple Day. Some of these boughs are then placed outside the village houses and the rest are carried in the procession later. A large oak bough is adorned with coloured ribbons and hauled to the top of the church tower. Known as the 'Marriage Bough', this is said to bring good luck to all who marry here in the ensuing year.

During the morning some of the villagers, led by the Rector and including four women carrying sprigs of oak, go to Salisbury Cathedral. The women dance on the cathedral green, after which the whole party enters the cathedral and cry 'Grovely, Grovely, Grovely and All Grovely' before the High Altar. Everyone then returns to Great Wishford, and a procession starts at Town-End Tree at the south end of the village. The celebrations continue through the afternoon.

When: *29 May.*
Map: *page 305, SU03.*

From the top down: Garland Day at Castleton, Padstow's Hobby Horse, Cheese Rolling at Cooper's Hill, Helston's Furry Dance, and Garland Day at Abbotsbury in Dorset

Above: a great tit

Halnaker Mill

West Sussex

Sussex poet and windmill enthusiast Hilaire Belloc wrote a poem about this mill, seeing in its desolation the death-knell of England. He must, therefore, have been gratified by the mill's restoration in 1934. Today, with sweeps and fantails, it is a striking landmark as it sits on top of 416ft Halnaker Hill and, although the machinery is no longer inside, the ¾-mile walk up the hill is well worth the effort. With its brick and unusual tile-hanging it has a rustic, even crude, appearance – a reminder that it is the oldest tower mill in Sussex, built in 1740.

Open: at all times.
Location: 5 miles NE of Chichester, off A285 just NE of Halnaker village.
Map: page 306, SU09.

Hamsterley Forest

County Durham

Hamsterley is the largest piece of woodland in County Durham. Unlike many commercial forests, Hamsterley has a very varied terrain and a wide variety of tree species, making it a most attractive place to visit.

The Forestry Commission has provided a number of waymarked walks in the forest between half-a-mile and eight miles in length. The walks are designed to show visitors the range of trees and wildlife, and some of the features of the Grove Estate and the valley of the Bedburn Beck around which the forest grows. There is also a forest drive, which follows the course of the Bedburn Beck.

Roe deer are always likely to be seen on these walks and in among the large areas of Scots pine there is a good population of red squirrels.

Because of the variety of conifers and broadleaved trees a wide range of birds occurs. Specialities include siskin and crossbill. The small and colourful siskin is increasing as a breeding species, as is the much larger and highly specialised crossbill. These big finches, with their sec-

ateur-like beaks, snip fir cones off and dissect them to get at the seeds. When crossbills are busy feeding it is quite common to be showered with fir-cone debris as they work through the treetops.

Open: all year. Visitor centre. Car parks. Picnic sites. Small toll for forest drive. FC.
Location: 7¼ miles W of Bishop Auckland. W of A68; 1½ miles W of Hamsterley village.
Map: page 310, NZ02/03.

Hardwick Park

Derbyshire

Within a few years of the death of that remarkable Elizabethan, Bess of Hardwick, her descendants the Cavendishes made the great house at nearby Chatsworth their family home. Hardwick became one of those houses which encapsulate a period – in

Blue tits – residents of garden and countryside

this instance the early 17th century. As with the house, so with the park, which lacks the formal shapes of the 18th century 'improvers', retaining a less sophisticated charm which Bess would have recognised.

However, the world has moved on, and the nature walk through the park (now a country park very popular with Midlan-

Hardwick Hall and its park

ders) begins and ends beside the M1 motorway. The 400-year-old Hardwick Oak is the first of many magnificent trees along the walk. After the Millers Pond with moorhen, coot and mallard, there is an area of natural regeneration. Oak and hawthorn are becoming established in the rough grass where pheasants strut and partridges scurry. On Broad Oak Hill the roundel of young trees contains willow and sweet chestnut.

Grazing throughout the park are the now rare Longhorn cattle and the white-faced woodland horned sheep, a hardy breed developed in the High Peak area. They have declined, partly because they produce insufficient lambs to satisfy modern farming practice, and the carpet industry, in which their wool was used, has contracted.

The walk passes a series of fish ponds first created over 300 years ago to provide fish for eating, not only at religious feasts, but as a winter replacement for meat. One of these ponds is now a wildlife refuge, and close by is an old duck decoy. On the last section of the walk, which includes the Great Pond, reed and willow warbler sing in summer and marsh plants like reedmace and common spike rush are plentiful.

Open: park all year daily. Car park charge (except NT members). (House open Apr to Oct, Wed, Thu, Sat, Sun and bank holiday Mon, pm only. NT.
Location: 5 miles NW of Mansfield; 2 miles S of M1.
Map: page 310, SK46.

Harlow Car Gardens

North Yorkshire

Owned by the Northern Horticultural Society, these magnificent gardens offer something for everyone throughout the year. Covering an area of about 60 acres and laid out on a variety of soils with a backdrop of woodland, they contain a vast array of flowers, shrubs and trees. A stream which divides the woodland from the open gardens adds even more interest to the site, and supports a great variety of moisture-loving plants along its banks. Grey wagtails can regularly be seen hunting aquatic insects in this part of the garden.

In contrast to the time when it was part of the ancient forest of Knaresborough, the woodland contains many introduced varieties of trees and is the place where wildlife is at its most abundant. Many of the commoner species of birds occur here including blackbirds, song thrushes, robins, chaffinches and blue and great tits but the woods are also good for less common species such as that delightful little woodland bird, the tree-creeper, and the much larger and more colourful great spotted woodpecker.

The shrubs, rock gardens, and flower beds of the open gardens are interspersed with expanses of lawn and are designed to provide as big a variety as possible, with year-round interest. The natural acid soil of the area is ideal for the large collection of rhododendrons but in addition there are limestone rock gardens, a sandstone rock garden and even peat terraces which provide suitable conditions for plants which otherwise would not grow here.

Open: all year daily. Admission charge. Picnic area. Refreshments. Shop. Suitable for disabled visitors. No dogs.
Location: in Harrogate, 1½ miles W of town centre, in Crag Lane off B6162 Otley Road.
Map: page 310, SE25.

Hartland

Devon

The dramatic cliffs around Hartland Point and Hartland Quay are among the most spectacular in the country. The coast cuts at right angles to the bedding of the rock, creating extraordinary geological formations. With the sheer height, up to 500ft in places, it is a recipe for magnificent views.

The coast south of the point faces the full extent of the Atlantic Ocean and the effect of the heavy seas can be seen in the jagged rocks breaking through the waves at the tide's edge. The area has been notorious for its shipwrecks over four centuries – a theme traced in the fascinating little museum at Hartland Quay. The remains of the quay can still be seen here, and to either side are cliffs where the different coloured rock strata give a brilliant striped effect.

In May and June the area is a delightful patchwork of cliff flowers, with extensive areas of pink thrift and the blue of spring squill. Later in the season there are many butterflies, including pearl-bordered fritillaries and grayling, in an area where once there could be found the now extinct large blue butterfly.

This is a very good place to see ravens. These large crows have wedge-shaped tails and can often be recognised by their harsh 'crup' call.

Location: 12¼ miles N of Bude. Access to the coast at Hartland Point and Hartland Quay.
Map: page 305, SS22.

Hartlebury Castle Museum

Hereford & Worcester

The medieval castle of Hartlebury was largely destroyed in the

The lighthouse on Hartland Point

Civil War, but the local red sandstone was used to build a mansion in its place. Part of that is still the Palace of the Bishops of Worcester, but the north wing now houses the County Museum. It makes a pleasant and historic setting for some notable collections, including some interesting rural displays. Victorian and Edwardian costume, kitchen equipment and furniture are featured, and a very well-presented gallery depicts aspects of 19th-century social life. The nearby Black Country is represented by displays of hand-forged scythes, needles and other ironwork. Outside there are blacksmith's and wheelwright's shops together with various carts and wagons.

Less than a mile to the south-west lies Hartlebury Common, a remarkable heathland with some of the best examples of moving sand dunes to be found inland in Britain. It is managed by the county council as a Local Nature Reserve.

Open: Mar to Oct daily (except Sat), pm only. Admission charge. Picnic area. Refreshments.
Location: 1½ miles E of Stourport-on-Severn, off B4193.
Map: page 309, SO87.

Hartsholme Country Park

Lincolnshire

This 88-acre park formerly belonged to the Earl of Liverpool, but his great house, Hartsholme Hall, is no longer standing. What remains is classic parkland including some splendid mature trees and a large lake.

The old trees, with much dead wood, immediately suggest woodpeckers, and indeed both great and lesser spotted are found here. The latter is surprisingly small, sparrow-sized, but is still capable of loud drumming. It is one of those birds that make a good day out for the bird-watcher, being not only attractive, but elusive and a bit of a challenge. The lake holds wild-fowl in winter and kingfishers often visit. Nightingales can be heard most years, which is a bonus, as this is getting towards the north of the range of this warmth-loving species.

Hartsholme's natural history interest is continued in displays in the information centre, housed in the stable block.

Open: *park all year; information centre Mar to Oct daily except Tue and Thu. Picnic area. Refreshments (Apr to Sep). Suitable for disabled visitors.*
Location: *on outskirts of Lincoln, 2½ miles SW of city centre. Entrance off unclassified Skellingthorpe Road, off A1180.*
Map: *page 310, SK96.*

Hastings Country Park

East Sussex

Established in 1971, Hastings Country Park covers some 500 acres and includes one of the most unspoilt stretches of the Sussex coast. The varied wildlife habitats within the park include woodlands, streams, heath, sea cliffs, chalk grassland and beach. Hastings Borough Council, which runs the park, has planned five nature trails to introduce visitors to the park's wildlife. Leaflets on the trails point out where numerous species, from beetles to bank voles, might be seen.

Stretching for four miles east of Hastings there are cliff walks with superb views of East Sussex and the English Channel.

Open: *park at all times. Interpretive centre summer only. Picnic and barbecue areas.*
Location: *stretching for 4 miles E of Hastings. Interpretive centre on Coastguard Lane, S of Fairlight Church.*
Map: *page 306, TQ81.*

Hatfield Forest

Essex

For the fallow deer gliding silently among the trees Hatfield is a tranquil haven. Yet its history is full of turbulence, of kings and commoners bitterly contesting rights, and later, proud families skirmishing as they struggled to assert those same rights. 'Forest' to the Norman kings meant any area of country to which they could apply the harsh and restrictive 'forest laws'. Virtually the whole of Essex became such a forest, but through opposition it was reduced by the 19th century to the forests at Epping, Hainault and Hatfield. Hainault was lost to the developers, Epping saved by the Corporation of the City of London, and in a dramatic last-minute rescue in 1924 Hatfield too was preserved.

Hatfield today consists of various coppices and broad stretches of open grassland. Dotted about these open chases are trees such as pollarded hornbeams, which are perhaps the most notable trees here now that the great old oaks have been removed. Silver birch, maple and poplar are to be found in the coppices, and beneath them blooms the false oxlip, a hybrid between cowslip and primrose. The single green flower of the strange-looking herb Paris may be found in damp ground, and several species of orchid grow in a restricted marsh area near the lake. In summer Hatfield is full of warbler song, and the nightingale still breeds here. Around the lake 18 species of dragonfly have been observed; boating and fishing are allowed here and large pike and tench have been caught.

Location: *3 miles E of Bishop's Stortford, on S side of A120. Access at Bush End. Parking charge (except for NT members). Information centre. NT.*
Map: *page 306, TL52/53.*

Haugh Wood

Hereford & Worcester

This large tract of woodland covers the centre of a remarkable rock formation known to geologists as the Woolhope Dome. An elongated upfold of Silurian rocks has had its top eroded away, leaving a series of exposed ridges of limestone separated by softer bands of shale. At the centre older sandstone is exposed. The result is an attractive area of varied topography, much of it wooded. Largest of the woodlands is Haugh Wood itself, which covers nearly 1000 acres.

Apart from a narrow strip of common land running through the centre which belongs to the National Trust, the whole wood is the property of the Forestry Commission. Since they acquired it in 1925 the Commission has carried out a great deal of felling and replanting but a lot of the previous oak woodland still survives alongside the younger oak, beech and a variety of conifers. Waymarked walks have been laid out by the Commission, taking in the different types of woodland and offering views over Hereford and beyond to the Welsh mountains.

In recent years the Commission have co-operated with conservation organisations to maintain the surviving natural features, in particular the butterflies and moths for which this is a very good locality. The flora is also of interest; in the autumn this is a good place to look for the striking pink flowers of the meadow saffron, one of Britain's most uncommon plants.

Location: *5½ miles SE of Hereford on unclassified Mordiford–Woolhope road, off B4224 at Mordiford. FC. Part NT.*
Map: *page 305, SO53.*

Hawksmoor Nature Reserve

Staffordshire

Hawksmoor should be visited more than once – if only because there are four different walks in addition to a nature trail. Three are one-and-a-half miles long, one is two miles, and between them they cover farmland, railway and disused canal as well as the River Churnet.

The nature reserve is mostly moorland covered in bracken and heathers, with some woodland. Lapwing twist and tumble over the slopes to the river, their sharp 'pee-wit' calls the clearest indication of how they received their vernacular English name, as is the haunting, bubbling 'cur-li' of the curlew. Perhaps the loss of suitable habitat has caused the nightjar to become rarer outside East Anglia, but it still breeds at Hawksmoor, and hunts at dusk during the summer months.

The Forestry Commission has been responsible for a major replanting of trees in the area. As part of its policy of adding colour to commercial plantings, the edges of the wood at Hawksmoor include red oak, whose leaves turn a splendid dark red in autumn. Among the conifers the lodgepole pine has been

planted; it is growing in popularity for commercial planting as it tolerates poor soil, and its upturned branches with their 'thin' covering of bright green foliage mean it occupies less space. It was popular, too, with the North American Indians as it was used as the centre pole of their tepees or 'lodges'.

Location: *2 miles NE of Cheadle, on N side of B5417. NT.*
Map: *page 309, SK04.*

Ancient pollarded hornbeams in Hatfield Forest

Bank Vole

As its name suggests, the bank vole is most likely to be found on banks along hedgerows and in broadleaved woodland. It can be told from its more common cousin, the short-tailed vole, by its longer tail and chestnut-coloured back. Like all mammals bank voles are shy, and patience is required for anything more than a fleeting glimpse. They sometimes climb shrubs to reach choice leaves, which form the major part of their diet along with such things as hips and haws and the occasional insect.

Haxted Mill

Surrey

In the Domesday survey of 1086, some 7000 Saxon watermills are listed. With the rise in population in the Middle Ages many more watermills were built, whereas windmills were unknown until they were introduced from Holland in the 12th century.

Built in the 16th and 18th centuries on early 14th-century foundations, Haxted Watermill now contains a museum which provides a vivid record of milling throughout the ages. Its own history is that of a flour-mill, but watermills down the ages have served many functions all over the country. Cornwall has its tin-mine wheels, the Weald its hammer-mills – used in the iron industry – while North Kent specialised in rag-pulping mills which provided raw materials for the making of paper.

All these different kinds of watermill, and more, are represented at this watermill museum. Exhibits inside and outside the mill tell the story of all kinds of watermills, which for over 1000 years were the principal source of mechanical power. Many of the exhibits (including Haxted's own water-wheel) are still working, and paintings, old photographs and audio-visual presentations help bring to life the background of this fascinating industry.

Open: *Apr to Sep weekends, also Mon to Thu, pm only, July to Sep. Admission charge. Refreshments (weekends). Shop.*
Location: *1½ miles W of Edenbridge on unclassified Lingfield Common road, between B2026 and B2029.*
Map: *page 306, TQ44.*

Left and below; the exterior and interior of Haxted's mill

Hayle Estuary

Cornwall

This tiny estuary provides some good opportunities to get close to waders and wildfowl. Even when the tide is out, the birdlife is still within range of binoculars. Although the numbers are not as great as on famous estuaries such as the Wash or Morecambe Bay, there is great variety and the density is high. The estuary's position, right in the south-west tip of England, also attracts unusual birds, occasionally from the USA.

The Royal Society for the Protection of Birds have an unmanned information hut here, and there is a hide which is open to the public.

A walk around the tidal pool of Carnsew, at the western end of Hayle, is also well worth while as there are often grebes or divers on its sheltered waters, ex-

cept in summer when there is the chance to see terns hovering and diving for fish.

Location: *Just W of Hayle along A30.*
Map: *page 304, SW53.*

Heacham: Norfolk Lavender Garden

Norfolk

An unusual feature of the west Norfolk countryside, near the holiday resort of Hunstanton, is the 100 acres of lavender fields at Heacham. They provide the raw material for a family business based in Caley Mill, a former watermill built in about 1800. The Miller's cottage is now an attractive tea-room. The most interesting time to visit is early July to mid August when harvesting takes place – the exact date depending on the weather. The lavender is either dried or distilled, and a conducted tour of the distillery is available during harvest. The perfume of lavender fills the air, and other traditional scents can be enjoyed in the herb garden.

Open: *June to Sep daily; Oct to May Mon to Fri. Admission charge. Refreshments. Shop. Suitable for disabled visitors.*
Location: *on E side of A149 King's Lynn–Hunstanton road at Caley Mill, Heacham.*
Map: *page 311, TF63.*

Headley Heath

Surrey

For centuries Headley was used to graze sheep, and although this practice ended in 1882 there was little change to the open heathland until the Second World War. Then it was used as a training area, and the soil was considerably disturbed, creating the ideal conditions for dormant birch seed to germinate. Within a short time the few remaining birch trees were surrounded by saplings. More recently, oak and beech have become established and great effort and ingenuity have been devoted to controlling their own growth and re-establishing the purple or bell heather, once a feature of the open heathland.

Headley, like its near neighbour, Box Hill, attracts many visitors; none the less wildlife abounds. All three woodpeckers, the acrobatic tits and many finches including linnet and goldfinch – joined in winter by siskin and redpoll – frequent the woods. A series of fires in recent

Musk mallow – a flower of waysides and banks. It is in the same family as the hollyhock

years has reduced the butterfly and moth population, but it is recovering; chalkhill blue, several skippers and the comma are all to be found in their preferred habitats. The birch-feeding orange underwing is one of the common moths. Both chalk and heathland orchids have survived, and the tall spikes of dark mullein and the pink-flowered musk mallow both flourish on Headley's chalk.

There are some fine wild cherry trees, but the brilliant white blossom in May, a month after the others have flowered, is the snowy mespil, an American arrival still probably better known as amelanchier. Another 'American', not common, but becoming established at Headley, is the black cherry, whose glossy dark green leaves are among the latest to appear each spring.

Location: *3 miles SE of Leatherhead, astride B2033. NT.*
Map: *page 306, TQ25.*

Hebden Water & Hardcastle Crags

West Yorkshire

The combination of mixed woodland with a Pennine river and feeder streams running through a steep-sided ravine makes this a special place at any time of the year. The National Trust owns a sizeable area of the woodland, together with the picturesque Hardcastle Crags, an escarpment above the trees.

Spring is an especially marvellous time in the old woodlands, with the fresh green of the trees complemented by the shimmering carpets of bluebells on the woodland floor. This is also the time of year when the woodland birds sing at their very best and make the walk to the tiny chapel at Black Dean a great pleasure.

An alternative walk in the area is the Slurring Rock trail, laid out by the local district council. It takes about two hours to walk, and several suggested stopping places are indicated. A ruined mill – one of many examples of industry depending on the fast-flowing Pennine streams – can be seen across the river, while later on the trail passes a charcoal pit – a reminder of a different kind of industry in the area.

The streams are also havens for wildlife; one bird which exploits them very successfully is the dipper. The power of the streams may be enough to run mills, but it is not enough to wash away

this little bird. Dippers can stand head-on into the stream and probe for food, mostly tiny invertebrates, among the stones on the stream bed.

The Slurring Rock trail offers a fine array of wild flowers. A largely inaccessible rock outcrop harbours many moisture-loving plants – pink claytonia and the not dissimilar herb Robert, golden saxifrage and wood sorrel – all in flower in early summer. In early spring and summer the leaves of the passion dock or bistort may be gathered – an ingredient of the local delicacy 'dock pudding'. The pink bells of bilberry adorn the part of the trail known as the Woodman's Haulage Road. Here also the delicate corydalis trails up the bank; a climber with pale cream flowers in bloom from early summer.

Grey and red squirrels both live in the area and the trail passes several wood-ant hills. These ants are unusual in Yorkshire. They prevent defoliation of woodland by eating insect pests.

At the highest point of the trail is the Slurring Rock, so called because local children once slid or 'slurred' down its slopes in their wooden clogs. Locally grown alder is often called clog-wood because clog soles were carved from it; there is an example of this tree beside the weir.

Location: *NW of Hebden Bridge. Access on W side from car park at Greenwood Lee on unclassified Blake Dean road beyond Heptonstall and Slack or from car park on E side of A6033 at Midgehole.*
Map: *page 309, SD92.*

Hele Mill
Devon

This fascinating 16th-century watermill, with its 18ft overshot water wheel, has been painstakingly restored to full working order and is now producing wholemeal flour. It also contains much information and many interesting items of mill machinery including an early porcelain roller mill and a 1928 diesel engine.

Open: *Easter to Oct, Mon to Fri daily; Sun pm only. Admission charge. Shop. No dogs.*
Location: *1 mile E of Ilfracombe on A399 Ilfracombe – Combe Martin road.*
Map: *page 305, SS54.*

Helford River
Cornwall

The Helford River is claimed by some to be the most picturesque of all Cornish estuaries. Set in a deep valley with stone and slate cliffs sometimes reaching the water's edge, it is similar to the nearby Fal in having extensive woodlands all along its banks. The sheltered nature of the area and its mild climate make it a pleasant place to be in, even in midwinter, which often seems more like spring.

The valley of Gweek Drive at the head of the estuary is just one of the large wooded areas which include the ancient oak woods at Merthen. Its winding creeks are good places to see waders such as the greenshank, which has a distinctive, three-note 'piu piu piu' call.

The National Trust has many separate holdings on both north and south banks of the Helford estuary. They vary greatly in size and description. Several small wooded coves and creeks, such as Frenchman's Creek, made famous by Daphne du Maurier, are more easily accessible by boat.

The Trust's most well-known property at Helford is the beautiful valley garden of Glendurgan – with water gardens, tender shrubs, specimen trees and a maze – all designed around one of the many streams that spill into the estuary.

Bosloe, south-west of Mawnan Smith, gives access to the coastal footpath and a beach; there are wooded cliffs at Mawnan Glebe, and mixed woodland on the south bank of the estuary and up the east bank of Vallum Tremayne Creek.

At nearby Gweek, the Seal Sanctuary cares for injured and orphaned seals which are kept in large pools until they are fit to return to the sea. An aquarium and a nature trail are also to be found here.

Open: *Glendurgan Garden Mar to Oct, Mon, Wed and Fri (closed Good Fri). Admission charge. NT. Seal Sanctuary open daily. Admission charge. Refreshments. Shop. Suitable for disabled visitors.*
Location: *5 miles SW of Falmouth. The tidal creeks can be explored using minor roads off B3291 between Gweek and Falmouth on N side, or on minor roads off B3293 on S side. Helford and Helford Passage are linked by passenger ferry.*
Map: *page 304, SW72.*

Hermitage
Tayside

Originally part of the ancient Caledonian pine forest, this area on the north bank of the River Braan had degenerated, after centuries of felling and burning, into a bleak and barren wilderness when the Second Duke of Atholl began to create a tree garden here in the 18th century. Today, thanks to his efforts, and the work of subsequent dukes, it is a richly wooded place with a great variety of trees. One of the finest is an immense Douglas fir – over 180 ft tall – said to be the tallest tree in Britain. Many trees native to the area can be seen alongside exotics like the monkey puzzle. The diversity of tree species, and the varied habitats of dense woodland, open glades and river banks, encourage a wide range of plants and animals. Red squirrels may be seen, as may more secretive creatures like voles, mice and shrews. Birdlife includes many members of the tit family, and, by the river, dippers and yellow wagtails. Two follies, Ossian's Hall and Ossian's Cave, can be seen along the woodland walk laid out by the National Trust for Scotland.

Open: *all year. Ranger/naturalist service. Access for disabled. NTS.*
Location: *2m W of Dunkeld, off A9.*
Map: *page 313, NO04.*

The Helford River at Gweek. Below Gweek the river becomes a wide estuary with many creeks

High Force
Co Durham

Rising high on the slopes of Cross Fell in the Pennines, the River Tees flows for 90 miles, reaching the North Sea beyond Middlesbrough. No stretch along that 90 miles is more spectacular than where the river thunders over a great whinstone cliff at Middleton-in-Teesdale to

Common Shrew

Shrews are naturally vociferous, and during the mating periods – early spring and late summer – their shrill, angry-sounding squeaks can be one of the dominant sounds of wayside and woodland. When not courting, they are solitary creatures, and the squeaks really are angry – shrews are extremely aggressive and will not tolerate other shrews in their territories.

become High Force. The 70 ft fall is set in a long, deep gorge, carved by the river over thousands of years. The sheer force of the dark peaty water as it pours over the cliff is astonishing, particularly after heavy rain.

Across the B6277 from the High Force Hotel a path leads down the slope of the gorge through coniferous woodland to the falls. Grey wagtails provide a splash of colour as they hunt insects along the river bank, while higher up the slope, spotted flycatchers sally out from exposed perches to catch flies, and where alders grow along the riverbank pied flycatchers can be found. Both flycatchers are summer visitors to Britain.

Open: *all year. Admission charge.*
Location: *4½ miles NW of Middleton-in-Teesdale off B6277.*
Map: *page 313, NY82.*

High Ham Windmill
Somerset

A splendid local landmark, this tower mill is unusual in that it has a thatched roof or cap. Thatched mills were never common and now High Ham is believed to be the sole survivor. Built in 1822 of local blue lias limestone and standing on a little 'platform' of earth, the mill is 28 ft high. The sail blocks remain, but the original sails and most of the machinery have gone. To the north are the flat expanses of King's Sedge Moor.

Open: *Apr to end Sep, Sun and bank holiday Mon, pm only. By appointment with the tenant. Admission charge. NT.*
Location: *2½ miles N of Langport, ½ mile SE of High Ham village.*
Map: *page 305, ST43.*

Hindhead Commons
Surrey

In a series of connected common, heath and woodland properties the National Trust owns nearly 1400 acres in this beautiful and much visited area. Nature walks have been laid out over both the Devil's Punch Bowl and Gibbet Hill, giving excellent introductions to their quite different delights. The Punch Bowl walk is a stiff 2½ miles, while the 1¾-mile walk on Gibbet Hill is easier.

Starting from the car park at the southern rim of the Punch Bowl the walker can enjoy the sweep of the land before descending steeply to cross the Smallbrook stream in the wooded valley. The walk down is through mixed woodland where the strikingly beautiful whitebeam gives colour for most of the year, its silvery green leaves and creamy white flowers giving way to red berries and gold foliage in autumn.

Superb views are the major feature of the Gibbet Hill walk. From the various viewpoints it is possible to take in a panoramic area that sweeps from the Chilterns past the Hampshire chalk hills to the South Downs. This walk is mainly across open heathland.

Location: *Just E of Hindhead on both sides of A3, 11 miles SW of Guildford. NT.*
Map: *page 306, SU83.*

Hobby Drive

Devon

This extensive broadleaved woodland area is situated on the North Devon cliffs near Clovelly. Mature native oak and ash is mixed with planted areas of beech. A private drive runs for almost three miles through this landscape, with superb views over the sea below and the famous little fishing village of Clovelly. The drive itself was built in the 19th century as a hobby by a previous owner, hence the name.

The woods support a rich variety of typical birdlife, and buzzards are often seen as they circle overhead on broad outstretched wings. The cliffs below are inhabited by herring gulls, fulmars, jackdaws, and by one or two pairs of the largest British member of the crow family – the raven.

Open: *daily Easter to Oct. Admission charge, which also covers parking at Clovelly village.*
Access: *traffic is one-way only westward from entrance at Hobby Lodge, on A39, ¾ mile W of Buck's Cross.*
Location: *7¾ miles SW of Bideford.*
Map: *page 305, SS32.*

Holkham

Norfolk

Pines and the sea make a pleasing combination here. The trees, which grow on the landward dunes, were planted in the 19th century, and most of those that survive are Corsican pines. In summer the glades here are full of flowers and butterflies, and there are many birds to be seen. Autumn is perhaps the best time to visit; many different kinds of fungi can be found, and bird-watchers scan the birch and blackberry thickets which are inland of the pines for rare migrants, some of which come from as far away as Siberia. Easier to find are goldcrests. Britain's smallest birds, they are present here all year, but their numbers are swelled by migrants in autumn and winter. Large flocks of brent geese gather around Wells harbour in winter.

Stretching west and east of Holkham, between Overy Staithe and Blakeney, is Holkham National Nature Reserve, a vast area of sand dunes, salt marshes and intertidal sand and mud flats.

Access: *unrestricted, but keep to paths and off farmland. W part of reserve is accessible on foot along sea wall from Overy Staithe and from beach at Wells. A private road, Lady Ann's Drive, leads from Holkham to Holkham Gap; admission charge for cars on this May to Sep. Footpath access to saltmarsh between Wells and Stiffkey. NCC.*
Map: *page 311, TF84/94.*

Holme Pierrepont

Nottinghamshire

Holme Pierrepont is unique, for it is the National Water Sports Centre as well as a country park. Most visitors come to see first-class water skiers, power boat races, canoeing and sailing regattas on the 90 acres of water and international standard courses. But as a change from all this frantic activity, it is possible to wander peacefully through the trees and lawns around the lake, or hope to catch a glimpse of a king-fisher along the reed-fringed banks in the undisturbed corners. There are 1½ miles of waterside with many places secluded enough to attract anglers, including the disabled, who can fish from wheelchairs on specially prepared platforms.

The open water attracts a variety of birds. Binoculars or telescopes are needed to identify the different gulls and ducks which are particularly numerous in the quieter winter season. Other birds such as grebes are more easily seen near the edges where they feed underwater on insect larvae and small fish, diving below for several seconds and popping up a few yards away.

Open: *all year.*
Location: *2½ miles E of Nottingham city centre, access off A52 Radcliffe road.*
Map: *page 310, SK63.*

Holy Island

Northumberland

Apart from the busy summer months, Holy Island, or Lindisfarne, is a place of great tranquillity and has been so for centuries. A religious pilgrimage to the priory, following the stakes of the old Pilgrims Way, is sometimes made by thousands of Christians, for this was once the home of St Aidan and St Cuthbert. For those not wanting to walk, a modern causeway provides an easy drive on to the island. Even with this road it must still be remembered that the is-

Below: purple sandpiper, a wader which is a winter visitor to coastal places such as Hunstanton

land is cut off by the tide twice a day and can be a dangerous place at high tide.

Between the island and the mainland are vast stretches of inter-tidal mud flats which provide a winter home for tens of thousands of wildfowl. The largest flock of wigeon in Britain, the only regular flock of pale-bellied brent geese in Britain and a substantial herd of who-oper swans, are all found here in winter. Because of these internationally important populations and the high botanical interest on the island, most of the area is a National Nature Reserve.

A walk round the shoreline of the main part of the island takes in most of the main features. The harbour just east of the village is overlooked by the castle on its crag. Along the northern shore the low cliffs give way to sandy bays. There are views to the Farne Islands and Bamburgh Castle from the east shore.

Open: *at all times; check tide-tables before crossing causeway. Part NCC.*
Location: *causeway to island, 2 miles E of A1 at West Mains on unclassified road 1 mile beyond Beal.*
Map: *page 313, NU14.*

The cliffs at Hunstanton

Hornsea Mere

Humberside

The northern and western shores of this shallow mere are well wooded; mainly with oak, ash and sycamore. Alder and willow grow in the wetter areas. These woodlands are dangerous due to the presence of silted-up ditches, and no public access to them is allowed. A public footpath, some distance back from the water's edge, runs through the farmland on the southern side of the mere and gives visitors the chance to see the other main habitat here – the reed swamp at the western end.

Well used for dinghy sailing, the mere is nevertheless an excellent place for birds, especially wildfowl. Particularly outstanding are the late spring gatherings of goldeneye and in late summer a large herd of moulting mute swans. This is also the time of year when the mere attracts good numbers of little gulls, an uncommon species in the British Isles.

The reed swamp, at the shallowest end of the mere, supports the most northerly breeding population of reed warblers on the east side of Britain. Water rails are common in this area in winter, though their skulking habits make them hard to see, and in recent years sparrowhawks have taken to hunting the starlings and other species that roost in the reeds. Fifteen species of butterfly occur regularly at Hornsea Mere, but in summer months the most noticeable insect is likely to be the mosquito!

Open: _escorted visiting all year Mon & Sat from information centre (admission charge for RSPB non-members). Reserve information centre also open weekends May to Aug. No dogs. RSPB._
Access: _public footpath on S side of mere, starting in Hull Road._
Location: _on W side of village of Hornsea, signposted off B1242._
Map: _page 310, TA14._

Hunstanton

Norfolk

The only resort on the east coast that faces west (into the Wash), Hunstanton has other unusual features. The famous cliffs are banded in four colours: brown carstone at the base, then rich red, fossil-bearing limestone, white chalk and a thin cap of brown soil. Beautiful in themselves, to the birdwatcher they have the added attraction of nesting fulmars, small relatives of the albatrosses. From the beach these sturdy grey and white birds can easily be seen on their nesting-ledges, but the best view can be had from the grassy cliff-top near the old lighthouse, where their extraordinary powers of flight can be appreciated at eye-level and close range.

In winter a telescope is really needed to view the large flocks of sea-ducks that gather offshore, but the waders on the beach are much more obliging. The best of them, the purple sandpiper, with dark plumage and orange-yellow legs, hunts for small animals around the groynes to the south of the town-centre.

Location: _on the A149 13¼ miles NE of King's Lynn. The cliffs lie at the N end of the town._
Map: _page 311, TF64._

APPLEBY HORSE FAIR

Appleby, Cumbria

This huge and extraordinary annual gathering attracts gypsies from all over Britain, who meet for the purpose of buying and selling horses, bringing colour and spectacle to this otherwise quiet market town and tourist centre. The travelling people set up camp on Fair Hill – some in their traditional brightly painted horsedrawn caravans, others in huge, shiny mobile homes. Appleby Horse Fair is certainly the largest event of its kind in the world, and has survived since 1685 under the protection of a charter granted by James II for horse-trading.

When: *second Tue and Wed in June.*
Map: *page 310, NY62.*

ALE TASTING AND BREAD WEIGHING CEREMONY

Ashburton, Devon

The purpose of this ceremony – believed to be of medieval origin – is to taste and approve the wares of the local taverns and bakeries. The taverns are visited by a procession led by the Portreeve, the Ale Tasters and other worthy members of the town including members of the Courts of Leet and Baron. If the ale is judged to be satisfactory, then the landlord is handed an evergreen sprig to put over his door. The procession is joined by the town's official Bread Weighers, who visit the local bakeries and test two loaves in each shop.

When: *Thu evening of Carnival Week, which starts on the fourth Sat of June.*
Map: *page 300, SX76.*

COMMON RIDINGS

Hawick and Selkirk, Borders

The origins of the various common ridings held in Scotland's border counties go back to the times when it was essential for townsfolk to prevent encroachment on to their common lands by neighbouring landowners. These ancient ceremonies were given added potency when they also became memorial celebrations to battles fought against the English.

The common riding at Hawick is a case in point. In 1514, a year after the Scottish defeat at Flodden, the young men of Hawick defeated an English force at Hornshole, and rode back proudly bearing a captured English banner. Since then a flag symbolising that banner has played an important part in the common riding. The boundaries, or marches, of the burgh are traced by mounted townsmen, led by the 'Cornet', a young man elected by the town council, whose main duty is to carry and care for the banner. Many ceremonies, meals and dances ensue, all made the more stirring by the full-throated rendering of 'Teribus', Hawick's anthem and ancient war song.

Selkirk's common riding has similar origins. The banner carried commemorates an English banner captured at the Battle of Flodden. It is said that of all the Selkirk men who rode away to fight at Flodden, only one returned alive, and he brought back the banner, which he flung down in the market place. The action is echoed today when the various standard-bearers of the town's guilds and trades dip their flags in respect. As many as 400 horsemen take part in the common riding itself. Games and Highland dancing take place the following day.

When: *Hawick Fri and Sat after first Mon in June. Selkirk Fri and Sat after the second Mon in June.*
Map: *Hawick page 312, NT51. Selkirk page 312, NT42.*

Stonehenge – scene of the Druids' midsummer rites

DRUIDS' CEREMONY

Stonehenge, Wiltshire

Stonehenge was undoubtedly constructed as the focus for now-forgotten ceremonial or religious purposes, and although it makes a most dramatic setting for this famous ceremony, it is most unlikely that the original druids ever gathered here to worship. Stonehenge is older by some 2000 years than the historical druids and, in any case, they preferred oak groves.

Nevertheless, the Stonehenge ceremony has become one of our most familiar midsummer customs. Held by the Companions of the Most Ancient Order

'Cavaliers' and 'Roundheads' at Robert Dover's Games

of Druids, it is a romantic reconstruction of rites once held to mark the summer solstice. The actual ceremonies are held at midnight, dawn and noon among the huge stones of Europe's most spectacular henge monument. From midnight a silent vigil is kept until the first rays of sunshine strike the altar stone or 'Hele Stone'. The dawn service then starts in order to greet the sunrise, with the white-robed 'druids' processing round the circle of stones amid much chanting. The midday ceremony is a celebration of summer and here the Presider is crowned. He is usually someone of the Druid Order who has done something especially beneficial for humanity. 'Lady Ceridwen' brings a gift of cider, symbolising the earth's life stream.

When: *on the summer solstice, usually 20/21 June.*
Map: *page 302, SU14.*

ROBERT DOVER'S GAMES & SCUTTLEBROOK WAKE

Chipping Campden, Gloucestershire

It was as a protest against puritanism that Captain Robert Dover decided to found his very own version of the Olympic Games in 1604. The games continued as an annual event until 1852, when they were prohibited because they became so rowdy. The games were revived in 1951 and now include such rural sports as tug of war, greasy pole, coursing, cudgel and slingback together with the ancient Cotswold sport of shin-kicking. There is also morris dancing, Scottish dancing, sideshows and other entertainment. The games are held on Dover's Hill, a splendid natural amphitheatre which rises to 800 ft.

The following day, Scuttlebrook Wake, a revival of the old spring fair, provides a traditional finale to the games. Here the Scuttlebrook Queen is crowned before riding in a floral cart, accompanied by four attendants and a page boy, in a procession headed by a fancy dress parade and floats, to the town square. This is followed by morris dancing, fancy dress competitions, races and other events before the parade makes its way to the fair.

When: *Fri and Sat after Spring Bank Holiday.*
Map: *page 304, SP13.*

WELL-DRESSING

Derbyshire and Staffordshire villages

The ancient and beautiful custom of celebrating the gift of water by decorating wells and springs still flourishes today, particularly in the villages of Derbyshire. Well-dressing has been traced back to medieval days and may even date back to the Roman occupation, when it was believed to be associated with the pagan rites of Fontus, god of wells and streams. Originally the decorating was by means of simple garlands, but today elaborate pictures are constructed depicting a religious scene, sometimes incorporating a text. The picture is composed entirely of flowers and other natural materials, pressed on to a clay-spread wooden background.

When: *well-dressing takes place in over 20 villages in Derbyshire and Staffordshire during the summer. In June it can be seen at Ashford, Hope, Litton, Rowsley, Tideswell, West Hallam, Wyaston and Youlgreave.*

Well-dressing at Buxton in the 19th century

Ickworth

Suffolk

Two splendid walks have been laid out by the National Trust in the magnificent grounds of Ickworth House. Trees are the prime object of the Albana Woodland walk; unusual species grow alongside the familiar plantings. English, sessile and turkey oaks are joined by the attractive round-headed evergreen holm oak, known as 'holly' oak in some areas. A shorter route passes through a fine avenue of yew.

The main walk circles Round Hill with its two superb clumps of trees; the southern of Wellingtonia, the northern of coast redwood – 'the tallest tree in the world' – although it rarely grows to great heights in this country. In addition to splendid specimens of Cedar of Lebanon (also much in evidence around Ickworth House) and sweet chestnut, you will also find hornbeam, ash, beech and sycamore along the walk.

As with the Albana Walk, the Canal Walk is of particular interest to the tree 'spotter', but it includes a walk around the 'canal', which is in reality a lake. Early in the walk the path passes between labelled specimens of Lucombe oaks and holm oaks. Both are evergreen, the Lucombe having a knobbly, corky bark and more typically oak-like leaves which appear lighter in colour than those of the 'holly' oak. Throughout the deer park are signs of the wild fallow and roe deer which feed here at night.

The church and its churchyard are worth a detour, but the view of these, and of the Rotunda of the house, from the canal is a highlight of the walk. The canal was dredged in 1981, and is now

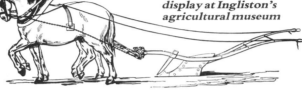

Early ploughs like this are on display at Ingliston's agricultural museum

home to a number of water birds including mallard, swans, coots and moorhens. In winter their numbers are swelled by teal and tufted duck. The trees along the bank are hornbeam – a tree with a great tradition of usefulness over the centuries, whether coppiced or pollarded. But it is perhaps the oaks which stay in the memory, whichever walk one takes at Ickworth.

Open: park daily all year. Car park charge. House open Apr to mid Oct all pms except Mon (unless bank holiday) and Fri (but open Fri June to mid Sep). Admission charge. Refreshments. NT.
Location: at Horringer, 3 miles SW of Bury St Edmunds on W side of A143.
Map: page 306, TL86.

Ingliston: Scottish Agricultural Museum

Lothian

Rural life in Scotland in the 18th and early 19th centuries is faithfully reproduced in this collection, the result of more than twenty years of acquisition and restoration work by the National Museum of Antiquities of Scotland. Fully furnished rooms show the interiors of homes in the Lowlands, Borders and

Inverpolly National Nature Reserve and the peak of Stac Polly

Ickworth's Rotunda

Highlands as they appeared over a hundred years ago. The changing patterns of farming are depicted by contrasting pieces of hardware from simple hand tools to complex machines. The development of ploughing begins with the Lowland ox teams and progresses to the light horse ploughs of later years, while the sowing process is demonstrated by hand-held sheets and drills and broadcast machines. Threshing, winnowing and milling methods throughout the ages are also shown, with transport ranging from creels, pack ponies and carts to the hydraulic powered tractors of our own generation. The first floor has displays of country trades.

Open: May to Sep, Mon to Fri and first Sun (pm only) in each month.
Location: 7 miles W of Edinburgh, off A8.
Map: page 313, NT17.

Inkpen Hill & Coombe Gibbet

Berkshire

There is excellent downland walking along the ridge of the chalk from East Woodhay Down in the east to Inkpen Hill and beyond in the west. The views to the north, across the valley of the River Kennet to the Berkshire Downs and the Ridgeway are particularly spectacular on clear days. The long, north-facing chalk scarp contains many typical downland plants including several species of orchid. Butterflies such as gatekeepers, meadow browns, various species of blues and lovely little skippers abound.

Half way between Walbury Hill (at 974ft the highest point in Berkshire) and Inkpen Hill, on Gallows Down, is the famous

Coombe Gibbet, with a fine long barrow at its foot. The gibbet is a replacement of others which have stood here before, the original having been erected to display the disintegrating corpses of executed criminals.

Location: *7 miles SW of Newbury; 4¼ miles SE of Hungerford. Access by unclassified roads from A338, A4 and A343.*
Map: *page 306, SU36.*

Inverewe Gardens

Highland

Now over 120 years old, these world-famous gardens are highly recommended for a visit. To come upon such an oasis and, in season, such a riot of colour in this otherwise rather barren area is a surprise, until one realises that the garden succeeds because it enjoys the kindly climatic influence of the North Atlantic Drift in this part of Scotland – and because its founder wisely planted a shelter-belt of trees on the headland. It has a magnificent collection of plants from many

countries, such as eucalyptus, azaleas, Himalayan lilies and many African and South American species.

Open: *all year daily. Visitor centre Apr to mid Oct daily; pm only Sun. Admission charge. Refreshments. Suitable for disabled. Seasonal ranger service. NTS.*
Location: *5 miles NE of Gairloch off A832; ¾ mile NE of Poolewe.*
Map: *page 314, NG88.*

Inverpolly National Nature Reserve

Highland

This superb reserve covers nearly 27,000 acres of remote, rugged country in the old county of Wester Ross. It has a very wide range of habitats, with seashore, sea islets, inland lochs with birch-clad islands, burns, bogs, birch and hazel woodland, rolling moorland, scree slopes and three great sandstone summits, Cul Mor (2786ft), Cul Beag (2523ft) and Stac Pollaidh – 'Stac Polly' (2009ft). Loch Sionascaig is the largest water area within the reserve. Red and roe deer are common here and other mammals present include otters, pine martens, badgers, foxes and wild cats – most of which are, unfortunately, unlikely to be seen on a short visit. The rich bird life of the reserve includes buzzards, ravens and dippers, with eiders,

red breasted mergansers and black guillemots around the coastal parts.

At Knockan Cliff, on the east side of the A835, the limestone outcrop and its fertile splash of greenery present a sharp contrast to the drab, acidic peat country to the west, and on the cliff itself there is an assortment of lime-loving plants, including moss campion, globe flower, mountain avens and yellow mountain saxifrage. The cliff itself is of tremendous interest, and yielded evidence which enabled geologists to unravel some of the origins of mountain chains throughout the world.

Open: *all year. Information centre at Knockan Cliff open May to Sep, Mon to Fri. NCC.*
Location: *W of A835, 10 miles N of Ullapool. Information centre on A835, 12 miles N of Ullapool.*
Map: *page 314, NC11.*

Irchester Country Park

Northamptonshire

The hills and dales of this attractive park were formed by the quarrying of ironstone. Evidence of this industry can be seen in many places, but much of the park is now wooded. Trees here include Scots pine and larch. Both are conifers, but the latter is not an evergreen: it changes colour and sheds its needles in autumn. There is a variety of other trees, including alder and poplars, and in one place rooks use a group of ashes for the untidy stick nests of their rookery: spring is the best time to see them. Areas of scrub, with blackberry and wild rose, are excellent for flowers and butterflies. The easiest mammals to see in the park are rabbits and grey squirrels; the presence of the latter can be detected by the dropped pine cones, whittled away to their centres by the sharp teeth of these rodents. There are the usual woodland birds, especially in the deciduous trees; learning the calls and songs of these birds is perhaps the best way of locating them. A nature trail leads through the park's varied habitats.

Open: *all year. Picnic areas. Nature trail.*
Location: *1¾ miles SE of Wellingborough off B570 midway between A509 and Irchester.*
Map: *page 306, SP96.*

Grey Squirrel

Introduced from America in the 1870s, the grey squirrel quickly spread through southern Britain and Wales. It has always had a mixed press – being regarded as a pest by foresters and gamekeepers, but as an endearing character by most of the public. It lives mostly in broadleaved woodland, whereas the red squirrel prefers conifers.

Isle of Wight

Lying just off the south coast, the Isle of Wight is England's largest island. Despite its proximity to the mainland, and its popularity as a holiday resort, it has its own special character and much of it is unspoilt. The island scenery is very varied: there are cliffs and estuaries, rolling downlands, woods, marshes, secluded valleys and fast flowing streams in their ravines or 'chines'. Picturesque villages and historic buildings and parks add further variety.

The famous chalk stacks called the Needles, and the lighthouse at their western end

The Needles are undoubtedly the island's most famous feature. They are made of chalk, and the same rock stretches eastwards along the coast in a series of high cliffs. These cliffs are the haunt of seabirds such as gulls, guillemots and razorbills. Puffins may also be seen. From Compton Bay eastwards there is a dramatic change in scenery, with softer cliffs of marls, shales and sandstones, terminating in St Catherine's Point. Among the unusual plants to be found along this coast are white horehound, wild stock and subterranean trefoil, which takes its name from the fact that after flowering, the flower-heads droop to the ground and the pods become buried. The Glanville fritillary butterfly is one of the rare insect specialities of this coast.

On the island's northern and eastern coasts there are several estuaries and coastal marshes – the Yar Estuary and Brading Marshes, the Medina Estuary, Newtown Harbour, and in the west, the island's other Yar Estuary and Freshwater Marshes. Between them they have such features as shingle and flint splits, mud flats, lagoons, salt

marshes and reed beds. Many wading birds can be found in these places, especially in the winter, while reed and sedge warblers are summer visitors in the reed beds.

At King's Quay oak and hazel wood extends to the shore, and there is an understorey of bluebells and primroses. There are woodland walks in Parkhurst Forest, and at Fort Victoria Country Park.

A great ridge of chalk extends from the Needles across the centre of the island to Bembridge Down in the east, and these downlands contain a wide variety of chalk loving plants. Their extreme southern location and the influence of the sea sprays make the plant communities somewhat different from those on the mainland. Compton, Mottistone, Garstons and Bembridge downs are among the best for wild flowers.

A coastal path can be followed round the whole island, and the county council has also established eight long-distance paths (two of which are described in this feature) which explore the island's interior. As well as these, there are numerous nature trails.

What to See

BARTON MANOR GARDENS AND VINEYARD

Although Barton Manor itself can be traced back as far as the Domesday Book, its 20-acre gardens have evolved since 1846, when Queen Victoria bought the manor as part of her Osborne estate.

The vineyard is a much more recent addition, having been planted by the present owners in 1977. It covers five acres and is planted with several varieties of grapes, all especially well suited to England's unpredictable climate. The estate's modern, scientific winery uses the grapes to produce dry and medium dry wines, usually white. Apple wine is also made here. The wines can be sampled in the wine bar during licensing hours, and are on sale by the bottle in the gift shop.

The varied gardens are well worth exploring, and a network of paths leads to enchanting corners such as the water garden (once Queen Victoria's skating

rink) and the secret garden, specially laid out with many kinds of sweetly scented plants. There is a lake with black swans and other waterfowl; a cork and ilex plantation; and a woodland garden which is a mass of daffodils in spring.

Open: *May to Sep daily, also Sun in Apr. Admission charge (House not open). Refreshments. No dogs.*
Location: *off A3021 at Whippingham (next to Osborne House).*
Map: *page 306, SZ59.*

BEMBRIDGE & CULVER DOWNS

The most prominent feature in the east of the island, the downs rise 343 feet before dropping sheer to the sea at Culver Cliffs. Over these dizzy heights gulls and other seabirds hang on the wind, and on the narrow ledges they make their nests. On the downs, once grazed by sheep, several types of downland grasses mix with a wide variety of

chalk-loving plants. One of the earliest of summer migrants, the wheatear, is a visitor here from late March onwards, its white rump prominent as it flits low across the ground.

Close to the downs is Bembridge Windmill, the last windmill remaining on the island. Built in 1700 of local stone, it was one of the last tower mills whose cap, the top section of sails and their gearing, was turned by means of a chain wheel. By the 1950s the mill was derelict, but it has since been restored to full

Green winged orchid. This little orchid flowers on open ground between April and June

working order, and much of the original 18th-century machinery survives.

Open: *downland all year; windmill Apr to Sep. Admission charge to mill. Shop. NT.*
Location: *windmill ½ mile S of Bembridge.*
Map: *page 306, SZ68.*

Bembridge Windmill is the Isle of Wight's only remaining windmill

BEMBRIDGE TRAIL

Quite early on in this 15-mile walk, which begins at the Royal Spithead Hotel, Bembridge, the path passes Bembridge Windmill. Along the edge of Brading Marshes look out for ducks – particularly in winter, and waders and warblers in the summer months. The views from Brading Down are among the finest on the island, although some might prefer the panorama to both the north and south from St George's Down. History enthusiasts will wish to visit the Iron Age settlement at Knighton – once a much bigger village than today. For much of the walk the plants are typical of downland, but between Kern and Knighton the moist conditions encourage the growth of a variety of ferns, including harts-tongue and buckler.

Location: between Bembridge Point and Shide, Newport.
Map: page 306, SZ68.

CALBOURNE WATER MILL AND MUSEUM OF RURAL LIFE

From before the time of Domesday Book until its closure as a working mill in 1955, the mill at Calbourne ground flour. Through most of its thousand or so years of its operation the craft of milling changed very little – it was basically a case of crushing grain into flour between heavy millstones.

Sophistication arose through the way in which power – in this case derived from water – was captured and utilized to move the stones. To this end complex and efficient machinery was evolved which needed to be housed in a sturdy building. Great change came in the 19th century with the development of 'roller mills'. These produced flour that was very much finer and whiter than the old stoneground type. At Calbourne both types can be seen almost side by side. All stages in the production of flour can be seen at the mill, as can all the machinery, including the splendid iron water wheel that was installed in 1881. Many other fascinating pieces of equipment can be seen in the mill itself, while a recently completed museum of rural life contains a wealth of interesting bygones.

Open: Easter to Oct daily. Admission charge. Picnic area. Refreshments. Shop.
Location: at Calbourne.
Map: page 306, SZ48.

FORT VICTORIA COUNTRY PARK

Centred around one of three forts built in the 19th century to defend the waters of the Solent, this country park consists largely of woodland on slopes leading down to the water. A nature trail has been laid out through the park, and makes its way through woodland, an area rich in species of fern, areas where damp-loving trees and plants thrive, and along the Solent shore.

Location: Off A3054, between Yarmouth and Totland.
Map: page 306, SZ38.

NEWTOWN

A nature walk has been laid out at Newtown, and there are various other footpaths which the visitor to this large National Trust property can explore. The full three-mile walk may be shortened by omitting the woodland section.

It is the saltings here which make Newtown so interesting, and the effectiveness of plants in stabilising mud to allow the marsh level to build up is well demonstrated here. The prime coloniser is the useful marsh samphire, which, in addition to its value in 'binding' mud, can be pickled or cooked like asparagus, and was also used for centuries in the production of glass. Another plant used in glass making, the saltwater-loving annual seablite, flourishes here as does sea purslane, which so often grows along the edges of salt-marsh creeks.

Over 170 species of bird have been seen at Newtown and the area attracts large concentrations of waders in winter. Inland, in summer, most of the common warblers and the resident birds of mixed woodland breed here. Inland too the butterfly population is large and varied – with speckled wood, white admiral, orange-tip, purple hairstreak and tortoiseshell – names as colourful as their owners.

Location: midway between Newport and Yarmouth, 1 mile N of A3054. Part NT.
Map: page 306, SZ49.

SHANKLIN CHINE

Most famous of the island's chines, or deep, narrow ravines, Shanklin has seen many changes since it was 'discovered' in Victorian times. However, it is still a good place to see many of the plants and animals which live in such habitats, and a short nature trail passes the most interesting features. Of special interest in the chine is the great variety of non-flowering plants that can be found. For example 25 species of mosses have been recorded here, some very rare, and there are also liverworts, ferns and lichens.

Location: on S side of Shanklin.
Map: page 306, SZ58.

TENNYSON TRAIL

Covering about 15 miles from Alum Bay to Carisbrooke, this trail gives a fine impression of the island and its flora and fauna. It is sometimes known as the 'island's roof' route.

From Alum Bay there is a climb to the Tennyson Monument (NT), but the views, first of the Needles and then, from the monument, of both the Solent and the English Channel, justify the exertion involved. Fortunate visitors may find several species of orchid – bee orchid and lady's tresses among them – as well as common downland plants. The whole of the area between Alum Bay and Tennyson Down, where the poet remarked that 'the air was worth sixpence a pint' is a bird sanctuary. Summer is a particular delight here with many seabirds including fulmar and puffin nesting on the cliffs.

Beyond Freshwater Bay the trail climbs on to East Afton Down. Along this section the violet blooms of the clustered bellflower are common. The grayling butterfly found here is worth studying. Always a complex species, with many sub-species and colour variations, specimens found along the Tennyson Trail tend to be lighter than those on another trail, the Hamstead, which heads north from Brook Down.

Brighstone Down (NT) rises to 701 feet and can provide quite spectacular views over the whole island. The trail joins a Forestry Commission nature walk in Brighstone Forest, and on rare occasions it is possible to see red squirrels here. The final part of the journey to Carisbrooke is through a mixed landscape of farm fields and copses.

Location: Nodgham Lane, Carisbrooke, to Alum Bay. Part NT.
Map: page 306, SZ38.

YAFFORD MILL

This lovely old 18th-century watermill was operated until 1970. In recent years it has been restored to full working order, and its interior contains much of the original milling machinery as well as tools and equipment related to the milling trade and way of life. Agricultural bygones are displayed here and in special display sheds.

Outside, rare breeds of sheep, cattle and pigs live alongside a waterfowl collection and a number of grey seals. A nature trail leads beside the mill stream.

Open: Easter to Oct. Admission charge. Refreshments. Shop. No dogs.
Location: off B3399, between Brighstone and Shorwell.
Map: page 306, SZ48.

The interior of Yafford watermill, showing the restored milling machinery

Isles of Scilly

Sometimes known as the Fortunate Isles, the Scillies are a group of over 100 islands and islets some 28 miles west of Land's End. They are a continuation of the granite spine of Cornwall, and consist for the most part of many reefs and rocky outcrops which have been worn down by the action of the ocean.

The islands are low-lying and windswept, being the first landfall of the prevailing westerly winds and acting as a breakwater against the force of the Atlantic. The warm gulf stream currents ensure a mild climate and frosts are rare. The shallow seas around the Scillies are rich in marine life and the clear waters are superb for skin-diving and underwater study. Most of the islands are owned by the Duchy of Cornwall and parts are designated as National Nature Reserves managed by the Nature Conservancy Council. Five of the larger islands – St Mary's, Tresco, St Martin's, St Agnes and Bryher – are inhabited. St Mary's is the biggest. It has the group's main port, and boasts 14 miles of roads.

The major industry in the islands, apart from tourism, is the cultivation of early spring flowers and potatoes. To provide shelter from the Atlantic winds the tiny fields are sheltered by high hedges planted as windbreaks. Shrubs used for this purpose include tamarisk, pittosporum, escallonia and fuchsia, tender plants fairly uncommon on the mainland. In early spring the fields of daffodils make a very fine sight.

Tresco is famous for its Abbey Gardens. Here sub-tropical plants have been gathered from all over the world. But exotic plants are not confined to grand gardens in the Scillies; they burst out of cottage gardens and spill over cliffs, dunes and fields. Among the more spectacular are echiums – incredibly tall members of the borage family – and mesembryanthemums, great drifts of which cloak many shores and cliffs. Many flowers originally grown as crops now grow wild, so that agapanthus, arum lilies and gladioli are likely to be encountered anywhere. Truly wild flowers are also to be found in abundance – there are heath, down, marsh, meadow and coastal habitats, and even a few woodlands, though these are uncommon.

Breeding seabirds are of particular interest in spring, and although the main breeding colonies on the uninhabited island of Annet cannot be visited, there are regular boat trips which provide good views of birds. Puffins, razorbills, guillemots, shags, cormorants, kittiwakes and other gulls are among the most likely to be seen. Such trips

John Muir Country Park

Lothian

Situated on a beautiful stretch of coastline, this country park extends south-eastwards from the Peffer Burn across Ravensheugh Sands, Tyne Sands and the broad expanse of Belhaven Bay into the pleasant small resort of Dunbar, to include the castle remains.

Dunbar was the birthplace, in 1838, of John Muir, a pioneer of conservation, after whom the country park is named. It was largely as a result of his writings that America's first National Park, Yosemite, was established in 1890. His house in the High Street has been restored and is open to the public.

For those wishing to stroll awhile the park has marked walking routes; perhaps the most interesting of these is the self-guided nature trail laid out along the cliffs. From here are magnificent views of the Isle of May, the Bass Rock and the ranges of hills away to the south.

The park's wide variety of wildlife reflects the richness and diversity of its habitats, which include cliff, dunes, saltmarsh, woodlands, scrub and grassland. Along the shore, rockpools contain starfish, shore crabs and bright red anemones and there is also a wide variety of shells to be found. Twelve species of butterfly have been recorded and the common blue and meadow brown can be seen in July and August. Among some of the plants commonly found here are thrift on the saltmarsh, marram grass and bird's-foot trefoil on the dunes and sea campion by the cliffs.

Open: *park at all times. John Muir House daily, July and Aug only. East Lothian District Council.*
Location: *lies on W side of Dunbar and stretches NW along the coast. Access to the two main car parks, situated on Belhaven Bay, is off A1087 on W outskirts of Dunbar or from car park close to castle and harbour in Dunbar.*
Map: *page 313, NT67/68.*

Coastline and sea at John Muir Country Park, on Belhaven Bay

The tail and hindquarters of the brown rat

Kelburn Country Centre

Strathclyde

Kelburn Castle, the historic seat of the earls of Glasgow, overlooks the country centre from private grounds, but the spectacular glen of the Kel Burn is accessible and is served by several walks, the longest of which lead up to open moorland. The view across the Firth of Clyde from the top is absolutely magnificent. The burn itself drops 700 feet in half a mile, via waterfalls and steep gorges, through a mixture of wild and cultivated areas. Kelburn has a notable series of gardens, famed for rhododendrons and azaleas and full of interesting and exotic plants and shrubs from around the world. It is also famous for its trees, which include yews which are at least usually also encounter basking seals, seemingly not bothered by the boatloads of staring faces. Evening trips provide the chance to see Manx shearwaters, long-winged seabirds which only come to their nesting burrows at night, but rest on the sea in hundreds just before dusk. Not many species of perching birds are represented on the Scillies, but the commonest – blackbirds, thrushes, sparrows and robins – are remarkably tame and some will even feed from the hand.

The islands have a deserved reputation as the place to see rare birds, most of them passage migrants, and in spring and autumn bird watchers flock to the Scillies because of the regular discovery of unusual birds, especially from

St Agnes, Isles of Scilly

North America. Not all of them have such odd names as the yellow-bellied sapsucker found on one occasion.

There are two excellent nature trails on St Mary's, one across freshwater marshland with open water, and the other alongside a little stream through woodland of elm – a sight now rare in Britain.

Location: *the islands can be reached by the regular sailings of m.v.* Scillonian *from Penzance, or by helicopter from Penzance Heliport. By 'plane from Plymouth, Exeter and Newquay in summer. Travel between the islands is by regular inter-island launches from St Mary's. Part NCC.*
Open: *Tresco Abbey Gardens: all year.*
Map: *page 304, SV91.*

1000 years old, an extraordinary weeping larch (which has to be seen to be believed), the oldest and tallest Monterey pine in Scotland and a dozen huge Californian redwoods – still young at about 130 years of age! Other attractions include an imaginative centre, based on a complex of farm buildings; a pet's corner and a children's playground. Of interest also are the museum and the audio–visual programmes on the area and its wildlife.

Open: *Easter to Sep daily; winter Sun pm only. Admission charge. Picnic areas. Refreshments. Shop.*
Location: *2 miles SE of Largs. Entrance off A78 Largs to Fairlie road.*
Map: *page 312, NS25.*

Kenfig Pool and Dunes

Mid Glamorgan

Kenfig Pool, a freshwater lake amid a huge expanse of sand dunes, is the focal point of a 1200-acre Local Nature Reserve run by the Mid Glamorgan County Council. It is a winter refuge for Bewick and whooper swans, pochard, teal, goldeneye and other wildfowl. Summer residents include mute swans, coots, moorhens, tufted ducks, and great crested grebes. Away

from the reed-fringed lake, dunes provide nesting places for such birds as the meadow pipit, stonechat and skylark.

On the northern edge of the reserve, sands beside the Afon Cynffig conceal the old town of Kenfig. It was a flourishing port in the 12th century, but was later buried by storms which swept vast amounts of sand eastwards from Swansea Bay. A 16th-century visitor described ruins 'almost choked and devoured with the sands that the Severn Sea there casteth up'. Although abandoned, the town retained borough status until 1883.

Open: *all year. Information centre (weekends only). LNR.*
Location: *3 miles N of Porthcawl, on unclassified road off B4283.*
Map: *page 305, SS78.*

Kennet Valley

Berkshire

The Kennet Valley – particularly east and west of Newbury – is full of interesting features.

At Chilton Foliat (on the B4192) many species of bird can be seen from the bridge; one of the most regular residents is the little grebe and one of the most interesting is the gadwall – a duck which looks rather like a mallard; one distinctive feature is the orange line along the bill. Teal, tufted duck, pochard, mallard and occasionally shoveler and wigeon, together with riverine species such as grey wagtail, reed bunting and sedge warbler can also be seen.

Freeman's Marsh at Hungerford is a mixture of fields and

Canal locks in the Kennet valley

unspoilt water meadows dominated by sedges and rushes, yellow flag, marsh orchids, water forget-me-nots, brooklime and ragged robin. Birds which might be seen include redshank, snipe, grey wagtails, kingfishers, teal, tufted duck and little grebes.

Between Kintbury and Newbury are wonderful wetland habitats – unfortunately access to the estates is limited, but there is good canal-side walking giving excellent views. Bitterns have been heard and the configuration of woods and fields makes them good for sparrowhawks. In autumn through to spring several of the fields contain flocks of lapwings and golden plovers, with large parties of fieldfares and redwings in winter.

East of Newbury are the extensive riverine reed beds of Thatcham Moor. These are a good habitat for grasshopper, reed, sedge, and willow warblers, and in some years parties of bearded tits. Many old gravel pits can be found from Thatcham to Theale and these harbour waterfowl and are particularly good for ducks, kingfishers, sand martins and wagtails.

Access: *on public footpaths.*
Location: *east and west of Newbury from A4.*
Map: *page 306, SU36/46.*

Brown Rat

Found throughout Britain, but usually not far from man and his crops and buildings, the brown rat is a successful, and very unpopular, opportunist. Brown rats arrived on ships from central Asia in the 18th century, rapidly displacing the black rat (itself an immigrant).

Keyhaven, Pennington & Hurst

Hampshire

Much of the North Solent shore is still relatively unspoilt and contains extensive tracts of wild marsh, as well as salterns, mud flats and creeks. From Milford-on-Sea a vast shingle spit runs south-east into the Solent and terminates at impressive Hurst Castle, a fort built by Henry VIII. Good views over the marshes and the Solent can be obtained from the top of the spit.

The North Solent marshes are best known for their bird life and, in winter, good numbers of dark-bellied brent geese can be seen all along this coast. Other wildfowl include mallard, wigeon, teal and shelduck. Along the shingle banks turnstones are the most widespread of the wading birds, but several other species are more numerous. Oystercatchers, lapwings, dunlins, black-tailed godwits, ringed plovers and redshanks, with smaller numbers of spotted redshanks and greenshanks, are regularly seen, particularly from autumn to spring. Curlews, grey plovers, snipe and ruff are also to be found. Predatory birds are at-

tracted to this large potential food source. Most are to be found in the winter months; merlins, hen harriers and sparrowhawks are all regulars, and occasionally the rare marsh harrier may be seen in the spring or autumn. Out to sea, cormorants, shags, scoters, red-breasted mergansers, great crested and red-necked grebes, kittiwakes and the occasional fulmar can be seen, particularly outside the breeding season. The shingle spits provide nesting sites for colonies of terns and gulls. Although these are protected areas, there are still impressive sights to be seen as the birds hunt for food

along the shore and shallow coastal waters. Little, Sandwich and common terns all breed in colonies, and the black-headed gull colonies, particularly at nearby Beaulieu, are some of the largest in the country.

Open: *all year, but keep away from sanctuary areas in breeding season. CNT.*
Location: *from B3058 at Milford-on-Sea lanes lead down to the shore and Hurst beach; also lanes from A337 at Lymington and Pennington.* **Map:** *page 306, SZ39.*

Keyhaven, with the marshes beyond

Killiecrankie

Tayside

At Killiecrankie the River Garry makes its way through a dramatic gorge, and this forms the focus for a large Royal Society for the Protection of Birds reserve and an extensive National Trust for Scotland property. The densely wooded gorge is cloaked in sessile oakwoods which also contain such trees as birch, ash and wych elm. This marvellous habitat is rich in birdlife; buzzards, kestrels, sparrowhawks, woodpeckers and crossbills can be seen all year, while summer

visitors include wood warblers, garden warblers and redstarts. Above the oakwoods, which give way to birchwoods, are heather moorlands. Living on the moorland edge are black grouse, the male of which is more commonly known as blackcock. These handsome birds, much larger than a red grouse, have lyre-shaped tails, under which is a white rump. This is displayed at the famous 'leks', where males gather at dawn and dusk to court females.

The flora of the reserve is as rich as its birdlife, and among the plants found are grass of Parnassus, which favours boggy

ground, and has five white petals, and globe flower, a member of the buttercup family with very large yellow flowers.

Open: *NTS visitor centre Apr to Oct daily. Admission charge. Walks. Ranger/naturalist service. RSPB reserve open for escorted walks on woodland and moorland paths Apr to Aug by prior arrangement with warden. Admission charge for RSPB non-members. No dogs. NTS. RSPB.*
Location: *3 miles NW of Pitlochry on A9. RSPB reserve ½ mile W of Killiecrankie on unclassified road.*
Map: *page 315, NN96.*

Kincraig: Highland Wildlife Park

Highland

All the animals to be seen here are either living in the Highlands today, or did so at some point in the past. It is an exciting collection, made all the more pleasurable by the fact that all the creatures are kept in surroundings that are as like their natural habitats as is possible. A drive-through section of the park enables visitors to see such animals as red deer, Highland cattle, wild

Wild cats, pine martens, badgers, foxes and golden eagles are all present-day Highland residents, but they are usually elusive, and the park gives the opportunity to see them at close quarters. The park is also home to such animals as rabbits, stoats, hedgehogs and many species of bird which are entirely wild and live in the park because it suits them to do so.

Open: daily Mar to Nov. Admission charge. Picnic area. Refreshments. Shop. No dogs (but free kennels at entrance).
Location: 4 miles NE of Kingussie. Entrance off B9152 between Kingussie and Aviemore.
Map: page 315, NH80.

Kingley Vale

West Sussex

Whether the yews at Kingley Vale were planted to celebrate the victory of Saxons from Chichester over marauding Danes in AD 859 or whether they are the descendants of sacred trees planted even earlier by the Druids is the stuff of legend. Today the Vale contains the largest yew forest in Europe and because it is now a National Nature Reserve there is every opportunity for it to continue as one of the few remaining examples of a once common habitat.

Until the reign of Queen Elizabeth I, yew was a tree protected by law because it provided the English infantryman's basic weapon – the longbow. In addition yew wood was made into furniture, drinking vessels, floor blocks, skewers and the working parts of machines, such as cogs for mills and axles.

In its management of this nature reserve the Nature Conservancy Council is anxious to ensure that the yew forest is rejuvenated. In winter huge flocks of redwings and fieldfares gorge on the bright red berries of the female trees and thus spread the seeds. However, the young seedlings are very vulnerable and many that survive do so because they grow protected beneath the prickly branches of juniper bushes. Management, therefore, must include maintenance of a healthy juniper population.

Other habitats of interest here are mixed woodland, chalk grassland and chalk heathland – all habitats that are disappearing at an alarming rate. Each must be managed to prevent its degeneration. For example, grazing animals must be introduced to prevent scrub plants such as bramble taking over all the available space and shading out the interesting and increasingly precious community of small herbs and grasses. It is here that several species of orchid grow: late June and July are the times to see the best displays of these.

Open: all year. Nature trail. Field museum (weekends only). NCC.
Location: at West Stoke, 3 miles NW of Chichester on unclassified road, off B2178. Car park at W end of West Stoke and then footpath of approximately 1 mile.
Map: page 306, SU81.

Kingsbury Water Park

Warwickshire

Worked-out gravel pits often provide a marvellous opportunity to create much-needed lakes in areas where few occur naturally. This idea has been developed admirably at Kingsbury, where a series of pits has been turned into a really exciting park with a wide range of facilities.

Visitors can sail, canoe, windsurf, fish, camp, climb, jog, walk, keep fit or ride. Or they can simply enjoy the view. But one of the best things about Kingsbury is the wide variety of birds and other wildlife that can be seen here.

The pools, streams, marshes, woods and the river provide homes for all sorts of plants, insects, birds and other animals. Each season has something different to offer. In summer as many as nine different kinds of warbler breed here, together with ducks, grebes and kingfishers. Coastal birds such as oystercatchers, shelducks, ringed plovers and – most unusual of all – a colony of common terns may also be seen. These are easily identified by their black and red bills, black caps and long forked tails.

In winter large numbers of ducks come here to rest and feed and many unusual species have been recorded. This is a good place to see pochard, a resident duck whose numbers are swelled considerably by winter immigrants from northern Europe and Siberia.

Open: all year. Admission charge. Information centre.
Location: 5 miles S of Tamworth, 1 mile W of Kingsbury on unclassified road, off A4097 at Bodymoor Heath.
Map: page 309, SP29.

horses, and bison (which became extinct in the Highlands thousands of years ago, but were still found truly wild in other parts of Europe until 1925. Today, all European bison are descended from animals kept in zoos). Other animals which once lived in the Highlands are brown bears, wolves and the lynx. All these, and many others, can be seen in the park's walk-through area. The white-tailed eagle may soon be on the list of birds living in the Highlands today, since it is the subject of a reintroduction programme in the Western Isles.

Golden eagle at Kincraig

Kingswear

Devon

One of the National Trust's more recent acquisitions, this 3½-mile strip of South Devon coast with a large acreage of wood and farmland behind, has remained surprisingly unspoilt.

A path from the northern car park near Woodhuish Farm leads to Man Sands, a charming bay between cliffs of unstable Staddon grit. Scabbacombe Sands, reached from the next car park, has, unusually for this area, a waterfall. Just south is Scabbacombe Point, with breeding colonies of kittiwake, fulmar and guillemot. As elsewhere on the coast, visitors are asked to take particular care to avoid disturbance in the breeding season between March and June.

Ivy Cove is reached from the Coleton Fishacre car park, and the route crosses the South Devon Coast Path (see page 261) which may be followed southwest to the old gun battery at Inner Froward Point. Along the path are good views of the wooded slopes of Coleton Fishacre valley, while further on is the Mew Stone, an offshore island with gulls, cormorants and shags, watched by basking grey seals at low tide. Near the battery are clumps of hardy Monterey, Corsican and maritime pine. This latter part of the walk may also be reached from the car park at Higher Brownstone Farm.

Location: *between Kingswear and Brixham, E of B3205. NT.*
Map: *page 305, SX94/95.*

Kingussie: Highland Folk Museum

Highland

There can be few better ways of recapturing something of the old Highland way of life than visiting this excellent and varied museum, originally set up on Iona but now permanently established at Kingussie in the Spey valley. The reception building introduces the museum and includes notable collections of Highland costume (working as well as formal attire) and musical instruments. A short walk leads to a reconstruction of a Lewis black house, with its low, thick, drystone walls, central peat-fire hearth (with no chimney), byre for the cattle – which shared the house with the crofters in winter – and 'best room'. Nearby there is another relic from Lewis – the Clack Mill, which was water-driven, requiring a good flow to make it work well. Many forget that the Vikings dominated the Western Isles until the 13th century: this mill is of Norse design and was brought to Scotland during the period of Norse influence in the islands. Next comes the farming museum, where not only tools are shown but the whole system of crofting, with crops and animals, and peat as fuel, is carefully explained. The circuit is completed at MacRobert House, with its fine displays of textile technology and craft and a superb collection of furniture. There are varied outside exhibits and periodic special exhibitions.

Open: *Apr to Oct daily, but pm only Sun; Nov to Mar Mon to Fri only. Admission charge. Picnic area. Shop. Suitable for disabled visitors.*
Location: *Duke St, Kingussie.*
Map: *page 314, NH70.*

Kintail & Morvich

Highland

This superb mountain area lies at the western end of Glen Shiel. The scenery is spectacular and takes in the Five Sisters of Kintail, four of which are over 3000ft, with Beinn Fhada (Ben Attow) at 3385ft. Some 12,800 acres here are owned by the National Trust for Scotland. Glen Shiel is a good place to drive slowly, with stops every so often, to look for golden eagles over the tops; other birds include peregrine falcons, ravens, red grouse, ptarmigan, common sandpipers and dippers, with eiders, red-breasted mergansers and black guillemots on Loch Alsh at the far western end of Loch Duich. Red deer are numerous and there are herds of wild goats; Ratagan Forest, above Loch Duich's south-western end, is a good place for the rare and elusive pine marten, especially around the litter bins in the car park at dawn and dusk. This spot also presents a breathtaking view across to the Five Sisters.

At Morvich is a National Trust for Scotland visitor centre, where full details on the area can be obtained.

Open: *NTS countryside centre (Morvich Farm) June to Sep.*
Location: *14 miles SE of Kyle of Lochalsh, N of A87. Morvich is 2 miles NE of Shiel Bridge on unclassified road off A87. Part NTS.*
Map: *page 314, NG91/92.*

Kintail and Morvich, showing the mountains around Loch Duich

Kinwarton Dovecote

Warwickshire

'Dovecote' is a misnomer, because doves do not return to roost in the same place each night. This is the habit of pigeons, which led the Romans to develop the idea of special buildings for pigeons to sleep and nest in. Kinwarton is an example of the practical form which the pigeon house could take – circular, with walls almost four feet thick, it contains over 500 nest holes. The tiled roof has dormer windows and is topped by a lantern. Inside, the *potence* has survived. This ingenious contraption consists of a central pivoted upright beam with horizontal beams leading to and supporting a sloping ladder set close to the wall. The ladder can move around the wall, allowing access to all the nests.

Open: *all year daily. Admission charge. NT.*
Location: *1½ miles NE of Alcester, just S of B4089.*
Map: *page 309, SP15.*

Kinwarton's dovecote may date from the 14th century; it is certainly one of the oldest of its kind in the country

Kinver Edge

Staffordshire

Rising steeply above the valley of Kinver, this sandstone escarpment has fulfilled various functions for man from Iron Age hill-fort to 20th-century dwelling place. Although the earthworks of the hill-fort are still visible, the most spectacular reminders of man's occupancy of the soft sandstone are the cave dwellings at Holy Austin's Rock, inhabited until the 1950s. Empty shells now, some of them had brick fronts and tiled gables in the 19th century.

The acid soil which is typical of sandstone localities means that plant life is limited, but on Kinver may be seen the whole range of heath, scrub and woodland development. Lizards live on the heath and adders are quite numerous on the Edge. Usually seen basking on the sandy soil, they rarely attack man, preferring swift retreat.

Location: *W of Kinver village 4 miles N of Kidderminster and 1½ miles W of A449. NT.*
Map: *page 309, SO88.*

Knole

Kent

For the visitor who leaves the often crowded streets of Sevenoaks, and steps into the 1000 acre deer park at Knole, there is a complete contrast of worlds. Although the area enclosed by Archbishop Bourchier in 1456 was considerably smaller than the present acreage, those who have added to it, including King Henry VIII, have not materially changed its character. Here a clump of trees has been planted to enhance a viewpoint – there an avenue of oaks leads the eye towards the great house which, by sheer size, dominates the landscape. But the walker moving through the park is travelling in a world barely altered by the passage of centuries.

Moving freely about the park and up to the walls of the house, is the large herd of fallow deer. Remaining close to the wooded area are the sika deer, a more modern addition to the park. Although colours of deer in enclosed herds can be very variable, the fallow generally has more white than the sika, is a little larger, and has palm-shaped as opposed to branched antlers.

Open: *park daily (free to pedestrians; charge for motorists). (House Apr to Oct Wed to Sat and bank holiday Mon, also Sun, but pm only. Garden open May to Sep, first Wed in month only. Admission charge.) NT.*
Location: *at S end of Sevenoaks, just E of A225.*
Map: *page 306, TQ55.*

MIDSUMMER BONFIRE

Whalton, Northumberland

Many believe that this old and unique custom has survived from the days of pagan worship. It is also known as 'The Midsummer Eve Baal Fire' which links it with Baal, an ancient god of fertility. For hundreds of years the fire has burned on the same spot in the main village street – only heavy rain halts the custom. Accordion music accompanies the fire, encouraging couples to make-merry and dance in the street. Traditionally, children are given coppers and sweets during the evening and a tray of drinks is brought out from the 'Beresford Arms' Inn to toast 'The Whalton Baal's'.

When: *4 July (Old Midsummer Eve).*
Map: *page 313, NZ18.*

PADLEY PILGRIMAGE

Grindleford, Derbyshire

The origins of Padley Pilgrimage lie in the religious struggles of the 16th century when priests ordained abroad were punishable by death. Such a penalty was also inflicted upon any who harboured or assisted them. During this period Padley Hall, a manor house owned by the Fitz Herbert family, became a Catholic stronghold and was frequently raided by zealots seeking Catholic priests. A raid in 1588 found two priests hiding in the chapel fireplace who, together with the tenants, were brought to trial. The priests were condemned to be hanged, drawn and quartered, and today the restored chapel at Padley Hall is a memorial to them. Every year pilgrims meet at Grindleford Station and walk through the woods to the now derelict hall. An open-air service is conducted behind the chapel in remembrance of the martyrs.

When: *Sun nearest 12 July.*
Map: *page 310, SK27.*

RUSH-BEARING

Ambleside, Cumbria

This custom appears to be medieval in origin, although its first occurrence in Ambleside is unknown. During the Middle Ages churches were built with hardened earth floors which had rushes strewn upon

them to alleviate damp and to make them more pleasant to walk on. The rushes were replaced every year amid great celebrations and most of the day's traditions have survived despite the modern floor, without rushes, in St Mary's Parish Church. A procession, led by the town band, commences at 2.30pm when adults and children carry rushes and 'bearings'. These are special frames adorned with flowers and rushes in variety of shapes including crosses and the Harp of David. The participants proceed through the town, pausing only at the Market Place, where the Rush-bearers' Hymn is sung. After this they enter the church for the Rush-bearing service and deposit their rushes and 'bearings' for the Sunday services. As the children leave the church each one is given a piece of gingerbread. The event concludes on Monday afternoon with a tea and children's races.

When: *first Sat in July.*
Map: *page 313, NY30.*

BLACK CHERRY FAIR

Chertsey, Surrey

This custom is thought to date from the Middle Ages, when Chertsey was granted a Charter to hold local fairs. The name 'Black Cherry Fair' was revived several years ago by the local Chamber of Commerce and probably derives from the fruit trees that once grew in the abbey grounds.

It is officially opened by a procession of floats through the town, and the crowning of the Black Cherry Princess. The fair takes place in the abbey fields recreation ground and consists of local craft stalls, fancy dress parades and various displays.

When: *second Sat in July.*
Map: *page 306, TQ06.*

A print of 1835 showing the rush-bearing ceremony at Ambleside. The proceedings are very much the same today

KILBURN FEAST

Kilburn, North Yorkshire

Nobody really knows how this custom originated, although it is thought to be connected with the fertility rites of a pagan festival. It has since become Christianised and lasts for a period of four days. The feast commences on Saturday afternoon with sports events including children's races open to both residents and strangers, and a mini-Marathon of approximately 4½ miles. There is a dance in the evening and on Sunday afternoon an open-air service takes place in the village square. The main feature of Monday is a game of quoits, while Tuesday is another sports day incorporating races for local children. During the evening the Lord Mayor rides through the village in a handcart fining people for whatever he wishes. He is ac-companied by the 'Lady Mayoress' – actually a man dressed as a woman – who kisses as many women as possible. After this the feast is brought to a conclusion in the pub.

When: *second week in July.*
Map: *page 310, SE57.*

SWAN UPPING ON THE THAMES

Today there are only two non-royal swan-owners on the Thames, the Dyers and Vintners companies, who were both granted swan marks in the late 15th century. Swan marking, or 'upping' as it is known, takes place on various stretches of the Thames between Surrey and Berkshire and lasts for several days. It is carried out by the Royal Swanherd for the Crown and the Swan Wardens of the Dyers and Vintners with their assistants. They travel in six boats with flags from the three bodies on display and catch and examine about 600 swans. The cygnets are also marked by them to show the owning company – one nick in the beak for Dyers and two nicks for Vintners. All unmarked swans are the property of the Crown.

When: *third full week in July.*
Map: *page 306.*

BLESSING OF THE WATERS

Reeves Beach, Whitstable, Kent

It is not known when this custom first began, although it has connections with the past observance of St James's Day – a saint highly respected by the local fishermen. A religious service, sponsored by the Association of the Men of Kent and Kentish Men, is held on the foreshore amid numerous visitors. There is also a gathering of boats whose crews include fishermen and sea scouts.

When: *25 July.*
Map: *page 306, TR16.*

EBERNOE HORN FAIR

Ebernoe, West Sussex

Many believe that this fair, held on St James's Day, has existed for several centuries. It is organised by the Ebernoe Cricket Club, which receives all proceeds from the day's events. However, this money is beneficially used as it permits any person to watch cricket free of charge for the rest of the year. Proceedings begin with the roasting of a sheep donated by Lord Egremont. A cricket match takes place at 11am between Ebernoe and a local village nominated during the previous year. This stops at 1pm when all the cricketers partake in a hot mutton lunch. Play is then resumed and at 6pm the highest scorer on the winning side is presented with the head and horns of the sheep by Lord Egremont. During the afternoon two more sheep are roasted.

When: *25 July.*
Map: *page 306, SU92.*

Swan upping at Marlow. Queen Elizabeth I granted the Dyers' and Vintners' companies the right to mark swans

The Lake District National Park

The largest of our National Parks, the most spectacular, and one of the most accessible because of its proximity to the M6 motorway, the Lake District is a fascinating mixture of water and mountain scenery.

The seasons play their part, bringing an extra dimension of colour to the land. The green of the summer oak woods changes to the brilliant reds and russets of autumn, while at the same time the bracken-covered lower slopes of the mountains become a rich brown, contrasting with the early snows on the high tops. The lakes and tarns provide a perfect series of mirrors to reflect this exciting landscape.

The Lake District – a sublime mixture of mountains, lakes, wild uplands and gentle pastures

It is the Lake District mountains which are most dramatically reflected in the waters of the lakes, and one of them is Scafell Pike. At 3210ft it is England's highest peak, and since it is also

Wast Water and its scree slopes

an easy walk on a fine day, it is one of the most popular peaks. It should be remembered that more often than not the weather is not fine on the tops and the unwary can be caught on the mountains. Using common sense and checking the weather forecast before leaving brings its own reward, with some of the finest hill walking in Britain. The best route to the top of Scafell Pike, certainly for spectacle, is from the Seatoller to Styhead Pass and then by track on the west side of the Pike.

It is the accessibility of even the highest fells which makes the Lakes such a good place for the walker and this is perhaps best

illustrated by Helvellyn. Easily the most popular of the mountains, a walk to its highest point can be as challenging as you want to make it because of the choice of paths available. Helvellyn is in fact at the centre of a fell range between Thirlmere and Ullswater. It contains much of what is typical Lakeland scenery. The very steep western slopes give way to the craggier and more bare eastern side, and outstanding features are the high glacial corries, or combes. One of these, which holds Red Tarn, is astonishingly situated between two narrow ridges of the mountain. The northern one is Swirral Edge, but the better known of the two, and the one which adds something special to this approach to the mountain, is Striding Edge. This very narrow ridge can be dangerous in certain weather conditions, particularly ice or high winds, but is the most popular route to the top of the mountain.

Climbing the two high fells of Helvellyn and Scafell Pike will certainly vividly illustrate the rugged character of the Lake District mountains, but the special quality of this place is that there are plenty of lower fells accessible from the main centres like Windermere and Keswick without any problem. Leave the car behind and use the Mountain Goat bus service to get to the main passes like Honister, Hard Knott, Wrynose and Kirkstone and then walk the fells, or simply stick to the valley bottoms, follow the lake shores and appreciate the scenery as it unfolds.

Wildlife

The oak woods of the Lake District, covering the lower slopes of the mountains, and in many places coming right down to the shoreline of the lakes, have a special atmosphere of their own, and are the richest wildlife habitats in the Park, even though overgrazing by sheep is preventing regeneration in many of them. Redstarts are the typical small songbirds of these woodlands, and the male is one of the most beautiful of all the birds occurring in Britain. Summer migrants, redstarts spend the winter in Africa before journeying north in the spring, and can be found in the Lake District oak woods from April through to September. The favourite small mammal of the woodlands is the red squirrel. Grey squirrels do not occur in the Park and this in itself is good news for the red squirrels. The likely places to see them are in the woods around Windermere, and probably best of all in the Borrowdale woods, but wherever someone regularly feeds nuts to the birds the chances are high that red squirrels will be there as well. Their natural food supply comes from the bountiful crop of acorns, as well as the seeds of Scots pines, and it is this food supply which also attracts some of the more colourful birds such as great spotted woodpecker and jay, which stores acorns very much like a squirrel.

Another attractive woodland mammal, common throughout the Park, is the elegant roe deer. This shy little animal is best seen in the early hours of the day when the Park is quiet and very few people are about. In fact this is the best time of day to see and hear all the wildlife, particularly of the woods and lakes.

Life by the Lakes

The lakes and tarns from which the Park derives its name vary in character enormously. Some, like Esthwaite Water, are rich in nutrients and are teeming with life; others, like Buttermere and Wast Water, are deep, cold, almost devoid of nutrients and pretty well lifeless. It was not always so. The deep cold lakes were invariably carved by great glaciers, and when they were first formed they were full of life, the initial nutrients being supplied by silts which the glaciers left behind. Further nutrients were washed off the land around into the lakes. The life which settled in these lakes eventually exhausted all the goodness they contained, leaving them barren.

The lakes that are rich in life are themselves constantly changing. Their edges are often marshes or fens, slowly invading the open water. This process, called succession, happens as plants stabilise an area of mud; more mud accumulates round their roots, and more plants grow on that mud. Eventually the lake is entirely filled up, as can be seen at Rusland Moss, between Windermere and Coniston Water. These marginal areas are often very exciting places to look for plants and animals. Skullcap and gipsywort are two of the unusual flowers that might be found, while snipe, which live and breed in boggy areas, are sometimes encountered. Much commoner are herons, while present, but very rarely seen, is the otter.

A very characteristic Lakeland plant is the mountain parsley fern, which grows abundantly in rocks and dry stone walls all over the fells. The high tops themselves are a hostile environment for all but the specialists, but one of these, the tiny yellow tormentil, brings colour to the most inhospitable places. Wetter areas are home to two other specialists, the sundew and the butterwort. Woe betide the unwary insect that lands on the leaves of either of these deceptively mild looking insectivorous plants.

The birds of prey are another group of specialists, and the commonest is undoubtedly the buzzard. Nesting in many of the woodlands, and on some of the crags, these birds are often mistaken for golden eagles. The National Park does have the only golden eagles nesting in England, but with only two pairs, you need a certain amount of luck to see them. The other special bird of the Park is the peregrine, and its numbers have increased considerably in recent years; in fact the Park has the highest known breeding density of peregrines in the world. Found in the same habitats is the largest of Britain's crows, the raven. The 'kronk-kronk' call of these birds is a characteristic sound of the fells.

Ennerdale

GRIZEDALE FOREST
Established in 1937, Grizedale Forest was the first Forestry Commission holding in which special efforts were made to provide interpretive and recreational facilities for visitors. The visitor and wildlife centre here has dioramas illustrating deer and other wildlife, history, industrial archaeology, geology, ecology and forest management. Numerous waymarked nature trails and

A roebuck. Roe deer live in nearly all Lake District woods and forests

What to See

CONISTON WATER
Something over five miles long, Coniston is the third largest of the lakes. It is surrounded by woodlands, especially on its eastern shore, and many footpaths can be followed beside and around it. From Coniston village paths lead up to The Old Man of Coniston, the most prominent peak in this area. On the lake's east shore is Brantwood, John Ruskin's home for many years, and here several nature trails have been laid out. They lead among great banks of azaleas and rhododendrons, with sheets of daffodils below then in spring, to excellent views of the lake and its encircling mountains.

Open: *Brantwood, daily mid Mar to mid Nov. Admission charge.*

ENNERDALE WATER
Ennerdale is a Lake District exception – it is the only lake with no public road along its shore. For that reason it is one of the quietest and most peaceful of the lakes. The conifers of the Forestry Commission's Ennerdale Forest cloak the sides of the lake, and the many forest trails and tracks make ideal walking routes.

Part FC.

FRIAR'S CRAG NATURE WALK, KESWICK
This exceptionally attractive nature walk is about two miles in length, and is, for some of its route, accessible to those in wheelchairs. Like much of the area it is very popular at all seasons but is best seen in early spring or late autumn.

From the public car park on Lake Road, south of Keswick, the walk leads to the shore of Derwent Water, and on to the superb viewpoint of Friar's Crag, passing a memorial plaque to the co-founder of the National Trust, Canon Rawnsley. It was his tireless efforts which ensured the purchase of many of the Trust's early Lakeland properties, and surely his true memorial is in the views over Derwent Water and the great mountains mirrored in the lake.

Each of the islands in Derwent Water has a fascinating history, but the view of Lord's Island, just to the south of Friar's Crag, awash with yellow daffodils in the spring, is one no photographer can resist. In recent years the National Trust has had to bring soil to the Crag area to replace that eroded by weather and walkers.

From Broom Point waterfowl can be studied. Many will be familiar, but look for the attractive red-breasted merganser sitting low in the water, and for the equally distinctive goldeneye. (Wheelchairs cannot go beyond this point.)

A fascinating relative of the salmon, the vendace, lives in Derwent Water, Bassenthwaite and other deep, cold mountain lakes in Scotland, Ireland and Europe. The very similar poivan or schelly is found in Ullswater and Haweswater. It is generally accepted that the original sea fish were 'stranded' in these lakes after the Ice Age, and have developed their variations over the centuries.

Leaving the shore, the track enters Great Wood, where there are red squirrels – the grey has never reached the Lake District. Both red and roe deer also live in Great Wood.

The path turns back to Keswick through a series of small woods, home to a wide range of hardwoods, many planted in recent years. The trees shelter numbers of birds which are preyed upon by sparrowhawks.

NT/CNT.

forest walks have been laid out here, all of them providing excellent views.

Open: *visitor centre daily all year. FC.*

HAY BRIDGE DEER MUSEUM
This museum was established to explain the principles of deer conservation, and to provide red and roe deer with an area containing all their needs, without pressure. There are two trails here, one including the deer enclosures, woodland craft areas and many aspects of natural history; the other with a greater emphasis on scenic variety, including woodland, marsh and two tarns.

Open: *daily (except Sun) Apr to end Oct. Admission charge.*

LAKE WINDERMERE

This is the largest lake in England and certainly the most intensively used in the Park for recreation. With all the boating, water skiing and other activities which take place here, it could be assumed that the whole area is spoilt, but that is far from being the case. It is still one of the most beautiful places in Britain and the place most visitors eventually make for when visiting the Lake District. The views across the lake are magnificent, and a steamer trip or a row on the lake from either Bowness or Ambleside is an ideal way to appreciate the diversity of lake and mountain scenery. An out of season visit is always worthwhile and this is also the time when Windermere plays host to an internationally important population of visitors from Iceland. They are goldeneye – among the

Windermere, popular beauty spot for two centuries

most beautiful ducks to be found in Britain. The lake supports a large population of them during the winter, here to escape the severe weather further north.

Excellent walks can be made at many points round the lake; some of the best are on the west shore, beneath the Claife Heights. Here broadleaved woodlands, with fine sweet chestnut trees, can be found close to the water, while conifers are dominant on the higher slopes.

On the east side of the lake is Brockhole, the National Park's excellent visitor centre. There are displays and films on the Lake District's geology and natural history, and a lakeside nature trail, which always gives superb views of the surrounding hills, and sometimes gives glimpses of red squirrels, while underfoot, in summer, may be seen the lovely yellow blooms of globe flower.

Open: *Brockhole visitor centre daily late Mar to early Nov. Admission charge.*

LOUGHRIGG FELL

Loughrigg Fell can be reached from a two-and-a-half mile walk which starts in Ambleside. A range of habitats and some splendid views justify the unavoidable amount of climbing necessary.

After leaving the town by following Stock Beck the walk turns into the Rothay valley with its large rock outcrops, green fields and several varieties of oak. The River Rothay is crossed at the high-arched pack-horse bridge, Miller Bridge. Climbing up the bridle path to Loughrigg the walk passes a wood with a fine mix of broadleaved and con-

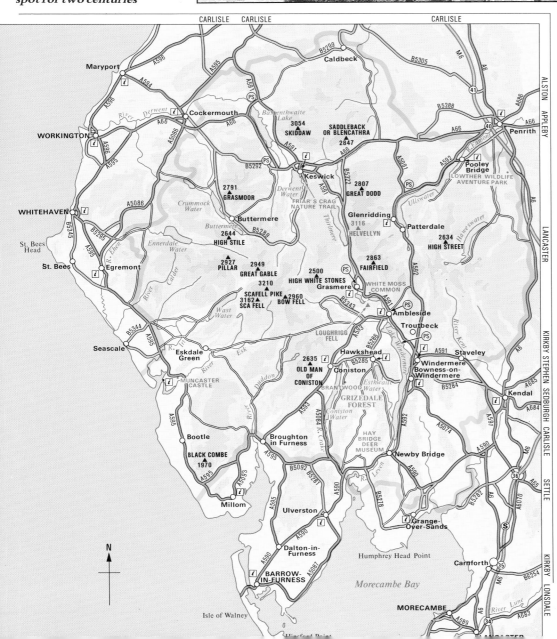

iferous trees. The area is both damp and acid, and woodland plants like wood sorrel and fox-glove, together with mosses, confirm this.

From Browhead is a splendid view of Ambleside. The path passes drystone walls with clumps of parsley and lady ferns, and continues over several streams and past a variety of trees. The range of habitats is extended when the walk passes several bogs and a tarn. Look for heath bedstraw, sphagnum moss and several species of rush in and around the bog, while, in addi-tion to waterlilies, bog-bean grows in the acid waters of the tarn. This most attractive plant was aptly described by a 16th-century herbalist as 'having a bush of featherlike flowers of a white colour, dasht over slightly with a wash of light carnation'.

The path returns to Miller Bridge and it is possible to make a detour to Rothay Park and the parish church of Ambleside, or to return direct to the town.

NT.

LOWTHER WILDLIFE ADVENTURE PARK

Many species of European ani-mals and birds are kept here, in near-natural surroundings. Larger creatures like deer, cattle and sheep roam in big enclos-ures, while smaller animals such as otters and badgers can be seen close to. Also here are a coun-tryside museum and outdoor ac-tivity centre. These provide op-portunities for individuals and groups to study many aspects of life in the countryside, including a section on plants and animals, rocks and soil formation.

Open: *Apr to Oct daily. Admission charge.*

MUNCASTER CASTLE

Rhododendrons are the most famous feature of this historic castle and its grounds. A nature trail leads through the rhododen-dron gardens – notable also for azaleas – to one of the largest heronries in England.

Also here is a bird garden, with many exotic species, and a number of Himalayan bears.

Open: *Easter to Sep. Closed Mon, except bank holiday. Admission charge.*

ULLSWATER

Many consider Ullswater to be the most beautiful of all the lakes. Towering above its west-ern shores is Helvellyn, destina-tion of many walkers. The com-mon lands between Helvellyn and the lake shore at Glenridding are criss-crossed by many paths

and are excellent places for studying upland wildlife and in-dustrial archaeology, since this was once a busy mining area.

The north shore of the lake is where Wordsworth was inspired to write his poem 'Daffodils', but although the scenery is impres-sive, there are few daffodils here today. A footpath from a car park just east of the A592/A5091 junction leads through woodland to Aira Force, a lovely 60ft fall. The journey is well worth it, not only for the spectacle of the fall itself but for the beauty of the woodland. On the other side of the lake lie the slopes of Martin-dale Forest. There are no trees on these bare fells, which are home to a herd of red deer. These up-lands are among the most remote in the park, being reached only by a long walk. On this side of the lake a road goes as far as the small village of Howtown, and from here an excellent footpath, through varied country, follows the lakeside contours to Patter-dale at the head of the lake. The views from this path are among the finest in the park.

WAST WATER

Dark and forbidding, with the smooth grim walls of the Wast Water Screes forming the south-ern shore, this is one of the Lake District's least friendly, but grandest, lakes. Its waters are cold and almost devoid of life, a condition encountered in many upland waters where the lack of nutrients in the water and in the surrounding rocks prevents plants and animals gaining a foothold. Even the shores of Wast Water are for the most part bare, plants being washed away before they can become estab-lished. On the great scree slopes lichens and mosses manage a pre-carious existence, but little else grows. Much of the country round the lake is for experienced walkers only, but there are gen-tler walks to be enjoyed at Was-dale Head, at the lake's eastern end.

WHITE MOSS COMMON

The nature walk at White Moss Common traverses typical Lake District country, through both outgrown scrub and mature woods and over open fell. It has the advantage of being short, taking only about 45 minutes, and is much less taxing than the Loughrigg walk, just down the road.

Cars should be parked in the quarry or on the common, and the walk begins along the edge of the River Rothay. The area be-fore the bridge is boggy, with rushes, cotton grass and bog-myrtle, which grows in aromatic clumps, usually in association

Above: Ullswater with the Lady of the Lake, which has been operating here since 1877. Below: view from Muncaster Castle, in the fells above the River Esk

Mountain fern, common on acid soils throughout the Lake District. It is also called the lemon-scented fern, and its leaves do have a citrus smell if rubbed

with sphagnum mosses. The orange-yellow male, and red female, catkins present an attractive picture.

Beyond the Bridge is woodland with a wide variety of broadleaved trees and some conifers. Part of the wood was probably planted as a hedge, but some trees, like the birch, are self-sown. In the open parts of the wood grow several ferns and damp-loving plants such as yellow pimpernel, which flowers from May to September.

The fell land is almost covered in a sea of bracken – and the views are the major interest, both from a conveniently sited seat, and from a little higher up the hill. Here it is possible to look out over Rydal Water and Grasmere Lake.

On the journey back down the fell wet patches are visible among the bracken. Here grows common butterwort, its pretty mauve flowers blooming from May to July among a starlike pattern of bright yellowy leaves. On their sticky surfaces insects are caught and 'digested' to supplement the plant's supply of nitrates and other mineral salts. The lousewort also grows in these wet patches – it has most attractive bright pink flowers.

The second wood through which the walk passes on the return leg, consists mainly of oak, beech and birch, and is altogether more ordered than the first. Tits are common to both woods, but woodpeckers prefer the first, and pied flycatchers are colonising the nest boxes in the second. A short stroll through riverside pasture completes the walk, but it can be extended by following an alternative route along Loughrigg Terrace; double the time allowance for this.

NT/CNT.

Land's End

Cornwall

The famous south-west extremity of England is best known for the journeys to John O'Groats which start and finish here – a total distance of about 873 miles. The wild granite cliffs overlook wave-washed rocks and reefs with the Longships Lighthouse one mile offshore, and the Wolf Rock eight miles away in the distance. On the far horizon are the Isles of Scilly, but they can be seen only in the clearest weather.

Stretching out into the western approaches, Land's End is in the path of Atlantic seabird migration, and onshore winds can bring a variety of seabirds close in to the shore. The large black and white gannet is the most obvious, but shearwaters, skuas and even storm petrels are seen.

In summer, Land's End is one of the busiest and most crowded 'honeypots' in England, but the magnificent cliffs on either side, although popular, are almost empty by comparison. To the south, Gwennap Head is the site of breeding seabirds in spring and early summer. North are the cliffs of Mayon and Trevescan, owned by the National Trust.

The visitor centre at Land's End has an informative series of displays and exhibitions about the area, including its wildlife and history.

Open: *visitor centre Mar to Nov daily. Admission charge.*
Location: *9 miles SW of Penzance at end of A30.*
Map: *page 304, SW32.*

Langstone Harbour

Hampshire

Along the south coast between Chichester and Gosport are three extensive basins open to the sea by narrow mouths and interconnected by tidal channels in the north. Although they have many similarities and their wildlife and wildlife habitats are closely related, perhaps the most exciting is Langstone Harbour, with the expanses of Farlington Marshes at its northern end.

There are major concentrations of wildfowl and waders and these are seen to their best advantage on a rising tide from the sea-wall surrounding Farlington. One of the biggest concentrations of dark-bellied brent geese in the south is to be found feeding on the eel grass on the flats or in fields on nearby Hayling Island. Several thousand dabbling ducks can be seen in winter with teal, wigeon and mallard being most numerous. At times shelduck (up to 3000) outnumber the other duck species. Pintail are an attractive species, with red-breasted merganser, great crested and some of the rarer grebes frequenting the deep water channels within the harbour.

Wading birds fly from the mudflats on to the marshes as high tide approaches. Dunlins, curlews and redshanks form the bulk of the numbers and there are significant numbers of grey plovers. It has been estimated that between 10 and 15% of the British wintering population of black-tailed godwits gather here. In all, over 40 species of wader have been recorded, including one or two notable rarities. Over 25 species can regularly be seen.

Access: *from A3023 Langstone to Hayling Island road; harbour lies to W of road. Views can be had from A2030 (on W side of harbour) and along the shores of Eastney Lake S of harbour. RSPB.*
Location: *2 miles SW of Havant, bordered by Hayling Island and Portsea Island.*
Map: *page 306, SU60/70.*

Langstone Harbour. In winter this is a superb place to watch wildfowl and waders

Lanhydrock

Cornwall

The burning down in 1881 and subsequent rebuilding of Lanhydrock has resulted in an unusual mixture of styles. The sense of the Victorian and Edwardian periods is particularly strong with billiard room, smoking room and grand kitchens a lasting reminder of those 'Upstairs, Downstairs' times.

Leave the house, strolling through the Victorian formal garden, under the attractive two-storey gatehouse and into the park, and it is possible to imagine oneself a guest enjoying a quiet walk. Pause and admire the great avenue of ancient beech and sycamore, then study the variety of trees, many planted this century, which grace the park and lead down to the River Fowey.

An alternative to the walk is to park the car at Respryn Bridge and explore the river by the

Lanhydrock – a grand house set in superb parkland

many footpaths shown on maps at the entrance to the car park. Over the pretty old bridge a path leads beside the clear, hurrying waters of the Fowey. The mixed woodland canopy ensures a degree of coolness even on the hottest days. In summer the woods are filled with birdsong, and in quiet moments the dipper may be seen pausing on a rock before walking under the sparkling water surface. The dampness of the riverside land is confirmed by the numbers of fungi to be found, and by the smell of the white-flowered wood garlic.

Open: *park at all times; house daily Apr to Oct only; gardens all year. Admission charge to house and garden. Refreshments. Shop. NT.*
Location: *2¼ miles SE of Bodmin on S side of A30 Bodmin bypass; signposted from A38 or B3268.*
Map: *page 304, SX06.*

The Bittern

Persecution and destruction of its habitat led to the bittern becoming virtually extinct in Britain in the latter part of the 19th century. Thankfully, this extraordinary bird now breeds here regularly once more, but only in a few sites, and it is still rare. It is likely that if it were not for protected sites such as the RSPB's Leighton Moss reserve it would disappear from Britain as a breeding species.

Lee Valley Park

Hertfordshire/Essex

The River Lee (or Lea) has been an important waterway since AD896 when the Danes sailed up from the Thames to establish a fort at Ware. During the Great Plague the narrowboat-men of Ware travelled regularly to London to maintain supplies. Rivers became less important as commercial links with the advent of railways and efficient road systems, and 15 years ago the valley of the River Lee was little more than derelict land. To help meet recreational needs in a densely populated area, the 23-mile-long valley was developed to provide facilities for water sports, riding at Lea Bridge, two sports centres – Pickets Lock and Eastway, and Hayes Hill Farm, which is open to the public.

Although mostly situated between London suburbs, much of the Lee Valley Park is attractive countryside: try Amwell Walkway for wild flowers, see 50 varieties of trees at Waltham Abbey, watch birds from hides at Rye House Marsh (managed by the RSPB), enjoy a riverside picnic at Dobbs Weir, or climb to the highest point of Eastway cycle circuit to see St Paul's Cathedral in the distance.

Open: *all year. Part RSPB (reserve open Sat and Sun all year; Mon and Tue Apr to Oct).*
Location: *E of A10 between Hackney Wick and Ware*
Map: *page 306, TQ39.*

Leighton Moss

Lancashire

Tucked away in a beautiful corner of England that is easily missed by those hurrying north on the M6, the Moss occupies the floor of a small attractively wooded valley close to Morecambe Bay. The valley was originally an arm of the bay before being cut off by an embankment. This transformed the area into a freshwater marsh fed by several streams from the surrounding low limestone hills. On these limestone slopes grow hawthorn, blackthorn and ash scrub, giving way to ash, oak and yew dominated woodland. The wet floor of the valley is covered in reed swamp and open, very shallow meres. In this marvellous variety of habitats live a rich selection of birds, mammals, insects and plants. The breeding population of birds is very large, with some specialities, particularly reed warblers and bearded tits, but best of all are the bitterns, among our rarest birds. The Leighton Moss population accounts for 25% of the entire British population. In the breeding season the continuous 'booming' of the males is a characteristic sound of the Moss. By sitting patiently in one of the hides strategically placed around the reserve, it is even possible to see this strange and secretive member of the heron family.

The hides are also the most likely places to see two of the very special mammals of the Moss. Red deer regularly lie up in the reeds or browse and drink around the fringe of the reeds, but the real stars are the otters. These delightful animals have been on the reserve for many years and are regularly seen, particularly in the mornings and evenings, swimming across the meres. The reserve's visitor centre has displays on the wildlife of the reserve and the surrounding areas.

Open: *Apr to Sep Sat, Sun, Wed and Thu; Oct to Mar Wed, Sat and Sun. Admission charge for RSPB non-members. Visitor centre. Public hide on causeway always open. No dogs. RSPB.*
Location: *3 miles NW of Carnforth on E edge of Silverdale village. Car park and visitor centre just S of Silverdale station off unclassified Silverdale-Yealand Redmayne road.*
Map: *page 309, SD47.*

Leith Hill

Surrey

In 1766 a 64ft tower was built on the summit of Leith Hill by the then owner of Leith Hill Place, Richard Hull. He was buried beneath the tower in 1772. Leith is, at 965ft, the highest point in south-west England – and the tower takes it to more than 1000ft. Hull intended it to be a place where he and others might enjoy the view – and what a view it is! Panoramic seems the only way to describe a prospect which takes in as many as 13 counties, and St Paul's Cathedral on a clear day.

If the weather is unkind you may like to explore one or more of the properties which make up the National Trust holding here. Leith is known for the thick carpet of bluebells which extends down the hill in spring. Rhododendrons are well established around Leith Hill Place and in Mosses Wood. Fine old oaks and beechs are joined in places by young conifers intended to give protection to new generations of hardwoods. There is always something to see on Leith – in every season. Spring flowers, dappled shade in summer, autumn colour, and when the last leaf has fallen, the branches of the great trees form natural frames for a succession of pictures of the rolling Weald.

Open: *free access; small admission charge to Leith Hill Tower. NT.*
Location: *4½ miles SW of Dorking; bounded by A25, A24, A29 and B2126.*
Map: *page 306, TQ14.*

Lepe Country Park & Calshot

Hampshire

Commanding views across the Solent to the Isle of Wight and the continual passage of shore and sea-birds, make this park an interesting spot. The vast colonies of black-headed gulls from Gull Island and the Exbury Marshes, at the mouth of the Beaulieu River, which can be seen from here, make it especially exciting. Inland, the valley of the Dark Water with its marshy areas provides a marked contrast. Further to the north-east is Calshot Spit with its castle and the Calshot marshes. The marshes of Spartina or cord grass are interesting scientifically as the place where the prolific hybrids between native and introduced species first occurred. The bird-life is also interesting, with some important roosts and feeding

The view from the top of the tower on Leith Hill

areas for waders and wildfowl. Ringed plovers, grey plovers, lap-wings, curlews and dunlins are characteristic and can be seen in quite large numbers.

Location: *Lepe Country Park is 3 miles S of Fawley on unclassified road; Calshot is 2 miles SE of Fawley on B3053. Areas linked by unclassified road.*
Map: *page 306, SZ49/SU40.*

Lightwater Country Park

Surrey

Lightwater Country Park lies close to that area where Surrey, Hampshire and Berkshire meet; an area dominated by heath and largely used as an army training ground. The country park, however, is given over to the public, for recreation and sport.

In the past, the heathland scene was preserved by grazing and burning, which prevented the seedlings from reaching maturity and developing into woodland. Many of the Surrey heaths are now overgrown with silver birch, and the severe fires during the droughts of 1976 damaged both flora and fauna. Lightwater has a mixture of habitats which demonstrate the transition from

heather to woodland.

A nature trail leading from the car park explores the habitats to be found here. Heather is often the dominant feature; keen botanists will be able to distinguish between the delicate ling which grows over most of the drier ground, and the more bell-like cross-leaved heath of the boggier parts.

The bogs form the richest habitat on the heath; providing a haven for numerous insects and the birthplace of dragonflies and damselflies. The dragonflies patrol up and down in search of prey or hover before darting out to grab a passing insect. In turn the dragonflies become prey themselves; victims to plant or bird.

The plant is a sundew; which feeds by closing the filaments on its sticky leaves around any insect that alights on it. The insect is absorbed through the leaves, its nutrients supplementing the plant's diet on the poor soil.

The bird that catches dragonflies is the hobby; a dashing little falcon that is a summer visitor to

Below: work horses. Pulling a plough early in the century (left) and at Littlewick's Courage Centre today (right)

the heaths. A few pairs breed in this area; mainly on army training grounds where they are largely undisturbed. Apart from dragonflies, hobbies feed mainly on birds, catching even swifts in flight!

Open: *all year.*
Location: *at Lightwater, off A322. Picnic area. Nature trails.*
Map: *page 306, SU96.*

Limpsfield Common

Surrey

There are similarities between Limpsfield Common and Headley, some miles to the west near Leatherhead. For centuries both were places where commoners grazed their animals and obtained fuel for cottage fires in the form of turves and dead wood. Both commons were, as shown on the 1860s' Ordnance Survey maps, almost treeless. Headley was much changed by military use in the Second World War, but at Limpsfield it was a shift in village, and national, economy which altered the appearance of the common.

Grazing virtually ceased in the 1920s – today one commoner has

grazing rights and another estovers, or the right to take firewood – and gradually the heather encroached, followed by gorse and bracken. Silver birch began to spread and oak and beech became established.

The National Trust owns 'chunks' of the common, including Moorhouse Bank, a small common encircled by trees, which is probably a miniature of how the whole area once looked. About 50 acres in the middle of Limpsfield Common are leased to a golf club, although open to the public. For absolute safety from flying golf balls you may choose to visit Limpsfield on summer Sunday afternoons, when play is suspended!

Location: *SE of Oxted and S of A25. NT.*
Map: *page 306, TQ45.*

Lings Wood

Northamptonshire

This area was, in the 16th century, a ling (or heather) and gorse heathland with birch copses and common grazing land. Today, as a result of afforestation, it provides an interesting mixture of

conifers and broad-leaved woodland with numerous grassy clearings. Probably the most delightful experience is to visit the woods in May and June when the rhododendrons are in bloom.

The animals are varied and exciting and especially valuable so near to expanding Northampton. There are squirrels, badgers, foxes, deer and rabbits; and birdwatchers can see all three species of woodpeckers, treecreepers, nuthatches, magpies and many species of finches, tits and warblers. The clearings are an excellent habitat for butterflies, and as many as 15 different species may be seen during an hour's visit.

Lings House, at the centre of the reserve, is the headquarters of the Northamptonshire Trust for Nature Conservation. An exhibition area here gives an introduction to seeing wildlife in the county; guides and nature trail leaflets are available. One of the trails is around Lings Wood itself, where there is a picnic site.

Open: *all year. Information centre open weekdays and Sun pm only. CNT.*
Location: *3¾ miles NE of Northampton city centre. In Lings Way, off A4500 Wellingborough Road. N of old A45 to Wellingborough.*
Map: *page 306, SP86.*

Littlewick Green: Courage Shire-Horse Centre

Berkshire

Although the centre exists primarily to show off Courage's magnificent work horses – weighing about a ton each – there are also other farm animals, fighting cocks and birds. There are drays, agricultural equipment and a display of harnesses, together with a cooperage and examples of country crafts. The blacksmith can sometimes be seen at work and on some weekends there are working traction engines and threshing machines. Other attractions include the Shire Horse Inn.

The Courage Shire Horses are well known at agricultural shows, including the Horse of the Year Show, and in the Display Room there are numerous prize rosettes won at shows.

Open: *Mar to Oct daily except Mon unless a bank holiday. Admission charge. Picnic area. Refreshments. Shop. Suitable for disabled visitors.*
Location: *2 miles W of Maidenhead on S side of A4; ¼ mile W of A423 (M)/A4/A423 junction.*
Map: *page 306, SU88.*

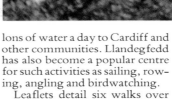

The Lizard

Cornwall

Many would argue that some of the best landscapes in Cornwall are to be found around the Lizard Peninsula. As a result the area is very much visited, but somehow retains its character.

On grey, misty days the Lizard Peninsula can be a sombre, eerie place, full of half remembered memories of wreckers and drowned men, of quicksand and strange Celtic legends, but on fine days the flowers seem brighter, more varied and more numerous than anywhere else in the land. This may seem fanciful, as may the claim of the Rev. Charles Johns, headmaster of Helston Grammar School and a fine Victorian naturalist, that he could find 12 wild plants in an area covered by his hat: but it is close enough to the truth. The mixture of soils and habitats ensures a unique variety of plants; many of them rare and local. The lavender blue of spring squill is common, and the strangely exotic, many-petalled red and yellow flowers of the Hottentot fig brighten the cliffs from May to August. Honey-scented clumps of thrift and bright yellow tormentil delight the eye, and the botanist will look for the delicate flowers of Cornish heath.

One of the major attractions on the Lizard is Kynance Cove, with its serpentine rocks – red-brown or grey-green, with veins of red, white, yellow and black. Much loved by the Victorians, it was enthusiastically 'mined' from the moors above the cove. A mile or so along the cliffs is Lizard Point itself, with magnificent views up the whole length of the Cornish Coast. Much of the area around Kynance Cove is leased by the Cornwall Trust for Nature Conservation as a nature reserve.

Location: *W and E of A3083, at end of Lizard Peninsula. Part NT/CNT.*
Map: *page 304, SW61/71.*

Llandegfedd Reservoir & Farm Park

Gwent

This 434-acre reservoir, nestling amid low, wooded hills between Pontypool and Usk, marks the 'border' between the industrialised valleys of South Wales and the essentially rural landscapes of eastern Gwent. Completed in 1964, it supplies 30 million gallons of water a day to Cardiff and other communities. Llandegfedd has also become a popular centre for such activities as sailing, rowing, angling and birdwatching.

Leaflets detail six walks over fields and through woods to the south of the lake and cover about 20 miles of public footpaths. The walks range from one-and-a-half miles to five-and-a-half miles. The longest visits the church of St Tegfedd.

Llandegfedd is Gwent's most important inland site for water-loving birds. Knots, oystercatchers and greenshanks are seen in spring and autumn, while winter visitors include tufted duck, wigeon and teal.

The 22-acre farm park at Coed-y-paen has splendid views across the reservoir to peaks in the Brecon Beacons National Park. It was established in 1976 to preserve rare breeds like Soay sheep and Old English Longhorn cattle. Other features include a nature trail which visits an excavated badger's set.

Open: *reservoir all year. Farm park May to Sep daily. Admission charge to farm park. Picnic areas. Refreshments.*
Location: *4 miles E of Pontypool, on unclassified road off A4042.*
Map: *page 305, ST39.*

Far left: Polpeor Cove, on the southern tip of the Lizard Peninsula

Llangollen Canal

Clwyd

Britain has many beautiful inland waterways, but none can quite match the last ten miles of the Llangollen Canal. Part of the Shropshire Union system, it crosses the Welsh border at Chirk, then runs along the lovely Vale of Llangollen to the Horseshoe Falls on the River Dee. Near Llangollen the canal is overlooked by the dramatic limestone cliffs of Creigiau Eglwyseg, and the gaunt ruins of Castell Dinas Bran, perched on a conical hill high above the town, are another memorable landmark.

Superb views are matched by spectacular reminders of Thomas Telford's civil engineering genius. The canal crosses the River Ceiriog on a lofty aqueduct, burrows through a 460-yard tunnel and sails 121ft above the Dee on the 336-yard Pontcysyllte aqueduct. Sir Walter Scott described Pontcysyllte – 'The Stream in the Sky' – as the finest work of art he had ever seen. It cost £47,000 and was completed amid great pomp and

Above: Pontcysyllte viaduct on the Llangollen Canal
Right: Llanrhaeadr Waterfall, hidden away in the Berwyn mountains

ceremony in 1805.

Although not officially designated as such, the canal is virtually a linear nature reserve whose water, banks and canopy of trees provide habitats for a great variety of plants and wildlife. Dragonflies flit above the slow-moving surface where frogs and newts can sometimes be seen. Birds include coots, moorhens, mallard, herons, wagtails and flycatchers. The vivid plumage of a kingfisher is a sight for the fortunate.

All aspects of canals and the Canal Age are brought out at the Canal Museum in Llangollen. In the exhibition area clear displays explain every aspect of life and work on the inland waterways. There is even a reconstruction of a coal mine to help in the explanation of coal transport.

Open: Canal Museum Easter, then Whitsun to Sep daily. Admission charge.
Location: Canal runs parallel to A5 between Chirk, Llangollen and Horseshoe Falls.
Map: page 309, SJ24.

Llanrhaeadr Waterfall (Pistyll Rhaeadr)

Clwyd

The peat-stained Afon Disgynfa rises high in the Berwyn Mountains before plunging over a wooded cliff to become the highest waterfall in Wales or England. It tumbles 120 feet into a natural cauldron of glistening, mossy rock, then foams through a natural arch before falling another 120 feet into a deep pool overlooked by a footbridge. The fall is one of the traditional 'Seven Wonders of Wales' and was formed about 10,000 years ago, at the end of the last ice age.

Mighty glaciers were responsible for the smooth profile of the deep, steep-sided valley through which the river runs towards its confluence with the Tanat below the village of Llanrhaeadr-ym-Mochnant. Water, trees and meadows make the valley a refuge for such birds as dippers, grey and pied wagtails, willow warblers, chiff-chaffs, green and great spotted woodpeckers, tree pipits and redstarts. Buzzards and kestrels may be seen on the higher ground. Ravens nest on the crags above a lead mine whose workings were abandoned at the end of the 19th century.

A footpath zig-zags steeply to the top of the waterfall and is also the starting point for a strenuous walk to the summit of Moel Sych, 2713ft above sea level and the highest point in the Berwyn range. Its neighbour, Cadair Berwyn, is only one foot lower. The mountains are less rugged than their counterparts in Snowdonia, but can be just as hazardous. Walkers must be prepared for fickle weather that can reduce visibility and temperature in a matter of minutes.

Location: at end of unclassified road, 4 miles NW of Llanrhaeadr-ym-Mochnant.
Map: page 309, SJ02.

Llanymynech Hill

Powys/Shropshire

The main street of Llanymynech is actually on the line of the ditch of Offa's Dyke. Just to the north of the village the dyke climbs steeply up the southern end of a long hill and follows the side of it for a while. This is Llanymynech Hill, the southern tip of a ridge of carboniferous limestone which continues intermittently northwards to Llandudno.

The Romans mined copper here, and for centuries the pure limestone has been quarried for lime-burning and building stone. The old quarries, mines and lime-kilns still exist as a reminder of those busy industrial times, but nature has taken over the limestone cliffs and screes and the hill today is wild and beautiful. All kinds of lime-loving plants occur here, including the bee orchid and the diminutive autumn lady's tresses – also a kind of orchid. Wild thyme and marjoram abound on the warm southern slopes and are visited by large numbers of butterflies and other insects. Among these is the grayling butterfly, whose markings merge with the stony ground on which it likes to settle. It has the curious habit of leaning over when at rest, thus avoiding casting a shadow and making it even more difficult to see.

There are numerous walks on the hill and two nature reserves managed by the Shropshire Trust for Nature Conservation may be visited. One of these is on the west side of Llanymynech Rocks; the other to the north at Llynclys Common.

Location: 5½ miles SW of Oswestry, W of A483. Part CNT.
Map: page 309, SJ22.

Lleyn Peninsula

Gwynedd

Lleyn is a world apart from the rest of North Wales. Unlike neighbouring Snowdonia, dominated by great mountain ranges, the peninsula is a patchwork of fields hemmed by narrow, high-banked roads which thread their way to clifftops, coves and long, dune-backed beaches. Outcrops of ancient rock rise to no more than 1850ft at the highest peak of Yr Eifl, but the hills stand in isolation and are superb vantage points on a clear day. Mynydd Mawr, for one, belies its modest 524 feet with breathtaking views down the graceful sweep of Cardigan Bay. Foel Fawr, topped with the ruins of an 18th-century windmill, overlooks Abersoch and the anchorage of St Tudwal's Road.

Carn Fadryn, 1217ft high, was fortified during the Iron Age. So was Tre'r Ceiri – 'The Giants' Town' – which towers nearly 1600 feet above Llanaelhaearn on the northern coast. Traces of about 150 stone-walled huts have been found on the hilltop where views embrace parts of Ireland,

Bardsey Island from Braich-y-Pwll, on the Lleyn Peninsula

the Isle of Man, the whole of Anglesey, Snowdonia, Cader Idris, the Cambrian Mountains and high ground in the Pembrokeshire Coast National Park, 70 miles away to the south-west.

Great sweeps of sand march westwards from Porthmadog to Pwllheli – Lleyn's unofficial 'capital' since the Middle Ages – and on beyond Abersoch, a popular holiday resort. The northern coast, officially designated an Area of Outstanding Natural Beauty, provides a delightful contrast. There are extensive sands at Nefyn, Morfa Nefyn and elsewhere, but cliffs and coves are more typical. At Porth Neigwl, on the south side of the peninsula, four miles of sand are framed by lofty headlands. When strong winds rage in from St George's Channel the bay lives up to its other name – Hell's Mouth – as awe-inspiring surf recalls the many ships driven ashore and pounded to matchwood in the days of sail.

Aberdaron, at the seaward end of the peninsula, is the departure point for Bardsey Island where Celtic monks found refuge in the 6th and 7th centuries. Bardsey's abbey became so famous that three pilgrimages to the remote island equalled one to far-off Rome. Scheduled as a Site of Special Scientific Interest by the

Nature Conservancy Council, Bardsey is an important nesting place for choughs, kittiwakes, guillemots, Manx shearwaters and many other seabirds. Ynys Enlli, as it is called in Welsh, is also said to be the last resting place of 20,000 saints – pilgrims who never returned to the mainland.

Location: peninsula to W of A487 between Caernarfon and Porthmadog.
Map: page 309, SH44.

Llyn Clywedog

Powys

Britain's highest dam, 237ft from base to parapet, holds back this man-made lake. The road along the western shore passes the start of a scenic trail which loops round a wooded peninsula with fine views of the lake and its backcloth of high, steep, rounded hills. The two-and-a-half mile walk, punctuated with places ideal for a peaceful picnic, can be cut short to make a gentle one-mile stroll.

The dam itself is overlooked by the tumbled stones of Pen-y-gaer, an Iron Age stronghold, and looms majestically above the restored Bryntail lead mine. The old workings are reached by a

footbridge which crosses the Clywedog as it swirls down a wooded gorge.

West of the lake, waymarked trails ranging in length from one to eight miles explore the Hafren Forest. The longest walk follows the River Severn – known in Welsh as the Afon Hafren – to its lonely source 2000ft up on the northern slopes of Plynlimon.

The short Cascades Trail visits a small waterfall which tumbles into a pool where sheep were dipped before the Forestry Commission started planting trees in 1937. Another walk passes the site of a lead mine where an antler-pick and other prehistoric implements have been found.

Location: NW of Llanidloes, off B4518
Map: page 309, SN88/98.

Llysyfran Reservoir Country Park

Dyfed

The summits of Mynydd Preseli, where prehistoric men quarried monoliths for Stonehenge, gaze down on the placid waters of this 187-acre reservoir. Fishing, sailing, canoeing and other activities, including sub-aqua swimming, take place here, but

pleasant walks can also be made along the shore. Rolling hills provide delightful backgrounds, and walks also reveal a rich variety of plant and animal life on land and in the water.

Llysyfran is an appropriate name for the reservoir and country park. It means 'Court of the Crows' in Welsh, and the area is indeed frequented by carrion crows, rooks, jackdaws and magpies.

Open: *all year. Picnic sites. Refreshments.*
Location: *off B4329, 12 miles NE of Haverfordwest.*
Map: *page 304, SN02*

Loch Garten

Highland

Originally made famous by the ospreys, which began their 'return' to Scotland by breeding here from the late 1950s (and indeed still nest), this RSPB reserve is now more widely recognised as an important conservation site for part of the old Caledonian pine forest of Abernethy, as well as for its lochs, bogs and adjoining moorland. The ospreys breed on the north side of Loch Garten. Access in that area is restricted to the signposted path leading to the observation hide where excellent

Loch Garten, most famous as nesting site of ospreys since the 1950s

views of the birds are to be had through the telescopes and binoculars provided. The ospreys rarely fish the lochs on the reserve, but are often to be seen in flight over the area. Otherwise, the reserve has all the characteristic breeding birds of the habitat, including capercaillies, crested tits, redstarts, siskins and Scottish crossbills. Blackcock are found on the moor edges, while Loch Garten and Loch Mallachie have breeding little grebes, teal, water rails, common sandpipers, and grey wagtails, and attract greylag geese, goldeneye and goosander in winter. Both red and roe deer are common, as are red squirrels. Otters and wild cats also live here – but are rarely seen.

Open: *reserve all year. If ospreys nest, observation post open daily approx mid Apr to late Aug. Shop. No dogs. RSPB.*
Access: *within statutory bird sanctuary strictly confined to marked path; elsewhere on reserve along pinewood paths.*
Location: *2 miles W of Boat of Garten. Signposted off B970 Coylumbridge – Nethy Bridge road.*
Map: *page 315, NH91.*

The osprey breeds at Loch Garten and a few other Scottish sites. It is a fish-eater, diving into the water and grabbing its prey with its claws. The nest is a huge construction of sticks.

Loch Insh & Insh Marshes

Highland

Loch Insh lies at the north-eastern end of the Insh Marshes, beside Kincraig, with the Spey flowing in at its southern end and out again beneath the bridge below Kincraig. Ospreys sometimes fish here and it is always worth stopping to look for goldeneye, goosanders and red-breasted mergansers. There are globe flowers on the shingle bank, and – if you are a very early riser – there is a chance of otters near the bridge.

The Insh Marshes form a broad flood plain along the southern side of the Spey between Kingussie and Kincraig and are among the most important inland wetlands in Scotland. Winter floods produce excellent conditions for wildfowl, with a regular flock of whooper swans being one of the main attractions. In spring and summer the pools and marshes attract a superb selection of breeding birds, including mallard, wigeon, teal, shoveler, redshank, snipe, curlew and water rail. There is also a large black-headed gull colony. The birch and juniper woods alongside hold breeding redstarts, willow warblers, tree pipits, redpolls and, sometimes, pied flycatchers. The whole area is excellent for birds of prey: hen harriers are regular visitors, and ospreys, peregrines, buzzards and sparrowhawks all occur frequently. As if that weren't enough, this is also a good place for great grey shrikes in winter.

Much of the RSPB reserve here is composed of sedge fen, and one of the sedges that grows here is the rare northern sedge. Another plant to be found in the fen is angelica, a stately member of the parsley family that takes its name from its 'angelic' properties, since it was once widely believed to be a superlative cure-all. Today it is used as a crystallised confection on cakes and sweets. There are drier areas on the reserve, and the RSPB is actively managing these to make them more attractive to birds and plants.

Open: *RSPB reserve visitor centre and hides Apr to July Wed, Fri and Sun; Wed only in Aug. Admission charge to RSPB non-members. All visitors should report to reception on arrival. RSPB.*
Location: *between A9/B9152 Kingussie to Aviemore roads and B970 Kingussie to Coylumbridge road. Reserve reception off B970 between Ruthven and Drumguish.*
Map: *page 315, NH80.*

Loch Leven & Vane Farm

Tayside

Throughout the autumn and winter months Loch Leven (which is a National Nature Reserve) is a birdwatcher's paradise. Large numbers of duck can been seen, the species including mallard, wigeon, pochard, goldeneye and tufted duck, but it is geese which are the special stars here. Thousands of them, mostly pinkfooted, but including large numbers of greylag, congregate here, feeding on farm fields during the day and flying into the roost on St Serf's Island in the evening. Other birds which might be seen include whooper swans, fieldfares and redwings.

A good many other birds can be seen around the loch and on the farm during the rest of the year. These include teal and herons on the water, with willow warblers, redpolls, tree pipits and spotted flycatchers in the wooded areas. Much of Vane Farm is managed to keep its fields open for the geese, but a lagoon has been created close to the RSPB's nature centre, and gorse is encouraged in some areas to provide nesting shelter for birds such as reed buntings and chaffinches, while in the wooded areas, mostly of birch, other trees are being introduced.

Those who enjoy wild flowers will not be disappointed; the woodland areas are bright with primrose, wood anemone and wood sorrel in spring.

Open: *National Nature Reserve all year (public access restricted to three areas: at Kirkgate Park (Kinross), Burleigh Sands and Findatie. In summer there are boat trips to Castle Island). Vane Farm Centre Sat and Sun Jan to Mar; daily (except Fri) Apr to Dec. Admission charge for RSPB non-members. Information centre. Shop. No dogs. RSPB. NCC.*
Location: *Loch Leven is at Kinross, E of M90 between Forth Road Bridge and Perth. Vane Farm is on B9097 on S side of loch.*
Map: *page 313, NT19/NO10.*

Loch Lomond National Nature Reserve

Strathclyde

The whole of Loch Lomond is of tremendous beauty and interest, even though it is one of Scotland's most popular tourist 'honeypots'. The winding A82, along the loch's western side, is especially good, as is the short stretch on the eastern bank from Balmaha to Rowardennan. This road also gives access to the fairly gentle walk to the summit of Ben Lomond.

Naturalists will be particularly interested in the National Nature Reserve, which is situated at the loch's south-east corner. The part of the reserve which is accessible to the public is Inchcailloch Island, reached by boat from Balmaha. The remainder of the reserve comprises four further islands and a block of mainland bounded by Endrick Water – all of which is privately owned. A nature trail explores all of the best features of Inchcailloch, which is especially noted for its rock formations and woodlands. The

Loch Lomond is the largest natural lake in Britain. This engraving dates from 1835

Highland Boundary Fault Line runs along the island, and in some places the change of rock can be clearly seen.

Oaks are the dominant trees on the island, but there is a good mixture of other tree species, including alders in a marshy area rich in ferns, sedges and grasses. Nearly all the alders were once coppiced, as were the oaks. Close to the island's summit, which gives superb views over the loch, is a fragment of Scots pine woodland. In all some 300 species of ferns and flowering plants have been recorded on the reserve's

variety of habitats.

Fallow deer live on the island, and it is possible that they may be seen, but it is more likely that their footprints will be found, or that trees will be seen which have been damaged by bucks rubbing their new antlers against them. Summer birds to be seen include buzzards, sparrowhawks, wood warblers, redstarts and woodcock, with redbreasted mergansers on the water. In winter the wildfowl includes wigeon, greylag geese and whooper swans.

Access: Inchcailloch reached by boat from Mac Farlane & Sons Balmaha boatyard. For trips on loch, Countess Fiona *sails daily from Balloch to Inversnaid and back.*
Open: *Inchcailloch all year. Organised groups should contact NCC regional office for permission. No dogs. NCC.*
Location: *Inchcailloch is opposite Balmaha, at end of B837 from Drymen, on SE shore of loch.*
Map: *page 313, NS48/49.*

Loch Ness

Highland

This long, narrow and very deep loch is the main water body in Glen Mor – the 'Great Glen' – which runs from Fort William in the south-west almost to Inverness in the north-east. The loch itself is generally a disappoint-ment to the naturalist, with often no more than a few red-breasted mergansers on the water and common sandpipers along the shore – unless, of course, you are lucky enough to spot the famous monster! The steep sides are usually more interesting. They are well wooded and likely birds include redstarts, tree pipits and wood warblers, with a good chance of buzzards and sparrowhawks and, above the higher tops, peregrines and, with luck, golden eagles. Siskins are found in the conifer plantations and are often easily seen in the town of Fort Augustus itself. Inchnacardoch Forest Trail, off the A82 just north of Fort Augustus, may give sightings of some of these birds; looking at the various trees and plants need present no problem.

At Drumnadrochit is the intriguingly named Official Loch Ness Monster Exhibition. Here the story of the attempt to find the beast from 1933 to the present day is described and illustrated with exhibits which include equipment used in the hunt, sonar displays and models of various underwater investigations.

Open: *Drumnadrochit, Official Loch Ness Monster Exhibition, Apr to end Oct daily. Refreshments. Picnic area. Shop.*
Location: *between Fort Augustus and Inverness.*
Map: *page 314, NH52.*

Loch of the Lowes

Tayside

The largest of a group of lochs east of Dunkeld, the Loch of the Lowes is a reserve of the Scottish Wildlife Trust. There is a good selection of the commoner breeding waterbirds, but at the loch itself the main attraction is a pair of nesting ospreys, the only ones on 'public show' apart from those at Loch Garten on Speyside. They can be seen well from the observation hide at the west end of the loch. The woodlands around the loch and nearby have an interesting range of breeding birds and likely species include sparrowhawk, buzzard, woodcock, green woodpecker, jay, tree pipit, redstart, wood warbler, coal tit, goldcrest and siskin. A well-equipped visitor centre has an exhibition on the ecology of the site and a booklet on the reserve is available here.

Open: *Apr to Sep daily. Visitor centre. No dogs. CNT.*
Location: *1¼ miles NE of Dunkeld.*
Map: *page 315, NO04.*

Lochore Meadows Country Park

Fife

Opened in 1976, Lochore Meadows covers an area of nearly 1000 acres and is set around the attractive Loch Ore. The park is itself at the heart of a massive reclamation scheme that has transformed coal mining wasteland into gently rolling grassland and young woodland. When the last pit closed in 1967 over four square miles lay derelict, the legacy of 70 years exploitation of coal.

Close to the park centre is the renovated winding gear of the Mary Pit, which stands as a monument to the area's industrial past. An old winding wheel standing at the main entrance is yet another reminder. Evidence of earlier history can also be found in the park.

Some 200,000 young trees have been planted as part of the landscaping endeavour and these have attracted hundreds of birds and mammals back to the area. A specially created nature reserve is located at the western end of the loch. Numerous trails and paths reveal the best that the park has to offer. The park has many other recreational facilities.

Open: *country park at all times; park centre daily. Picnic area. Refreshments. Suitable for disabled visitors.*

Location: *3 miles N of Cowdenbeath. Main entrance off B920 at Crosshill. Access also available from A909 or B996 roads.*
Map: *page 313, NT19.*

Lochwinnoch & Castle Semple

Strathclyde

Although it is close to large centres of population and has busy roads and a railway running close by, the RSPB reserve at Lochwinnoch is nonetheless rich in birdlife. The reserve includes Barr Loch, a shallow stretch of water, and Aird Meadow, where there are patches of open water and larger extents of sedge and reed grass. Lochwinnoch Nature Centre overlooks Aird Meadow, and has an observation tower equipped with telescopes. A nature trail leads to two hides with extensive views.

Breeding birds here include great crested and little grebes, mallard, shoveler, pochard and tufted duck; black-headed gulls and sedge and grasshopper warblers. There are also small numbers of snipe, redshanks and lapwings. Kestrels and sparrowhawks nest nearby and are seen regularly. Winter wildfowl can be memorable, and a day here might yield sightings of whooper swans, greylag geese, wigeon, teal, pochard, goldeneye and goosander.

Adjacent is the 180-acre Castle Semple Country Park, the centrepiece of which is Castle Semple Loch. In winter, goosander, goldeneye and smew might be seen on this loch; during summer it is a popular place to go sailing or rowing.

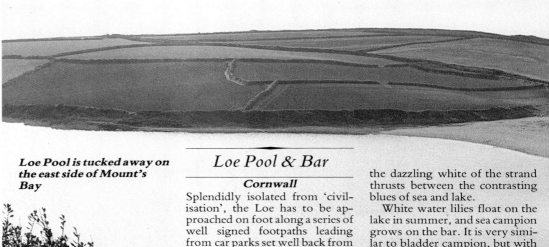

Loe Pool is tucked away on the east side of Mount's Bay

Loe Pool & Bar

Cornwall

Splendidly isolated from 'civilisation', the Loe has to be approached on foot along a series of well signed footpaths leading from car parks set well back from the lake. Loe Pool is the largest natural freshwater lake in Cornwall – divided from the sea by the great shingle and sand beach of Loe Bar. The effect can be memorable on sunny days when the dazzling white of the strand thrusts between the contrasting blues of sea and lake.

White water lilies float on the lake in summer, and sea campion grows on the bar. It is very similar to bladder campion, but with a sprawling habit. The landward side of the lake is fringed by woods, considered by many to be among the most beautiful in the county. Largely consisting of oak, sycamore and pine, with rhododendron providing extra

Open: *country park all year. Lochwinnoch reserve Thu, Fri, Sat and Sun. Admission charge for RSPB non-members. RSPB.*
Location: *S and E of Lochwinnoch, off A760.*
Map: *page 313, NS35.*

Loggerheads Country Park

Clwyd

Birds, flowers, industrial archaeology and links with famous names from the past are features of this fascinating country park whose 67 acres are overlooked by the eastern slopes of Moel Famau, the highest of the Clwydian peaks. It is carved by the River Alyn, which sometimes vanishes down 'swallow holes' in the limestone during dry weather. It also used to flood the lead mines that operated here. The site of a water wheel, built in the 1700s to pump water from the workings, can be seen from the park's one-and-a-half mile nature trail. Water still powers the restored Pentre corn mill by the information centre, where displays describe the park's ecology, geology and history.

River and woodland habitats encourage a wide variety of birdlife. Species likely to be seen in different parts of the park include heron, moorhen, herring gull, green and great spotted woodpecker, dipper, grey wagtail and goldcrest. Siskins, small members of the finch family, may also be seen. They are particularly fond of prising the seeds from alder cones.

Loggerheads was a popular beauty spot long before the country park was established. It inspired at least one famous composer, Felix Mendelssohn, and was admired by Richard Wilson, the landscape painter who lived nearby until his death in 1782. It also has a link with King Arthur. According to legend a stone on the park's southern boundary marks the point where his horse landed after leaping across the valley from Moel Famau.

Open: *all year. Information centre. Picnic area. Nature trail.*
Location: *at Loggerheads on A494 between Mold and Ruthin.*
Map: *page 309, SJ16.*

patches of colour in spring, they can be explored along numerous paths. It is possible to walk right round the Loe and the experience is worth the effort, although the journey is about six miles.

Location: *2 miles S of Helston, 1 mile E of Porthleven. NT.*
Map: *page 304, SW62.*

Green Woodpecker

Common in wooded places, and also often seen on rough grassland, where it searches for ants, the green woodpecker is the largest native British woodpecker. It is a handsome bird – green, with a yellowish rump and a red crown. Some country people call it the yaffle, after its loud ringing cry, which can sound like mad laughter. It has another commonly heard call, a sharp *quip quip* of alarm. The bird in the illustration has braced its tail against the tree to give it extra support.

London

At first glance London seems an unpromising place for wildlife. Of course, everyone knows about the pigeons and the sparrows, which are everywhere. But these are only the most obvious 'wild' inhabitants of the city. In London's parks, gardens, reservoirs, building sites and neglected areas can be found a varied and exciting cross-section of Britain's wildlife.

St James's Park

London is no more 'unnatural' than the countryside which surrounds it. Man has adapted and changed nearly all landscapes to suit his needs; London differs principally in that much of the original land surface has been covered by brick, tarmac, concrete and other materials. Even these inhospitable surfaces have been readily colonised – kestrels have nested on buildings in Westminster, black redstarts achieved fame when they nested in bomb sites throughout London after the Second World War, Oxford ragwort grows wherever it can gain a roothold, rosebay willowherb blooms in profusion on any disturbed site – the list of plants and animals which thrive in the 'concrete jungle' is long and impressive.

Waste places, forgotten corners, traditional sewage farms

What to See

The list of places to visit given here is intended to give a flavour of some of the more notable formal areas. London has thousands of acres of parks, and thousands more of what might be described as marginal land – any of which might repay exploration.

BARN ELMS RESERVOIR
In winter this reservoir is an especially good place for duck. Species likely to be seen include pochard, gadwall, wigeon, smew and tufted duck. During the spring and autumn migrations waders and terns of several species might be seen. Access to this reservoir, which lies on the south side of Hammersmith Bridge, is by permit only from the Metropolitan Water Board.

HYDE PARK AND KENSINGTON GARDENS
As is the case with the other parks in central London, Hyde Park and Kensington Gardens do not have many mammals, though hedgehogs are sometimes seen.

However, the flowerbeds are attractive to butterflies, moths and other insects, and there are many kinds of birds. These are at their greatest concentrations around the Long Water, the Serpentine and the Round Pond. Among the more common species are song thrushes, blackbirds, great tits, blue tits, wrens, greenfinches and chaffinches. There are also records of osprey, avocet and hoopoe from these parks – an indication of the surprises that might be in store for the diligent birdwatcher.

KEW GARDENS
Outstanding among botanical gardens, Kew is a 'must' for any-one interested in plants. Within the 300-acre grounds can be found every conceivable kind of plant from every corner of the globe. Many will find the hot houses, with their astonishing tropical plants, the highlight of a visit, but there are surprises and delights along every path at Kew. Part of the gardens, Queen's Cottage Grounds, are set aside as a 'wild' area, and here typically British wild flowers such as bluebells and primroses grow beneath mighty oaks. Birdwatchers will not be disappointed here, for nuthatches, treecreepers, woodpeckers, warblers and many others are commonplace.

where they can still be found – all of these can yield exciting discoveries. A slow worm might be basking in a sunny spot, butterflies feeding on buddleia, or a blackbird's nest might be found in a tangle of bramble. It is even possible to find foxes far into the heart of the city.

London's parks are more traditional hunting grounds for the city naturalist. Birds such as starlings, sparrows, blackbirds and gulls search among the grass for food, and roost in trees and on buildings. A variety of diving and dabbling ducks live on the lakes and ponds. The annual species list of birds in Regent's Park is about 100, and it includes herons, which breed in the park. The Long Water in Kensington Gardens has coots, moorhens and great crested grebes. St James's Park has a fine collection of wildfowl; a good many are pinioned, but they are joined by

many hundreds of truly wild birds. Greenwich Park, on the east side of London, has foxes, hedgehogs, a captive herd of fallow deer, and up to 60 species of birds. The three westerly royal parks – Richmond, Bushy and Hampton Court – are almost large enough to qualify as 'real' countryside, and the variety of creatures which either live in them or visit is correspondingly big. Richmond Park is famous for its badgers, and it also has red and fallow deer. The variety of habitats in Richmond Park attracts a great many species of birds; among the more unusual which might be seen are wheatears, woodcock, goosanders and tree pipits. Barn, tawny and little owls nest here, as do

several species of warbler. Green woodpeckers, nuthatches and treecreepers are among the many birds that can be seen in Bushy Park and Hampton Court. Finally, no London park would be complete without its complement of grey squirrels, many of which will feed from the hand.

In recent years the Thames has become dramatically cleaner, and the numbers and variety of fishes in water that was once poisonous is increasing all the time. Even salmon have returned. There have been sightings of porpoises and seals in the Pool of London, but it is birds that are the most frequent vis-

itors on the Thames in central London. Cormorants can often be seen perching on the cutwaters of bridges, and gulls are nearly always present. London's reservoirs can be superb places to watch for water birds – among the best are Barn Elms and Staines.

REGENT'S PARK
Within the park's 487 acres is the widest range of habitats in any of central London's parks. This diversity is reflected in the high number of bird species to be found. Of outstanding interest is the heronry on the lake. Kestrels are frequent visitors. Most common birds of park and garden are also present. Within the grounds of Regent's Park is London Zoo, so any visit is likely to be accompanied by the howling of wolves or the roaring of lions.

ST JAMES'S PARK
Created from a marshy waste to become a deer park for Henry VIII, this is the oldest of Lon-

don's royal parks. It was transformed into a formal garden during the reign of Charles II, but remodelled by John Nash in 1828. It is especially noted for the wildfowl on the lake. Here, exotic water birds from all over the world are joined by wild mallard, tufted duck, pochard and gulls. Other birds in the park include pigeons, sparrows, blackbirds and starlings – many of them so tame that they will feed from the hand.

STAINES RESERVOIR
This is one of the best reservoirs for wildfowl in England, and consequently it is an extremely popular place with birdwatchers.

During the winter months there are many species of duck here, including smew, shoveler, goldeneye and wigeon. Black terns can often be seen in spring and autumn, and a regular flock of black-necked grebes is one of the special treats in the period from August to October.

WILLIAM CURTIS ECOLOGICAL PARK
Opened in 1977, on the 100th anniversary of Curtis's *Flora of London*, this urban nature reserve lies on the South Bank just above Tower Bridge. It was created from an area of derelict wasteland and illustrates the plants and animals that will thrive in Lon-

don given the opportunity and a little encouragement.

Open: *all year daily. Information centre.*

WIMBLEDON COMMON
Heathland and large expanses of grass are the principal components of Wimbledon Common and adjoining Putney Heath. Skylarks and yellowhammers predominate on the open areas, while in areas of scrub, willow warblers and whitethroats are among the birds likely to be seen. There are also areas of mature woodland, where woodpeckers might be seen, and areas of open water, which attract wildfowl.

Longleat

Wiltshire

Longleat is famous for its safari park and its stately home, and it is these that most people come here to see, but the ancient parkland and the surrounding woods are of great interest for their native trees, plants and animals. Some of the oaks in the park may be several hundred years old, and they are of tremendous importance for indigenous wildlife since oaks support more kinds of life than any other British tree. The surrounding woodlands were once some of the finest in southern England, but much has been felled to make way for conifer plantations. Nevertheless, enough remains to be of value.

The safari park itself has lions, Siberian tigers, wolves, giraffes and many others in large enclosures which approximate to their natural territories. Boat rides can be taken on a lake complete with hippos and sealions, while an island is occupied by gorillas.

About two miles north-east of Longleat, close to the A362, is Cley Hill, a distinctively shaped dome of chalk that is a landmark for miles around. It belongs to the National Trust. On its slopes are the banks of an Iron Age hillfort, and a profusion of chalk-loving flowers. These include horseshoe vetch, chalk milkwort, several species of orchid and the oddly named bastard toadflax, an uncommon plant which is partly parasitical on other plants.

Open: *safari park Apr to Oct daily. Admission charge. Picnic Area. Refreshments. Shop. Cley Hill, free access. NT.*
Location: *3 miles W of Warminster, on unclassified road off A362.*
Map: *page 305, ST84.*

Right: Longleat in 1881. Today it is best known for its lions (above) but the grounds also harbour much indigenous wildlife

The Long Mynd – a heather-covered plateau of ancient rocks

Long Mynd & Carding Mill Valley

Shropshire

In 1881 the Carding Mill Valley was described as 'a favourite resort of excursionists'. Over 100 years later this is still the case as the valley is now historically and geographically the central point of the area of the Long Mynd managed by the National Trust. It is possible to 'explore' the Long Mynd by parking the car in one of the parks scattered around the hill, but the splendour, the peace, and the wildness are best revealed to the walker.

From Carding Mill there are three walks of varying length and difficulty. The first explores the valley and the second concentrates on prehistory, taking in the Iron Age fort on Bodbury Ring.

The third walk gives a splendid introduction to the variety of the Long Mynd; it includes the Light Spout waterfall, rolling moorland, a perpetual spring and the triangulation point on the summit of Pole Bank. On fine days the view extends from Snowdonia to the Cotswolds, and from Cader Idris to the Clent Hills. This walk is not an easy stroll, in common with other paths crossing the Long Mynd from the valleys south of Carding Mill.

The wildlife is typical of the uplands, with ravens and buzzards often the most obvious birds. Wheatears and ring ouzels (very like blackbirds but with white chests) visit in summer and the dipper is a resident of the clear streams. Brown trout and bullheads are the only fish which live in the cold, clear streams of the Long Mynd.

Heather grows in a patchwork of plots on the upper slopes. Long Mynd is the most southerly grouse moor in the country and nowadays regular mowing has superseded the traditional spring burning of old heather. The plots you see are at various stages in the regenerative process, which supplies the needs of the red grouse – young shoots for food, clearings for sunning and mature plants for cover. The red grouse themselves are often to be seen, usually exploding away across the heather with loud alarm-clock calls.

Location: *15 miles S of Shrewsbury, W of Church Stretton. NT.*
Map: *page 309, SO49.*

Brown Trout

This the only species of trout native to Britain. Brown trout are found in lakes and large rivers, and they are characteristic of smaller upland streams like those of the Long Mynd. Trout in larger waters can grow very big, but in the small, fast-flowing upland streams, fully-grown adults may be less than 10 inches long. Crustaceans, snails and insects form the major part of their diet in such streams.

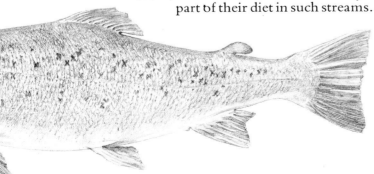

Lowestoft

Suffolk

Lowestoft is, of course, a fishing-port and a notable holiday resort with a sandy beach and all the amusements and amenities. It would probably not occur to most people as a place to watch birds. And yet it is, because of, rather than in spite of, man's activities. Fishing-boats always attract gulls, and it was probably the fishing industry that brought Lowestoft's most notable birds, the kittiwakes, to the town. These gentle gulls make a fine sight nesting on the incredibly narrow ledge at the end of the buildings on the south pier – the nearest equivalent they can find to their normal cliffs! In the cold months, the fishing-boats return with hordes of gulls in attendance, and most winters bring such unusual species as a glauc- ous gull from the north or a Mediterranean gull from the south.

Occasionally, a real rarity turns up, usually at the decidedly unglamorous waste-disposal bins of the frozen food factory north of the harbour! If this is too much, a short walk further north will usually give good views of purple sandpipers dodging crashing waves at the point.

Location: *South pier and harbour in Lowestoft.*
Map: *page 307, TM59.*

Ludshott

Hampshire & Surrey

Ludshott consists of typical Surrey heathland, supplemented by the three ponds known as Waggoners' Wells. It is generally thought that these were hammer ponds used in connection with the Wealden iron industry. There seems little doubt that the earliest of the lakes was originally used as a fish pond.

There are a number of nature walks around the lakes, and Ludshott is criss-crossed with paths and rides, so the walker may easily avoid the most visited areas. Inevitably the lakes attract most attention, and some of the plants surrounding them are becoming scarcer. In early spring, bright yellow marsh marigold is the harbinger of better days and by May the deep blues of brooklime and water speedwell appear. A wide range of trees grows around the ponds and along the streams which feed them. Farmyard ducks join tufted duck on the water, and kingfishers visit to feed on the shoals of sticklebacks. The middle lake is stocked with trout, and there are fine specimen carp in the third lake; on sunny days their grey shapes are visible just below the surface.

Following a fire on the heath in 1980, ling and bell heather are becoming re-established. The meadow brown butterfly, common but very welcome since it flies in dull as well as bright weather, has survived in numbers. On the drier soils common lizards openly bask, but although the rabbit population is recovering well, they, like the deer, are wary in an area where many dogs and humans exercise. The bird population is large and excitingly varied; over 90 species have been recorded in recent years – some are comparative rarities like the red-backed shrike, a bird which is declining in numbers in Britain.

Location: *1½ miles W of Hindhead, S of B3002. NT.*
Map: *page 306, SU83.*

Lulworth Cove

Dorset

Scenically and geologically, the coastline at Lulworth is fascinating. Lulworth Cove itself is almost circular, its waters protected from the open sea by a narrow mouth. It was formed by the sea wearing through a hard band of limestone to softer rocks behind. The wearing process continues all the time, and Mupe and Worbarrow bays, immediately to the east, were formed in the same way, but have worn away much more. The remarkable Durdle Door, a natural arch which is one of Bri-

The Lulworth skipper is found only on coastal hillsides in Dorset and Devon

tain's most famous topographical features, lies to the west, and is a fragment of the limestone band which has almost worn away at this point. Further west still limestone and softer rocks have gone entirely, leaving chalk cliffs. The changing nature of the rocks is illustrated graphically at Stair Hole, immediately to the west of Lulworth Cove. Here the rock strata are exposed, revealing contorted limestone beds

Stair Hole and Lulworth Cove

battered by the sea on one side and dipping dramatically beneath softer rocks on the landward side.

The downlands around Lulworth are rich in chalk-loving plants, and in butterflies, one of which, the Lulworth skipper, was first recognised in this area. It is very similar to the more common small skipper. Footpaths criss-cross the entire area, but immediately to the east of Lulworth is a military training ground, which is frequently closed to the public.

Location: *9 miles SW of Wareham on B3070.*
Map: *page 305, SY87.*

Lundy

Devon

Set on the western approaches to the Bristol Channel, Lundy is a bleak and windswept island about three miles long and three quarters of a mile wide. It draws thousands of visitors each year. Not all succeed in landing but, of the many who do, those with a love of solitude will return again and again.

In the old Norse language 'Lund-ey' means 'puffin isle', but although these birds still nest in the north of the island they are no longer common; their decline is probably connected with oil pol-

The CASTLE, *in the* ISLE *of* LUNDY.

lution. Over 400 species of bird, including rare vagrants from America, have been listed at Lundy. Kittiwake, fulmar and that great oceanic navigator, the Manx shearwater, nest here. Ravens still nest on Lundy, as does the largest and fastest of our falcons – the peregrine. Lundy ponies are now a recognised breed and the island boasts three unique breeds – a rat, a pygmy shrew and the Lundy cabbage. Soay sheep and wild goats are more likely to be seen, while the small Sika deer is very elusive.

Open: *all year. Landing fee, except for passengers on the* Polar Bear *or island helicopter. NT members admitted free. Refreshments. No dogs. NT/Landmark Trust.*
Location: *11 miles N of Hartland Point.*
Map: *page 304, SS14.*

Lyme Park

Cheshire

The exterior of Lyme Hall is an imposing blend of classical architectural motifs. Set in a superb walled moorland park, it almost certainly stands at a higher elevation than any other great house in England. The beauty of the interior matches the exterior.

Lyme's attraction is not, however, restricted to the house. Within the park it is still possible to glimpse the descendants of the herd of red deer which were famous at the time of the first Queen Elizabeth. Look, too, for fallow deer among the fine woods of both coniferous and deciduous trees. Aptly, lime grows well here, and both small- and large-leaved varieties can be identified.

Open: *House daily Apr to Oct except Mon (open bank holiday*

Lundy – wildlife haven and guardian of the Bristol Channel

Mon). Park and gardens all year. Admission charge to house. Refreshments. Shop. Grounds suitable for disabled visitors. NT.
Location: *S side of A6, 6½ miles SE of Stockport, entrance on W outskirts of Disley.*
Map: *page 309, SJ98.*

Lymington River & Reed Beds

Hampshire

From the Bridge Road bridge, which crosses the river on Lymington's eastern edge, there are good views upstream of reed beds that are the haunt of reed warblers and other little birds. Further upstream still are wet meadows where snipe are often seen. Views can be had from the minor roads and footpaths on either side of the river.

Downstream from the bridge the river opens up, with large mudflats on both banks. This is an excellent site for birdwatching, with kingfishers, little grebes, cormorants, black-headed gulls, and various species of tern and duck often feeding on the open water. Herons, redshank and, sometimes, spotted redshank feed on the muddy areas and at the water's edge. Where the river enters the Solent there are superb coastal marshes; these merge with the marshes of Keyhaven and Pennington to the west (see page 142). Footpaths follow the coast from Lymington right round to Keyhaven.

Location: *Lymington River flows on the E side of Lymington.*
Map: *page 306, SZ39.*

ST WILFRID'S FEAST PROCESSION

Ripon, North Yorkshire

St Wilfrid's Feast originated in 1108 with a charter granted by King Henry I to the Archbishop of York for a four-day Fair. It has since been extended to two weeks and takes place during the last week of July and the first week in August. During this fortnight there are sporting and other events to entertain both residents and visitors.

The main attraction of the feast, however, is the procession which was added to the celebrations several hundred years ago. This commences at 2pm when carnival floats leave the town hall led by a man dressed as St Wilfrid on a white horse. The procession makes its way through the city and arrives at the cathedral about 4pm, where 'St Wilfrid' is met by the Dean of Ripon. A short service is then held in the cathedral.

When: Sat before first Mon in Aug.
Map: page 310, SE37.

Ripon in the 19th century

CRANHAM FEAST AND DEER ROAST

Overton Farm, Cranham, Gloucestershire

This custom is thought to date from the mid-15th century. Its origins may have been to give the lord of the manor an opportunity to meet the commoners and 'beat the bounds' of the parish. This allowed them to claim their right to the common land. Afterwards everybody shared in a feast of venison.

The custom lapsed just before the Second World War, but was reintroduced in 1951 and has since been organised by the Cranham Feast and Deer Roasters Committee. During the afternoon a meal takes place which is attended by the lord of the manor, various guests and villagers. In the evening a deer which has been slowly roasting all day is made available to all. Villagers also enact, in mime, the meeting of the lord of the manor and the commoners.

When: first Mon after 4 Aug.
Map: page 305, SO81.

MARHAMCHURCH REVEL

Marhamchurch, Cornwall

Like many customs, this one almost died out, has been revived, and probably combines elements from several customs and ceremonies. As enacted today it consists of a little girl, the 'Queen', being crowned by 'Father Time' on the spot where St Marwenne (who brought Christianity to the village in the 6th century) had her cell. A procession follows the crowning, and the day is completed with competitions, sports and dancing.

When: *Mon after 12 Aug.*
Map: *page 305, SS20.*

Faces and flames during the Burning of Bartle. Like many such ceremonies, this one probably has very ancient roots

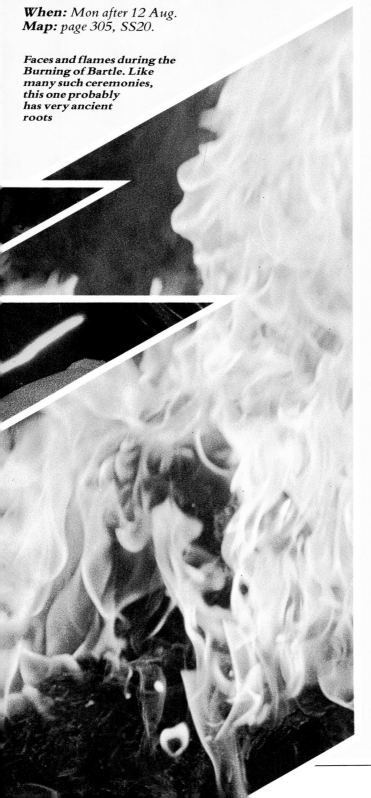

THE BURNING OF BARTLE

West Witton, North Yorkshire

An unnamed thief and sheep stealer is the central character in this centuries-old custom. He was eventually caught and brought to trial on St Batholomew's Day, which gave him the nickname 'Bartle'. He was subsequently burnt at the stake and an annual fire now takes place in remembrance of his fate. An alternative interpretation of this ceremony is that it may once have been a fertility rite, held at harvest time to ensure a good crop.

Proceedings start at 9pm when an effigy of 'T'Owd Bartle' is carried through the village while a verse beginning 'In Penhill Crags he tore his rags, ... ' is chanted. The effigy is then thrown on to the village bonfire in Grassgill Lane.

The custom forms part of the West Witton feast activities which take place during the weekend and include children's sports and fancy dress competitions.

When: *Sat nearest 24 Aug.*
Map: *page 310, SE08.*

MARLDON APPLE PIE FAIR

Marldon, Devon

This 19th-century custom has been attributed to one George Hill, who owned a large apple orchard. Every year his apples were cooked in a huge pie at the Royal Oak (now a private residence). The pie was then drawn on a donkey and cart in the annual fair procession and afterwards it was cut into slices for the public to purchase. This custom was revived in 1958, and has taken place ever since, and the pie is still drawn on a donkey and cart in the fair's procession. As in Victorian times it is then cut into slices and served with cream. Other attractions at the fair include a band, side shows and many stalls selling country crafts.

When: *Aug Bank Holiday Sat.*
Map: *page 305, SX86.*

PLAGUE SUNDAY

Eyam, Derbyshire

Few ceremonies are as poignant as this. At the end of August 1665 a box of cloth was delivered to Eyam's tailor, George Viccars. Unbeknown to him, or anyone else, the cloth was infected with the plague, and very shortly the villagers began to fall ill. In order to try to contain the infection, the rector, William Mompesson, suggested that none of the people leave the village. None of them did, and for 13 horrible months the plague raged. Eventually, it burned itself out, leaving over 250 of the people dead.

Every year a procession led by clergymen is made from the village to a rocky hollow called Cucklet Dell. This was Eyam's open-air church during the plague, and a service is held here in memory of the victims.

When: *last Sun in Aug.*
Map: *page 310, SK27.*

Maiden Castle

Dorset

Occupied from Neolithic times right through to the Roman period, Maiden Castle is probably the most famous of Britain's hill-forts. Its most imposing ramparts date from the Iron Age.

As is the case with many hill-forts, its steep banks and ditches have never been ploughed, and were kept as cropped turf by grazing sheep for hundreds of years. This has meant that a good variety of chalk-loving plants have survived here when so many other downlands have either been ploughed or sprayed. A wide variety of butterflies can been seen here in the summer months, while the birds most likely to be seen are skylarks. Corn buntings might also be seen, but they are shy and not very common. They closely resemble yellowhammers, but their harsh repetitive song, said to be like the jangle of a bunch of keys, is quite unlike that of any other bird.

Location: *2 miles SW of Dorchester on W side of A354.* **Map:** *page 305, SY68.*

Maidenhead & Cookham Commons

Berkshire

The greens and commons of Maidenhead and Cookham range in size from eight to 368 acres and include an area beside the Thames, Cookham Dean village green and an Iron Age farm enclosure.

Maidenhead Thicket is the largest of the commons and includes Robin Hood's Arbour – the prehistoric farm – a large clearing beside the main path carpeted in spring with primroses. The Thicket is also an area where nightingales may be heard singing on summer evenings. Among other birds are blackcap, whitethroat, willow warbler, chiffchaff and other members of the warbler family, while all three British woodpeckers live here throughout the year. Tits are always present, including family parties of long tailed tits, twittering excitedly as they move through the trees, often ignoring the walkers or riders below them.

Location: *N and W of Maidenhead, and near Cookham; area bounded by the Thames, A404 and A4. NT.* **Map:** *page 306, SU88.*

Malvern Hills

Hereford & Worcester

The 'hog's-back' of the Malvern Hills runs north to south for nearly ten miles and forms one of the most prominent physical features of the Midland Plain. It is hardly surprising, therefore, that the ridge was settled at an early date and there are many hill-forts, camps, ancient trackways and other features.

The central spine of the main ridge is composed of granites and related rocks of the pre-Cambrian period. These are among the oldest rocks in Britain, being somewhere between 600 million and 1000 million years old. Thin, dry soils, on which grows a sparse turf of grasses, with bilberry and gorse, cover much of the terrain. There are also extensive natural woodlands, particularly on the steeper slopes, and bracken is common. In a number of places the granites have been quarried, mainly for building and road-stone, leaving huge scars on the flanks, but these exposures are of great value to geologists in showing how the hills were formed.

Numerous footpaths run along each side of and over the main ridges of the hills, and there are several superb viewpoints. One of the best is 1394ft Worcestershire Beacon, to the west of Great Malvern. From here, in clear weather, the Black Mountains, the Wrekin, the Clee Hills and the Cotswolds can all be seen. On the south-western slopes of the beacon are the old West of England quarries, which were purchased by the Malvern Hill Conservators in 1931 and have been landscaped in several stages since. They are an example of the work undertaken by the conservators to preserve the beauty of the Malverns. Car parks here make a good base from which to explore Worcestershire Beacon.

Further south is 1114ft Herefordshire Beacon, also known as the British Camp. Crowning this summit are earthworks and fortifications dating from Iron Age times right through to the medieval period. A great linear earthwork can be seen running north and south of the beacon along the ridge of the Malverns. This is Red Earl's Dyke, or Shire Ditch, constructed in the late 13th century to mark the boundaries of the hunting forests of the Bishop of Hereford and Gilbert de Clare, Earl of Gloucester.

On the plain to the east of Herefordshire Beacon is Castlemorton Common, 600 acres of ancient grazing land owned and managed by the Malvern Hill Conservators. About 200 acres of it is a Site of Special Scientific Interest, of greatest value for its plant communities and birdlife.

South of Herefordshire Beacon are three further hills – Midsummer, Ragged Stone and Chase End. Midsummer Hill belongs partly to the National Trust, and it is crowned by an Iron Age hill-fort.

The Malverns are administered by the Malvern Hills Conservators, created by Act of Par-

The Malvern Hills are ridges of very ancient rocks separating the plains of Worcestershire and Herefordshire

Corn Bunting

Closely related to the yellowhammer, the corn bunting is found in very similar, open, habitats – like that of Maiden Castle. It does not have any of the yellowhammer's yellow plumage, and is a slightly larger bird.

liament in 1884 for the purpose of safeguarding the extensive commons from enclosure and damage. However, their most important function now is to provide facilities for public recreation and enjoyment and generally to cater for visitors while maintaining the character and atmosphere of the hills. Being so close to Worcester, the Black Country and Birmingham, they have been a popular 'lung' since Victorian times. Despite this and their increasing popularity, walkers can still find here the beauty and solitude which inspired three of Britain's best-loved composers – Holst, Vaughan Williams and Elgar.

Location: *W of Great Malvern.*
Map: *page 305–9, SO74.*

Mapledurham House & Mill

Oxfordshire

Mapledurham House and Watermill are tucked away under the foothills of the Chilterns on the north bank of the River Thames. In addition to the Tudor house and mill there are almshouses and a church. The house has many fine plaster ceilings, oak staircases and paintings collected over three centuries, and is surrounded by quiet parkland. Adjacent to the house is a 24-acre country park comprising riverside meadows and including the mill, which is the last one on the Thames to use wooden machinery. It has been restored and still grinds local grain into flour.

One of the attractions of this little bit of 'Old England' is that the approach is either down a 'no through road' leading only to the Mapledurham community, or by boat up the Thames from Caversham Bridge at Reading. The boat trip offers the possibility of seeing herons, kingfishers, little and great crested grebes and several species of duck. A public footpath leads up through beech woods, where woodpeckers, nuthatches and other woodland birds may be heard and seen.

Open: *Easter Sun to end Sep, Sat, Sun and bank holidays, pm only. Admission charge. Ground floor and gardens suitable for disabled visitors. Shop. No dogs. By river the Caversham Lady leaves promenade adjoining public car park near Caversham Bridge, Reading, at 2.15pm on days when house open.*
Location: *on Thames 3 miles NW of Caversham. Road access via unclassified roads off A4074.*
Map: *page 306, SU67.*

Marazion Marsh

Cornwall

The remains of a submerged forest provide the basis for this freshwater marsh with its reed beds, pools and damp grassland. Many migrant birds use the marsh as a nesting and feeding place, and its westerly position makes it an ideal place to watch for rarities from across the Atlantic.

Spring and autumn are ideal times to visit, but the autumn passage begins in late July, so there is only a short period when things are quiet. Springtime is especially notable for migrant yellow wagtails and wading birds, while in autumn more or less anything is possible, and normally elusive birds such as spotted crake and water rail may be seen. Herons nest in the reeds in summer; an unusual sight since these strangely prehistoric-looking birds normally nest in trees.

The wide sweep of Mounts Bay is another good area for birds, with grebes and divers out in the bay in winter. There is also likely to be a variety of interesting gulls on the beach, including, perhaps, some uncommon ones.

Access: *viewable from road. Car park opposite marsh.*
Location: *¼ mile east of Longrock, 1 mile NW of Marazion. Leave Penzance on A30 Redruth road, and at Longrock branch right on to an unclassified road and cross railway.*
Map: *page 304, SW53.*

Marbury Country Park

Cheshire

Marbury Country Park was formerly the estate of a minor stately home, now demolished. The parkland is being restored and landscaped by Cheshire County Council. The work being carried out includes the reinstatement of an overgrown arboretum. Other features of interest include fine oak woods, and the Trent and Mersey Canal, which skirts the park boundary.

The northern boundary of the park is formed by Budworth Mere, a lake notable for its bird-life. There is a hide in the park, overlooking a reed bed which is a reserve of the Cheshire Conservation Trust. Here it is possible to see nesting great crested grebes, little grebes, coots and moorhens, as well as reed warblers at the north-western limit of their range. In the winter, large numbers of wildfowl can be seen on the mere.

Open: *all year daily. Part CNT.*
Location: *2 miles N of Northwich on Comberbach road.*
Map: *page 309, SJ67.*

Margam Country Park

West Glamorgan

Margam Castle, a 'Gothick' mansion built in the 1830s and now a ruined shell, is the focal point of this award-winning 850-acre country park whose wide-ranging attractions include a unique herd of Glamorgan cattle and the largest herd of fallow deer in South Wales. Near the mansion, much older buildings recall the Abbey of Margam which was founded in 1147 and flourished for nearly 400 years. Another notable link with the past is the magnificent, 327ft-long orangery. It was completed in 1790 and restored in the 1970s.

The park's steep, wooded hills provide superb views across Swansea Bay and are known to have been farmed during the Bronze Age. Later settlers were responsible for the banks and ditches of Mynydd-y-Castell, a seven-acre Iron Age hill-fort. The higher ground combines with lakes and streams to provide habitats for a rich variety of birds and mammals. These include foxes, hares, badgers, skylarks, stonechats, buzzards, kestrels and sparrowhawks. The lakes and streams attract mute swans, pochard, tufted duck, kingfishers and other species, while Margam also has a heronry on Furzemill Pond.

Open: *all year: Apr to Oct Tue to Sun (also Mon in Aug and bank holidays); Nov to Mar Wed to Sun. Admission charge. Information centre. Waymarked walks. Picnic areas. Refreshments. Shop. Suitable for disabled visitors.*
Location: *on A48 SE of Port Talbot.*
Map: *page 305, SS88.*

Marlborough Downs

Wiltshire

This great expanse of rolling chalk downland lies between Marlborough and Swindon and extends north-eastwards to the Lambourn Downs. This area is rich in archaeological remains, particularly from the late Bronze Age, with impressive enclosures and lynchets (banks of soil created by ploughing on slopes), especially on Ogbourne Down; long barrows south of Avebury; round barrows; stone circles; and the astonishing man-made mound of Silbury Hill, whose function and purpose is not known.

During the 18th century a number of 'white horses' were cut in the chalk turf, giving this part of Wiltshire the name 'White Horse Country'. Lying on the surface over several areas of downland are 'fields' or 'streams' of sarsen stones, many of which were worked for building stone in the past. These blocks of sandstone are the remains of strata which once overlay the chalk. They take their name from saracen – a reference to their foreign-looking appearance. They are also known as grey wethers. Wethers are sheep, and the stones can indeed look like flocks from a distance. The best grouping of sarsens is on Fyfield Down.

Botanically the Marlborough Downs are not as rich as those further south (see Pewsey Down, page 226), but in winter they are well known for large flocks of finches, buntings and thrushes. Golden plovers are also often seen on the downlands at this time of year. Visiting short- and long-eared owls and resident kestrels may be seen quartering the ground for food. (Also see the Ridgeway, page 235.)

Access: *by public footpaths.*
Location: *W of A345 N of Marlborough and W of Marlborough N of A4.*
Map: *page 305, SU17.*

The grey heron is a familiar character by water throughout Britain. It spends a good deal of time standing quite still, but it can move very fast when stabbing at a fish with its long bill

Silbury Hill, an enigmatic monument on the west side of the Marlborough Downs

An engraving of Marsden Rock

Marsden Rock & Marsden Bay

Tyne & Wear

This spectacular stack of magnesian limestone stands less than 100 yards from the mainland cliffs just three miles south of the entrance to the River Tyne. Battered by the winter storms of the north-east coast, it is heavily eroded and a natural arch has been formed which gets larger in succeeding winters. The top of the stack is now inaccessible except to the most foolhardy, but early in this century brass bands used to hold concerts on top.

Their place these days has been taken by a thriving breeding colony of cormorants. These large black seabirds occupy the entire flat top of the rock during the spring and summer months and have as neighbours on eroded ledges lower down both fulmars and kittiwakes. Most of the kittiwakes, however, of which there are over 4000 pairs, nest on

the mainland cliffs. This colony is one of the most accessible anywhere in Britain: a staircase down the cliffs to the beach, passes very close to the nesting birds. The long sweeping sandy bay is bounded by rocky outcrops where the rock pools are rich in marine life. This richness of species is also evident in the flora of the cliff tops where they have been left unmown. Another unusual feature of the bay is the public house built into the limestone grottos of the mainland cliff.

Location: *alongside A183 between South Shields and Whitburn.*
Map: *page 310, NZ46.*

Primrose and bugle – two wild flowers often found in woodlands such as The Mens

grazed grassland which has become overgrown with scrub; this in turn eventually becomes woodland. Where the trees have not yet taken over, gorse and bracken thrive. Such places are attractive to a large variety of birds, insects and other animals. Bullfinches, chaffinches, linnets, long-tailed tits and many different warblers find ideal nesting sites in the bushes and dense herbage. Sparrowhawks and kestrels live and hunt their prey here. Adding even greater variety are ponds where newts and dragonflies may be seen.

Open: *all year. CNT.*
Location: *5¼ miles N of Shrewsbury on unclassified road on W side of Merrington between A528 and B5067.*
Map: *page 309, SJ42.*

Martin Mere

Lancashire

The rich farmland south of the Ribble Estuary is based on peat which in places reaches depths of 20ft. Martin Mere sits in the middle of this area and, although parts of the land hold water in severe weather, it is a far cry from the days when the mere was the largest in Lancashire, being three miles long and two miles across. The first serious attempt at drainage was in 1692 when about two thousand men were employed to cut a drainage channel from the mere to the sea. Persistence has eventually paid off for the farming enterprises of the area, but not everyone wants to see the area dry.

The Wildfowl Trust acquired 360 acres of the most primitive part of the old marsh in 1972 and set about re-creating some of the open water habitats. A variety of small ponds as well as an extensive lake are home to more than 1600 wildfowl from all over the world.

In addition to the formal collection there is a 300-acre wild refuge overlooked by spacious hides. Thousands of pink-footed geese from Iceland visit this area in winter together with large numbers of pintail and teal from northern Europe. The refuge is also a good place in winter to see whooper swans (also from Iceland) and, most exciting of all, the Bewick's swans, which have travelled some 2600 miles from Siberia.

Open: *all year daily (except 24 and 25 Dec). Admission charge. Refreshments. Information centre. Picnic site. Shop. Parts suitable for disabled visitors. No dogs. WFT.*
Location: *2 miles NW of Burscough Bridge on unclassified road between Burscough Bridge and Holmeswood.*
Map: *page 309, SD41.*

The Mens

West Sussex

Most woodland in the Weald has been managed as coppice or coppice-with-standards (the traditional practice where an understorey of smaller trees and shrubs is cut down on a rotational basis, while some trees, the 'standards', are allowed to grow on to maturity before felling). The Mens is unusual in having been left unmanaged for many centuries except for the removal of mature timber trees and, in this way, has developed the character of primaeval 'high forest'.

Where the Wealden clays are lighter, great beech trees tower above and shade a dense shrub layer of holly and young beech. On heavier clays oak and beech share a more open canopy and in these lighter conditions the understorey contains a wider range of shrubs and small trees including ash, crab apple, hazel, holly, Midland hawthorn, spindle and yew with a herb-rich ground cover of wood anemone, bluebell, bugle and many other wild flowers. There are also areas of birch and bracken.

This combination of high forest and glades is an excellent habitat for woodland birds and butterflies: most notable of the latter is the purple emperor, which spends much of its time flying high among the upper branches. Three species of deer are found: roe are abundant, while fallow and muntjac are seen less frequently. In autumn the Mens is especially rich in fungi; some of the species are found nowhere else.

Access: *only on footpaths and rights of way. CNT.*
Location: *alongside A272 road 3¼ miles E of Petworth.*
Map: *page 306, TQ02.*

Merrington Green Nature Trail

Shropshire

Merrington Green is an area of common land, grazed for centuries by commoners' cattle. Such places were often used by pigs, goats and geese as well. Now it is no longer economic for commoners to keep animals in that way and, ironically, while farming intensifies on private land, commons everywhere are growing wild through lack of management. The Merrington Trail is one of several established by the Shropshire Trust for Nature Conservation. It illustrates vividly the changes that take place when grazing ceases.

Here a typical story unfolds of the development of long un-

Minsmere

Suffolk

This internationally famous reserve is the showpiece of the Royal Society for the Protection of Birds. No other area of comparable size in Britain can boast so many types of breeding bird – over 100 species are regularly recorded.

This richness comes from careful management of a variety of habitats; within the reserve's 1500 acres there are woodlands, heaths, reed beds, pasture, beaches and dunes. One of the most exciting places on the reserve is the Scrape. This is an entirely man-made addition to the diversity of habitats and consists of a shallow lagoon with areas of wet mud and islands with surfaces of shingle, moss or grass. It is on the Scrape that the RSPB's emblem – the avocet – breeds. These elegant black-and-white birds had not bred in Britain for something like 150 years until they began to breed on Havergate Island (further down the coast) in the years after the end of the Second World War. Their unmistakable up-turned bills are used to skim tiny creatures from the water surface.

Overlooking the reed swamp, visitors might see the spectacular aerial food-pass of the marsh harrier. This takes place during the breeding season; the male catches food for the female and the brood, and passes it to the female in mid-air. Bitterns are also regularly seen in the reed beds, but visitors are more likely to hear their extraordinary booming calls. Spoonbills and purple herons are occasional visitors.

A pylon hide, with its top high in the tree canopy, gives intimate glimpses into the lives of woodland birds, and views across the reserve. Many nightingales sing, and in the evening the strange churring of the nightjar rolls across the heath. There are many other hides dotted strategically across the reserve, giving the best possible views of the birds and their habitats.

As well as birds, Minsmere has a varied and interesting list of plants, especially in the damp pasture, where marsh orchids, lousewort, yellow rattle and much else can be found. Red deer live in the woods, hares are often seen around the Scrape, and otters have been known to breed here. Less welcome are coypus and mink – both species originally escaped from fur farms.

The RSPB controls the number of visitors to Minsmere very carefully, but if the reserve is full there are excellent free public hides overlooking it from the beach.

Open: *Apr to mid Sep, Sat, Sun, Mon and Wed; mid Sep to end Oct, Sun only; Nov to Mar, Sun and Wed. All Suns and bank holiday periods, including Wed, members only. Permits issued on 'first come, first served' basis. Admission charge for RSPB non-members. Information centre. Shop. Picnic area. RSPB.*
Location: *E of B1125 Leiston-Blythburgh road, 2 miles SE of Westleton.*
Map: *page 307, TM46.*

Minsmere at Sunset. A tremendous variety of bird species is attracted to this famous reserve

Moel Famau Country Park

Clwyd

This 2000-acre country park takes its name from the highest peak in the Clwydian Range, which forms the 'spine' of north-east Wales. Walkers who reach the summit of Moel Famau on a clear day are rewarded with majestic views embracing Snowdonia, the Isle of Man, the Lake District and the Pennines. Many of Liverpool's biggest buildings can also be identified, while the bridge linking Runcorn and Widnes is another landmark.

The path to the summit, 1817 feet above sea level, climbs through Forestry Commission land where willow warblers, goldcrests, wrens and many other tree-loving birds may be seen. Higher up the mountain, kestrels and buzzards hover above open moorland where red grouse and meadow pipits breed. Skylarks and ring ouzels bring song to the summit, where the base of the ill-fated Jubilee Tower makes a fine viewing platform. The tower was planned to mark the 50th year of George III's reign, and thousands of people climbed Moel Famau when the foundation stone was laid in 1810. It never reached its intended height of 150 feet and collapsed during a storm in 1862.

Open: *all year.*
Location: *3½ miles NE of Ruthin. N of unclassified road between Loggerheads and Llanbedr-Dyffryn-Clwyd.*
Map: *page 309, SJ16.*

Morecambe Bay

Lancashire

Morecambe Bay's vast expanses are feeding grounds for the largest population of waders wintering anywhere in Britain. A very high proportion of them can be found on the RSPB's 6000-acre reserve, which lies on the east side of the bay. But this is not just a place for teeming throngs of birds; it is a giant panorama of cloud and sky, shifting sands and glistening sea, a sea which seems to retreat to the horizon at low tide. In fact the tide dictates the day in the bay for both the human population and the birds. Humans must be wary of the advancing tide – particularly on the salt marsh, where the channels become full of deep water in minutes. The same tides mean that twice a day the birds lose valuable feeding areas. During this period the birds must find a safe roost and one of the largest of these is at Hest Bank, near the railway signal box. Here waders such as knot, dunlin, oystercatcher, curlew, bar-tailed godwit, ringed plover and redshank can be watched at close range. Shelduck and pintail feed or roost off-shore, while wigeon graze the salt marsh. Merlins hunt the area during the winter months, but the most exciting birds of prey in the area are peregrines, here to hunt the waders. They can be seen perched on posts around the bay, or in pursuit as the waders whirl around the sky in panic. At the northern end of the reserve, where limestone cliffs back the marsh, a rich collection of flowers includes bloody cranesbill, rock rose and rock samphire.

Open: *all year. Information centre. RSPB.*
Location: *off A5105 Morecambe to Carnforth road at Hest Bank (over level crossing beside main road).*
Map: *page 309, SD46.*

Morgan's Hill

Wiltshire

It is in Wiltshire that England's largest remaining tracts of unploughed and unimproved chalk downland can be found. Even though the sites may be close to each other, there is often a tremendous difference in the character of the places, and in the kinds of plants and animals to be found in them. Morgan's Hill is an excellent example. It is especially noted for its orchids, and has one of the most diverse assemblies of these lovely flowers in Wiltshire. Among the many species are fly, bee and musk orchids, and the only colony of marsh helleborine (usually found in marshes and fens) on open downland in the country. Many other spectacular chalk downland plants can be found here, including round-headed rampion, whose brilliant blue flowers bloom in July and August. A small stand of juniper, a prickly shrub whose berries are used to flavour gin, can also be seen.

Morgan's Hill is part of the North Wessex Area of Outstanding Natural Beauty, and from it there are superb views of sweeping downland slopes. The Wansdyke, an earthwork built in the post-Roman period, runs across the hill and can be seen in places stretching away to the south-east, while to the east are numerous prehistoric tumuli, earthworks and barrows – monuments very typical of the Wiltshire landscape.

Location: *between Devizes and Calne, off unclassified road linking A4 and A361. Footpath leads across a golf course from small car park on E side of road.*
Map: *page 305, SU06.*

Morte Estate

Devon

Along the north Devon coast between Croyde and Ilfracombe the National Trust has a splendid range of properties known collectively as the Morte Estate. At Woolacombe is perhaps the finest sandy beach in the country. Behind it is grassland rich in flowers and butterflies. Around Baggy Point, at the south end of Morte Bay, it is possible to enjoy fine views of the coast from a path which those with no head for heights will be pleased to know does not run close to the edge of the 300ft-high cliffs!

In spring, autumn and winter there is a splendid sense of isolation on the paths to Morte Point, north of Woolacombe. A few sheep and cattle, seabirds and the churning sea far below are the visitor's companions. The long Atlantic rollers continually crash against the knife-edged slate columns, and twice each day the tidal surge called the Morte Race charges around the point.

From Bull Point to Lee the coastal path follows the cliff edge. Beyond Lee it climbs inland before descending to the edge of Ilfracombe and joining Torrs Walk and possibly the best of all the views of the coastline around Ilfracombe.

Location: *between Ilfracombe and Croyde, 4 miles W of A361 Barnstaple–Ilfracombe road. NT.*
Map: *page 305, SS44.*

Mortimer Forest

Shropshire/Herefs & Worcs

For excellent views of this ancient hunting forest first go to the village of Wigmore, on the A4110 road between Leominster and Knighton. Here there is a castle mound, all that remains of a stronghold built by the Mortimers, powerful Marcher lords whose base was at Ludlow.

Covering some 5000 acres, the forest is of as much interest for the rocks which underlie it as for the plants and animals that live within it. It stands on top of a crest of very ancient limestones and shales, laid down by the sea some 400 million years ago, and its north-eastern extremity is formed by the River Teme at Ludlow, where a famous 'bone bed' is located. The remains of a primitive fish that had no jaws are among the discoveries that have been made here. A trail guide produced by the Nature Conservancy Council is available from Ludlow Museum (where examples of local rocks and fossils can be seen); it points out the most interesting geological features. Two waymarked trails beginning from a car park 1½ miles west of Ludlow's Ludford Bridge explore other aspects of the forest. On these a Mortimer Forest speciality might be spotted – a unique variety of fallow deer with a long coat. One of Britain's prettiest woodland butterflies, the silver-washed fritillary, might also be seen.

Open: *Ludlow Museum, Easter to Sep, Mon to Sat, also Sun June to Aug.*
Location: *forest is 2 miles SW of Ludlow, off Ludlow to Wigmore road. Part NCC.*
Map: *page 309, SO47.*

Morwellham Quay

Devon

Once the greatest copper port in Queen Victoria's Empire, Morwellham fell into forgotten retirement until it was transformed by a charitable trust into a vivid reconstruction of the heyday of Victorian prosperity and success. Visitors will see the blacksmith, assayer, quay workers and many others in authentic surroundings and in authentic costumes. It is possible to travel underground into a copper mine and to ride on a horse-drawn wagonette.

For all those who love a taste of the past, Morwellham is an excellent destination, and it is also of interest to those who enjoy the countryside. A nature trail explores the secrets of a Devon valley, taking in a typical lane and its

Morecambe Bay. Wildfowl and waders feed on the bay's sandflats and salt marshes

varied wildlife, especially rich in ferns. The woodland visited includes both conifers and broad-leaved trees with their resident birds – principally tits and finches. The trail leads to the tow-path of the Tavistock Canal, where frogs frequent the shallower areas. The trail ends at the Tamar, tidal to Morwellham, and here such birds as herons and kingfishers might be seen. Kingfishers often perch on branches over the water – waiting for unwary fishes to swim below.

Open: *all year. Admission charge. Refreshments. Shop. Picnic area.*
Location: *on N bank of Tamar 4 miles SW of Tavistock.*
Map: *page 305, SX46.*

Curlew

The curlew, Britain's largest wader, uses its long, curved bill to probe in mud for worms. It also searches shallow water and rocky places on the shore for other creatures. Curlews nest inland, but non-breeding birds can be seen on the coast at almost any time. After the breeding season huge numbers of them may gather to feed and roost in Morecambe Bay.

Mount Edgcumbe Country Park

Cornwall

A magnificent setting on a promontory overlooking Plymouth Sound makes this country park particularly memorable. Perhaps the most enjoyable way to visit the park is by passenger ferry from Plymouth. The grounds are a mixture of formal gardens, which have fountains and statues in several styles, and open parkland. The old deer park leads south towards the coast and there are several follies as well as superb views. Tree-lined walks pass marvellous evergreen oaks – hybrids of cork and Turkey oaks raised in the West Country in the 18th century. In spring primroses and daffodils provide a scatter of yellow on the open grasslands.

A more remote and wilder part of the peninsula on which the park lies is to the west, where the Cornwall Coast Path borders the park and the Sound and continues round Penlee Point and Rame Head to Whitsand Bay. Here there is always the chance of seeing seabirds, especially in spring and autumn.

Open: *all year daily. Information centre. Refreshments.*
Location: *3 miles E of Millbrook, at the extreme SE corner of Cornwall. Passenger ferry to the main Cremyll entrance from Admirals Hard at Stonehouse, W of Plymouth city centre. By road off the B3247, at the Maker entrance.*
Map: *page 305, SX45.*

The 18th-century folly that crowns Mow Cop

Mow Cop

Cheshire/Staffordshire

Mow Cop rises about 1100ft above sea level, and appears at first glance to be a very natural landmark, but man is responsible for much of what we see today. Formed of gritstone, the top has been extensively quarried, while both coal mining and limestone quarrying have altered the sides, and the mount is crowned by the most obviously artificial of edifices.

The castle-like Gothick folly was built in 1754 by the owner of the Rode Hall estate, Randle Wilbraham, to create a focal point on the skyline three miles to the east of the hall. Originally used as a summerhouse, it stands exactly over the boundary between Staffordshire and Cheshire. Below the folly is a stone monument recording an extraordinary twelve-hour long prayer meeting held on Mow Cop in 1807 from which rose the religious movement known as Primitive Methodism. One hundred years later over 70,000 disciples of the movement gathered to worship on their 'Holy Mount'. An unusual rock formation called the Old Man of Mow adds further interest to this spot, and it is here that the Mow Cop Spur Trail – part of the Staffordshire Way footpath – begins.

The view from the triangulation station at the top of the hill is dramatic and extensive. To the north, beyond the ridge of Alderley Edge lies Manchester, while to the north-east is the Peak District. Looking south the view extends from Cannock Chase to the North Shropshire Plain with the South Shropshire Hills visible 50 miles away. To the west, over the Cheshire Plain, the view is to the Berwyn Mountains in Wales.

Location: *at Mow Cop village, 2 miles NE of Kidsgrove, 4 miles S of Congleton, 2 miles W of Biddulph. NT.*
Map: *page 309, SJ85.*

Muirshiel Country Park

Strathclyde

Country parks are often set in domestic landscapes, but Muirshiel lies at the wilder end of the spectrum. Set in a high valley amid rolling moorland, it is reached by single-track road up the lovely Calder Glen from the village of Lochwinnoch. It consists of the policy, or enclosed woodland, of the former Muirshiel Estate. Trails and walks radiate from its information centre, and many will enjoy walking beyond the park to the peak of Windy Hill, over 1000ft high, for a view of the moors and the Firth of Clyde, or to a waterfall on the River Calder.

The park brings together moorland, woodland and river, which provide several different kinds of habitat and therefore a profusion of plants and a large population of birds, small animals and insects. Among the plants, the rhododendrons are always lovely in June; while more common mammals include rabbits, hares, woodmice, stoats, field voles, weasels and shrews. Roe deer are also residents and there is a chance of seeing the kids in early summer. The park's birdlife best illustrates the diversity of habitats, with buzzards, kestrels, hen harriers and sparrowhawks hunting over the moorland. Grey wagtails and dippers are to be seen along the river. Coal tits and goldcrests are common throughout the conifer plantations and the mixed woodland has bullfinches all year round.

Open: country park at all times.

Information centre. Ranger service.
Location: 4 miles NW of Lochwinnich. Signposted along unclassified road off B786 from Lochwinnoch.
Map: page 313, NS36.

Mull of Galloway

Dumfries & Galloway

Situated at the extreme south-western corner of Scotland, this rugged granite headland is of considerable interest. The RSPB has a reserve on the cliffs at the end of the headland, which illustrates much of the interest of the area. On the cliffs are small colonies of breeding seabirds, including fulmars, cormorants, shags, guillemots, razorbills, kittiwakes and herring and great black-backed gulls, with black guillemots around the rocks below. With a major colony to the north at Ailsa Craig, and a smaller one to the east on the Scare Rocks, gannets are almost always passing to and fro offshore. Manx shearwaters are often seen too, with the best numbers passing in late summer and autumn. As well as birdlife the reserve is rich in wild plants. Among them, purple milk vetch and spring squill can be found on the clifftop turf, while on the rocks below notable species include golden and rock samphires, rock sea spurrey, rock sea lavender, and Scots lovage.

Luce Bay, to the east, can be good for various species of seaduck during the winter months, while Loch Ryan at Stranraer often has divers and grebes.

Open: RSPB reserve at all times.
Location: 5 miles S of Drummore via B7041 and unclassified road.
Map: page 312, NX13.

Mull

Strathclyde

The Isle of Mull has been described as 'the Highlands in miniature'; perhaps it is more than that, representing all that is best in western Scotland in microcosm. It has a lovely coastline and mountains, and a character which is part West Highland and part Hebridean.

Armed with the 1:50 000 Ordnance Survey map, the visitor can explore most of the island by road. Inland, the route from Craignure through Glen More to the Ross of Mull is particularly recommended for wild scenery in the glen itself and the truly Hebridean nature of the landscape towards Bunessan and Fionnphort. An alternative to the Ross is to leave Glen More on the B8035, crossing the base of the Ardmeanach peninsula and following the coast road round to Loch na Keal: on a good day the panorama from this road is superb, with Staffa and the Treshnish Isles clearly visible. From Gruline the coast road around the north-western part of the island is equally fine and, ultimately, brings you to the delightful little town of Tobermory. The circuit is completed by heading south again via Salen.

The waters around Mull are good for seabirds. Auks, shags, fulmars, gannets and kittiwakes are usually all seen from the ferries, and Manx shearwaters are not uncommon. Look out, too, for common dolphins and basking sharks. The sheltered inshore waters are excellent for common seals. Eider duck, red-breasted mergansers and black guillemots seem to be everywhere. Common gulls and oystercatchers are among the most typical shorebirds – and in the early mornings and evenings there is always a good chance of seeing an otter on any of the sea-lochs. Red-throated divers are frequent along the coast, and there is always a possibility of the much less common black-throated diver; wintering great northern divers often stay until early summer and may even be seen in full breeding plumage.

It will be an unlucky visitor who fails to see red deer along the way and, with a little patience, blue hares should be seen too. Buzzards, hooded crows, wheatears and stonechats are all common 'roadside' birds and in the wilder areas it is worth keeping an eye open for merlins, hen harriers and ring ouzels. Golden eagles are numerous on Mull and might be seen almost anywhere in the more mountainous areas or along the wilder stretches of coast: even the day visitor will be unlucky if he or she leaves the island without having seen at least one!

A visit to the Information Office in Tobermory is recommended for information on the many historical and archaeological spots on the island. Aros Park and Gardens (one mile from Tobermory on the Salen road) is worth a visit; there are about five miles of footpaths here, among superb rhododendrons and azaleas. Torosay Castle, on the road from Craignure to Lochdon, has superb gardens which are open all year. For the really energetic, there is a stiff walk (five miles) from the east end of Loch Scridain along the southern shore of the Ardmeanach peninsula to 'the Wilderness': this area is owned by the National Trust for Scotland. At the Burg stands the 40ft MacCulloch's Tree, a fossil estimated to be 50,000,000 years old and accessible at low water.

Access: ferries from Oban all year daily; ferries from Lochaline all year daily except Sun. Part NTS.
Open: Aros Park and Gardens all year daily. Torosay Castle May to Sep daily. Admission charge. Shop. Refreshments. Picnic area.
Map: page 312, NM63.

Near Aridholas, Ross of Mull

HOP HOODENING

Canterbury, Kent

Today this ceremony is a bright and cheerful affair, but it originated as a fertility custom that was taken very seriously and could have been frightening to encounter. Virtually all that remains of the original is its name; the Hoodening (or Hooden) Horse appeared at Christmas in many parts of the country. It was a man disguised as an animal, and he carried a horse's head, usually an actual horse's skull, on the end of a long pole. This weird creature visited all the houses in the neighbourhood to bring luck.

Now the ceremony takes place in September and begins in the dignified surroundings of the precincts of Canterbury Cathedral. It consists of dances by morris men and other country dancers in the presence of the 'Hop Queen'. Later the dancers move to the nearby village of Wickhambreaux, where they dance in front of The Rose pub, which displays the sign of the defunct Hooden Horse pub, which once stood in the village. In the afternoon the dancers perform in Faversham's West Street, after which they return to Canterbury, where they dance in the St George's area. In the evening a barn dance takes place at Wickhambreaux village hall.

When: *first Sat in Sep.*
Map: *page 306, TR15.*

September

CORNISH GORSEDD

Cornwall

The Cornish Gorsedd was founded at Boscawen Un on 21 September 1928 and is allied to the gorsedds in Wales and Brittany. It exists to maintain the national Celtic spirit of Cornwall, to encourage the study of Cornish history, language, art, music and literature and to promote peaceful co-operation among those who work for the honour of Cornwall.

Abbots Bromley horn dancers past and present

Much of the colour of the ceremonies of the gorsedd is lent by the bards, dressed in blue robes. Proceedings open with groups of young dancers, followed by the commemoration of bards who have died during the previous year. Afterwards the Grand Bard welcomes and bestows bardic names upon new bards who are initiated into the gorsedd. In order to qualify for membership the nominee should have manifested the Celtic spirit or have rendered some outstanding service to Cornwall or Cornish people.

The event is concluded by a public concert in the evening and a church service in the appropriate parish church on Sunday afternoon.

When: *first Sat in Sep.*
Map: *various locations in Cornwall – it is held at a different place every year.*

RUSHBEARING

Sowerby Bridge, West Yorkshire

This ancient ceremony originated to provide rushes for covering church floors. During the 17th century they were transported on a rushcart, which today forms the centrepiece of the celebrations.

For many years the custom had lapsed at Sowerby Bridge, but in 1977 it was revived, and has taken place annually ever since. Because of its popularity the route has been extended to include more churches – all of which receive a token branch of rushes.

On Saturday morning a procession, including the rushcart and morris dancers, leaves the Mason's Arms pub near Warley and during the afternoon stops are made at different locations including various churches and hostelries. The remainder of the route from Sowerby to Ripponden is covered on Sunday afternoon in a similar fashion.

When: *first Sat and Sun in Sep.*
Map: *page 310, SE02.*

ABBOTS BROMLEY HORN DANCE

Abbots Bromley, Staffordshire

Several theories about the origins of this dance are offered, but the most usually accepted one is that it is descended from very ancient fertility rites. The dancers consist of 12 men – six carry reindeer antlers weighing between 16 and 26lbs. They are accompanied by 'Maid Marion', 'Hobby Horse', 'Jester', a boy carrying a bow and arrow, another carrying a triangle and a musician playing an accordion.

The event commences early in the morning when the dancers collect the horns from the parish church. The horns are then 'danced' in front of the church and outlying farms on the way to Blithfield Hall for refreshments. After this the dancers return to the village, arriving about tea-time. From then until dusk the dance moves along Bagot Street, past the Butter Cross to the High Street and Lichfield Road and back to the church where the horns are carefully stored away until the following year.

When: *Mon following first Sun after 4 Sep.*
Map: *page 309, SK02*

WIDECOMBE FAIR

Widecombe-in-the-Moor, Devon

According to records the first fair at Widecombe was held on 25 October 1850. It is one of the most famous fairs in the world owing, largely, to the song about 'Old Uncle Tom Cobbleigh and all'.

Nowadays it is primarily a pleasure fair attracting large crowds and includes traditional games as well as the selling of sheep and ponies from Dartmoor.

When: *second Tue in Sep.*
Map: *page 305, SX77.*

Painswick's clipping ceremony

PAINSWICK ANCIENT CLIPPING

Painswick, Gloucestershire

The clipping ceremony may have descended from a pagan Roman festival. It later became Christianised and has been held in Painswick annually since 1897 to commemorate the dedication of the church to the Blessed Virgin Mary. The name 'clipping' is taken from the ancient word 'yclept' which means embracing. The ceremony is not (as is often thought) connected with the 99 ancient clipped yew trees which are such a famous feature of Painswick's churchyard.

The ceremony begins when the clergy, choir and children from Painswick and neighbouring parishes process round the churchyard. Hands are then joined in an unbroken chain to encircle and embrace the church and a traditional hymn is sung while dancing to and fro. Many adults watch the proceedings from the churchyard and take part in the thanksgiving service that follows. Afterwards each child is given a traditional Painswick bun and silver coin.

When: *first Sun after 19 Sep.*
Map: *page 305, SU80.*

Naphill Common & Bradenham Woods

Buckinghamshire

Set on the plateau and dip slope of the Chilterns, these woods have several interesting and unusual features. Most people will associate the Chilterns with beech woods, but on Naphill Common, oaks, both sessile and pedunculate, are the predominant trees over large areas. Between 150 and 200 years ago Naphill was a much more open and grazed common, but with the reduction in grazing natural regeneration has taken place. There are some large holly and cherry trees within the woodlands and in patches beech does occur. The understorey and shrub layers are mainly of holly, cherry, whitebeam, rowan, yew, willow, elder, bramble with honeysuckle, bracken and some heather. In Bradenham Woods beech is dominant although oaks and whitebeam do occur. As in many of the Chiltern dip-slope woods the ground flora is relatively poor, with wood-sorrel and foxgloves being two of the more obvious species. In nearby Park Wood there is a more diverse flora in both the shrub and ground layers.

Access: on public paths.
Location: 4 miles NW of High Wycombe on the A4010 Princes Risborough Road; turn off to Bradenham village; woods are on either side of road beyond village.
Map: page 306, SU89.

Nap Wood

East Sussex

Although a visit to Nap Wood involves obtaining a permit, the effort is well worth making, for it is an excellent example of a Wealden oak wood. It is bordered by two little streams, running through ravines which they have gouged in the soft sandstone. A pond adds to the variety of habitats.

Oak may be studied in a range of development, from old coppiced areas through fine mature specimens to comparatively young trees. Unlike the oak, the birch and rowan need little encouragement to grow here, and there are good specimens of yew and wild cherry in the drier parts of the wood.

Along the wet valleys of the streams, alder and ash flourish, and ferns are prominent in a climate which closely resembles that of the south-western areas of Britain. Look for the hay-scented buckler fern, found now almost exclusively in the West Country and believed to be a relic of the time some 7000 years ago when the whole country had a damp, cool but humid climate.

Open: Sun Apr to Oct; applications for permits to visit the reserve at other times should be made to the Conservation Officer, Sussex Trust for Nature Conservation, Woods Mill, Henfield. No dogs. NT. CNT.
Location: 4 miles S of Tunbridge Wells on A267.
Map: page 306, TQ53.

Newborough Warren National Nature Reserve

Gwynedd

Millions of tons of sand, swept inland by exceptionally violent storms, created this wilderness of dunes and marram grass during the 14th century. The 'desert' now forms part of a 1565-acre Nature Conservancy Council reserve which sweeps up the Anglesey coast at its southern end to include Llanddwyn Island, part of Newborough Forest, and an extensive salt marsh on the eastern side of the River Cefni's broad estuary.

As its name indicates, New-

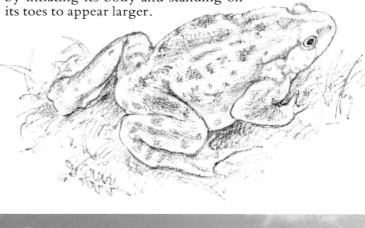

Common toad

Toads are still quite common, but they, like newts and frogs, have suffered through the loss of ponds and wetland areas, their natural spawning grounds. The toad's warts contain one of its defensive mechanisms – a poison which is released if it is attacked. It can also deter attack by inflating its body and standing on its toes to appear larger.

borough Warren swarmed with rabbits until myxomatosis started taking its toll in 1954. As a result, the vegetation has increased and formed a natural carpet to stabilise inland dunes where orchids and many other plants now flourish. The reserve is also a breeding ground for toads and lizards. Birds likely to be seen include herring gulls, oystercatchers, lapwings, curlews, skylarks and meadow pipits. Shags and cormorants breed near Llanddwyn Island, which is joined to Anglesey at low water. The Cefni salt marsh and Malltraeth Pool attract many wildfowl and waders.

The little town of Newborough was 'new' 700 years ago when it was settled by people who had been driven from their homes on the far side of Anglesey when Edward I started building Beaumaris Castle. Felling trees to create farmland removed a natural shield and enabled the sand to be driven inland by south-westerly gales. During the

Newborough Warren and the distant peaks of Snowdonia

reign of Elizabeth I a law was passed to ban the harvesting of marram grass. The plant has long, matted roots which help to stabilise the dunes. Despite the law, Newborough later became a marram-weaving centre where mats, ropes and baskets were made. The area between the dunes south of Newborough and the Cefni estuary is now occupied by the Forestry Commission's Newborough Forest, which has forest walks and picnic sites on Llanddwyn Bay.

Access: through Newborough Forest to car park on shore. (Permit required away from public rights of way.) NCC. FC.
Location: SW of Newborough (on A4080 between Menai Bridge and Rhosneigr).
Map: page 309, SH46.

Newent: Birds of Prey Centre

Gloucestershire

Founded in 1966, the Birds of Prey Conservation and Falconry Centre specialises in breeding, displaying and training birds of

prey from all over the world. Its success has been such that more species of birds of prey have been bred in captivity here than anywhere else in the world. Among the birds that can be seen are owls, falcons, eagles, buzzards, kites and vultures.

Perhaps the most important part of the centre is the breeding aviaries, where the young birds can be seen being reared in spring and summer. It is possible that visitors may be invited to photograph, and even handle, baby owls in the Baby Aviary.

Conservation is the keynote of the centre's philosophy. Endangered species from all over the world are sent here to breed in safety, then released into their natural habitat in the hope that they will re-establish themselves.

Undoubtedly one of the highlights of a visit here will be to watch a flying demonstration. Eagles, buzzards and falcons are put through their paces to show just how precise and deadly their hunting skills are. Many of the demonstrated birds are 'stars', and have appeared in films and

An evocative poster from the early years of the 20th century advertising a tractor binder

advertisements.

A museum attached to the centre shows through exhibits and photographs the development of falconry, the conservation of raptors and related subjects.

Open: Feb to Nov daily except Tue. Admission charge. Picnic area. Refreshments. Shop. Suitable for disabled visitors. No dogs.
Location: 1¼ miles SW of Newent, on unclassified road to Clifford's Mesne.
Map: page 305, SO72.

Newton: Hunday National Tractor & Farm Museum

Northumberland

Situated on the northern ridge of the Tyne valley, the Hunday museum is housed in a typical stone-built Northumbrian farmhouse together with its surrounding buildings. It contains the most comprehensive collection of agricultural machinery in Europe including over 140 tractors. Pride of place goes to the Ivel, dating back to 1903 and one of the world's oldest internal combustion tractors.

Many of the tractors are American and reflect the loss of horses on the land during the two world wars and the need for self-sufficiency in food. Thousands of these machines were shipped from America to help achieve this. Some are remarkably small, and many are little more than engines on wheels; there are certainly no 'driver comforts'.

While the tractors are inevitably a big attraction, perhaps the most remarkable item in the whole collection is the Bingfield steam engine with its threshing drum, millstones and straw chopper. Originally built around 1835 and unique in threshing design, it has been rebuilt and is in full working order.

The entrance to the museum is a Northumbrian wheel house better known as a Gin Gan. These strange round houses were designed to provide motive power on farms. Two, three or four horses would laboriously trudge round yoked to a central gear mechanism which provided power for threshing, milling and chaff cutting.

Open: all year (except Sat, Christmas to Apr). Refreshments. Shop. Picnic area. Narrow gauge railway. No dogs. Parts suitable for disabled vistors.
Location: at Newton, N of A69 Newcastle-Hexham road, 3 miles E of Corbridge.
Map: page 310, NZ06.

Gnarled oaks and beeches, some of them very ancient, are an essential part of the New Forest landscape

New Forest

Hampshire

145 square miles of woodland, open heath, bog, pond and river, together with villages, roads and some agricultural land make up the New Forest. The woods, heaths and bogs form one of the most extensive tracts of unsown or semi–natural vegetation in southern Britain.

The forest, unlike much of wild upland Britain, has probably been much the same for the past 900 years, ever since King William I created his 'new' forest in about 1079. Almost certainly, it was a hunting preserve of Saxon and Danish kings before that. William enacted his Forest Laws, mainly to protect the beasts of the chase, notably the stags, which the Anglo-Saxon chronicles say he loved 'as if he were their father', and the forest has been controlled by a succession of Acts since then. The latest, in 1964 and 1970, protect features and interests within the boundary or perambulation. Most of the forest is now managed for the Crown by the Forestry Commission.

Fallow are the most common deer in the forest

The Forest Landscape
The forest is essentially a low lying mass of sand, gravel and clay deposits in the centre of the area known as the 'Hampshire Basin'. The relatively flat landscape is dissected by broad, shallow valleys and slow flowing rivers with impeded drainage. It is here that acid peats form in the boggy areas and along the valley sides. In the valley bottoms, intricate mosaics of woodland, carr, scrub, bog, grass and wetland habitats create a very different scene from the extensive views of wild heath and ancient wood to be had from the broad, flattened crests of the ridges between the valleys. Many of these landscapes probably evolved after Bronze Age man had impoverished the thin forest soils with cut-and-burn agricultural techniques, after which much was only fit for rough grazing.

Woods, Heaths and Rivers
There is great diversity of woodland type in the forest. The most interesting from a wildlife and conservation viewpoint are the unenclosed woodlands known as the 'Ancient and Ornamental' woodlands. There are a number of partially enclosed ancient woods of native species and in addition, the 'Statutory Inclosures' which are mainly planted and managed commercially.

Of the semi-natural and ancient woods the most extensive are composed of beech, pedunculate and sessile oak and mixtures of oak and beech. The main understorey trees are holly, yew and hawthorn. Along the river valleys alders are common and birches are scattered throughout the forest.

The woodlands are mainly of a wood pasture type – which means that forest animals grazed beneath trees that were relatively widely spaced. The trees themselves were pollarded; branches were sawn off them higher than the animals could browse, which enabled new branches to grow without being eaten. This process was repeated on a regular basis, and could be continued almost indefinitely. The timber was used for every conceivable purpose – including feeding the stock in winter. Some of the pollard beeches and oaks are of great antiquity and beauty. Many of the alders, and some other species, have also been coppiced.

Another feature of the woodlands is the varied age structure from the very ancient overmature trees – with much dead and dying timber both on the trees and in the form of fallen hulks – to young saplings a few years old. It is this great variety of type, age and structure which

helps make the area of international importance to biological science.

The remaining acid heaths within the forest form the largest habitat of their kind in lowland Britain. The heaths are mainly of heather, or ling, and cross leaved heath with gorse, but as the heaths become wetter, then species such as bog myrtle become common. Frequently, dry heaths grade into wet heaths, bogs and valley mires. The effects of past and present land use, particularly grazing, burning and cutting result in heaths of differing structure. Where soils are deeper large areas of bracken may be found.

Another feature of the forest is its 'lawns', many of which are found on the stream sides. The rivers and streams are base-poor and in many respects similar in structure to upland rivers, but with a flora and fauna differing from their upland counterparts. In this respect they are another of the forest's unique features.

Deer and Other Creatures
The New Forest is home to a large number of wild animals. The most common deer of the forest are the fallow, but there are also several hundred roe and a number of red, as well as Japanese sika deer. Badgers, foxes, stoats and weasels are present, as are several species of rodent and smaller insectivorous mammals. Most British reptiles and amphibians occur, including the adder and the very rare smooth smake and sand lizard. Although it is usually possible to see the fallow deer on a drive or a walk through the forest, most deer are shy and can be missed easily. The Bolderwood Deer Sanctuary (four miles west of Lyndhurst) is a good place to see them and special observation towers may be reserved for a fee by application to the Forestry Commission. Amphibians and reptiles can be observed in the reptiliary at Holidays Hill (off the A35 three miles west of Lyndhurst).

Birds
The New Forest is a marvellous place for birdwatchers. Two of the specialities are the woodlark, on the more grassy heaths, and the Dartford warbler on the gorse-covered heaths. Other heathland species are the stonechat, whinchat, hobby and nightjar. Tree pipits favour areas

Pollarded trees near the Lymington River

with scattered trees. In winter hen harriers can be seen frequently quartering the heather for small birds.

The wooded areas contain all the main woodland species: great, lesser and green woodpeckers; treecreepers; nuthatches; redstarts, wood warblers, hawfinches, stock doves and several species of tit. In the conifer woods, crossbills, goldcrests and siskins are among the birds that may be seen.

In the wetter areas, redshank, snipe, lapwing and curlew will breed and feed. Several species of bird of prey hunt over the forest as a whole; buzzard, sparrowhawk, kestrel, and tawny owl are examples. In winter, in addition to the hen harrier, merlins may be seen occasionally.

Invertebrates
The forest is home to several interesting invertebrates. The New Forest cicada is found nowhere else in Britain and the large marsh grasshopper is another speciality. There are several species of dragonfly and damselfly, including some exceed-

ingly rare species. There are many butterflies; woodland, heath and grassland species all occur.

A small selection includes white admiral, silver studded blue and grayling. The Emperor moth (distinguishable from all other British moths by the conspicous eye spots on its wings), with its spectacular green caterpillar, can often be seen on the heaths. The forest is internationally known for its range of beetles, especially those associated with the very old trees and dead wood.

Wild Flowers
The wild gladiolus is found in the New Forest and is restricted to Hampshire. However, the heavily grazed wood pastures generally contain few plant species, but in some of the oldest woods, bluebell, violets, wood anemone, wood spurge and butcher's broom can be found in quantity. In wetter woods such rarities as touch-me-not balsam and Hampshire-purslane may be found. The plant list for the forest is impressive, but this is largely as the result of the extent of the forest rather than great diversity in any one part.

What to See

BOLDERWOOD WALKS
Several walks laid out by the Forestry Commission explore woodlands off the unclassified road from the A31 to Lyndhurst. The Radnor Walk leads through majestic Douglas firs. The Mark Ash walk is named after one of the oldest woodlands in the New Forest, the name being derived from a traditional boundary marked by ash trees. The walk passes an enclosure of planted beech and oak and this contrasts sharply with the ancient woodlands of the forest and the Douglas fir plantations on the Radnor Walk.

The Arboretum Walk explores an arboretum planted in 1860 where species of cypress, spruce, cedar, fir, larch, pine, redwood, poplar, hemlock and yew can be seen.

GODSHILL AREA
The forest's north-western boundary overlooks the River Avon, and there are excellent views across the valley from Castle Hill, on the unclassified road

from Godshill to Woodgreen. The castle from which the hill takes its name is a Norman motte-and-bailey structure. Godshill Wood and Godshill Inclosure, east of Castle Hill, have good walks through coniferous and broadleaved woodland along gravelled forestry tracks. Further east still are heathlands cut by little valleys with bleak names like Deadman Bottom and Black Gutter Bottom.

NEW FOREST BUTTERFLY FARM, ASHURST
Freely flying exotic butterflies and moths in an indoor tropical garden are the unusual attractions of this very different 'farm'. Species from Malaya, Africa, Brazil, Australia or Japan can be seen among banana and lemon trees. Many other exotic invertebrates can also be seen. There is a British butterfly area and a dragonfly pond.

Open: *Apr to Oct daily. Admission charge. Picnic area. Refreshments. Shop.*

New Forest Heaths

The New Forest heaths are among the largest in lowland Britain, and are internationally important. Once forested, the heaths were probably cleared of their tree cover by prehistoric man, and his grazing animals kept them clear by eating the saplings that grew. The commoners' animals that roam the forest today – cattle and the famous ponies – still help to keep the heaths open. Heathers are the commonest heathland plants, with cross-leaved heath (left) dominant in wetter areas.

PAULTONS COUNTRY PARK AND BIRD GARDENS

Beautiful parkland on the edge of the New Forest at Ower is the setting for this country park. Among the magnificent cedars are large aviaries containing many species of British and foreign birds including finches, macaws, eagle owls, Carolina ducks, geese, swans, cranes and flamingoes. There are mammals too, including wallabies and deer. At the village life centre are a blacksmith's forge, wheelwright, dairy and other craft exhibits.

Open: *all year daily. Admission charge. Picnic area. Refreshments. Shop. No dogs.*

PIPER'S WAIT AREA

At 422ft, Piper's Wait is the highest point within the New Forest Boundaries. It is also an excellent place from which to explore the north-eastern parts of the forest. It lies north of the B3078 Brook to Redlynch road. To the east is Bramshaw Wood, one of the 'Ancient and Ornamental' woodlands, with superb beech trees and a good cross section of the forest's bird life. Longcross Pond, to the south and on the other side of the B3078 from Piper's Wait, is a man-made dew pond and is also excellent for forest animals and birds. South is the little forest village of Fritham, where pigs wander at will during the 'pannage' season.

A little over a mile to the west, along the B3078, is Bramshaw Telegraph, where there was a semaphore station during the Napoleonic Wars. Paths from here lead south into Studley Wood and Island Thorns Inclosure.

WILVERLEY WALKS

The Forestry Commission has laid out a walk through the woodlands of Wilverley Inclosure. A shorter walk from the car park on Wilverley Plain is suitable for the disabled. Most of the trees here are coniferous, but there are also stands of oaks and sweet chestnuts. On Wilverley Plain, towards the A35, is the Naked Man. This is the gaunt ruin of an ancient oak, almost hidden by tall bracken in summer. It stands on the old Lymington Ridgeway, and may once have served as a gallows, but it is more likely that its name is derived from its pale and bleached appearance. Wilverley Plain itself gives extensive views towards Rhinefield House and over the northern part of the forest.

OBERWATER WALK

This walk forms part of a network of walks demonstrating features within the forest; in this case a typical forest streamside with its surrounding land use and associated wildlife. Information plaques are located throughout the length of the walk and there are two car parks, one at Whitefield Moor and one at Puttles Bridge. It is an excellent walk on which to see a cross-section of forest habitats.

The wetter parts of the Oberwater system are some of the most important for delicate elements of the forest's flora and fauna. From the marked footpaths the transitions from these fragile habitats through grassy lawns to tussocky wet heaths and bog to dry open heath and then to woodland can be seen.

ORNAMENTAL DRIVES

Rhinefield and Bolderwood Ornamental drives have been laid out along an unclassified road which links Brockenhurst to the A31. Several walks have been waymarked from the drives for those who wish to see the forest at closer quarters (see also Bolderwood walks). Black Water Walk, Tall Trees Walk and Brock Hill Walk originate from the Rhinefield drive. Many types of commercial and ornamental trees can be seen, together with other features of the forest. Off the Bolderwood drive is the Knightwood Oak Walk, the focus of which is the venerable Knightwood Oak – one of the forest's oldest and most famous trees. Explanatory panels point out much else of interest on this fascinating little walk. Though the drives are busy during the afternoon – especially in summer and at weekends – they can be good places to watch for wildlife in quieter periods.

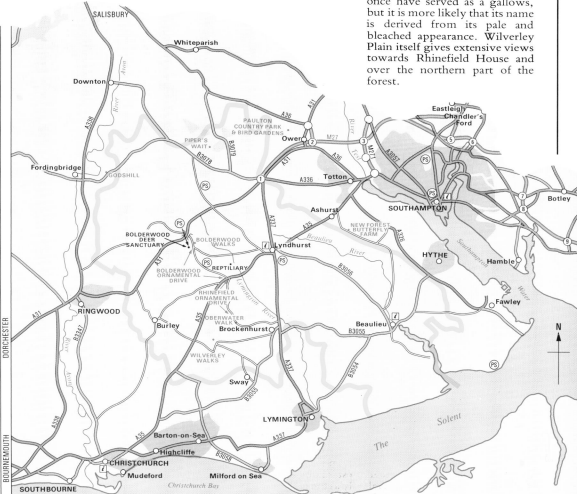

Norfolk Broads

Norfolk

It is not easy to know the Norfolk Broads. They give up their secrets only after many visits by land and by water. These large shallow lakes were peat-diggings in medieval times and first became flooded during the 14th century as sea levels rose. They lie along five main rivers, amid damp fens (where reed and saw-sedge are still grown for thatching), wide grass marshes divided by dykes, and wet woodlands, known as carrs.

The Broads are many things – an irreplaceable landscape and wildlife habitat with many rare species, a unique and extensive navigation system, a fishery for roach, bream and huge pike, a holiday centre. Visitors will be looking for different things, but the flavour of Broadland can best be enjoyed from the water. Motor launches may be hired (including by the day) from the towns of Wroxham, Horning and Potter Heigham on the River Bure, from Stalham on the River Ant and Brundall on the River Yare. Cruising the narrow rivers and wide broads gives a fine illusion of remoteness mainly because access from the land is limited and difficult in most places. The motorist can nevertheless enjoy the landscape too. The A149 and A1064 cross the unspoilt Ormesby/-Rollesby/Filby chain of broads and parking is available on the east side of both crossings: rowing boats may be hired. The magnificent wide grazing-marshes, dotted with cattle and punctuated with old wind-pumps, can be best seen from the A47 Acle to Great Yarmouth road and, mid-way, the Stracey Arms windpump can be visited in summer.

Wetlands are among Britain's richest wildlife habitats, and the Broads comprise some of the largest remaining wetland areas. A typical broad will have open water surrounded by a dense growth of reeds; further from the water will be fen vegetation, dominated either by herbaceous species such as willow herb, purple loosestrife, meadow-sweet and various sedges, or sallow and alder-dominated carrs. Most of the broads are now devoid of aquatic plants, owing to the excessive quantities of nutrients in the water, but the fens possess a wealth of species, including a number of rarities such as marsh fern, greater spearwort and marsh pea. The variety and richness of plant life draws a myriad insects to the Broads – of these dragonflies are perhaps the most spectacular of the common species. The bird life of the region is prolific, with coots, moorhens, great-crested grebes, reed and sedge warblers and other common water-loving species, together with several national rarities, including the bearded tit, bittern and marsh harrier.

There are numerous wildlife reserves on the Broads. One of the best is at Hickling, where the rare and gorgeous swallowtail butterfly is on the wing in June, and many scarce birds breed. The reserve is managed by the Norfolk Naturalists' Trust, which also runs the unique, floating Conservation Centre at Ranworth (off the B1140 from South Walsham), with fine views and a display which explains the interest of the Broads and the many problems which they face. Ranworth Broad itself forms part of the Bure Marshes National Nature Reserve, and the Centre is reached via a nature trail, which affords the visitor an opportunity of seeing the adjoining fen vegetation and birdlife. Boat-borne visitors can also walk a nature trail in the vicinity of Hoveton Great Broad, at the other end of the Bure Marshes Reserve. The Royal Society for the Protection of Birds has a re-

Horsey Mere is nearer the sea than the other broads. It belongs to the National Trust.

serve at Strumpshaw, on the River Yare east of Norwich. This is one of the places where a marsh harrier might be seen.

Open: *Stracey Arms Windpump, May to Sep. Broadlands Conservation Centre Ranworth, Apr to Oct (closed Mon and Sat am, but open bank holiday Mon). Information centre. Shop. No dogs. CNT. NCC. Hickling Broad Nature Reserve, Apr to Oct (closed Tue) Admission charge. Information centre. No dogs. CNT. Hoveton Great Broad nature trail (moorings provided opposite Salhouse Broad) weekdays May to Mid Sep. No dogs. NCC. Strumpshaw Fen Reserve, all year Mon, Wed, Thu, Sat and Sun. Admission charge. Information centre. RSPB.*
Location: *main area lies in triangle Norwich/Stalham/Great Yarmouth. Outliers in S are River Waveney upstream to Beccles and Bungay, Oulton Broad and Lowestoft.*
Map: *page 307/311.*

Marsh Harrier

Loss of their favoured fenland habitats reduced the numbers of marsh harriers dramatically in the last century. Today their breeding stronghold is East Anglia. Marsh harriers are associated almost exclusively with reed beds and shallow open water; they can often be seen on the Norfolk Broads. Birds' eggs, frogs, voles and mice are among the prey. The marsh harrier usually searches for these by carefully quartering an area from a few feet above the reeds.

Norfolk Wildlife Park

Norfolk

If the best way to see animals and birds is living free in the wild, then the next best thing must be to see them in natural surroundings. This park is the largest collection of European mammals and birds in such conditions. The emphasis here is on conservation, and the park has a fine breeding record. Some of the creatures born here have been returned to the wild; others are kept as breeding stocks so as to ensure the survival of species.

Besides such familiar creatures of our own countryside as badgers, deer and foxes, there are such rare European animals as bison, wolf and lynx. The otters are particularly attractive, and there are many types of bird. Of special interest are the stone curlews, rare British breeding birds of open country, and the owls, of which the most spectacular are the enormous European eagle owls. Some of the mammals, and also the owls, are mainly nocturnal and patience is often needed to see them well. However, specially built houses enable visitors to view the private lives of some of the animals, even during the daytime. Among the many other fascinating animals and birds here is an unrivalled collection of rare pheasants.

Open: *all year daily. Admission charge. Shop. Refreshments. Picnic area. No dogs.*
Location: *1 mile NW of Great Witchingham, off A1067.*
Map: *page 311, TG01.*

Norsey Wood Country Park

Essex

That this is a very ancient wood is proved by the fact that it is shown and described on the earliest maps and records. Indeed, several archaeological sites in the park trace the history of the area as far back as the Bronze Age. In more recent times the wood was, like many others, managed for its timber by coppicing. The sweet chestnut was the most important tree here in this respect, and it is still coppiced in the park. The aim now is not so much to provide timber (although woodcraft items are on sale here) but to encourage the rich plant and animal communities which flourish in coppices. The glades in the park are good for flowers and butterflies and there is a good mixture of woodland birds, including the brilliant, but elusive, green woodpecker. The great spotted woodpecker uses resonant branches for the loud drumming which is its 'song' (searching for food and excavating its nest-hole are quieter affairs).

Open: *all year daily. Information centre. Nature trail.*
Location: *from Billericay follow Norsey Road towards Ramsden Heath; in 1 ¼ miles turn right into Outwood Common Road for country park.*
Map: *page 306, TQ69.*

Northaw Great Wood

Hertfordshire

This fine wood was declared a country park in 1968, but its recorded history goes back more than 900 years – it was already woodland when the Normans took their inventory. This antiquity has, as in other ancient woods, resulted in a rich wildlife which recently planted woods cannot match. Among many mammals, badgers and foxes occur – although the only real chance of seeing these is early morning or late evening. Far more obliging are the birds, and there is a good variety of common species. As in other woods, a good way of finding birds is by listening for and learning their calls. Some birds are very difficult to see at all, like the nightingale, which pours its lovely song out from the depths of blackthorn thickets in the wood. There are fine native trees here, although it will be some years before losses due to felling during the Second World War are made up by the replanting which has taken place.

Open: *all year daily. Waymarked trails. Picnic area.*
Location: *N of B157, Cuffley to Brookman's Park road.*
Map: *page 306, TL20.*

Mouflon, wild sheep from Corsica and Sardinia, at Norfolk Wildlife Park

North Downs Way

Kent & Surrey

The North Downs of Kent and Surrey have a distinct character of their own, quite unlike the bare downs of Wessex or the South Downs. Being well-wooded, they more closely resemble the Chilterns; but perhaps their dominant feature is the view across the Weald from the ridge.

Other downland ridges tend to fall straight to a plain; this enhances the feeling of elevation but reduces the interest of the view. Except for the Hog's Back (not itself on the route of the Way, which runs to the south across Puttenham Heath), so narrow that it gives views both north and south, the view from the North Downs Way is to the south, across to the dome of Ashdown Forest, and sometimes across that to the South Downs.

The route of the officially designated long-distance footpath call the North Downs Way runs along the crest of the downs for much of its way, deviating only to cross the rivers that cut through the chalk (only five in 140 miles) or where a right of way has yet to be negotiated. The whole length, from Farnham to Dover, is reckoned to take about 10 days to walk, but any section is easily reached and will give pleasure simply for the view from the top.

Two stretches of the Way can be mentioned as being especially characteristic and lovely; they are the ridge between Dorking and Guildford, with a vista across to the South Downs, and the last section from Etchinghill to Dover, with all the excitement of glimpses of the sea until the cliff-tops are finally reached.

Bird life is varied along the Way, and on the grassier parts which have not been ploughed, re-seeded or treated with chemicals, orchids and some of our scarcer butterflies may be found.

Access: *along waymarked footpaths.*
Map: *page 306, SU84/TR34.*

North Kent Marshes

Kent

Famous as the setting for parts of Dickens' *Great Expectations*, the North Kent Marshes retain a degree of wildness and a hint of malice that belies their proximity to London. The dominant forces here are still sky, wind, and water. It is an area for those who appreciate solitude and are prepared to walk reasonable distances.

There are three main points of access: at Cliffe, High Halstow and Stoke. An ideal outing is to make a three-sided walk, starting at any one of the access points and walking out to the Thames across the grazing marshes, then along the sea-wall with an accompaniment of river traffic a mile off, then back across the marshes to the next access point (this way of walking requires transport to be laid on at the finishing point).

Apart from the wide marsh landscapes, birds provide the greatest interest here. Spring and autumn are similar in that the key birds are passage waders and waterfowl; in autumn the wildfowl numbers are building up towards the winter high, while in spring numbers are dwindling, but there is more chance of seeing that elusive little duck, the garganey. At both times of the year black terns and freshwater waders are likely.

Summer is the quietest time, but redshank and shelduck are always present, and there are summer visitors like sedge and reed warblers and yellow wagtails to enliven the scene. It is worth remembering, too, that about the time the smaller birds stop singing (around the end of June) is when the return passage of waders begins. Non-breeding ducks might also be seen at this time and terns will be venturing farther afield to find food for their growing young.

Winter is bleak scenically, but rich in birds: short-eared owls and hen harriers quarter the marshes; large numbers of waders and wildfowl come close inshore on a rising tide, and the lucky observer may find a party of bearded tits or the white-fronted geese that spend winter here.

Location: *between Cliffe and Allhallows on the Kent side of the Thames estuary. Take unclassified* roads off A228 Rochester – Isle of Grain road, or B2000 to Cliffe from Rochester.
Map: *page 306, TQ77/87.*

North Leverton Windmill

Nottinghamshire

Old windmills are a striking but not particularly rare sight in parts of Britain. However, only a tiny number are still working and operated commercially and North Leverton is one of them. It is a tower mill, built of brick in 1813 and heightened in 1884. Its thirty-foot sails weigh a ton apiece, yet so delicately are they balanced that a light breeze turns them. An attractive device known as a fantail keeps the sails turned into the wind. The flour ground here may be bought from the cottage by the mill.

North Leverton village has attractions other than its mill, with several interesting 17th- and 18th-century buildings; some with 'tumbling', a triangular brickwork design at the edges of the gables. It has a functional purpose in that bricks laid at right angles to the slope of the roof give better weather protection. 'Tumbling' was originally introduced from Holland, as were the pantile roofs so frequently seen in the counties on England's eastern side.

Open: *weekends, and some weekdays, pm only.*
Location: *5 miles E of East Retford on unclassified road.*
Map: *page 310, SK78.*

The owl's talons

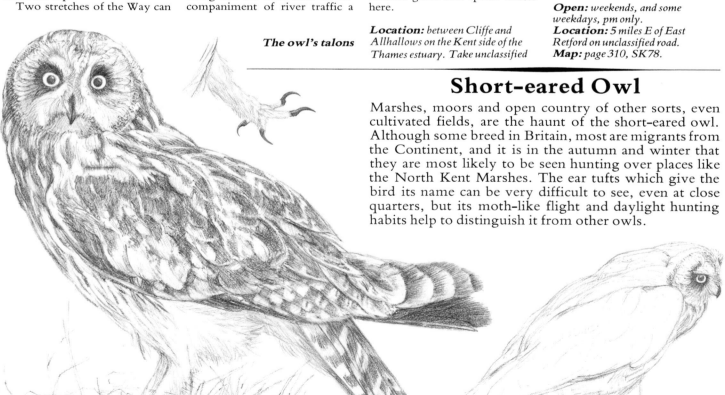

Short-eared Owl

Marshes, moors and open country of other sorts, even cultivated fields, are the haunt of the short-eared owl. Although some breed in Britain, most are migrants from the Continent, and it is in the autumn and winter that they are most likely to be seen hunting over places like the North Kent Marshes. The ear tufts which give the bird its name can be very difficult to see, even at close quarters, but its moth-like flight and daylight hunting habits help to distinguish it from other owls.

Northumberland Coast

Northumberland

A good starting point to see this Area of Outstanding Natural Beauty, with its peaceful sandy bays and magnificent castles, is at Warkworth, a village nestling in a bend of the River Coquet and dominated by a ruined castle. Warkworth is at the southern end of Alnmouth Bay, and from here a coastal footpath can be followed all the way to Bamburgh, the only detour being at Alnmouth, to cross the river. The shoreline is a mixture of sweeping sandy bays and flat rocky promontories. Cliffs are encountered at Cullernose Point, just south of Craster. These have small colonies of kittiwakes and fulmars, but the most interesting birds here are house martins. All house martins were originally cliff nesters before adapting to nesting under the eaves of houses, and Cullernose has one of the few cliff colonies left.

The three-mile walk between the fishing villages of Craster and Low Newton embraces some of the best scenery in Northumberland. This part of the coast is an outcrop of the doleritic rock formation known as the Great Whin Sill. In winter, birds such as turnstone and purple sandpiper move along the foreshore. They often feed together, and in their winter plumage are difficult to identify, but the purple sandpiper is a much faster feeder, dashing around while the turnstone investigates each pebble with care. In spring and summer the bright black and white plumage of the oystercatcher is common, but this above all else is the land of the eider, that most attractive and charming of ducks. Look among the rock pools in June and July for groups of chicks, watched over by non-breeding females.

In addition to truly panoramic views north and south from Dunstanburgh Castle, the cliff on which it stands has a large breeding colony of kittiwakes and fulmars with a few shags usually present. Beyond Dunstanburgh are the wide sands of Embleton Bay.

Close to Low Newton village is Newton Pool, now managed by the National Trust as a nature reserve. It supports a great variety of bird life, with a large black-headed gull colony dominating from early spring to summer. In autumn and spring waders pause at the pool during their migration. Redshank, ruff and snipe are common, but rarer species also occur. Winter visitors to the observation hides at the pool will not be disappointed, as the resident mallard and teal are joined

On the Northumberland Coast: Lindisfarne from Budle Bay, Bamburgh. Inset: an engraving of Bamburgh Castle.

by pochard and large flocks of goldeneye. One of the hides at the pool is suitable for disabled visitors, as is the path from here into Low Newton village.

Beyond Beadnell Bay is Seahouses. The view from the harbour at Seahouses is a memorable one, with the Farne Islands out to sea and the long sweep of sand

north to the castle at Bamburgh, and further north again to the smaller castle on Holy Island, or Lindisfarne (see page 133). Boats leave Seahouses daily in spring and summer for trips to the Farnes (see page 103).

Bamburgh is the pick of all the villages along this coast. It has a village green, a beautiful church, and, most memorable of all, a great castle on a rock.

Open: *Bamburgh Castle Apr to Oct daily, pm only. Admission charge. Refreshments. Shop. Dunstanburgh Castle all year Mon to Sat, and Sun pm. Admission charge. Part NT.*
Map: *page 313, NU22.*

Northumberland National Park

The most northerly of Britain's ten National Parks, Northumberland is the least populated and least visited. The fact that it also contains some of the most diverse and beautiful countryside in Britain is the surprise that awaits those who explore it.

From the Roman Wall near its southern boundary, to the Cheviot Hills on the border with Scotland at its northern extremity, the Park provides a continually changing panorama. The wild country north of the Wall gives way to the softer lands in the valleys of the Tyne, Rede and Coquet, before changing once again to the harsher upland landscapes of the Cheviots.

Even now, standing on the Roman Wall or the ridge of the Whin Sill on which the Wall runs, it is not difficult to imagine how the Romans must have felt when they were posted to this extreme northern outpost of their Empire. Although the landscape has changed over 2000 years, the bleak rolling countryside to the north is uninhabited for mile after mile through

Northumberland and into the Scottish border counties. Largely covered in serried ranks of Forestry Commission conifers, it forms part of the great Border Forest Park (see page 34).

Walkers on the Wall cannot fail to notice a succession of reed fringed lakes just to the north, the loveliest of which is Crag Lough, tucked in below the Wall near Steel Rigg. This group of

loughs provides a haven for whooper swans from Iceland during the winter months, but the best place to see these magnificent birds is on a shallow, easily overlooked lough at Grindon, just south of the Wall.

Following the old Roman road, the Stanegate, gives a viewpoint overlooking the lough, with its swans, wildfowl and waders. The lough is a reserve of the Northumberland Wildlife Trust; there is no access to the lough itself. The main road running parallel to the Wall is a General Wade road, built to try to move an army to cut off Bonnie Prince Charlie in the rebellion of 1745.

Several miles north of the Wall the River North Tyne winds its

way through the Park for a short distance, and beyond it the land begins to rise into the Cheviot and Simonside Hills. The major landowner in this part of Northumberland is the Ministry of Defence, whose Otterburn Range covers one-fifth of the Park. Access is barred when the red warning flags are flying, but the part of the range north of the River Coquet is accessible by right of way at all times and offers some of the finest upland walking in northern England.

The River Coquet

The valley of the River Coquet is not only the most beautiful in the Park, there are few better in northern England. The best approach is from the south-west

through the village of Elsdon. The vicarage here is an old pele tower, one of many in villages in the Border Marches where defence was a high priority. The villagers could retreat into the tower in the event of a raid by the Scots. Climbing the steep hill north out of the village brings one of the finest views in the Park. At the top of the hill the whole of the valley of the Grasslees Burn, a tributary of the Coquet, lies in the immediate foreground with the Simonside Hills on the right and the Cheviots on the left. On a clear day the view extends as far as the north Northumberland coast. The road descends to follow the Grasslees Burn to its confluence with the River Coquet. A minor road off

to the left to Holystone continues on to Alwinton, a tiny village tucked in against the foothills of the Cheviots. From here a single-track road pushes on for a further nine miles or so, always alongside the infant River Coquet, to the hamlet of Blindburn and then on to the Roman camp of Chew Green, high in the hills and right on the border with Scotland.

North of Rothbury the Park is concentrated entirely on the Cheviot Hills. A succession of valleys give access to these famous Border hills and the best known and most visited is the Breamish valley. The River Breamish rises high in the hills on the flank of Cairn Hill and runs through some of the Park's wil-

dest country before rushing and tumbling into the broader and more cultivated part of its course. Visitors are encouraged to use the main valley and the National Park has a small information centre at Ingram.

The whole of the Park offers excellent walking and is crossed by the Pennine Way (see page 225). Entering the Park at Greenhead, down in the south-west corner, the Way follows the Roman Wall for several miles before turning north through Wark Forest to the village of Bellingham in the valley of the North Tyne. The wild country between the Noth Tyne and the River Rede is crossed before the Way reaches the Border near Carter Bar. From here it follows the

Border along the north-western boundary of the Park before its end at Kirk Yetholm.

Wildlife
The diversity of wildlife over the Park as a whole is the result of the great diversity of landscape. Roe deer are common because of the coniferous woodland; foxes and badgers are widespread, and that delightful little animal, the red squirrel, is a common resident in suitable parts of the Park. Dippers are found on the rivers and streams in large numbers, as well as common sandpipers and grey wagtails, but the bird of the Park, and its symbol, is the curlew. Its long bubbling call is heard all over the Park in the spring and is a sound which perfectly evokes this wild and remote part of Britain.

What to See

THE CHEVIOT
Highest of the Border hills, The Cheviot gives superb views from its plateau-like summit, especially to the east, where the Farne Islands and Holy Island can seem only a stone's throw away. All around are moorland slopes – north is the Scottish border and a group of hills crowned by Iron Age hill-forts. The largest of these is on Yeavering Bell.

Peat covers much of The Cheviot itself and the tops of the hills around; in drier areas heather grows, while in wetter areas sedges are the dominant plants. In a few rocky ravines on The Cheviot slopes can be found plants such as hairy stonecrop and starry saxifrage, flowers that became established here at the end of the Ice Ages.

The Cheviot can be approached along the valley of the Harthope Burn, on the southeast side of the hill. An unclassified road leads up the valley to Langleeford, from where a track continues up to Langleeford Hope, about a mile from the summit. A track from Hethpool, north of The Cheviot, also leads towards the summit; it follows the College Burn up to its headwaters. The Pennine Way, close to its northern terminus at Kirk Yetholm, makes a detour on to the summit of the hill.

COQUET HEAD
Wild and remote, Coquet Head makes an ideal destination for all those exploring the National Park. It can be reached by several routes; the road which snakes all the way up the Coquet valley ends at Makendon, about a mile short of the Head, the Roman road called Dere Street can be followed northwards across the moors from Rochester, and the Pennine Way also makes its way northwards from Byrness, before passing Coquet Head and travelling on to follow the border across the Cheviots.

Landscape in the upper reaches of the River Coquet

HARBOTTLE CRAGS

This large heather moor, owned by the Forestry Commission, is managed as a nature reserve by the Northumberland Wildlife Trust. The geology of the area consists of sandstone which, in places, outcrops to form a series of north-facing crags.

Bilberry, cowberry, crowberry and bell heather are among the plants that can be seen on the crags, while occasional damper areas allow the growth of bog myrtle. Peat bogs have formed in the wet basins. There is an information centre at the reserve.

Access: *by footpath.*
Open: *information centre weekends Whitsun to Sep, pm only. CNT/FC.*

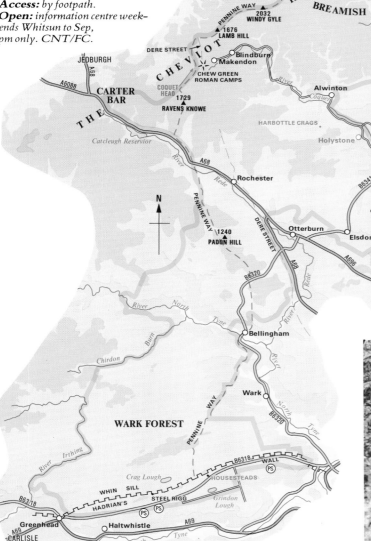

HOLYSTONE

This is a pretty little village, set beside a burn which shortly enters the River Coquet. The line of a Roman road can be followed westwards from here out on to the moors.

The Forestry Commission has laid out several walks here. One makes its way through spruce plantations, along part of the Roman road and across open farmland to the Lady's Well. This may have associations with St Ninian. Another walk leads to Dove Crag, a fine viewpoint, and to a lovely waterfall.

Part FC/NT.

HOUSESTEADS

Perhaps the most famous of the Roman forts along Hadrian's Wall, Housesteads was built at the beginning of the 2nd century AD to house an infantry unit of about 1000. The ruins are remarkably evocative, and a small museum houses some of the finds which have been made here. As well as being an excellent goal in its own right, Housesteads can be a base from which to explore the Wall and the countryside in this southern part of the National Park. The three loughs near the fort – Crag, Greenlee and Broomlee – attract water birds, while meadow pipits and wheatears are common in the open countryside. Further to the north are the dark and forbidding conifer plantations of Wark Forest.

Open: *all year daily except Sun am, Oct to Mar. NT.*

Starry Saxifrage

Quite common in mountainous areas of northern England, Scotland and Wales, starry saxifrage grows in wet rocky areas and on ledges. The leaves are low and close-set to avoid winds and conserve moisture. The flowers are carried on leafless stems.

North York Moors National Park

Most compact of the National Parks, the North York Moors is largely high plateau moorland, with the vales of Pickering and York along its southern boundary and the flat expanse of the Plain of Cleveland to the north. Isolated in this otherwise flat landscape, the visual effect of the Moors is very striking – never more so than in August and September, when a great purple sea of heather is in full bloom over most of the Park.

Above: the white horse at Kilburn. Below: North York Moors landscape

Deep valleys, known as dales in this part of the world, cut into the northern and southern flanks of the plateau, while on the western side sandstone cliffs are exposed in many places. On its eastern side the Park ends abruptly at the North Sea with a spectacular coastline.

The few roads in the Park are, in the main, very narrow and mostly run north and south, taking advantage of the dales or of the long ridges. The best dales are those which have been cut by rivers flowing south from the Park, and of these Farndale is by far the most popular – largely because of its springtime display of daffodils. Visitors tend to concentrate on the very popular walk between Low Mill and Church houses, where the banks of daffodils are certainly impressive. However, they bloom throughout the dale in equally large concentrations and in any case Farndale is beautiful in all other seasons.

On the High Moors
A little to the east is Rosedale, evoking memories of the Rosedale Railway, built originally to exploit the iron ore of the valley. With a need to connect with the existing network to Ferryhill, the railway ran across the high moors from Bank Top above Rosedale, past the head of Farndale and down an astonishing incline to Ingleby Greenhow

14 miles away. Although the trains no longer run, a walk along the track is an experience never to be forgotten, particularly the views into Farndale and Rosedale. This high country, dominated by heather, is the stronghold of Britain's smallest bird of prey, the merlin. This tiny falcon, little bigger than a blackbird, needs large expanses of well managed heather, both as nesting sites and hunting areas. The moors are also important places for curlews and golden plovers, the bubbling call of the former and the plaintive cry of the latter being typical sounds of spring on the high moors.

On the western side of the Park the high sandstone cliffs at Sutton Bank stand out very prominently, while just below Whitestone Cliff lies the glacial Gormire Lake, with a steep footpath leading down to it through woodland growing up the slope below the cliff.

The other main attraction in this corner of the Park is the Kilburn White Horse. Cut in the 1850s, the horse is a landmark for many miles around, as it should be because of its great size. It is 314 ft long and 228 ft high, so it is not so surprising that it can be seen from the city walls of York, 19 miles away, and even as far as Leeds, some 30 miles away.

Just to the north of the White Horse runs the Cleveland Way long distance footpath (see page 61), and for several miles it follows the very edge of the escarpment, giving magnificent views

west into the Yorkshire Dales (see page 296). Follow the Cleveland Way around the very rim of the Park and Roseberry Topping, one of the most distinctive features of the North York Moors, comes into view. Looking as it does like a miniature Matterhorn, it has proved irresistible to thousands of people. This is Captain Cook country, and it is highly likely that he also climbed Roseberry. He went to school at Great Ayton nearby and his father worked at a farm on the slopes of the Topping.

Along the Coast
In spite of being dominated by moors, the Park has many miles of spectacular coastline containing some of North Yorkshire's most picturesque villages, and one of the loveliest, Staithes, is another with Captain Cook connections. Like so many of the villages along this coast, Staithes seems to be engulfed by the towering coastline, in this case by

two arms of the crumbling cliffs. Just to the north of the village, at Boulby Head, the highest sea cliffs on the east coast of England rise to over 680ft. The whole of this coast rewards the explorer and is accessible over its length through the Park by following the Cleveland Way.

Ancient and Modern
The symbol of the Park is a moorland cross, and nothing could be more appropriate since the Moors contain the highest concentration of old stone crosses in Britain. Over thirty of these ancient monuments can be found in the Park, some merely stumps, but many complete. The oldest, Lilla Cross, dates from the 7th century and is situated on Fylingdales Moor near Ellerbeck Bridge. Another of man's monuments, the giant 'golf balls' of Fylingdales Early Warning Station, are not far away. The domes sit as comfortably in the landscape as do the crosses.

What to See

BRIDESTONES MOOR NATURE RESERVE
The impressive sandstone outcrop known as the Bridestones is the main feature of this moorland reserve owned by the National Trust and managed jointly with the Yorkshire Wildlife Trust. These Jurassic rocks have been eroded at different rates, produc-

ing curious shapes, and as softer rocks form the lower strata, they are mostly top-heavy. A half-mile walk takes the visitor to Low Bridestones, from which most of the reserve can be seen. The walk continues through woodland consisting mainly of sessile oak. Above the woodland is an open moorland plateau.

Heather or ling, the main cover, is usually controlled by burning, and supports a population of red grouse. Other breeding birds here include meadow pipits and curlews.

Beyond Low Bridestones the path crosses Bridestones Griff – the local name for a small steep-sided valley. After High Bridestones the path turns south down a wider valley and then follows the course of Dovedale Beck. The path crosses the beck and continues along the edge of Staindale Wood, back to the main entrance.

Open: *all year daily. Picnic area. NT/CNT.*

BRANSDALE

A group of five delightful and largely unspoilt dales – Bilsdale, Bransdale, Farndale, Rosedale and Newtondale – run north from the A170 between the high moors at the western end of the National Park. Through all these dales run rivers, or becks, creating green oases along the floors of the valleys, from which cultivated land, broken by drystone walls, fans out up the sides of the dales until it gives way to the bracken and heather of the high moors. The smallest of the five, and least accessible, is Bransdale.

The best way to enjoy this gem of a dale by car is to take one of the unclassified roads which run from around Kirkbymoorside towards Fadmoor. At the head of the valley two streams tumble down from Bransdale Moor, joining just south of the road. The major stream, Hodge Beck, continues along Bransdale, eventually joining the River Dove below Kirkby Mill. After turning south, the road clings to the steep sides of Bilsdale East Moor, giving fine views across Bransdale. It then climbs out of the valley onto open moorland before descending through gentler wooded country and farmland, rejoining the A170 on the edge of Helmsley.

NT.

DALBY FOREST

Owned by the Forestry Commission, Dalby Forest stretches northwards from the south-eastern corner of the National Park. The Dalby Forest Drive can be followed for 10 miles through a variety of scenery. To the north are the forests of Langdale and Broxa, which has forest trails, and to the east across Trout Dale, is Wykeham Forest, which also has trails.

Open: *Dalby Forest Drive all year. Toll charge. Forest trails always open. Picnic area. FC.*

DANBY: MOORS CENTRE

Situated east of the village of Danby, in the north of the National Park, this is the Park's principal information centre. Literature, displays, films and talks cover every aspect of the Park. There are also 13 acres of meadow and woodland to be explored here.

Open: *Easter to Oct daily. Oct to Easter Sun pm only. Picnic area. Refreshments. Shop. Suitable for disabled visitors.*

ESK VALLEY WALK

This long-distance footpath stretches 33 miles from Farndale Moor to Whitby, following the route of the Esk Valley railway. It begins on the high moors before joining the Esk to pass Westerdale, Castleton and Danby. Farmland and woodland are encountered as path, railway and river make their way to the sea at Whitby.

Stone walls and farm buildings in the North York Moors

The Esk Valley Railway itself makes a marvellous journey. Part of the line was originally established by George Stephenson in 1836.

Open: *trains all year except Sun Sep to May.*

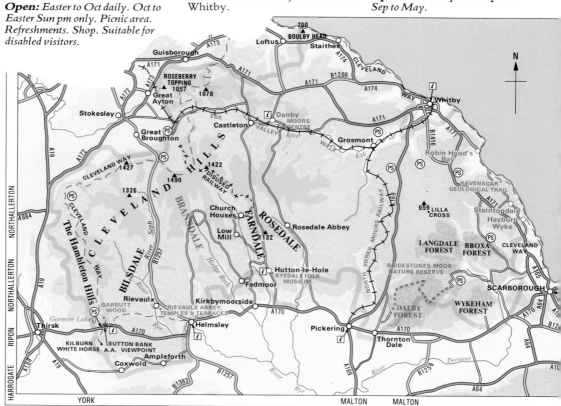

Rabbits were probably introduced to Britain during the 13th century. At first they were confined to warrens, but wild populations soon became established. Myxomatosis killed 99% of rabbits in the 1950s; their numbers have since recovered somewhat

GARBUTT WOOD

Whitestone Cliff, a sheer sandstone cliff, is the most conspicuous feature of this nature reserve. It rises from Gormire Lake, and near the lake may be found a rich variety of marsh plants. Bracken-covered slopes dotted with groups of birch, hazel and sallow comprise much of the rest of the reserve. There is an information centre here, and there are marked paths and nature trails.

FC/CNT.

NORTH YORKSHIRE MOORS RAILWAY

Running from Pickering up to Grosmont (where it joins the Esk Valley Railway), this line passes through some of the most splendid scenery in the National Park, and is a superb and relaxed way to sightsee. Historic steam and diesel locomotives pull trains through landscapes that range from wooded Newton Dale to wild Goathland Moor.

Open: *Apr to Oct, and 'Santa trains' Dec. Admission charge. Refreshments. Picnic area. Shop.*

RAVENSCAR GEOLOGICAL TRAIL

The Ravenscar Trail displays the unique geological formations and faults of the area. There is, in addition, much of interest for the industrial archaeologist, while the varied habitats through which the trail passes ensure a rich supply of plant and bird life. The full walk is about four-and-a-half miles long and includes a steep climb, but a shorter two-and-a-half mile walk is easier.

The walk starts by an information centre and proceeds along the route of the old Scarborough to Whitby railway. There are fine views over Robin Hood's Bay before disused quarries, where alum was dug and processed from the 17th to the 19th century, are reached. The trail briefly joins the Cleveland Way close to where the alum was processed, then turns back towards Ravenscar. The longer trail continues to the sea while the shorter route turns right, returning to the start past the Raven Hall Hotel. The trail follows the course of the major geological fault, known as the Peak Fault, down a shallow valley to the sea shore. The final part of the route, along the base of the cliff, gives an opportunity to see the 'Mermaids' Dining Tables' – a group of hard limestone rocks.

This area is rich in fossils and it is possible to find a wide variety along the path to and from the sea and in the quarries.

Open: *all year. Information centre and shop Apr to May, weekends and bank holiday Mon; Jun to Aug daily; Sep weekends only. Part NT.*

RIEVAULX TERRACE & TEMPLES

Overlooking the graceful ruins of Rievaulx Abbey, the terrace and temples were built in 1758 by Thomas Duncombe to complement a similar arrangement at his home three miles down the River Rye, which runs in a loop around Duncombe Park.

The recommended route from the car park plunges the visitor straight into a woodland walk of great charm, particularly in spring when early purple orchids mingle with masses of bluebells. Beyond the old entrance gate the walk emerges close to the Doric or Tuscan Temple.

There are twelve prepared views along the walk, most giving views of the abbey ruins, framed by the branches of oak, ash and sycamore trees. In early spring the grassy slopes of the walk are covered with primroses, forget-me-nots and wild violets, while in autumn the changing colours of the leaves on the trees bring fresh beauty.

The final view of the abbey is from beside the Ionic Temple, which has an almost austerely classical exterior and, by contrast, an elaborately decorated interior. The basement holds an exhibition depicting the development of English landscape design in the 18th century.

Open: *Apr to end Oct daily (closed Good Fri). Admission charge. NT.*

ROBIN HOOD'S BAY: STAINTONDALE & HAYBURN WYKE

The Cleveland Way passes through or close by a group of properties owned by the National Trust in the area between Robin Hood's Bay and Hayburn Wyke. From the north the property includes Bay Ness Farm, sited on the superb cliffs which form the northern headland of the village of Robin Hood's Bay. The bay, from which the village takes its name, sweeps on to Ravenscar, ending at Old Peak. The Trust owns over 250 acres on these spectacular coastal cliffs.

Another exceptional area for cliff top walking is to be found near Staintondale at Rigg Hall Farm. Accessible only on foot along the Cleveland Way, the Trust's property runs for over a mile, partly above the great mass of Beast Cliff. The views are memorable, but landslips are an ever-present danger along this section of the long-distance path – care must be taken.

Very different, much less hazardous, but quite delightful, is the path leading down to Hayburn Wyke, a mile to the south. From the cliffs the path runs through a small wood where the variety of damp-loving plants has led to the setting up of a nature reserve by the Yorkshire Wildlife Trust. Beside the path runs the Thorny Beck, a fast-flowing stream which creates a series of little waterfalls as it rushes down to a small but very attractive bay. The final waterfall drops into a pool on the rocky beach which fringes the bay. The path is steep and can become slippery, but the walk to the bay repays the effort.

NT/CNT.

RYEDALE FOLK MUSEUM

Collections of household equipment, craftsmen's tools and agricultural implements are housed here in a variety of buildings. Some of the buildings, like the Elizabethan manor house, were saved from demolition and re-erected here. The aim of the museum is to show how ordinary people of north-east Yorkshire lived and worked in the past. The museum is set in the centre of Hutton-le-Hole, one of Yorkshire's prettiest villages.

Open: *end Mar to Oct daily. Admission charge. Shop. Ground floor suitable for disabled visitors.*

Dragonflies

Almost any area of water is likely to be visited by a dragonfly at some time. They are also frequently seen a long way from water, even in city streets. Dragonflies rest with their wings open, unlike their relatives the damselflies, which rest with closed wings. The illustration is of a common darter dragonfly.

Northward Hill

Kent

Northward Hill guards the North Kent marshes, which lie along the Thames estuary east of Gravesend. It is a National Nature Reserve, managed by the RSPB, and supports Britain's largest heronry. Something like 400 of these elegant fishing birds congregate here.

Formerly dominated by elms, the reserve is now a mixture of oak wood and hawthorn scrub – the elms having been cut back by Dutch elm disease. Apart from the herons, which are present from February to August, Northward Hill's glory is a multitude of song birds, of which the nightingale is supreme. April to May is the best time to visit, for then the bird song is at its height. Three kinds of woodpeckers and three kinds of owls live at Northward Hill; of these the long-eared owl is the most noteworthy, but the one least often seen.

An insect speciality of the reserve is the white-letter hairstreak butterfly. This butterfly is dependent on the elm; now only the secondary growth of suckers from the still-live roots keeps the population going.

Access: *at all times along paths in southern part of reserve. NCC/RSPB.*
Location: *off Northward Avenue in High Halstow village.*
Map: *page 306, TQ77.*

North Warren

Suffolk

The coastal heaths of Suffolk, known as the Sandlings, once stretched in a virtually unbroken line from Lowestoft to Ipswich. Agriculture, forestry and other developments have reduced them to a few small fragments, one of which is this RSPB reserve. Beside the heath is oak and

birch woodland, and an area of fen, another rare habitat these days. Nightingales nest in deep cover here and there are also reed and sedge warblers. There is also a length of disused railway-line, a habitat that has been colonised by interesting plants and numerous butterflies.

Open: *at all times along marked nature trail. RSPB.*
Location: *from Aldeburgh follow B1122 Leiston road N for 1 mile. Entrance to RSPB car park on E of road, between houses.*
Map: *page 307, TM45.*

Nower Wood

Surrey

A variety of soils and slopes, including clay-with-flints capping the ridge which Nower Wood straddles, and exposures of chalk on the steep slopes, make this a fascinating area to visit.

The lower slopes on or near the chalk carry stands of ash, beech, field maple, yew and wild cherry, with a ground flora of bugle, woodruff and yellow archangel. On the acid soils over the clay, oak and sweet chestnut are the dominant trees, with birch, holly and rowan above a sward of bracken and a magnificent display of bluebells in spring.

Five ponds near the top of the hill are surrounded by open areas of marsh with wetland plants such as lesser spearwort and soft rush. Towards evening, roe deer and badgers may come to drink at the willow-fringed water's edge. There is a day field centre here run by the Surrey Trust for Nature Conservation.

Open: *at all times, but parking limited in locked car park: keys available from keyholders listed on notice board in car park. CNT.*
Location: *½ mile NW of Headley on N side of B2023.*
Map: *page 306, TQ15.*

Nutley Post Mill

East Sussex

Set on the edge of Ashdown Forest, Nutley village grew up when farms and smallholdings were carved out of the forest in the 14th century. Here cottage gardens merge into the heath, and this straggly settlement presents a landscape that has barely changed since the 17th century. Nutley's post mill, an important legacy from those bygone times, was built in 1670, but from 1908 until 1968 it was unused, and had become derelict.

Thanks to the initiative and hard work of local preservationists, the mill has been restored and is now the oldest and only working open-trestle mill in Sussex. Its sails are of the earliest type, a lattice of wood covered by canvas. Inside, the machinery is intact and includes two pairs of mill stones.

Open: *most weekends and bank holidays. Admission charge.*
Location: *1 mile N of Nutley to E of A22, on unclassified road.*
Map: *page 306, TQ42.*

Oakham: Rutland Farm Park

Leicestershire

Traditionally, the chief delight of the British landscape has been its variety. A few miles travelled can bring great differences in the scene. Modern agriculture, however, tends to bring uniformity in the name of efficiency. This is true of landscapes themselves and of elements within them, such as livestock. Some once-familiar animals, such as hens and pigs, have virtually disappeared from view into intensive units. Cattle and even sheep are increasingly kept indoors in winter. Alongside this process, the breeds themselves have become less varied. If these losses are inevitable, at least we may still see the variety that once was in a few places, such as Rutland Farm Park.

This is a collection of both rare and commercial breeds of cattle, sheep, pigs and poultry. Among the most attractive of the animals are splendid White Park cattle, which closely resemble the original wild cattle. The farm buildings date from mid-Victorian times and there are 18 acres of park and woodland.

Open: *May to Sep and bank holidays, closed Mon and Fri. Admission charge. Shop. Refreshments. Picnic site. Nature trail.*
Location: *on A6003 S of Oakham.*
Map: *page 306, SK80.*

Offa's Dyke

Welsh Border counties

Offa's Dyke was constructed by the Mercian King Offa towards the end of the 8th century. It runs for 150 miles from near Prestatyn in the north to the Severn at Chepstow in the south, and al-

though it is not continuous it can readily be traced for a total of about 80 miles. At the time of its construction the dyke formed the frontier between England and Wales.

An official long-distance footpath, waymarked by the Countryside Commission, follows roughly the line of the dyke. While some stretches of it cross exposed moorland where special care is needed, for much of its length the path passes through lowland farmland and woodland and offers pleasant and easy walking.

The route crosses a considerable variety of rocks, including limestones, sandstones and hard ancient rocks, so the scenery and wildlife are correspondingly diverse. For example, in the Wye valley are steep oak, lime and beech woods as well as impres-

A stretch of Offa's Dyke at Furrow Hill, near Knighton

sive cliffs. Further north, in the Black Mountains, heather, bilberry and cotton-grass predominate on the open hills. South of Oswestry the path runs over Llanymynech Hill, where carboniferous limestone supports a wealth of colourful flowers (see page 159).

Access: *by waymarked paths.*
Map: *pages 305, 309.*

Old Oswestry

Shropshire

Old Oswestry is a large, elaborate and well-preserved Iron Age fort. It is thought to have been one of the most important strongholds of the Cornovii, a Celtic tribe which settled in Shropshire in the 7th century BC. Finds made here suggest that the fort may have continued in use some time after the Roman occupation.

Ancient monuments such as this often provide a refuge for plants and animals that are unable to survive on neighbouring agricultural land managed by modern methods. Old Oswestry's sheep-grazed ditches and banks support a wide variety of wild flowers, which in turn attract many butterflies and other small creatures. Also at home here is the skylark, whose lovely song, delivered from high in the sky, creates much of the atmosphere of such places.

Location: *1 mile N of Oswestry, on unclassified road off A483.*
Map: *page 309, SJ23.*

Old Winchester Hill

Hampshire

Old Winchester Hill, a National Nature Reserve on the east side of the Meon valley, is one of those now-rare areas of chalk downland which still retains a great diversity of wild flowers, butterflies, birds and mammals. Habitats here range from open grassland through to mixed woodland, but it is the short, sheep-grazed downland that has the richest mixture of flowers. These include cowslip, devil's bit scabious, felwort, roundheaded rampion and 14 species of orchid. Perhaps the best time to visit the reserve is on a sunny day in June or July. It is then that the greatest variety of flowers will be found, and it is also the best time for insects such as grasshoppers and butterflies. Among the many birds on the reserve are nuthatches, goldcrests and green woodpeckers, often seen searching for ants among the short turf.

Open: *all year. Dogs must be kept on lead. NCC.*
Location: *off unclassified road E of Warnford, which is on A32.*
Map: *page 306, SU62.*

Orkney

Orkney comprises 65 islands, only half of which are inhabited, and despite its proximity to mainland Scotland it is barely 'Scottish' in character, reflecting much more closely its historical ties with Scandinavia and with the Norsemen who ruled here until the islands became part of Scotland in 1468–69.

The Orkneys as seen from Thurso Bay

The islands are at once rugged, with fine coastal cliff scenery; barren, with wide stretches of open moorland; and green and fertile, with some very rich farmland. Everywhere there is evidence of a way of life which also lies balanced between farming and seagoing. For many visitors, the main area explored will be Mainland, perhaps plus the easily accessible islands of Burray and South Ronaldsay, reached via the road over the Churchill Barriers – originally built in 1939 to close off the south-eastern approaches to Scapa Flow.

Orkney has some of the best prehistoric remains in Europe. On the road from Kirkwall is Maes Howe, Britain's finest megalithic tomb. Six miles north-north-west of Stromness, at the Bay of Skaill, lies Skara Brae, the beautifully preserved remains of a Stone Age village – certainly one of the most amazing things to see in Orkney. Two other easily identifiable and always accessible sites are the Ring of Brodgar, a superb circle of standing stones about four miles north-east of Stromness on the B9055, between the Loch of Harray and the Loch of Stenness, and nearby, on the southern shore of the Loch of Harray, the Stones of Stenness.

A fascinating insight into life on an Orkney farmstead around the middle of the 19th century can be gleaned at the Corrigall Farm Museum, off the A986 south of Dounby. The 18th-century farmhouse is divided in two by a large central hearth; one half being called the 'oot-by' and the other the 'in-by'. The 'oot-by' was originally where animals were kept – pig stalls and recessed goose nests can still be seen – but in the 19th century, livestock was relegated to another building and the pig stalls became stands for dairy equipment. The 'in-by' was where the family lived, and it was divided in two. One part served as a living room, while the other contained box beds, behind which was an ale-store. Close to the house are the other buildings which make up the farmstead. These include the byre, stables and barn.

Orkney's wildlife can best be sampled by exploring Mainland and, in particular, by visiting the RSPB reserves there. Some of the special birds are widespread and common and there is generally little difficulty in seeing such species as red-throated diver, shag, black guillemot, eider, hen harrier and great and arctic skuas. There is an easily accessible seabird colony at Marwick Head, on the west coast, where the impressive 280ft cliffs are overlooked by the grim-looking monument to

Lord Kitchener, who was drowned off Birsay in 1916 while on his way to Russia. Guillemots, razorbills, fulmars and kittiwakes are all abundant here and there is always a good chance of seeing both ravens and truly wild rock doves. This reserve is always accessible and lies 15 miles north of Stromness and seven miles north-west of Dounby.

One of the best remaining wetlands is preserved at The Loons; there is no access on to the marsh itself, but the area, which lies by the Loch of Isbister between the A967 and B9056 roads, can be seen well from the road. This basin mire marsh with its

associated pools holds eight species of breeding ducks, including wigeon and pintail, nesting lapwings, ringed plovers, curlews, redshanks, snipe and dunlin, many breeding common gulls and a colony of up to 250 pairs of Arctic terns. A tremendous variety of interesting plants includes bog pimpernel, northern marsh orchid, grass of Parnassus, knotted pearlwort, small bladderwort and alpine meadow rue. It is also an excellent site for Orkney's only amphibian, the common toad.

Two RSPB reserves have been established to preserve the characteristic Orkney moorland habitats of varying wet and dry

heath. At Birsay Moors and Cottasgarth Reserve, five miles north of Finstoon (an area best viewed from the road but also accessible from the farm at Lower Cottasgarth) there are breeding merlins, hen harriers and short-eared owls. Red-throated divers can be seen on the hill lochans, and golden plover, dunlin and great and Arctic skuas on the open moor. Breeding duck include wigeon, teal and red-breasted merganser.

The Dee of Dirkdale is one of the best botanical areas. Here plants of particular interest include bog whortleberry, lesser twayblade and heath spotted, northern marsh and early marsh orchids – with 15 species of sedges awaiting the really keen plant-spotter! This is one of many places where there is a chance of seeing the Orkney vole, mainstay of the hen harrier and short-eared owl population; this mammal may originally have been introduced to Orkney, but at any rate has been present here since Neolithic times.

A broadly similar range of birds and plants can be found on the Hobbister Reserve – five miles south-west of Kirkwall on the A964 – an area which owes its present character to the fact that it has remained ungrazed and unburned for many years. There is access at all times to that part of the reserve lying between A964 and the sea.

Open: *Corrigall Farm Museum Apr to Sep daily; Sun pm only. Shop. Suitable for disabled visitors. No dogs. RSPB reserves open at all times (but no access to The Loons, which is viewable from road).* **Map:** *page 315, HY31.*

Part of the interior of Corrigall Farm Museum

Otter Estuary

Devon

This little estuary is one of the smallest in the county and a reserve of the Devon Trust for Nature Conservation. The shingle ridge which forms an extension of the beach at Budleigh Salterton bars the mouth of the estuary and there is a small salt marsh running for half a mile inland.

From the footpath alongside the west side of the estuary good views can be obtained of the birdlife, which can include a flock of Canada geese and parties of large brown, black and white shelduck.

Just below the first bridge crossing the river, is a small reed bed on the west side of the path. This is the haunt of reed and sedge warblers in summer and shy and elusive water rails in winter. The path continues upstream, where the river gradually begins to wind and is set in a sheltered valley with overhanging trees, quickly losing its tidal influence. Here is the chance to find typical riverside birds such as grey wagtails, kingfishers and even dippers.

Access: *by path from car park on E side of Budleigh Salterton. CNT. Map: page 305, SY08.*

Although it is small, the Otter Estuary provides habitats for many water-loving birds and a wide range of plants

Ot Moor

Oxfordshire

Examine a map of the area to the north-east of Oxford and you will find a large circle of road through the villages of Islip, Oddington, Charlton-on-Otmoor, Murcott, Boarstall, Studley, Beckley and Noke, with no communities in or roads across the intervening land. This wild basin of land, through which the River Ray passes, is Ot Moor, a large area of low lying, poorly drained farmland which still retains its many broad green lanes with tall hedges and hedgerow trees and many wide ditches full of fascinating water plants. It is the essentially open nature of Ot Moor, with lapwings, reedbuntings, corn buntings and yellowhammers which make walking across it such an enjoyable experience. (See also Boarstall Duck Decoy, page 31.)

Access: *by footpaths and green lanes; from Charlton, Fencott, Noke, etc.*
Location: *NE of Oxford, N of B4027.*
Map: *page 306, SP51.*

Ouse Washes

Cambridgeshire/Norfolk

The East Anglian fens once held uncountable numbers of birds, but man drained this land and most of the interest was lost. Ironically, though, the very drainage works themselves created a new wildlife habitat. A new landscape was formed, with arrow-straight watercourses (called drains) and straightened rivers. One of the most dramatic sections is north-east of Ely. Here the Old Bedford River and the New Bedford River run parallel with each other for something like 20 miles. They are about 1000yds apart, and the land between is called the 'washes'. These store the winter floods between high banks, and are emptied in summer to expose rich grassland. Unlike the intensively cultivated peat farmland beyond the drains, the washes are rich in plants (more than 260 species have been recorded) and are a haven for birds of many species.

The winter waters of the Ouse Washes provide a home for hordes of ducks and swans, driven from their frozen breeding-grounds in Scandinavia and Arctic Russia. In summer, the damp grasslands are ideal for nesting ducks and waders, including the rare and charming black-tailed godwit, which has its British stronghold here.

In all, over 3000 acres of this marvellous area is managed by three conservation bodies. The Wildfowl Trust section, at Welney, provides spectacular views of ducks and three types of swan from comfortable hides in winter. Further south, the RSPB and county conservation trust sections, also with hides, are excellent in the breeding season and during migration times. Birds which can be seen include, in winter, Bewick's swan, whooper swan, wigeon, teal, pintail, mallard, golden plover and lapwing. Hen harriers might also be seen; a conspicuous white rump patch helps to identify these graceful birds. In spring or early summer, as well as the black-tailed godwits, there are ruffs, snipe, shoveler, gadwall garganey, warblers and many more besides.

Open: *Wildfowl Trust: daily except 24, 25 Dec. Admission charge. Information centre. Picnic area. Shop. Suitable for disabled visitors. No dogs. RSPB/CNT: at all times (except 24, 25 Dec; Sep to Jan Sun preferred) by marked paths. Centre open weekends. No dogs WFT/RSPB/CNT.*
Location: *Wildfowl Trust, turn north from A1101 by suspension bridge 1 mile S of Welney. RSPB/CNT, at Welchers Dam signposted from Manea, on B1093.*
Map: *page 306, TL48/59.*

Outer Hebrides

(North and South Uist) Western Isles

The southern half of the 'Long Island', as the Outer Hebrides are called locally, comprises the Uists, with Benbecula sandwiched between them, and the small islands of the Barra group off the southern tip of South Uist.

There are two points of access by car ferry, from Oban to Lochboisdale in South Uist, or from Uig in Skye to Lochmaddy in North Uist. It is possible to drive round the greater part of North Uist, with excellent views of the coast and the inland area with its peat bogs and huge complex of lochs and pools. The western half of Benbecula is well served by roads, while a single main road, with many small side roads and drivable tracks leading off, runs

Rueval, on Benbecula

north and south for the whole length of South Uist.

There is a tremendous contrast between the fertile, shell-sand enriched western, Atlantic side of the island and the acidic moorland, with its bogs and dubh-lochans, on the eastern side. It is the fertility of the Atlantic side which concentrates the crofting communities down that half of the island – and produces an incredibly rich variety of wildlife. The flowers on the machair are among Britain's greatest natural wonders – great carpets of daisies and buttercups, with many other interesting species intermingled. These include wild thyme, eyebright, milkwort, fairy flax, field gentian and frog orchid, to name just a few. There are many small

Padarn Country Park

Gwynedd

Snowdon's majestic crags dominate views from this lakeside country park, whose 350 acres embrace a rich variety of natural history, industrial archaeology and scenic splendour. Its focal point, the Welsh Slate Museum, originally housed workshops built to serve the vast Dinorwic Quarry which closed in 1969. At its peak, Dinorwic employed 3000 men and was the biggest source of slate anywhere in the world.

The narrow-gauge Llanberis Lake Railway, one of the park's main attractions, uses two miles of the track built to take slate to Port Dinorwic on the Menai Strait. The abandoned Vivian Quarry – impressive in itself, but only a small part of the vast Dinorwic workings – contrasts with Coed Dinorwig, a beautiful wood whose sessile oaks cover steep slopes above the lake. This fragment of ancient forest gives a vivid impression of how much of North Wales looked shortly after the Ice Age, and is a Local Nature Reserve of considerable importance.

Open: *country park all year. Refreshments. Picnic site. Welsh Slate Museum April to Sep daily. Admission charge. Picnic area. Shop. No dogs. Llanberis Lake Railway operates Easter to Sep. Admission charge. Suitable for disabled visitors. Refreshments.*

Shop. Picnic area. No dogs.
Location: *above Llyn Padarn opposite Llanberis. Part LNR.*
Map: *Page 309, SH56.*

Pagham Harbour

West Sussex

Pagham Harbour is a nature reserve run by West Sussex County Council, which has laid out a nature trail and built an information centre on reclaimed land near Sidlesham Ferry. Across the road from the ferry is the ferry pond, on which in July shelduck with enormous creches of young may be seen. In winter there are Brent geese and various species of duck here. Over 40 species of waders have been recorded, among them avocets, and little stints and wood sandpipers in autumn and spring.

The one-and-a-half-mile trail skirts the harbour to the village of Sidlesham and returns through farmland. The tidal mud of the harbour contains countless tiny animals on which birds feed, and in winter it is a feeding ground for wading birds, ducks and geese. In summer there is a colony of little terns on the shingle. These beautiful seabirds nest in colonies and are very vulnerable to disturbance, so access is restricted in the breeding season. In summer at high tide the terns can be seen feeding in the harbour. In places where the currents are slow, plants have managed to establish a foothold in the mud and thus a salt marsh has been created. Cord grass dominates here, but other plants include sea purslane, seablite and glasswort, a strange-looking plant with scale-like leaves.

Location: *5¼ miles S of Chichester, E of B2145. LNR (West Sussex County Council).*
Map: *page 306, SZ89.*

Brent Goose

Pagham Harbour is one of the places on the coast where Brent geese spend the winter. Wherever these small geese are found there is bound to be eel grass, their principal food. When the eel grass all but disappeared in the 1930s, so too did the geese. Brent geese have prominent white sterns that show up clearly in flight and when the geese are swimming.

lochs and marshes, with iris, bogbean, cotton grass, ragged robin and northern marsh and early marsh orchids growing around them. Beautiful beaches of white sand, refreshingly devoid of people, lie between the land and the sea.

The machair supports the highest breeding densities of some wading birds, such as dunlin and ringed plover, found anywhere in Britain. It also holds large numbers of breeding corncrakes, a bird you may not see but will most certainly hear (non-stop, all night!) with no difficulty. The call is a continually repeated 'crek, crek'. The corncrake is fast disappearing from all but the most remote

parts of Britain, where traditional and less intensive methods of farming are still practised – it is in an embattled position now, even in the Outer Isles.

There are seals along the coast, along with eiders, black guillemots and common, Arctic and little terns. Other breeding waders present in very large numbers include lapwings, oystercatchers, redshanks, curlews and snipe; while nesting duck include wigeon, teal and gadwall. Arctic skuas nest inland and forage along the coast, and birds of prey likely to be seen include merlins, hen harriers and short-eared owls. There are a few pairs of golden eagles along the quieter eastern side of the island. Both

red-throated and black-throated divers occur, and breed on undisturbed waters inland. Small birds include stonechats, wheatears and twites. Relatively few people will visit the Uists in winter, but at this time great northern divers are common, and there is every chance of seeing small flocks of barnacle geese, while northern species such as glaucous and Iceland gulls are frequently encountered.

Reserves to Visit
Two nature reserves are of special interest: both provide a fascinating insight into the rich and varied wildlife of the islands. The RSPB reserve at Balranald in North Uist presents a perfect cross-section of machair habitats, from beach to freshwater marsh. While much that is natural is preserved here, it is also possible to see how increasing drainage and the conversion of grazed machair to arable land is slowly eroding the valuable wild habitats in the islands. Most of the typical birds can be seen here,

Left: on the shores of Loch Maddy, North Uist

with a chance, too, of spotting a red-necked phalarope, now confined to only one or two sites in the Outer Hebrides. The Loch Druidibeg National Nature Reserve in South Uist presents a complete contrast, lying as it does on the fringe of the acidic, western zone. Compare it with the rich machair with its pools and marshes in the Grogarry area immediately to the west. Druidibeg is best known for its inland heronry and for the largest remaining breeding colony (about 65 pairs) of truly wild greylag geese in Britain.

Open: Balranald, at all times. Contact summer warden (Apr to Aug) at Hougharry on arrival. Visitors should keep to waymarked trails. RSPB. Loch Druidibeg, at all times. Contact the NCC warden at Stilligarry, South Uist, on arrival. Access is restricted when geese are nesting. NCC.
Location: Balranald reserve on unclassified road to Hougharry township, W of A865 on W side of North Uist. Loch Druidibeg, E of A865 between Howmore and Stilligarry in centre of South Uist. Map: page 314.

Pamber Forest & Silchester Common

Hampshire
Pamber Forest is an extensive ancient oakwood on acid soils which has been managed as hazel coppice with oak standards. Within the forest are massive oaks which are well over 200 years old. Heather is characteristic of the acid sandy gravel deposits in the Thames Basin, and this habitat can be seen on adjacent Silchester Common to the north, where heathers and gorse predominate.

In addition to the oak and heathland communities, there are small areas of other kinds of woodland, such as alder wood, and a small valley bog with bog asphodel and cotton grass. Nightjars, green woodpeckers and woodcock are some of the birds that can be seen here, while

silver studded blue and white admiral are two of the more interesting butterflies.

Access: by footpaths. Part LNR.
Location: N of Basingstoke, off A340 E of Tadley.
Map: page 306, SU66.

Pang Valley

Berkshire
The River Pang flows from springs on the chalk for about 13 miles to the River Thames. It is like many another southern stream, but with special charms of its own. Between Stanford Dingley and Bradfield there are pleasant views across unspoilt countryside with streams, woods, pastures and old water meadows. Plants in the river include water-milfoil, fennel-leaved and Canadian pondweeds, starworts, water-dropwort, and masses of water

crowfoot. The water fern, a plant introduced from America, may also be seen. On some stretches sweet flag and the great bur-reed grow in profusion. On the banks comfrey, purple loosestrife, and ragged robin are among the plants to be found.

Kingfishers, grey and pied wagtails are often seen along the water courses, and redshanks, snipe, curlews and occasionally, in autumn and winter, one or two migrant green sandpipers can be seen.

Access: along public footpaths.
Location: N of A4 between Newbury and Theale.
Map: page 306, SU57.

Parke

Devon
It is very easy for the first time visitor to Parke to be deceived as to the pleasures it offers. The main entrance, near the Lodge, leads into a spacious parkland which falls gently to the River Bovey. A late Georgian mansion sits comfortably in these surroundings, and a large formal car park seems to suggest a slightly clinical visit to a fairly typical National Trust house. But the house is not open, and the joy of Parke lies in its many well-marked footpaths.

Past the farm buildings, where the Dartmoor National Park Authority and the National Trust

jointly run an interpretation centre (although the estate does not lie within the National Park), one path leads into Lodge Wood. The walker plunges immediately into a thick broadleaved wood of considerable age. Impossible to cultivate because of the steepness of the slope, the only changes it has seen are the planting of a few clumps of conifers in recent years.

An alternative is to walk down to the Bovey valley, crossing a mill leat. It is possible to walk upstream along the length of the river from here to the edge of the estate at Wilford Bridge, passing the weir where the water for the mill leat is drawn off. The return to Parke Bridge can be made along the tracks of the old Moretonhampstead railway branch line. North of the line is Parke Wood, a lovely beech wood full of colour from spring to late autumn.

Near the farm buildings is a rare breeds farm – not managed by the National Trust – where some of the oldest and rarest of British breeds of cattle, goats, sheep, pigs, horses and poultry are being reared.

Open: parkland all year; admission free. NT. Rare Breeds Farm, Apr to Oct daily. Admission charge. Refreshments. Shop. Picnic area. Dogs in parkland only.
Location: W of Bovey Tracey on N side of B3344 to Manaton.
Map: page 305, SX87.

The Peak District

The Peak District is a significant British crossroads. Here, the landscapes of the South and the Midlands change to the harsher, more dramatic shapes of the Pennines. This is a land visibly dominated by the rocks which lie just under, and sometimes at, the surface. The natural division of the area into the White Peak and the Dark Peak reflects the two principal rock types – light-coloured limestone in the south and centre of the area, dark gritstone round the edges and to the north.

There is another way in which the Peak District marks a change in the British scene; it is at the heart of the sprawl of cities, factories, mines, quarries, mills and endless strings of houses, which are the legacy of industrial Britain in the North Country. Less than twenty miles to the west of the centre of the Dark Peak lies Manchester; its satellite towns – Romiley, Glossop, Stalybridge – are much closer. To the northeast is Huddersfield. On the east is Sheffield, its outer reaches touching the boundary of the National Park.

Industry and Farming

The Peak District itself has not been left untouched by industrial man. There are vast limestone quarries around Buxton, in Peak Forest and at Stoney Middleton Dale; one of the largest quarries in Europe with a face over two miles long, and growing every year, is at Tunstead, right on the border of the National Park.

Lead mining over the centuries has also taken its toll of the landscape, yet the greater part of the Peak District remains unaffected by the works of industrial man. It is pastoral man whose works have been very much more far-reaching – and infinitely more subtle. Some of these are easily seen and understood – the marching miles of drystone walls creating chequerboard patterns of field and pastures; the wide range of ancient monuments, religious and otherwise – such as Arbor Low (see page 212) – which was probably built by the earliest prehistoric farmers as a gathering point for local tribes; the stout stone farmhouses and their little groups of outbuildings. Less easily appreciated is the fact that the appearance of moorland and mountain, forest and woodland is due to man's activities through something like

Peak District landscape

6000 years. The single most significant change has been the loss of the woodland which once covered most of the landscape. This has vanished as a result of a mixture of felling and constant nibbling by sheep. Now the predominant landscape is open moors, hillside meadows and valley pastures.

Peak Rivers

The River Dove is the most famous of the Peak District's rivers, and by far the most popular. It lies west of Tissington, itself famous for its fascinating well-dressing ceremonies. There is car parking below Thorpe Cloud, the hill guarding the entrance to Dovedale, but no roads penetrate this most celebrated stretch of the river.

On the east side of the National Park are three more beautiful and renowned rivers: the Derwent, Wye and Lathkill. Perhaps the Lathkill is the least known, and yet it should be famous, especially for the limestone terraces and cliffs which mark its upper reaches. Footpaths lead across the moors from Monyash down to the infant river's limestone source.

The Wye has its source to the west of Buxton, through which it flows before threading across the centre of the National Park.

Its most picturesque stretches are Chee Dale, Millers' Dale and Monsal Dale. Chee Tor is surely the most dramatic limestone crag in the whole Peak District. Between Bakewell and its confluence with the Derwent, the Wye flows past Haddon Hall, one of Britain's loveliest mansions.

To follow the course of the River Derwent is to traverse virtually every kind of scenery in the Peak District. It rises among the lonely moorlands and peat hags of Bleaklow. At 2061ft this is the second highest point in the Peak District. Close to the Derwent's source is charmingly named Featherbed Moss, which owes its name to the nodding seed heads of cotton grass, which look like blobs of cotton wool. Even these landscapes, which seem so quintessentially wild, have in part at least, been created by man. The river soon enters Derwent Dale, now filled with three huge reservoirs – Howden, Derwent and Ladybower – and cloaked in Forestry Commission

plantations. Beyond the reservoirs the Derwent flows down through wooded valley sides with several sizeable villages on each side. To the east of Grindleford Station is Longshaw Country Park. The river continues on its journey down to Chatsworth. This glorious stately home is surrounded by splendid parkland and the river forms its central theme. On this brilliant fanfare the Derwent leaves the boundaries of the National Park.

Natural History

The immensely varied pattern of plant and animal life within the Peak District National Park is due, in large measure, to its two distinct landscapes of gritstone and limestone.

On the high plateaux in the north of the area, very little grows on the vast tracts of peat which cover the remains of once extensive forests. Only cotton grass grows well, with occasional patches of cloudberry and, even more rarely, in areas of bog, sundew and bog rosemary. Sheep and blue hares constitute the mammal population, while meadow pipits, golden plovers and grouse are the only common birds, the latter carefully husbanded for the shooting season.

Heather shoots provide food for grouse and moor burning is widespread, creating a patchwork effect on the gritstone moors.

Woodland has virtually disappeared from the gritstone country, but small clumps remain as reminders of the great sessile oak and birch forests which once covered the hills. On high ground they mix with holly and rowan, while lower down the slopes, streams are edged with alders and willows. Here, violets and bluebells flower in spring and early summer. The shelter given by the trees encourages lichens and mosses to grow, and, if not grazed by sheep, bilberry is common.

Stone walls are a feature of the upland limestone landscape where trees occur only as windbreaks of beech and sycamore around farms. While wildlife is not plentiful on the plateau, the dales are full of interest. The woods which clothe them are of ash, wych elm and sycamore with an extensive shrub layer. Some older and more varied woods occur – Dovedale has fine oaks, Ilam a superb stand of small-leaved lime.

Limestone grasslands are often full of flowers and the Peak District is no exception. Mountain pansy is common on the upper slopes, while the fescue grasses of the pasture land are covered in spring with cowslips, and later by great numbers of lime-loving plants like bird's foot trefoil, purging flax and salad burnet.

and rocks tower above the water which enters the valley at Mill Dale under the packhorse bridge.

Part NT.

EDALE
The National Trust is one of the biggest landowners in Edale, with several farms along the valley and hill country which includes Mam Tor and the Winnats.

The River Noe winds through the Vale of Edale – a lush and, in summer, gentle place, dotted with charming small villages. But from the floor of the valley rise steep hills, often topped by bleak, inhospitable moorland. Behind the hamlet of Edale, at Grindsbrook Booth, the most gruelling of all the long-distance walks, the Pennine Way, begins – a walk to test the most experienced rambler (see page 225).

Part NT.

HOPE WOODLANDS
To the west of the three large Derwent Dale reservoirs, the ground rises steeply through a fringe of Forestry Commission trees to open moorland. Here, where grouse rise sharply before the walker and the bubbling cry of the curlew floats across the moor, the National Trust owns the 16,500 acre Hope Woodlands Estate. Paradoxically, only some 400 acres are now woodland, the remainder being untamed and often frighteningly inhospitable moors – Alport, Ashop, Ronksley and the seemingly aptly named Bleaklow Moor. The latter's name is indeed descriptive for it means 'dark-coloured hill', and Bleaklow, like most of the moors, is black because of its peat cover. There are no roads allowing easy access to these moors, and only very fit and experienced walkers should attempt to explore them. Even the Pennine Way, crossing the A57 Snake Pass (the western boundary of the estate) above Lady Clough Valley, is not for beginners.

Access: *at all times, except for occasional notified days for shooting, between Sep and Dec. NT.*
No part of this estate is accessible by car.

ILAM
Close to the joining of the rivers Manifold and Dove is the picturesque village of Ilam, grouped around its Gothic cross. Nearby is the imposing Ilam Hall and its church. Although there has been a settlement at Ilam for centuries, the present cottages and the Hall are all of 19th-century construction. The church alone is older, but even that was much altered

What to See

ARBOR LOW
Arbor Low was probably constructed, at least in part, towards the end of the Neolithic period by one of the Beaker tribes who were beginning to cut and clear the trees of the high plateau. It consists of a roughly circular bank, its sides dotted with flowers, enclosing a 10ft deep ditch and level central area. On this lie about thirty large limestone boulders. Some are slightly raised, adding credibility to the theory that once, as at Stonehenge, the stones stood upright. The monument has a peculiarly evocative character.

Open: *at all times. Parking charge.*

DOVEDALE
The valley of the 'silver shining Dove' is indisputably outstanding, even in an area where much of the scenery is remarkably beautiful. It must be stressed, however, that it is among the most over-visited of 'honeypots' in the country. The best times to visit are early morning and late evening, but if your visit must be made during 'peak hours' consider the walk from Mill Dale towards Hartington. Not strictly Dovedale, it contains much superb scenery.

There are car parks near the villages of Ilam and Thorpe to the south of the valley and paths lead into Dovedale between the

The Dove Valley
guardian heights of Bunster Hill and Thorpe Cloud. Once over the stepping stones, take the worn path through grassy meadow banks leading to the spectacular heart of the dale. Above the slopes, thickly wooded with ash and alder, rise hills, tors and great weathered limestone formations. On the left bank is the crag known as Dovedale Castle and soon the first of the famous rocks appear. Most of these have legends appropriate to their names – the Twelve Apostles, Jacob's Ladder, Lovers' Leap and Tissington Spires. Over the centuries the river has carved great caves in the soft limestone rock: Reynard's Cavern, with its 30ft high interior, and Dove Holes are particularly impressive. More hills

imposed on five of the six people arrested, public opinion began to swing behind the campaign. A weak Act of 1939 was replaced ten years later by the National Parks and Access to the Countryside Act. This led to the setting up of ten national parks, including, in 1951, the Peak District National Park. Much of the land in these parks remained in private hands, but 'access' agreements were reached with landowners allowing the public to walk, with certain provisos, on open land such as Kinder. In 1982 the final step in securing the future of public access to Kinder Scout was taken when over 3000 acres of the massif were purchased by the National Trust.

What then is this land which has such a strong symbolic significance for so many lovers of open country? A great high plateau of virtually featureless moorland, it includes, but by only a few feet, the highest point in the Park. By common consent it is neither as bleak nor as menacing as Bleaklow Moor. Certainly there is never the same sense of being alone in the world, for the Kinder plateau is crossed by the 'M1' of long distance walks, the Pennine Way.

Yet Kinder remains 'the' place for many who climb its steep

by the Victorians.

Walkers often think of Ilam as a splendid place from which to begin long expeditions to the Dove and Manifold valleys, but it has some gentle and attractive walking within its own park. The Paradise Walk leads alongside the Manifold, past the so-called 'Boil Holes' where the river reappears after flowing underground for four miles. The walk affords a splendid view of the far bank of the river – a natural wooded amphitheatre. This is Hinckley Wood, which has its own sometimes slippery path. The small-leaved lime grows here in sufficient abundance to justify the wood's classification as a Site of Special Scientific Interest.

Open: *Ilam Park all year. Small car park charge. Shop and information room Apr to Oct daily, Nov to Mar weekends only. Dogs must be on leads. Picnic area. Teas from Easter to end Sep. Hall open only to Youth Hostellers. NT.*

KINDER SCOUT

Kinder has a special place in this country's social history, for it was following a 'mass trespass' here in 1932 that the movement to allow public access to hill and mountain land gathered impetus. The actual trespass by a few hundred walkers was minimal, but when prison sentences were

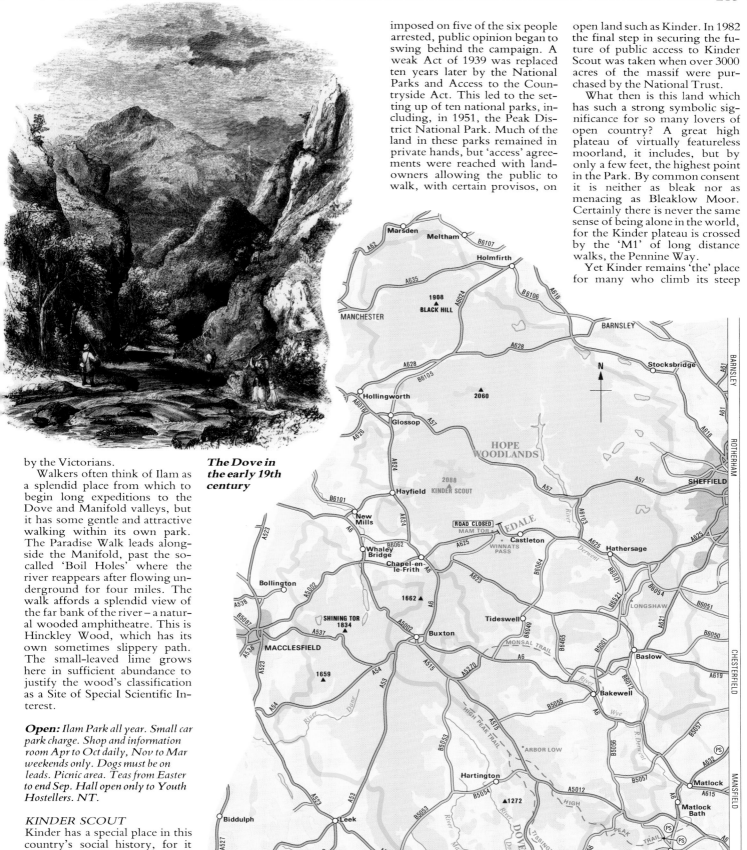

The Dove in the early 19th century

Caves

Inside the steep hillsides overlooking Castleton are the Peak District's most celebrated caves. Blue John Cavern, Treak Cliff Cavern and Speedwell Cavern were all carved out of the limestone hills by the action of underground rivers (although parts of Speedwell were made by miners). Blue John is the name of an extremely beautiful and rare mineral which occurs in the limestone and is fashioned into ornaments. Peak Cavern is under the ruined Peveril Castle, and its huge entrance cave leads to numbers of smaller chambers. It can be reached on foot, whereas the glories of Speedwell are seen by boat. All these caves have stalactites and stalagmites, and other features created by the action of water against rock.

Pendant of Blue John stone

grass-clad slopes and tramp across its peat-covered plateau. Most will visit the splendid 'Downfall', where the River Kinder plunges 100ft through a split in the rock, or is turned by the wind to a huge spray seemingly blowing endlessly back on to the plateau.

Kinder Scout is never a place to be treated lightly, however gentle the day may seem in the vale of Edale far below. Appropriate clothing and footwear and a reasonable standard of fitness are essential.

Open: at all times except for a few days each year during the shooting season. In winter it is essential to contact the Peak National Park Information Centre at Edale (which has a daily weather forecast) before walking on Kinder Scout – and this is advisable at all times. NT.

LONGSHAW

The Longshaw Estate covers 1500 acres of unspoilt moorland, grassland and woodland and includes a country park. Through the centre of the estate runs the Burbage Brook, for much of the year a noisy, quarrelsome torrent which can almost disappear in summer, leaving a dry stone bed.

The country park has many good paths which make access to the numerous points of interest relatively simple for the walker. Several make for the area known as Lawrence Field where, in addition to the Rocking Stone, there are the outlines of an ancient village settlement with the remains of defensive walls and hut sites. The Rocking Stone, a large smooth boulder perched precariously on a group of rocks, is one of several weird gritstone rock formations dotted around the estate. There are a number of fine viewpoints within the estate and from ridges above the Derwent and Burbage Brook.

Open: at all times (Longshaw Lodge not open). Shop/cafe/information centre open on varying days from Apr to Oct. Dogs must be on leads. NT.

MAM TOR & WINNATS PASS

The local name of 'Shivering Mountain' is splendidly appropriate, for down the sheer eastern face grit and shale may still be seen sliding or 'shivering'. In fact the landslip has blocked the A625 road here. At close quarters Mam Tor resembles nothing more than a gigantic quarry, and may appear somewhat overpowering. The views from the summit are superb.

Less than a mile to the south is Winnats Pass, a narrow winding gorge best approached from Chapel-en-le-Frith.

NT.

MANIFOLD & HAMPS VALLEYS

The Manifold rises on Axe Edge, source of four other rivers including the Dove. Although the two rivers flow at times down deep and dramatic gorges, the Manifold seems gentler – more a river of the lowlands where cattle stand in fertile water meadows and flowers grow in profusion. For the visitor the Manifold possesses important advantages over the Dove. With the exception of the area around Wetton Mill, it is never as crowded and the motorist can drive through some of its best and most typical scenery between Hulme End and Wetton – unlike the valley of the Dove, which is inaccessible to the motorist.

For a different perspective there is a fine, and very popular, trail for cyclists and walkers which follows the route of the old light railway from Hulme End to Waterhouses. It runs close beside the Manifold until it reaches Beeston Tor, where it turns along the narrow gorge of the River Hamps. There are no roads along this delightful river, but leave your car in the large car park at Weag's Bridge just above Beeston Tor.

Hamps means 'summer-dry' and shortly after joining the Manifold both rivers disappear during dry summers into the rocky river bed to reappear at Ilam some miles downstream.

NT.

MONSAL TRAIL

There can be little dispute that the Monsal Trail passes through some of the best and most consistently beautiful scenery of the White Peak area. It follows the route of the old Midland railway line from Coombs Road Viaduct, just south of Bakewell, to

Red grouse are more or less confined to heather moors, and heather forms the greater part of their diet. In the Peak District, and other upland areas, the moors are carefully managed so that they are most suitable for grouse

Monsal Dale from Monsal Head

Blackwell Mill Cottage at the top of Chee Dale. There are several tunnels along the route which are considered to be unsafe and have been sealed. The trail is therefore divided into four sections of varying length which can be enjoyed separately or walked as an entity, using the linking footpaths around the tunnels. Some of these paths, particularly the river path between Millers Dale and Chee Dale, contain difficult sections, but the trail itself is easy walking and includes two stretches which are suitable for the disabled.

The trail starts at Coombs Road Viaduct, but is usually joined at Bakewell Station where there is a car park. This is the longest unbroken section of the trail, running for four miles up to Little Longstone through a gentle rolling landscape. From Monsal Head, where the limestone dome breaks above the shale, the scenery becomes progressively more dramatic, culminating in some breathtaking examples of limestone cliffs in Chee Dale. The linking path to the final one-mile section along Chee Dale passes the spectacular Chee Tor, probably the best example of a limestone crag in the Peak District.

TISSINGTON & HIGH PEAK TRAILS

In 1968 the Peak Park Board purchased 11½ miles of the old Ashbourne-Buxton railway line and began the task of converting it into a trail for walkers, cyclists and pony trekkers. Called the Tissington Trail, it was opened to the public in 1971 and a further 1½ miles were completed the next year. In the same year the Board bought a section of the former Cromford and High Peak line which, when completed, linked with a similar development outside the National Park to create a 17½-mile trail from the Cromford Canal to Dowlow near Buxton. At the quaintly named Parsley Hay, the High Peak Trail meets the Tissington Trail for the final mile of the route. The trail can be joined at the sites of the old stations dotted along the line.

The paths run up and across the rolling southern limestone plateau of the White Peak area and provide a series of outstanding views over the country. Bird and plant life are abundant on both routes and some areas are now nature reserves. Devotees of industrial archaeology will explore Cromford with its memories of Richard Arkwright and the first water-powered cotton mill.

Peakirk Waterfowl Gardens

Cambridgeshire

The Wildfowl Trust, which owns the gardens, is internationally famous for its conservation and research work, especially at Slimbridge in Gloucestershire (see page 252) and Welney in Norfolk. The atmosphere at Peakirk is a different one. It is true that the gardens serve a serious purpose in holding populations of rare birds (some of which breed) away from other collections, so that an epidemic is much less likely to destroy all of the trust's vital stock. But the main purpose is to show the public the beauty and fascination of the birds. Naturally, wildfowl are the principal interest. They range from the tiny teal to the huge trumpeter swan, the rarest swan in the world. These are descended from three pairs presented to the Queen by the Government of Canada in 1951, and whose care was entrusted by Her Majesty to the Wildfowl Trust. Between these extremes there are wildfowl of many kinds. The rare species are intriguing, but no less so are the common ones, since good views of what are proverbially shy birds are easy here. Wild ducks do fly in to join the captive birds (probably for the free food!) and Chilean flamingoes add a brilliant touch of colour.

Car Dyke, a canal built by the Romans, passes through the 15 acres of old osier beds on which the gardens are sited. A series of ponds in woodland settings makes the gardens attractive, and they have a secluded atmosphere appreciated by both birds and human visitors. There are pens for particularly quarrelsome or rare birds, and also for ducklings that are reared by foster-hens.

Open: *all year except 24, 25 Dec. Admission charge for Wildfowl Trust non-members. Refreshments. Shop. Picnic area. No dogs. WFT.*
Location: *signposted from Peakirk village, on B1443, E of A15 N of Peterborough.*
Map: *page 306, TF10.*

Peckforton Hills

Cheshire

The Triassic sandstones which occupy much of north Shropshire and Cheshire are generally covered by thick deposits of clay, sand and gravel left behind by the last Ice Age. But, in a number of places the underlying sandstones have been fractured and tilted by ancient earth movements and lifted up above the surrounding plain. This is the origin of the group of hills near Peckforton and Bickerton, 10 miles southeast of Chester. Although the highest point, Raw Head, is only 680ft above sea level, these hills are the most prominent feature of central Cheshire.

Peckforton Hill itself is mainly wooded, with both semi-natural woods of oak, birch and rowan – especially on the steep west-facing slopes – and forestry plantations. There is more semi-natural woodland on the cliffs below Raw Head and on the eastern slopes of Bulkeley Hill.

Further south, Bickerton Hill also gives the impression of being wooded, but look closely and you will see that most of the trees are less than 50 years old and the ground vegetation is largely heather and bilberry. In fact this hill was grazed by sheep until 1930 and it provides an excellent demonstration of how quickly birches and oaks will re-colonise heathland when grazing ceases. If the attractive heathland is to be retained the encroaching trees will have to be removed and grazing reintroduced.

Man has not only modified the vegetation of these hills but he has also dwelt here for a very long time. From the remains of the Iron Age fort, Maiden Castle, in the south, to the 13th century Beeston Castle which sits commandingly on Beeston Crag at the north end of the hills, a wide range of buildings is to be seen. These include rock caves, charming cottages of red sandstone and half-timbering such as Peckforton and Beeston and the 19th-century Peckforton Castle.

Another large 19th-century castle, Cholmondeley Castle, lies in a deer park five miles to the south and its gardens may be visited during opening hours in the

Ruddy-headed geese at Peakirk

summer months. On the estate is a 13th-century chapel containing 17th-century box pews and a fine carved screen dated 1655.

A long-distance path – the Sandstone Trail – follows the hills on its way from Grindley Brook, near Whitchurch, to

The Fox

For some the countryside's arch-villain, for others the victim of needless cruelty, the fox is certainly Britain's most controversial animal. Although found everywhere, from mountain top to city street, many people have never seen one. Their reputation as the scourge of the hencoop is legendary, but it is salutary to discover that the greater part of their diet is often earthworms.

Beeston Castle, in the Peckforton Hills

Head of the fox

Pembrey Country Park
Dyfed

Beacon Hill at Frodsham, a distance of 30 miles. Information boards at various points on the trail give details of the route and of local shops where the trail booklet can be bought.

Open: *Cholmondeley Castle Gardens Easter to Sep Sun and bank holidays. Admission charge. Shop. Picnic area.*
Location: *10 miles SE of Chester.*
Map: *page 309, SJ55.*

Opened in 1980, this 520-acre country park on the eastern shore of Carmarthen Bay caters for a remarkably wide range of activities and interests. They include land yachting and parascending on the seven-mile sweep of Cefn Sidan Sands, horse-and-carriage rides, pony trekking, orienteering and four nature trails, one of which is suitable for disabled visitors. Among the other facilities are barbecue sites and guided walks.

Conifer plantations, sand dunes and other habitats also make Pembrey a refuge for wildlife. Migrant birds feed on Cefn Sidan during the winter months, and seals have also been spotted on the sands. More than 30 species of butterfly have been recorded, and the park is also noted for orchids. Mammals include foxes, hares, and badgers.

Many visit Pembrey just to relax on the dune-backed beach which is patrolled by lifeguards during the summer months.

Open: *all year. Admission charge. Visitor centre with exhibition and sea aquarium. Refreshments. Picnic area. Nature trails.*
Location: *off A484 1 mile W of Burry Port.*
Map: *page 305, SN40.*

Pembrokeshire Coast National Park

Giraldus Cambrensis, the priest and chronicler who travelled throughout Wales at the end of the 12th century, hailed Pembrokeshire as the finest part of the principality's most beautiful province. Despite many changes, notably Milford Haven's development as an oil port, his words ring as true today as they did 800 years ago. Even the old county name has been kept alive by the 225-square-mile National Park which embraces some of Britain's finest coastal scenery and beautiful inland areas steeped in history and folklore.

Large numbers of Manx shearwaters can be seen on Skomer Island, off the Pembrokeshire coast

This lovely corner of Wales is basically a rolling plateau which was raised about 200ft above the sea less than 20 million years ago. Volcanic rocks, much harder than their neighbours, now form such dominant features as the long arm of Mynydd Preseli and the steep, crag-topped hills which make superb viewpoints on the coast near St David's. The massive Pen Caer peninsula, Fishguard Bay's great bulwark against Atlantic storms, is also the result of volcanic action.

Different types of rock run right across the National Park from east to west and account for its ever-changing coastal scenery. The great sweep of St Bride's Bay, for instance, is the result of waves pounding relatively soft coal measures which extend all the way to Saundersfoot and Amroth. The spectacular limestone ramparts between Stackpole Quay and Linney Head contrast with dark cliffs at Cemaes Head and elsewhere which have been bent through 180 degrees by titanic natural forces.

The final touches were added barely 10,000 years ago when melting Ice Age glaciers made the sea level rise once more. Water swirling up what had previously been river valleys created

safe anchorages. The most outstanding example, Milford Haven, was described by Nelson as one of the two finest natural harbours in the world. Hills were cut off from the mainland to form islands where Celtic saints sought refuge during the Dark Ages.

The monastic tradition is maintained by the Cistercian monks who farm Caldey Island, while Grassholm, Skomer and Skokholm have become important bird sanctuaries. Caves and coves make Ramsey Island one of Britain's main breeding grounds for the grey seal.

Prehistoric and Roman Settlers

Pembrokeshire's first settlers are believed to have arrived at the end of the Ice Age. Their hunting grounds included forests which were gradually submerged by the rising sea. Petrified tree stumps can still be seen at Amroth and on several other beaches when the tides are at their lowest.

Later generations built the *cromlechs* or burial chambers with huge capstones weighing many tons. Pentre Ifan, on the hills above Nevern, and Arthur's Quoit near Whitesand Bay are two of the most evocative reminders of that period. Whitesand Bay was also the seaward end of a major Bronze Age highway used by traders taking copper and gold from Ireland to England.

Before the coming of the Romans, steep hills and high, wavelashed headlands attracted Iron Age dwellers who built walls and dug ditches to strengthen natural defences. There are fine examples on St David's Head and at Foel-drygarn, the Preseli range's eastern summit.

The 'Age of Saints' which followed the Roman retreat from Britain mingles delightful folk tales with the hard facts of recorded history. David, Justinian, Brynach and other monks encouraged a great flowering of Celtic art. It is epitomised by the tall, 'wheel-headed' crosses at Nevern and Carew whose sides are carved with elaborate, interlaced patterns and geometrical motifs. Most of the religious settlements were pillaged by Norsemen whose raids are recalled by such Scandinavian placenames as Skomer, Ramsey and Gateholm.

It was the Normans who changed Pembrokeshire's political and cultural character by creating a north-south division that has survived to this day. Pembroke became the centre of 'Little England beyond Wales' and Welsh was rarely spoken below a line from Newgale to Narberth. The Normans also built mighty castles to guard their western province and to serve as bases for the invasion of Ireland.

Harbours Great and Small

Until the middle of the 19th century, when the railways arrived, the sea was Pembrokeshire's main link with the outside world. One of the National Park's many attractions is the way in which reminders of the long age of sail have survived in many a sandy bay and rocky cove. The most common relics are lime-kilns built at virtually every point where a small coaster could discharge its cargo in safety. The most outstanding examples are at Porth-clais and Solva, on the northern coast of St Bride's Bay, where clusters of kilns resemble the truncated towers of miniature castles. Abereiddi, Abercastle and Porth-

gain, isolated hamlets on the formidably rugged coast between St David's and Pen Caer, also have links with the industrial past. Ships built locally carried granite, slate and other cargoes to ports as far afield as North America.

Supertankers from the Persian Gulf now nose in and out of Milford Haven, and Fishguard is a ferry port for Ireland, but the Park's character is essentially 'natural'. Dramatic cliffs frame broad, sandy bays where surfers pit their skill and courage against the Atlantic waves. Narrow lanes, sunk between grassy banks, wriggle down to remote coves, while Marloes Sands, Barafundle Bay and several other exceptionally attractive beaches can be reached only on foot. Long stretches of the southern coast, with its caves, blow-holes and wave-sculpted arches, are also reserved for walkers. A sea-washed chasm near Bosherston – itself famous for lily ponds – clasps a tiny chapel dedicated to St Govan and built during the Middle Ages.

Inland, a detached part of the National Park surrounds the upper waters of Milford Haven and its two main tributaries, the Eastern and Western Cleddau, which flow through a tranquil patchwork of fields and woodlands. One of the haven's many creeks is overlooked by the romantic ruins of Carew Castle, built at the start of the 14th century. The water powers the twin wheels of a restored tidal mill.

Despite its name, the Pembrokeshire Coast National Park also includes Mynydd Preseli, the hills which run westwards from Crymmych to Fishguard Bay and are crossed by a prehistoric track whose evocative Welsh name – *Yr Hen Ffordd* – means The Old Road. For reasons unknown, the men who built Stonehenge had more than 80 huge stones transported all the way to Salisbury Plain from this remote corner of Wales. They are believed to have been hauled down to Milford Haven on rollers, then shipped to England by way of the Bristol Channel and West Country rivers.

What to See

BOSHERSTON

Footpaths from the car park beside Bosherston's church lead to a series of freshwater pools, and to Broad Haven, a safe and sandy beach. The pools, formed when a dam was built across the mouth of a little estuary, are famous for their white water-lilies, which bloom in June. They are also excellent places to watch for birds such as swans, moorhens, kingfishers and herons.

The lowest pool has a path right round it and makes an excellent walk. Longer walks can be made to the east across Stackpole Warren, to the cliffs of Stackpole Head, where seals can often be seen. Further round the coast is Barafundle Bay, only accessible by footpath, but always popular in summer.

CALDEY ISLAND

Tenby, still with its medieval walls, is the starting point for visits to this 600-acre island where Cistercian monks farm and make perfume from gorse flowers. The monastery was founded in 1929, but Caldey's history as a religious centre goes back 1400 years to the time of St David. A walk from Priory Bay follows a lane to a lighthouse and medieval priory buildings.

Open: *May to Sep (closed weekends). Refreshments. Shop.*

CAREW

The ivy-covered ruins of Carew Castle dominate this pretty little village. In its shadow is one of the finest carved crosses in Wales. It dates from the 11th century and commemorates a prince of South Wales. Castle and village stand beside a tidal arm of Milford Haven – a few hundred yards downstream is Carew Mill, one of the few working tidal mills remaining in Britain.

The many inlets of the Carew River are good places for birdwatching. Among the species that might be seen in the winter months are greenshank, blacktailed godwit, common sandpiper, and a variety of duck species.

Open: *castle and mill Easter to Sep (closed Sat). Admission charge. Information centre. Picnic area.*

GWAUN VALLEY

The little Afon Gwaun has its source high in the Preselis and makes its way through a delightful valley, wooded for much of its length, to the sea at Fishguard. Dippers and grey wagtails can be seen by the water, while birds such as wood warblers and redstarts are summer visitors to the woods. Buzzards are usually to be seen gliding above the valley. Footpaths can be followed from the unclassified road that threads through the valley; other paths lead up on to the Preselis.

MANORBIER

The Normans built more than fifty castles in the south-west of Wales and many, as at Manorbier, survive, albeit in ruins. It was always a little too remote to hold a key position, and it seems clear from the writings of its favourite son, Gerald of Wales (Giraldus Cambrensis), that it was less a fortress and more a well maintained home. Manorbier, described by Gerald as 'the most delectable spot in all Wales', is a small village which seems rather dominated by the romantic ruins of its castle.

Nearby is the church of St James, parts of which are older than the castle. From the National Trust-owned cliffs to the south of the church there are views to

St Govan's Head across Manorbier Bay.

Open: *Whitsun to Sep daily. Admission charge. Shop. Gardens suitable for disabled visitors.*

The monastery on Caldey Island

Marloes Sands

southern end. A new barrier, in the form of a high stone wall, was built across the neck of the promontory early in the 19th century. The owners' intention was to create a deer park, but the scheme was never completed – fortunately, as it is difficult to imagine a less suitable home for deer than this flat, treeless plateau.

What the deer park does possess, for the lover of wild places and things, is a great wealth of natural beauty in a relatively small area. From the National Trust car park beside the valley a path leads into the park and up to the highest point – the coast-guard lookout. From here are fine views north over the great sweep of St Bride's Bay to the St David's Head peninsula. South across Broad Sound lies the famous island bird reserve of Skokholm. Due west, and as well-known to birdwatchers, is Skomer. A variety of seabirds may be seen from the cliff, while the centre of the headland holds such birds as meadow pipits and stonechats.

NT.

MYNYDD PRESELI

Buzzards and ravens patrol the skies above these steep, smooth-flanked hills, which rise to 1760ft above the hamlet of Rosebush. A ridgeway track, which can be joined from the B4329 north of Rosebush, leads across the centre of the hills. Walkers who follow the track, which dates from pre-historic times, are rewarded with breathtaking views which extend from Bardsey Island in the north to Somerset and Devon.

The hills are mostly sheep-walks, their vegetation dominated by heather, gorse, bilberry and coarse mountain grasses. It is a landscape where the sky plays an important part, and it is a fitting setting for the hundreds of prehistoric remains that can be found here.

Carnmenyn, where most of the 'bluestones' for Stonehenge were quarried, can be reached by following the ridgeway westwards from a lane one mile south-west of Crymmych. The walk takes about 30 minutes and skirts Foeldrygarn, a rocky summit fortified during the Iron Age. On the north edge of the hills, overlooking the valley of the Nyfer, is Pentre Ifan, the best-preserved prehistoric burial chamber in the area. The views from here are superb.

PEMBROKESHIRE COAST PATH

Apart from a few unavoidable breaks, this 167-mile path runs all the way from St Dogmaels in the north to Amroth on what used to be Pembrokeshire's southern boundary with Carmarthenshire. The coastal scenery along many stretches is spectacular; particularly invigorating are the lengths from Freshwater East to Bosherston, around St David's Peninsula and from Fishguard to St Dogmaels.

The whole walk can be completed in about two weeks and there is no better way to experience the National Park's magic. The path also enables the coast to be explored by taking relatively short strolls from virtually every point where roads meet the shore.

MARLOES DEER PARK

The western tip of the Marloes peninsula, already formidably protected by natural barriers, was further defended by Iron Age men building a bank and ditch at its

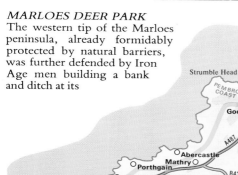

SKOMER ISLAND

This internationally important seabird breeding site stands off the end of the Marloes peninsula. It is a reserve of the West Wales Trust for Nature Conservation. The island, over 700 acres in extent, is mainly a windswept plateau intersected by rocky ridges and surrounded by cliffs and steep grassy slopes.

Skomer holds one of the finest seabird colonies in north-western Europe, with fulmars, kittiwakes, razorbills and guillemots breeding on the cliffs, while puffins, storm petrels and Manx shearwaters nest in burrows beneath the turf. The population of shearwaters is immense, probably over 100,000 pairs.

Predatory mammals are absent so that rodents are numerous. Particularly noteworthy is the Skomer vole, an island race of the bank vole, which is larger and lighter in colour than its mainland cousin.

The island is covered by a fine range of maritime plant communities which, together with old farmland, marshland and

RAMSEY ISLAND

The island is served by a boat which sails from St Justinian, west of St David's. Visitors can spend about six hours ashore, exploring an island where seabirds nest on cliffs rising 300ft above the waves. Boat trips can also be made round the island and these often provide superb views of seabirds and also seals.

Ramsey, like Skomer, is the haunt of the grey seal. Pups have white fur and weigh about 28lbs at birth, but the female's rich milk enables them to more than treble their weight in about three weeks.

Open: *Easter to Sep daily, weather permitting (landing fee) from St Justinian Lifeboat Station.*

ST DAVID'S HEAD

Two miles west of St David's, the B4583 ends in a car park at Whitesand Bay. Popular in summer with those who come to surf and bathe, the mile-long beach is attractive to passage waders on quiet days. Choughs sometimes visit the car park, from which the Pembrokeshire Coast Path runs north to St David's Head. Just beyond the car park a stone marks the site of the chapel from which St Patrick is thought to have sailed for Ireland. Further on are clear signs of an Iron Age field system, and, on the headland, the remains of a village of the same period, sheltered behind a massive stone wall known as Warrior's Dyke. Close to the footpath leading back to Whitesand Bay is a Stone Age burial chamber called Coetan Arthur.

Along the length of the walk a succession of flowers and shrubs add colour from spring to early autumn. The cliff top areas are particularly full, with ling and bell heather, gorse and bramble, thrift and sea campion.

Part NT.

Sea spleenwort is the only British maritime fern. It grows in rocky crevices

St Justinian's lifeboat station

pools, harbour over 200 species of wild plants, including spring squill and sea spleenwort.

The sea around Skomer and the Marloes peninsula has become a marine nature reserve because of the need to protect the spectacular underwater scenery and abundant marine life.

Open: *Apr to Sep, Tue to Sun, and bank holiday Mon. Boats between 10.00 and 12.00 weather permitting (landing fee) from Martinshaven. Information centre at Martinshaven. NCC/CNT.*

STACKPOLE

The National Trust owns 2000 acres at Stackpole – part of what was once a vast estate of great diversity owned by the earls of Cawdor. Happily the diversity remains, with cliffs, woods, beaches, freshwater lakes and open country – all within walking range of one of the two car parks at Stackpole Quay and Bosherston village.

Stackpole Quay was built to serve a nearby limestone quarry. Close to the quay the sandstone which forms the low cliffs to the east gives way with dramatic suddenness to towering limestone cliffs. Across these a path leads to Barafundle Bay, a well protected beach of sand and marram-covered dunes which, though remote, is popular with summer visitors. A few sycamores have established themselves at the south end of the beach, protected by the cliffs of Stackpole Head. These isolated stacks are alive in spring with colonies of breeding kittiwakes, razorbills and guillemots. Beneath them, where ancient caves have collapsed from the action of the sea, blow-holes have been formed, and in rough weather sea water thrusts up through them with awesome strength.

Behind the Head is Stackpole Warren, a lonely place populated by a few cows grazing the grass which has re-colonised this once extensive area of sand dunes. Its character lightens in summer, as sheets of violet-blue viper's bugloss colour the ground. (Also see Bosherston.)

Part NT.

Pencarrow Head

Cornwall

The breadth of the view from 447ft-high Pencarrow Head can scarcely be described by the bald statement that it extends from Bolt Head in the east to Lizard Point in the west – a distance of nearly 70 miles. Some 200ft below the triangulation pillar on the summit, the Cornwall Coast Path follows the curve of the headland, and it is possible to reach the beautiful sheltered bays of Lantic and Lantivet.

At Lansallos Beach it is easy to imagine the smugglers who haunted this area. Among the shingle the non-climbing sea bindweed trails its pink and white striped flowers. In August and September the aptly named Autumn Lady's Tresses orchid shows tiny white flowers which spiral up its stems among the cliff-top grasses. In contrast to these easily overlooked blooms, thyme grows in profusion on the downland turf. The bright pink of both common and slender centaury add to the colours of the headland.

Rabbits have returned here in strength in recent years. With them have come buzzards, weasels and foxes to join the ravens and kestrels who make their homes in this delightful and unspoilt place.

Access: *footpaths from Polruan-Lansallos and Polruan-Pont roads. NT.*
Location: *between Polruan and Polperro.*
Map: *page 305, SX15.*

Penistone Hill Country Park

West Yorkshire

This park is in the heart of Brontë country, set as it is on Penistone Hill immediately above the village of Haworth, where the Reverend Patrick Brontë was curate of the church of Saint Michael and All Angels. This is where Anne, Charlotte and Emily wrote their novels, and it is not

difficult to see where their inspiration came from.

Heather moorland has a very special quality, and where it is easily accessible, as in this country park, it brings a special range of wildlife within reach. The commonest small bird is the meadow pipit, a small, thrush-like insect eater. But, the most interesting of the small insect eaters occurring here is the whinchat. This handsome little bird is a summer visitor from Africa where it spends the winter. It feeds on insects as large as the emperor moth. This large and beautifully marked moth is Britain's only silk moth and can be found flying over heather moorland in the spring, while the large green caterpillars with their black and yellow spots feed on the heather in the summer months.

An excellent detour from the country park is to Top Withins Farm or Wuthering Heights. On the way the track passes through lovely country including a series of small waterfalls, and to complete the Brontë connection, Haworth has the Brontë Parsonage Museum.

Open: *Brontë Parsonage Museum, all year except 3 weeks in Dec.*

Admission charge. Shop. No dogs. Penistone Hill Country Park all year. Picnic area.
Location: *W of A6033 Hebden Bridge to Keighley road. B6142 leads to Haworth. Country park is ¾ mile beyond village.*
Map: *page 310, SE03.*

Penmon

Gwynedd

Penmon is the start of a toll-road, free to walkers, which leads to Black Point, the rocky spur on Anglesey's heel. A favourite spot for fishermen, it overlooks uninhabited Puffin Island, where St Seiriol, a Celtic monk, founded a sanctuary in the 6th century. Much later, the island became a link in a chain of signalling stations which enabled shipping news to cover the 70 miles between Holyhead and Liverpool in less than a minute. The narrow channel between Black Point and the island is guarded by a delightfully picturesque little black-and-white lighthouse complete with battlements. It was built in 1837 and would not look out of place on a giant's chessboard. Seabirds that might be seen from the point include kittiwakes, razorbills, shags, cormorants and guillemots. All these nest on Puffin Island, where there are also puffins!

Puffin Island from Penmon

At the start of the toll-road stand a medieval church, the remains of a 13th-century priory and a 400-year-old dovecote with nesting places for nearly 1000 birds. Nearby, trees cluster round a well dedicated to St Seiriol. The lower walls of the tiny building which shelters the pool of cold, clear water are believed to date from the earliest days of Christianity on Anglesey.

Location: *from Beaumaris follow B5109 Llangoed road for 1¾ miles, then turn left onto an unclassified road, turning right after another 1¼ miles to reach Penmon (road to Penmon may be covered briefly by high spring tides).*
Map: *page 309, SH68.*

Pennine Way

Northern England

From Edale in Derbyshire this 250-mile long-distance path runs right up the Pennine Chain to the Scottish border. On the way it crosses some of the wildest moorland in Britain. Here, typical sounds are the calls of grouse and curlew, while a typical sight is cotton grass blowing in the wind. Very pleasant on a fine day, but these are exceptional, and the weather can quickly change to wind, mist and rain. Only experienced walkers with correct equipment should attempt these stretches. The beginning of the path is through the Peak District (see page 210). Where the route runs through the Yorkshire Dales, it crosses some of the finest limestone scenery in Britain. Especially noteworthy is Malham Cove, whose cliffs rise sheer for 300 feet due to a geological 'fault'. Also of interest are the limestone 'pavements', areas of limestone blocks exposed by the action of glaciers and now weathered so that the joints form deep fissures. These 'grikes' and 'clints' as they are called are extremely dangerous but they provide a shaded and sheltered habitat for a great variety of plants. These include various ferns, such as the limestone polypody, and a northern relative of the buttercup, the baneberry. This has small white flowers followed by large poisonous shiny black berries.

Further north the Way meets Hadrian's Wall, near the A69 west of Greenhead, and follows the wall for some distance.

The path climbs over the Cheviots (see page 197) where it runs along the Scottish border before dropping down to Kirk Yetholm, and its finishing point.

Map: page 309, 310, 313.

A limestone pavement at Malham Cove, on the Pennine Way

Penrhos Nature Reserve

Gwynedd

The sheltered 'inland sea' between Holy Island and Anglesey laps the shores of an exceptionally interesting nature reserve notable for encouraging conservation-minded attitudes in young people. Penrhos was established in 1972 by a local policeman, Ken Williams, on land owned by Rio Tinto Zinc and the Kaiser Corporation, whose aluminium smelter with its 420ft-high chimney dominates inland views. The reserve includes an animals' hospital whose patients have included badgers stunned by passing cars, and an exhausted peregrine falcon rescued from a hillside in Snowdonia. Two young ravens, taken to Penrhos after their parents had been poisoned, were later presented to the Tower of London.

Several walks explore the reserve, which covers low ground between the Stanley Embankment – built to carry Thomas Telford's London-Holyhead road – and a grassy headland overlooking the sand and shingle of Llanfawr Bay. The oyster-catcher is the emblem of Penrhos, but the reserve has also attracted such unlikely visitors as a sacred ibis.

Species more likely to be seen at various times of the year include Slavonian grebes, ringed plovers, greylag, snow, barnacle and Canada geese, cormorants, puffins, herons, blackbirds, goldcrests, wigeon, teal and mallard. Four varieties of tern nest on nearby islets – one set a record when it was 'logged' in Australia just seven months after being ringed at Penrhos.

The reserve's many other interesting features include one of Telford's 19th-century toll-houses and the remains of a gun battery built to defend Holyhead during the Napoleonic Wars.

Open: *all year. No charge, but box for donations. Picnic area. Suitable for disabled visitors.*
Location: *on A5, 2 miles SE of Holyhead.*
Map: *page 308, SH28.*

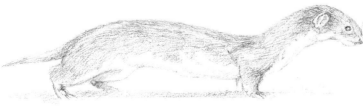

The Weasel

Despite its diminutive size and charming appearance, the weasel is a deadly and efficient killer. Its prey ranges from mice and voles to rabbits. Although most active at night, the weasel is frequently seen during the day – often scrutinising the human observer with obvious curiosity. The weasel and its close relative the stoat can be told apart by the stoat's much larger size and black-tipped tail.

Pentire Head

Cornwall

From just above New Polzeath – an example of the dangers of unchecked property development – to Portquin, the National Trust owns some 700 acres of coast and farm land. The most striking features are the great headlands, or points, of Pentire and The Rumps.

There are fine views from Pentire Point south and south-west to Stepper Point and Trevose Head, while to the north-east the view on clear days is to Hartland Point. It is difficult to imagine that the land round which one now walks so freely was once divided into building plots, and was saved only by public appeal in 1936.

Off the coast lie the small islands of Newland and the Mouls. Formed, like Pentire, of solidified lava, they are home to puffins and grey seals. The Mouls is the nearest to the coast, lying just off Rumps Point where the defences of an Iron Age fort are still clearly visible, guarding the neck of the prong-shaped peninsula.

The attractive walks on the Pentire headland lead the walker over good paths through beautifully maintained farms and across cliffs carpeted with short turf and bracken. Foxgloves, red campion and poppies add to the pleasure of these walks, while past Doyden Castle, an 1830s folly perched on the cliff edge, lies Portquin, a film maker's dream Cornish fishing village. However, appearances are often deceptive – it is not a fishing village, and the old story of the lost fishing fleet of Portquin is merely a legend.

Access: *by footpaths. NT.*
Location: *6 miles NW of Wadebridge, off B3314. Follow signs for New Polzeath or Portquin.*
Map: *page 304, SW98.*

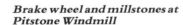

Petworth Park

West Sussex

Petworth House is justly famed for its contents and in particular for its great picture collection. Supreme among the many paintings are those by Turner, two of which depict the park, believed by many to be the finest work of Lancelot 'Capability' Brown.

Size, grand design, above all the sheer confidence of Brown's best achievements, are perfectly demonstrated at Petworth. Visit it on a crisp winter's day, entering the car park one-and-a-half miles north of the town – the only one open in winter – and the first impression is of towering beeches dwarfing the cars. Walk across the crackling beech leaves and study a typical Brown landscape, still very much as he would have envisaged it. The ground falls away gently, and the eye follows the curve up across the shallow valley, past the gleam of water in the small lake to the ridge beyond, surmounted by magnificent clumps of mature

Petworth House and Park from an engraving of 1830

Brake wheel and millstones at Pitstone Windmill

chestnut, oak and beech. It is surely a tribute to Brown's genius that today these wholly unnatural plantings are accepted as part of his 'natural landscape' theory.

There is a multitude of tracks and paths across Petworth Park; the major path from the car park leads over the ridge to reveal the serpentine lake, and beyond it the house.

On the lake are mallards and moorhens, while black-headed gulls wheel overhead. On the way back study some of the 400-strong herd of fallow deer, and note the leading stag – not feeding but watchful. Pause again before returning to the car park to absorb the tranquil scene and you will appreciate why Petworth is said to represent so completely the age of nobility.

Open: *park every day; free access. House open from spring to autumn at specified times. Dogs allowed in park only, under control. NT.*
Location: *Car park for park only on A283, 1½ miles N of Petworth.*
Map: *page 306, SU92.*

Pewsey Downs National Nature Reserve

Wiltshire

This National Nature Reserve is situated on the steep south-facing scarp slope which runs along the northern side of Pewsey Vale. Fine views can be had from the down across the vale to Salisbury Plain in the south and, from the western end of the reserve, there are views northwards to Silbury Hill (see Marlborough Downs, page 176) and beyond.

Pewsey Downs are among the richest downland slopes for wild

flowers in Britain, with chalk milkwort, horseshoe vetch, round-headed rampion, bastard toadflax, early gentian, devil's-bit scabious, saw-worts, and several orchids, including burnt-tip, among the species to be found. With so many wild flowers, grassland butterflies can be seen in profusion on a windless day in high summer. Chalk-hill, common and small blues, marbled whites, brown argus, Duke of Burgundy, and several skippers are but a few of them. The reserve is well known for its badgers and their young can often be seen playing alongside fox cubs on early summer evenings.

Access: *on public footpaths. NCC.*
Location: *from A4 W of Marlborough take Lockeridge/Alton Barnes Road; reserve is on either side of road just N of Alton Barnes.*
Map: *page 305, SU16.*

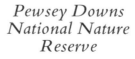

Pitstone Windmill

Buckinghamshire

Pitstone is a post mill – that is to say its rectangular wooden body is supported by a massive upright post. The body pivots on this post, enabling the mill to be turned so that the sails face the wind. A long pole, which projects from the base of the movable part of the mill, is used as a lever to push the mill round. At Pitstone this pole ends in a cartwheel, making it easier to turn the mill.

The age of this very early mill is not fully established. A date on one of its timbers, once believed to be 1697, was later proved to be 1627, making Pitstone the earliest dated English windmill. It is almost certainly much older than this, since the county records of 1624–8 refer to structural work being carried out for the tenants. It seems clear that this included repair work to an already existing building.

Whatever its age, the mill continued operating commercially until 1902, when a freak storm caused very extensive damage to the machinery and outside walls. The next 41 years saw its almost continuous decline, although the National Trust carried out some 'first aid' repairs after acquiring the mill. In 1963 a complete overhaul was undertaken, and in 1970 the mill once again ground corn, using the 19th-century machinery with new grindstones.

Open: *May to Sep Sun and bank holiday Mon, pm only. Admission charge. NT.*
Location: *¼ mile S of Ivinghoe, 3 miles NE of Tring, just W of B488. Reached along track.*
Map: *page 306, SP91.*

Pixey & Yarnton Meads

Oxfordshire

There has been over 900 years of recorded hay cutting on these ancient meadows, which retain a diversity of neutral grassland flowers and grasses unique in the British Isles. That they have survived when most other herb-rich meadows have either been ploughed or re-seeded, is due to their complex ownership, called 'movable freehold', whereby various owners hold definite acreages, which are, however, not fixed on the ground. The hay cutting is followed by late summer and winter grazing and it is the continuity of this form of land use which makes the meads so interesting to botanists.

Among the interesting plants

Pitstone Windmill and its modern neighbour

to be found here are yellow rattle, devil's-bit scabious, pepper-saxifrage and adder's-tongue fern. Meadow foxtail and the delicate quaking grass are two of the most abundant grasses. In early spring large numbers of moles can be seen burrowing out from the dryer, higher margins of the meads towards the centre. They are forced out of the lower ground by winter flooding, but can return when the water levels fall in spring.

Access: *on footpaths.*
Location: *Pixey Mead can be seen to W of A34 Oxford by-pass alongside the Thames. Yarnton Mead can be approached from a track on N side of A40 1 mile S of Yarnton which leads to a public footpath.*
Map: *page 306, SU41.*

Plessey Woods Country Park

Northumberland

While strolling through the woodlands which form the core of this lovely park, it is hard to believe that industrial Tyneside is less than ten miles away. In fact industry of one sort or another has influenced this site since the beginning of the 13th century, although few signs of these activities remain today. Those that do are interpreted for visitors who follow the history trail (one of several colour-coded trails), which shows that mining, milling, quarrying and forestry have all been major sources of employment here at one time or another.

Another route through the park, opening up entirely new vistas, is to follow the riverside trail. The River Blyth is only a few miles from its source here, but being fed by a number of smaller rivers and streams, it becomes a major river by the time it reaches the sea at Blyth. In the park it winds through dense woodland and provides a rich wildlife habitat. The exquisite song of the wren is characteristic of the area in the spring, a time when grey wagtails flit along the river, and the commonest of our wildfowl, the mallard, finds a nest site in the damper areas.

These are just two of the trails marked out in the park; the whole area is managed and interpreted in such a way that visitors can easily discover for themselves how Plessey Woods have developed.

Open: *all year. Refreshments. Information centre. Picnic area. Disabled persons electrically powered car available for visitors.*
Location: *entrance on A192 Morpeth road, 1¼ miles SW of Bedlington.*
Map: *page 313, NZ28.*

Plym Bridge Woods

Devon

A fascinating mixture of industrial archaeology and natural history can be found here. There are delightful walks through the woodland, and by the river, the remains of old slate quarries, a canal and the tracks of three railways – all in an area of 124 acres.

Many of the walks, of which there are several miles, were originally railway lines or slate extraction tracks. They run through a mainly broadleaved woodland of oak with beech and hornbeam. In the wet areas the trees are mostly willow and alder, and there is a large amount of laurel in which fallow deer lie up. Jays, spotted and pied flycatchers, treecreepers, buzzards and sparrowhawks live in or visit the woods. Along and under the river dippers may often be seen – and, very occasionally, otters. Butterflies flutter in the woodland clearings, and adders warm themselves on sunny days.

Beside the remains of the Cann Quarry Canal runs a 4ft 6in gauge railway; both are of interest to botanists and industrial archaeologists. One of the main attractions of the walk along this track is the Cann viaduct, high over the river and the only way across, other than Plym Bridge itself, just at the start of the walk, and not National Trust property.

Location: *3¼ miles NE of Plymouth. NT.*
Map: *page 305, SX55.*

Plynlimon

Dyfed/Powys

Plynlimon's summit, 2468 feet above sea level and littered with the remains of Stone Age burial cairns, is the highest point in Wales between the Snowdonia National Park and the Brecon Beacons. In late August and early September it is a resting place for dotterels on their way to spend the winter in North Africa. They are members of the plover family. Small numbers of them breed in the central Highlands of Scotland and a few other areas. Late summer is also the time of year when red kites, among the rarest birds of prey in Britain, are most likely to be seen wheeling and hovering in search of prey. The kite, easily identified by its forked tail, breeds in the so-called 'Desert of Wales' to the south of Plynlimon. Buzzards and skylarks may also be seen on the mountain.

Plynlimon is the source of the Severn, Wye and fast-flowing Rheidol which races down to the sea at Aberystwyth. Its western slopes overlook the 680-acre Nant-y-Moch Reservoir, which provides water for the power station in Cwm Rheidol.

Grey wagtails can be seen at Plessey Woods; this one is a female

Wood Mouse

Confusingly, this little creature is also called the long-tailed field mouse. To make things even more confusing, its favourite haunts are probably hedgerows. It also likes gardens, and is often the culprit when seeds, apples and potatoes disappear. Like most mice, the wood mouse is largely nocturnal, and the best times to look for it are late evening or very early morning.

On a clear day, views from the summit embrace all but three of the 'old' Welsh counties (Anglesey, Flintshire and Glamorgan are the exceptions) together with hills in Shropshire and Herefordshire.

Access: *two footpath routes lead to summit; both become ill-defined on upper stages. Sensible safety precautions should be taken on mountain.*
Location: *on A44 between Llangurig and Aberystwyth.*
Map: *page 309, SN78.*

Polegate Windmill and Milling Museum

East Sussex

Once windmills were a common sight on hilltops in south-east England. While many were built only in the last century, the industrial revolution eventually caught up with milling and by the end of the First World War it

was clear that the days of local mills supplying flour for local use from locally grown corn were numbered. Polegate mill lasted longer than most, working up to the Second World War, so that it had been derelict for less time than most when it was restored in 1967, 150 years after it was built.

Restoration of windmills relies on the enthusiasm of local people – the owner, local residents or the

local authority. At Polegate it was local residents who were responsible, launching an appeal in 1964. The restoration, undertaken by a skilled millwright, took two years. Ironically, mills are sited to make the most of the wind, which in turn makes working on them very difficult. Rebuilding the cap at the top of a 47-foot tower in high winds must have been frightening, and in 1965 when work began there were extremely high winds that slowed progress.

The internal machinery was repaired and renewed so that now the sweeps (the Sussex name for sails) can be seen working. There are several types of sweep; the ones at Polegate are Sir William Cubitt's patent sails. One of the problems of working windmills was to control the speed of the sails: like sails on boats there had to be some method of reefing or reducing canvas. If the sails were allowed to turn without control, the consequent friction would start a fire and the mill would burn down.

On the lower floor and in the old store room there is now a milling museum, where the visitor can learn about the history of windmills with particular reference to Sussex, and see such arcane utensils as a maize and bean kibbler, a bran ring and a grain dresser.

Open: *Easter to Sep, Sun pm only. Also Easter Mon, bank holiday Mons in May and Aug and all Weds in Aug, pm only.*
Location: *W of A22, 4 miles N of Eastbourne.*
Map: *page 306, TV50.*

Pont Pill

Cornwall

In 1960 the National Trust carried out a rebuilding programme at the head of Pont Pill Creek. Included in the work was the restoration of two quays and a connecting footbridge. As a result the circular walk from Fowey along both banks of the charming and largely unspoilt creek has been re-opened. The walk is three miles long and includes two ferry crossings at Bodinnick and Polruan.

From Bodinnick Ferry the walk goes steeply uphill and along Hall Walk, where Charles I was almost decapitated by a cannon shot from Fowey during the siege of the Parliamentarians. On this beautiful north bank of Pont Pill, woods of oak, sycamore,

hazel and chestnut sweep down to the edge of the creek. The hamlet of Pont is now so quiet it is difficult to imagine it as a busy offshoot of Fowey port, but it was – less than a century ago! Over the footbridge the walk turns back along the south bank of the creek and back to the ferry at Polruan. On summer evenings the songs of warblers float over the creek, and herons stalk across the mud, or stand, shadow-like, waiting for fish. The tranquillity is broken only by the sounds of human voices and cars carrying over the water from Fowey.

Access: *reached from Fowey by Bodinnick Ferry. NT.*
Location: *at entrance to Fowey Harbour.*
Map: *page 304, SX15.*

The wooded banks of Pont Pill Creek, with Fowey in the background

Porthkerry Country Park

South Glamorgan

Fossil-rich limestone cliffs, rising to 150ft, and a lofty viaduct built in 1898 for the Vale of Glamorgan Railway, are dramatic features of Porthkerry Country Park. Oak and ash dominate clifftop woodlands where springtime's primroses, violets and bluebells give way to wild strawberries during the summer months. Green woodpeckers, chiffchaffs, willow warblers and great tits are among the woodland birds that can be seen here, while mammals include foxes, and smaller hunters such as the stoat.

Oystercatchers, searching the shore for food, and several species of gull are frequent sights from the beach of smooth shingle. Maidenhair fern grows on the cliffs where it was first recorded by Edward Llwyd, a pioneering Welsh botanist, at the end of the 17th century. Meadow-sweet, yellow flag and other freshwater plants grow beside streams as they make their way down to the shore.

Porthkerry is said to be named after Ceri ap Caid, a local ruler in the pre-Christian era. It also witnessed the first Norman invasion of South Glamorgan, in 1093. Other links with the past include the remains of a kiln where lime was burned to make fertiliser, and a 19th-century sawmill overlooked by Mill Wood.

Open: all year. Small car parking charge on Sun and bank holidays in summer. Picnic areas. Refreshments. Shop.
Location: on coast, 2 miles W of Barry.
Map: page 305, ST06.

Portland

Dorset

All but an island – it is joined to the mainland only by shingle beaches – Portland has a rugged, even ugly, quality. The Portland stone which creates this massive outcrop gives the houses and villages an austere appearance, and the treeless scenery with fields flanked by grey stone walls adds to the bleak atmosphere. But the landscape has special features, since some of the fields are still farmed in the medieval strip system that once covered a good deal of England.

Portland Bill, at the south end, extends fully six miles out into the English Channel, and offshore there is a fierce tidal race.

Portland's wildlife interest is mainly birds, although there are interesting flowers along the rocky shore. In spring, seabirds breed along the west side of the cliffs, including some guillemots and a few puffins. The prime interest is, however, migration, and Portland Bill is ideally placed as a landfall for migrant birds in spring and autumn. The old lighthouse, inland from the present one, is a bird observatory, and up-to-date information on migrants is normally available here.

A museum providing interesting background information, including good fossils from Portland's quarries, is at the southern end of Easton village.

Open: museum Jun to Sep daily, Oct to May Tue to Sat. Admission charge. Shop.
Location: follow 'Portland A354' signs from Weymouth.
Map: page 305, SY67

Port Lympne

Kent

The land on the Romney Marsh side of the Royal Military Canal is about 15ft above sea level; on the other side the ground rises steeply to 350ft; and at the top of this ridge lies Port Lympne, a Dutch Colonial mansion set in terraced gardens with 270 acres of woodland and paddocks.

John Aspinall, famous for his wildlife collection at Howletts, chose this superb setting as a place to found a second collection. If herd animals are to thrive in captivity then they need to live as herds, reasons Mr Aspinall. So successful has this technique been

Cave Hole, carved from limestone on Portland's east side

that the animals at Howletts had outgrown their first home. Here was the ideal site for the expanding herds and colonies of wild animals.

Mr Aspinall also set about restoring the house and gardens, which had been neglected since the outbreak of the Second World War. There are terraces, a vineyard, striped, chequer-board and clock gardens and a herbaceous border that took 200 tons of elephant manure before planting! From the gardens can be seen Romney Marsh and the English Channel, with a view to France on a clear day.

Inside the mansion there are wildlife paintings and an exhibition of animal photography.

To see the animals there is a choice of a circular walk, a two-and-a-half mile ramble or a short direct walk. Specialities here are tigers and a chimpanzee colony. In the paddocks are various antelope, deer and bison, and elephants and rhinos. Beautifully marked snow leopards, ocelots, Barbary lions and cheetahs are among the cats to be seen.

Open: all year daily, except 25 Dec. Admission charge. Picnic area. Refreshments. Shop. Suitable for disabled visitors. No dogs.
Location: 3 miles W of Hythe on B2067, off A261.
Map: page 306, TR13.

Portsmouth Harbour

Hampshire

Portsmouth Harbour is one of the complex of shallow intertidal 'harbours' along the south coast. Although not so impressive as Langstone Harbour or Chichester Harbour, it nevertheless supports considerable numbers of waders and wildfowl, with several hundred dark-bellied brent geese in autumn and winter. On the incoming tide considerable numbers of waders can be seen, especially at the north end of the harbour near Portchester Castle. Among the birds that might be seen in winter are wigeon, teal, goldeneye, redshanks and curlews. The curlews are also here in spring and autumn, along with grey plovers. Portsmouth Harbour is designated as a Site of Special Scientific Interest by the Nature Conservancy Council.

Location: *W of Portsmouth.*
Map: *page 306, SU60.*

Priston Watermill

Avon

Many watermills have very long histories, and this one is no exception, records in Domesday Book indicating that corn was being milled here over 1000 years ago. The present mill building dates from the early 18th century, but some of its machinery, including the waterwheel, which turns two sets of grindstones, was replaced in 1850. The long tradition of milling is continued here today, with the mill working commercially as part of a mixed arable and dairy farm. Flour, wholemeal bread and other produce can be purchased in the farm shop, and farm visits can be arranged.

Open: *by arrangement with the owner only, Easter to Oct, weekdays and some evenings. Shop.*
Location: *4 miles SW of Bath, NW of B3115.*
Map: *page 305, ST66.*

Purbeck Heaths

Dorset

The Purbeck area, on the southern side of Poole Harbour, is one of the most undeveloped and unspoilt areas of Dorset. Much of the countryside is heathland and it includes superb examples of this special habitat, which is so sadly reduced over other parts of southern England. The views across the rolling heaths of Arne, Studland and Godlingston to the sheltered waters of Poole Harbour are superb and unlike almost anywhere else in Britain. The preservation of the heaths is mainly due to the establishment of nature reserves on the major sites. Arne is an RSPB reserve, while Studland, Godlingston and Hartland are National Nature Reserves managed by the Nature Conservancy Council. Two of these, Studland and Godlingston, together with a third – Middlebere – have belonged to the National Trust since it acquired the 7294-acre Corfe Castle Estate in 1982. These reserves constitute some of the largest and most important tracts of lowland heath remaining in Britain.

The heaths are at their best in late summer when no less than four species of heather are in flower. The various shades of purple interspersed with the rich yellow of gorse create a veritable riot of colour.

The wildlife quality of the area is very special indeed. All six British reptiles occur on the heaths, while the insect life is outstanding, with dragonflies having some of the best sites in the country, and butterflies, moths and crickets occurring in great numbers.

The birdlife is also full of specialities related to the heathland habitat. Probably the most well known is the Dartford warbler. Although this little bird can be very shy, it is still possible to see one, especially where there are dense patches of gorse. It is dark brown with a dull red breast and a cocked tail. Because of its specialised habitat, the bird is at risk from heath fires or the effects of cold winters, but on these carefully protected heaths it has been able to recover from the last disastrous winter of 1963. One of the birds more likely to be seen is the green woodpecker, its yellow back showing as it flies ahead.

Great flocks of wintering ducks visit the freshwater lagoons, while the shoreline and sea attract waders and numbers of migrant sea birds, including skuas and shearwaters.

Access: *keep to marked trails and public footpaths.*
Open: *permits are required to visit the RSPB reserve at Arne, but a public nature trail and hide are situated at the end of the peninsula; these are open May to Sep. Guided walks on reserve Apr to Aug; admission charge to RSPB nonmembers, advance booking required. No dogs. Permit required for Hartland reserve. RSPB. NCC. NT.*
Location: *SE of Wareham, off A351 and B3351.*
Map: *page 305, SZ08.*

Birdwatchers on the Purbeck Heaths

Quantock Hills & Fyne Court

Somerset

The Quantocks comprise a well-wooded ridge running from just west of Bridgwater towards Taunton and reaching a height of 121ft at Wills Neck. Views open up to the west towards the rolling hills of Exmoor. The ancient woodlands are predominantly of oak and are rich in typical woodland birds, especially woodpeckers and redstarts. Buzzards are often seen circling high overhead on rising currents of warm air. Other wildlife habitats include areas of open heathland and sheltered combes. Red deer can sometimes be seen in these areas. Hodders and Holford combes, at the northern end of the range, are two excellent examples of typical wooded valleys. Also providing an introduction to Quantock woodlands is the two-and-a-half mile Quantock Forest Trail from Seven Wells Bridge or Ramscombe Picnic Place. It makes its way through Forestry Commission woods that are a mixture of conifers and broadleaved trees.

At Fyne Court, in the scattered village of Broomfield, the Somerset Trust for Nature Conservation has established its headquarters and an interpretation centre containing displays illustrating the wildlife of the Quantock Hills. The buildings that house the Trust are all that remains of the Manor House, burnt down in 1898, and are rented from the National Trust.

There are clear signs that Broomfield was once a much larger community which has fallen victim to the rural depopulation of the last two centuries. The area has a long history, demonstrated by a Bronze Age urn ploughed up on a local farm, an Iron Age hill enclosure site and traces of medieval buildings. This was, until this century, almost exclusively stock-rearing country, but now milk cattle have joined the sturdy Red Devons and the Dorset Horned sheep, while barley and oats are the main crops in fields first cultivated during the world wars.

Most visitors to Fyne Court take one of the walks or nature trails through pleasantly varied habitats. The STNC has prepared leaflets describing the walks. Within easy reach of the car park and a picnic area is the lakeside, where oak, hazel and beech are replacing sycamore and laurel. The path runs beside the leat – a channel carrying water to the lake – through a valley which is white with snowdrops in February. Spring colour is continued in the beech wood, where bluebells provide great mists of colour each year.

Perhaps the most attractive trail is that through Five Pond Wood. Little more than quarter of a mile in length and quite narrow, this is a near perfect example of English woodland. Beech, ash, elder and hawthorn are all present, and red campion, primroses and bright gold kingcups, which are massed beside the stream through the wood, add still more to the richness of colour. The area known as Quarryland once provided Morte slate for building large houses like Fyne Court, but now it is home to the badger, symbol of the STNC. In Deadwood many of the beech trees are well past maturity and are dying. Here

The Butser Hill Ancient Farm Project at Queen Elizabeth Country Park

over 100 species of fungi have been recorded. Around the pond are alder and goat willow, and beyond the house is the Arboretum, a mixture of mature and young trees.

A five-mile walk round the parish provides splendid viewpoints and affords an excellent insight into the history and character of the village and its surrounding lands.

Access: *to hills from car park above West Quantoxhead off A39. Also at Crowcombe Park Gate on unclassified road between Nether Stowey and Crowcombe.*
Open: *Fyne Court grounds all year daily. Shop daily Apr to Dec, pm only; Jan to Mar Thu to Sun, pm only. Interpretation centre. Nature trails. Picnic site. No dogs. NT/CNT. There is an information centre run by Somerset County Council at Nether Stowey, open Mon, Wed and Fri.*
Location: *Fyne Court is at Broomfield, 6 miles N of Taunton.*
Map: *page 305, ST13/ST23.*

Queen Elizabeth Country Park

Hampshire

Modern beechwoods and ancient downlands are the two principal features of this country park, which covers 1400 acres at the westernmost end of the South Downs.

Though the beech plantations, established by the Forestry Commission, are not old, there are older trees scattered among them. Some of these are dead or dying, and provide valuable habitats for a range of animals, insects and fungi; woodpeckers excavate their nest holes in decaying wood, as do willow tits – both these birds can be seen in the woodlands. Roe deer are also commonly seen, their numbers having increased substantially within the park since the 1960s.

It is the downland slopes, especially on Butser Hill (the highest point of the South Downs) that form the richest habitat within the country park. Here the turf is very short, and is cropped, as it has been for centuries, by sheep. A great diversity of downland flowers and plants can be found, and these attract a wide variety of butterflies and other insects. There are a number of deep combes on the slopes of Butser Hill; yew woods and individual ancient yew trees can be seen in these. These combes are managed as nature reserves by the Hampshire and Isle of Wight Naturalists' Trust by agreement with Hampshire County Council.

A special component of the country park is the Butser Hill Ancient Farm Research Project. Ancient ways of life are recon-structed here, and archaeological theories tested. A demonstration site close to the park's information centre shows aspects of the fascinating research carried out here into the way ancient man lived and farmed. The information centre itself has displays and literature which help to interpret and explain many aspects of the country park. There are numerous waymarked trails throughout the park, and demonstrations of traditional crafts and many other events take place regularly.

Open: *country park all year daily. Park centre Mar to Oct daily; Nov to Feb Sun only. (Butser Hill Ancient Farm Project demonstrations Apr to Sep daily. Admission charge.) Information centre. Refreshments. Picnic area. Tree trail suitable for disabled visitors.*
Location: *3 miles S of Petersfield on A3.*
Map: *page 306, SU71.*

Radipole Lake & Lodmoor

Dorset

It is perhaps surprising that two RSPB nature reserves should be so close to the centre of a large seaside town like Weymouth. Despite the proximity of roads and houses both retain a very natural feeling and attract a wealth of wildlife.

Radipole Lake is really the estuary of the River Wey, but the river has been dammed and it is more a freshwater reed marsh with sheltered open water areas. The RSPB have a large purpose-built reserve centre here overlooking the lake. It has imaginative displays of the birds likely to be seen on the reserve. These are often surprisingly tame and close views can frequently be had of colourful ducks such as teal and shoveler. The reeds and scrub have some special residents. Bearded tits can be traced by their 'pinging' alarm calls, while the resident Cetti's warblers have a song that is produced in loud bursts. This small brown warbler has only recently become established as a British breeding bird, but is fairly common here.

The open grassland at Lodmoor, to the east of Weymouth, is one of the newest RSPB reserves. Its wet meadow habitat is particularly attractive to wading birds, especially flocks of lapwing and snipe. A series of paths and hides is being established.

Open: *Radipole, paths and hides all year daily. Reserve information centre Apr to Sep daily; weekends Oct to Mar. Suitable for disabled visitors. Lodmoor, path and hides all year daily. Refreshments. Picnic area. No dogs. RSPB.*
Location: *Radipole is on W side of Weymouth; reserve centre at far end of main swannery car park. Lodmoor on A353, 1 mile NE of Weymouth.*
Map: *page 305, SY68.*

Ramsey: The Grove Rural Life Museum

Isle of Man

Museums that give intimate glimpses into the everyday life of yesterday are usually delightful, and the Grove is no exception. It is an almost wholly Victorian house, built around an earlier, much smaller cottage, by a Liverpool merchant as a holiday home for his wife and family. The house remained the property of the same family, the Gibbs, until it was left to the Manx Museum in 1976. Many of the furnishings are original and there are many personal belongings of the Gibb family. As far as possible the house and contents reflect the life and times of a typical Victorian villa, from the dining room with its portraits and formal furniture down to the pots and pans in the kitchen and the soaps and scouring materials in the scullery. The main bedroom, sewing room, costume gallery and toy room are packed with objects and displays which make Victorian times seem very close and very homely.

Outside is a yard which served as a centre for the farm that was an important aspect of the villa's life. A special exhibit here, among the farming tools and early vehicles, is a horse-driven threshing mill. This is one of the few of its kind to survive in working order. The gardens are also in keeping and are bright with flowers throughout the year. To add further interest to the museum there are displays explaining bee-keeping, with many different kinds of hives, the tools used to extract honey and beeswax, and, of course, bees!

Open: *May to Sep; Mon to Fri, Sun pm only. Admission charge. Shop. No dogs.*
Location: *Andreas Rd, Ramsey.*
Map: *page 309, SC49.*

Shoveler

The broad bill – used to sieve tiny plants and animals from shallow water and mud – helps to distinguish the shoveler from all other ducks. The drake has a green head, white chest and chestnut flanks. The duck is predominantly brown. Radipole Lake is a good place to look for shovelers.

Ravenshill Wood

Hereford & Worcester

This mixed coniferous and broadleaved woodland is a reserve of the Worcestershire Nature Conservation Trust and covers an east-facing hillside. From the top of the hill there are magnificent views of the Malvern Hills, Temeside and the Severn Valley. The wood is divided into sections dominated by different trees; in addition to native species such as oak, ash, birch and beech there are considerable areas of Corsican pine, western hemlock, larch and Douglas fir, which together form a varied habitat for plants and animals.

The soil is a calcareous clay and, under the broadleaved trees, supports a rich and varied ground and shrub layer including spurge-laurel, spindle, hazel, herb-Paris and broad-leaved helleborine.

During spring and early summer, the wood is full of the sound of birdsong, particularly of warblers. The roding flight of woodcock should be listened for and wetland birds looked for by the pool near the entrance. Small mammals are abundant and include the dormouse, while foxes and badgers are also present. Insects are plentiful and the wood white butterfly is one of the rarer species that may be seen.

The reserve has particularly well-laid paths for pleasant walking, with informative labels identifying many trees and plants. The small 'discovery' centre is designed especially for children, who find its nature table irresistible.

Open: *Mar to Oct. Small charge for car park. Information centre. Picnic area. Refreshments. CNT.*
Location: *7 miles W of Worcester. Entrance at Raven emblem on left of unclassified Alfrick to Knightwick road ¼ mile N of Alfrick village.*
Map: *page 305, SO75.*

Ribble Estuary

Lancashire

When this outstanding area of salt marsh and tidal flats came under threat of reclamation a few years ago, the resultant public outcry was enough to persuade the government of the day to provide the money that allowed the Nature Conservancy Council to purchase the site and establish a National Nature Reserve.

Situated on the south shore of the estuary, the expanse of salt marsh affords wide open views to the north with the famous tower of Blackpool only 10 miles away. Good as the distant views may be, the real grandeur of this place is in the number and variety of birds it supports.

To begin with a remarkable statistic: about 30 per cent of the world population of pink-footed geese can be found here in winter. Wildfowl such as shelduck, pintail, teal and wigeon are also to be found in very large numbers. Waders though, are the group which make the Ribble quite outstanding, and here again the importance of the place is shown by the fact that 25 per cent of the British wintering population of black-tailed godwits, 15 per cent of the wintering bar-

Hythe, on the eastern edge of Romney Marsh

The Ridgeway, busy highway since Neolithic times

tailed godwits, 35 per cent of the knots, 25 per cent of the sanderlings, 15 per cent of the grey plovers and dunlins, and seven per cent of the redshanks, are found here.

The spectacle of all these birds, albeit often at a distance, can be seen from the minor road along the south side of Marshside Marsh and the sea wall bounding this and Banks Marsh.

Access: *public footpaths lead N at various points from unclassified*

The Ridgeway

Wilts, Oxon and Bucks

The Ridgeway is an ancient highway dating from prehistoric times, and is probably one of the oldest routes in Britain. A long-distance path starting near Avebury in Wiltshire follows the course of the track to the Thames at Goring Gap. From there it follows the Icknield Way, another ancient track, all the way to Ivinghoe Beacon in Buckinghamshire, making a total distance of 85 miles. Chalk downland typifies the landscapes crossed on the western part of the path, while much of the eastern part of the walk is through well-wooded, hilly countryside.

Throughout its length the pathway offers excellent walking with many spectacular views, especially on the downland sections.

An outstanding feature of the Ridgeway is the great wealth of prehistoric and historic monuments which can be seen directly from the route or by making short detours from it. Hundreds of tumuli, ancient field systems, strip lynchets, dykes, hill forts, long barrows, standing stones, settlements and other archaeological features remain. Such well-known sites as Avebury stone circle, Silbury Hill, Windmill Hill (with its three concentric rings of earth banks constructed over 4500 years ago), and the ancient forts at Barbury,

Liddington and Uffington are but a few of the important remains. At Uffington is the famous White Horse, thought by some to be the carved emblem of a prehistoric tribe. Not far away is Wayland's Smithy, a Neolithic burial chamber. It is the continuity of man's constructions over the centuries that gives the walker many thoughts to ponder over. A good illustration (although not the most exciting or aesthetically pleasing), is where the Ridgeway crosses both the M4 and, within a few hundred yards, the Roman Ermine Way. Three transport and communication systems spanning 5000 years of history!

Several spectacular geomorphological features are to be

found along the route. There are great 'fields' and 'streams' of greywethers or sarsen stones in the west, particularly on Fyfield Down; many great combes, of which the Devil's Punch Bowl is one of the most impressive; and Goring Gap with the Thames cutting through the chalk. Most of the common and several rare downland plants can be found along the path. Birdlife includes all the common species; stone curlews and quails are very far from common, but lucky walkers might see one, or both, of these, although both are secretive birds at the best of times.

Access: *along waymarked paths; can be joined or left at many points.*
Map: *page 305, 306.*

Banks to Hesketh Bank road. Other viewpoints are from Marine Drive, N of Southport. NCC.
Location: *from A565 at Southport take minor road to Marshside and Banks.*
Map: *page 309, SD32/42.*

Romney Marsh

Kent

This famous marsh was once open sea. The sea itself began the land-building process, throwing

up a barrier of sandbanks behind which marshes slowly developed. Men have been reclaiming these marshes for a very long time – the Saxons drained several thousand acres for example – and by the end of the 17th century most of the land had been drained. Today the marshes are marshes in name only, and form some of the best sheep pastures in the country.

The landscape is quite flat, criss-crossed by an intricate network of ditches. It is in these that

some of Romney's most celebrated inhabitants live. These are marsh frogs, a few of which were released into a garden pond in 1934 because they were surplus to laboratory requirements. Since then they have spread throughout the whole marsh, and the loud croaking of the males (they can be heard 600yds away) adds an extraordinary quality to the place from May to June.

Since the Royal Military Canal from Rye to Hythe was com-

pleted in 1840, Romney Marsh has virtually been an island, adding more to its 'different' quality. Wide skies and the ever-present sheep are essential components of this atmosphere.

Access: *public footpaths link many of the roads crossing the marsh, and there are footpaths along stretches of the canal.*
Location: *within a triangle bounded by Dungeness, Rye and Hythe.*
Map: *page 306, TQ92.*

Privet, a shrub at Roundway Hill Covert

attractive features of the park is its craft centre, where there are first-class exhibitions of traditional and contemporary craftwork and a shop. The centre is also the base for an imaginative programme of guided walks.

Open: *all year. Centre, shop and cafe open weekends only in Jan, Feb and closed Mon (except bank holidays) in Apr, May, Jun, Sep. Daily in other months. Refreshments. Picnic area. Guided walks. No dogs in craft centre.*
Location: *on A614, 17 miles N of Nottingham, 2 miles S of Ollerton.*
Map: *page 310, SK66.*

Rutland Water

Leicestershire

An important public water-supply, this is one of Europe's largest man-made lakes, with a surface area of 3100 acres and a perimeter 24 miles long. In places it is 110ft deep. As a sailing centre, it attracts craft ranging from sail-boards to the boats of the English Olympic team. Each year, fly-fishermen catch about

Roswell Pits, Ely

Cambridgeshire

In medieval times Ely (Eel Island) was an island of land surrounded by the vast watery wastes of the fens. The island, like most in the area, is made of Kimmeridge clay capped by lower greensand.

This clay has been dug for centuries as a source of material for repairing the banks of the nearby River Ouse and its tributaries. The resulting pits have become filled with water, and a rich and varied vegetation has grown up round their margins, dominated by a variety of willows and such water-edge plants as common reed, hard rush, gipsywort, water mint and purple loosestrife. Away from the water there are extensive areas of ash, hawthorn and maple interspersed with open, grassy areas.

This variety attracts a good range of birds. Breeding species include tufted duck, shoveler, great-crested grebe, reed and sedge warblers and reed buntings, with such woodland birds as blackcap, chiffchaff and redpoll. Winter visitors include pochard and a few goldeneye.

The pits are a reserve of the Cambridgeshire and Isle of Ely Naturalists' Trust. A nature trail starts in Springhead Lane, Ely, off the B1382 road to Prickwillow.

Access: *nature trail at all times along well marked paths. CNT.*
Location: *to the NE of Ely Cathedral between Prickwillow road and River Ouse.*
Map: *page 306, TL58.*

Roundway Hill Covert

Wiltshire

Roundway Hill Covert is on a steep west-facing scarp with extensive views over the Wiltshire Plain to Salisbury Plain and the distant Mendip Hills. A prominent feature near by is the Iron Age hill-fort known as Oliver's Castle. Small areas of original chalk downland and scrub form sheltered glades around the margins of beechwoods originally planted by Lord Roundway. Many of the original trees were felled in 1949 and replanting was done in the early 1950s.

Clematis (or old man's beard), native box, wild privet, wayfaring tree, cowslip, violet, rock-rose, carline thistle and autumn felwort are but a few of the shrubs and plants found here. Ash, hazel and birch, as well as beech, are some of the main kinds of tree. Several butterfly species may be seen on fine, warm days. These include such grassland species as small and large skippers, common blue, marbled white and meadow brown. In the scrubby areas brimstones, small tortoiseshells and peacocks are all relatively common. In sunny glades within the woods the speckled wood butterfly is a resident that is frequently seen. Grasshoppers and beetles are plentiful – including the large, black, bloody-nosed beetle. It takes its name from the fact that if attacked it exudes red blood from its mouth, and also from its body joints. This usually deters the attacker. Typical birds of scrub and woodland abound in the covert.

Bloody-nosed beetles might be seen at Roundway Hill Covert

Open: *all year. Countryside trail. FC.*
Location: *1 mile N of Devizes, W of A361. Trail starts in picnic area N of wood.*
Map: *page 305, SU06.*

Rufford Country Park

Nottinghamshire

Rufford Abbey was built in 1147 by an order of Cistercian monks who sought seclusion within Sherwood Forest. The abbey has long been a ruin, and the great country house that replaced it is also largely derelict. The surrounding park and woodland are still beautiful, however. The woodland, which is known as The Wilderness, contains an old ice-house, where ice, cut in winter, could be stored for use the following summer. In the parkland, rare breeds of sheep graze one of the meadows. The attractive lake is the home of a varied collection of waterfowl, some of which come readily to be fed.

One of the most important and

60,000 trout here.

There are attractive woodlands, particularly at Barnsdale, on the north shore, which has primroses and bluebells in spring. There is a chance of seeing roe deer here, and a one-mile nature trail is laid out between the Whitwell and Barnsdale picnic-sites. A 350-acre nature reserve at the western end of the lake is run by the Leicestershire and Rutland Trust for Nature Conservation (access from Egleton). The public can visit part of this from Easter to October, via the new visitor centre at Lyndon (open only at weekends). Spring and autumn are best for large numbers of wildfowl and waders, although a good variety of birds breed and can be seen from the specially provided hides.

Open: *all year. Four large car parks (charge) at Barnsdale, Whitwell Sykes Lane and Normanton. Refreshments Sun and bank holidays, pm only (not at Barnsdale car park). Picnic areas. Information centre and adventure playground at Sykes Lane. Part CNT.*
Location: *between A47 and A606 W of A1. Sykes Lane is on N shore between Empingham and Whitwell.*
Map: *page 306, SK80/90.*

Rye Harbour

East Sussex

By contrast with the delightful town of Rye the settlement at Rye Harbour is rather ugly, but beyond it is a nature reserve well worth visiting. Lying to the west of the estuary of the River Rother are 585 acres of shingle beach, wet gravel and farmland belonging to the Southern Water Authority and run by a voluntary management committee as a Local Nature Reserve.

This landscape began to evolve after the River Rother changed its course during a terrific storm in 1287; its new alignment slowed the movement of shingle across Rye Bay towards Dungeness, creating a shingle beach. Successive shingle ridges built up through the centuries, gradually creating more and more dry land. The shingle ridges, or rather their outlines, can be seen quite clearly in the sheep pasture on the seaward side of the castle.

While the 400-year-old shingle is now grazed, the newest ridges are practically bare. One of the first plants to colonise new shingle is the sea pea, which carpets the ridges with pink flowers in June. Other characteristic plants are the yellow horned poppy, scentless may-weed, which has large daisy-like flowers, and wall-pepper, which grows in bright yellow patches in June and July.

The shingle is where common and little terns breed. These seabirds migrate north from the warm waters in the Atlantic off Africa to nest here. Little terns have suffered severely from accidental disturbance by holidaymakers and it is largely because of protection schemes and nature reserves that they are still breeding in Britain. Man's activities have led to great fluctuations in the little tern population. It doubled during the war when the area came under military control and was relatively little disturbed, but disturbance by post-war holiday makers caused the population to plummet. It is only recently that the pre-war levels have been regained, thanks to protection.

Once the wheatear was a common breeding bird on the South Downs, but modern farming practices have so altered the chalkland that probably no pairs can be found breeding there today. A few pairs breed on the Sussex coast and one of the strongholds is the Rye Harbour area. Oystercatchers nest on the shingle and can be seen and heard as they fly overhead. Another breeding wader of the shingle is the ringed plover.

On the large gravel pit on the reserve there are two hides for the use of visitors. The pits attract large numbers of waders and wildfowl in autumn, winter and spring and there are breeding wildfowl and grebes in the summer.

Because of the danger of disturbing the breeding birds it is important that visitors do not stray from the marked paths. There is an information centre in the car park. Sensible shoes are advisable because the walk across shingle can be difficult. Without binoculars visitors cannot expect to see some of the birds very well.

Access: *footpaths lead from car park at Rye Harbour. LNR.*
Location: *¼ mile S of car park at Rye Harbour.*
Map: *page 306, TQ91.*

Rutland Water is one of Europe's largest man-made lakes

BELL RINGERS' FEAST

Twyford, Hampshire

In 1754 local landowner William Davis bequeathed in his will the sum of £1 per annum to be paid to the bell-ringers of the parish for a peal of bells to be rung on the morning and evening of 7 October each year. This was to commemorate his narrow escape from death when riding home in dense fog one night. His horse changed direction at the sound of the bells just before it would have plunged into a deep chalk pit.

Today the bells are rung in the early morning and in the evening, followed by a supper attended by the bell-ringers and their guests.

When: *7 Oct.*
Map: *page 306, SU42.*

PACK MONDAY FAIR

Sherborne, Dorset

This ancient fair is heralded by a unique parade known as Teddy Roe's Band. At midnight a group of between five and six hundred people, generally led by the town's dignitaries, march through the town banging tin cans, blowing horns, bugles and whistles, singing and generally making a great deal of noise. The finishing point is reached about 1am and is followed by a further half hour of old songs, traditional music and dancing. Local tradition has it that the custom commemorates the completion of Sherborne Abbey in 1490 when workmen were granted a holiday to celebrate. A foreman of the stonemasons called Teddy Roe led the merrymaking by heading a march through the streets, and his name has been associated with the event ever since.

The fair itself was once a major hiring and horse-trading venue for the region. Today it attracts a large number of street traders who set up their stalls in the main street, staying until late in the evening. The funfair is also a popular feature.

When: *first Mon after 10 Oct.*
Map: *page 305, ST61.*

MOP FAIR & RUNAWAY MOP FAIR

Stratford upon Avon, Warwickshire

Mop Fairs or 'Statutes' date from the years following the Black Death (1348–49) when a severe shortage of labour forced a wage spiral which threatened the stability which the landowning classes enjoyed. The Establishment attempted to peg agricultural wages to pre-plague levels by the Statute of Labourers in 1351, but in the competitive work market this attempt at an incomes policy failed. However, a kind of order was eventually established when wages for the coming year were set on a regional basis and announced at Michaelmas. Employers and workers alike gathered to hear the new rates and the opportunity was then taken by farmers to hire their workforce for the next year at the same time. Enterprising traders and entertainers were soon there to take advantage of the situation and the tradition of 'hiring fairs', a day for business and pleasure, was born.

October

The Stratford Mop was once the main hiring fair for the district and achieved a certain notoriety in the mid-19th century because of its reputation for encouraging drunkenness and debauchery amongst the young. The sight of so many youngsters enjoying themselves was too much for the local clergy, who attempted to have the event abolished. The Mop has survived, however, although today it is primarily a funfair and carnival. The Runaway Mop was established so that labourers who had made a bad deal or were unhappy with their new situation had a chance to run away and be rehired before the fair left the area.

Other mops that have survived include one at Cirencester and another at Warwick.

When: *12 Oct, unless it falls on Sun, then 13 Oct. Runaway Mop Fair held a week later.*
Map: *page 305, SP25.*

Below: archive photographs of Stratford's Mop Fair

CONKER KNOCKOUT COMPETITION

Ashton, Northamptonshire

Unlike many other British customs this has only existed since 1964. It originated in October of that year when four local men put down their fishing tackle and 'strung up' conkers from the village green. The resulting games were so successful that 18 stalwarts contributed towards a trophy and declared it an annual event. In 1965 rules were devised and the competition began in earnest. Numbers are limited to 64 entrants of any nationality who compete for the trophy bought by the original 18 members. This is on permanent display in 'The Chequered Skipper' pub which overlooks the green where the competition still takes place. The whole event is presided over by the champion known as 'King Conker'. He wears a very distinctive costume complete with strings of conkers around his neck – each string representing a year of the competition's existence.

When: *second Sun in Oct.*
Map: *page 306, TL08.*

Judging on Punkie Night (below) and a punkie (right)

TITCHFIELD CARNIVAL

Titchfield, Hampshire

This carnival starts with a procession of floats which threads its way through the village and culminates with a bonfire, fireworks display and funfair in the evening. The festivities are organised by the Titchfield Bonfire Boys Society, formed in 1880. However, the tradition of bonfires here goes back to the years following the Reformation, when the earls of Southampton were granted the abbey estate.

The third Earl contained the sea within Titchfield Haven as a land improvement measure, so denying the villagers use of the estuary of the River Meon. To show their displeasure they burnt his effigy outside the Place House, then seat of the estate. The custom of burning effigies was revived during the Napoleonic Wars and later developed into the carnival it is today.

When: *last Mon in Oct.*
Map: *page 306, SU50.*

PUNKIE NIGHT

Hinton St George, Somerset

This custom is said to date from the Middle Ages, when legend has it that some local men got the worse for drink at the nearby Chiselborough Fair and failed to return home by nightfall. Their womenfolk went out to search for them using for light 'punkies', candle-lanterns made from mangold-wurzels.

Today, the children commemorate the event by holding a procession and visiting houses around the village carrying their 'punkies' and singing the 'Punkie Night Song'. At the end of the procession a competition is held to judge the best 'punkie'.

When: *last Thu in Oct.*
Map: *page 305, ST41.*

St Abb's Head

Borders

The superb cliffs between St Abbs and Pettico Wick rise to over 300ft on this promontory. St Abb's Head is the most important location for cliff-nesting seabirds in south-east Scotland; there are over 15,000 pairs of kittiwakes and some 17,000 guillemots, as well as smaller numbers of fulmars, shags, razorbills, herring gulls and puffins. The location makes the Head a good landfall site for autumn migrants, and in recent years a number of rarities have been recorded, including wryneck, red-breasted flycatcher, yellow-browed warbler and bluethroat.

Sea campion and thrift, two plants specially adapted to surviving in exposed situations, can be found here, and add much to the beauty of the cliffs.

St Abb's Head, which also has historical and archaeological interest, was declared a National Nature Reserve in 1983; the offshore waters are part of Scotland's first voluntary marine reserve, declared in 1984 to protect the area and its wildlife.

Nearly 200 acres around St Abb's Head are owned by the National Trust for Scotland and managed jointly with the Scottish Wildlife Trust.

Access: *from car park on approach road leading to St Abb's.* NTS/CNT/NCC.
Location: *4 miles NW of Eyemouth, along B6438 road from A1107.*
Map: *page 313, NT96.*

St Bees Head

Cumbria

The great red sandstone cliffs forming this double headland are the most prominent feature of the Cumbrian coast, and give extensive views to the west and north. Thirty miles away to the south-west lies the Isle of Man and the mountain of Snaefell, while away to the north-west are the mountains of Dumfries and Galloway in south-west Scotland.

Beginning at the sea front car park in the village of St Bees, a footpath winds its way north, following the cliff edge most of the way to Whitehaven. About one-and-a-half miles along this path, at the mouth of a stream, lies Fleswick Beach. The beach is composed mainly of pebbles, the direct result of cliff erosion and subsequent pounding by the Atlantic storms. Half a mile further on is the St Bees Head lighthouse. Just beyond it the views open out, with Workington along the coast and the distant hills of Scotland on the other side of the Solway Firth.

The Head is famous for its seabird colony – the largest on the west coast of England – comprising guillemots, razorbills, puffins and a number of black guillemots. These stout birds, black with a broad white wing patch and bright red feet in the summer months, have their stronghold in the Orkneys and Shetlands. This is their only English breeding site.

Access: *on public footpath. Parking at St Bees seafront. Part RSPB.*
Location: *W of B5345 at St Bees, 4¼ miles S of Whitehaven.*
Map: *page 313, NX91.*

Calm sea along the north Cornwall coast near St Agnes

St Agnes

Cornwall

Between St Agnes Head and Chapel Porth, high cliffs, topped by windswept moorland, look down on sandy beaches across which the advancing tide sends great breakers to crash against the base of the cliffs. The area is dotted with the remains of tin and copper mines, relics of Cornwall's wealthy industrial past. The National Trust owns 450 acres here, including St Agnes Beacon and most of the disused mines around Chapel Porth.

The views from the 630ft St Agnes Beacon are among the most magnificent in a county renowned for spectacular vistas. On a clear day it is possible to see a sweep of 26 miles of the north Cornwall coast extending from Carn Naun near St Ives to Trevose Head. Inland, the view takes in the high plateau of Bodmin Moor, and continues across the peninsula to the south coast. In late summer the bright yellow of western gorse and purple of heather flowers produce great sheets of colour to cover the beacon.

Between St Agnes and Chapel Porth is Newdowns Head, with more fine views north over Perran Bay. The narrow valley of Chapel Coombe leads down to the two-mile-long sandy beach at Chapel Porth. The best known of the ruined mines owned by the Trust is probably Towanroath Shaft, perched high on a cliff edge overlooking the beach. Gaunt and grey, the crumbling mines have now become an essential component of this wild and beautiful country.

Location: *½ mile W of B3277 Truro to St Agnes road. NT.*
Map: *page 304, SW64.*

St Fagans: Welsh Folk Museum

Mid Glamorgan

Buildings that would have been demolished or fallen into ruins have been rebuilt in the 100-acre grounds of St Fagans Castle since it was given to the National Museum of Wales by the Earl of Plymouth in 1946. Set in a beautiful park, they illustrate many aspects of Welsh life over some 500 years, and are supplemented by exhibits covering everything from clothes and musical instruments to agriculture and religion.

Hendre'r-ywydd Uchaf, a farmhouse from the Vale of Clwyd, dates from the end of the 15th century, while parts of the Stryd Lydan barn, also from North Wales, are only about 60 years younger. Among the many other buildings are an 18th-century, water-powered woollen factory, a corn mill, the last oak-bark tannery in Wales, a cockpit and a Unitarian chapel – also used as a school – whose ministers included a great-uncle of Dylan Thomas, the turbulent, Swansea-born poet.

The castle itself is 16th-century and has a fine collection of period furniture and recalls life in a Welsh mansion during the past 400 years. Adjoining buildings house a cooper and a wood turner who makes traditional spoons, bowls and other utensils from sycamore.

Museum staff have spent more than 25 years interviewing and tape-recording people about every aspect of Welsh life, but with particular emphasis on the home, farming, folklore and age-old rural crafts.

Open: Mon to Sun, Sun pm only (but closed 24–26 Dec and 1 Jan). Admission charge. Museum shop. Restaurant. Suitable for disabled visitors. No dogs.
Location: signposted from A48, 4 miles W of Cardiff.
Map: page 305, ST17.

St Leonard's Forest

West Sussex

The central plateau of the Weald is the Forest Ridge. Largely composed of sand, this ridge is between 500 and 800 feet above sea level and its western end begins east of Horsham in St Leonard's Forest. Here the plateau is split by deep valleys clothed in birch and pine. Other trees have been planted: more recent is the larch grown for commercial forestry, but oak, ash and other hardwoods had previously been

Top: using an apple mill at St Fagans. The two engravings show that the process has hardly changed

planted to provide material for tools, fencing and fuel.

Perhaps the greatest influence on the landscape here came in Tudor times, when the forest stretched across 9000 acres, with 2500 acres let for farming. Before the industrial revolution of the 17th and 18th centuries, the Weald was the centre of the iron industry, and in St Leonard's Forest plenty of evidence of the industry remains. For example, the streams in their narrow valleys were dammed to provide water for the industry. These lakes – known as furnace or hammer ponds – can still be seen in several places, providing magnificent views to the walker who comes across them suddenly. Near the furnace ponds there are often ironmasters' houses, confident Elizabethan and Jacobean residences, sometimes grander than the house of the local squire.

Conservation has a long history here. Indeed, objections to the devastation of the woodland by the depredations of the ironmasters and charcoal burners led to much comment during Tudor times, and within 100 years John Evelyn was writing of the need to plant trees to make up for the devastation. In reality, the main deforestation happened in the Middle Ages rather than during the 16th and 17th century: by the time Elizabeth I came to the throne less than a third of St Leonard's Forest remained.

Much of the heathland in the forest was planted with conifers during the 18th century, a practice that was abhorred by landscape designers such as Repton and Brown, even though the heathland was regarded as waste and wilderness by many of their contemporaries.

The Sussex Trust for Nature Conservation manages three small areas within the forest, partly in order to protect rare mosses and plants.

A wonderful landscaped garden exists on the edge of the Forest at Leonardslee, in Lower Beeding. Here Sir Edmund Loder, who acquired the estate in 1888, created a spring garden with azaleas and rhododendrons, clothing the banks of a series of 15th-century hammer ponds.

Open: Leonardslee, mid Apr to mid Jun and Oct weekends. Admission charge. Picnic area. Refreshments. Shop. Suitable for disabled visitors. No dogs.
Access: to forest on footpaths. FC/CNT.
Location: forest is 1½ miles E of Horsham. Bounded by A264 to N, and A281 and A279 to S. Leonardslee is 4 miles SE of Horsham on A281.
Map: page 306, TQ23.

Salcey Forest

Northants and Bucks

This is a 'mixed' forest, containing both deciduous and coniferous trees. Some of the oaks are hundreds of years old, though most were planted from 1847 onwards. They grow alongside beech, cherry and other hardwoods, as well as two softwoods, Corsican pine and Norway spruce, which have been planted since the Second World War. The forest is managed by the Forestry Commission and the woodland blocks are divided by rides. As is often the case, the 'edge' thus provided between two habitats is very good for wildlife. Pheasants may be seen crossing the rides and, in the twilight, the secretive woodcock performs its territorial 'roding' flight, regularly patrolling the same boundaries, with odd grunting and sneezing calls. Dusk is also a good time to hear the familiar, wavering hoot of the tawny owl. Much easier to see is its relative, the little owl, which sometimes emerges by day from the hollow oaks which it loves. Nightingales sing both day and night from the thickets.

Fallow deer and the introduced muntjac, an Asian deer, live in the forest, but are difficult to find. Butterflies are still common: though some species have been lost in recent years, two unusual ones surviving are the purple hairstreak, which flies high around the oaks, and the delicate-looking wood white. There are many flowers, including bluebells and the delightfully-named wood goldilocks under the trees, and ragged robin in the rides. Part of the forest is leased as a nature reserve jointly by the Northants Naturalists' Trust and the Berkshire, Buckinghamshire and Oxfordshire Naturalists' Trust.

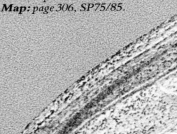

Open: all year. Picnic sites. Forest walk. FC/CNT.
Location: W of B526 on Hartwell road, about 8 miles S of Northampton.
Map: page 306, SP75/85.

Sandringham

Norfolk

Sandringham House is, of course, a favourite home of Her Majesty the Queen and the royal family. The house, its grounds, the museum and the church of St Mary Magdalene are of great interest, with innumerable royal associations.

To the west of the house lies Sandringham Country Park, a fine area of woodland – mainly conifer and rhododendron – and heath. The northern part, in particular, is very popular, but there are numerous quiet corners. One of the most attractive birds here, the crossbill, has probably always been indifferent to human presence; these attractive finches often feed in the larches around the main car park. Rhododendrons, being exotic and therefore poor in native species, do, however, give shelter to the similarly introduced and fantastically colourful golden pheasant. To glimpse this shy bird, early morning visits are best, when there is also a chance of fallow deer. At other times there are plenty of the commoner woodland birds and large numbers of squirrels.

Open: house and grounds usually late Apr to late Sep (except last 2 weeks Jul). House and church closed Fri and Sat. All closed when royalty present. Check by telephoning King's Lynn 2675. Admission charge. Refreshments. Shop. No dogs. Country park all year. Nature trail and picnic area late Apr to late Sep.
Location: 7 miles NE of King's Lynn, E of A149.
Map: page 311, TF62.

Sandwich Bay Area

Kent

The Kent Trust for Nature Conservation manages two excellent, but very different, reserves in the Sandwich area. The smaller, Gazen Salts, has been carefully developed to provide a wide diversity of habitats within a restricted area sited at the edge of the town. A freshwater lake and reed-beds now occupy land which was for centuries an area of rough grazing land subject to winter flooding. Plants – including a number of uncommon species – trees and shrubs have been introduced, not only for their attractiveness, but also for their value as food sources for insects and birds. As a result of this policy many butterflies and over 150 species of birds have been recorded in or about the reserve.

The Sandwich Bay Nature Reserve – one-and-a-half miles from the nearest car park – has a similar diversity of plant and animal life in its various habitats. But here a largely uncontrolled evolution is taking place, as the growing sand and shingle spit of Shellness forces the River Stour further into Pegwell Bay.

Those prepared to undertake the walk to the reserve will experience a splendid sense of isola-

Almost certainly you will hear the sharp pebble-clicking call of the stonechat, and see one, tail and wings flicking, on its favourite gorse.

To the east of Salcombe the National Trust owns more coastline from Mill Bay to Gammon Head, with 'outcrops' at Prawle and Woodcombe Points. In spring and autumn Prawle Point is a good place to watch migrating birds, but there is always some bird activity along this coast. Kestrels, ravens and buzzards patrol the cliff edges; cormorants fly low and swiftly over the waves, or stand 'drying' their wings at Gara Rock.

Open: *Overbecks Museum Apr to Oct daily. Admission charge. Overbecks Gardens always open. Parking charge refundable on purchase of entrance ticket. Shop. NT.*
Access: *by coastal path along cliffs. NT.*
Location: *either side of Salcombe Harbour.*
Map: *page 305, SX73.*

Salisbury Plain

Wiltshire

This vast, elevated plain is situated to the north-west of Salisbury between Amesbury, Warminster, Westbury, Devizes and Pewsey. It has a gentle tilt to the south-east and is divided by the rivers Avon, Wylye, Nadder and Ebble, which converge on Salisbury.

Much of the Plain is used for military training, which has prevented many areas from being devastated by the plough, so that large tracts of country remain as grassland with a great diversity of grassland plants, insects and birds. Another feature resulting from the military use is that in many areas the grass has not been grazed by sheep or cattle to the same extent as many other downland areas. The longer tussocky grass is ideal for small mammals together with the birds which prey upon them, and for butterflies. Short-eared owls, merlins and hen harriers are regularly seen in winter, while stonechats and whinchats are summer specialities.

Most of the typical plants of the chalk are to be found, together with many species of grassland butterfly such as chalk-hill blue, marbled white, skippers and browns. Cowslip, vetch, milkwort, scabious, dropwort and orchids abound.

Most of the rivers are typical chalk streams, famous for their trout, and for their aquatic plants. In the derelict water meadows, lusher vegetation attracts such birds as redshank and snipe.

No description of Salisbury Plain would be complete without a mention of its tremendous wealth of prehistoric remains. In Neolithic and Bronze Age times this was the most densely populated part of Britain, the 'capital' of a sophisticated civilisation that has left behind traces of its fields, houses, graves and great ceremonial structures. The most famous is, of course, Stonehenge, but there are hundreds of other sites. Many of these, especially earthworks of one sort or another, have not been ploughed or sprayed and are excellent places to look for the flowers and insects of chalk downland.

Access: *on public path. Keep out of military training areas when red flags flying.*
Location: *N of Salisbury. Lanes and bridleways lead from A303, A360 and W of A345.*
Map: *page 305, SU04.*

The wood white butterfly is found in Salcey Forest

Salcombe

Devon

Visitors to Salcombe have a wonderful opportunity to contrast the sub-tropical splendour of the garden at Overbecks with the very English cliff walks to the west. A six-mile stretch of coast here, and the Overbecks Garden (which has a fascinating local museum) are owned by the National Trust.

Car parks are available at points along the way, but the cliff walks remain unspoilt. Wind, waves and seabird cries will accompany you as you explore the cliffs and coves along the coast. On Cathole Cliff, the delicate flowers of spring squill give an almost bluebell-like sheen to the slopes. English stonecrop grows on the stony ground, its pretty white flowers flushed with pink.

tion, particularly on winter days when the sea roars in across Sandwich Flats, and the Stour struggles towards the bay. On the dunes, marram, sea spurge and sea holly can be found, joined in summer by bedstraw and broomrapes. In wetter areas the white flower heads of water dropwort precede the reddish-brown seed pods of the rare sharp rush, while the salt marshes support such plants as sea lavender and sea aster.

The Kent coast is famed for its migrants, and both birds and butterflies pass through the reserves in large numbers in spring and autumn. In winter, parties of ducks and waders feed in Pegwell Bay and the occasional rarities-which make a landfall here attract attention from birdwatching enthusiasts.

The less active can gain a good overall view of the area and its natural history from the Kent County Council car park and picnic site at Pegwell Bay.

Access: *unrestricted, but visitors should avoid those areas indicated by notices. NT/CNT.*
Location: *Gazen Salts: NW edge of Sandwich next to A257; Sandwich Bay & Pegwell Bay: 2–3 miles N of Sandwich.*
Map: *page 307, TR36.*

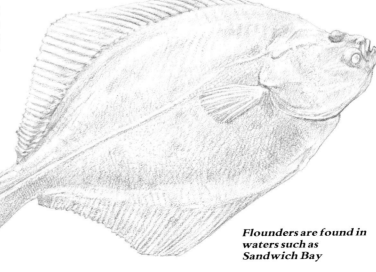

Flounders are found in waters such as Sandwich Bay

Sandy: The Lodge

Bedfordshire

The countryside along the A1 in east Bedfordshire is generally not very attractive – but there are exceptions. An outcrop of the rock known as lower greensand has given a name to the small town of Sandy, and an element of height and variety to the landscape. On this ridge stands The Lodge, built by a son of Sir Robert Peel and since 1961 the headquarters of the Royal Society for the Protection of Birds. It is in pleasant honey-coloured buildings, with grounds that consist of gardens, woodlands and heath. The gardens are bright with flowers in summer, when the huge carp in the old swimming pool will take bread from visitors' fingers. The woods have a varied bird life, including warblers, woodpeckers and tits. As elsewhere, these can be elusive, although many birds come to drink at the Lake, and at another small pond, where hides have been provided. The heath is scientifically important, being one of only a few areas of its kind left north of the Thames. It holds birds such as the tree pipit, with its 'parachute' song flight, as well as the rare natterjack toad, which has recently been reintroduced here. Autumn is a fine time for fungi and in winter there are flocks of finches.

Open: *all year, Mon to Sat. (Sun and bank holiday weekends, RSPB members and guests only and members of Beds and Hunts Naturalists' Trust). (Reserve closed 25 and 26 Dec. Shop closed 21 to 31 Dec.) Admission charge for RSPB non-members. Information centre. Nature trails. Shop. Picnic site. No dogs. Facilities for disabled visitors. RSPB.*
Location: *1½ miles E of Sandy on Cambridge road, B1042.*
Map: *page 306, TL14.*

Savernake Forest

Wiltshire

Once an extensive medieval royal forest, Savernake still retains many aspects of its former glory, with relicts of the mid-18th-century woodland together with areas of scattered scrub and grassy glades. Massive sessile oaks, some of the largest sweet chestnuts in the country and beeches are the main forest trees. It is the open nature of much of the forest which makes it so good for birds and insects, particularly beetles and moths. Mosses, lichens and fungi also abound.

Although such unusual birds as the roller (a bright-blue visitor from the Continent) have been recorded in the forest, it is the more common scrub and woodland species such as nightingales, turtle doves, tree pipits, woodpeckers, nuthatches, treecreepers, six species of tit and several warblers for which the forest is best known. With a bit of luck wood warblers and redstarts may also be seen.

Open: *all year. Forest trail. Picnic sites. FC.*
Location: *SE of Marlborough between A4 and A346.*
Map: *page 305, SU26.*

Saxtead Green Windmill

Suffolk

This 18th-century mill combines elements of both earlier and later windmill design. Our oldest mills, dating from the 12th century, were post mills, which revolved around a strong central wooden pillar. To keep the sails into the wind the miller had to turn the whole structure by leverage on a long beam. In later designs, only the top or 'cap' of the mill actually turns and is kept into the wind by a 'fantail' – a small wheel of sails extending behind. Saxtead Green is in the middle ground – it is a post mill, but it also has a fantail. When first built it probably had canvas-covered sails. These would need to be stopped to adjust them to the strength of the wind. A 19th-century invention, the 'patent' sail, had shutters which could be adjusted while in motion, and these are now fitted to this mill. The sails of a windmill drive an upper grindstone against a fixed lower stone, through a series of gears, which can be disengaged at will. This mill is unusual in having two sets of stones.

Open: *Apr to Sep Mon to Sat daily. Admission charge.*
Location: *W of Framlingham on A1120 Yoxford to Stowmarket road.*
Map: *page 306, TM26.*

Scarlett Visitor Centre

Isle of Man

The Manx Nature Conservation Trust's Scarlett Visitor Centre is set in a area of fascinating geology and high botanical interest. The centre has been constructed in a restored building which was originally an office for a limestone quarry near Castletown. Carboniferous limestone is rare in the Isle of Man, but in this area there is an exposure showing an abundance of fossils. Further along the coast, there is spectacular evidence of volcanic activity.

Displays in the centre explain the geology of the area, and also give information on the birds, flowers and inter-tidal life. There is a good collection of fossils, and also an explanation of the local industrial archaeology, including a nearby lime kiln. A nature trail can be followed along the coastal footpath.

Open: *late May to early Sep Thu, Sat and Sun pm only. Admission charge. Shop. Nature trail. CNT.*
Location: *1 mile SW of Castletown on coastal road.*
Map: *page 308, SC26.*

Saxtead Green Windmill

Scolton Manor Country Park & Museum

Dyfed

Scolton Manor, one of the most attractive country houses in the old county of Pembrokeshire, was built in 1840 for James Higgon, Mayor of Haverfordwest, whose family had owned the Scolton estate since the end of the 16th century. It cost £3000 – considerably more than expected – and was designed by two local architects, the brothers William and James Owen. They also made the furniture.

The house is now the focal point of a 40-acre country park

whose eastern flank is sheltered by an arboretum where trees include the evergreen holm oak, Japanese umbrella pine and the beautiful Chilean firebush. Another area was planted with cherry laurel in the 1930s, while elsewhere in the park are Douglas fir, Norway spruce – the traditional Christmas tree – and other conifers. Scolton, like so many Victorian estates, is also notable for rhododendrons, many species of which were introduced to Britain in the 19th century.

A saddle-tank locomotive, built in 1878 to serve the nearby Rosebush slate quarries, is part of

Left: sweet chestnut trees like these can be seen in Savernake Forest

a display which illustrates Pembrokeshire's railway history. It is overlooked by the exhibition hall whose exhibits include a collection of dairy equipment made by Llewellin's Churn Works, a Haverfordwest company whose products were sold all over the world during the Victorian and Edwardian periods.

Open: *country park all year. Nature trail. Tree trail. Guided walks for organised parties. Butterfly garden. Countryside centre and Scolton Manor Museum Jun to Sep, Tue to Sun. Refreshments. Shop. Picnic area. Facilities for disabled visitors. No dogs in house.*
Location: *on B4329, 5 miles N of Haverfordwest.*
Map: *page 304, SM92.*

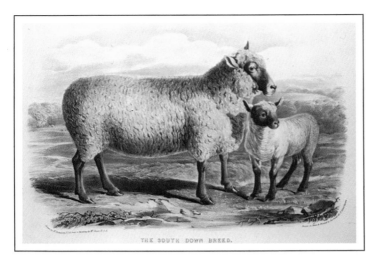

THE SOUTH DOWN BREED.

Seaton Cliffs

Tayside

The sandstone cliffs to the north of Arbroath are spectacular and colourful, the rich red of the rock contrasting with the blues and greens of the sea. The Scottish Wildlife Trust has produced a nature trail guide to the cliffs, and the trust owns a stretch known as the Seaton Cliffs Nature Reserve.

The action of the sea on the rocks has produced coves, blow holes and stacks, and the coves and ledges provide nesting places for fulmars, herring gulls, rock doves and house martins. The old red sandstone contains a certain amount of lime, and hence supports a wide variety of plants: clustered bellflower, birdsfoot trefoil, purple milkvetch, and early purple and heath spotted orchids are all present. There is also a good variety of butterflies, including the uncommon small blue, which has the kidney vetch as its food plant.

Access: *cliff-top footpath passes through reserve. CNT.*
Location: *footpath leads from N end of promenade at Arbroath.*
Map: *page 313, NO64.*

Selborne Hill

Hampshire

If Gilbert White, the most celebrated of amateur naturalists, had not existed, it is probable that Selborne and the famous wooded hill under which it shelters would still have become a centre for nature lovers. The 700ft-high beech-clad hill consists mainly of chalk, but there is clay beneath it and grey and black malm in the surrounding fields and valleys. The richness of the black malm in particular, combined with the contrasting soils and a high humidity in the woods, ensures a profusion of

Southdown sheep graze on the downs and meadows at Seven Sisters Country Park

plants and animals which White described in the letters gathered together as *The Natural History of Selborne.*

There are many walks – shown in a leaflet prepared by local National Trust members – of which the most renowned is the Zig-Zag path (built for White) leading up through the woods to the hill top. The paths become very slippery in wet weather. Not an easy walk, but it is possible to take the Bostal path along the edge of the woods, which gives good views of the mellow brick-ed houses in the valley below. It would be pleasant to think that little has changed since White's time, but some things certainly have. He refers to 'two rocky hollow lanes . . . they look more like water courses than roads.' One of those roads, from Alton, now brings visitors to Selborne every day of the year. If possible, however, climb the Zig-Zag early on a summer morning. At that time, when there are few other people about, the spirit of Gilbert White may join you – that spirit which, said W. H. Hudson, 'shines in every page' of 'this little cockle-shell of a book'.

Access: *from car park signed in Selborne village. Selborne Hill is criss-crossed by paths. NT.*
Location: *4 miles S of Alton between Selborne and Newton Valence, W of B3006.*
Map: *page 306, SU73.*

Seven Sisters Country Park

East Sussex

The South Downs meet the sea at the Seven Sisters. Viewed from either the sea or the land, this part of the Sussex coast is of un-

doubted outstanding scenic value. Now 692 acres go to make up the Seven Sisters Country Park and cover a wide variety of habitats – chalk cliffs, shingle beach, fresh water, brackish water, salt marsh, wet meadow, downland and scrub.

Fulmars, herring gulls and jackdaws nest on the cliffs. Other species can be seen on the sea and in spring and autumn migrants make landfall here.

On the shingle, the plants are those that have developed a high tolerance to salt and an ability to grow with little or no topsoil. Among them are sea kale, yellow horned poppy and sea beet.

The fresh water in the park is provided by the old course of the Cuckmere River. Although the course of the river has been changed, the old meander can be seen lying like a silver snake across the water meadows. This is the place to look for wildfowl and wading birds in winter.

Southdown sheep are grazed on the early grass in the meadows in early summer. Later in the summer the sheep are taken up to the downs during the day and moved to recently harvested arable fields at night. In winter they are fed on root crops.

There is a fine selection of fescues and prostrate herbs on the chalk downland. These include thyme and squinancywort as well as both stemless and carline thistles. Orchids grow here too – early purple, common and pyramidal. Grassland butterflies and moths can be seen on the wing during sunny days in high summer.

Details of the farming regimes in the area are graphically described in the excellent information centre at the tiny village of Exceat. Here, in beautifully converted 18th-century farm buildings, are an exhibition about the Downs, a library of reference books for visitors to consult, and a 'Living World' exhibition which has living specimens of butterflies, bees, spiders, snails, moths and marine life in settings that are as nearly natural as possible. There is also an interesting shop. Among the items for sale are nestboxes for bats and several species of birds, and live insects at various stages of development with equipment to rear them. Other facilities include a nature trail and a hide from which birds can be seen.

Open: *Easter to Oct daily. Oct to Easter Sat and Sun only (closed 25 Dec). Information centre. Picnic area. Shop. Facilities for disabled visitors.*
Location: *1¼ miles E of Seaford at Exceat.*
Map: *page 306, TV59.*

Shallowford: Izaak Walton's Cottage

Staffordshire

The name Izaak Walton is usually associated with 'The Compleat Angler', which he wrote in 1653 and which is still widely read today. In fact, he was a well-known biographer of his time and wrote several other notable books. Fishing, however, was a favourite pastime. He did a lot of it on the River Lea in Hertfordshire, but he also fished the Dove with his friend Charles Cotton, who lived at nearby Beresford Hall.

Walton was born in Stafford in 1593, and although he moved to London and subsequently to Winchester, where he died in 1683, he retained his links with his home town. Around 1654 he bought a farm at Shallowford

and the cottage that now bears his name appears to have been part of it. A note by him dated 23 October 1676, states that he then held title to it.

In his will he left the farm to the town of Stafford for charitable purposes, together with various other bequests. In 1920 it became the property of Staffordshire County Council, who sold the farm, and the cottage was bought by the Izaak Walton Cottage Trust. They restored it and

The cliffs at Seven Sisters

opened it as a museum in 1924. After that the cottage was twice damaged by fire, resulting in the thatched roof being replaced by tiles in 1939.

The cottage is now managed as a museum by the Staffordshire County Museum Service on behalf of Stafford Borough Council. Although it contains no authentic objects associated with Walton, it is furnished in the style of the period. The garden is planted with the kinds of flowers and herbs that would have been cultivated for decoration and use in the 17th century.

Open: Apr to Sep Wed to Sun and bank holidays. Oct to Mar Sat and Sun pm only. Admission charge. Picnic area. Shop. No dogs. Facilities for disabled visitors.
Location: 5 miles NW of Stafford, off A5013 from Little Bridgeford, or off B5026 from Norton Bridge.
Map: page 309, SJ82.

Fulmar

Offal thrown from trawlers has greatly increased the fulmar's food sources, enabling it to expand from one British nesting site (St Kilda), a hundred years ago, to suitable breeding places all round the coast today. Seaton Cliffs and Seven Sisters Country Park are two of the very many places where they nest. Outside the breeding season, the fulmar is a bird of the open sea, and rarely comes to land.

Shardlow: The Clock Warehouse

Derbyshire

This handsome 18th-century building is the setting for Britain's largest permanent canal exhibition and several related ventures. The warehouse itself, built beside a basin off the Trent and Mersey Canal, is of considerable architectural interest and was saved from virtual dereliction in 1976. Its most prominent feature is the semi-circular opening which enabled barges to enter the warehouse and unload directly on to the floors.

The exhibition explains all aspects of canals and the canal age in a series of colourful and informative displays and reconstructions. One exhibit, for example, gives a vivid feeling of what it was like to live on a cramped narrow boat, while another is of a fully equipped blacksmiths' forge – very much a part of canal life in the age of horse power. A shop, restaurant, marina, boat trips and boat-hire facilities complete the attractions offered here.

Open: *Apr to Oct daily. Nov to Mar weekends only. Admission charge. Picnic area. Refreshments. Shop.*
Location: *at Shardlow, 7 miles SE of Derby, off A6.*
Map: *page 310, SK43.*

Sherborne: Worldwide Butterflies & Lullingstone Silk Farm

Dorset

This is a very special kind of enterprise. Butterflies and moths from all over the world can be seen here in settings as close as possible to their natural habitats. Some species, like the giant Edward's Atlas moth – over 12 inches across – are spectacular indeed. Others, including many British species, are less startling, but equally beautiful. Conservation is the keynote, so that in the Breeding Hall caterpillars are raised to become butterflies here, or to be sold, or to be supplied to lepidopterists across the world. In the Butterfly House rare and not-so-rare British species can be seen alongside tropical species. The Jungle, a specially-prepared area of tropical plants, holds more gorgeous tropical butterflies.

The conservational tone is continued outside. Worldwide Butterflies is housed in Compton House, a lovely old stone manor house, and its grounds and gardens are specially managed to en-

The swallowtail is one of the rare and beautiful butterflies reared by Worldwide Butterflies at Sherborne

courage native butterflies. Some areas are planted with flowers that attract butterflies such as tortoiseshell, peacock and red admiral, while other areas are carefully controlled semi-wild plots to provide habitats for grassland and woodland species.

As well as live specimens, there are many displays of mounted butterflies and moths, and much related material. Lullingstone Silk Farm has been an integral part of Worldwide Butterflies since 1977. Here all stages in the life-cycle of silk moths can be seen, and silk-weaving demonstrations are given. The reeling machine on which the silk for the Princess of Wales' wedding dress was prepared is a prime attraction.

Open: *daily Apr to end Oct. Admission charge. Shop. No dogs.*
Location: *at Compton House, on A30 between Yeovil and Sherborne.*
Map: *page 305, ST51.*

Sherwood Forest

Nottinghamshire

Surely the most famous forest in Britain, thanks to a hero who may or may not have once hunted deer, and rich men, here. Today, those interested in the legend of Robin Hood can see an unusual and attractive exhibition near the visitor centre at Edwinstowe, which tells the story of the most famous outlaw of them all.

The forest itself is surprisingly varied. In some places the trees stand close together, but elsewhere there are broad glades covered with grass, heather and bracken. The most famous tree is the Major Oak, perhaps 500 years old and over 30 feet in girth, which stands beside one of the waymarked walks through the forest. There are still deer here and a wide variety of woodland birds. The dead and dying wood, which does not occur in younger and tidier forests, is one reason why Sherwood Forest is important for unusual insects. Information on the wildlife can be had from the excellent visitor centre.

Open: *Edwinstowe visitor centre all year (except 25 & 26 Dec). Shop. Refreshments. Picnic area. Facilities for disabled visitors.*
Location: *forest visitor centre on B6034, ¼ mile N of Edwinstowe, between A6075 and A616, 20 miles N of Nottingham.*
Map: *page 310, SK66.*

Ducks and geese on Ellesmere, one of the Shropshire Meres

Shropshire Meres

Shropshire

Much of Shropshire north of the River Severn consists of a gently undulating plain. This is relieved by a few ridges of sandstone, but otherwise the Triassic rocks are hidden by deposits of clays, sands and gravels left behind by retreating glaciers at the end of the last ice age, some 15,000 years ago. These 'drift' deposits, as they are called, vary greatly in thickness and contain frequent hollows, many of which were formed when large detached

Shipley Country Park

Derbyshire

This country park, covering 570 acres, lies mainly on land affected by coal mining for over 200 years. But Derbyshire County Council and the National Coal Board have carried out an ambitious scheme of landscaping, including restoration of Shipley Lake. The result is a very pleasant park with a wide range of facilities including nature trails, fishing and sailing, as well as informal walking and picnicking.

Adjacent to the park lies Britannia Park, a further 330 acres around the south and east sides of Shipley Lake, which is being laid out by private developers as a leisure park. This will include extensive sports facilities, amusements and thematic displays. There will be a large inn providing overnight accommodation and restaurants.

Shipley and Britannia Parks together make up a large and important leisure facility within easy reach of many people.

Open: *Shipley Country Park, all year. Information centre. Picnic area. Britannia Park, all year daily. Admission charge. Information centre. Shop. Refreshments. Picnic area. Suitable for disabled visitors. No dogs.*
Location: *1½ miles N of Heanor.*
Map: *page 310, SK44.*

Shipley Mill

West Sussex

One of the more recently built of the mills in West Sussex, Shipley Mill is nevertheless the largest mill in the county and also the only working smock mill. The mill acquired several other names (Vincent's Mill, King's Mill, Belloc's Mill and even Mrs Shipley) during its comparatively short working life. By 1926 it had ceased to grind corn.

For almost 50 years the mill belonged to that cosmopolitan lover of Sussex, Hilaire Belloc, who bought King's Land, a nearby house, and its adjoining land in 1906. Belloc was born in France in 1870 and educated in England. However, as a Frenchman he had to serve for a period in the French army, after which he returned to Balliol College, Oxford, where he read history. He married an American and took British citizenship in 1903. For four years from 1906 to 1910 he was a Member of Parliament, but it was as a writer, journalist and historian that he was best known. Belloc was a windmill enthusiast, and between the wars he was at pains to keep the mill in good repair, but the difficulty of obtaining materials and labour during the Second World War proved too much for him and the mill fell into disrepair.

When Belloc died in 1953 it was decided that a fund be set up to restore the mill as a memorial. The response was generous and a committee of local people was formed. They managed to interest West Sussex County Council in helping. Major repairs have been carried out from time to time and in order to maintain the building the Shipley Committee makes a small charge to visitors.

Open: *first weekend in each month from May to Oct, pm only. Admission charge. Shop.*
Location: *in Shipley village, W of B2224, 5 miles S of Horsham.*
Map: *page 306, TQ12.*

---

blocks of ice melted, leaving steep-sided holes.

Some of the lakes which formed in these hollows have gradually filled up with the accumulated remains of vegetation and become peat bogs. However, many deep lakes still survive, particularly around Ellesmere, and – together with very similar lakes found further north in Cheshire – they are one of the most important groups of freshwater lakes found anywhere in Britain. A good way to see some of these is to follow the 'Meres Trail'. This starts from the car park by The Mere at Ellesmere, where there is an excellent interpretative centre, and makes use of the tow-path of the Shropshire Union Canal to explore the nearby lakes. These include Blakemere, Kettlemere and, finally, Colemere. The latter and its surrounding woodlands make up an excellent country park managed by the Shropshire County Council.

All of these lakes and woods are most attractive and abound in wildlife. Breeding birds include Canada geese, herons, great crested and little grebes, coots, moorhens, mallard and many others. You may even see the North American ruddy duck, which has escaped from waterfowl collections and established itself in a number of places including this area. The drake is deep chestnut red in colour with a dark cap and tail and a conspicuous white patch each side of the head. In winter many more ducks arrive on migration, including tufted duck, pochard, teal, wigeon and goldeneye.

Fishing is available in many of these lakes and, as well as fish, the waters support an abundance of plant and animal life of all kinds. Some of the smallest of the plants – the microscopic 'blue-green' algae – are responsible for the local phenomenon 'the breaking of the meres', when vast numbers come to the surface and form a crust similar to yeast breaking the surface of a vat of beer.

Open: *Meres Visitor Centre Apr to Oct. Picnic area. Refreshments. Colemere Country Park all year. Picnic area. Waymarked walks.*
Access: *some meres are totally private, but others may be visited using public footpaths, including the Meres Trail.*
Location: *Meres Visitor Centre, at Ellesmere, 16 miles NW of Shrewsbury. Colemere Country Park, 14 miles NW of Shrewsbury, E of A528.*
Map: *page 309, SJ43.*

Singleton: Weald & Downland Open Air Museum

West Sussex

Many of the buildings in the Weald and on both the North and South Downs have been so altered by succeeding generations that it is difficult to visualise how they must have looked when they were first built. A visit to the Weald and Downland Museum soon changes that and at the same time gives the visitor a greater understanding of the way in which country people once lived.

Set on a slope of the South Downs, the museum has plenty of space – all of which is needed to accommodate the 50-odd buildings that have either already been erected or are in store awaiting reconstruction. The museum was set up by a group of enthusiasts anxious to preserve the vernacular buildings of the south-east, and all the buildings here have been rescued. For example, when Bough Beech Reservoir was created in 1967 several interesting buildings would have disappeared beneath the water had not the East Surrey

Inside Bayleaf House, at Singleton's Weald and Downland Open Air Museum

Skye

Highland

Perhaps through its historical and romantic associations with the Young Pretender, Charles Edward, and certainly through the splendour of its scenery, the Isle of Skye features on most tourists' itineraries when they are in the Western Highlands. The largest of the Inner Hebrides, it is noted for its geology and botany as well as its rich history and folklore.

The island is accessible by ferry from Mallaig (to Armadale) and Glenelg (to Kylerhea) – both offering scenic routes to the main part of the island – but for most the journey 'over the sea to Skye' is from Kyle of Lochalsh to Kyleakin. Visitors arriving via Armadale will find a diversion to Ord, six miles to the north, rewarding for the spectacular view of the Cuillins: these great hills dominate the southern part of the island and are renowned for some of the best climbing in Scotland. They are best approached from Sligachan, nine miles south of Portree, or Glenbrittle, seven miles south-west of Sligachan.

Fifteen miles from Kyleakin on the A850 lies Luib, where the

Black House Folk Museum depicts life as it was on Skye in the early part of this century. The black house itself has the low, thick walls and turfed roof characteristic of these buildings, but is of a relatively late design with a chimney and small windows. It is furnished and equipped with farm and domestic implements of the period. Near the Three Chimneys Restaurant, four miles from Dunvegan on the Glendale road (B884) is the Skye Black House at Colbost, a much older form of dwelling, again equipped with period furniture and implements, and burning a peat fire throughout the day.

There is another excellent museum at Kilmuir, north of Uig on the scenically superb Trotternish peninsula. Dunvegan Castle, the seat of the chiefs of Clan MacLeod for 700 years, is well worth a visit for its collection of historical items, relics and curios – including the clan's famous Bratach Sith (fairy flag) and a lock of Bonnie Prince Charlie's hair.

Nowhere on Skye is more than six miles from the sea and there are boat trips to be had from several townships, including Uig (good for seeing puffins around the Ascrib Islands) and Dunvegan, for the seals in the sea-loch there; longer cruises are also available (details locally), including right around the island. As elsewhere in the Inner Hebrides, birdwatchers will find shags, eider duck, red-breasted mergansers, black guillemots and oystercatchers all round the is-

Portree, Skye, in 1815

Water Company presented them to the museum. These have been reconstructed in the way in which they would have been when first built.

The buildings of the south-east of England were traditionally constructed of the most readily available local materials – flint on the chalk downlands; wood, clay and sand in the Weald. The introductory exhibit, displayed in a late 18th-century barn from Hambrook in Sussex, shows in detail some of the building methods that were used in the area. Nearby is a treadmill from Hampshire, its huge wheel made so that a man or an animal could walk round inside it and thereby raise water from a well.

Romantic ideas of the way in which our ancestors lived will soon disappear after a look round Winkhurst Farm, a medieval timber-frame building with an open hall, a wood fire and unglazed windows. A photograph of the house as it appeared before

it was re-erected is in the museum's guidebook, and shows just how great a change the building underwent in 500 years.

Of course, much of the reconstruction must be based on conjecture, because the original has been changed so much. An excellent example of this is the Market Hall from Titchfield in Hampshire. It is typical of many market halls built in Tudor and Stuart times, with an open ground floor arcade where traders could set up their stalls and a first floor room where the town council would meet. Gradually these market halls were demolished or moved to other sites. Titchfield Market Hall was one that was moved, and rebuilt in the last century looking very different from the original. When its owners were served with a dangerous buildings notice that insisted on immediate demolition, it was decided to move it once again, this time to Singleton, where it forms

the centre-piece of a market place, alongside other town buildings.

The museum is not confined to buildings, and traditional industry has its place. In the coppiced woodland there is a charcoal burners' camp – visitors can buy the resulting charcoal in the museum shop. Also in the wood is a cattle shed with a display about woodland crafts and a reconstruction of a Saxon sunken hut.

In the village area there is a saw-pit, a smithy and a watermill where the visitor can buy stoneground flour. The mill-pond has a collection of waterfowl and carp which almost come out of the water in order to be fed.

Open: *Apr to Oct Tue to Sun daily. Also bank holiday Mons throughout summer. Nov to Mar Wed and Sun daily. Picnic area. Refreshments. Shop.*
Location: *S of A286 between Singleton and West Dean.*
Map: *page 306, SU81.*

Skegness: Church Farm Museum

Lincolnshire

First and foremost a popular seaside resort, Skegness may seem an unlikely home for this historic farm and its collection of agricultural bygones. Ironically, the farm was part of the estate of the family responsible for developing Skegness as a resort – the earls of Scarborough.

The buildings have been restored to show a typical Lincolnshire farmstead, with a farmhouse dating from about 1760, and fully furnished in the style of about 1900. The associated farm buildings include a barn, cow byre and stables, now used to display old farm machinery and reconstructed workshops including a blacksmith's, a wheelwright and a saddler's. In 1980 the museum acquired a complete timber-framed cottage which was systematically dismantled and brought to the museum from its original site at Withern, near Louth. It has been carefully reconstructed here and its original appearance preserved.

Open: *May to Oct daily. Admission charge. No dogs.*
Location: *in Church Road South, Skegness.*
Map: *page 310, TF56.*

The Cuillins from Elgol, Skye

land. Gannets, puffins, guillemots and razorbills occur in good numbers offshore, while with their breeding grounds on Rhum so close, Manx shearwaters are abundant. Inland, the mountainous parts of the island have ravens and peregrines and are excellent for golden eagles. Watch out too for the huge white-tailed sea eagle around the south-west facing coastline. The exciting reintroduction of this bird is based on nearby Rhum and wandering birds occur on Skye – appropriately, since the island held the very last native pair before their final extinction as breeding birds in 1916.

Open: *Luib Black House Museum Apr to Oct daily. Admission charge. Skye Black House Folk Museum, Colbost, Easter to Oct daily. Admission charge. Skye Cottage Museum, Kilmuir, mid–May to Sep Mon to Sat. Admission charge. Shop. Facilities for disabled visitors. Dunvegan Castle Easter to Oct; late May to Sep Mon to Sat daily, Easter to late May and during Oct Mon to Sat pm only. Admission charge. Refreshments. Shop.*
Map: *page 315.*

Slapton Ley

Devon

This freshwater lagoon is separated from the sea by the wide shingle bar of Slapton Sands. Inland it is surrounded by picturesque hills and on either side stretch the impressive cliffs of the South Hams.

The ley is a nature reserve managed by the Field Studies Council and at the field centre there is a countryside information unit. The ley is divided in two by the road from the field centre to the coast, and the higher ley to the east is mainly overgrown reed swamp with scrub. It is not surprising that this dense cover is one of the few remaining sites on the coast for otters. Nowadays though, mink are much more likely to be seen. They have thrived in the wild since they began to escape from mink farms in the 1950s and are regarded by most as unwanted and destructive pests.

The lower ley has much more open water and is the place to look for wildfowl and, in particular, great crested grebes. Several pairs of these attractive diving birds breed on the lake.

A good selection of plants can be found on the shingle – among the more colourful are viper's bugloss, restharrow and yellow horned poppy.

Open: *reserve all year. Information centre. Picnic area. Marked trails. Facilities for disabled visitors. Guided walks mid-Jun to mid-Sep (admission charge). Field centre, residential courses Mar to Oct.*
Location: *A379 Dartmouth to Kingsbridge road runs alongside ley. Field centre is a short way along road to Slapton village.*
Map: *page 305, SX84.*

Slindon Estate

West Sussex

Slindon village is signposted from the A29, but for many, hurrying to reach the coast, it is all too easy to miss. The National Trust owns 3500 acres here including much of the village. Within the estate is contained a fascinating microcosm of English history.

In Palaeolithic times, the sea, now a shimmering light five miles away over the roofs of the village, came up to this point of the South Downs. Today it is possible to study part of the shingle beach, 'stranded' 130ft above sea level in Slindon Park. The Neolithic causewayed camp at Barkhale lies within the estate, and there are also Bronze Age round barrows. Three-and-a-

Bewick's Swan

This lovely bird is the smallest of the three swan species seen in Britain. It breeds in the far north of Europe and in Russia, north of the Arctic Circle, and flies south to spend the winter months in warmer climates. A large herd of Bewick's swans is one of the most exciting winter attractions of the Wildfowl Trust at Slimbridge.

half miles – the longest surviving section – of Stane Street, along which the Roman Legions marched to Chichester, passes Bignor Hill, where a strange sense of timelessness persists undisturbed by the modern radio masts. In medieval times this was an important estate of the archbishops of Canterbury, although the majority of the houses that stand in the village today are 17th-century. Many of them are of the brick and flint construction typical of this area.

Walkers on the path which makes its way past the famous Slindon beeches, are likely to hear the calls and songs of hundreds of birds from warblers to woodpeckers. In spring wood anemones flower above the thick beech leaf carpet, while in the autumn the Horn of Plenty, an edible fungus looking rather like

a battered trumpet, grows close to the tree roots.

The very familiarity of the plants, animals and birds on the estate is one more example of the attractiveness of the English landscape – its sense of continuity so beautifully epitomised at Slindon.

Slimbridge: Wildfowl Trust

Gloucestershire

Bordering the River Severn at Slimbridge, the headquarters and grounds of the Wildfowl Trust are well worth a visit at any time of year. The world's largest collection of ducks, geese and swans is complemented by the presence of thousands of wild birds which seek refuge here, especially dur-

Access: *park and Bignor Hill open daily. Access to rest of estate by public footpath only. Dogs must be on leads. NT.*
Location: *6 miles N of Bognor Regis on A29.*
Map: *page 306, SU90.*

Horn of plenty

ing the winter months.

A visit to Slimbridge may take the following pattern. Directly through the main entrance you first come to an exhibition hall with displays depicting the history of the work of the Wildfowl Trust. Huge picture windows look out over the outdoor enclosures so that even in the coldest and wettest weather unusual and attractive waterfowl can be watched in comfort and from a distance of just a few feet! From the entrance hall walk straight out into the collection, a series of pens and pools each containing colourful ducks and geese from around the world. Some are common in their native countries, some far less so. The Wildfowl Trust here plays a very important role in international wildfowl conservation and takes part in vital programmes to breed and re-introduce birds to their natural habitats.

Beyond the wildfowl collection, in its attractive setting of pools, islands and ornamental shrubs, stretch the flat expanses of fields and saltings beside the River Severn, and beyond them the mudflats and sandflats of the estuary itself. Several hides overlook this area, which is frequented in winter by many thousands of wild birds which migrate south from cold northern countries. Most conspicuous are white-fronted geese and Bewick's swans. Hides overlooking the aptly named 'Swan Lake' near the main buildings give excellent views of the wild Bewick's swans, together with hundreds of tufted duck, pochard and wigeon and many other species.

Open: all year (closed 24 and 25 Dec). Admission charge (to non-Wildfowl Trust members). Refreshments. Shop. Nature trails. Picnic area. Facilities for disabled visitors. WFT.
Location: 10 miles S of Gloucester; signposted from A38 3½ miles S of Junction 13 of M5 motorway.
Map: page 305, SO70.

Snelsmore Common

Berkshire

Part of Snelsmore Common is a country park with good facilities for car parking and picnics. The common is an extensive area of open heath, birch woodland and valley bog, about 250 acres in extent.

A wide selection of characteristic heathland plants and animals can be found here. Ling, bell heather, cross-leaved heath and bilberry are present, together with three kinds of gorse – common, western and lesser. In the boggy areas, cotton grass, bog asphodel and heath-spotted orchid can be seen, as can marsh violet, bog pimpernel and sundew, making this an exciting place for botanists. Under the trees, bluebells, wood anemones, dog violets and early purple orchids are some of the flowering plants. Closer inspection of the ground cover below the trees may lead to the discovery of moschatel, a little plant scarcely four inches tall. It takes its other common name, townhall clock, from the way in which the flowers are clustered at the top of the stem; there are usually five, one pointing upwards, and the others facing outwards in different directions. Among the birds that may be seen here are woodcock, tree pipit, grasshopper warbler and various species of tit.

Access: most of common is Public Open Space and there are many paths.
Location: car park 2½ miles N of Newbury, W of B4494.
Map: page 306, SU47.

Snettisham

Norfolk

This reserve of the Royal Society for the Protection of Birds lies on the east shore of the Wash, a huge bay which is one of the best estuaries in Britain, indeed in Europe, for birds. The mud and sand of the Wash is the home of enormous numbers of marine worms, shellfish and crustaceans. At low tide, these become available to the wading-birds, each adapted to different foods according to the length and shape of its bill. Scattered over the huge flats, these birds are difficult to see well, but at high tide they are pushed nearer the shore and, best of all, over the sea-wall on to the pits that make up part of this reserve. On daylight high tides in winter the spectacle is quite staggering, as thousands upon thousands of birds crowd on to the banks and islands of the pits. There are often ten wader species present and these difficult-to-identify birds can be compared at point-blank range from hides, without disturbing them. At the same time, the waters of the pits may be covered with ducks, the males in a variety of colourful plumages, and wild geese fly overhead. In summer, things are quieter, but terns and gulls nest on the islands, and redshanks on the nearby salt marsh. The hides on the reserve give excellent views of this wealth of wildlife.

Access: public footpath passes through reserve. No dogs.
Location: beach signposted W of A149 in Snettisham: reserve a short walk S of car park. RSPB.
Map: page 311, TF63.

Snowdonia

This 845-square-mile National Park takes its name from the highest mountain in Britain south of the Scottish border. Snowdon rises 3560 feet above sea level and is typical of a region whose majestic cliffs have challenged the skill, stamina, courage and determination of countless climbers. Valleys with lakes, rivers, woods and pastures add a more gentle beauty.

Snowdonia was 'discovered' by climbers when the sport first became popular, towards the end of the 19th century, and the youth hostel at Pen-y-Pass, between Capel Curig and Llanberis, was originally a climbers' inn. The nearby Pen-y-Gwryd Hotel was a training base for many of the men who conquered Everest in 1953.

The Llanberis Pass, notable for some of the most rugged scenery in Britain, has many of the National Park's most difficult climbs. An information board in the parking area at Pont-y-Gromlech indicates some of the classic routes. But the scale of the crags is difficult to appreciate until you realise that specks of apparently natural colour are in fact climbers. Proper training and equipment is essential for tackling the cliffs, but most of the summits can be reached by well-walked tracks, although it is absolutely essential to observe the basic mountain-safety rules.

Trails on Snowdon
Relatively 'soft' options are provided by the Park's numerous waymarked walks, guided walks and landscape trails, many of which start from picnic places in valleys washed by streams and waterfalls. The trails combine ample exercise with a wealth of information about Snowdonia's natural history, farming methods and industrial heritage. The Miners' Track on Snowdon is a good example which provides the best of both worlds. This nature trail starts at the head of the Llanberis Pass and follows a broad path used by 19th-century copper miners who delved deep into the heart of Y Wyddfa. The trail climbs gently for one-and-a-half miles to Llyn Llydaw, a mile-long lake dominated by formidable crags forming Snowdon's mighty 'horseshoe' of cliffs and saw-toothed ridges.

Moorland Wildernesses
The Park's most dramatic features are high mountains and deep valleys – some with relics of ancient oak woods – but there are also vast tracts of open moorland where curlews cry and trout breed in lonely pools. Migneint is an outstanding example of such country. The wilderness rises to the south-west of Pen-machno and is crossed by an unfenced, little-used road which reaches almost 1600 feet before dropping down to Ffestiniog. In the depths of winter, Migneint's isolated peaks look like icebergs in a frozen sea.

'The Swampy Place' has defied generations of farmers and foresters, to remain little changed for thousands of years. It is a strange, solitary tract of country with a rare, haunting beauty. Another expanse of high, open ground lies between Trawsfynydd and Bala Lake or Llyn Tegid, the largest natural lake in Wales. It is traversed by a narrow, gated road with superb views of Cader Idris and the Rhinog, Aran and Berwyn ranges.

Elsewhere, mountains and moorland contrast with mile after mile of sandy, dune-backed beaches on a long coastline, carved by estuaries, between Harlech and Aberdyfi. Some features are very new in geological terms. The broad Dysynni valley, running inland from Tywyn, may well have been a tidal inlet as recently as the Middle Ages. It has a huge cliff, known as Craig-yr-Aderyn, where cormorants still nest, far from the sea. Morfa Harlech, formed by sand and pebbles swept up Cardigan Bay by tidal currents, has developed in less than 700 years and was open water when Harlech's mighty castle was built.

Man in the Landscape
Man has wrested a living from Snowdonia for a very long time, once grazing cattle on the lowland meadows, now tending sheep in the mountains, mining for gold, copper and other metals, and sending slate to destinations as far afield as South America. Royal wedding rings have been fashioned with gold from mines near Dolgellau.

Stone circles, burial chambers, standing stones, ancient trackways, the remains of prehistoric dwellings and a few traces of the Roman occupation recall the region's early inhabitants. Snowdonia was a natural fortress during the Middle Ages, when native princes battled with England's kings. Llewelyn the Great was born in Dolwyddelan Castle and became ruler of virtually the whole of Wales before his death in 1240.

Geology
Great complexity makes the Snowdonia National Park a paradise for geologists. Rocks formed during the Cambrian period, between 500 and 570 million years ago, include the purple, grey and green slates which gave this part of North Wales its most thriving industry in the 19th century. Cambrian rocks form the great 'dome' whose limits roughly coincide with Harlech, Barmouth, Dolgellau and Blaenau Ffestiniog.

It includes the Rhinog range, where rocky peaks rise to 2475 feet, and is surrounded by Snowdon, Cader Idris and other mountains formed during the 'Ring of Fire' period some 500 million years ago.

In relatively recent times, Ice Age glaciers sculpted the valleys and scooped out the great cauldrons of rock, known as cwms in Welsh, which contribute so much to the mountains' rugged grandeur.

Wildlife
Walkers and climbers share Snowdonia's mountains with many winged predators that were once common sights in England. The raven, for one, is an impressive bird which sometimes flips itself upside-down in flight. It patrols the uplands in search of food that may be anything from a beetle to a dead sheep. The buzzard has a similar diet. Among other birds of prey in the National Park are the kestrels, merlins, sparrowhawks and peregrines.

Rocky slopes and gullies are the haunts of the wheatear, the ring ouzel – sometimes dubbed the mountain blackbird – and the tiny wren, whose probing beak seeks small insects. The Berwyn Mountains and other tracts of high, open country carpeted with heather are the home of the grouse, while lakes attract mallard, teal, the common sandpiper and colonies of black-headed gulls.

Snowdonia's oak woods cover many acres of hillside, providing shelter for such birds as pied flycatchers, nuthatches and woodpeckers.

Mammals include the polecat and pine marten, although both are largely nocturnal and are not often seen. Otters still survive in lakes and rivers; they, too, are more likely to be heard at night than seen during the day.

What to See

ABERGLASLYN PASS
Pont Aberglaslyn, a small stone bridge across the River Glaslyn, attracts summer visitors in great numbers, many eager to be photographed against the backdrop of the Aberglaslyn Pass. This extends one-and-a-half miles to the mountain-enclosed village of Beddgelert, and consists of a steep-sided, narrow valley through which the Glaslyn rushes in an impatient torrent.

The trees which clothe the slopes are mostly firs, but bracken provides a range of colour during the year and both alpine and water-loving plants bloom here during the summer months. More than 500 acres on both sides of the pass are owned by the National Trust, which is also responsible for 300 acres of common land at nearby Moel Dyniewyd.

NT.

Llanberis Pass, north of Snowdon, in 1830 and today. Its scenery is unfailingly rugged

BALA
Bala, sheltered by the heights of Arennig and Berwyn, is a fine centre for exploring the southern part of the park. It overlooks the deep waters of Bala Lake, the largest natural lake in Wales, where visitors sail and swim. Grebe, cormorant, heron and swan feature prominently among the lake's birdlife. The southern shore has a narrow-gauge railway.

BEDDGELERT FOREST
Walks in this forest can be started from the Forestry Commission car parks a mile north of Beddgelert off the A4085. The forest has been planted on the northern slopes of Moel Hebog, which can sometimes be glimpsed through the trees. Paths and trails lead through conifers up to little Llyn Llywelyn, hidden among the trees. One of the routes up Snowdon begins on the east side of the A4085; parking is provided.

FC.

BISHOP MORGAN TRAIL (TY MAWR)
Bishop William Morgan was born in the farmhouse at Ty Mawr, probably in 1541, and grew up in this very attractive part of Gwynedd where Welsh cultural roots run deep. While studying at Cambridge, Morgan began the translation of the Bible into Welsh, virtually ensuring the survival of the oldest European language, and laying the foundations of modern Welsh literature.

A short trail, starting and finishing at Ty Mawr farmhouse, and less than a mile in length, provides an opportunity to study a Welsh upland landscape and its natural history. Part of the walk is along an old drovers' track bounded by drystone walls, marking the division between enclosed land and open moor. The Forestry Commission manages much of the land, and different phases in forest development can be seen. About halfway round the walk there are good views of the little Wybrnant valley with its broadleaved woods and old farm buildings. Near the larger of the two streams along the trail, the Afon Gwybernant, is a mixed wood of silver birch, sessile oak, ash, Japanese larch and several pine species. Birds of the area include woodpeckers, tits, goldcrests and jays.

The farmhouse, rebuilt in the 1560s, is a fine example of North Wales architecture. Stone-built with a slate roof, the house contains 17th- and 18th-century furniture on loan from the Welsh Folk Museum. Ty Mawr is part of the vast Ysbyty estate, the largest owned by the National Trust.

Open: *Apr to Sep: Tue to Fri and bank holiday Mon (pm only) Oct by appointment only. Admission charge to house. NT.*

CASTELL-Y-BERE
This ruined castle, set on a rocky spine in a valley of great beauty, is an ideal place for a tranquil picnic or a short walk. The

stronghold was built by Llewe-lyn the Great, early in the 13th century, and was the last bastion of the Welsh when Edward I completed his conquest of Snowdonia in 1283. The lane which skirts the ruin eventually peters out into a track leading to the summit of Cader Idris.

COEDYDD MAENTWROG
This splendid relic of the once widespread oak woods of the valleys of North Wales is a National Nature Reserve which is owned by the National Trust and managed jointly by the Nature Conservancy Council and the North Wales Naturalists' Trust. The reserve extends for nearly two miles along the north side of the hills high above the Vale of Ffestiniog and occurs in three blocks of which the smallest, Coed Llyn Mair, is open to the public.

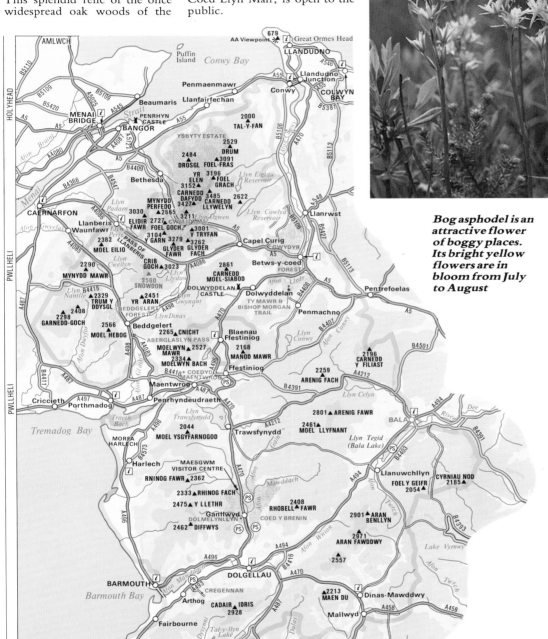

Bog asphodel is an attractive flower of boggy places. Its bright yellow flowers are in bloom from July to August

The reserve also has several small grassy clearings and exposures of rocky heathland with a dense cover of bilberry and heather. Above the wood there is a marshy area dominated by grey willow.

Within, and about, the wood there is a rich variety of breeding birds including buzzards, jays, green and great-spotted woodpeckers, nuthatches, pied flycatchers, redstarts, treecreepers and wood warblers.

Open: *at all times. Access by footpaths along nature trail laid out by NCC. Picnic area. NT/NCC/CNT.*

COED-Y-BRENIN
With an area of over 16,000 acres, this forest embraces all the woodlands around and to the north of Dolgellau. A good place to begin exploring is the Maesgwn Visitor Centre, off the A470 eight miles north of Dolgellau. Here displays and exhibitions explain all aspects of life and work in the forest, and a network of waymarked trails can be followed. There are more forest trails at Tyn-y-groes, reached from the A470 six miles north of Dolgellau; also reached from this road, one mile east of Tyn-y-groes, is the Glasdir Arboretum, where a wide range of forest tree species can be seen in a secluded setting beside the Afon Las.

The trees are mainly sessile oak with a scattering of alder, birch, rowan and sycamore. Under the trees, mosses, ferns and lichens form an almost continuous carpet through which a variety of flowers emerge: lesser celandine, primrose and common dog-violet in spring, followed by common cow-wheat.

Open: *Maesgwn Visitor Centre Easter to Sep (all year for schools; prior booking). Parking charge. Information centre. Picnic area. Refreshments. Suitable for disabled visitors. Glasdir Arboretum all year daily. FC.*

CREGENNAN

About 1000 feet above the little valley of Arthog, on the southern bank of the Mawddach estuary, the National Trust owns more than 700 acres of rough grazing and moorland with two hill farms and twin lakes – Llynnau Cregennan. This is wild, untamed country, lying under the northern slopes of Cader Idris, with magnificent views north over the estuary to Barmouth and across Cardigan Bay to the Lleyn Peninsula. Inland, the skyline is dominated by the great rolling bulk of Cader Idris rising behind the dark waters of the lakes. There is a great sense of history in this area and both Bronze and Iron Age artefacts have been found on the Trust's land. The old drovers' road known as Ffordd Ddu or the Black Road runs by the property, while the privately let bungalow close to the lakes was one of the first prefabricated buildings built in the country.

NT.

CWM IDWAL (CARN-EDDAU) NATURE TRAIL

The National Nature Reserve of Cwm Idwal forms only a fraction of the Carneddau estate, which itself is part of the much larger Ysbyty estate in the ownership of the National Trust. The valley was hollowed out of the mountain by glacial activity during the Ice Age. At its centre lies the brooding Llyn Idwal; legend has it that no birds will fly over its surface. The nature trail runs around the lake, a distance of two miles, and is relatively easy, but sensible clothing and good shoes are necessary.

From the first 'station' or stopping place the geological interest of Cwm Idwal becomes apparent, with a panoramic view over the lake to a striking range of geological features including the 'Devil's Kitchen', a great cleft in the cliff in which the arrangement of the rock strata can clearly be seen. The range of common and rare plant life is an indication of the influence of both geological and soil variations; look for mat-grass, bent grass and sheep's

fescue, all of which dominate at points along the trail. Because of its great scientific interest the cwm has been extensively studied since the 17th century; Charles Darwin published notes on its glacial features in 1842.

The vegetation of Snowdonia is greatly affected by the grazing of domestic animals, and the Nature Conservancy Council is carrying out continuous studies in the reserve, where there are numbers of small enclosed plots. The regeneration of heather is a very noticeable feature within these protected areas. By the lake and the nearby boggy ground, plants like marsh cinquefoil and the insect-catching sundew flourish. On steeper ground, bilberry and rowan grow, safe from the attention of sheep. Close to the waterfall at the far end of the lake are purple saxifrage, mountain sorrel and alpine meadow-rue. From a study of peat deposits beside the lake it is clear that Cwm Idwal was once a heavily wooded area – greater woodrush, normally a woodland plant, still grows on ledges near the waterfall.

Llyn Idwal contains both trout and minnow and, in defiance of the legend, is flown over and fished by gulls, herons and occasional cormorants. Whooper swans, pochard and goldeneye are frequently recorded in winter, and common sandpiper breed here in summer. The earliest summer visitors to the higher ground are wheatears, closely followed by ring ouzels. The deep croak of the raven can be heard throughout the year. This large, black bird frequently performs magnificent flying displays.

NT/NCC.

DOLMELYNLLYN

Much of the 1250 acres owned by the National Trust around the village of Ganllwyd is rough grazing land on the slopes of Y Garn. But there are riverside meadows beside the Afon Mawddach, and a short walk away from Ganllwyd is one of the most spectacular features in Wales – the Rhaiadr Ddu, or Black Waterfall. Behind the village is Y Llethr, at 2475ft the highest part of the Rhinogau, where the National Trust owns more land adjoining two sheep walks on the Dolmelynllyn es-

tate. From its slopes the little River Gamlan flows down to a point about half a mile above Ganllwyd village, where it makes two steep, linked drops. For much of the year the result is a cascade of rushing white water, trapped between moss-covered black rocks. The damp conditions created by the spray under the trees near the falls are ideal for many species of moss and fern, including some rarities, and a part of the area is now a nature reserve.

The river continues down to join the Mawddach, passing through a pleasant and well-maintained wood of mostly sessile oak. Tits and woodpeckers are present in the wood all year, and in summer it is home to warblers, redstarts and pied flycatchers.

NT/NCC.

GWYDYR FOREST

Including much of the country around Betws-y-coed, this forest offers a very wide range of walks and excursions, both through conifer woodlands and across wild, open hillsides. Waymarked trails can be followed from here. At Clogwyn Cyrau and Bwlch Gwynant, both in the forest south of the centre, hides are provided for birdwatchers. The former is in broadleaved woodland, the latter beside a small lake. Llyn Geirionydd and Llyn Crafnant, reached by narrow roads from Trefriw, have walks with superb views of forest, lake and mountain.

FC.

SNOWDON

The dramatic massif from which the National Park takes its name is one of the most memorable viewpoints in Britain. There are five main paths to the summit. The walk from Llanberis runs roughly parallel to the Snowdon Mountain Railway and has superb views of Clogwyn du'r Arddu. The Pyg Track starts at the head of the Llanberis Pass,

Polecat

The forests and wild uplands of North and Mid Wales are the stronghold of the Polecat. Once it was common throughout Britain, but its attacks on poultry and game made it very unpopular with farmers and gamekeepers, who nearly exterminated it. Now, as a result of the conifer forests planted in Wales since 1915, which are an ideal habitat for polecats, they are increasing their range. They are mainly nocturnal. Ferrets are a domesticated form of polecat, and the two can be confused.

1170ft above sea level, while the Watkin Path is perhaps the most interesting route, but involves climbing about 3300 feet and negotiating steep scree slopes near the summit. The Rhyd Ddu and Snowdon Ranger walks climb Snowdon's western slopes from starting points on the Caernarfon-Beddgelert road. They offer relatively easy walking – but no route up the mountain should be undertaken lightly.

YSBYTY ESTATE
This is the largest property of the National Trust, totalling 41,727 acres, but divided into four smaller properties located in three separate and distinct areas.

Penrhyn Castle is the outstanding example of the strange neo-Norman revival of the 19th century. It is a curiosity, but a curiosity on a vast scale, set, as all the best castles are, in magnificent surroundings, with a fine garden full of rare and beautiful trees and shrubs.

The Carneddau estate contains some of the wildest, most remote mountain country remaining in Britain. Nine of the highest mountains in Snowdonia lie within its boundary, several reached only by the most determined climber. For motorists, the best way to see the property is by driving along the A5 over the Nant Ffrancon Pass. The Carneddau Estate lies on either side; it is an ever changing, always dramatic landscape at all times of the year.

South of Betws-y-coed, and on the south side of the A5, is the Ysbyty Ifan estate, nearly 26,000 acres of beautiful hill, moorland and valley country. From Llyn Conwy, a lake almost 1500ft above sea level, flows the infant Afon Conwy, which runs through a narrow valley beside the B4407, one of two outstanding scenic roads – the B4406 to Penmachno is the other – which provide the motorist with an excellent opportunity to view much of the estate in comfort. Also see the descriptions of Bishop Morgan Trail and Cwm Idwal Nature Trail.

Nant Gwynant, one of the loveliest of Snowdonia's passes

Open: *Carneddau and Ysbyty Ifan at all times. Penrhyn Castle Easter to Oct daily, pm only (closed Tue). Admission charge. Information centre. Picnic area. Refreshments. Shop. Facilities for disabled visitors. NT.*

Solway Coast

Cumbria

Driving west out of Carlisle on the minor road to Bowness-on-Solway, it is not until you are beyond Burgh-(pronounced bruff) by-Sands that the Solway Firth comes into view. Just out of the village the road runs along the southern boundary of the salt marsh; high tides regularly come up over the road here to a depth of two or three feet in places.

From here easy walking is possible all along the southern shore of the Firth, with many attractive detours on the way. A special activity to watch out for along this coast is haf netting. It is a unique method of salmon and sea-trout fishing whereby men standing in the flood of the rising tide hold large square nets mounted on poles in which to catch the fish. Sometimes the water reaches as high as the men's shoulders.

The Firth is a marvellous place for birdwatchers, with huge numbers of waders using it as a staging post in spring and autumn. At high tide, enormous roosts of waders, especially oystercatchers, can often be seen. Some of these roosts form close to the coast road, particularly on the stretch between Port Carlisle and Cardurnock Flatts. Just beyond Cardurnock the road begins to turn east, and after passing the giant wireless masts at Anthorn it twists around the shore of the large bay of Moricambe. At Abbeytown a detour is needed to get out on to Grune Point, but it is worth the effort to reach this isolated tip of the Solway, with its distant views of Galloway and its sense of loneliness and tranquillity.

A note of caution should be added here, since estuaries like the Solway can be dangerous places, especially when the tide is coming in. The water can rise very fast, and there are also many hidden and potentially hazardous channels in the salt marshes.

Location: *follow minor road leaving B5307 1¼ miles W of Carlisle, signposted Burgh-by-Sands/Bowness-on-Solway.* **Map:** *page 313, NY15/16/26.*

Somerset Levels & Moors

Somerset

Recent controversies over proposed land-drainage schemes for some of the grazing marshes and meadows which make up the Somerset Levels and Moors have brought this lovely area into the focus of public attention.

Although much has already been drained, large expanses are still subject to winter flooding, and where this continues along with the traditional pattern of summer grazing and hay-making, a tremendous variety of wild flowers, animals and birds is preserved. Much of the character of these low-lying, open farmlands is provided by the irrigation ditches (known locally as rhynes) which criss-cross them, and by the pollarded willows which stand alongside many of the roads.

In spring, the hay meadows can be a riot of colour, the yellow of marsh marigold being followed by the pinks and purples of ragged robins and marsh orchids. A good field may contain an astonishing 70 plant species. Later in the summer, the rhynes have aquatic plants; some, like frogbit and water violet, floating on the water, others like bur-reed and flowering rush, growing along the margins. The sounds of the levels and moors in spring and summer are the calls of the marsh birds. One of the most evocative is the bubbling song of the curlew.

Another is the *pee-wit* call of the lapwing (country people often call lapwings peewits after this song). Often it is accompanied by the lapwing's spectacular, tumbling display flight.

Despite the changes in land use in some areas, the Levels remain the best place for breeding waders in south-west England, and in winter it plays host to large numbers of birds, especially wildfowl and waders.

The miles of waterways are rich in amphibians, especially frogs; and dragonflies are everywhere on warm sunny days in late summer.

Some of the best remaining

On the South Downs Way – view from the Devil's Dyke, south-west of Poynings

Somerset & North Devon Coast Path

Somerset and Devon

From Minehead in Somerset to Marsland Mouth on the Devon/Cornwall border, this exceptionally varied coast path winds for almost 100 miles. It forms part of the 510-mile South-West Peninsula Coast Path, which runs from Minehead right round to South Haven Point in Dorset.

For the first part, the cliff path is within the Exmoor National Park (see page 96) and is very comprehensively signposted. The terrain slopes down from high moors through well wooded areas before reaching the cliffs, making the Exmoor coast very different from the open, sheer cliffs beyond the Taw-Torridge estuary. There is sometimes a choice of routes between a high-level broad track and a lower, narrow path: the low path is often only for the more energetic, but it does bring walkers closer to the cliffs. Some of these reach over 1000ft; Great Hangman is 1043ft, and worth the climb for its glorious views.

The main seabird colony along the coast is at Woody Bay, west of Lynton, where there are kittiwakes and guillemots. Beyond Westward Ho! the path follows the route of an old narrow-gauge railway and remains well wooded until coming out into open country beyond picturesque Clovelly.

The open cliff path from here onwards is good for flowers and butterflies. Buzzards and kestrels nest on the cliffs and are often seen gliding and hovering on upcurrents of air.

Access: path is waymarked and can be joined or left at many points.
Map: page 305.

South Devon Coast Path

Devon

Part of the South-West Peninsula Coast Path, the South Devon Coast Path winds for 93 miles from Lyme Regis (actually just over the county border in Dorset) to Plymouth through exceptionally attractive coastal scenery. The first section, from Lyme to the River Exe, includes the East Devon Heritage Coast, which has been specially waymarked. Informative display boards have been erected at several points. This section includes landslips and the Axmouth-Lyme Regis Undercliff, which is

a National Nature Reserve, rich in plants and butterflies. (This section is only accessible at each end.) The chalk cliffs of Beer give way beyond Sidmouth to red sandstone, with a colony of cormorants and shags at Ladram Bay.

The other main section of the coast path is in the South Hams, beyond Torbay, and takes in the rugged cliffs of Start Point and Prawle Point, Bolt Head and Bolt Tail. This stretch of coast is designated as an Area of Outstanding Natural Beauty and is rich in wildlife.

This is where the cirl bunting has its main stronghold in Britain. A close relative of the yellowhammer, it breeds on the coastal farmland with its deep hedges and sunken lanes. Out of an estimated British population of 150 pairs, over 100 are found on this stretch of coast.

Access: coast path is waymarked and can be joined or left at many points. Part NCC.
Map: page 305.

South Downs Way

East Sussex and West Sussex

The 80 miles that make up the South Downs Way form the first long distance bridleway accessible to cyclists and horse riders as well as to walkers. The South Downs have been designated as an Area of Outstanding Natural Beauty, and the path runs along the ridge of the downs, crossing the valleys of the Cuckmere, Ouse, Adur and Arun in its course from Eastbourne and Beachy Head (see page 23) in the east, to Harting and the Hampshire border in the west. The landscape is very beautiful, and in summer the chalkland flowers and butterflies will delight the naturalist.

Exceptional views are among the highlights of the Way, and outstanding viewpoints include Bostal Hill and Firle Beacon, between Alfriston and Lewes, Ditchling Beacon (see page 83), near Saddlescombe, and Chanctonbury Ring (see page 55) near Washington. At 837 feet, Littleton Down, east of Singleton, is the highest point of the Way. Among the outstanding monuments on the route are the Long Man of Wilmington (see page 290) and a stretch of the Roman Stane Street near Bignor.

It is planned to extend the Way another 30 miles, to Winchester, and this stretch may be open by 1986.

Access: path is waymarked and can be joined or left at many points.
Map: page 306.

areas are Tealham and Tadham Moors, Kings Sedgemoor and West Sedgemoor. The first two areas are the most easily observed from roads which cross the flat, open landscape. West Sedgemoor, where there is an RSPB reserve, is further away from roads and visiting is limited at present. Breeding birds of these moors include snipe, lapwing, redshank, curlew, yellow wagtail, sedge warbler and whinchat. In winter there are golden plovers and Bewick's swans as well as redwings and fieldfares, especially where shallow flooding occurs. Where the meadows are unimproved there are fine displays of wild flowers in spring and summer, and the mammals present include foxes, badgers and roe deer.

Location: Somerset Levels and Moors can be explored on roads off A361 Glastonbury to Taunton Road and B3151 Glastonbury to Cheddar road. RSPB reserve is N of A378 Langport to Taunton road, E of North Curry.
Map: page 305, ST32/43/44.

South Stack Cliffs

Gwynedd

Nearly 800 acres of the western-most part of Anglesey are a re-serve of the RSPB. The tremen-dous cliffs here form the visual highlight of the reserve, and pro-vide nesting places for thousands of seabirds, but there are also two areas of maritime heathland – Holyhead Mountain and Pen-rhos Feilw Common – which are important both for their birds and for their plant communities.

On the cliffs, breeding birds include over 1500 guillemots and several hundred razorbills and puffins. There is also a colony of kittiwakes on Penlas Rock, and a few pairs of choughs nest in the sea caves which cut into the cliffs. The choughs, members of the crow family with bright red bills and feet, can sometimes be seen searching for insect food on the clifftop sward and on Holyhead Mountain.

A flight of 403 steps leading down to South Stack lighthouse provides excellent views of the birdlife, and the RSPB informa-tion centre overlooks the seabird colony. Walks along the cliffs to-wards Holyhead overlook rocky coves where grey seals may be seen. There are superb views of Anglesey and Snowdonia from the summit of Holyhead Moun-tain, and in clear weather it is also possible to see Ireland.

The remains of a 'village' of circular huts, said to have been built between 1600 and 1800 years ago by Irishmen trading for gold, are close to the car park.

Open: *all year. Information centre Apr to Sep daily. RSPB.*
Location: *at end of well-signed minor road, W of Holyhead.*
Map: *page 308, SH28.*

South Swale

Kent

Along the North Kent coast there are extensive areas of tidal mudflats and salt marshes; land-scapes which can appear bleak and cheerless, but which are of great value and importance for their wildlife. At South Swale, west of Seasalter, the Kent Trust for Nature Conservation has a 500-acre reserve which protects some of these marshes, along with smaller areas of grazing land and a shell bank.

Birds are of the greatest inter-est here, especially in winter, when waders and wildfowl of several species are present. These include dark-bellied brent geese, here to feed on the eel grass growing on the mudflats, and wigeon. Less common migrants

South Stack Lighthouse in winter

Yellow horned poppy grows at South Swale and South Walney

include shore larks and snow buntings. A variety of birds also breed on the marshes.

The reserve is excellent for plants, with such species as gold-en samphire on the marshes and yellow horned poppy on the shell bank. An uncommon plant that might be seen on the sea wall is sea clover, which is restricted to southern England and Wales.

Access: *reserve can be visited at all times from footpath running along sea wall; access to other areas is by permit only (no permit required for bird watching). CNT. LNR.*
Location: *2¼ miles NE of Faversham; reached via unclassified road through Graveney, meeting coast W of Seasalter.*
Map: *page 306, TR06.*

South Walney

Cumbria

Walney Island is a large area of shingle deposits, on top of which has grown up a sand dune sys-tem. It lies directly off the coast from Barrow-in-Furness, and is connected to the mainland by road. The southern part of the island is a nature reserve of the Cumbria Trust for Nature Con-servation, incorporating a wide variety of different habitats – mudflats, salt marsh, freshwater marsh, meadowland, shingle, dunes and open water. This di-versity of habitats is reflected by the variety of plants to be seen; there are such attractive species as sea lavender and sea aster on the mudflats, and sea holly, yellow horned poppy and thrift on the sand and shingle. Where the ground has been disturbed by gravel workings, other species are found. One of these is hen-bane, a sticky, hairy plant with an unpleasant smell. It is ex-tremely poisonous.

The area is also very good for birds, with a large breeding col-ony of gulls, particularly lesser black-backed and herring gulls. Several other birds nest on the reserve, including eider duck, shelduck, oystercatchers, and ringed plovers. In winter, there are large flocks of ducks and waders to be seen. Booklets and nature trail leaflets are available from the site office at South End, Walney Island.

Open: *all year, except Mon, but entrance by permit only (available on site). Parties should notify warden of intended visits in advance. Admission charge. Nature trail. Dogs allowed on lead outside breeding season (breeding season is 1 Apr to 31 Aug).*
Location: *on Walney Island, 4 miles S of Barrow-in-Furness.*
Map: *page 309, SD26.*

South Woodham Ferrers: Marsh Farm

Essex

This 320-acre farm is set in the flat, featureless lowlands of Essex, an atmospheric landscape cut by drainage ditches and bounded only by sea walls and salt marshes. Purchased as a country park by the County Council, it has been kept as a working farm on a commercial basis. Several British breeds of sheep, pigs and beef cattle are raised. Visitors can watch the animals and farming activities from specially constructed walkways in the buildings. The highlight of a visit might be to see the 'farrowing', or birth, of a litter of piglets. The stockmen are happy to talk to visitors, and a display area in the visitor centre gives more background information.

The eastern end of the park is designated a nature conservation zone, and here the demands of agriculture come second to the needs of wildlife conservation. Pesticides and artificial fertilizers are banned, and as a result, a far greater variety of plants and insects is found here. These fields are a favourite feeding ground for geese in winter and a roosting place for wading birds.

To add further interest to this part of the farm, an area of open water has been created. This attracts many kinds of birds, especially duck such as teal and wigeon.

Open: all year. Car park charge Sat pm, Sun and bank holidays. Admission charge to farm. Visitor centre. Picnic areas. Marked trails. Farm buildings suitable for disabled visitors. No dogs in farm buildings; elsewhere on lead.
Location: S of South Woodham Ferrers on N side of River Crouch.
Map: page 306, TQ89.

Sowley Pond

Hampshire

Open water, marshy areas and mixed woodland make Sowley Pond and its surroundings attractive to a wide variety of birds. The waters of the Solent are less than half a mile away, adding further to the diversity of species. With so much water about, duck are bound to be the main attraction, with mallard, teal, pintail, tufted duck, shoveler, gadwall, pochard and wigeon being some of the regulars. On the Solent, brent geese and scoter, along with the occasional merganser, are winter visitors. Little and great crested grebes are usually present on the fresh water and lucky observers may see Slavonian or red-necked grebes on the sea. Warblers are common around the pond and in the marshy areas, while in the woods, woodpeckers, nuthatches and treecreepers, together with tits and goldcrests, are almost certain to be seen or heard. Swallows, martins and swifts skim over the water during the summer and there is a heronry close by. In all, it is possible for the birdwatcher to see well over 60 different kinds of birds here in the course of a year.

Location: 3 miles E of Lymington, ¾ mile SE of East End village. Reached on unclassified roads off B3054 Lymington to Beaulieu road.
Map: page 306, SZ39.

Spurn Head

Humberside

Few places in Britain give the feeling of isolation produced by Spurn Head. Set across the mouth of the Humber, this four-mile-long sand and shingle spit begins at the tiny village of Kilnsea and sweeps round in a great curve until it ends facing in a south-westerly direction, pointing towards Cleethorpes, five-and-a-half miles away across the estuary.

Subject as it is to North Sea currents, and to the force of the waters of the Humber, Spurn Head has changed shape many times through the centuries, the sand and shingle from which it is made being pushed now one way, now another. Great efforts have been made to stabilize it in recent years, principally by placing hundreds of tons of rubble on the seaward coast.

Near the end of the spit is a lifeboat station which has the only professional lifeboat crew in Britain. The crew and their families are the only residents of the tiny hamlet at Spurn, and although plenty of people find their way down the spit during the summer months, for most of the year they have the place to themselves.

Most of Spurn Head is a reserve of the Yorkshire Wildlife Trust, which has undertaken much of the work of protecting it from the sea. On the estuary side of the spit there are salt marshes and mud flats, while facing the sea are narrow beaches of sand and shingle. There are also sand dunes – the older, fixed dunes with a short turf of low-growing plants.

Because the east coast of Britain is well used by migrant birds in the autumn, as they move down into southern Europe and Africa, Spurn is well visited by birdwatchers, and the Spurn Bird Observatory at the north end of Spurn Head, maintained by the Yorkshire Wildlife Trust, records many of the rarest birds seen in Britain, as well as huge numbers of the commonest migrants.

An autumn morning when huge numbers of Scandinavian thrushes and other migrants are pouring in off the North Sea is a memorable experience and helps to underline Spurn's unique qualities.

Open: all year. Admission charge to reserve for cars. Information centre. No dogs. CNT.
Access: road to Spurn Head is private, but public footpath runs along spit.
Location: 18 miles SE of Hull. From A1033 at Patrington take B1445 to Easington, then unclassified road to Kilnsea.
Map: page 310, TA41.

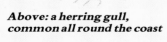

Above: a herring gull, common all round the coast

Right: eiders can be seen at such places as South Walney

Stiperstones

Shropshire

The Stiperstones ridge, with its prominent rock 'tors' rising to over 1700ft, is the most easily recognized of all the South Shropshire hills. Its jagged skyline is in marked contrast to the smoothly rounded outlines of other Shropshire landmarks such as the Long Mynd, or the long thin shapes of the Lawley and Caer Caradoc.

Many legends have gathered round the Stiperstones. The Devil is said to have sat on one of the largest of the rock outcrops – the 'Devil's Chair' – and dropped the thousands of sharp rocks which spread out over the ridge and down the hillsides. When the summit is hidden by cloud and rain, as it frequently is, the local people say the Devil still sits in his chair. There is no doubt that the hill does have a special atmosphere; the novelist Mary Webb spent much time here and featured it in her novels.

The ancient rocks which make up the Stiperstones were formed in the Ordovician period, some 500 million years ago, and consist of a series of shales and sandstones, including a hard, pale quartzite which outcrops along the ridge. It is the weathering of the latter which has produced the tors and associated screes which give the hill its special character. The rocks are also rich in minerals, especially lead, which was worked here for centuries. The remains of several of the old mines are still to be seen at Snailbeach, Shelve and other places.

Much of the open hill is covered in heather and bilberry and other moorland plants. Birds that might be seen include ravens, grouse, meadow pipits and curlews. The main part of the hill was declared a National Nature Reserve in 1982.

Location: 10 miles SW of Shrewsbury, E of A488. Car parking places at various points on unclassified road from Shelve to Bridges. NCC.
Map: page 309, SO39.

Stithians Reservoir

Cornwall

Set in the rugged and bleak Cornish uplands, this large windswept reservoir is nearly 500ft above sea level. As there are few large expanses of fresh water in the far south west, the reservoir draws large numbers of wildfowl and wading birds. Its geographical situation has also proved an attraction for rare migrant birds, with a number being recorded – some from as far afield as North America.

As with most reservoirs, the water level is an important factor in determining the kind of birds which may be seen. After dry weather in late summer the water levels may be low and a variety of wading birds can be attracted to the mud along the shoreline. This is perhaps the best time to look for a rarity. Among those recorded in recent years have been the long billed dowitcher and the lesser golden plover. Both these birds breed in Siberia and Alaska. Casual visitors to the reservoir would be very lucky indeed to see such celebrated visitors. Birds which *are* likely to be seen include lapwings and golden plovers and among the duck, teal and wigeon, which are best seen from the causeway at the south end of the reservoir.

Open: at all times (the South-West Water Authority issues birdwatching permits for the reservoir).
Location: W of Stithians village; SW of A393 Redruth to Penryn road on unclassified roads or N of A394 Penryn to Helston road.
Map: page 304, SW73.

Stockgrove Country Park

Beds and Bucks

The builder of Stockgrove House certainly knew a beautiful site when he saw one. Undulating heath and woodland on the colourful Lower Greensand rock made this an exceptional area to which the owners of the estate added lakes and more trees. They have gone now, the house has become a school, and part of the estate forms a pleasant country park.

One of its most interesting features is the ancient woodland – important enough to be classified as a Site of Special Scientific Interest. The trees are a good mixture, dominated by oaks, and, as expected in a wood which grew up so long ago, there is a carpet of interesting wild flowers, including bluebells, lily-of-the-valley and wood vetch. The nut-bearing hazel bushes are of interest to grey squirrels and to the nuthatch, a bird which chisels the nuts open, after wedging them securely in a bark crevice.

The open ground has its own birds, among them the green woodpecker which, if disturbed in its hunt for ants' nests, flies off in deep undulations, showing green plumage with a brilliant yellow rump. Adding to the diversity is a lake with lilies, water birds and frogs as well as dragonflies.

Open: all year. Picnic area.
Location: off A418, 2¼ miles N of Leighton Buzzard.
Map: page 306, SP92.

Hazel catkins – harbingers of spring

Stock Hill

Avon

A variety of walks can be taken here through an area of conifer plantations and open grassland. Stock Hill itself is Forestry Commission woodland which is part of Mendip Forest. The wide woodland rides provide good walking with the chance of seeing a variety of wildlife. Roe deer frequent the area and several may run quickly across the rides. Among the birds jays make themselves conspicuous by their raucous calls. Groups of silver birches add variety and may harbour flocks of finches or tits, which move about the woodland in mixed parties outside the breeding season.

On the west side of the road, the open country of North Hill has several shallow pools called the Priddy Pools, formed in old quarry workings. They are excellent for dragonflies and damselflies in midsummer. Dragonflies are larger, with wings held out at right angles to their bodies when at rest, whereas damselflies close their wings. Pipits and stonechats are the most characteristic birds in this area. Adders might be seen basking on warm days; they are best left well alone.

Open: *at all reasonable times. FC.*
Access: *to Stock Hill plantation along forestry tracks.*
Location: *E of Cheddar. From junction of B3135 from Cheddar and B3134 from Churchill take minor road to S. Parking areas along road after short distance.*
Map: *page 305, ST55.*

Stodmarsh

Kent

Lying in the valley of the River Great Stour, Stodmarsh, as its name implies, has always been a marshy area. Now, as a result of subsidence caused by coal-mining at Chislet, there is a large area of open water and an even larger reed bed, the largest freshwater marsh in Kent. Upstream towards Fordwich are reed-fringed gravel workings, downstream are the water meadows of Grove Ferry. All in all it is a wonderful wildlife sanctuary, all the more pleasing because it has been created in part from what were once disfiguring industrial processes.

Stodmarsh itself has been the scene of two remarkable colonisations in recent years. Savi's warbler, which was first identified in 1824 and was extinct as a British breeding bird 32 years later, reappeared at Stodmarsh in 1960 and has bred annually from the year after. Its strange history is more interesting than its appearance – olive brown all over. It sings a distinctive reeling song which is rather like the stridulating of a grasshopper.

The voice of the second colonist, Cetti's warbler, is also quite distinctive, loud and far-carrying. This warbler stays at Stodmarsh all year round, and sings throughout the year, as it holds a winter territory as well as a breeding one. Cetti's warblers first bred in 1972 and are now much more numerous than Savi's.

Adding exotic colour, and considerable surprise to any visit to Stodmarsh, are two glossy ibis which roost here each evening and spend their days in the area. For three months of the year they spend their time at Elmley on the Isle of Sheppey (see page 93). Some doubt has been cast as to the origins of these birds, but at present they are regarded as genuinely wild birds.

In summer, from the causeway that crosses the reserve, bearded tits can be seen flitting among the reed-heads and warblers chatter in the undergrowth. Autumn sees hosts of wagtails, swallows and martins, while marsh harriers and garganey pass through in spring.

In winter it is worth carrying on along the river bank towards Grove Ferry for wildfowl. As a splendid finale, hen harriers may be seen coming to roost in the reed bed at dusk.

Access: *at all times along public footpath between Stodmarsh and Grove Ferry. NCC.*
Location: *5¼ miles NE of Canterbury, between A257 and A28 roads.*
Map: *page 306, TR26.*

Stoke Bruerne: Waterways Museum

Northamptonshire

Two centuries of working boats on the waterways are commemorated in this museum, housed in an attractive old grain warehouse, beside the Grand Union Canal in the village of Stoke Bruerne. The lives of the boatmen and their families were rigorous, but there is a pleasing

A barge moored at Stoke Bruerne's Waterways Museum

contrast between the heavyweight equipment they used (such as the lock crane and the boat-weighing machine) and the traditional designs, often of flowers, painted in brillant colours on a dark background, used to decorate the boats themselves and much of their equipment. These are well shown in the replica of a 'butty boat' cabin, which also has its kitchen range, brassware and lace drapes. Among many other items of interest are contemporary prints and photographs. No canal enthusiast will be able to resist the museum shop, with its wide selection of books about the canal system, posters, models and miniatures of canalware, hand-painted in the traditional style.

Open: *Easter to Oct daily; Oct to Easter Tue to Sun. Admission charge. Shop. No dogs.*
Location: *S of Northampton; off A508, 1 mile S of Roade, on unclassified road.*
Map: *page 306, SP74.*

Raven

Largest member of the crow family, and also the biggest perching bird (or passerine) in Britain, the raven is a bird of mountain, moor and coast in the north and west. The Stiperstones, in Shropshire, is a typical haunt.

Stonor Park

Oxfordshire

Stonor Park has been the home of the Camoys family for over 800 years. Situated in the Chilterns, in a narrow valley north of Henley, the impressive house is one of the oldest examples of domestic architecture in Oxfordshire and is surrounded by a deer park and extensive wooded hillsides.

The deer park has a herd of fallow deer, while in the surrounding woods and thickets are roe and muntjac. The latter is a tiny deer, scarcely 18 inches tall at the shoulder and weighing little more than 20lbs. Introduced to Britain from India and China (the two races are thought to have interbred in this country) from about the turn of the century onwards, these deer soon began to escape from the animal collections in which they were first confined, and are now established in the wild. Being very small, and also extremely shy, muntjac are seldom seen.

In the area surrounding the park are many lanes, bridleways and public footpaths which provide excellent walking. Many of the woods are typical Chilterns beechwoods, but others contain oak, hazel, birch, ash, field maple, yew, holly, hawthorn and whitebeam. There are small areas of coppice, which is generally rare in the Chilterns. There are many localised or rare plants in the district, including orchids and herb Paris. Diligent searchers might also find Mezereon, a rare shrub belonging to the daphne family. Its fragrant pink flowers bloom between February and April. Interspersed among the woodlands are banks of chalk covered in herb-rich turf and supporting many species of butterfly.

Open: Stonor Park and House Apr to Sep, Sun, Wed and Thu pm only. Also Bank Holiday Mon and Sat pm in Aug. Admission charge. Refreshments. Shop. Footpaths and bridleways in surrounding countryside always open.
Location: off B480 between Watlington and Henley-on-Thames.
Map: page 306, SU78.

Stour Estuary

Essex and Suffolk

There are four river Stours in England. This one is pronounced 'Stoor' by the people of Suffolk and Essex, and it divides these two counties as it flows through the beautiful Dedham Vale – universally known as Constable Country – driving Flatford Mill as it goes. It enters the sea as a long broad estuary where the silt it deposits provides a home for countless small invertebrate animals. In winter these are the food of a fine variety of wading birds, notably the scarce and elegant black-tailed godwit. Wildfowl, such as the pintail, a beautifully streamlined duck, visit the estuary at the same season.

On the Suffolk shore, the mouth of the river at Shotley Gate is dominated by the imposing naval training headquarters of HMS Ganges, now disused. Waders and wildfowl, including brent geese, can be viewed from the car here. The more active can enjoy a pleasant walk further west, from Stutton church down to Stutton Ness. On the Essex side, many mute swans feed on waste grain by the quay at Mistley. Further east there are two fine coppiced chestnut woods rich in plants, butterflies and moths, at Copperas Wood (a reserve of the Essex Naturalists' Trust) and Stour Wood, part of an RSPB reserve which also includes mudflats.

Access: all year on public footpaths. Footpaths run along much of shoreline. Access to footpaths from B1352 in Essex and from B1080, B1456 and unclassified roads in Suffolk. RSPB/CNT.
Location: 7 miles S of Ipswich, W of Harwich.
Map: page 306, TM13/23.

Stover Country Park

Devon

The woods and heaths which make up this country park were originally laid out in the late 18th century as the landscaped grounds adjacent to Stover House. The house is now a school, and nearly all of the landscaping has disappeared under plantations, but since the grounds were purchased by Devon County Council, tremendous efforts have been made to restore some of their former character.

The lake which forms the centrepiece of the park is the most prominent survivor of the 18th-century landscaping. It has water lilies and many other kinds of water plants, and has such water birds as moorhens and swans; but it is of especial interest for dragonflies, 19 species having been recorded here. Perhaps the most spectacular of these is the Emperor dragonfly, which is almost certain to be flying here on sunny days in high summer. Several species of butterfly may be seen along the woodland rides in similar weather conditions.

The woodlands themselves have an excellent variety of trees, especially at the west end of the lake. Here may be found uncommon firs, pines and spruces, all part of the original landscaping scheme. A pinetum has been established on one of the islands in the lake to commemorate the Queen Mother's 80th birthday.

Open: during daylight hours. Picnic area. Waymarked paths.
Location: NE of Ashburton. Main entrance on A382, ¼ mile SE of junction with A38.
Map: page 305, SX87

Strata Florida

Dyfed

Founded by Cistercian monks in 1164, the 'Vale of Flowers' abbey flourished for nearly 400 years before it was closed by order of Henry VIII. Its ruins, scant but evocative, overlook an ancient yew which marks the grave of Dafydd ap Gwilym, who died in about 1385 and was one of the greatest Welsh poets of any century. The setting is peaceful – a sleepy, river-washed valley overlooked by high, wooded hills.

The moorlands of Mid Wales surround the ruins, but the wildest landscapes stretch away to the south and east. Even the recently planted forests and huge new reservoirs have done little to dispel the isolated, secret atmosphere of these windswept uplands. There are tracks and footpaths across the moors and hills, but they are remote and potentially dangerous and should only be undertaken with care and the correct clothing.

Open: abbey all year. Mon to Sat all day, Sun pm only. Admission charge.
Location: signposted from minor road which leaves B4343 at Pontrhydfendigaid, between Devil's Bridge and Tregaron.
Map: page 309, SN76.

Stowmarket: Museum of East Anglian Life

Suffolk

Here is an interesting collection of buildings, some old, some new and some which were brought here from different parts of Suffolk and reconstructed on the site. The oldest of these is a 13th-century tithe barn. There is also a 14th-century medieval hall, a watermill and an 18th-century smithy.

These fine old buildings, and two purpose-built new ones, house a wide-ranging collection of items connected with rural life in Suffolk. Huge harvest waggons are reminders of the historic and continuing importance of Suffolk as corn land, as is a Victorian steam engine that once turned mill machinery to make flour in Wickham Market. Times have certainly changed on land, but perhaps less so at sea, judging by the exhibition of fishing-gear, a reminder of Suffolk's long attachment to this industry. Reconstructions include two cottages dating from 1709.

Open: *Apr to Oct daily (Sun pm only). Admission charge. Refreshments (Sun only; daily during school holidays). Picnic area. Shop. Suitable for disabled visitors.* **Location:** *in Stowmarket.* **Map:** *page 306, TM05.*

A fire engine from Stowmarket's Museum of East Anglian Life, and (below) the reconstructed wheelwright's shop

Stratford-upon-Avon Canal

Warwickshire

When the Queen Mother reopened the southern section of the Stratford-upon-Avon Canal in 1964, it marked a significant stage in the struggle to restore some of Britain's most attractive but neglected waterways. The thirteen-and-a-half-mile length of canal had been lying derelict for many years when rescued by the National Trust in 1960. The programme of work then initiated was carried out by a force of voluntary workers, and was the first to be completed by voluntary labour. The success of the scheme has proved an inspiration and a model for those attempting to reclaim other stretches of waterways around the country.

Quite soon after leaving Stratford on its journey to Kingswood Junction, the canal enters the quiet rural landscapes of Warwickshire. It would be foolish to suggest that the region has not changed since Shakespeare's time, but this is probably the best way to see and enjoy his country. At Wootton Wawen the route passes through the heart of the Forest of Arden, although the original trees which Shakespeare knew have long since been cut down. The ideal way to travel the canal is clearly by boat, but for the walker, the towpath provides a splendid alternative, although it is a little rough in places.

Open: *Navigation throughout year subject to stoppages for maintenance purposes. Tolls payable; no reduction for NT members. Details available from Canal Office, Lapworth, Solihull. Towpath open all year as footpath; no charge. NT.* **Location:** *southern section: extends from Lapworth to Stratford-upon-Avon.* **Map:** *page 309, SP17/SP25.*

Strathclyde Country Park

Strathclyde

Not very long ago this was an exhausted industrial landscape of the ugliest kind, dominated by rubbish tips and disused pit workings. It has been transformed into an exciting country park, with many leisure facilities and an exciting range of wildlife.

The most spectacular creation is the loch, nearly two miles long and entirely artificial. It even has two beaches. Looking over the loch, and over the motorway which runs across the park, is the Hamilton Mausoleum. This famous monument, 120ft high, was built for the 10th Duke of Hamilton and was completed in 1857.

North-west of the mausoleum are areas set aside as reserves. These are of considerable importance for their plants, birds and animals. They are perhaps best known for their wintering wildfowl, including whooper swans, wigeon, pintail and goldeneye, but there are also breeding great crested grebes and a flourishing heronry. Permits are required to enter the nature reserves, but the park has many other areas where access is not restricted and which have a good cross section of trees, plants, birds and insects.

Open: *country park all year; visitor centre and Hamilton Mausoleum Easter to end Sep daily, Oct to Mar weekends only. Field studies centre. Waymarked trails. Picnic area.*
Location: *between Hamilton and Motherwell. Approached from M74 junction 5 or 4 and A725 or A723 roads.*
Map: *page 313, NS75.*

Stretton Mill

Cheshire

Forming part of a delightful group of rural buildings, Stretton Mill is a gem. Its setting is superb and its atmosphere magical.

There was a mill here as long ago as the 14th century. The present building, which has been greatly altered since it was constructed in the 17th century, was in use until 1959. Cheshire County Council rescued it from decay in the 1970s and carried out a most imaginative restoration scheme. The two water-wheels and the machinery have been thoroughly overhauled and can be operated for visitors. The external fabric has been faithfully restored, the pond cleared and the sluices repaired. The whole effect is so authentic that it is easy to imagine the days when corn was brought here by wagon from the surrounding farms.

Open: *Easter to Sep, Tue to Sun pm only, also bank holiday Mon. Admission charge.*
Location: *at Stretton, 3 miles E of Farndon, S of A534.*
Map: *page 309, SJ45*

The coot is found on ponds, lakes, canals and slow moving rivers. Its enormous lobed toes help it to swim and to walk on mud and vegetation

Studley Royal Park

North Yorkshire

The park has a large and varied deer herd. Some 200 fallow deer form the bulk of the herd, but there are about 80 of the much larger native red deer and a small group of sika, which superficially resemble the red, but are a little smaller. The deer move freely about the 300-acre park, often feeding beside one of the splendid specimens of sweet chestnut, beech and wild cherry. Great avenues of lime and oak run beside the road and lead to St Mary's Church in the park.

The lake by the car park is home to Canada geese, mallard and coot – all fearless in their approach to humans. The violent splashing at the water's edge in spring is probably caused by spawning roach, while trout rise at most seasons. A walk around the lake and down the Skell valley, crossing and recrossing the river by small bridges, is delightful in all seasons.

A bonus for the visitor to this landscaped park is the truly magnificent ruin of Fountains Abbey, 400 yards away. Linking park and abbey are the formal gardens, with temples, man-made ponds, canals and waterfalls.

Open: *deer park all year during daylight; abbey & grounds all year except 24 and 25 Dec and Good Fri. Admission charge to abbey and garden. Refreshments. Shop. Suitable for disabled visitors. NT.*
Location: *2 miles W of Ripon off B6265.*
Map: *page 310, SE26.*

Summercourt: Dairyland & Cornish Country Life Museum,

Cornwall

Modern farming is often very efficient, and it is increasingly automated. Once, and it seems an age away, but it was a lot less than a hundred years, all cows were milked by hand. At Dairyland, which has one of Europe's most advanced milking parlours, the cows are milked by machines in a rotary parlour. The whole operation, from the time the cows enter the collection yard to the time they go out into the dispersal yard, is controlled by one man from a central control panel. He has an electric 'dog' which herds the cows into the parlour; he can determine the

Roach are among the fish in the lake in Studley Royal Park

amount of food each cow receives while being milked; he can tell from the central console which cows are pregnant, which ones are due to calve, and much more besides. Visitors can watch all stages of the milking and see just how hygienic a modern milking unit can be. The milk herd is made up of some 170 Friesian cows, each one of which yields some eight gallons a day at the height of her production. Besides the rotary parlour there is much else to see here, including an old dairy and a buttery containing equipment that pre-

Inside Dairyland, near Summercourt

ceeded the automatic machinery of today.

Open: *Easter week, bank holidays and Jun to Sep daily; late Mar to May and Oct to early Nov pm only. Admission charge. (Milking starts at 3.15.) Shop. Refreshments. Picnic area. Dogs in car park only.*
Location: *on A 3058 between Summercourt and Newquay, 2 miles NW of Summercourt.*
Map: *page 304, SW85.*

Sutton Bingham Reservoir

Somerset and Dorset

This large reservoir lies right on the Somerset/Dorset borders only a short distance south of Yeovil. There are relatively few large freshwater areas in the West Country, so Sutton Bingham attracts a wide variety of wildfowl in winter, especially dabbling ducks and including the attractive pintail. It is a good place for migrant birds in spring and autumn, with waders along its shoreline if levels are low. Breeding birds of the lake include two species of grebe. The diminutive little grebe (or dabchick) is constantly diving, and seems to spend more time under water than above. The much larger great crested grebe was once uncommon, but in recent years its numbers have greatly increased and it is now an extremely attractive feature of many lakes.

A causeway crosses the reservoir, providing good views over two areas, while further south on the same road, the Wessex Water Authority has provided a bird-watching hide overlooking the long southern arm of the lake.

Location: *3 miles S of Yeovil, on unclassified road off A37.*
Map: *page 305, ST51.*

SOUL-CAKING PLAY

Antrobus, Cheshire

It used to be thought that at Halloween the souls of the dead came back to mingle with the living in the place where they had lived. With them also came the evil spirits, and these had to be expelled, so gangs of men were despatched to perform special rites and chants to lead the unwelcome visitors away from the district. For this service the men were awarded a piece of soul cake, specially baked for the occasion, and a draft of strong ale.

In Cheshire this ritual took on a unique character with the performance of a play, the characters in which included the Wild Horse, the Letter Inn, King George, the Black Prince, Old Mary and Quack Doctor, who depicted the fight between good and evil. The fight is re-enacted annually.

Today the players gather at the Antrobus Arms and from there they tour the district, performing their play at clubs, pubs, village halls and even private houses. Their arrival at any venue is heralded by the singing of chants.

When: *31 Oct and Thu, Fri and Sat for the following 2 weeks.*
Map: *page 309, SJ67.*

CARRYING THE TAR BARRELS

Ottery St Mary, Devon

Proceedings here start at 5.45am with the firing of 'rock cannons'. This is performed by a hand-held metal tube resembling a gun in which gunpowder is ignited by a hot iron. Other events take place throughout the day. At 4pm the boys' barrel-rolling takes place; five nine-gallon barrels are rolled by school children at different venues in the town. There is a Carnival Procession at 7.30pm, followed by a bonfire and the burning of the guy.

November

The tar-barrel ceremony itself begins after the procession. Eight barrels, holding between 18 and 70 gallons and coated with coal tar or bitumen, are successively set alight. Each one is carried by a man with a greased face and protective clothing to prevent scorching. When he becomes exhausted, others take turns until the barrel burns out.

This celebration has caused much anxiety through the years, as the flaming barrels are carried among the crowds. However, a Tar-Barrel Committee exists to prevent disasters, and accidents are rare.

When: *5 Nov.*
Map: *page 305, SY09.*

Carrying the Tar Barrels at Ottery St Mary

TURNING THE DEVIL'S BOULDER

Shebbear, Devon

This ceremony centres on a stone located just outside the east gateway of the churchyard, under an ancient oak said to be 1000 years old. The event is enacted by the village bellringers. Before the actual stone-turning they ring a loud peal of bells from the belfry of the church – this is done to frighten away any demons. They then make their way to the stone and, by the light of torches and lanterns, turn it.

The origins of the ceremony are uncertain, with several differing stories as to its beginnings, including the legend that the stone was dropped by the Devil and that harm will come to the village should it not be turned each year.

When: *5 Nov.*
Map: *page 305, SS40.*

Firing the Poppers in Lean Park

The church was built between 1724 and 1730 and the poppers are believed to date back to this period, but it is not certain when they were first used. In 1859 the Fenny Poppers were re-cast so that the custom could continue.

When: *11 Nov.*
Map: *page 306, SP83.*

WROTH SILVER

Knightlow Cross, Warwickshire

The payment of Wroth Silver is thought to originate from the payment of taxes from the parishes of Knightlow Hundred to the Duke of Buccleuch, Lord of that Hundred, or as payment in lieu of military service, or even as a wayleave-payment to enable farmers to drive their cattle over Dunsmore Heath.

Before sunrise, representatives of each parish gather in a field at a stone which is all that remains of the Knightlow Cross. Money is dropped into a hollow in the stone while a Charter of Assembly is read by the Duke's agent.

Afterwards, the assembly returns to the Dun Cow Inn at Stretton-on-Dunsmore for a breakfast of 'rum and milk', courtesy of the Duke of Buccleuch. Nowadays, a specially made clay 'churchwarden' pipe is given as a souvenir to all who take part in the ceremony.

When: *11 Nov.*
Map: *page 306, SP47.*

The Devil's Boulder, Shebbear

FIRING THE POPPERS

Lean Park, Bletchley, Bucks.

Throughout St Martin's Day six cannons called 'poppers' are fired in Lean Park to commemorate the death of Sir Thomas Willis. Up to a quarter of a pound of gunpowder is used in each cannon, and they are fired at intervals throughout the day.

In order to perpetuate his grandfather's memory, Browne Willis funded the building of St Martin's Church, Fenny Stratford, where he paid for a sermon to be read in conjunction with the firing ceremony.

COURTS LEET & BARON

Ashburton, Devon

The Court Leet is composed of elected Freeholders from within the Borough who have the power to make 'presentments' to the public on matters of general interest. A meeting to elect the officers of the Court takes place annually in St Lawrence's Chapel, where the Borough Court has met for over 600 years.

When: *4th Tue in Nov.*
Map: *page 305, SX76/77.*

Tamar Estuary & St John's Lake

Devon and Cornwall

Taken together with its tributaries, the Lynher River and the River Tavy, the Tamar forms the largest estuarine complex in the West Country.

The large bay on the Cornish side below Torpoint is known as St John's Lake, and it is one of the major areas for wading birds and wildfowl. One of the most distinctive waders that might be seen here in winter is the black-tailed godwit, a long-billed bird with a white rump and black tail. Oystercatchers, curlews, turnstones and dunlins are among the other birds usually present.

Above the Tamar Bridge, the estuary is undeveloped and scenically attractive, with fringing fields and woodlands. Six miles of foreshore at Landulph, on the west bank of the Tamar, are a nature reserve of the Cornwall Trust for Nature Conservation. These mudflats and salt marshes are good for wildfowl and waders, especially in winter and during the migration periods. Weir Quay, further up the Tamar on the east bank, is one of the best birdwatching places on the estuary. Bere Ferrers, on the west bank of the Tavy, is another excellent spot. The flock of avocets that is such a speciality of the estuary in winter might be seen at any of these places.

Access: by public footpaths and minor roads. Part CNT.
Location: immediately W of Plymouth. St John's Lake reached by Torpoint ferry from Plymouth, or from A374. Upper Tamar reached on unclassified roads E of A388 N of Saltash. Weir Quay and Bere Ferrers reached on unclassified roads S of A390, or W of A386 from Tavistock.
Map: page 305, SX45/46.

Tamar Lakes

Devon and Cornwall

These two lakes are close to the headwaters of the River Tamar, and like that famous river, they lie astride the Devon and Cornwall border.

The lower lake was constructed as a reservoir, but it is now a bird sanctuary, and its job of water supply has been taken over by a new reservoir built just upstream in 1975.

There are car parks here, and a public footpath runs along the

western side of the lower lake, overlooking good areas of lakeside marsh. These marshy areas are good for damselflies and dragonflies, which are at their most active on calm sunny days in high summer. Among the many attractive wild flowers growing here are ragged robin, blooming between May and July, yellow flags, in bloom from May to August, and purple loosestrife, flowering from June to September.

The birds of the lakes are mainly wildfowl and waders, but other water birds are likely to include herons and coots. Bird-watching hides have been provided.

Location: just N of Bude on minor roads E from A39. Permit to visit hides obtainable from South West Water Authority Lodge. Picnic area.
Map: page 305, SS21.

Tatton Park

Cheshire

Tatton is usually very busy; the garden regularly attracts more visitors than almost any other owned by the National Trust.

The house, with its fascinating contents, is always full, and both deserve their popularity, but those wishing to escape the throng will find uncrowded peace in the magnificent parklands.

Of the 2000 acres which make up the estate, visitors are free to wander over about 1000. For more structured explorations of the park, follow the medieval village trail or the Melchett Walk, a historical nature trail showing the natural history of the area and indicating the effects of subsidence in the landscape.

The present form of the park was largely determined by the work of the great 18th-century landscape gardener Humphry Repton, and probably closely resembles what he envisaged 200 years ago. One of Repton's ideas was for a mere where Melchett Mere is today. As a result of pumping by a salt extraction company, brine from beneath Tatton was drawn away, and the land subsided, leaving the mere to form naturally. The then owner, Lord Egerton, rather pointedly named it after Lord Melchett, owner of the company! The mile-long Tatton

Gardens at Tatton Park

Mere was planned and forms a wonderful oasis of tranquillity so close to Manchester. To it flock fishermen, seeking roach, perch and pike. It is said that the fish in Tatton Mere grow faster than in any other freshwater lake in the country. The mere also attracts large numbers and varieties of wildfowl during the winter.

A large number of fallow deer and a good-sized herd of red move in stately fashion through the park. Look out too, for the small dark brown Soay and black St Kilda sheep.

Open: park and garden daily, except 25 Dec (gardens pm only, but from mid-morning during high season). House, farm and Old Hall daily Apr to Oct, pm only (farm from mid-morning during high season); Nov and Mar Sun only. Admission charge. Refreshments. Shop. Suitable for disabled visitors. NT.
Location: 2 miles N of Knutsford, 4 miles S of Altrincham. Reached via Rostherne Lodge on Ashley Road, 1½ miles N of junction of A5034 and A50.
Map: page 309, SJ78.

plovers. As with most estuaries, it is best visited within several hours of high tide, when the birds are close in to the shore and can be viewed easily.

Access: *by public footpaths. Part NCC.*
Location: *W of Barnstaple and N of Bideford. There are many good vantage points, including the Skern at Appledore; beside park at Bideford; Fremington Pill and quay; and also at Ashford and Heanton. Northam Burrows is reached via Northam on A386 and B3236 from Bideford, while Braunton Burrows is reached via Braunton on A361 from Barnstaple.*
Map: *page 305, SS42/43/53.*

Tegg's Nose Country Park

Cheshire

Tegg's Nose is a rocky outcrop on the eastern fringes of Cheshire, where the land rises up on to the wild heather-clad moors leading over towards Buxton and the High Peak. The millstone grit here has been extensively quarried for building in the past, but all that ceased in 1955 and in 1972 the area became a country park.

The handsome brick-built tower windmill at Thaxted, built by a local farmer in 1804

Taw/Torridge Estuary

Devon

This estuary of two rivers is the only one on the North Devon coast. The Taw has a more open character and a larger area of mudflats. Beyond Bideford, the banks of the Torridge are quite thickly wooded.

The mouth of the estuary is very sandy and there are extensive sand dunes on either shore. On the south side is Northam Burrows, a country park run by Devon County Council and on the north side is Braunton Burrows, 2400 acres of dunes partly managed as a National Nature Reserve by the Nature Conservancy Council. These dune systems are exceptionally rich in wild flowers, including many rare ones. Sand toadflax is one of the most uncommon of these, and there are also several varieties of marsh orchids and gentians.

Like most estuaries, the Taw/Torridge supports a wealth of wading birds and wildfowl, and the sheer variety makes any walk along its banks an adventure. Perhaps the commonest birds here are curlews and ringed

This is a fine place to walk, to savour the atmosphere of the nearby hill country and to obtain spectacular views of the Cheshire Plain to the west and the Bollin valley to the south. Informative displays in the country park explain the geology of the area and tell the story of quarrying.

A nature trail explores the park, and shows that although poor soils limit the range of plant species able to live here, moorland such as this has its own special plant and animal communities.

Open: *at all times. Nature trail. Picnic area.*
Location: *2 miles E of Macclesfield, off A537. Car park at Windy Way on minor road from Macclesfield to Walker Barn.*
Map: *page 309, SJ97.*

Thaxted Windmill

Essex

Thaxted's windmill still bears the name of John Webb, a farmer, who built it in 1804 with bricks from his own works. It is a tower mill, five floors high, the great height making room for huge sails that could drive three pairs of stones. It replaced six earlier and smaller post mills and catered for a rapidly growing population, particularly in London, which could be reached via the expanding canal network of the times. The mill is in the pro-

cess of being restored: its main machinery is intact, the cap now turns and the sails will hopefully do so in the future. The ground and first floors have a museum of rural bygones.

Open: *May to Sep Sat, Sun and bank holidays, pm only. Admission charge. Shop. Picnic area.*
Location: *Thaxted lies on B184 Great Dunmow to Saffron Walden road; mill is behind church.*
Map: *page 306, TL63.*

Theale Gravel Pits

Berkshire

Set in the Kennet Valley between Theale and Reading, this series of gravel pits is of great interest for its bird life. Some of the pits are still in use, others are flooded, and some have thick vegetation round them – a variety of habitats which in turn attract a variety of bird species.

Where pits are being worked, colonies of sand martins excavate nest holes in the recently exposed vertical surfaces. In the spring and autumn they are joined by their relatives – house martins, swallows and swifts – all hunting for insects over the water surfaces. Little ringed plovers breed on some of the dryer pits. These birds, about six inches long, have only nested in Britain since 1938; before that they were rare visitors. They nest almost exclusively in gravel pits, and seem to prefer those still being worked, despite the disturbance. They do not find pits with vegetation in attractive. Little ringed plovers are summer visitors to Britain, flying south for the winter. In autumn, green sandpipers, spotted redshanks and lapwings can also be seen here.

Where disused pits have become filled with water, large concentrations of duck can be seen in winter. These might include pochard, wigeon, goldeneye and tufted duck, along with mallard and teal. Canada geese and great crested grebes are two of the many breeding species. Fish-eating birds such as heron and kingfisher can also be seen. Where bankside vegetation has developed, reed buntings and reed and sedge warblers breed. Nightingales might be found in areas where the vegetation has become thick scrub.

Access: *many of the pits can be seen from public roads. A public footpath running on S bank of the Kennet and Avon Canal gives good views.*
Location: *from A4 at Theale take road over railway to Sheffield Bottom. Pits are on either side of road.*
Map: *page 306, SU67.*

Therfield Heath

Hertfordshire

Despite the name, Therfield Heath is an area of chalk grassland – one of the most important in eastern England. It has survived the plough because it is common land which has been used for many years as a golf course and for training racehorses: there are also some outstanding archaeological features including a Neolithic long barrow.

The ancient turf is extraordinarily rich in plants; over 200 species have been recorded, with up to 30 in a single square yard. Pride of place goes to the pasque flower, with deep blue, bell-like flowers, which colours the sward in April, but many other rare species also occur, including spotted cat's-ear, bastard toadflax, wild candytuft, field fleawort, and five species of orchid.

This variety provides food plants for an extensive list of insects, especially the butterflies. Among the most notable are chalkhill blue, holly blue and brown argus, as well as four species of skipper.

Typical birds of the open heath are meadow pipits, skylarks and yellowhammers. Grasshopper warblers may be heard along the woodland edge on the south side, while kestrels hover overhead. James I had a palace nearby and hunted with hawk and falcon on the heath when great bustard, rock thrush and dotterel still occurred; of these only the dotterel now breeds in Britain (but only in small numbers) and the other two are very rare visitors.

Open: at all times. Public car park near pavilion at Royston, at east end of heath. CNT.
Location: on S side of unclassified Baldock road, on W side of Royston.
Map: page 306, TL34.

Thetford Forest

Norfolk and Suffolk

The great sandy heaths of Breckland, which once covered mile after mile of central East Anglia, have gone. Man has replaced them with enormous plantations of pine. Something has certainly been lost, but the forest has very positive attractions of its own. Its strong point is its variety. Scots pines have pinkish trunks, Corsicans are blue-grey; roads are lined with a varied mixture of deciduous trees; forest-management produces clear-felled areas alongside thickets and lines of mature trees. All this makes for a varied landscape and

Among the conifers in Thetford Forest

wildlife. Roe deer are common and there is still a chance of seeing the rapidly declining red squirrel. Crossbills, the males dark red and brilliant crimson, have beaks specially adapted for opening the pine-cones to get at the seeds. Nightjars are widespread in the clearings, their liquid, churring song a feature of summer twilight.

Most of the forest can be explored along rides and tracks, and good centres are the picnic-places at Hockham, Lynford, Santon Downham and Mildenhall. Brandon Country Park is convenient, and offers a chance of seeing the shy, but brilliantly colourful, golden pheasant.

A remnant of the old Breckland landscape with specialised flowers, the rare and curious-looking stone curlew and rabbits galore, is the Norfolk Naturalists' Trust reserve at Weeting. The Trust's reserve at East Wretham has two very beautiful meres. Grime's Graves, a fascinating series of excavations where Neolithic men dug flint

with tools of bone and stone, provides a historical continuity stretching back 6000 years.

Open: forest all year, subject to forest management. Information centre at Santon Downham open Mon to Fri daily. Waymarked walks. Picnic area. FC. Brandon Country Park, all year. Visitor centre. Tree trail. Picnic area. Shop. Facilities for disabled visitors. Weeting Nature Reserve, open only during summer (times flexible). Admission charge. CNT. East Wretham Nature Reserve, daily except Tue (permits available from Warden's house on reserve). Admission charge. Trail guide. CNT. Grime's Graves, Mon to Sat daily, Sun pm only all day Apr to Sep. Admission charge.
Location: forest is mainly W and N of Thetford, on the A11, 30 miles SW of Norwich. Brandon Country Park is on B1106, ¾ mile S of Brandon. Weeting Nature Reserve is on unclassified road 1¼ miles W of Weeting. East Wretham Nature Reserve is on A1075 4 miles NE of Thetford. Grime's Graves are off unclassified road 3¼ miles NE of Brandon.
Map: page 306, TL88.

Thorndon Country Park

Essex

Unusually, this park is in two parts, north and south, separated by half a mile of farmland, but connected by signposted footpaths and bridleways. The northern half is mainly wooded and there are both conifer and broadleaved plantations. The southern section is also wooded, but has meadowland too, and a large pond. As is always the case, the native deciduous trees have much more wildlife associated with them than the alien conifers. The main reason for this is probably that native trees, plants and animals have had thousands of years to become adapted to each other. Woodland animals, such as the grey squirrel, and birds, such as woodpeckers, tits and warblers, are all likely to be seen. But one speciality of Thorndon, the hawfinch, is very shy and elusive. There is a good show of flowers here, especially in spring, when wood anemones, primroses and bluebells flower in that order, before the trees have put out their leaves and cast the woodland floor into shade.

Open: all year. Picnic area. Car parking charge Sat and Sun in summer, pm only.
Location: N section signposted W of A128 1¼ miles S of Brentwood. S section entrance just NW of junction of A127 and A128.
Map: page 306, TQ69.

Threave Garden & Threave Wildfowl Refuge

Dumfries & Galloway

The superb gardens at Threave, owned by the National Trust for Scotland, are noted for the great variety of plants on show, especially in the rock and water gardens. The spring show of daffodils here is outstanding. Threave Wildfowl Refuge, on the River Dee, is well worth a visit in winter for its greylag geese, whooper swans, wigeon, teal, mallard and other wildfowl.

Open: Threave Gardens all year daily. Admission charge. Visitor centre (open Apr to Oct). Refreshments (Apr to Sep). Suitable for disabled visitors. NTS. Threave Wildfowl Refuge, open Nov to Mar. Admission charge.
Location: Threave Gardens off A75, 1 mile W of Castle Douglas. Threave Wildfowl Refuge on either side of A75 close to Bridge of Dee.
Map: page 313, NX76.

Thursley Common
Surrey

When, many centuries ago, men cleared the woodland on the sandy soils of Surrey, the areas developed instead into heathland which supported a different variety of wildlife. One of the most important of these areas remaining today is Thursley National Nature Reserve, owned by the Nature Conservancy Council and managed in association with the Surrey Trust for Nature Conservation. As well as the large areas of dry heathland, there is an extensive bog, open pools, and woodland.

This variety of habitats supports a wide range of different plants and animals. Over 140 species of birds have been noted, including, as a breeding species, the rare Dartford warbler. It is also a very good site for reptiles and for insects, supporting the largest variety of dragonfly species in southern Britain.

The 'GLASGOW' Farm Tractor

Access: by public footpath (some of these can become flooded and difficult to negotiate after rain).
NCC/CNT.
Location: accessible from A3, 2½ miles SW of Milford, or from minor road between Elstead and Churt. Free car park at The Moat, 1½ miles S of Elstead.
Map: page 306, SU94.

Tilford – Old Kiln Agricultural Museum
Surrey

In general, the exhibits in this fascinating collection are grouped by use, which includes yard machinery, corn and grain handling equipment, tillage and hand tools. Much of the collection is shown outside in ten acres

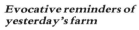

Evocative reminders of yesterday's farm

of woodlands and fields. Displays on various aspects of village life from the late Victorian age to the 1940s give an insight into such topics as trapping, shepherding and pharmacy.

Certainly the most evocative displays are the smithy and the wheelwright's shop. The latter is shown as a live workshop, halted in time. The wheel is partially constructed, with tools, felloes and patterns strewn on the benches. A vast array of tools hangs ready to use.

The collection of tools in the forge is no less formidable. Hammers and tongs, anvil, forge and bellows lie in readiness for use, and indeed this is a working smithy, with practical demonstrations of the blacksmith's art. Shoeing horses was only one of a wide array of skills the smith needed to meet the demands of the bygone age.

The dairy exhibit next to the wheelwright's shop also shows the skills of the farmer's wife. Milk-, butter- and cheese-handling equipment is shown, and an old-fashioned milk float with churn and jugs can be seen.

Open: Wed to Sun (and bank holidays) Apr to Sep. Admission charge. Picnic area. Shop. Suitable for disabled visitors.
Location: on Reeds Road, between Frensham and Tilford.
Map: page 306, SU84.

Titchfield Haven
Hampshire

The Local Nature Reserve at Titchfield Haven is managed by Hampshire County Council in such a way that visitors get the most value from their trip. There is a small exhibition, at which the Ranger (who gives guided tours) meets visitors. The reserve is only open when the wildfowl are most numerous.

A mixture of shallow lagoons, islands, reed beds, damp meadows and scrub woodlands makes up the reserve, encouraging a wide variety of bird species. Among the most common or interesting wildfowl that might be seen are wigeon, mallard, teal, pintail and shoveler. In summer, reed and sedge warblers breed in the reed beds and adjacent scrub. Occasionally, parties of bearded tits can be seen feeding on the edges of the reed beds. Ringed plovers and redshanks, together with other waders, frequently visit the shallower pools and muddy areas. Part of the area is owned by the Hampshire and Isle of Wight Naturalists' Trust.

Open: Aug to Mar (by prior arrangement only) Fri, Sat and Sun. Admission charge. Guided tours. Information centre. Suitable for disabled visitors. No dogs. LNR (Hampshire County Council). CNT.
Location: 4 miles SW of Fareham.
Map: page 306, SU50.

Titchwell Marsh

Norfolk

Much of the beautiful north Norfolk coast is protected as nature reserves. But protection is not enough – wildlife communities must be managed to keep their interest. The RSPB has actively followed this policy at Titchwell Marsh, and has also created new habitats. These have been quickly found by birds, and this is now one of the best places to see them on the whole coast.

The sea is the home of mussel-eating eider ducks and scoters in winter. At low tide, from autumn to spring, many types of wading birds forage on the exposed mud. The beach is the nesting-ground of ringed plovers, oystercatchers and, best of all, common and little terns. These can be enjoyed at close range and almost at eye-level from a hide sunk in the dunes. Other hides overlook a brackish and a freshwater marsh, often so full of activity, particularly during migration, that happy bird-watchers don't know which way to look. Rare birds breed in the reedbeds – bittern, marsh harrier and the delightful bearded tit.

Open: *public footpath all year. Visitor centre and hides Apr to May and Oct weekends only; June to Sep Sat, Sun, Mon and Thu, (at time of going to press. It is hoped to open every day mid July to end Sep from 1985 on). Nov to Mar only open for organised groups. Picnic area. Shop with reserve literature. RSPB.*
Location: *car park signposted N of A149, 6 miles E of Hunstanton, 1¼ miles W of Brancaster.*
Map: *page 311, TF74.*

Tondu: Glamorgan Nature Centre

Mid Glamorgan

This centre, which stands in open countryside north-west of Bridgend, is the headquarters of the Glamorgan Trust for Nature Conservation.

The building and car park were acquired as a gift from the Opencast Executive of the Coal Board and opened to the public in 1982 by HRH the Prince of Wales. Inside, an exhibition area provides an introduction to the wildlife of the county and the work of the Trust.

There is a small nature reserve with its own trail adjacent to the centre: a well-constructed path leads across a stream to a pond

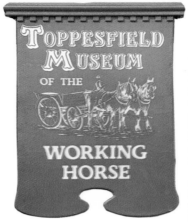

Signboard at Toppesfield

fringed with willows and a marshy area with wild angelica, great willow-herb and bittersweet. Snipe feed on the marsh, while tits and finches shelter in the willow scrub. Further on, the trail reaches a wooded area dominated by oak, with some ash, elm

and several mature small-leaved limes.

Grayling and common blue butterflies feed on clover in a grassy picnic site behind the centre.

Open: *most weekends from Easter to Sep, pm only. Also some weekdays. Shop. Waymarked trails. Dogs in centre building and car park only. CNT.*
Location: *3 miles NW of Bridgend, 1 mile W of Tondu.*
Map: *page 305, SS88.*

Toppesfield Museum of the Working Horse

Essex

It is difficult today to realise the former importance of the horse in both rural and urban Britain. A few breweries still keep their huge and magnificent dray-horses for special occasions, but otherwise most of us see working horses very rarely. And yet, not long ago, the muscle-power of these animals was a vital element of such essential jobs as ploughing, driving machinery and pulling vehicles of all kinds from crude carts to the most elegant of carriages. A variety of rural industries provided support. This museum houses a wheelwright's shop, a harness-maker's, a working forge, saw-pit and a variety of horse-drawn vehicles and farm implements. It is a most interesting record of the fascinating relationship between man and working horse.

Open: *Apr to Oct, Sat, Sun and Bank Holidays, pm only. Admission charge. Shop. Picnic area.*
Location: *at the Wheatsheaf, Toppesfield, on minor roads W of A604 at Great Yeldham.*
Map: *page 306, TL73.*

Torridon Countryside Centre

Highland

Torridon lies immediately west of the Beinn Eighe National Nature Reserve (see page 25) and is conveniently situated in an area where the visitor can take in these two sites as well as Inverewe Gardens (see page 137). The mountain scenery here is superb, with several peaks approaching or exceeding 3000ft. There is a National Trust for Scotland Visitor Centre at Torridon, and a fine deer museum. Both red and roe deer occur in the area and blue hares and wild goats are usually seen fairly easily. Although also present, wild cats and pine martens are very elusive. The birds are marvellous, with good opportunities for seeing black-throated and red-throated divers, golden eagles, peregrines, red grouse, ptarmigan (on the highest ground only), common sandpipers, ring ouzels, dippers and wheatears.

Open: *visitor centre and deer museum Jun to Sep daily (Sun pm only). Audio-visual display. Ranger/naturalist service. NTS.*

Lovely Highland landscape near the Torridon Countryside Centre

Location: *at junction of A896 and Diabaig road, near Torridon.*
Map: *page 314, NG95.*

Wildcat

Once widespread throughout Britain, the wildcat now lives only in parts of the Highlands of Scotland, although there are signs that it is extending its range. Although similar in appearance to a large tabby, the wildcat is not closely related to domestic cats. If it feels threatened, the wildcat is the personification of hissing, spitting fury.

Toys Hill

Kent

For centuries Toys Hill was part of the commons of Brasted Chart, and very much a working area. Pigs and cattle were kept here, beechwood cut for charcoal and churtstone quarried for roads. Today it is a peaceful area, with the bonus of lovely views across Kent.

Plants are scarce among the hill-top beeches, but fungi are plentiful in autumn. The apricot-yellow chanterelle is edible and one of the most attractive, but the olive capped death cap is decidedly neither of these – it is very poisonous. Picking any fungi, unless you are an expert, can be dangerous.

Lower down the hill are the greatest concentrations of flowers, with fine displays of bluebells in spring. All through the spring and summer resident birds are joined by migrants. Blue, great and coal tits are always to be seen and heard, but the greater spotted woodpecker, despite its smart red, white and black plumage, can be very elusive. Migrants include chiffchaffs, willow warblers, garden warblers and black caps.

There is a well-marked circular walk of about 1¼ miles round the top of the hill and additional longer walks branch from it to points of interest lower down the hill.

Location: *2¼ miles S of Brasted, 2 miles N of Four Elms, on unclassified road. NT.*
Map: *page 306, TQ45.*

Tredegar House & Country Park

Gwent

Tredegar House, one of the finest mansions in Wales, stands in a 90-acre estate notable for its walled garden, avenue of 200-year-old oaks, extensive woodland, shrubberies bright with rhododendrons and an ornamental lake now used for boating and fishing. The country park's other attractions include an aquarium and a bird garden. The days when Tredegar House was virtually self-contained are recalled by a children's farm devoted to rare breeds of cattle, pigs, sheep and poultry.

Open: *country park daily. (House Good Fri to end Sep Wed to Sun and bank holidays. Admission charge. Refreshments. Shop. Suitable for disabled visitors. No dogs in house.) Visitor centre daily except 25, 26 Dec and 1 Jan.*
Location: *off junction 28 of M4, 2 miles W of central Newport.*
Map: *page 305, ST28.*

Tregaron Bog
Dyfed

This huge bog on the upper reaches of the Afon Teifi is one of the natural wonders of Wales. Its origins go back to the end of the Ice Age, about 10,000 years ago, when stones and soil dropped by a melting glacier turned the river into a shallow lake whose sediments and plants were gradually compressed into a thick carpet of peat. The area includes three raised bogs, but their contours are lost in a wilderness whose flatness contrasts vividly with the hilly landscape around.

Abandoned peat cuttings share the bog with willow, birch and many other plants which thrive in wet, acidic conditions. In summer it is white with great masses of nodding cotton-grass. Birdlife includes curlews, lapwings and sedge warblers. Fortunate visitors may also see a red kite – one of Britain's rarest birds of prey – flying overhead.

Most of the bog is now the Cors Caron National Nature Reserve and may be explored only after obtaining a Nature Conservancy Council permit (permits, which are free, are essential, as parts of the bog are dangerous and permits show safe paths). No permit is needed to walk along the part of the abandoned railway track which runs beside the road from Tregaron to Pontrhydfendigaid.

Open: *all year. Information boards in lay-bys. Permits and leaflets from warden at Minawel, Ffair Rhos, Ystrad Meurig. NCC.*
Location: *2 miles N of Tregaron, W of B4340.*
Map: *page 309, SN66.*

Trelissick
Cornwall

Standing at the head of the Carrick Roads where the Fal estuary begins to narrow, it is possible to obtain magnificent views of the river from the garden of this estate. For those wishing to explore part of the estuary, there is a three-mile circular walk through park and woodland beside the river.

After leaving the garden, the walk heads inland and then turns down to Lamouth Creek which is both beautiful and quiet. The walk passes through thick oak woods close to the water and round to King Harry Ferry. It is possible to walk back to the car park at Trelissick along the main road here, but it is a busy road. The walk continues past a Celtic cross, from which a pleasant path leads back to the garden and on to

The speckled bush cricket might be seen at Treswell Wood

the Carrick Roads. It then turns away back inland and up the valley to the house. In summer the woods are filled with bird song, while in winter it is possible to see waders feeding on the beaches. The garden itself is full of colour from spring to autumn.

Open: *woodland walk at all times; garden Mar to Oct daily (Sun pm only). Woodland free; admission charge for garden. Dogs admitted to park and woodland only, on leads. Refreshments. Shop. Suitable for disabled visitors. NT.*
Location: *4 miles S of Truro on both sides of B3289 above King Harry Ferry.*
Map: *page 304, SW83.*

Trencrom Hill
Cornwall

The people of Cornwall have a strong Celtic tradition of folklore, and several stories are told concerning the giants who lived on Trencrom Hill. The tales provide an explanation for the great weathered granite outcrops and stone ramparts which are the major features of this 500ft high outpost on the edge of the Land's End peninsula.

Although no formal excavation work has been undertaken on the hill, it seems probable that the first of many human occupiers were Neolithic farmers. Polished greenstone axes of the period have been found on the lower slopes. Around the top of the hill, a rampart encloses the remains of a number of Iron Age huts. There are sweeping views from the gorse-covered summit of the hill.

Access: *via unclassified road through Lelant Downs from junction with A30 and A3074. Footpaths to summit. Part NT.*
Location: *3 miles S of St Ives, 4½ miles NE of Penzance.*
Map: *page 304, SW53.*

Treswell Wood
Nottinghamshire

Treswell Wood, a reserve of the Nottinghamshire Trust for Nature Conservation, was first recorded in the Domesday Book, and over the centuries has provided local people with wood for building and fuel, mainly by the ancient practice of coppicing. This method of woodland management, cutting the trees right down to their bases so that they throw up many fast-growing stems, was discontinued at the beginning of this century but is now being carried out again by the Nottinghamshire Trust. Coppicing is beneficial to wildlife, and the restoration of more open conditions is allowing fine spring displays of bluebells, primroses, wood anemones and wood-sorrel. The antiquity of the wood is shown by the presence of uncommon plants like the wild service tree and herb Paris, and by the localised speckled bush cricket, as well as other insects. The wood also has a good range of birds.

Open: *nature trail open to public on 2nd Sun of month from Apr to Sep; access is by permit only at other times. CNT.*
Location: *3 miles ESE of Retford, on unclassified Grove-Treswell road.*
Map: *page 310, SK77.*

Trosley Country Park
Kent

Lying on the scarp slope of the North Downs, Trosley encapsulates the landscapes of the Kent Downs, having a mixture of woodland and grassland with a fine range of plants and animals.

Woodland runs the one mile length of the park, with beech the dominant tree. However, the glory of Trosley is the downland turf. No less than eight varieties of orchid grow here, in some years more. This is because the flowers set variable amounts of

seed from year to year, and because it can take anything up to ten years between seed germination and flowering. Look for the flowers from May to July, a time when more inconspicuous plants such as fairy flax, milkwort and rock rose are also in flower.

Open: *country park daily, except 25 Dec. Information centre weekends, pm only, and bank holidays. Picnic area. Waymarked walks.*
Location: *2 miles NE of Wrotham, off A227.*
Map: *page 306, TQ66.*

The Trossachs & Queen Elizabeth Forest Park
Central

As an area of considerable beauty and wildlife interest close to Glasgow, the Trossachs are probably only surpassed by Loch Lomond itself, which adjoins the area to the west. The historic small town of Aberfoyle is in the heart of the region and makes an ideal centre from which to explore.

To the south-east, bounded by the A873, A811, B8034 and B822 roads, lies Flanders Moss, a large tract of bog and moorland where such birds as hen harriers, golden plovers, curlews and black grouse might be seen. In winter pink footed geese are also likely to be present here – they may also be seen flighting into the nearby Lake of Menteith late on winter afternoons.

Much of the rest of the Trossachs region lies within the vast Queen Elizabeth Forest Park, which comprises some 25,000 acres of forest land and 20,000

acres of mountain and moorland extending west to the shores of Loch Lomond. As well as extensive commercial conifer plantations, there are mixed woodlands, large and small lochs, rivers and burns and high tops, including both Ben Lomond and Ben Venue. Red and roe deer are plentiful, golden eagles still occur in the more remote northern section, and other likely birds include buzzards, hen harriers, sparrowhawks, peregrines, red and black grouse, common sandpipers, short-eared owls, dippers, ravens, ring ouzels, red-

starts, wheatears, whinchats, wood warblers, siskins and crossbills.

Along the eastern shores of Loch Lomond, the road to Rowardennan is well worth exploring; there are camping and picnic sites here and the relatively easy walk up to the summit of Ben Lomond begins at Rowardennan (stout footwear and warm, waterproof clothing essential). From Aberfoyle, two routes can be recommended. The first is via the Duke's Pass, leading to Loch Katrine, Loch Venachar and Callander. A short way beyond Aberfoyle is the excellent Forestry Commission Visitor Centre at David Marshall Lodge, which has comprehensive local information and literature and a superb view. Details are obtainable here for the forest walks in Loch Rad Forest and Buchan Forest, Drymen, and also for the caravan and camping site at Cobleland, Aberfoyle. A short, picturesque drive leads to Loch Achray and then Loch Katrine, with Ben Venue away to the

west. The steamer trip on Loch Katrine is recommended: watch for golden eagles over the slopes above the southern shore and also over the high ground north of the turning-point at Stronachlachar.

The alternative route to Stronachlachar is by road, the B829 west from Aberfoyle. This offers the chance to stop and explore the woods and hillsides from Loch Ard along to Loch Chon; it is worth stopping at the junction above Stronachlachar and walking down to the pier. A short stretch of quite wild country alongside Loch Arklet runs down to the road end at Inversnaid, high above Loch Lomond: you can go no further, but refreshments are available and the view across to Ben Vorlich and Ben Ime on the far side of the loch makes the journey worthwhile.

Around the Trossachs – church beside Loch Achray (left) and the Falls of Leny

Open: *David Marshall Lodge mid Mar to Oct daily. Information centre. Nature trails. Picnic area. FC. Loch Katrine steamers sail daily in summer.*
Location: *David Marshall Lodge is 1 mile N of Aberfoyle off A821.*
Map: *page 313, NN40/50.*

Tummel & Pitlochry

Tayside

There are several sites worth visiting in the Pitlochry area, which can be included in a general tour taking in Killiecrankie just to the north and Loch Rannoch and the Black Wood of Rannoch (see page 29) to the west.

In Pitlochry itself, clearly signposted from the main street, is the famous fish ladder, where salmon can be observed closely, through windows, as they climb up from the River Tummel to Loch Faskally, which was created when the Pitlochry Dam was built.

The Linn of Tummel comprises 50 acres owned by the National Trust for Scotland, near to their land at Killiecrankie (see page 142). Woodland nature trails explore about two miles of the River Garry to the former Falls of Tummel, which disappeared when the dam raised the water level to create Loch Faskally. Above Loch Tummel lies the Tummel Visitor Centre, which has a good interpretative display on the area and its forests, as well as a series of woodland walks of varying lengths.

The whole area is good for birds. Canada geese nest on the lochs, while the conifer woods and plantations hold buzzards, sparrowhawks, coal tits, goldcrests and siskins. In mixed woodland, redstarts, wood and garden warblers and green and great spotted woodpeckers may be encountered.

Open: *Tummel visitor centre Easter to end Sep daily. Audio-visual display. Picnic area. Forest walks.*
Location: *Pitlochry is on A9. Tummel is NW of Pitlochry; Visitor centre is off B8019 4 miles W of A9 at Garry Bridge. Part NTS.*
Map: *page 315, NN85/95.*

Thomas Bewick

Thomas Bewick was born at Cherryburn, near what is now Tyne Riverside Country Park, in 1753. His delightful engravings, some of which are shown on this page, often depict Northumberland scenes.

Tyne Riverside Country Park

Northumberland and Tyne & Wear

This long, narrow park is based on a footpath which winds its way along the banks of the River Tyne for six miles. It begins its journey in the pleasant countryside of Northumberland and ends on the outskirts of the city of Newcastle upon Tyne.

Thomas Bewick, the great wood engraver, would still recognise many of the scenes he depicted here, although things have changed a lot since he drew his inspiration from this countryside. His old home at Cherryburn is close to the beginning of the footpath and he and his wife are buried in Ovingham churchyard, just across the river.

There is an abundance of wildlife to see in this varied park, and the river has a great influence on this. Unusual species such as the goosander are not uncommon in winter, and cormorants can regularly be seen flying inland to

various reservoirs. Sand martins nest in several places and even kingfishers may be seen.

As the river valley opens out, the city of Newcastle comes into view, but at Newburn the river can be crossed and the return journey made by a different path.

Open: *at all times. Picnic areas.*
Location: *on both banks of Tyne between Ovingham and Newburn; 5 miles W of Newcastle upon Tyne.*
Map: *page 313, NZ16.*

Upper Hamble Country Park

Hampshire

There are many quiet walks along the banks of the River Hamble and through this country park's ancient woods. Barnfield picnic area is surrounded by trees and a walk from here through Catland Copse leads to the wooded shore of the river. The views up and down the river are spectacular. Within the park is an old manor farm which is being restored to house the Hampshire Farm Museum. Also in the park is the Queen Elizabeth II Jubilee Activities Centre for the Handicapped.

Not far away is the Royal Victoria Country Park, with its wide range of leisure facilities. This park is also well equipped for use by the handicapped. Further down the estuary are extensive areas of salt marsh, where such plants as sea purslane, sea lavender, thrift, and sea aster may be found; there are also large reed beds here, good for a variety of birds.

Open: *Upper Hamble and Royal Victoria country parks all year. Admission charges for cars Apr to Sep. Information centres. Picnic areas. Refreshments. (Royal Victoria has a shop.) Both suitable for disabled visitors.*

Location: *Upper Hamble Country Park ¼ mile E of M27 junction 8, 1½ miles SE of Hedge End. Royal Victoria Country Park 1 mile NW of Hamble, off B3397.*
Map: *page 306, SU41.*

Upton Country Park

Dorset

This 54-acre country park is situated on the shores of Poole Harbour and consists largely of the grounds of historic Upton House. These are a mixture of formal gardens and parkland. Fine trees are a special feature of the parkland. The views over Holes Bay and across Poole Harbour are superb; in the distance are the Purbeck Heaths (see page 231).

The tidal areas alongside the park are good for wading birds at the right state of the tide and there are often good numbers of wildfowl offshore. These are excellent places to see diving ducks such as red-breasted merganser or goldeneye in winter, and often a few grebes.

Open: *all year daily. Information centre. Picnic area. Refreshments. Suitable for disabled visitors.*
Location: *S side of A35 just N of Poole.*
Map: *page 305, SY99.*

Usk Valley Walk

Gwent

A waymarked walk of just over 25 miles explores the lovely Vale of Usk between Abergavenny and Caerleon. The river, famous

River and canal viaduct in the Usk Valley

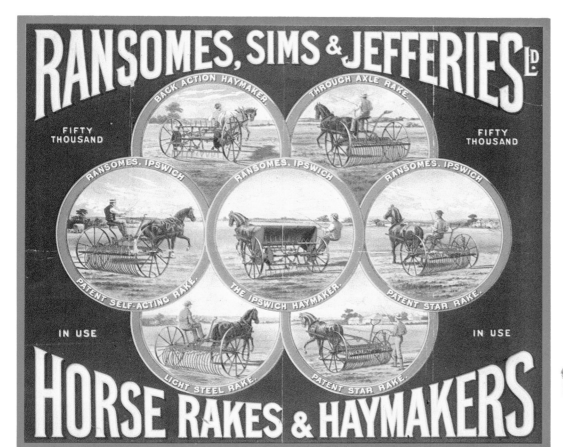

The Viking Way

Lincs and Leics

A long-distance footpath stretching 125 miles from the River Humber in the north to Rutland Water in the south, the Viking Way is unusual in that it runs mainly through intensively-farmed countryside. At the northern end of the path is the Humber Bridge with its 4626ft span – the longest suspension bridge in the world. Moving southwards, the Way passes through the beautiful Wolds: among many items of interest are the Melton Gallows, just west of Barnetby on the A18, still kept in good repair as a reminder of an ancient feud. The church of All Saints, high on the hillside above Walesby, is known as the 'Ramb-

for its salmon and trout, meanders seawards through a landscape of rolling, wooded hills overlooked from the west by the Brecon Beacons National Park. Fine views reward those who climb Ysgyryd Fach, which rises to 830 feet above Abergavenny.

South of Abergavenny, an old market town with the remains of a medieval castle, the Usk Valley Walk follows a stretch of the

Ransomes is one of the most famous names in agricultural machinery. Posters like this are in the Rutland County Museum at Oakham, on the Viking Way

The goosander is a member of the 'sawbill' group of ducks. Tyne Riverside Country Park is one place where goosanders might be seen

lers' Church', with an appropriate stained-glass window and a 'Ramblers' Service' every summer.

Southwards again the path joins the Roman Ermine Street and, at Woolsthorpe, follows a different highway, the towpath of the old Grantham canal. The last stretch of the walk crosses into Lincolnshire, passes through Exton, one of Rutland's prettiest villages, past Rutland Water (see page 236) and on, finally, to Oakham, where the Rutland County Museum has a nationally important rural life collection.

canal built between 1797 and 1812 to forge a link between Brecon and the Bristol Channel. The route's other attractions include glimpses of Clytha Castle – a folly built at the end of the 18th century – the Gwent Rural Life Museum in Usk and the Roman amphitheatre in Caerleon.

Open: Gwent Rural Life Museum Apr to Sep Fri to Sun and bank holidays pm only; mid-Jul to mid-Sep daily; Mar and Oct Sun pm only. Admission charge. Caerleon Amphitheatre and Barracks all year daily, Sun pm only, but daily Apr to Sep. Admission charge.
Map: page 305.

Open: Rutland County Museum Tue to Sat daily, also Sun pm Apr to Oct. Closed Good Fri, 25, 26 Dec. Suitable for disabled visitors.
Access: path is waymarked by Viking helmet symbols and can be joined or left at many points.
Map: page 306, 310.

December

The Crookham Mummers – in 1905 and today

BURNING THE ASHEN FAGGOT

Dunster, Somerset

Thought to have originated in the early 1600s, this custom is continued each Christmas Eve in the Luttrell Arms at Dunster. A log composed of bundles of ash sticks neatly bound together, and measuring three feet in length and eight inches in diameter, is placed on the open fire shortly before midnight, and mulled cider is served to all.

When: *24 Dec.*
Map: *page 305, SS94.*

FIREBALL CEREMONY

Stonehaven, Grampian

Originally thought to have been a ritual to ward off evil spirits for the coming year, this custom continues each Christmas Eve when young men from the village parade down the High Street swinging flaming balls of fire above their heads. These fireballs consist of wire netting cages full of burnable material attached to long wire ropes. They are lit about one minute before midnight. Over 30 fireballs are swirled skilfully through the air as the procession makes its way through the old town.

When: *24 Dec.*
Map: *page 315, NO88.*

RINGING THE DEVIL'S KNELL

Dewsbury, West Yorkshire

Ringing the Devil's Knell is a custom dating back to the Middle Ages, when a tenor bell was given to Dewsbury Parish Church by Sir Thomas de Soothill in expiation of a murder he had committed. It is said that Sir Thomas requested that the bell be tolled every Christmas Eve, once for each year passed since the birth of Christ and timed to finish at midnight.

This act was thought to free the village of the Devil for the coming 12 months, but others believe it was to celebrate the birth of Christ and the defeat and death of the Devil. Until recently the bell was known as 'Black Tom of Soothill'.

When: *24 Dec.*
Map: *page 310, SE22.*

DISTRIBUTION OF NEW PENNIES

Sherborne Castle, Sherborne, Dorset

At 9am on Christmas Day every year the owner of Sherborne Castle gives a small gift of money to the townsfolk who gather in the Castle Estate Yard. Adults receive ten pence and children are given five pence each, always in brand new coinage.

Once called 'Up to Lodge', records for this custom date back to 1881, though some say it is older.

When: *25 Dec.*
Map: *page 305, ST61.*

MEN AND BOYS' BA' GAMES

Kirkwall, Orkney

This custom takes place each Christmas Day and New Year's Day. It consists of two games of 'football'; a boys' game starting at 10.30am, and a men's game beginning at 1pm. There are sides for each game – 'Uppies' and 'Doonies'. 'Uppies' are those born above the market cross, and 'Doonies' those born below it.

A cork-filled leather ball is thrown among a loose scrum formed by the players, and this denotes the start of a game, the boys' game lasting about two hours, while the men's game could last up to seven hours. There is no limit to the number of participants in each team and the end of the game is called when one side reaches its 'goal' – Mackinson's Corner or the sea front. Finally, the successful team appoints one member as the winner of the 'Ba', kept as a cherished prize.

When: 25 Dec and 1 Jan.
Map: page 315, HY41.

CROOKHAM MUMMERS' PLAY

Crookham Village, Hants

Once performed all over the south of England, mummers plays were thought to have derived from the St George Death and Resurrection plays, showing the fight between good and evil, which date back to medieval times. The 'Saint' is replaced by the 'King' in Crookham's play.

The Crookham mummers' play is enacted on the village green and outside various pubs and begins with the players walking around in a circle to bring good luck to the village. The troupe consists of seven characters – Father Christmas, Bold Roamer, Bold Slasher, Doctor, Johnny Jack, Turkish Knight and King George.

A fight takes place between King George and the Bold Roamer, ending in victory for King George, who goes on to slay the Bold Slasher. Doctor is called and the two are resurrected by a magic potion. After this King George is challenged by the Turkish Knight, whom he defeats after a lengthy battle, but does not kill. Finally, Father Christmas enters into a duel with Johnny Jack, also known as Trim Tram, and is slain.

Five of the actors are covered in strips of coloured wallpaper, leaving Father Christmas in traditional red garb and the Doctor recognisable in black clothing and carrying a black bag. The Turkish Knight also has a blackened face and wears a fez or turban.

When: 26 Dec.
Map: page 306, SU75.

GREATHAM SWORD DANCE

Greatham, Cleveland

A mixture of sword dancing and spoken words, this tradition is performed annually on Boxing Day at several venues in Greatham, firstly at the entrance to the church hall and afterwards at the Smith Arms and the Bull & Dog public houses. The event involves dancing, as well as a short play usually enacted by six players.

Many spectators enjoy the tradition and witness the celebration of the end of the old year and the beginning of the new, symbolised by the death and resurrection of one of the characters in the play.

When: 26 Dec.
Map: page 310, NZ42.

Vyrnwy, Lake

Powys

This vast artificial lake covers 1120 acres and is a superb example of the Victorians' ability to blend civil engineering with natural beauty. The dam, 144 feet high and one-fifth of a mile long, looks like the wall of a medieval castle, while the tower on the lake's northern shore would not be out of place perched on a crag above the Rhine. The lake itself is complemented by pine forests which give way to mountains more than 2000 feet high.

The lake is the focal point of the Royal Society for the Protection of Birds' largest reserve. It covers 16,000 acres where pied flycatchers, wood warblers, crossbills, ravens, buzzards, long-eared owls, goosanders, great-crested grebes, herons, dippers, common sandpipers and many other species may be seen or heard.

Birds can be watched from hides on the two RSPB nature trails, one of which provides an energetic walk of three-and-a-half miles, while the other covers a more gentle one-and-a-quarter miles. There is also an information centre near the southern end of the lake. It reveals what the area was like before the lake was formed, tells why the valley was flooded, and has a large display devoted to wildlife.

Open: *information centre Easter to Spring Bank Holiday, weekends pm only; Whitsun to Sep daily, pm only. Audio-visual displays. Picnic sites around lake. Nature trails. Centre suitable for disabled visitors. RSPB.*
Location: *on B4393 11 miles W of Llanfyllin.*
Map: *page 309, SJ01, SH92.*

Wallington

Northumberland

There is a pleasing dignity about Wallington, standing among its charming 100 acres of woodland and lakes, in country which seems surprisingly remote, although only 20 miles from Newcastle.

The interior of the house is a particular delight, displaying the treasures acquired in three centuries of occupation by two families – the Blacketts and the Trevelyans – and often reflecting the personal interests of the collector.

The National Trust has designed three walks in these extensive grounds. Two are 'mixed' walks in that they include part of the formal landscape while drawing attention to the wild plant and bird life. The third, longer walk, is an extension of the second and includes a lengthy section of path beside the River Wansbeck.

Wallington's grounds are open all year and there is always something of interest to be seen along the walks. In winter, look for the seemingly delicate but surprisingly tough snowdrop, forcing its head above the snow. It will continue to flower in great clumps throughout the Wallington woods well into March. In spring, daffodils, primroses, wood anemones and celandines abound, followed in early summer by comfrey, which may be pale yellow, white, pink or purple. The water lilies here are particularly fine and there are splendid examples of the great, rhubarb-like gunnera, by the garden pond. Autumn colour is provided by the leaves of such trees as beech, oak and maple.

The birds are typical of mixed woodland – tits, finches and woodpeckers – and of ponds, with ducks, moorhens and coots. A kingfisher is usually resident along the Wansbeck, and on summer days trout will be seen, rising lazily to the insects on and above the surface of the river.

Lake Vyrnwy, a huge reservoir created in the 1880s

Open: *house Apr to Sep Wed to Mon, pm only; Oct Wed, Sat and Sun, pm only; walled garden and grounds every day. Admission charge. Dogs must be on leads in walled garden. Suitable for disabled visitors. Refreshments. Shop. NT.*
Location: *13 miles W of Morpeth on B6342; 6 miles NW of Belsay, N of A696.*
Map: *page 313, NZ08.*

Washburn Valley

North Yorkshire

Crossing Blubberhouses Moor, and just beyond the space-age 'golf balls' of the United States communications station at Menwith Hill, a side road leads south into the deep valley carved by the River Washburn. Here there is a great contrast to the open moor-

The Washburn Valley and its reservoirs

land. The lower part of the valley has been dammed to form two reservoirs, Swinsty and Fewston, and the slopes are clothed in trees, producing a much softer landscape.

A system of footpaths provides the opportunity to explore fully this delightful area. The reservoirs are well used as a roosting area by gulls, mainly black-headed, and by wintering wildfowl. Canada geese, an introduced species in Britain, also use these reservoirs, both as a

breeding and roosting site.

Following the path through the woodland along the eastern side of Swinsty is a good place to practise being a nature detective. Grey squirrels live in these woods and the distinctively nibbled cones can be found everywhere. Nearby, where the water is shallow, grey herons can often be seen standing patiently waiting for eels or other food to come within reach of their long necks and sharp beaks.

Ancient packhorse bridges are

found throughout this part of Yorkshire and there are two within the valley, with another crossing Timble Ghyll. The latter is a replica and was built in 1967 in memory of a 'lifelong rambler', just one of many who know the beauty of this area.

Access: along public footpaths.
Location: from A59 Harrogate to Blubberhouses road take B6451 to Otley. After 1 mile turn W to Fewston along unclassified road.
Map: page 310, SE15.

Wandlebury

Cambridgeshire

This estate is in a commanding position on the crest of the Gog Magog Hills – on a clear day the towers of Ely Cathedral may be seen across the fields. The outlines of an Iron Age hill-fort are visible here and a display room shows the tools and jewellery which have been excavated.

Over the last 10 years the Cambridge Preservation Society has managed part of the estate as a nature reserve. From the well-marked nature trail there is an opportunity to see reserve management in practice. Some of the undergrowth in the mixed woodland has been cleared, fallen trees are allowed to decay slowly, and sheep have been reintroduced to crop the chalk meadow turf. Many chalk-tolerant species of trees have been planted. All this has led to more flowers and insects. Those visiting in summer are now more likely to see warblers and spotted flycatchers, and hear nightingales on the estate for the first time for many years.

Open: estate all year. Display room Apr to Oct daily; Sun pm only. Picnic area. Nature trails. Dogs on leads only.
Location: 4 miles SE of Cambridge, off A1307.
Map: page 306, TL45.

Washington Waterfowl Park

Tyne & Wear

An integrated part of the new town of Washington, the waterfowl park (a reserve of the Wildfowl Trust) is situated on the north bank of the River Wear, the southern boundary being the river bank itself. At this lower end of the park is the Wild Refuge, where a combination of ponds and low woodland forms an irresistible attraction to a wide variety of species passing over the landscape and through the river valley.

A nature trail winds through the hawthorn woodland and, part way along, a hide overlooks a well frequented feeding station where the 'customers' range from blue and great tits, as well

as the occasional great spotted woodpecker, to pheasants. The range of ponds created in the wild part of the park includes a shallow wader pond which is very attractive to the commoner waders such as redshank and snipe. During spring and autumn, when wader passage is at its height, they are joined by smaller numbers of less common birds.

The main attraction is the large collection of ducks, swans and geese which occupy most of the park's 103 acres. Wildfowl from every continent are included in the collection, but special emphasis is given to North America because of the connections between George Washington, first president of the United States of America, and Washington Old Hall nearby.

Open: all year daily (except 24, 25 Dec). Admission charge. Shop. Lecture Theatre. Picnic area. Facilities for disabled visitors. No dogs. WFT.
Location: S side of A1231 Sunderland to Washington road. 1 mile W of junction with A19.
Map: page 310, NZ35.

Weald Country Park

Essex

Part of this country park was a fort in the Iron Age. The abbots of Waltham Cross managed a deer park here before the Norman Conquest. Their monastery was dissolved by Henry VIII in 1540 and the estate became private property. Its hall, built in the same century, is thought to have played host to Mary Tudor: she may well have seen, as young trees, ancient oaks which survive today. The hall itself stood until 1950 when a fire was the final cause of its demolition. During the last war the park was used for military training. At present, it provides quiet enjoyment of the countryside for all. There is a wide selection of common plants, animals and woodland birds and two lakes.

Open: all year daily. Car park charge Apr to Oct. Information centre. Picnic area.
Location: at South Weald, reached via minor roads 1 mile W of A12 at Brentwood.
Map: page 306, TQ59.

Wellington Country Park & National Dairy Museum

Hampshire

Stratfield Saye House is the home of the Duke of Wellington, and the country park is situated in part of the estate, some distance from the house.

The lake is the main attraction of the park. A varied shoreline with grassy banks, areas of woodland, peninsulas, bays and islands gives it a varied and interesting appearance. Many woodland birds, particularly great spotted and green woodpeckers, nuthatches, treecreepers and several species of tit, may be seen or heard in the trees.

The National Dairy Museum is housed in buildings near the house. Its displays show 150 years of change within the industry. A charcoal burner's camp gives an insight into another early industry which has all but died out in Britain.

Open: *country park and National Dairy Museum Mar to Oct daily. Nov to Feb weekends only. (House Easter and weekends in Apr, then May to Sep daily (except Fri). Admission charge. Shop. Refreshments. Picnic area. Nature trails. Suitable for disabled visitors.* **Location:** *7 miles N of Basingstoke. Country park near Riseley E of A33. House W of A33.* **Map:** *page 306, SU76.*

Wembury Bay & the Yealm Estuary

Devon

The National Trust owns land on both sides of the Yealm Estuary. Unfortunately the ferry which used to cross the deep, tidal Yealm (pronounced Yam) has not functioned in recent years, so the visitor wishing to explore both properties is faced with a lengthy but pleasant drive.

Wembury Cliffs are probably best explored by parking near the church and walking out to Warren Point. The path loops round the Point then returns to Wembury along the cliff top. The views here are superb, with the Yealm winding away north through tree-covered slopes, Dartmoor beyond, and, in the other direction, the sea. Look for the tall Monterey pines growing beside the path. This is a low, shrubby tree in California where it grows wild, but it appears to thrive on the exposed south-west coasts of Britain. The cones of this pine can remain on the tree for more than 20 years, falling

only when the branch is broken by weight of snow, or by high winds.

Across the river, the long five-to seven-mile walk round the Yealm Woods and the Warren Cliffs provides more splendid river and coastal views and a variety of habitat. Passage Wood is a fine example of a hanging wood, while the alternative loop along the cliff edge in Brakehill Plantation can be a little hair-raising. In this part of Devon there were numbers of commercial rabbit-breeding sites and, both here on Warren Cliff and on Warren Point, the warreners' cottages remain. The strange parasitic plant called dodder grows on gorse hereabouts; when firmly attached its root withers and it takes its nutrition from its host.

Location: *5–6 miles SE of Plymouth. Wembury reached on minor roads S from Plymstock. Noss Mayo (for Yealm Woods and Warren Cliffs) reached on B3186 S from Yealmpton, then along minor roads. Car park beside coast road ¼ mile E of Worswell Farm, W of Noss Mayo. NT.* **Map:** *page 305, SX54.*

A cart in the National Dairy Museum. The inset shows an early milking machine

Wenlock Edge

Shropshire

The Edge runs in a straight line from Much Wenlock to Craven Arms, its mainly wooded scarp face being one of the best known features of the Shropshire landscape.

In marked contrast to the older and mainly acid rocks of which most of the Shropshire hill country is composed, the Edge consists entirely of Wenlock limestone. This supports a relatively diverse flora, including lime-loving plants such as thyme, rock rose, with its delightful buttercup-yellow flowers, yellow-wort, centaury and many others. Several species of orchid also

occur in the woods. Of these the broad-leaved helleborine and twayblade are frequently found. Another orchid, the bee orchid, does not grow in the woods, but favours dry, sunny banks including areas disturbed by quarrying.

A good road runs along the crest of the ridge for several miles in the northern section and affords spectacular views to the west and north. The National Trust owns some of the scarp woodland near to Much Wenlock and the Manor House at Wilderhope. Further south, at Edge Wood, is a nature trail provided by the Shropshire Trust for Nature Conservation.

Running parallel to Wenlock Edge to the south east is a second scarp, separated from the first by a pleasant valley called Hope Dale. This second ridge is higher but less continuous, being composed of softer Aymestrey limestone, which has been broken through by a series of streams feeding into the River Corve. This is a delightfully unspoilt area with many pretty villages and historic features. At Aston Munslow there is a country life museum in a house of great age and character.

Open: *White House Museum of Buildings and Continuous Family Life: Easter Sat to end Oct, Sat, Wed and bank holidays. Admission charge. Picnic area. Shop. Garden centre.*
Location: *Edge is between Much Wenlock and Craven Arms. Reached on B4371 from Church Stretton or Much Wenlock; B4368 from Craven Arms or Much Wenlock. White House Museum is on B4368, 6 miles NE of Craven Arms. Part NT. Part CNT.*
Map: *page 309, SO48/58/59.*

Wentwood Forest

Gwent

Jays, goldcrests, wrens and wood pigeons are among the common birds likely to be seen or heard while exploring this 2700-acre forest in the hills of Gwent. They share its sanctuary with badgers, grey squirrels and other mammals.

Wentwood was a royal hunting ground for the rulers of Gwent long before the coming of the Normans. In later years, strict laws governing the forest and its animals were enforced by the 'Speech Court' held at Foresters' Oaks, which is now one of Wentwood's four main picnic places. It was at Foresters' Oaks in 1829 that a man was last hanged for stealing sheep.

The forest's character has changed considerably since the 17th century, when thousands of its oaks were felled to provide timber for warships. It is now dominated by Japanese larch, Sitka spruce and other fast-growing species which produce marketable timber much faster

than the native hardwoods.

Wentwood's six waymarked walks range in length from one to four miles. They include a climb to the summit of Gray Hill – a splendid vantage point just over 900 feet above sea level – which passes a stone circle dating from the Bronze Age.

Access: *along public footpaths and forestry tracks.*
Open: *all year. Picnic areas. Waymarked walks. FC.*
Location: *on minor roads, N of A48 between Chepstow and Newport.*
Map: *page 305, ST49.*

West Runton & Beeston Regis Heath

Norfolk

South of the A149, between Cromer and Sheringham, the land achieves a height of 330ft – the highest point in Norfolk. The National Trust owns 110 acres of the attractive heath and woodland here, which includes some of the best views in Norfolk.

For centuries beacons formed the only 'early warning system' against possible invasion, and one of the twelve established in the county was sited here. All that remains of the site which, in this century, has acquired the name 'Roman Camp', is a small earthwork containing samples of a crude form of iron slag. Research has shown that the many overgrown pits in the area yielded ironstone which, from Saxon to medieval times, was smelted in primitive furnaces.

Within the relatively sheltered valleys of the area many trees have seeded themselves naturally, and small clumps of ash, oak, beech, mountain ash, wild cherry and holly can be found. The most common species are Scots pine and silver birch, the latter a constant problem due to its habit of encroaching rapidly on open land.

The mixed nature of the woods ensures that most com-

mon woodland species of birds are present. One attractive species which is increasing is the redpoll; in summer it is possible to see several males performing their slow, looping display flights together. No longer widespread, but, happily, surviving in the woods here, is the red squirrel. For the adder and the slow worm, open heath is an ideal habitat; fortunately the adder is usually observed in retreat from human contact!

Access: *on public footpaths through woodlands. Part NT.*
Location: *¾ mile S of West Runton station, between A149 and A148 roads.*
Map: *page 311, TG14.*

West Stow Country Park

Suffolk

This pleasant park lies on the southern edge of Breckland. Part is still heathland, a reminder of the vast sheep-walks and rabbit-warrens which once occupied nearly all of this part of East Anglia. The heath is bordered by deciduous and conifer woodland; there is a man-made lake and the River Lark forms the southern boundary. Men settled in this spot some 4000 years ago, and about 1500 years ago an Anglo-Saxon village was built here. The village came to an untimely end because its inhabitants had to abandon it as it was being inundated by windblown sand – a fate which befell many Breckland settlements through the centuries. Its foundations have been excavated and replicas of some of its buildings, reconstructed using Anglo-Saxon methods, can be visited.

No doubt much of the existing wildlife would have been familiar to those ancestors of ours. One bird, however, is a newcomer. The gadwall was introduced into Breckland in about 1850 and has since spread to many other regions. Look for a grey (male) or brown (female) duck with a brilliant white 'speculum' – a patch of feathers at the rear inner edge of the spread wing.

Open: *country park all year. Shop. Picnic areas. Suitable for disabled visitors. Reconstructed village Apr to Oct, Tue to Sat pm only; Sun and bank holiday all day. Admission charge. Nature trail. Waymarked walks in King's Forest just to NE.*
Location: *6 miles NW of Bury St Edmunds. Main car park on unclassified road from A1101 ¾ mile N of Lackford.*
Map: *page 306, TL77.*

Jay

The jay is one of the most colourful members of the crow family. It is common throughout England and Wales, but not so widespread in Scotland. Acorns are an important part of its diet; the jay often buries them, retrieving them when other food is scarce. Its harsh alarm call often betrays the presence of humans to other woodland residents.

Weyhill: the Hawk Conservancy

Hampshire

The Hawk Conservancy aims to encourage an appreciation of the beauty of birds of prey – a group which has been, and still is, under threat from pollution, game keeping activities, illegal egg-collecting and the unlicensed taking of birds for falconry. Disturbance and habitat loss have also played a part in their losses in previous decades.

At the Hawk Conservancy there are opportunities for photographing hawks, falcons, owls, eagles, vultures and kites from Britain and many other parts of the world. Some of the British species that can be seen are little, tawny and barn owls, peregrines and buzzards.

Weather permitting, some of the birds are exercised at regular intervals throughout the day so that visitors can enjoy and appreciate the skills of some of the finest flyers in the bird kingdom. A breeding programme is carried out at the Trust.

Open: *Mar to Oct daily.*
Admission charge. Shop. Suitable for disabled visitors.
Location: *Signposted off A303 ½ mile W of Weyhill roundabout (junction with A342).*
Map: *page 306, SU34.*

Wey Navigation

Surrey

Flowing from the Hampshire/Surrey border through Godalming and Guildford to Weybridge and the Thames, the River Wey pursues a serpentine course toward the end of its journey, and is not, perhaps, the obvious choice for canalisation. But Sir Richard Weston, who began the process in 1635, was a far-sighted and ingenious man – not the least of the many remarkable occupants of Sutton Place, the superb Tudor mansion which graces the north bank of the river near Guildford.

Some ten miles of artificial channel were dug; twelve locks, based on the Dutch system, were constructed, and the project was completed at a cost of £15,000 in 1653, a year after Weston's death. The four-mile section to Godalming was added in 1760. Commercial traffic reached its peak in the early years of the 19th century, but began to decline, as elsewhere, with the completion of the London to Guildford railway line. By the end of the First World War, traffic, mainly in agricultural produce, had virtually

Falconry yesterday, and today at the Hawk Conservancy

ceased, although grain continued to be transported to Coxes Mill until 1983.

Today the traffic is in pleasure boats, which in summer line the banks of this most attractive waterway. Surprisingly quiet and unspoilt almost before it has left Weybridge, the river is soon slipping through alder-fringed banks, beyond which stretch fields and water meadows. Close to the river are two fine and relatively unspoilt Norman churches at Wisley and Pyrford. The Anchor Inn, which is near both churches, is very popular at most seasons, with both river and road travellers. In contrast, a short distance away, the ruins of Newark Priory can seem very desolate on winter mornings when grey, cold mist cloaks the meadows.

The simplicity of lock-keepers' cottages contrasts with the magnificence of Sutton Place, and the route through Guildford is full of interest. Beyond the town are more water meadows and a quiet passage to Godalming, marked only by an occasional schoolboy using the tow path for running practice.

Location: *between Godalming and Weybridge, via Guildford. NT.*
Map: *page 306, SU94/TQ05/06.*

Wicken Fen

Cambridgeshire

The existence of Wicken Fen is a double tribute to the ingenuity of man. The success of the schemes to drain the great East Anglian fens has caused a contraction of the peaty soil, leaving Wicken as an 'island' some feet above the surrounding fields. To maintain this level the windmill on the site pumps water into, not out of, the fen. The result is one of the most important 'wetland' reserves in Western Europe. There is no need to follow a specific route at Wicken; the paths are broad and clearly defined, each giving a clear impression of the fen. A word of warning: by its very nature the ground here becomes wet at times and the local mosquitoes, of which there are many varieties, are merciless!

The mosquito is just one of an estimated 5000 insect species, including 700 butterflies and moths, and 200 spiders, of which six are restricted to Wicken. Perhaps the most spectacular of the insects is the British swallowtail butterfly. Nowadays it is confined to the fens, and the first sight of this lovely creature, with its bright yellow and black wings, is always memorable.

There are over 300 species of flowering plants at Wicken, in addition to large reed and sedge beds. These beds need constant control, as does the blackthorn and alder scrub known as 'carr'; left to themselves they would choke back other vegetation and pave the way for larger trees and a change of habitat to woodland.

This variety of habitats encourages the enormous variety of bird life. Almost 200 are listed in a recent pamphlet, and the range of species ensures that the bird-watcher will find something of interest at every season.

Wicken is not the most easily accessible of National Trust properties, but once discovered it draws visitors again and again. The richness of its wildlife is matched by its weather. On dark days, when huge banks of cloud are hurled across the wide East Anglian skies, the reeds hiss and groan as if in torment, but on soft, sunlit days when nothing stirs, tranquillity replaces violence, isolation becomes gentle seclusion.

Open: *all year daily. Admission charge. Dogs must be under control. NT.*
Location: *3 miles SW of Soham, 7 miles NW of Newmarket. On S side of A112 at W end of Wickham village.*
Map: *page 306, TL57.*

Willington Dovecote & Stables

Bedfordshire

Sir John Gostwick, Master of the Horse to Cardinal Wolsey, built a large mansion at Willington in the 16th century. All that can be seen today are the dovecote and barn (known as Henry VIII's stables). 'Seen' is the operative word, for, in the flat Bedfordshire farmland the dovecote is visible for some miles. It is a rather curious building with the appearance of one roof perched on another. It is also interesting in that the structure of the building consists of two square shapes 'pushed' together to make a rectangle.

The three-foot-thick walls have kidney-shaped nesting boxes for 1500 pigeons – not doves, which do not always return to the same place to sleep. Very little imagination is needed to realise the amount of damage this number of birds would do to crops, and it has to be remembered that local tenants were almost invariably forced to supply part of their crop to the lord of the manor. As he owned the pigeons, the tenants were, in effect, 'paying' twice. Naturally this was resented, particularly as the lord was unlikely to provide

The superb dovecote at Willington

any pigeon carcasses for the peasants during the winter months when fresh meat was doubly valuable. It says much about the British character that, in the face of this resentment, the practice of keeping dovecotes continued as long as it did, slowly dying out from the 18th century onwards.

The similarly designed barn or stable stands a few yards away, its main interest the inscription 'John Bunyan, 1650' carved in the stone fireplace in the loft.

Stacked reed at Wicken Fen

Open: *Apr to end Sep by written appointment only; and on some weekends without appointment. Admission charge. Accessible to wheelchair users, though floors are uneven. Dogs in car park only. Refreshments at weekend openings only. NT.*
Location: *in Willington village, 4 miles E of Bedford, just N of A603 Sandy road.*
Map: *page 306, TL14.*

Willoughbridge

Staffordshire

The Dorothy Clive Memorial Garden at Willoughbridge dates from 1939, when Colonel Harry Clive started to develop a woodland garden in a former sand and gravel quarry. Conditions were ideal for azaleas and rhododendrons, the soil being acid and freely-drained. A magnificent collection of these shrubs was planted, together with a large number of trees, including many rare cultivars.

Subsequent developments included shelter-belts, walls, screes and a water garden, and since 1967, a very wide variety of shrubs and flowering plants have been introduced.

Situated on the flanks of the Maer Hills, this is not only a lovely garden in itself, but is in a very pleasant situation with excellent views over the farmland to the south.

Open: *Mar to Nov daily. Admission charge.*
Location: *off A51, 1 mile W of junction with A53; 8 miles SW of Newcastle-under-Lyme.*
Map: *page 309, SJ73.*

the Saxons, and evidence of their presence can clearly be seen to the south of the village. Cut into the downs on the north side of Windover Hill is the largest representation of a human figure anywhere in Europe. This is the famous Long Man of Wilmington – 230 feet long and holding two staffs. No one is quite sure of the origins of the figure. Local legend says that it is where the giant of Windover Hill fell when he was killed by the giant of Firle Beacon. The earliest reference to the figure is a picture in an 18th-century manuscript showing it carrying a scythe and a rake, which might suggest an Iron Age fertility symbol. The figure has been elongated on the ground so that when viewed from the floor of the valley it takes on normal proportions – a remarkably subtle use of perspective.

South of the Long Man are

several round barrows which date back to 1700–1400 BC. Even older are the flint mines just over the crest of the hill and a long barrow dating back to 3500–2500 BC.

Wilmington Priory was founded in the 13th century by Benedictines. The priors built no church of their own, being content to use the parish church of St Mary and St Peter. The priory contains a mixture of architecture – the undercroft and the porch are 14th-century; the windows are Elizabethan; and there is an 18th-century staircase with a Chippendale balustrade. The Sussex Archaeological Society, which cares for the priory, has a small museum of agricultural implements here.

Open: *priory mid Mar to mid Oct, weekdays (except Tue) and Sun pm.*
Location: *Long Man ½ mile S of Wilmington village. Priory in Wilmington, 5 miles NW of Eastbourne.*
Map: *page 306, TV50.*

The garden at Mary Arden's House, Wilmcote, and (left) one of the outbuildings

Wilmcote: Mary Arden's House

Warwickshire

Shakespeare's mother, Mary Arden, was the daughter of a farmer called Robert Arden, who lived at Wilmcote near Stratford-upon-Avon. Their Tudor farmhouse is now one of a number of Shakespearian properties managed by the Shakespeare Birthplace Trust and visited by tourists from all over the world.

The house is well preserved and simply furnished and gives an authentic flavour of the period. In front is a delightful cottage garden with clipped box hedges, old-fashioned roses, lilacs and laburnum. Although most of the plants are more Victorian than Tudor, they provide a pretty setting for the picturesque half-timbered farmhouse.

The associated stone barns contain one of the best museums of rural life in the country.

Open: *all year daily (except Good Fri, 24–26 Dec and Sun Nov to Mar). Admission charge. Shop.*
Location *in Wilmcote, 3 miles NW of Stratford-upon-Avon.*
Map: *page 309, SP15.*

Wilmington Priory & the Long Man

East Sussex

Wilmington village was founded by the Saxons and taken over by the Normans. However, man had been active here long before

Wilton Windmill & Crofton Beam Engines

Wiltshire

Originally built in 1821, Wilton mill is constructed of brick and is five storeys high. It is Wiltshire's only remaining working windmill.

Just north of Wilton village is Wilton Water, which provides water for the Kennet and Avon Canal and attracts several species of waterfowl, including shoveler duck and a resident population of Canada geese.

Housed in Crofton Pumping Station, north-west of Wilton, are the famous Crofton Beam Engines. These two mighty steam engines are the oldest working beam engines in the world. One dates from 1812 and the other from 1845. The engines are operated from time to time and it is well worth a visit to see the six ton, 29ft beams rocking slowly and pumping water at the rate of six-and-a-half million gallons in a 24-hour period.

Open: *Wilton Windmill Easter to end Sep Sun and bank holidays pm only. Admission charge. Picnic area. Shop. Crofton Beam Engines Apr to Oct, Sun only (not working). In steam several weekends Apr to Oct (no specific times available). Admission charge for steam weekends only. Picnic area. Refreshments. Shop.*
Location: *windmill ¼ mile E of Wilton village, 6 miles SW of Hungerford. Crofton Beam Engines ¾ mile NW of Wilton on N side of Kennet and Avon Canal.*
Map: *page 306, SU26.*

Wimpole

Cambridgeshire

Wimpole Hall is the largest and most spectacular country house in Cambridgeshire. It stands in a landscaped park which still bears witness to the work of three great designers, and, as a bonus, the Home Farm is now grazed by rare breeds of livestock.

The house is set on a slight rise in surrounding flat countryside. Until Dutch Elm disease destroyed it in recent years, there was a magnificent double avenue of elm trees running from the road towards the house. This South Avenue is being replanted by the National Trust, using lime trees grafted from those in the park. Continuity is thus being maintained, as the limes were planted by Charles Bridgeman, who also conceived the South Avenue. Among other designers who influenced Wimpole Park as it is today were the ubiquitous 'Capability' Brown and Humphry Repton.

The National Trust has established circular walks in the park, and a walk from the car park leads to the Home Farm. Here the impressive thatched buildings designed by Sir John Soane have been restored. In the Great Barn is a superbly refurbished collection of farm machinery and implements of the last two centuries.

Several rare breeds of farm animals can be seen grazing in the park. These and others may be studied more closely in the paddock in the walled garden on the way to the farm, where more are kept in the outbuildings. Look out for the attractive White Park and British White cattle. The British White forms the largest herd at Wimpole and may be descended from wild or feral stock. Among several horned breeds of sheep at the farm are Hebridean, Herdwick and the spectacularly horned Portland, which arrived with the Spanish Armada, swimming ashore from the wrecks. Goats, pigs and poultry are kept in and around the farmyard.

Open: *Apr to Oct (limited opening early and late in season). Closed Fri. Admission charge. Refreshments. Picnic area. Shop. Suitable for disabled visitors. NT.*
Location: *at Arrington, 8 miles SW of Cambridge, off A603; 6 miles N of Royston, off A14.*
Map: *page 306, TL35.*

Windsor Great Park

Berkshire and Surrey

The remnants of what was once a vast royal hunting forest, Windsor Great Park and Forest still gives an impression of what this ancient tract of heath, woods, streams, glades and thickets must have been like in medieval times.

Of outstanding interest are the oaks. Some of these gnarled giants, which were once pollarded, may be 800 years old; many are certainly over 500 years old. Most of these trees are now hollow hulks with a 'stag-headed' appearance, but still carrying shoots of leaves each summer. The first record of oaks being planted at Windsor was in 1580 in order to maintain timber for the fleet. Some of these 'younger' trees can be seen today in Cranbourne Park, between Cranbourne Tower and Rangers Lodge. As well as oaks, there are many ancient beeches in the park.

Such trees play a vital role in supporting Britain's insect population. Nearly 300 different insect species feed on oak, and many more are associated with it, including the spectacular white admiral butterfly and many moths and beetles. Britain's largest beetle, the stag beetle, is found at Windsor, along with over 2000 other kinds of beetle. Many of these are dependent upon the ancient oaks and beeches; some of them are only found in Windsor Forest and in the Great Park, and some only in the rotting wood of the oldest trees. Many other invertebrate groups such as flies, bees, wasps, crane flies and moths are well represented.

With so many insects, it is not surprising that insectivorous birds are also numerous, especially warblers and woodpeckers. On the more heathy areas, nightjar, hobby, stonechat and woodlark can be found. There is a well-studied population of sparrowhawks scattered throughout the forest. All the dead wood provides excellent habitats for fungi, although flowering plants are not too well represented.

Among the mammals that can be seen here are red deer, which were removed from the park during the Second World War, but have recently been reintroduced. Roe deer are common, especially in the southern area of the forest, and muntjac are also resident. Fallow deer occasionally pass through the area.

The beautifully coloured mandarin duck, which has become naturalised in Britain since the 1920s, can be seen on Virginia Water. Shoveler, teal, wigeon, pochard, tufted duck and gadwall can also be seen, along with mallard.

Within the park are the Savill Garden and the Valley Gardens. Both are woodland gardens, and both have superb displays of shrubs such as rhododendrons, magnolias and camellias.

Open: *all year. Admission charge for Savill Garden; Car park charge for Valley Gardens.*
Location: *extends S from Windsor to A329 at Virginia Water. The A332 Windsor to Bagshot road passes through park and has parking at several places.*
Map: *page 306, SU96, 97.*

Wirral Country Park

Cheshire and Merseyside

Step into the booking hall at Hadlow Road Station, near Willaston on the Wirral peninsula, and you are back in the 1930s. The timetables, tickets and furnishings are all authentic. On the platform are milk churns and wooden trolleys. The atmosphere is so real that you expect to hear the hiss of steam and a train whistle. But there are no trains!

In fact, this preserved railway station is one small part of a 12-mile-long country park that follows the long-disused railway from West Kirkby to Hooton. From West Kirkby to Neston the old line runs along the Dee Estuary, the haunt of vast congregations of ducks and wading birds outside the breeding season. Beyond Neston the track turns inland.

As well as the estuary sands, the park has mud flats, cliffs, open embankments and wooded clearings – a range of habitats that is home to a variety of wildlife.

There are numerous access points, car parks and picnic sites, a visitor centre at Thurstaston and a Ranger service to help the visitor.

Open: *all year daily. Visitor centre. Picnic sites.*
Location: *on W side of Wirral Peninsula, W of A540; Willaston section is E of A540, S of B5133.*
Map: *page 309, SJ 27/28/37.*

Witley

Surrey

It is rare for the depradations of modern man to have an advantageous effect on the wildlife community of an area, yet this has happened at Witley. Until the First World War it had a limited range of habitats and vegetation, but in both wars the commons of Witley and Milford were used as army camps. The importing of soil and materials for use on these sites changed considerably the ecology of the area.

As an example of the variety of species, look in high summer for the purple flowers of bell heather and, close by, wild majoram – typical acid-loving and alkali chalkland plants respectively. The same variation is apparent in the tree and shrub population; the mixture of deciduous and pine woods encourages a wide range of bird species. Among the large variety of insects, the butterfly family is particularly well represented. Expect to see small heath, common blue, red and white admiral, peacock and many others during the spring and summer seasons.

From August to November Witley is a mecca for mycologists – those who study fungii – for they will probably find many interesting species, from the tiny, delicate mycena to the large beefsteak, firmly attached to deciduous trees.

Open: *information centre Apr to Oct daily (except Mon and Fri); Nov weekends, pm only. Parking charge for NT non-members. Shop. Nature trails. NT.*
Location: *7 miles SW of Guildford, between A3 and A286 roads.*
Map: *page 306, SU94.*

Wittersham: Stocks Mill

Kent

Stocks Mill is a fine example of a post mill, and is believed to date from 1781. There is some evidence, however, that the mill may have been transferred to its present site from East Kent at that time; it being not uncommon for a mill of this type to be moved to take advantage of prevailing winds.

The construction explains how a mill of this sort could be moved cross-country without too much difficulty. The mill itself is balanced on a huge oak post, which in turn is supported by a framework of wooden bars and beams known as a trestle. The trestle rests on brick piers,

and so stable is the mill that there is no need for the trestle to be anchored. So the mill could be dismantled, removed, and reconstructed leaving only the brick piers behind. At Stocks Mill the trestle was later enclosed in a brick roundhouse.

Certain parts of the interior have had to be reconstructed, but enough of the original remains to see how the milling was done. The main interest, however, is the functioning of the post mill; and the new sails even show the twist that was necessary to increase the power of the wind. In its early days, the sails would have been covered with sail cloth, but the mill finished its working life with spring sails, where the framework of the sail is fitted with louvres which adjust to the force of the wind by the tension of the springs.

Open: *Jun to Sep Sun pm only. Admission charge.*
Location: *4¼ miles N of Rye on B2082 road.*
Map: *page 306, TQ92.*

Also known as lady's smock and milkmaids, the cuckoo flower is found in damp areas such as at Woods Mill

Wolvesnewton Model Farm

Gwent

The name may suggest a quaint cluster of large-scale toy buildings, but Wolvesnewton – nestling amid the rolling hills of Gwent – is a model in the other sense of the word. It was built for the Duke of Beaufort at the end of the 18th century and then represented the ultimate in 'modern' agricultural architecture. The farm is dominated by a huge, cross-shaped barn.

The farm buildings house a wide-ranging collection of folk exhibits covering many aspects of country life since the Victorian era, from a horse-drawn wagon to toys and saucy postcards. They are complemented by a maker of traditional corn dollies and other craft workers.

Open: *Jul to Sep daily; Easter to Jun Sat, Sun and Mon. Also Oct and Nov Sun pm only. Admission charge. Refreshments. Shop. Suitable for disabled visitors.*
Location: *4¼ miles SE of Usk, on unclassified road off B4235.*
Map: *page 305, SO49.*

Wolves Wood

Suffolk

This RSPB reserve is an ancient woodland, one of the few surviving fragments of the vast forests that once covered the country. With such an ancestry, it has many interesting plants and animals. There are five species of orchids, including the odd-looking bird's nest orchid and the violet helleborine. Over twenty kinds of butterfly live here.

Nightingales thrive in the areas of coppice especially managed for them. They are easily heard day and night in May and June, but very quiet thereafter. Patience is needed to see them and the same is true of the hawfinch, despite its bulk, as it sits in the tops of the hornbeam trees. The pools are a good place to wait for bathing and drinking birds. The woodland is damp, and mud and mosquitoes should be allowed for.

Open: *at all times.*
Access: *along marked trails. No dogs. RSPB.*
Location: *2 miles E of Hadleigh, N of A1071 Ipswich road.*
Map: *page 306, TM04.*

The Wrekin

Kingfisher

Usually seen as a flash of iridescent blues and greens as it flies low and fast over water, the sight of a kingfisher is bound to be a highlight of any outing in the countryside. When perching, often on a branch projecting over the water, it can be much more difficult to see. Then its bright plumage blends remarkably with its surroundings. The kingfisher often uses the same perches, where it watches and waits for fish or water-living insects.

Woodbury Common

Devon

Woodbury Common is the collective name for several commons that lie on a five mile long heathland ridge to the north of Exmouth. Although the heaths are largely open, covered for the most part by heather and gorse, there are also scattered clumps of trees and a few plantations.

Insects are numerous on the common, and include dragonflies, moths and butterflies. One of the most attractive of the latter is the silver-washed fritillary. Stonechats are often seen perching on the gorse, and nightjars are to be found here in summer. Their churring call is most likely to be heard in late evenings between May and August.

One of the commons in this group, Aylesbeare, is an RSPB reserve. Another, Colaton Raleigh, is a firing range and care should therefore be taken.

Location: 4 miles NNE of Exmouth. Part RSPB.
Map: page 305, SY08.

Woods Mill

West Sussex

This 18th-century water mill is the headquarters of the Sussex Trust for Nature Conservation. It contains an extensive exhibition and information centre illustrating many aspects of the wildlife and geology of Sussex and of the natural history of the nature reserve in which it lies.

A nature trail takes the visitor through a typical Wealden wood where an area is managed as a demonstration of coppice-with-standards. The trees here include oak, ash, beech, birch, field maple, hawthorn, hazel, holly and wild service tree over a carpet of wood anemones, bluebells, celandines and primroses.

Lime-rich water draining from the downs has produced a fine range of wetland habitats, including streams, ditches, marshes, a lake and a reed bed. The marsh and lake edge are particularly rich in plants, including wild angelica, cuckoo flower, yellow iris and hemp agrimony.

The lake attracts kingfishers and herons, while the alders and willows at its edge provide winter food for flocks of finches. The reedbed is alive with the songs of reed buntings and sedge-warblers in spring and summer. Dragonflies and damselflies are the most spectacular of the many kinds of insect which flourish in this area.

Open: Easter to end Sep Tue, Wed, Thu and Sat pm only; Sun and bank holidays all day. Admission charge. Information centre. Shop. CNT.
Location: 1½ miles S of Henfield on A2037, at junction with Horn Lane.
Map: page 306, TQ21.

Wormley Wood

Hertfordshire

Ancient woodlands are among Britain's most endangered habitats; it has been estimated that between 30 and 50 per cent of them have been lost since 1939. Wormley Wood is almost entirely ancient, and is the largest oak-hornbeam woodland still largely remaining in its semi-natural state. Designated as a Grade 1 Site of Special Scientific Interest, Wormley is especially important for the structure of its woodland, rather than for the diversity of its flora. However, the range of mosses here is unique and there is also an interesting stream system.

Fortunately, Wormley's future is secure, as it is a property of the Woodland Trust. The Trust's work in conserving the wood includes replanting with deciduous trees an area that was clear-felled and planted with conifers in the 1970s.

Access: on public footpaths. WLT.
Location: W of A10 between Cheshunt and Hoddesdon, on unclassified roads.
Map: page 306, TL30.

The Wrekin

Shropshire

One of the best known and most conspicuous features of the Shropshire landscape, the Wrekin is a hill of solidified volcanic lavas and ashes formed in the pre-Cambrian era. Rising 1334ft above a flattish plain, it is not surprising that it formed a link in the chain of bonfires which were lit to warn of the sailing of the Spanish Armada in 1588.

The steep slopes of the Wrekin and of adjoining Ercall Hill are largely covered in woodland of sessile oak, birch and rowan. There are many pleasant walks through these woods and up to the summit, which offers magnificent views all around. At the summit is a large Iron Age fort.

Location: W outskirts of Telford New Town, 2 miles SW of Wellington.
Map: page 309, SJ60.

Wye Valley

Welsh Borders

Britain has many beautiful rivers, but few can match the tranquil beauty of the Wye. It rises in the heart of Wales then flows 130 miles to join the Bristol Channel near the Severn Bridge. The lower reaches, from Symond's Yat to Chepstow, are particularly attractive and can be explored by following the waymarked Wye Valley Walk which runs northwards to Ross-on-Wye.

Rich in natural and human history, the Wye Valley Walk combines superb scenery with the opportunity to visit Goodrich, Chepstow and other medieval castles built to guard the border. Much older attempts to hold the Welsh in check are recalled by stretches of Offa's Dyke (see page 204), the earthwork whose name recalls an 8th-century King of Mercia.

South of Symonds Yat, where Yat Rock is the Wye's most famous viewpoint, the river has spent the past two million years carving itself a series of spectacular gorges. Woodlands clamber up steep slopes punctuated by such dramatic crags and cliffs as the Seven Sisters and the great ramparts of naked rock overlooking Longhope Reach, upstream from Chepstow. Another rock, the Devil's Pulpit, is said to be the point from which Satan yelled insults at the monks of Tintern Abbey.

The Seven Sisters tower majestically above St Martin's Pool, where kingfishers bring splashes of vivid colour to the gorge, and are reached by paths through the oaks and beech trees of Lord's Wood. Buzzards, jackdaws, woodpeckers and ravens nest in the wood, sharing its secret places with fallow deer.

On the eastern side of the river as it nears the tidal Severn, is the Forest of Dean (see page 107).

Elsewhere, other paths make it equally easy to explore the Wye's lower reaches. Three of the most popular walks start at the former railway station between Tintern Parva and Brockweir in the heart of the Wye Valley Area of Outstanding Natural Beauty. Opened in 1876, the line stopped carrying passengers in 1959 and was completely closed five years later. Tintern station was eventually restored and is now an attractive picnic area and information centre with information on the area, including walks and an exhibition devoted to the Wye Valley Line. The walks are from one to two and a half miles and take from 30 to 75 minutes to complete. One provides fine views of Tintern Abbey, the lower Wye's most celebrated ruin.

Further downstream is Wynd Cliff, a carboniferous limestone cliff which rises 700ft above the River Wye on its west banks above Chepstow. The view from the top is spectacular. A fairly steep path through ancient woodland (or more shortly by numerous steps) leads to a famous viewpoint – the Eagle's Nest. From here the confluence of the Wye with the Severn, and the distant Cotswold and Mendip hills, can be seen.

The walk passes through sessile oak and small-leaved lime woods on the lower gentler slopes, but then gives way to yew and beech on the steeper scree slopes and on the cliff face. Scattered amongst these dominant trees are occasional maple and wych elm as well as several species of whitebeam. The varied ground flora includes a number of rare and local plants including

Wye & Crundale Downs

Kent

Wye and Crundale Downs are very steep; doubtless this is how they escaped the plough when lesser slopes went under cultivation. But without grazing by sheep and rabbits, the downs rapidly become hawthorn scrub and, later, woodland, just as they once were thousands of years ago when Neolithic man began to clear them of their tree cover. Fortunately grazing has been resumed at Wye to encourage the chalkland specialities, particularly orchids and butterflies.

From the top of the escarpment is a fine view towards the High Weald. The upper slopes are wooded with ash and hawthorn, home in summer to whitethroats, nightingales and turtle doves. Hawthorn is attractive to many insects, and here can be found all sorts of shield-bugs and spiders, as well as butterflies and moths.

Out on the grassy slopes above the Devil's Kneading-trough, one of those strange dry combes so typical of the chalk, one may see the superbly camouflaged dark green fritillary butterfly, or one of the rare blue butterflies.

Carefully protected against sheep and man alike are the or-

Dark green fritillary, one of the grassland species of butterfly found on Wye and Crundale Downs

herb Paris, upright spurge, fingered sedge and common wintergreen.

On sunny days butterflies are abundant and about half the species known in Britain occur, including speckled wood, holly blue and silver-washed fritillary. There is a wide range of woodland birds, including buzzards and five species of tits. Herons (which nest in a colony below) may also be seen, as may cormorants, which roost in the trees and fish in the River Wye, which is tidal at this point.

Open: *Tintern Information Centre Easter to Dec daily. Shop. Refreshments. Picnic area. Tintern Abbey all year daily (except Sun am Oct to Mar). Admission charge.*
Location: *lower Wye Valley extends from Chepstow in S to Ross-on-Wye in N. Reached from A466 and B4228 roads.*
Map: *page 305.*

---

chids. They are somewhat erratic in their appearance from year to year, but a number of varieties may usually be seen.

Location: *4½ miles NE of Ashford; 1¾ miles SE of Wye on unclassified Hastingleigh road. NCC.*
Map: *page 306, TR04.*

Wye College Agricultural Museum

Kent

A magnificent black weatherboarded tithe barn houses this fascinating collection derived from the Wye Agricultural College.

Constructed towards the end of the 1300s, using oak timbers

that are even earlier, the barn housed produce paid as tithes to Christ Priory at Canterbury.

The central area of the barn is occupied by large items like harvesters and wagons. Notable are the hay wagons and a four-wheeled cart, which were used locally. In the bays around this collection are various smaller pieces of equipment, a number of which were used on the college farm. Although most of these were made in the last hundred years, they represent the last stage of a continuum where designs hardly changed in 400 years, until the tractor replaced the ox and the horse. Many hand tools are also on display.

Adjacent to the barn is a 19th-century oast-house, which has machinery relating to hop farm-

ing on the ground floor and hand tools in the loft.

Open: *May to Sep Wed pm only; also Sat in Aug pm only.*
Location: *in Brook, on unclassified road 4 miles NE of Ashford.*
Map: *page 306, TR04.*

Wyre Forest

Herefs & Worcs/Shropshire

A surprisingly large area of the former royal hunting forest of Wyre has survived and it now ranks alongside the New Forest and the Forest of Dean as one of the largest areas of ancient woodland left in England.

Formerly coppiced regularly to produce wood for charcoal

burning and oak bark for tanning, substantial areas have been converted to conifers, but more than 2500 acres of mainly oak forest still exist. Nearly 1000 acres of that is now a National Nature Reserve managed by the Nature Conservancy Council. The Council's main objective is to perpetuate the native woodland with its associated plants, birds, insects and other animal life. To achieve that it is actively regenerating parts of the area, while allowing other parts to grow to and beyond maturity for the benefit of plants and creatures that require old, dead or rotting timber.

Apart from the woodland itself, other special features of the reserve and the forest generally are the numerous old meadows and orchards around the fringes, and the Dowles Brook and its tributaries. Together, all these various habitats support a wealth of wildlife and are a superb place for the naturalist. The Forestry Commission's Information Centre at Callow Hill is the ideal introduction to the forest, its history, wildlife and crafts.

Open: *information centre all year, except public holidays. Picnic site. Suitable for disabled visitors.*
Access: *cars are not permitted in forest, but there is an adequate car park at Callow Hill and a number of smaller ones alongside B4194. Area is well served by public footpaths. Part NCC. Part FC.*
Location: *forest is W of Bewdley, reached from B4194 and A456 (information centre on A456).*
Map: *page 309, SO77.*

The Yorkshire Dales

Sweeping landscapes and a pattern of dry stone walls are essential components of the unique Dales character. Stone-built villages, farms and barns on valley sides and beside rivers are further elements in the composition. Dominating the western skyline is the backbone of England, the Pennines.

Yorkshire Dales National Park

Stretching from Stainmore Forest – close to the old Roman road from Brough to Barnard Castle (now the A66 and A67) – down to Skipton in the south, and across from Sedbergh westwards to Great Whernside, is the 680-square-mile Yorkshire Dales Na-tional Park. It encompasses the finest of the Dales scenery.

Swaledale
Largest of the Dales, Swaledale is a good place to begin to under-stand the landscape, the character of the villages and the people. The pattern of farming life shapes the land throughout the Dales, and in Swaledale sheep graze the fells, with cattle in the fields along the valley floor. The meadows here grow rich crops of hay and a few – too few – have never seen modern fertilizers, so still contain an impressive array of wild flowers in the spring and summer. Using the material that is easily available, all the build-ings in the dale are of stone and blend beautifully with the land-scape.

The road through the dale stays close to the River Swale from its birthplace on Birkdale Common in the Pennines, near Keld, all the way to the ancient market town of Richmond. A network of footpaths radiates out and through the dale and pro-vides excellent walking. One fea-ture which is immediately obvi-ous is the pattern of dispersed stone hay barns, particularly in the upper part of the dale. They originally had the double func-tion of storing hay in the top half and cattle in the lower half during the long winter months.

Progress along Swaledale is by way of the seemingly evenly spaced villages. All around is the typical wildlife of the dale: wheatears, summer visitors from Africa, feeding in the cropped grass, yellow wagtails in the damper meadows, dippers on the river and swallows, house mar-tins and swifts around the farm and village buildings.

High above Swaledale on the road from Thwaite over the moors to Wensleydale, are a series of deep holes known as the Buttertubs. Typical of limestone country, these water-formed holes are marvellous places for hart's-tongue and a variety of other ferns. Back in Swaledale itself is Gunnerside. The gill which gives the village its name can be followed northwards up through a beautiful little valley. High up the valley are many re-mains of the lead-mining indus-try which was once so important here. Men have lived and worked in the Dales for thousands of years, and evidence of that is to be seen in the huge earthwork called Maiden Castle on the fell-side near Reeth. The ideal way to discover the influence man has had more recently, particularly by mining and farming, is by a

visit to the Swaledale Folk Museum on Reeth Green (open Easter to October).

Wensleydale

Over the ridge to the south lies Wensleydale, completely different in character from its northern neighbour. Wensleydale is a broad farming dale with very little history of lead mining. The river that has carved its way out of the Pennines here is the Ure, so perhaps the dale derives its name from the former importance, in medieval times, of the village of Wensley.

One thing the two dales do have in common is the marvellous array of footpaths they both possess. Wensleydale is particularly well served, with access to its many side valleys, and a footpath running the full length of the dale, from the Moorcock Inn to Middleham. The first stop on this route should be Hawes, where, in the Station Yard, two information centres help visitors to appreciate the life of the Dales. The Upper Dales Folk Museum depicts life on the farms, while the Yorkshire Dales National Park Centre helps visitors understand the whole environment of the Park as well as providing details of current activities (both are open April to October).

A diversion on the unclassified road from Hawes over Buttertubs Pass to Thwaite, can be made to Hardrow Force; at 100ft said to be the highest unbroken waterfall in England. It is possible to walk behind the falls, which are set in a lovely natural amphitheatre. For a more strenuous walk, follow the path (part of the Pennine Way, see page 225) to the top of Great Shunner Fell, where the views are superb. To the west lie the Lakeland fells and to the south the classic Dales hills of Whernside, Ingleborough and Pen-y-ghent. Down in the dale again, a side road from Bainbridge leads to one of Yorkshire's two natural lakes, Semer Water.

Further on in Wensleydale, is Aysgarth, an attractive village given added beauty by Aysgarth Falls (see page 298). Wensley itself is a lovely little place with a delightful village green.

Wharfedale and Littondale

The River Wharfe has its source in several becks high up on the moors of Langstrothdale Chase. For its first mile it flows through remote Langstrothdale, entering Wharfedale at Buckden. It flows south past Kettlewell and the limestone crags at Kilnsey and on down through Strid Gorge (see page 301) to leave the National Park just beyond Bolton Priory. Littondale can be followed along unclassified roads leading northwestwards from Wharfedale to the north of Kilnsey. It is one of the most secluded of the Dales; at its head is Halton Gill, from where strenuous paths lead across to Pen-y-ghent.

Malham Cove

Limestone dominates the land formation in the Park and this is most evident in the west. Perhaps the best known of the natural features, and the most spectacular, is Malham Cove. This huge natural amphitheatre is the result of land movements millions of years ago on the Mid Craven Fault line. The top of Malham Cove is a superb example of limestone pavement, where, as in the Buttertubs, the grikes, or clefts in the rock, contain a wide variety of ferns. Malham village is nearby and the National Park Information Centre here (open April to October) helps to interpret the beauty of the surrounding landscape. From the village there are a number of circular walks to Malham Tarn (see page 300), two miles to the north.

Ribblesdale and the Three Peaks

Further west again lies Ribblesdale, curving its way between Pen-y-ghent and Ingleborough. Apart from the infant River Ribble, the dale carries the Carlisle to Settle railway line, one of the most spectacular rail journeys in Britain. The most famous stretch of the line is in the wild country of Blea Moor, where it travels over the 24 arches of the Ribblehead Viaduct. It is the cost of maintenance of this graceful structure which may eventually force the closure of the line.

Forming a triangle of flat-topped hills with Ingleborough and Pen-y-ghent is Whernside, sitting astride the border with Cumbria. Horton-in-Ribblesdale is the usual starting point for the Three Peaks Walk taking in these famous hills.

A walk in this limestone country is an experience never to be forgotten, not only for the beauty of the landscape, but for the wildlife which finds a home there. Curlews and lapwings are widespread, skylarks seem to be everywhere and wheatears and ring ouzels are common enough on the higher ground. The high ground is also the place for interesting plants such as bilberry and cloudberry, with the elusive bird's eye primrose a bonus on some of the fells where the soil is especially calcareous.

In spite of the last county boundary changes, meaning that Dentdale and Baugh Fell in the north-west corner of the Park became part of Cumbria, the Yorkshire Dales National Park is truly Yorkshire in every respect, and an area where the county of the broad acres truly lives up to its name.

What to See

AYSGARTH
One of Wensleydale's prettiest villages, Aysgarth has the attraction of a very picturesque waterfall. It tumbles over a series of limestone steps among wooded river scenery. Close by is the Yorkshire Museum of Carriages and Horse Drawn vehicles. Here, housed in an old stone-built mill, is a collection of over 50 coaches, carriages and other vehicles. Also in Aysgarth is a National Park visitor centre, where information is available.

Open: *Old Mill Carriage Museum July to Oct daily; Easter to June weekends and bank holidays. Admission charge. Refreshments. Shop. National Park Centre Apr to Oct daily.*

CLAPHAM: THE REGINALD FARRER TRAIL
Named in honour of Reginald Farrer, a famous botanist and plant collector who was born at Ingleborough Hall in 1880, this fascinating nature trail explores the valley of the Clapham Beck. It begins in Clapham village.

Near the start of the trail is the lake, created by the Farrer family as a landscape feature in the early 19th century. Among the many superb specimen trees that can be seen around the lake are holm oak, beech, Scots pine and holly. Less common trees include Weymouth pine, red oak and western hemlock. Further up the beck are dense stands of rhododendrons, planted by Reginald Farrer in pockets of acidic

An archive picture of a sheep fair at Settle (below) and an auction at Hawes today (above)

soil occurring naturally in the predominantly limestone rock.

At Beck Head is the entrance to Ingleborough Cave, one of the most impressive show caves in the North of England. It was opened up by Farrer and his brothers in 1837. The trail now returns, via Trow Gill, back to Clapham along a track on the other side of the beck. A footpath for the adventurous, and well-equipped, leads from Trow Gill up to Gaping Gill, a pothole 365ft deep. From there the path continues up to Ingleborough.

DODD FELL AND FLEET MOSS

An unclassified road from Hawes to Langstrothdale gives superb views of these wild landscapes, which include the highest fells in the Dales. A Roman road runs between Dodd Fell and Oughtershaw Side; this is as good a route as any to penetrate the moors. The Pennine Way runs along the Roman road from Cam Fell, veering off to run along the west side of Dodd Fell.

The wildlife here is typical of the Dales; meadow pipits are probably the commonest birds, and skylarks are frequent. In the breeding season, curlews, golden plovers, redshanks and lapwings are all likely to be present. Black-headed gulls might be seen on the tarns.

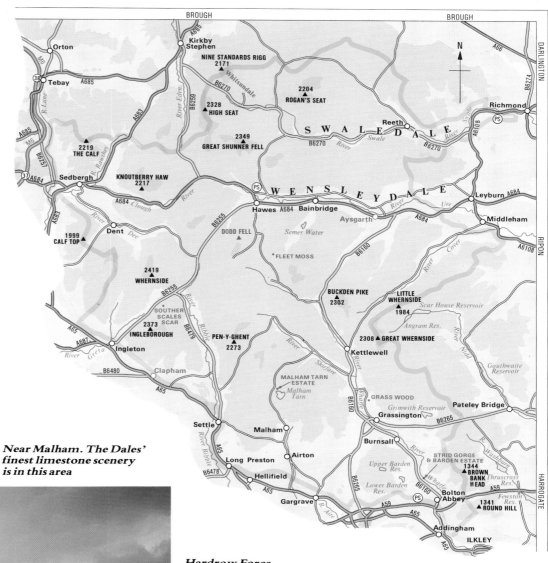

Near Malham. The Dales' finest limestone scenery is in this area

Hardrow Force

GRASS WOOD

This wood, on the east side of Wharfedale, consists largely of ash and it is an example of the kind of woodland that once covered many of the limestone slopes in the Dales. There is an interesting ground flora here, with such plants as mountain melick, stone bramble and lily-of-the-valley. Woodland birds are numerous, and since the River Wharfe is so close, water-loving birds are also to be seen. The wood is leased by the Yorkshire Wildlife Trust and lies just off the unclassified Conistone road, to the north-west of Grassington.

CNT/FC.

MALHAM TARN ESTATE

Man has a long connection with Malham. There is evidence that Stone Age man came to the tarn in summer, and there are extensive remains of field and hut systems dating from the Bronze and Iron Ages. Local place names suggest that Norsemen settled the wild country of Malham Moor during the Dark Ages. In the Middle Ages the Percy family handed the area to the monks of Fountains Abbey. Much later, in the 18th century, Malham Tarn was the site of an important cattle fair, while lead mines flourished in the moors. Today the estate consists of over 4000 acres including the tarn and Tarn House, both let by the National Trust to the Field Studies Council. In addition to organising a range of courses each year for those with an interest in natural history, the Council has provided a nature walk.

For much of its length the walk follows the route of the Pennine Way round the northern edge of the tarn, a natural lake formed some 10,000 years ago. The sheep which graze on the poor grass of the area are likely to be Swaledale or Dalesbred – believed to have been developed by the monks. There are few woodlands in the dale, but along the path are some groupings of sycamore, hawthorn, yew and larch.

In the boggy areas around the tarn are plants such as the beautiful grass of parnassus, with delicate white blooms on long stems from July to October. On the heavily grazed but unimproved pastures beside the path, wild thyme spreads its delightful scent, and yellow birdsfoot trefoil competes with the purple and yellow-splashed white flowers of eyebright – used as a cure for eye complaints by herbalists. Although tiny, eyebright can bloom in such profusion as to transform the area in which it grows. Where grazing is pre-

vented, tufted hair grass flourishes, smothering all but a few strong plants.

In winter the tarn attracts many water birds including ducks such as shoveler, pochard and goosander. Land birds tend to be concentrated in the area around Tarn House and the west boathouse, where young trees are growing. Here, swallows, warblers and spotted flycatchers join resident wagtails, tits and chaffinches in summer.

The estate can be approached by road from Settle or Malham village, but for the adventurous the old drovers' road known as Mastiles Lane runs for five miles over the moors from Kilnsey to the Tarn. The most popular route for walkers is from the village along the Pennine Way past the spectacular Malham Cove, and up the strange 'moonscape' of the dry valley beside Ewe Moor.

NT.

SEMER WATER

This is the largest natural lake in Yorkshire. It is over half a mile long and lies above Wensleydale, to the south of Bainbridge. Although very popular as a tourist destination and water-sports centre in summer, it is a quiet place outside the tourist season and can be excellent for wildfowl. The broad flat valley above the head of the lake is Raydale, enclosed by high and lonely fells, many of whose lower slopes are covered in extensive conifer plantations.

SOUTHERSCALES SCAR

Lying on the north-western slopes of Ingleborough, Southerscales Scar is a reserve of the Yorkshire Wildlife Trust and is primarily of interest for its limestone pavements. Great cracks, known as grikes, have been worn in the limestone by water over the course of millions of years, and in these grows a rich variety of flowers and ferns. There are also areas of limestone and acidic grassland and blanket bog on the reserve. Among the especially interesting plants to be found here are lily-of-the-valley, dark-red helleborine and baneberry. The bird life is typical of the Dales; among those that might be seen are golden plovers, curlews, wheatears and ravens. The reserve can be reached on public

Traditional farming pattern in Swaledale

moor, and therefore dogs must always be kept on leads. There are two 19th-century reservoirs on the moor; they can be seen on the exhilarating trek across to Rylstone Fell.

WHITSUNDALE

This small dale, formed by the Whitsundale Beck tumbling down the southern slope of Ravenseat Moor, is a miniature version of the two main northern dales, Swaledale and Wensleydale, and in fact it opens out into Swaledale close to Keld. A well-trodden footpath beginning at the River Swale follows the shoulder of the dale to the small packhorse bridge at Raven Seat, where it turns back along the beck following the opposite bank. Heading up the dale, the great bulk of Ravenseat Moor lies ahead, and just out of sight beyond it is Tan Hill, the highest inn in England.

The beck tumbles over small cascades on its way down the dale, with plenty of places to stop and picnic, or just to sit and enjoy the sights and sounds of the tumbling water. Pied wagtails are common along the beck, finding nest sites in dry stone walls and among rocks. The brighter grey wagtails are also present in smaller numbers and are very noticeable with their yellow and grey plumage and long tails.

The grassland of the dale is closely cropped by both sheep and rabbits, and this close sward is ideal for the wheatear.

footpaths from Chapel le Dale, but permits are required away from the paths.

CNT.

STRID GORGE AND BARDEN ESTATE

Between the ruins of 15th-century Barden Tower and the evocative remains of Bolton Priory, the River Wharfe rushes and tumbles through the Strid Gorge. Old woodlands stand on both sides of the river, and among the birds that might be seen are redstarts, pied flycatchers, woodcocks and dippers. A nature trail can be followed along the river.

Walks on to the moorland to the north-west of the river can be made by following the gloomily named Valley of Desolation. About a mile up the valley is Park Waterfall, a spectacular 50ft cascade. From here the path continues on to the open moors of Barden Fell and reaches Simon's Seat, which gives superb views over Wharfedale.

On the other side of the river is Barden Moor, much of which is accessible on public footpaths. Much of it is managed as a grouse

Lapwing

Lapwings are familiar autumn and winter visitors to many parts of Britain. They breed throughout the country, but as a result of changing agricultural practices the numbers nesting in the south have declined substantially. They still breed in large numbers in areas such as the Yorkshire Dales.

Yealmpton: Devon Shire Horse Centre

Devon

Until well into the 20th century nearly all farmwork now done by tractor was done with the assistance of heavy horses. Most famous of all heavy horses are the Shires – huge, immensely strong, yet gentle and patient. A big stallion might weigh as much as a ton and be nearly six feet tall from ground to withers. Such horses were used for all the really hard work on the farm – ploughing, harvesting, pulling laden carts and wagons. Tractors had replaced virtually all heavy horses by the mid 1950s, but some farms kept them on, and many were kept for recreational purposes. In recent years there has been a considerable revival of interest in the big horses, and they can be seen working on a good number of farms and demonstration areas up and down the country.

One such place is the Shire Horse Centre near Yealmpton. Here Shire horses can be seen all year round, whether working in the fields or at rest in the stables. As well as the charm and fascination of the horses, there are collections of tack and old farm machinery, farm walks across the 60-acre site, cart rides, and an active craft centre.

Open: *all year (except Christmas week). Admission charge. Refreshments. Shop. Picnic area. Suitable for disabled visitors.*
Location: *¾ mile SE of Yealmpton, S of A379 at Dunstone.*
Map: *page 305, SX55.*

Ynys-Hir

Dyfed

This 630-acre estate was a private nature sanctuary before it was bought by the Royal Society for the Protection of Birds in 1968. Overlooked by the Snowdonia National Park's southern hills, it runs down to the lovely Dyfi Estuary (see page 87) and provides a very wide range of habitats, from salt marsh and peat bog to mixed woodland and rocky outcrops.

Nearly 70 bird species breed at Ynys-Hir every year, mainly in and near the ancient oakwoods. They include pied flycatchers, blue, great, coal and willow tits, redstarts, nuthatches, goldcrests, treecreepers, wood warblers and woodpeckers. Buzzards, kestrels, sparrowhawks and other birds of prey may also be seen. The handsome red kite, recognised by its forked tail, is most likely to be spotted in spring and summer.

Many birds pause at Ynys-Hir during the 'passage' seasons, while winter brings such visitors as wigeon, mallard, teal, red-breasted merganser, tufted duck and white-fronted geese.

Open: *Apr to Sep Wed, Thu, Sat and Sun; Oct to Mar Sun and Wed. Admission charge for RSPB non-members. Reserve centre. Nature trails. RSPB.*
Location: *5 miles SW of Machynlleth off A487 road, in Furnace village opposite mill (entrance signposted).*
Map: *page 309, SN69.*

Zennor Head

Cornwall

In one sense it may seem illogical to include Zennor in a book where plant and animal life are stressed. No trees grow on this harsh land and the plant community has not yet recovered from the effects of a fire which raged some years ago in the peaty subsoil of the heathland. There is, however, a rare sense of communion with nature here, an almost eerie rapport with the ancient landscape.

On rough days the sea can rise 100ft through a blow hole below Zennor Head, while the sound of great boulders being bounced and crashed about in the water is clear and frightening above the wind. But, by contrast, the phenomena called the 'green flash' may be experienced. On quiet summer days when the clarity and purity of light and colour in sky and land seem matchless, watch the sun set and observe, if you are lucky, the flash of emerald green light which floods across the western sky. Most visitors are not privileged to see the 'flash', but Zennor itself will remain in the memory.

Access: *by public footpaths to cliffs and moorland. NT.*
Location: *4½ miles W of St Ives off B3306 at Zennor.*
Map: *page 304, SW43.*

Zennor Head

ATLAS KEY

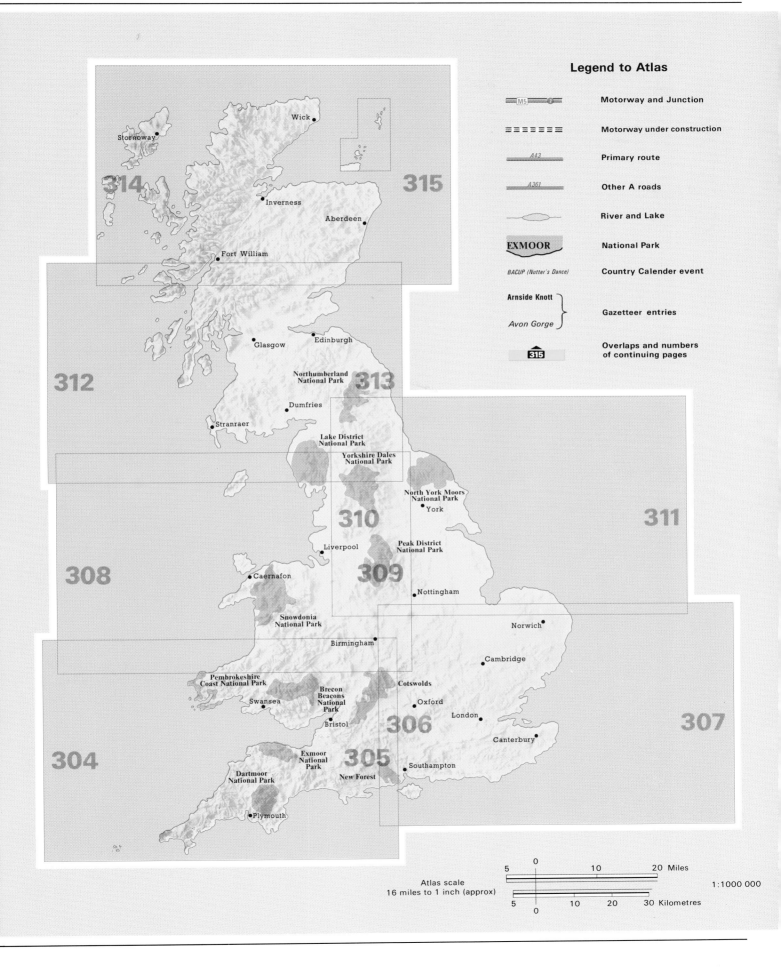

Legend to Atlas

M5 〔7〕	Motorway and Junction
▭▭▭▭▭▭	Motorway under construction
A43	Primary route
A361	Other A roads
⌇⬭	River and Lake
EXMOOR	National Park
BACUP (Nutter's Dance)	Country Calender event
Arnside Knott ⎫ ⎬ *Avon Gorge* ⎭	Gazetteer entries
▲ 315	Overlaps and numbers of continuing pages

314   315

Wick

Stornoway

Inverness

Aberdeen

Fort William

312

Glasgow   Edinburgh

Northumberland National Park   313

Dumfries

Stranraer

Lake District National Park

Yorkshire Dales National Park

North York Moors National Park

311

310

York

Liverpool

Peak District National Park

308

309

Caernafon

Nottingham

Snowdonia National Park

Norwich

Birmingham

Cambridge

Pembrokeshire Coast National Park

Brecon Beacons National Park

Cotswolds

Swansea

Oxford

London

Bristol

306

Canterbury

307

304

Exmoor National Park

305

Southampton

Dartmoor National Park

New Forest

Plymouth

Atlas scale
16 miles to 1 inch (approx)

5   0   10   20 Miles

5   0   10   20   30 Kilometres

1:1000 000

The letters and figures at the end of each entry are Ordnance Survey grid references.

Page
10 Afan Argoed Country Park *SS89*
11 Alscot Farm Agricultural Museum *SS41*
13 Arlington Court *SS64*
15 Ashleworth Barn *SO82*
16 Ashley Countryside Collection *SS61*
18 Avebury *SU17*
18 Avon Gorge & Leigh Woods *ST57*
19 Avon Valley Woods *SX74*
19 Axe Estuary *SY29*
27 Berry Head Country Park *SX95*
27 Bickleigh Mill Craft Centre & Farm *ST90*
28 Blackdown Hills *ST11*
29 Blagdon Reservoir *ST55*
32 Bodmin Moor *SX28*
36 Branscombe & Salcombe Regis *SY28*
37 Breamore House Countryside Museum *SU11*
37 Brean Down & Axe Estuary *ST25*
38 The Brecon Beacons
44 Brockhampton Woods *SO65*
44 Brokerswood: Woodland Park & Phillips Countryside Museum *ST85*
45 Brownsea Island *SZ08*
47 Burton Mere *SY58*
51 Caldicot Castle & Country Park *ST48*
51 Camel Estuary *SW97*
53 Castle Woods *SN62*
54 Cenarth Fishing Museum *SN24*
56 Cheddar Gorge & Caves *ST45*
57 Chesil & The Fleet *SY67*
57 Chew Valley Lake *ST66*
59 Christchurch Harbour & Hengistbury Head *SZ19*
62 Coate Water Country Park *SU18*
64 Cornwall Coast Path
65 Cotehele *SX46*
66 The Cotswolds
73 Cranborne Chase *ST91*
74 Cwmcoy: Felin Geri Mill *SN34*
75 Cwmllwyd Wood Nature Reserve *SS69*
75 Dart Estuary *SX84/85*
76 Dartmoor National Park
83 Dolaucothi *SN64*
83 Dolebury Warren *ST45*
84 Dorset Coast Path
87 Durlston Country Park *SZ07*
92 Ebbor Gorge *ST54*
92 Ebbw Forest *ST29*
95 Exe Estuary & Dawlish Warren *SX98/SY08*
96 Exmoor National Park
102 Fal Estuary *SW83/84*
103 Farway Countryside Park *SY19*
106 Fontmell Down *ST81*
107 Forest of Dean *SO60/61*
109 Fourteen Locks Picnic Area *ST28*
109 Fowey Valley *SX26*
114 Gelli Aur Country Park *SN51*
115 Glastonbury: Somerset Rural Life Museum *ST53*

117 Golden Cap Estate *SY39/49*
118 Gower Peninsula *SS48/49/58/59/68/69*
119 Grand Western Canal *SS91/ST01*
120 Great Haldon *SX88/98*
121 Gwenffrwd/Dinas Nature Reserve *SN74*
125 Hartland *SS22*
126 Haugh Wood *SO53*
129 Hayle Estuary *SW53*
130 Hele Mill *SS54*
130 Helford River *SW72*
131 High Ham Windmill *ST43*
132 Hobby Drive *SS32*
140 Isles of Scilly *SV91*
141 Kenfig Pool & Dunes *SS78*
144 Kingswear *SX94/95*
154 Lands End *SW32*
155 Lanhydrock *SX06*
158 The Lizard *SW61/71*
158 Llandegfedd Reservoir & Farm Park *ST39*
160 Llysyfran Reservoir Country Park *SN02*
164 Loe Pool & Bar *SW62*
168 Longleat *ST84*
170 Lulworth Cove *SY87*
171 Lundy *SS14*
174 Maiden Castle *SY68*
174 Malvern Hills *SO74*
176 Marazion Marsh *SW53*
176 Margam Country Park *SS88*
176 Marlborough Downs *SU17*
180 Morgan's Hill *SU06*
180 Morte Estate *SS44*
181 Morwellham Quay *SX46*
182 Mount Edgcumbe Country Park *SX45*
187 Newent: Birds of Prey Centre *SO72*
189 New Forest
204 Offa's Dyke
207 Otter Estuary *SY08*
209 Parke *SX87*
217 Pembrey Country Park *SN40*
218 Pembrokeshire Coast National Park
224 Pencarrow Head *SX15*
226 Pentire Head *SW98*
226 Pewsey Downs National Nature Reserve *SU16*
228 Plym Bridge Woods *SX55*
229 Pont Pill *SX15*
230 Porthkerry Country Park *ST06*
230 Portland *SY67*
231 Priston Watermill *ST66*
231 Purbeck Heaths *SZ08*
232 Quantock Hills & Fyne Court *ST13/ST23*
233 Radipole Lake *SY68*
234 Ravenshill Wood *SO75*
235 The Ridgeway
236 Roundway Hill Covert *SU06*
240 St. Agnes *SW64*
241 St Fagans; Welsh Folk Museum *ST17*
243 Salcombe *SX73*
243 Salisbury Plain *SU04*
244 Savernake Forest *SU26*
244 Scolton Manor Country Park & Museum *SM92*
248 Sherborne: Worldwide Butterflies & Lullingstone Silk Farm *ST51*
252 Slapton Ley *SX84*
252 Slimbridge: Wildfowl Trust *SO70*
260 Somerset Levels & Moors *ST43/44*

261 Somerset & North Devon Coast Path
261 South Devon Coast Path
264 Stithians Reservoir *SW73*
264 Stock Hill *ST55*
266 Stover Country Park *SX87*
269 Summercourt: Dairyland & Cornish Country Life Museum *SW85*
269 Sutton Bingham Reservoir *ST51*
272 Tamar Estuary & St John's Lake *SX45/46*
272 Tamar Lakes *SS21*
273 Taw/Torridge Estuary *SS42/43/53*
276 Tondu: Glamorgan Nature Centre *SS88*
277 Tredegar House & Country Park *ST28*
278 Trelissick *SW83*
278 Trencrom Hill *SW53*
280 Upton Country Park *SY99*
280 Usk Valley Walk *ST39/SO21*
286 Wembury Bay & The Yealm Estuary *SX54*
287 Wentwood Forest *ST49*
292 Wolvesnewton Model Farm *SO49*
293 Woodbury Common *SY08*
294 Wye Valley *ST59, SO50/51/52*
302 Yealmpton: Devon Shire Horse Centre *SX55*
302 Zennor Head *SW43*

COUNTRY CALENDAR
134 *Ale Tasting & Bread Weighing Ceremony SX76*
122 *Bread and Cheese Dole SO50*
282 *Burning the Ashen Faggot SS94*
113 *Candle Auction ST30*
270 *Carrying the Tar Barrels SY09*
122 *Cheese Rolling Ceremony SO81*
271 *Courts Leet & Baron SX76/77*
48 *Court of Purbeck Marblers SY98*
172 *Cranham Feast & Deer Roast SO81*
282 *Distribution of New Pennies ST61*
134 *Druid's Ceremony SU14*
123 *Grovely Forest Rights SU03*
122 *Helston Furry Dance SW62*
122 *Hobby Horses SW97 & SS94*
48 *Hurling the Silver Ball SW96*
173 *Marhamchurch Revel SS20*
173 *Marldon Apple Pie Fair SX86*

238 *Mop Fair & Runaway Mop Fair SP25*
238 *Pack Monday Fair ST61*
185 *Painswick Ancient Clipping SU80*
239 *Punkie Night ST41*
135 *Robert Dover's Games & Scuttlebrook Wake SP13*
271 *Turning the Devil's Boulder SS40*
21 *Wassailing the Apple Trees ST04*
185 *Widecombe Fair SX77*

25 Beltring: Whitbread Hop Farm *TQ64*
26 Bernwood Forest *SP61*
27 Bewl Bridge Reservoir *ST90*
27 Bix Bottom *SU78*
28 Black Down & Marley Common *SU93*
30 Blean Woods *TR16*
30 Blenheim Park *SP41*
31 Boarstall Duck Decoy *SP62*
33 Bohunt Manor *SY83*
33 Bookham Commons *TQ15*
35 Bough Beech Reservoir *TQ44*
35 Box Hill *TQ15*
35 Bradfield Woods *TL95*
36 Bradgate Park & Swithland Woods *SK51*
46 Burnham Beeches *SU98*
47 Burton Dassett Hills Country Park *SP35*
55 Chalfont St Giles: Chiltern Open Air Museum *SU99*
55 Chanctonbury Ring *TQ11*
58 Chichester Harbour & East Head *SU70*
58 Child Beale Wildfowl Trust *SU67*
60 Cissbury Ring *TQ10*
60 Clayton: Jack & Jill Windmills *TQ31*
63 Cogges Farm Museum *SP31*
64 Coombe Hill *SP80*
66 The Cotswolds
74 Cudmore Grove Country Park *TM01*
75 Danebury Ring *SU33*
82 Daventry Country Park *SP56*
83 Ditchling Beacon Common *TQ31*
85 Dungeness *TR01*
86 Dunstable Downs *TL01*
87 Dunwich Heath *TM46*
90 Earsham: The Otter Trust *TM38*
91 Easton Farm Park *TM25*
93 Elmley Marsh *TQ96*
94 Epping Forest *TQ49*
95 The Essex Way
95 Etchingham: Haremere Hall Shire Horses *TQ72*
104 Fence Wood *SU57*
105 Ferry Meadows Country Park *TL19*
105 Finchampstead Ridges *SU86*
105 Fingringhoe Wick *TM01*
106 Fleet Pond *SU85*
110 Fowlmere *TL44*
110 Frensham Common *SU84*
110 Friston Forest *TQ50*
111 Fritton Lake Country Park *TG40*
117 Goodwood Park *SU80/81*
119 Grafham Water *TL16*
120 Great Coxwell: The Great Barn *SU29*
120 Gressenhall: Norfolk Rural Life Museum *TF91*
124 Halnaker Mill *SU09*
126 Hastings Country Park *TQ81*
126 Hatfield Forest *TL52/53*
128 Haxted Mill *TQ44*
129 Headley Heath *TQ25*
131 Hindhead Commons *SU83*
136 Ickworth *TL86*
136 Inkpen Hill & Coombe Gibbet *SU36*
137 Irchester Country Park *SP96*
138 Isle of Wight *SZ58*
141 Kennet Valley *SU36/46*
142 Keyhaven, Pennington & Hurst *SZ39*

143 Kingley Vale *SU81*
145 Knole *TQ55*
154 Langstone Harbour *SU60/70*
155 Lee Park Valley *TQ39*
156 Leith Hill *TQ14*
156 Lepe Country Park & Calshot *SZ49/SU40*
156 Lightwater Country Park *SU96*
157 Limpsfield Common *TQ45*
157 Lings Wood *SP86*
157 Littlewick Green: Courage Shire Horse Centre *SU88*
166 London
169 Lowestoft *TM59*
169 Ludshott *SU83*
171 Lymington River & Reed Beds *SZ39*
174 Maidenhead & Cookham Commons *SU88*
175 Mapledurham House & Mill *SU67*
178 The Mens *TQ02*
179 Minsmere *TM46*
186 Naphill Common & Bradenham Woods *SU89*
186 Nap Wood *TQ53*
189 New Forest
192 Norfolk Broads
193 Norsey Wood Country Park *TQ69*
193 Northaw Great Wood *TL20*
194 North Downs Way *SU84/TR34*
194 North Kent Marshes *TQ77/87*
204 Northward Hill *TQ77*
204 North Warren *TM45*
204 Nower Wood *TQ15*
204 Nutley Post Mill *TQ42*
204 Oakham: Rutland Farm Park *SK80*
205 Old Winchester Hill *SU62*
207 Ot Moor *SP51*
207 Ouse Washes *TL48/59*
208 Pagham Harbour *SZ89*
209 Pamber Forest & Silchester Common *SU66*
209 Pang Valley *SU57*
216 Peakirk Waterfowl Gardens *TF10*
226 Petworth Park *SU92*
227 Pitstone Windmill *SP91*
227 Pixey & Yarnton Meads *SU41*
229 Polegate Windmill & Milling Museum *TV50*
230 Port Lympne *TR13*
231 Portsmouth Harbour *SU60*
233 Queen Elizabeth Country Park *SU71*
235 The Ridgeway
235 Romney Marsh *TQ92*
236 Roswell Pits, Ely *TL58*
236 Rutland Water *SK80/90*
237 Rye Harbour *TQ91*
241 St Leonards Forest *TQ23*
242 Salcey Forest *SP75/85*
242 Sandwich Bay Area *TR36*
244 Sandy: The Lodge *TL14*
244 Saxtead Green Windmill *TM26*
246 Selborne Hill *SU73*
246 Seven Sisters Country Park *TV59*
249 Shipley Mill *TQ12*
250 Singleton: Weald & Downland Open Air Museum *SU81*
252 Slindon Estate *SU90*
253 Snelsmore Common *SU47*
261 South Downs Way
262 South Swale *TR06*

263 South Woodham Ferrers: Marsh Farm *TQ89*
263 Sowley Pond *SZ39*
264 Stockgrove Country Park *SP92*
265 Stodmarsh *TR26*
265 Stoke Bruerne: Waterways Museum *SP74*
266 Stonor Park *SU78*
266 Stour Estuary *TM13/23*
267 Stowmarket: Museum of East Anglian Life *TM05*
273 Thaxted Windmill *TL63*
273 Theale Gravel Pits *SU67*
274 Therfield Heath *TL34*
274 Thetford Forest *TL88*
274 Thorndon Country Park *TQ69*
275 Thursley Common *SU94*
275 Tilford: Old Kiln Agricultural Museum *SU84*
275 Titchfield Haven *SU50*
276 Toppesfield Museum of the Working Horse *TL73*
277 Toys Hill *TQ45*
278 Trosley Country Park *TQ66*
280 Upper Hamble Country Park *SU41*
281 The Viking Way
285 Wandlebury *TL45*
285 Weald Country Park *TQ59*
286 Wellington Country Park *SU76*
287 West Stow Country Park *TL77*
288 Weyhill: The Hawk Conservancy *SU34*
288 Wey Navigation *SU94, TQ05/06*
288 Wicken Fen *TL57*
289 Willington Dovecote & Stables *TL14*
290 Wilmington Priory & The Long Man *TV50*
291 Wilton Windmill & Crofton Beam Engines *SU26*
291 Wimpole *TL35*
291 Windsor Great Park *SU96/97*
292 Witley *SU94*
292 Wittersham: Stocks Mill *TQ92*
292 Wolves Wood *TM04*
293 Woods Mill *TQ21*
293 Wormley Wood *TL30*
294 Wye & Crundale Downs *TR04*
295 Wye College Agricultural Museum *TR04*

COUNTRY CALENDAR
238 *Bell Ringers Feast* *SU42*
112 *Biddenden Dole* *TQ83*
146 *Black Cherry Fair* *TQ06*
147 *Blessing of the Waters* *TR16*
112 *Bottle Kicking & Hare Pie Scramble* *SP79*
239 *Conker Knockout Competition* *TL08*
283 *Crookham Mummers Play* *SU75*
147 *Ebernoe Horn Fair* *SU92*
271 *Firing the Poppers* *SP83*
113 *Hocktide Festival* *SU36*
184 *Hop Hoodening* *TR15*
49 *Olney Pancake Race* *SP85*
112 *Running Auction* *TF02*
49 *Shrovetide Football* *SP89*
88 *Skipping* *TQ50*
20 *Straw Bear Festival* *TL29*
147 *Swan Upping on the Thames*
88 *Tichborne Dole* *SU53*
239 *Titchfield Carnival* *SU50*
271 *Wroth Silver* *SP47*

Page
12 Andover: Finkley Down Farm & Country Park *SU34*
15 Arundel Wildfowl Trust *TQ00*
15 Ashdown Forest *TQ43*
16 Ashridge Estate *SP91*
16 Aston Rowant *SU79*
22 Barnwell Country Park *TL08*
23 Beachy Head *TV59*
24 Beaulieu River *SU04*
24 Bedgebury Pinetum *TQ73*

Page

10 Acton Scott Working Farm Museum *SO48*
11 Alderley Edge & Nether Alderley Mill *SJ87*
13 Arnside Knott *SD47*
22 Bardsea Country Park *SD37*
23 Beacon Fell Country Park *SD54*
31 Blithfield Reservoir *SK02*
45 Bromsgrove: Avoncroft Museum of Buildings *SO96*
47 Bwlch Nant-yr-Arian Forest Visitor Centre *SN78*
52 Cannock Chase *SJ91/SK01*
54 Ceiriog Valley *SJ23*
54 Cemlyn *SH39*
56 Cheddleton Flint Mills *SJ95*
60 Clee Hills *SO68*
61 Clent Hills Country Park *SO98*
73 Cregneash: Manx Open Air Folk Museum *SC16*
73 Croft Centre *SO44*
82 Delamere Forest *SJ57*
83 Devil's Bridge *SN77*
86 Dunham Massey *SJ78*
87 Dyfi National Nature Reserve *SN69*
90 Earl's Hill *SJ40*
91 Eaves Wood *SD47*
93 Elan Valley *SN96*
106 Forest of Bowland *SD65*
108 Formby & Ainsdale *SD20/21*
119 Graig Fawr *SJ08*
125 Hartlebury Castle Museum *SO87*
126 Hawksmoor Nature Reserve *SK04*

129 Hebden Water & Hardcastle Crags *SD92*
143 Kingsbury Water Park *SP29*
145 Kinver Edge *SO88*
145 Kinwarton Dovecote *SP15*
148 The Lake District National Park
284 Lake Vyrnwy *SJ01, SH92*
155 Leighton Moss *SD47*
158 Llangollen Canal *SJ24*
159 Llanrhaeadr Waterfall *SJ02*
159 Llanymynech Hill *SJ22*
160 Lleyn Peninsula *SH44*
160 Llyn Clywedog *SN88/98*
165 Loggerheads Country Park *SJ16*
169 Long Mynd & Carding Mill Valley *SO49*
171 Lyme Park *SJ98*
176 Marbury Country Park *SJ67*
178 Martin Mere *SD41*
178 Merrington Green Nature Trail *SJ42*
180 Moel Famau Country Park *SJ16*
180 Morecambe Bay *SD46*
180 Mortimer Forest *SO47*
182 Mow Cop *SJ85*
186 Newborough Warren National Nature Reserve *SH46*
204 Offa's Dyke
205 Old Oswestry *SJ23*
208 Padarn Country Park *SH56*
210 The Peak District
216 Peckforton Hills *SJ55*
224 Penmon *SH68*
225 Pennine Way
225 Penrhos Nature Reserve *SH28*

228 Plynlimon *SN78*
233 Ramsey: The Grove Rural Life Museum *SC49*
234 Ribble Estuary *SD32/42*
244 Scarlett Visitor Centre *SC26*
246 Shallowford: Izaak Walton's Cottage *SJ82*
248 Shropshire Meres *SJ43*
255 Snowdonia
262 South Stack Cliffs *SH28*
262 South Walney *SD26*
264 Stiperstones *SO39*
266 Strata Florida *SN76*
267 Stratford upon Avon Canal *SP17–SP25*
268 Stretton Mill *SJ45*
272 Tatton Park *SJ78*
273 Tegg's Nose Country Park *SJ97*
278 Tregaron Bog *SN66*
286 Wenlock Edge *SO48/58/59*
289 Willoughbridge *SJ73*
290 Wilmcote: Mary Arden's House *SP15*
291 Wirral Country Park *SJ27/28/37*
293 The Wrekin *SJ60*
295 Wyre Forest *SO77*
302 Ynys-Hir *SN69*
296 The Yorkshire Dales

COUNTRY CALENDAR

185 *Abbots Bromley Horn Dance SK02*
89 *The Nutters' Dance SD82*
270 *Soul-Caking Play SJ67*

The peaks of the Snowdon massif from Llanberis Lake

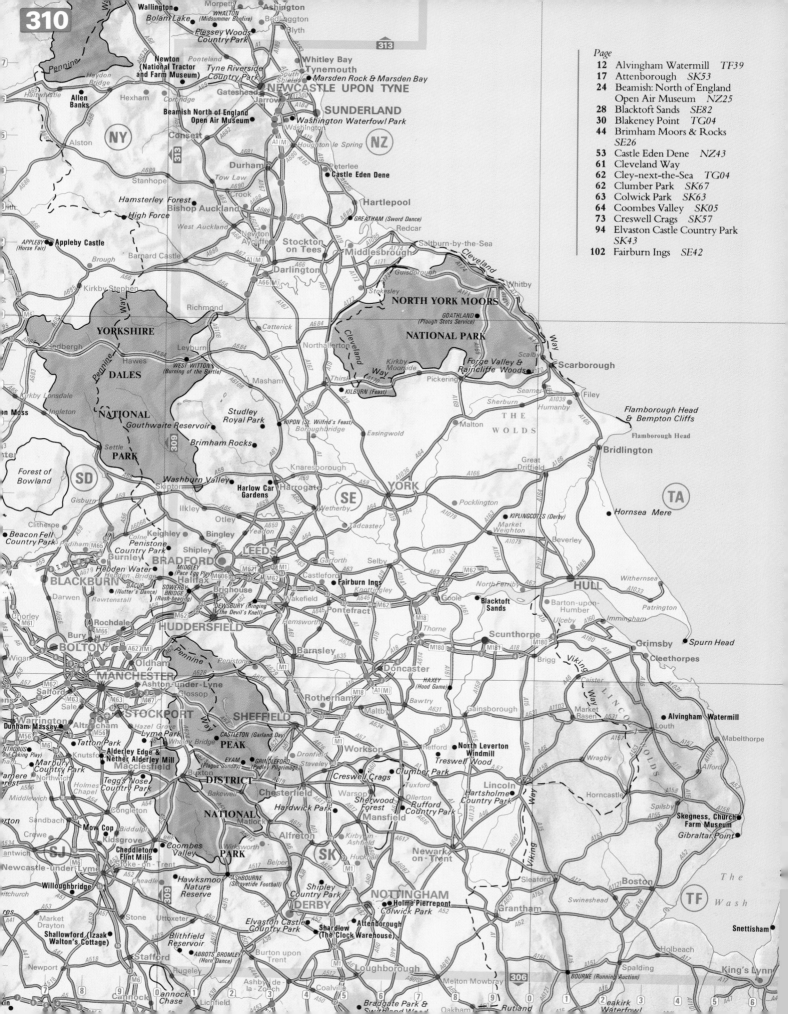

Page
12 Alvingham Watermill   *TF39*
17 Attenborough   *SK53*
24 Beamish: North of England Open Air Museum   *NZ25*
28 Blacktoft Sands   *SE82*
30 Blakeney Point   *TG04*
44 Brimham Moors & Rocks   *SE26*
53 Castle Eden Dene   *NZ43*
61 Cleveland Way
62 Cley-next-the-Sea   *TG04*
62 Clumber Park   *SK67*
63 Colwick Park   *SK63*
64 Coombes Valley   *SK05*
73 Creswell Crags   *SK57*
94 Elvaston Castle Country Park   *SK43*
102 Fairburn Ings   *SE42*

104 Felbrigg TG13
106 Flamborough Head &
    Bempton Cliffs TA17/27
108 Forge Valley & Raincliffe
    Woods SE98
114 Gibraltar Point TF55
117 Gouthwaite Reservoir
    SE16/17
124 Hamsterley Forest NZ02/03
124 Hardwick Park SK46
125 Harlow Car Gardens SE25
126 Hartsholme Country Park
    SK96
129 Heacham: Norfolk Lavender
    Garden TF63
132 Holkham TF84/94
132 Holme Pierrepont SK63
133 Hornsea Mere TA14
133 Hunstanton TF64
177 Marsden Rock & Marsden Bay
    NZ46
187 Newton: Hunday National
    Tractor & Farm Museum
    NZ06
192 Norfolk Broads

193 Norfolk Wildlife Park TG01
194 North Leverton Windmill
    SK78
196 Northumberland National Park
200 North York Moors National
    Park
210 The Peak District National Park
224 Penistone Hill Country Club
    SE03
225 Pennine Way
236 Rufford Country Park SK66
242 Sandringham TF62
248 Shardlow: The Clock
    Warehouse SK43
248 Sherwood Forest SK66
249 Shipley Country Park SK44
251 Skegness: Church Farm
    Museum TF56
253 Snettisham TF63
263 Spurn Head TA41
269 Studley Royal Park SE26
276 Titchwell Marsh TF74
278 Treswell Wood SK77
281 The Viking Way
285 Washburn Valley SE15

Dovedale and Ilam Rock, Peak District

285 Washington Waterfowl Park
    NZ35
287 West Runton & Beeston Regis
    Heath TG14
296 The Yorkshire Dales

COUNTRY CALENDAR

134 *Appleby Horse Fair* *NY62*
173 *The Burning of Bartle* *SE08*
123 *Castleton Garland Day* *SK18*
283 *Greatham Sword Dance*
    NZ42

20 *Haxey Hood Game* *SX79*
147 *Kilburn Feast* *SE57*
88 *Kiplingcotes Derby* *SE84*
89 *Pace Egg Play* *SE02*
146 *Padley Pilgrimage* *SK27*
173 *Plague Sunday* *SK27*
21 *Plough Stots Service* *NZ80*
282 *Ringing the Devil's Knell*
    SE22
185 *Rushbearing* *SE02*
172 *St Wilfrid's Feast Procession*
    SE37
49 *Shrovetide Football* *SK14*

The Norfolk Broads

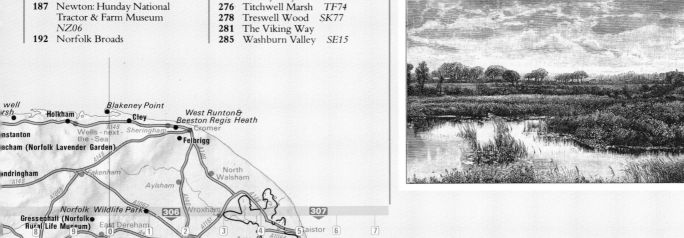

Page

10 Aberlady Bay   *NT48*
11 Allen Park · *NY76*
12 Appleby Castle Conservation
    Centre   *NY62*
13 Argyll Forest Park   *NS20*
14 Arran   *NR93*
17 Auchindrain Museum of
    Country Life   *NN00*
22 Bass Rock   *NT68*
25 Beecraigs Country Park
    NT07
26 Ben Lawers   *NN63*
33 Bolam Lake Country Park
    NZ08
34 Border Forest Park   *NY69*
51 Caerlaverock   *NY06*
58 Chillingham Park   *NU02*
72 Cragside Country Park   *NU00*
74 Culzean Country Park   *NS20*
84 Dollar Glen   *NS99*
91 East Linton: Preston Mill &
    Phantassie Doocot   *NT57*
92 Eden Estuary   *NO42*
103 Falls of Clyde   *NS84*
103 Farne Islands   *NU23*
114 Galloway Forest Park
114 Glamis: Angus Folk Museum
    NO34
120 Grey Mare's Tail   *NT11*
130 Hermitage   *NO04*
130 High Force   *NY82*
132 Holy Island   *NU14*
136 Ingliston: Scottish Agricultural
    Museum   *NT17*
183 Island of Mull   *NM63*
140 John Muir Country Park
    NT67/68
140 Kelburn Country Centre
    NS25
148 The Lake District National Park
162 Loch Leven & Vane Farm
    NT19/NO10
162 Loch Lomond National Nature
    Reserve   *NS48/49*
164 Lochore Meadows Country
    Park   *NT19*
164 Lochwinnoch & Castle Semple
    NS35
183 Muirshiel Country Park
    NS36
183 Mull of Galloway   *NX13*

195 Northumberland Coast
    NU22
196 Northumberland National Park
225 Pennine Way
228 Plessey Woods Country Park
    NZ28
233 Ramsey: The Grove Rural Life
    Museum   *SC49*
240 St Abb's Head   *NT96*
240 St Bees Head   *NX91*
246 Seaton Cliffs   *NO64*
260 Solway Coast   *NY15/16/26*
268 Strathclyde Country Park
    NS75

274 Threave Garden & Threave
    Wildfowl Refuge   *NX76*
279 The Trossachs & Queen
    Elizabeth Forest Park
    NN40/50
280 Tyne Riverside Country Park
    NZ16
284 Wallington   *NZ08*
296 The Yorkshire Dales

COUNTRY CALENDAR
134 *Common Ridings   NT42 &
    NT51*
48 *Jethart Ba'   NT62*
146 *Midsummer Bonfire   NZ18*
146 *Rush-Bearing   NY30*

In the Lake District

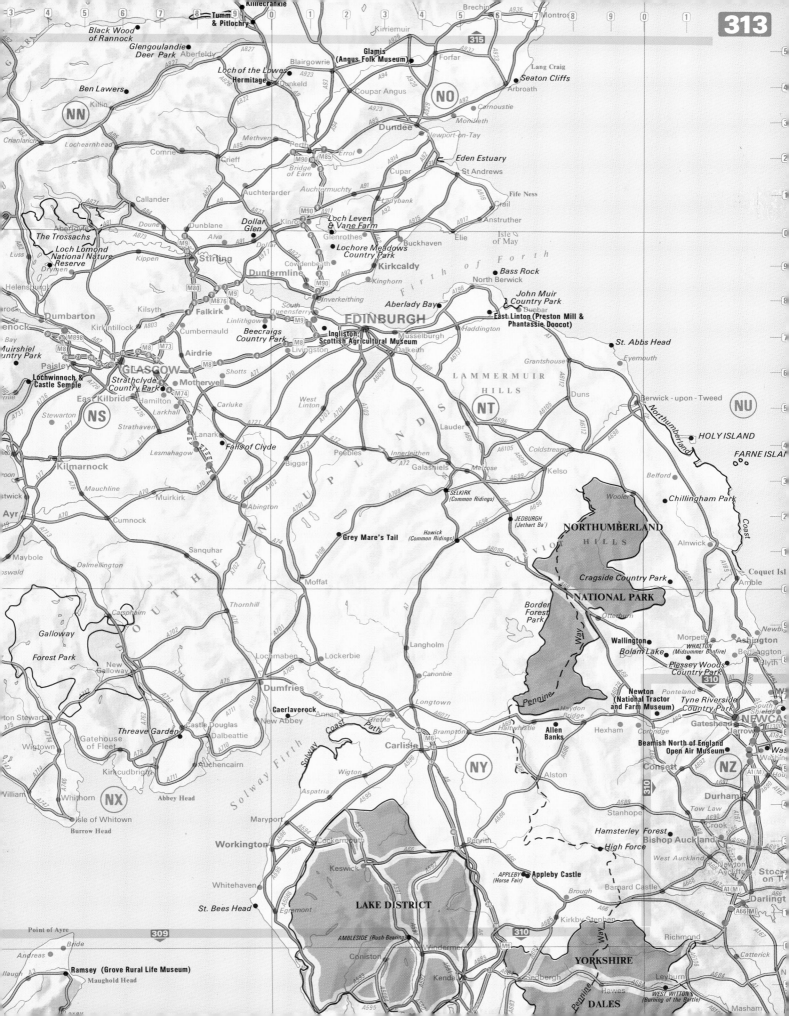

ISLE OF LEWIS

NB

Tolsta Head

Tiumpan Head

Broad Bay

Cape Wrath

Faraid Head

Whiten Head

Strathy P

Durness

A838

Bettyhill

Tongue

A836

NC

Handa

Laxford Bridge

A838

Altnaharra

A836

North Minch

Point of Stoer

Rubha Coigeach

A894

Unapool

A837

Lochinver

A837

Inverpolly National Nature Reserve

A837

Ledmore Junction

A838

Lairg

A839

Summer Isles

Priest Island

Horse Island

Greenstone Point

Ullapool

A835

Bonar Bridge

A9

Rubha Reidh

Inverewe Gardens

Corrieshalloch Gorge

A832

Braemore Junction

A835

A836

Longa

Gairloch

A832

A9

Inver

Beinn Eighe National Nature Reserve

Kinlochewe

A832

Garve

Alness

Torridon

A896

Achnasheen

A832

Dingwall

Shieldaig

A890

Strathpeffer

A832

HEBRIDES

Sound of Harris

NORTH UIST

BENBECULA

SOUTH UIST

Sound of Barra

Little Minch

Sound of Raasay

Rona

Inner Sound

Raasay

NG

ISLAND OF SKYE

Scalpay

A850

Lochcarron

A896

A890

Stromeferry

NH

A831

A862

Inverness

Kyle of Lochalsh

Balmacara

Dornie

Cannich

A831

Drumnadrochit

Broadford

A850

Kyleakin

Shiel Bridge

Kintail & Morvich

A87

Glen Affric

Loch Ness

Invermoriston

A887

A82

Ardvasar

A851

Sound of Sleat

Fort Augustus

A87

Invergarry

MONADHLIAT

MOUNTAINS

Kingussie (Highland Folk Museum)

Newtonmore

RHUM

Sound of Canna

Mallaig

Arisaig

A830

A82

A86

Laggan

A889

Eigg

Sound of Arisaig

A861

Kinlochmoidart

Spean Bridge

A86

Dalwhinnie

NM

Salen

A861

Corpach

Fort William

NN

Tobermary

Drimnin

Glencoe

Black Wood of Rannock

COLL

312

Salen

Lochaline

Sound of Mull

A848

A828

South Ballachulish

A82

Glengoulandie Deer Park

A827

TIREE

Portnacroish

Lismore

Ben Lawers

Page
22 Balmacara NG72
25 Beinn Eighe National Nature Reserve NH06
29 Black Wood of Rannoch NN65
50 Cairngorms National Nature Reserve NH90/NJ00/NN99/NO09
53 Carrbridge: Landmark Visitor Centre NH92
65 Corrieshalloch Gorge NH27
72 Craigellachie National Nature Reserve NH81
74 Culbin Forest & Sands NJ06
84 Dornoch Firth & Loch Fleet NH78/79/88/89
85 Dunbeath: Laidhay Croft Museum ND12
105 Findhorn Bay NJ06
115 Glen Affric NH12/22/32/33
115 Glen Coe NN15
116 Glengoulandie Deer Park NN75
116 Glen More Forest Park NH90/91
116 Glen Muick & Lochnagar NO38
137 Inverewe Gardens NG88
137 Inverpolly National Nature Reserve NC11
142 Killiecrankie NN96
142 Kincraig: Highland Wildlife Park NH80
144 Kingussie: Highland Folk Museum NH70
144 Kintail & Morvich NG91/92
161 Lock Garten NH91
162 Loch Insh & Insh Marshes NH80
163 Loch Ness NH52
164 Loch of the Lowes NO04
206 Orkney
208 Outer Hebrides
314 Skye
276 Torridon Countryside Centre NG95
280 Tummel & Pitlochry NN85/95

COUNTRY CALENDAR
21 *Burning of the Clavie* NJ16
282 *Fireball Ceremony* NO88
283 *Men & Boys Ba' Games* HY41
21 *Up-Helly-Aa* HU44

Highland scene

In order to make the book easier to use, entries that are listed in the gazetteer under the initial letter of their nearest town or village (e.g. Andover: Finkley Down Country Park) are included under their own name (e.g. Finkley Down Country Park) here. Individual entries in the 'What to see' sections of National Park and large area features are also indexed. Other important topographical features mentioned within entries are also indexed. Plants, animals and birds are indexed only if some description of them is given, so this is not a complete list of all the species mentioned.

A

Abbey Gardens, Tresco 140
Abbots Bromley Horn Dance 185
Abbots' Way 78
Abbotsbury Swannery 57
Aberdyfi 87
Aberfoyle 279
Aberglaslyn Pass 256
Ackling Dyke 73
Adder 111
Afon Mellte 39, 42
Agen Allwedd 39
Ailsa Craig 14, 183
Ainsdale Dunes 108
Aird Meadow 164
Alderman's Barrow Area 98
Ale Tasting and Bread Weighing Ceremony, Ashburton 134
Alyn, River 165
Ancient Oakwood 209, 255
Ancient Woodland 44, 104, 189, 264, 292, 293, 295
Angelica 162
Angus Folk Museum, Glamis 114
Annet, Island of 140
Appleby Horse Fair 134
Arbor Low 210, 212
Arctic Tern 54
Arlington Mill Museum, Bibury 68
Arlington Row, Bibury 68
Arne 231
Aros Park and Gardens 183
Arran Nature Centre 14
Autumn Lady's Tresses Orchid 224
Aviemore 72
Avocet 179, 272
Avoncroft Museum of Buildings 45
Axe Estuary 37
Aysgarth 298
Ayton Castle 108
Azalea 289

B

Badger 65
Badgworthy Water 98
Bagot Goat 12
Bala Lake 256
Balranald, North Uist 209

Bamburgh 195
Bank Vole 127
Bardsey Island 160
Barn Elms Reservoir 166
Barnacle Goose 51
Barden Estate 301
Barton Manor Gardens and Vineyard 138
Bearded Tit 28, 57, 62, 233, 276
Becky Falls 79
Beddgelert Forest 256
Bee Orchid 110
Beeston Castle 216
Beeston Regis 287
Bell Ringers Feast, Twyford 238
Belle Toute Lighthouse 23
Bellever Wood 79
Belloc, Hillaire 124, 249
Bembridge Down 138
Bembridge Trail 139
Bembridge Windmill 138
Bempton Cliffs 106
Benbecula 208
Ben Lomond 162, 279
Bere Ferrers 272
Berwyn Mountains 54, 159
Bewick's Swan 252, 253
Bewick, Thomas 35, 58, 280
Bibury 68
Biddenden Dole 112
Bignor Hill 252
Birds of Prey Centre, Newent 187
Birsay Moors and Cottasgarth Nature Reserve, Orkney 206
Bishop Morgan Trail 256
Bison 143
Bistort 129
Bittern 155, 179
Black Cherry Fair, Chertsey 146
Black grouse 142
Black Guillemot 240
Black-headed gull 24, 156
Black House Folk Museum, Luib, Skye 250
Black-tailed Godwit 92, 234, 266, 272
Blackmore Vale 106
Blessing of the Waters, Whitstable 147
Bloody-nosed Beetle 236
'Blue Hare' 34, 276
Blue John Cavern 214
Blue John Stone 214
Bog Asphodel 32, 257
Bog-bean 152
Bokerley Ditch 73
Bolderwood Walks 190
Bosherston 220

Bottle Kicking, Hallaton 112
Box 35
Bradenham Woods 186
Bradgate House 36
Brandon Country Park 274
Bransdale 202
Braunton Burrows 272
Bread and Cheese Dole, St Briavels 122
Breamish Valley 197
Breckland 274, 287
Brecon and Abergavenny Canal 42
Bredon Tithe Barn 68
Brendon Hills 98
Brent Goose 58, 105, 142, 154, 208, 231, 262
Bridestones Moor Nature Reserve 201
Brighstone Down 139
Britannia Park 249
Broadway Tower Country Park 69
Brockhole, Windermere 151
Brodick Castle 14
Brontë Parsonage Museum, Haworth 224
Broomfield 232
Brown, Capability 30, 226, 290
Brown Clee 60, 61
Brown Rat 141
Brown Trout 169
Buckler Fern 186
Bunting
 Corn 174, 175
 Cirl 261
Bure Marshes National Nature Reserve 192
Burning of Bartle, West Witton 173
Burning of the Clavie, Burghead 21
Burning the Ashen Faggot, Dunster 282
Burrator Reservoir 79
Bushy Park 167
Butser Hill 233
Butterfly
 Chalkhill Blue 111
 Clouded Yellow 85
 Grayling 159
 Large Heath 14
 Lulworth Skipper 171
 Marbled White 266
 Meadow Brown 169
 Purple Emperor 178
 Silver-washed Fritillary 180
 Swallowtail 192, 288
 White-letter hairstreak 204, 292
 Wood White 234, 242
Buttermere 149
Buttertubs, the 297
Butterwort, Common 153
Buzzard 41, 149, 232

C

Caban Coch Reservoir 93
Cader Idris 257, 258
Caerleon 281
Cairngorms 53
Calbourne Watermill and Museum of Rural Life 139
Calder Glen 183
Caldey Island 220

Callow Hill Information Centre, Wyre Forest 295
Calshot 156
Canal Museum, Llangollen 159
Candle Auction, Tatworth 113
Capercaillie 29, 50, 116
Car Dyke 216
Caratacus Stone, Winsford Hill 101
Cardigan Bay 47
Carding Mill Valley 169
Carew 220
Carlisle to Settle Railway Line 297
Carneddau Estate 259
Carmarthen Bay 217
Carn Fadryn 160
Carn Goch 41
Carnmenyn 221
Carreg Cennen Castle 42
Carron, Loch 22
Carrying the Tar Barrels, Ottery St Mary 270
Castell Dinas Bran 158
Castell-y-Bere 256
Castle Campbell 84
Castle Drogo 79
Castlemorton Common 174
Castle Semple 164
Castleton Garland Day 123
Cattle
 Highland 116
 Longhorn 12, 70, 91, 124
 White Park 12, 70
 Wild White 58
Cetti's Warbler 233, 265
Chains, The, Exmoor 98
Chalkhill Blue 111
Chanterelle 277
Chapman Barrows 98
Charcoal Burning 107
Charnwood Forest 36
Chedworth Roman Villa 69
Chee Dale 215
Chee Tor 211, 215
Cheese Rolling Ceremony, Copper's Hill 122
Cherryburn 280
Cheshire Plain 273
Cheshire Sandstone Trail 82
Chesil Beach 47, 57, 84, 230
Cheviot, The 198
Chew Valley Lake 29
Chichester Harbour 58
Chillingham Cattle 58, 59
Chiltern Open Air Museum 55
Chilton Foliat 141
Cholmondeley Castle 216
Chough 222, 262
Church Farm Museum, Skegness 251
Chwarel Wynne Mine and Museum 54
Cirl Bunting 261
Clachaig 115
Clapham 298
Claval Tower 84
Clayton Tunnel 60
Cleeve Hill 66
Cley Hill, Wiltshire 168
Clifton Suspension Bridge 18
Clock Warehouse, Shardlow 248
Clyde, Firth of 14
Coaley Park 71

Coberley 67
Coed Dinorwig 208
Coed-y-Brenin 257
Coedydd Maentwrog 257
Coed-y-paen 158
Coetan Arthur 222
Colemere 249
Colliford 32
Common Butterwort 153
Common Ridings, Hawick and Selkirk 134
Common Shrew 130
Common Tern 143, 237
Conishead Priory 22
Coniston, Old Man of 150
Coniston Water 150
Conker Knockout Competition, Ashton 239
Constable Country 95, 266
Cookham Common 174
Coombe Gibbet 137
Cooper's Hill Local Nature Reserve 69, 122
Coot 268
Copperas Wood 266
Coppice/coppicing 30, 35, 44, 91, 193, 278, 293
Coquet, River 197
Coquet Head 198
Coracle 54
Cord Grass 156
Cormorant 75, 177
Corn Bunting 174, 175
Corncrake 209
Cornish Gorsedd 184
Corrigall Farm Museum, Orkney 206
Cors Caron National Nature Reserve 278
Cotswold Countryside Collection 70
Cotswold Farm Park 70
Cotswold Stone 68
Cotswold Water Park 70
Cotswold Way 70
Cotton Grass 28, 79, 278
Countisbury 100
Courage Shire Horse Centre, Littlewick Green 157
Court of Purbeck Marblers, Corfe Castle 48
Courts Leet & Baron, Ashburton 271
Cowal Peninsula 13
Crag Lough 196
Craig Goch Reservoir 93
Craig-yr-Aderyn 255
Craig-y-nos Country Park 42
Cranham Feast and Deer Roast 172
Cranmere Pool 80
Cregennan, Gwynedd 258
Crickley Hill Country Park 71
Croft Ambrey 73
Crofton Beam Engines 291
Crookham Mummers 283
Crossbill 50, 124, 242, 274
Crundale Down 294
Cuckoo 32
Cuckmere River 246
Cuillins 250
Culver Down 138
Curlew 22, 51, 100, 126, 181, 198, 235, 260
Cwm Idwal Nature Trail 258
Cwm-yr-Argoed 10
Cwmcarn Scenic Drive 92

Dabchick 269
Dairyland & Cornish
  Country Life Museum,
  Summercourt 269
Dalby Forest 202
Damselfly 106, 190,
  265, 272
Dan-yr-Ogof and
  Cathedral Showcaves
  39, 42
Danby, Moors Centre 202
Dartford Warbler 189, 231,
  275
Darwin, Charles 52, 258
David Marshall Lodge
  Visitor Centre 279
Dawlish Warren 95
Death Cap 277
Dedham Vale 266
Dee of Dirkdale,
  Orkney 206
Deer
  Fallow 145, 163, 189,
    228, 242, 266, 269
  Muntjac 242, 266
  Red 13, 97, 101, 116, 232
  Roe 34, 149, 233, 266, 274
  Sika 45, 145, 269
Deer Museum,
  Torridon 276
Denfurlong Farm Trail 71
Derwent, River 108, 211
Derwent Water 150
Desolation, Valley of 301
Devil's Punch Bowl,
  Hindhead 131
Devon Shire Horse
  Centre, Yealmpton 302
Dinas Nature Reserve 121
Dipper 19, 81, 109, 129
Distribution of New
  Pennies, Sherborne 282
Ditchling Beacon 261
Dodder 286
Dodd Fell 299
Dolmelynllyn 258
Dorothy Clive
  Memorial Garden,
  Willoughbridge 289
Dorset Cursus 73
Dorset Fossils 84
Dorset Horn Sheep 106
Dotterel 50, 228, 274
Dove, River 211
Dovedale 212
Dragonfly 106, 157, 190,
  192, 204, 231, 265, 272
Druids' Ceremony,
  Stonehenge 134
Duck decoy 31
Duck
  Eider 30, 103, 195
  Gadwall 141, 287
  Garganey 17
  Goldeneye 62, 102, 116
  Mandarin 291
  Pochard 82
  Ruddy 57
  Shoveler 233
  Tufted 57, 82
Dunkery Beacon 99
Dunlin 58, 59, 234
Dunstanburgh 195
Dunster 98
Dunvegan Castle 250
Durdle Door 84, 170
Dyer's Hill 75
Dynevor Deer Park 53

Eagle
  Golden 13, 14, 50, 115,
    143, 149, 183,
    209, 251, 279
  White-tailed 143
Eagles Nest Viewpoint,
  Wye Valley 294
East Head, West Sussex 58
East Wretham Nature
  Reserve 274
Ebernoe Horn Fair 147
Echium 140
Edale 212
Edwards Atlas Moth 248
Edwinstowe Visitor
  Centre 248
Eider 30, 103, 195
Ellesmere 249
Emperor Dragonfly 266
Emperor Moth 190, 224
English Stonecrop 243
Ennerdale Forest 150
Ennerdale Water 150
Ermine Street 281
Erne Valley 80
Esk Valley Railway 202
Esk Valley Walk 202
Esthwaite Water 149
Ewyas, Vale of 43
Exbury Marshes 156
Exminster Marshes 95
Exmoor Pony 97
Exton 281
Eyebright 300

Fallow deer 145, 163, 189,
  228, 242, 266, 269
Falls of Clyde 187
Farrer, Reginald 298
Featherbed Moss 211
Felin Geri Mill,
  Cwmcoy 74
Fernworthy Forest 80
Fernworthy Reservoir 80
Fewston Reservoir 285
Fforset Fawr 285
Finkley Down Farm and
  Country Park 12
Fireball Ceremony,
  Stonehaven 282
Firing the Poppers,
  Lean Park, Bletchley 271
Firle Beacon 261
Five Sisters of Kintail 144
Flanders Moss 279
Flatford Mill 95, 266
Fleet Moss 299
Fleet, The 57
Flycatcher 131
Foel-drygarn 219
Foel Fawr 160
Fort Victoria Country
  Park 139
Forth, Firth of 10
Fossils, Dorset 84
Fountains Abbey 269
Fox 216
Fragrant Orchid 17
Freeman's Marsh,
  Hungerford 141
Frencham Great Pond 110
Frencham Little Pond 110
Friar's Crag Nature

Walk, Keswick 150
Frocester Hill 71
Fulmar 27, 133, 247
Fylingdales Moor 201
Fyne Court 232

Gadwall 141, 287
Gallants Bower 75
Galloway Deer
  Museum 114
Gannet 22, 100, 106, 183
Gaping Gill 299
Garbutt Wood 203
Garganey 17
Gibbet Hill, Hindhead 131
Glamorgan Nature Centre,
  Tondu 276
Glasdir Arboretum 257
Glen Mor (the 'Great
  Glen') 163
Glen Mor Forest Park 50
Glen Rosa 14
Glen Shiel 144
Glendurgan Garden 130
Glossy Ibis 265
Goat
  Bagot 12
  Guernsey 70
  Wild 34, 114, 121
Goat Fell, Arran 14
Goat Park, Talnotry 114
Godshill Area 190
Godlingston Nature
  Reserve 231
Gog Magog Hills 285
Goldcrest 132
Golden Eagle 13, 14, 50,
  115, 143, 149, 183, 209, 251,
  279
Goldeneye 62, 102, 116
Golden Pheasant 242, 274
Goodameavy 80
Goosander 31, 102, 116, 281
Goose
  Barnacle 51
  Brent 58, 105, 142, 154,
    208, 231, 262
  Greylag 209
  Pink-footed 10, 29, 234, 279
  Snow 33
Grand Union Canal 82, 265
Grasshopper Warbler 274
Grass of Parnassus 142, 300
Grass Wood 300
Grayling Butterfly 159
Great Barn Museum,
  Avebury 18
Great Barn, Coxwell 120
Great Crested Grebe 29,
  57, 62, 106, 119, 252, 269
Great Glen 163
Greatham Sword
  Dance 283
Great Shunner Fell 297
Great Spotted
  Woodpecker 125, 126,
    193, 277
Great Tit 124
Great Whin Sill 103
Green Hellebore 27
Green Sandpiper 209
Green-winged Orchid 138
Green Woodpecker 59,
  165, 193, 231, 264
Greenshank 102, 131
Greenwich Park 167

Grey Plover 234
Grey Seal 14, 103, 219,
  222, 226, 262
Grey Squirrel 137, 167, 264
Grey Wagtail
  109, 125, 228, 301
Greylag Goose 209
Grimes Graves 274
Grimspound 80
Grizedale Forest 150
Grouse
  Black 34, 100, 142
  Red 41, 100, 169, 214
Grove Rural Life
  Museum, Ramsey 233
Grovely Forest Rights,
  Great Wishford 123
Grwyne Fawr Valley 42
Guillemot 87, 230, 240,
  261, 262
Gull
  Black-headed 24, 156
  Herring 262
  Lesser blacked-backed 106,
    262
  Little 133
Gull Island 156
Gullane Bay 10
Gunnerside Gill 296
Gwaun Valley 220
Gwydyr Forest 258

Haddon Hall 211
Hadlow Road Station,
  Wirral Country Park 291
Hadrian's Wall 11, 34, 196
Hafnetting 260
Hallaton 112
Hambleton Hills 61, 117
Hamilton Mausoleum 268
Hamps Valley 214
Hampshire Farm Museum,
  Upper Hamble Country
  Park 280
Hampton Court 167
Harbottle Crags 199
Hardcastle Crags 129
Hardrow Force 297
Hare Pie Scramble,
  Hallaton 112
Haresfield Beacon 71
Haresmere Hall Shire
  Horses, Etchingham 95
Hartland Nature
  Reserve 231
Hartland Point 125
Hartland Quay 125
Hartlebury Common 125
Hawes Information
  Centre 297
Hawfinch 72, 274, 292
Hawk Conservancy,
  Weyhill 288
Hawick 134
Haworth 224
Haxey Hood Game 20
Hay Bridge Deer
  Museum 150
Haytor Down 80
Haytor Granite
  Tramway 80
Heath Fritillary 30
Heather 157
Heddon Valley 99
Helford, River 130
Helston Furry Dance 122
Helvellyn 148

Hembury 80
Hengistbury Head 59
Hen Harrier 28, 190, 265
Henrhyd Falls 39
Hentor 80
Herb Paris 126, 278
Herdwick Sheep 291
Herefordshire Beacon 174
Herring Gull 262
Hermitage Castle 34
Heron 41, 83, 176, 204,
  273, 285
Hest Bank 180
Hetty Pegler's Tump 66
Hickling Broad
  Nature Reserve 192
High Peak Trail 215
Highland Folk
  Museum, Kingussie 144
Highland Wildlife Park 142
Hinckley Wood 213
Hobbister Nature
  Reserve, Orkney 206
Hobby 157
Hobby Horses,
  Padstow and
  Minehead 122
Hoccombe Water 98
Hocktide Festival,
  Hungerford 113
Holidays Hill
  Reptiliary 189
Holm Oak 136, 245
Holne 80
Holnicote 97
Holyhead Mountain 262
Holystone 199
Honister Pass 148
Hop Hoodening,
  Canterbury 184
Hope Dale 286
Hope Woodlands 212
Hornbeam 94, 126
Horner Woods 99
Horn of Plenty 252
Horseshoe Falls 158
Horsey Mere 192
House Martin 195
Housesteads 199
Hoveton Great Broad 192
Humber Bridge 281
Hunday National Tractor
  & Farm Museum,
  Newton 187
Hungerford 113
Hurling the Silver
  Ball, St Ives &
  St Columb Major 48
Hurlstone Point 99
Hurst Castle 142
Huxley, Julian 110
Hyde Park 166

Ilam 212
Ibis, Glossy 265
Icknield Way 235
Inchcailloch 162
Inchnacardoch Forest
  Trail 163
Ingleborough 298, 300
Ingleborough Cave 299
Insh Marshes 162
Isle of Arran
  Heritage Museum 14
Ivinghoe Beacon 16
Izaak Walton's Cottage,
  Shallowford 246

J

Jack & Jill Windmills,
  Clayton   60
Jacob Sheep   13, 116
Jay   265, 287
Jeffries, Richard   63
Jethart Ba', Jedburgh   48
Jubilee Tower, Moel
  Famau   180
Jubilee Walk, The   47
Juniper   180

K

Katrine, Loch   279
Kelburn Castle   140
Kennet Valley   273
Kensington Gardens   166
Kestrel   103, 166
Kew Gardens   166
Kielder Castle   34
Kielder Water   34
Kilburn Feast   147
Kilburn White Horse   201
Kilmuir Museum   250
Kilmun Arboretum   13
Kincraig   162
Kinder Scout   213
Kingfisher   103, 159, 181,
               273, 284, 293
Kiplingcotes Derby   88
Kittiwake   106, 169, 177,
             240, 261, 262
Knightwood Oak   191
Knockan Cliff   137
Knot   234
Kynance Cove   158

L

Ladram Bay   261
Laidhay Croft
  Museum, Dunbeath   85
Landmark Visitor
  Centre, Carrbridge   53
Lansallos Beach   224
Lapwing   126, 260, 301
Larg Hill and
  Bruntis Forest Trail   114
Large Heath Butterfly   14
Lathkill, River   211
Leonardslee Gardens,
  Lower Beeding   241
Leigh Woods   18, 19
Lesser Black-backed
  Gull   106, 262
Lesser Spotted
  Woodpecker   126
Lindisfarne (Holy
  Island)   132
Ling   157
Linnhe, Loch   115
Little Dartmouth Cliffs   75
Little Grebe   141, 269
Little Gull   133
Little Owl   242
Little Ringed Plover
                      104, 273
Little Tern   114, 208, 237
Littondale   297
Lizard Point   158
Llanberis Pass   255, 256

Llanberis Lake
  Railway   208
Llanddwyn Island   186
Llangollen, Canal
  Museum   159
Llangorse Lake   43
Llanmodoc Hill   118
Llwyn-on Reservoir   43
Llyn Idwal   258
Llyn Pendam   47
Llywernog
  Silver-Lead Mine   47
Lochalsh, Kyle of   22
Loch an Eilein   50
Loch Druidibeg
  National Nature
  Reserve   209
Loch Eck   13
Loch Fleet   84
Loch Katrine   279
Loch Linnhe   115
Loch Lomond   162, 279
Loch Morlich   116
Lochnagar   116
Loch Ness Monster
  Exhibition   163
Loch Ryan   183
Loch Trool Forest
  Trail   114
Lodge, the, Sandy   244
Lodgepole Pine   126
Lodmoor, Weymouth   233
Lomond, Loch   279
Longham   95
Longshaw   214
Longships Lighthouse   154
Long-billed Dowitcher   264
Long-tailed Duck   30
Longhorn Cattle   12, 70,
                       91, 124
Long Man of
  Wilmington   290
Long Mynd   264
Loons, The, Orkney   206
Loughrigg Fell   151
Lousewort   153
Lowther Wildlife
  Adventure Park   152
Luce Bay   183
Lucombe Oak   136
Ludlow Museum   180
Lullingstone Silk
  Farm, Sherborne   248
Lulworth Skipper   171
Lydford Gorge   80
Lynmouth   100
Lynx   193

M

Machair, the   208, 209
Maen Llia   41
Maesgwn Visitor
  Centre   257
Maes Howe   206
Maiden Castle, Reeth   296
Maidenhair Fern   230
Major Oak,
  Sherwood Forest   248
Malham Cove   225, 297, 300
Malham Tarn Estate   300
Malltraeth Pool   187
Mam Tor   214
Mandarin Duck   291
Manifold Valley   214
Manorbier   220
Manx Loghtan Sheep   73
Manx Open Air
  Museum, Cregneash   73

Manx Shearwater
               141, 183, 218
Marbled White
  Butterfly   111, 266
Marhamchurch Revel   173
Marlborough Downs   18
Marldon Apple
  Pie Fair   173
Marley Common   28
Marloes Deer Park   221
Marloes Sands   221
Marsh Frog   235
Marsh Harrier   28, 142,
                179, 192, 276
Marsh Samphire   139
Martin
  House   195
  Sand   105
Martin Down   73
Marwick Head,
  Orkney   206
Mary Arden's House,
  Wilmcote   290
Mastiles Lanes   300
Meadow Brown
  Butterfly   169
Meadow Foxtail   227
Meadow Pipit   32, 224
Melchett Mere   272
Melton Gallows   281
Men and Boys Ba'
  Games, Kirkwall   283
Mendip Hills   29
Menteith, Lake of   279
Meres Centre,
  Ellesmere   249
Merlin   28, 101, 201
Mersea Island   74
Mesembryanthemum   140
Mezereon   266
Midsummer Bonfire,
  Whalton   146
Migneint   255
Minchinhampton   71
Mink   45, 252
Moel Famau   165
Monsal Head   215
Monsal Trail   214
Monterey Pine   141, 286
Moors Centre, Danby   202
Mop Fair and Runaway
  Mop Fair, Stratford
  upon Avon   238
Morecambe Bay   13, 22, 155
Morfa Harlech   255
Morlich, Loch   116
Morvich   144
Moschatel   253
Moth
  Edwards Atlas   248
  Emperor   190, 224
Mound Alderwoods
  National Nature
  Reserve   85
Mount's Bay   176
Mount Grace Priory   61
Mountain Fern   153
Mountain Hare   34
Mountain Parsley   149
Muich, Loch   116
Muncaster Castle   152
Muntjac   242, 266
Museum of East
  Anglian Life,
  Stowmarket   267
Musk Mallow   129
Mynydd Illtyd
  Mountain Centre   43
Mynydd Llangattock   39
Mynydd Maen   92
Mynydd Mawr   160
Mynydd Preseli   219, 221

N

Nant Ffrancon   259
Nant Gwynant   259
National Dairy
  Museum, Stratfield
  Saye House   286
National Water Sports
  Centre   132
Natterjack Toad   51, 109
Needles, The   138
Needs Ore Point   24
Nene Park   105
Nether Alderley Mill   11
New Forest
  Butterfly Farm   190
New Forest Heaths   189, 191
Newland Island   226
Newton Pool,
  Northumberland   195
Newtown, Isle of
  Wight   139
Nidderdale   117
Nightingale   30, 126, 242,
               273, 292
Nightjar   87, 120, 126,
                274, 293
Norfolk Lavender
  Farm, Heacham   129
Norfolk Rural Life
  Museum, Gressenhall   120
North Ronaldsay   70
North Yorkshire
  Moors Railway   203
Northam Burrows   272
Northleach   70
North of England
  Open-Air Museum,
  Beamish   24
Nuthatch   53, 232, 264
Nutters Dance, The,
  Bacup   89

O

Oak   168, 186, 291
Oare Church   98
Oasthouses   25
Oberwater Walk   191
Ochil Hills   84
Ogbourne Down   176
Ogof Ffynnon Ddu   39
Old Caledonian Pine
  Forest   25, 50, 115, 116,
                130, 161
Old Kiln Agricultural
  Museum, Tilford   275
Old Man of Mow   182
Olney Pancake Race   49
Orchid   27, 180, 278, 286,
                           292
  Autumn Lady's Tresses   224
  Bee   110
  Coral-root   29
  Fragrant   17
  Green-winged   138
Ornamental Drives,
  New Forest   191
Osprey   117, 119, 161,
                162, 164
Ossian's Cave   130
Ossian's Hall   130
Otter   50, 53, 90, 155, 162,
         183, 192, 193, 252
Otter Trust,
  Earsham   90

Overbecks, Salcombe   243
Owl
  Eagle   193
  Little   242
  Short-eared   34, 194
  Tawny   59, 242
Oxwich Bay   118
Oxwich Point   118
Oystercatcher   22, 24, 225,
             230, 237, 260

P

Pace Egg Play,
  Midgley   89
Pack Monday Fair,
  Sherborne   238
Padley Pilgrimage,
  Grindleford   146
Padstow   122
Painswick Ancient
  Clipping   185
Pant Mawr Pot   39
Park Wood   186, 209
Parkhurst Forest   138
Park Waterfall   301
Pasque Flower   68, 274
Pasture woodland   86, 189
Paultons Country
  Park and Bird Garden   191
Peak District Caves   214
Peak Rivers   211
Pegwell Bay   243
Pembrokeshire Coast
  Path   221
Pendennis Castle   102
Pennington   142
Penrhos Feilw
  Common   262
Penrhyn Castle   259
Pentre Ifan   221
Pen-y-Fan   38
Pen-y-Gaer   160
Pen-y-Garreg
  Reservoir   93
Peregrine Falcon   50, 121,
                149, 171, 180
Peveril Castle   214
Pewsey Vale   226
Phantassie Doocot,
  East Linton   91
Pied Flycatcher   44, 131
Pied Wagtail   301
Pike   104
Pine Marten   25, 144, 255
Pink-footed Goose   10, 29,
                   234, 279
Pinkworthy Pond   98
Pintail   266
Pitlochry Dam   280
Plague Sunday,
  Eyam   173
Plockton   22
Plough Stots Service,
  Goathland   21
Pochard   57, 82, 143
Poivan   150
Polecat   73, 255, 258
Pollard pollarding   46, 94,
                189, 190
Pontcysyllte   158
Pony
  Exmoor   97
  Lundy   171
  Shetland   13
Porlock Bay   99
Poole Harbour   280
Porpoise   167
Porth Neigwl   160

Porth yr Ogof 39
Portland Sheep 291
Portquin 226
Portland, Isle of 57
Powderham 95
Preston Mill,
  East Linton 91
Ptarmigan 115
Puffin 87, 103, 226, 230, 250
Puffin Island 224
Punkie Night,
  Hinton St George 239
Purple Emperor 178
Purple Hairstreak 242
Purple Loosestrife 272
Purple Moor Grass 100
Purple Sandpiper 133, 169, 195
Pwllheli 160

Q

Quail 235
Quaking Grass 227
Quantock Forest Trail 232
Queen Elizabeth Forest
  Park 279
Queen Elizabeth's Hunting
  Lodge 94

R

Rabbit 203
Ragged Robin 272
Raiders Road Forest
  Drive 114
Raincliffe Woods 108
Ramsey Island 222
Rannoch Moor 115
Ranworth, Broadlands
  Conservation Centre 192
Ratagan Forest 144
Raven 41, 44, 121, 125, 255, 265
Ravenscar Geological
  Trail 203
Ravenseat Moor 301
Raydale 300
Raw Head 216
Razorbill 262
Red Deer 13, 97, 101, 116, 232
Red Earl's Dyke 174
Red Grouse 41, 100, 169, 214
Red Kite 41, 47, 121, 228, 278, 302
Redpoll 287
Redshank 234
Red squirrel 11, 33, 34, 149, 274, 287
Redstart 97, 149
Reed warbler 43, 106
Regent's Park 167
Reginald Farrer Trail 298
Repton, Humphry 272, 290
Reynards Cavern 212
Rhaiadr Ddu (Black
  Waterfall) 258
Rheidol Forest 47
Rhinogs 255
Rhododendron 40, 152, 183, 245, 289
Rhossili Down 118
Ribblehead Viaduct 297

Ribblesdale 297
Richmond Park 167
Rievaulx Abbey 61, 203
Rievaulx Terrace and
  Temples 203
Ring of Brodgar 206
Ring Ouzel 97, 169
Ringed Plover 105, 114, 237
Ringing the Devil's
  Knell, Dewsbury 282
Robert Dover's Games,
  Chipping Campden 135
Robin Hood's Bay 203
Rock-rose 56
Rodborough
  Commons 71
Roe Deer 34, 149, 233, 266, 274
Roman Wall (see also
  Hadrian's Wall) 196
Roseberry Topping 61, 201
Rosedale 201
Rothay, River 151, 152
Rough Tor 32
Rowbarrow Warren 83
Rowley Station 24
Royal Military Canal 235
Royal Victoria
  Country Park 280
Ruddy Duck 57, 249
Rufford Abbey 236
Rumps Point 226
Running Auction,
  Bourne 112
Rural Life Museum,
  Usk 281
Rush-bearing
  Ambleside 146
  Sowerby Bridge 185
Rutland County
  Museum, Oakham 281
Rutland Farm Park,
  Oakham 204
Ryedale Folk Museum 203

S

St Anthony Head 102
St Bride's Bay 219
St David's Head 222
St George's Channel 160
St George's Down 139
St James's Park 31, 167
St John's Lake 272
St Kilda 116
St Mary's Nature Trails,
  Isles of Scilly 141
St Wilfrid's Feast
  Procession, Ripon 172
Salad Burnet 106
Salcombe Regis 36
Salmon 54
Sand Martin 105, 273
Sanderling 95, 234
Sandstone Trail 216
Sandwich Bay Nature
  Reserve 242
Sarsen Stones 176
Savi's Warbler 265
Scabbacombe 144
Scabious 71
Scafell Pike 148
Scare Rocks 183
Scaup 92
Schelly 150
Scots Pine 105, 274
Scottish Agricultural
  Museum, Ingliston 136
Scuttlebrook Wake 134

Sea Aster 262
Sea Bindweed 224
Sea Buckthorn 114
Sea Campion 164, 240
Sea Clover 262
Sea Eagle 251
Sea Holly 262
Seahouses 195
Sea Lavender 105, 262
Sea Pea 237
Sea Spleenwort 222
Seahouses 195
Seal 30, 141, 167, 183, 250
Seal, Grey 14, 103, 219, 222
Seal Sanctuary,
  Gweek 130
Seaton 19
Sedge Warbler 82
Selkirk 134
Selworthy 97, 100
Semer Water 300
Seven Sisters,
  Wye Valley 294
Sgwd yr Eira 42
Shag 75
Shanklin Chine 139
Shaptor Wood 81
Sheep
  Dorset Horn 106
  Herdwick 291
  Jacob 13, 116
  Manx Loghtan 73
  Portland 291
  Soay 70, 116
  Southdown 246
  Swaledale 296
  Woodland Horned 124
Shelduck 10, 59
Sheppey, Isle of 93
Shetland Pony 13
Shire Horse 10, 302
Short-eared Owl 34, 194
Shoveler 233
Shrew, Common 130
Shrovetide Football,
  Ashbourne and
  Atherstone 49
Shrubby seablite 30
Shugborough Park 52
Sika Deer 45, 145, 269
Silbury Hill 18, 176, 177, 235
Silchester Common 209
Silver-washed
  Fritillary 180, 293
Siskin 124, 163, 165
Sitka Spruce 47
Skara Brae 206
Skipping, Alciston 88
Skomer Island 222
Skomer Vole 222
Skye Black House,
  Colbost 250
Skylark 32, 41
Slade, Berkshire 104
Slow-worm 45
Slurring Rock Trail 129
Snipe 32
Snow Bunting 62, 144, 116, 262
Snowdon 255, 258
Snowdon Mountain
  Railway 258
Snowdrop 284
Snowy Mespil 129
Soay Sheep 70, 116
Solomon's Seal 27
Solway Firth 260
Somerset Rural Life
  Museum,
  Glastonbury 115

Soul-caking Play,
  Antrobus 270
South Hams 19, 261
South Hill, Exmoor 101
Southdown Sheep 256
Southerscales Scar 300
Sowerby Bridge 185
Spartina 156
Speckled Bush Cricket 278
Speedwell Cavern 214
Spey Valley 53
Spleenwort 56
Spotted flycatcher 131
Spotted Redshank 102
Spring Squill 119, 158, 243
Squirrel
  Grey 137, 167, 264
  Red 11, 33, 34, 35, 149, 274, 287
Stackpole 223
Staffordshire Way 182
Stag Beetle 291
Staines Reservoir 167
Staintondale 203
Stair Hole, Lulworth 170
Standish Wood 71
Stanpit Marsh 59
Starry Saxifrage 199
Steyning 55
Stocks Mill,
  Wittersham 292
Stoke Pero 100
Stone Curlew 193
Stonechat 109, 117, 243, 265
Stonehaven 282
Stonehenge 134, 243
Stour Wood 266
Stracey Arms
  Windpump 192
Strathspey 53
Straw Bear Festival,
  Whittlesey 20
Strid Gorge 301
Stroan Forest Walk 114
Stroudwater Canal 71
Strumpshaw Fen
  Nature Reserve 192
Studland Nature
  Reserve 231
Suffolk Punch Horse 91
Sugar Loaf, The 43
Sundew 32, 149, 157
Swaledale 296
Swaledale Folk
  Museum, Reeth 297
Swaledale Sheep 296
Swallowtail Butterfly 192
Swan
  Bewick's 178, 252
  Trumpeter 216
  Whooper 102, 117
Swan Upping 147
Sway Hood 20
Sweet Chestnut 193, 244
Swithland Woods 36
Swinsty Reservoir 285
Symonds Yat 294

T

Taf Fechan
  Reservoirs 43
Talnotry Forest Trail 114
Talybont Reservoir 43
Tamworth Pig 10
Tan Hill 301
Tarr Steps 100
Tatton Mere 272
Tatworth 113

Taunton, Vale of 28
Tawny Owl 59, 242
Teal 29
Teign Valley Woods 81
Tennyson Trail 139
Tern
  Arctic 10, 54
  Common 143, 237
  Little 114, 208, 237
Thames, River 147, 167
Thatcham Moor 141
Thorburn Birds
  Gallery, Dobwalls 109
Threave Wildfowl
  Refuge 274
Three Peaks 297
Thrift 240, 262
Thyme, Wild 47
Tichborne Dole 88
Tintern Abbey 294
Tintern Station 294
Tissington Trail 215
Tit
  Bearded 28, 57, 62, 233, 276
  Blue 124
  Great 124
Titterstone Clee 60
Toad
  Common 186
  Natterjack 51, 109
Tobermory 183
Topsham Bridge 19
Torosay Castle 183
Torridge Estuary 273
Traeth Maelgwyn 87
Treecreeper 125
Tree Pipit 244
Tre'r Ceiri 160
Tresco 140
Trumpeter Swan 216
Trundle, the 117
Tufted Duck 57, 82
Tummel, Falls of 280
Tummel Forest Centre 280
Tummel, Linn of 280
Turning the Devil's
  Boulder, Shebbear 271
Turnstone 195
Twayblade 71
Twm Sion Catti 121
Ty Mawr 256
Tyne Valley 11
Tyn-y-groes 257
Tywi, Vale of 38, 114

U

Uffington White Horse 235
Uist, North and South 208
Ullswater 152
Up-Helly-Aa, Lerwick 21
Upper Dales Folk
  Museum, Hawes 297

V

Vale of Ewyas 43
Vale of Rheidol
  Railway 83
Valley of Desolation 301
Valley of the Rocks 101
Vane Farm 162
Vendace 150
Viper's Bugloss 223

Waggoners' Wells 169
Wagtail
 Grey 109, 125, 228, 301
 Pied 301
Wallpepper 56
Walney Island 262
Waltham Abbey 155
Walton, Izaac 246
Wansdyke 18
Warbler
 Cetti's 233, 265
 Dartford 189, 231, 275
 Grasshopper 274
 Reed 43, 106
 Savi's 265
 Sedge 82
Warkworth 195
Warrens, The 80
Washington 55
Washington Old Hall 285
Wassailing the Apple
 Trees, Carhampton 21
Wast Water 149, 152
Water rail 15, 57
Watersmeet 100
Waterways Museum,
 Stoke Bruerne 265
Waylands Smithy 235
Weald and Downland
 Open Air Museum,

Singleton 250
Weasel 225
Webber's Post 99
Weeting Nature
 Reserve 274
Weir Quay 272
Well-dressing,
 Derbyshire and
 Staffordshire Villages 135
Wellington Monument,
 Blackdown Hills 28
Wellingtonia Avenue 105
Welney 207
Welsh Folk Museum,
 St Fagans 241
Welsh Miners'
 Museum 10
Welsh Slate Museum,
 Dinorwic 208
Wensleydale 297
West Kennet
 Long Barrow 18
West Lyn 99
West Webburn Valley 77
Whalton 146
Wharfedale 297
Wheal Betsy 77
Wheatear 47, 138, 237,
 296, 301
Whiddon 79
Whimbrel 92, 261
Whinchat 42, 109, 224
Whitbread Hop Farm,
 Beltring 25
White Admiral 45

White, Gilbert 110, 246
White Horse Museum
 of Buildings and
 Continuous Family
 Life, Aston Munslow 287
White Horse,
 Uffington 235
White-letter
 Hairstreak
 Butterfly 204, 292
White Moss Common 152
White Nothe 84
White Park Cattle 12, 70
White Rock-rose 37
White-tailed Eagle 143, 251
Whitebeam 100
Whitesand Bay 219, 222
Whitstable 147
Whitsundale 301
Whooper Swan 102, 117
Widecombe Fair 185
Wigeon 10, 262
Wild Gladiolus 190
Wild Goat 34, 121, 276
Wild Service Tree 28, 90,
 278
Wild White Cattle 58
Wildcat 25, 277
William I 189
William Curtis
 Ecological Park 167
Wilverley Walks 191
Wimbleball Lake 101
Wimbledon Common 167
Win Green Hill 73

Windermere, Lake 149, 151
Windover Hill 290
Winnats Pass 214
Winsford Hill 101
Wolf Rock 154
Wood-ant 129
Woodcock 234, 242
Woodland Horned
 Sheep 124
Woodland Park and
 Phillips Countryside
 Museum 44
Woodlark 189
Woodleigh Woods 19
Wood Mouse 228
Woodpecker
 Great Spotted 125, 126,
 193, 277
 Green 59, 165, 193, 231, 264
 Lesser Spotted 126
Wood White Butterfly
 234, 242
Woody Bay 101, 261
Woolacombe 180
Woolhope Dome 126
Woolly Thistle 71
Worcestershire Beacon 174
Wordsworth, William 152
Worldwide Butterflies,
 Sherborne 248
Worms Head 118
Wren 228
Wroth Silver,
 Knightlow Cross 271
Wringapeak 101

Wryneck 30
Wrynose Pass 148
Wych Elm 92
Wye, River (Peak
 District) 211
Wynd Cliff 294

Yafford Mill 139
Yarner Wood National
 Nature Reserve 81
Yarnton Mead 227
Yealm Estuary 286
Yellow Flag 272
Yellow Horned
 Poppy 237, 262
Yew 143
Y Gaer 41
Y Llethr 258
Ynyslas 87
Yorkshire Museum of
 Carriages and
 Horsedrawn Vehicles 298
Younger Botanic
 Garden 13
Yr Eifl 160
Yr Hen Ffordd 219
Ysbyty Estate 256, 258, 259

ACKNOWLEDGEMENTS

Ardea London J. Mason 17, 109, 242/3, 278.
R. Gibbons 257. A & E Bomford 262. Ardea 245.
Nature Photographers Ltd T. Andrewartha Cover
2/3. F. V. Blackburn 42, 100, 294. D. A. Smith 50. E. A.
Janes 53, 68, 72, 178, 228. P. Sterry 47, 71, 264.
A. Wharton 71, 79. N. W. Callow 81. D. Swindells 90.
A. Cleave 129, 153, 222, 236. D. Smith 103. D.
Washington 110. T. Tomlinson 119. R. Tidman 132/3.
D. Worthington 138. D. Sewell 170, 236. K. Carlson
175. R. Bush 191. C. Palmer 199. M. Gore 216. S. C.
Bisserot 252, 268/9. L. R. Knights 252/3. B. Burbidge 292.
Dog Rowe 49 (2), 88, 89 (2), 112, 113, 123 (5), 184, 239
(2), 172 (3) 270, 271 (2).
The Mansell Collection 21, 94, 96, 106/7, 112, 113,
135, 146, 168, 177, 190, 238/9 (2).
Mary Evans Picture Library 12/13, 18, 31, 46, 55, 78,
151, 162/3, 171, 173, 184/5(2), 195, 206, 213, 226, 234,
250, 256, 311 (2), 312, 315.
**Museum of English Rural Life, Reading
University** 35, 68, 108/9, 114, 136, 156/7, 186, 241,
246, 275 (2), 281, 286, 288.
Welsh Tourist Board 38, 40, 87, 256.
Bob Johnson 64, 204/5, 206, 223, 230, 234/5, 277, 302.
National Trust for Scotland 14.
Spectrum Colour Library 19.
David Simpson DAS Photos 20/21.
West Country Tourist Board 28/29.
A. D. Maddrell, Manx Museum 73.
Heart of England Tourist Board 107 (2).
J. Allan Cash 141.
British Tourist Authority 147 (2).
Peter Wenham 207, 215.
British Waterways Board 265.
Stan Knight 282/3 (2).

Courtesy of Scunthorpe Museum N. Salmon 20.
J. B. Tremain 46.
The Watermill Museum 128 (2).
Fritton Lake Country Park 111.
Worldwide Butterflies Ltd 248.
Thaxted Windmill 272.
Donna Hartley & Joan Ingliby 298.
AA Photo Library M. Adelman 105, 166/7, 183, 251.
R. Eames 217, 224, 272/3. R. Fletcher 170/1. S. King
148, 152, 279. Bowaters 1. R. Newton 168, 214.
C. Molyneux 82, 221, 281, 284. R. Surman 4/5, 69, 72,
86 (2), 176, 182, 212. T. Wood 82/3, 195, 266/7, 267, 289.
J. Wyand 28, 76, 79, 80. S & O Mathews 10/11, 15, 18,
23, 31, 35, 81, 104, 110, 120, 121, 126/7, 132/3, 136, 138,
156, 157, 226, 226/7, 244/5, 289, 292, 298, 299, 300/1.
Others 10, 24, 37, 42, 43, 45, 51, 52 (2), 55, 56, 57, 58/9,
59, 62, 90/1, 94, 106 (2), 124, 125, 134, 135, 138/9, 141,
142/3, 145, 150, 152/3, 158/9, 160, 161, 168/9, 188/9,
200, 208, 209, 220/21, 241, 262, 279, 285. H. Williams
11, 12, 13, 15, 16/17, 22, 25, 26/27, 27, 30 (2) 32/33,
34/35, (2), 36, 44, 46, 50, 54/55, 57, 60/61, 63, (2), 65, 69,
70 (2), 74, 84, 85, 90, 92/3, 95, 98/9, 100, 101, 102, 108,
114/5, 116, 117, 118, 119, 130/1, 133, 136/7, 139, 140/1
143, 144, 154, 155, 158, 159, 164/5, 174/5, 178/9, 180/1,
186/7, 192, 193, 198, 202, 210, 225, 229, 231, 232, 236/7,
240, 246/7, 248/9, 250, 259, 260/1, 264, 269, 274, 276,
286/7, 288, 290 (2), 295, 296, 298/9.